CONSTITUTIONAL LAW OF THE EU'S COMMON FOREIGN AND SECURITY POLICY

The Common Foreign and Security Policy (CFSP) of the European Union is a highly exceptional component of the EU legal order. This constitutionalised foreign policy regime, with legal, diplomatic, and political DNA woven throughout its fabric, is a distinct sub-system of law on the outermost sphere of European supranationalism. When contrasted against other Union policies, it is immediately clear that EU foreign policy has a special decision-making mechanism, making it highly exceptional.

In the now depillarised framework of the EU treaties, issues of institutional division arise from the legacy of the former pillar system. This is due to the reality that of prime concern in EU external relations is the question of 'who decides?' By engaging a number of legal themes, that cut across foreign affairs exceptionalism, executive prerogatives, parliamentary accountability, judicial review, and the constitutionalisation of European integration, the book lays bare how EU foreign affairs have become highly legalised, leading to ever-greater coherence in how Europe exerts itself on the global stage.

In this first monograph dedicated exclusively to the law of the EU's Common Foreign and Security Policy in modern times, the author argues that the legal framework for EU foreign affairs must adapt in a changing world so as to ensure the EU treaties can cater for a more assertive Europe in the wider world.

Volume 95 in the Series Modern Studies in European Law

Modern Studies in European Law

Recent titles in this series:

The Use of Force and Article 2 of the ECHR in Light of European Conflicts
Hannah Russell

Environmental Crime in Europe
Edited by Andrew Farmer, Michael Faure and Grazia Maria Vagliasindi

Questioning EU Citizenship: Judges and the Limits of Free Movement and Solidarity in the EU
Edited by Daniel Thym

The European Union under Transnational Law: A Pluralist Appraisal
Matej Avbelj

Illegally Staying in the EU: An Analysis of Illegality in EU Migration Law
Benedita Menezes Queiroz

Social Legitimacy in the Internal Market: A Dialogue of Mutual Responsiveness
Jotte Mulder

The EU Better Regulation Agenda: A Critical Assessment
Edited by Sacha Garben and Inge Govaere

Administrative Regulation Beyond the Non-Delegation Doctrine: A Study on EU Agencies
Marta Simoncini

The Interface Between EU and International Law: Contemporary Reflections
Edited by Inge Govaere and Sacha Garben

The Rise and Decline of Fundamental Rights in EU Citizenship
Adrienne Yong

The Court of Justice and European Criminal Law: Leading Cases in a Contextual Analysis
Edited by Valsamis Mitsilegas, Alberto di Martino and Leandro Mancano

The EU as a Global Regulator for Environmental Protection: A Legitimacy Perspective
Ioanna Hadjiyianni

Citizenship, Crime and Community in the European Union
Stephen Coutts

Critical Reflections on Constitutional Democracy in the European Union
Edited by Sacha Garben and Inge Govaere

For the complete list of titles in this series, see 'Modern Studies in European Law' link at www.bloomsburyprofessional.com/uk/series/modern-studies-in-european-law

Constitutional Law of the EU's Common Foreign and Security Policy

Competence and Institutions in External Relations

Graham Butler

• HART •

OXFORD • LONDON • NEW YORK • NEW DELHI • SYDNEY

HART PUBLISHING

Bloomsbury Publishing Plc

Kemp House, Chawley Park, Cumnor Hill, Oxford, OX2 9PH, UK

HART PUBLISHING, the Hart/Stag logo, BLOOMSBURY and the Diana logo are trademarks of Bloomsbury Publishing Plc

First published in Great Britain 2019

A catalogue record for this book is available from the British Library.

Library of Congress Cataloging-in-Publication data

Names: Butler, Graham, author.

Title: Constitutional law of the EU's common foreign and security policy : competence and institutions in external relations / Graham Butler.

Description: Chicago : Hart Publishing, 2019. | Series: Modern studies in European law ; volume 95 | Includes bibliographical references and index.

Identifiers: LCCN 2019021113 (print) | LCCN 2019021913 (ebook) | ISBN 9781509925957 (EPub) | ISBN 9781509925940 (hardback : alk. paper)

Subjects: LCSH: European Union countries—Foreign relations—Law and legislation. | Constitutional law—European Union countries.

Classification: LCC KJE5105 (ebook) | LCC KJE5105 .B88 2019 (print) | DDC 342.242/2—dc23

LC record available at https://lccn.loc.gov/2019021113

ISBN: HB: 978-1-50992-594-0
ePDF: 978-1-50992-596-4
ePub: 978-1-50992-595-7

Typeset by Compuscript Ltd, Shannon

PREFACE

In the production of a book, an author owes vast amounts of gratitude to many people. This is particularly so when it is an author's first book. Whilst it is impossible to list them all, a few will be singled out.

Primarily, the book would not been possible without Professor Helle Krunke at Det Juridisk Fakultet, *Københavns Universitet*. She has been the most exceptional mentor during the composition of this work, and I will forever be indebted to her. Without Helle and her encouragement, this book would never have come to fruition. Secondly, Professor M. Elvira Méndez Pinedo warmly embraced my research in Reykjavík at *Háskóli Íslands* and has also been an enormous support. The award of the Joint Fellowship for my years in Copenhagen by the University of Copenhagen and the University of Iceland has been a most rewarding experience and I owe a debt of gratitude to many individuals across both institutions for their collective embrace.

The trio of Robert Schütze, Bart Van Vooren, and Ramses A Wessel examined an earlier version of the manuscript that led to my award of a joint doctoral degree. In addition, Morten Broberg conducted an earlier evaluation and I wish to thank all four of them for their attentiveness, discussion, and debate.

At Aarhus University, I want to thank my colleagues Birgitte Egelund Olsen, Karsten Engsig Sørensen, Louise Halleskov Storgaard, Helle Hjorth Christiansen, Jytte Mønster, Tine Sommer, Michael Steinicke, Hanne Søndergaard Birkmose, Ole Terkelsen, Jens Vedsted-Hansen, and Pernille Wegener Jessen for their companionship and valour. Moreover, the Professor dr. jur. Max Sørensens Mindefond and the Aarhus University Research Foundation have supported my research over the years, for which I am very appreciative.

Thank you to Sinead Moloney at Hart Publishing for shepherding this book through the publishing process from beginning to end. Lastly, I am forever grateful to my parents, John and Yvette; my brother, Greg; as well as my own family, Katarina and Johan, for their support.

This book is dedicated to those who elucidate the role that law has played, and will continue to play, in the process of European integration. For otherwise, historians, economists, political scientists, and others would cast it aside and let it be forgotten.

Graham Butler
Aarhus, February 2019

CONTENTS

LIST OF ABBREVIATIONS

AFET	European Parliament's Committee on Foreign Affairs
BUDG	European Parliament's Committee on Budgets
CCP	Common Commercial Policy
CFR	EU Charter of Fundamental Rights
CFSP	Common Foreign and Security Policy
COPS	*Comité politique et de sécurité*
COREPER	Committee of Permanent Representatives
COREU	*Correspondence européenne*
COSAC	Conference of Community and European Affairs Committees of Parliaments of the European Union
CSDP	Common Security and Defence Policy
DAA	Draft Accession Agreement
DG	Directorate-General
ECA	European Court of Auditors
ECB	European Central Bank
ECSC	European Coal and Steel Community
ECOWAS	European Community of West African States
EDA	European Defence Agency
EDC	European Defence Community
EDF	European Development Fund
EEAS	European External Action Service
EEC	European Economic Community
EIB	European Investment Bank
EPC	European Political Cooperation
EPCA	Enhanced Partnership and Cooperation Agreement

ESM	European Stability Mechanism
EU	European Union
EUFOR	Operation Althea (European Union Military Operation in Bosnia and Herzegovina)
EULEX Kosovo	European Union Rule of Law Mission in Kosovo
EUNAVFOR Med	Operation Sophia (European Union Naval Force Mediterranean)
EUNAVFOR	Operation Atalanta (European Union Naval Force Somalia)
EUPM	European Union Police Mission
EUSR	European Union Special Representative
ECHR	European Convention on Human Rights
ECtHR	European Court of Human Rights
EUMC	European Union Military Committee
EURATOM	European Atomic Energy Community
E2I	European Intervention Initiative
FAC	Foreign Affairs Council of the European Union
FRA	European Union Agency for Fundamental Rights
FTA	Free Trade Agreement
ICJ	International Court of Justice
IGC	Intergovernmental Conference
MEP	Member of the European Parliament
MFF	Multiannual Financial Framework
NATO	North Atlantic Treaty Organisation
NAVFOR	European Union Naval Force
OCCAR	Organisation for Joint Armament Cooperation
OJ	Official Journal of the European Union
PA	Parliamentary Assembly
PCA	Partnership and Cooperation Agreement
PCA	Permanent Court of Arbitration

PESCO	Permanent Structured Cooperation
PJC	Police and Judicial Cooperation
PSC	Political and Security Committee
PTA	Pirate Transfer Agreement
QMV	Qualified Majority Voting
SatCen	European Union Satellite Centre
TEU	Treaty on European Union
TFEU	Treaty on the Functioning of the European Union
TSCG	Treaty on Stability, Coordination and Governance
UNHRC	United Nations Human Rights Council
VCLT	Vienna Convention on the Law of Treaties
WEU	Western European Union
WEU PA	Parliamentary Assembly of the Western European Union

TABLE OF CASES

Court of Justice of the European Union

Chronologically, by date of delivery

Opinions and Views of the Advocates General

Chronologically, by date of delivery

General Court of the European Union

Chronologically, by date of delivery

National courts of Member States

Chronologically, by date of delivery

1

The Constitutionalised Regime of the Common Foreign and Security Policy

The Common Foreign and Security Policy (CFSP) of the European Union (EU) is an exceptional policy in the EU legal order. This constitutionalised foreign policy regime with legal, diplomatic, and political DNA woven throughout its fabric is a distinct sub-system of law on the outer-most sphere of European supranationalism. When contrasted with other Union policies, it is immediately clear that there is a separate remit of decision-making within the Council, with the deliberate intention of shielding it from parliamentary involvement and judicial oversight.

There is constitutional significance to the choice of legal basis for foreign policy and external relations acts of the Union. Therefore, legal tension exists in EU external relations between CFSP matters and non-CFSP matters as the institutional competence differs in terms of decision-making, procedures, substance, and justiciability. Decision-making, in itself, is not a particularly appealing aspect of the law; however, in Union law, it is of critical importance, as it governs the direction and speed of integration.

Of central concern in EU external relations is the question of 'who decides?' Accordingly, it is a legal challenge to decipher the intricacies of how to operate a highly exceptional policy from an institutional perspective within the legal framework of the EU treaties. Post-Lisbon, in the proclaimed depillarised framework of the treaties, issues of institutional division arise in EU external relations because of the legacy of the former pillar system. Following this most recent significant overhaul of the treaties, this book sheds new light on the legal shape of CFSP matters, analysing and debating the parliamentary and judicial branches of the Union in the legal regime of EU foreign policy. In so doing, it brings forward the argument that the long-term sustainability of distinguishing between CFSP and non-CFSP matters in EU external action is cause for concern. Through discursive analysis, the book looks at the constitutional dimension of CFSP matters through a legal lens and outlines how the treaties can cater for a more assertive Europe in the wider world.

With the legal framework of the EU's external relations increasingly coming under the spotlight, the book analyses the current state of legal affairs in the EU's external action, with a particular focus on the constitutional law of CFSP matters.

It engages with legal themes of foreign affairs exceptionalism, executive prerogatives, parliamentary accountability, and the scope of constitutionalisation of European integration. Through an internal approach for external effect, the book lays bare, through gradual incrementalism, how the foreign affairs dimension of EU external relations has become highly legalised, leading to ever-greater coherence in how Europe exerts itself on the global stage. Simultaneously, the book reveals that the legal framework for the foreign policy element of EU external relations must adapt in a changing world, so Europe's internal processes neither limit nor constrain its potential externally.

1.1. Introduction

In Union law, it is assumed that the constitutional legal order is a single *acquis*. In fact, the reality paints a far more complex picture. The Union has its own foreign policy, separate and distinct from the Member States, and there is a need for a greater understanding of the constitutional nature of this foreign policy of the Union. From a legal perspective, CFSP matters are as much a legal conundrum for the Union as it is a policy manifestation. The link between the legal nature of the policy and the political context is undeniable, and institutional arrangements for CFSP matters and its procedural practice mark it as clearly distinguishable from normal EU policies.

The treaties allow for express external capabilities of the Union in the world, but this EU external action is categorised into two groups: CFSP matters and non-CFSP matters. The former, creates a 'world of its own'[1] and is the main subject of analysis in this book. CFSP matters possess legal, diplomatic and political characteristics, with each shining through in its own way. These two different external action regimes leave practitioners with a perplexing assortment of legal arrangements for the Union in a range of different areas when the Union acts externally. The divide between CFSP and non-CFSP matters, split across the two different treaties, remains a lingering source of confusion to non-lawyers. Thus, the presence of the distinctions and dissimilarities makes the ideal opening for legal analysis.

The coming about of CFSP as a legal field was 'an accident',[2] yet it embodies the constitutional uniqueness of foreign policy matters when legalised.[3] That accident

[1] Monica Claes and Bruno De Witte, 'Competences: Codification and Contestation' in Adam Łazowski and Steven Blockmans (eds), *Research Handbook on EU Institutional Law* (Edward Elgar, 2016) p 59.

[2] Piet Eeckhout, 'A Panorama of Two Decades of EU External Relations Law' in Anthony Arnull, Piet Eeckhout and Takis Tridimas (eds), *Continuity and Change in EU Law: Essays in Honour of Sir Francis Jacobs* (Oxford University Press, 2008) p 325.

[3] Peter Van Elsuwege, 'EU External Action after the Collapse of the Pillar Structure: In Search of a New Balance between Delimitation and Consistency' (2010) 47 *Common Market Law Review* 987 at 998.

is still with us and, to use a well-known axiom, it is an 'infant disease'[4] that has never been cured.[5] As a policy, CFSP matters are at the forefront of the EU's external action on both legal and political levels, yet sit alongside non-CFSP external action, contributing to an all-encompassing practice of the Union's external relations. CFSP matters have long been identified as different as they are contained within the Treaty on European Union (TEU).[6] The legal framework governing regular institutional process of law-making through the ordinary legislative procedure (OLP) is not applicable for CFSP matters, as will be highlighted in its nature as non-legislative law. As an evolutionary entity, in much the same manner as the Union is itself, CFSP matters are a unique aspect of Union law that can be labelled the 'CFSP *acquis*'.[7] However, this dilutes the wholeness of EU external action, artificially thwarting Europe's potential to act externally.

At every Intergovernmental Conference over the decades, the opportunity has arisen to get off to a fresh start, to clear the slate, and once and for all amend the provisions of the treaties, to chart a new course and streamline and simplify the legal framework governing EU external actions. The Treaty of Lisbon brought about several important changes to the functioning of a more modern international organisation of Member States,[8] but it retained the legal divide between CFSP and non-CFSP matters.

With the Union as international organisation being identified as an entity of states seeking closer cooperation, as opposed to a loosely defined collaboration,[9] CFSP matters emerge from the EU legal order scarred by distinction when compared to non-CFSP matters. Yet, what emanated from the Treaty of Lisbon process was the willingness to build a clearer, more coherent identity of the Union for the outside world to see, and for it to be put into force.

1.1.1. The Legal Nature of EU Foreign Policy

To achieve the EU's desired aim, it preaches many core principles within its treaties, applicable both internally and externally.[10] That sets high expectations for a polity that is governed by law beyond the state. To the outside world, CFSP matters

[4] See, Pierre Pescatore, 'The Doctrine of "Direct Effect": An Infant Disease of Community Law' (1983) 8 *European Law Review* 155.

[5] Robert Schütze, *European Constitutional Law* (Cambridge University Press, 2012) p 314.

[6] Bart Van Vooren and Ramses A Wessel, *EU External Relations Law: Text, Cases and Materials* (Cambridge University Press, 2014) pp 105 and 346.

[7] Christine Delcourt, 'The Acquis Communautaire: Has the Concept Had Its Day?' (2001) 38 *Common Market Law Review* 829 at 832.

[8] That being said, categorisation of the Union as fitting into either a state or international organisation model is a forced matter – neither of which are accurate. See, Robert Schütze, 'Two-and-a-Half Ways of Thinking about the European Union' (2016) 53 *Politique européenne* 28.

[9] Armin Von Bogdandy, 'The Legal Case for Unity: The European Union as a Single Organization with a Single Legal System' (1999) 36 *Common Market Law Review* 887 at 895.

[10] TEU, Preamble, Articles 2, 3, 8, 21 and 32, amongst others.

may appear fully normalised within the EU legal structure, but this is not the case when the legal and procedural intricacies are probed. Foreign policy in the EU has been peculiar due to the lack of a uniform legal framework in the overall scheme of EU external relations.[11] The Member States have mandated that the EU's external relations are handicapped between two different spheres – CFSP and non-CFSP matters. However, that does not sit well with the premise that aspiration for greater integration is inherent in the treaties.

EU foreign policy, whilst wide-ranging and not brief, creates purposeful norms through law.[12] CFSP law was born in what has been called 'a sub-system of EU law',[13] for it has a robust sense of 'other-ness' about it. Acts of foreign policy are in constant need of adjusting to ensure they align with their intended goal. This is what poses a challenge for law. By its very nature, foreign policy does not lend itself to be a close companion of the law. Foreign policy can often be reactionary, evoking itself to changing scenarios as its respective government sees fit. Putting foreign policy and law together, even within the same sentence, must be questioned[14] and, whilst they may be 'strange bedfellows',[15] when EU foreign policy is mixed with law, it brings about anxious levels of curiosity that deserve further investigation.

The assumption that there is little law-making in EU foreign policy is wholly incorrect, as CFSP matters entail legal tools that are built into the TEU. The law and politics in CFSP matters are explicitly intertwined on a practical level and the workings of the two are premised and dependent on one another.[16] CFSP matters demand attention and detail, in that there is policy on one side of the equation and decision-making on the other. Systematically, trying to separate the variances in CFSP matters is perplexing, given that legal instruments flow from the same equation.

Decisions on what positions the EU may take in foreign policy are political questions[17] and are decided upon by the political institutions. They require an understanding of many important traits of what are inherent in political deliberation – historical, social, economic, political, moral, and ethical reflections.

[11] Daniel Thym, 'Foreign Affairs' in Armin Von Bogdandy and Jürgen Bast (eds), *Principles of European Constitutional Law* 2nd edition, (Hart Publishing, 2009) p 311.

[12] See Chapter 3, Joris Larik, *Foreign Policy Objectives in European Constitutional Law* (Oxford University Press, 2016).

[13] Bruno De Witte, 'The Elusive Unity of the EU Legal Order after Maastricht' in Maartje De Visser and Anne Pieter Van Der Mei (eds), *The Treaty on European Union 1993–2013: Reflections from Maastricht* (Intersentia, 2013) p 61.

[14] See, Anne-Marie Slaughter, 'Are Foreign Affairs Different?' (1993) 106 *Harvard Law Review* 1980.

[15] Geert De Baere and Ramses A Wessel, 'EU Law and the EEAS: Of Complex Competences and Constitutional Consequences' in David Spence and Jozef Bátora (eds), *The European External Action Service: European Diplomacy Post-Westphalia* (Palgrave Macmillan, 2015) p 175.

[16] Damian Chalmers, 'Post-Nationalism and the Quest for Constitutional Substitutes' (2000) 27 *Journal of Law and Society* 178 at 192.

[17] See, Graham Butler, 'In Search of the Political Question Doctrine in EU Law' (2018) 45 *Legal Issues of Economic Integration* 329.

The law does not hugely contribute to such inclinations.[18] Yet, political decisions are ultimately encapsulated into the EU legal regime once such decisions are made. Therefore, whilst CFSP matters are an area where the Union performs legally, the treaties demand the absurd situation in that democratic involvement and judicial control is theoretically meant to remain at Member State level. Member States have wanted the distinction between CFSP and non-CFSP matters to be as black and white as possible, but in fact, it is nothing more than an entirely grey area. It thus may be surprising that legal arguments in EU *external* relations are, in fact, fought upon *internal* legal rules. This book fits into the category of analysing Union law through the lens of an autonomous and distinct legal order.

Despite seeming to be the contrary, CFSP matters are a legalised field. For lawyers, everything in EU external relations begins with a discussion on the legal basis for supporting actions. As the Union strives for more coordination, consistency and cooperation, the choice of legal basis is of profound importance. The law is only one element of EU external relations, but it is an integral component that caters for the execution of external action. This is even more so in CFSP matters where strict conditions for the procedural issues are set down in the treaties. This is not only in EU external relations law, but for all EU acts or measures, which must have a legal basis. Ensuring that a legal basis exists for any given act or measure ensures a level of institutional balance (*équilibre institutionnel*) in the Union and prevents, to varying degrees, the excessive use of incorrect legal basis by institutions for their own gain, to the impairment of others.[19] By using law as an instrument of the political debate between institutions and bodies, it is important to not forget that external relations law strikes the delicate balance between different institutions and their involvement in particular policies.

1.1.2. External Relations and International Agreements

Whilst the legal distinction between CFSP and non-CFSP matters is important, there are also distinctions to be made between the different types of international agreements that the Union is capable of entering into. Between bilateral and multilateral agreements, the Union is a party to well over 1,200 of them.[20] The deciding factors for determining if an international agreement relates *exclusively*

[18] The same argument has been made with respect to US foreign policy and the law. H Jefferson Powell, *The President's Authority over Foreign Affairs: An Essay in Constitutional Interpretation* (Carolina Academic Press, 2002) p 148.

[19] Koen Lenaerts and Piet Van Nuffel, *European Union Law* Robert Bray and Nathan Cambien (eds) 3rd edition (Sweet and Maxwell, 2011) p 112.

[20] See, 'Annotated Summary of Bilateral Agreements between, on the One Party, the European Union, the Former European Community or Euratom, and, on the Other Part, Third States or International Organizations (Treaties Office, Legal Affairs Division)' (European External Action Service 2018). 'Annotated Summary of Multilateral Agreements to Which the European Union Is a Contracting Party' (European External Action Service 2018).

to CFSP matters or not depends on a case-by-case assessment. Varying institutional interpretations exist for what this should entail. This book explores the changes that have occurred since the passage of the Treaty of Lisbon, and the direct impact it has had for international agreements the EU is concluding.

To achieve improved coherence in Union law,[21] particularly in external relations, the changes that have been made to the treaties over time have factored in minor improvements, but no great leap has been made. As a result, the book probes the continued divide between CFSP and non-CFSP matters, whether it has a future, and what effect a fragmented *internal* legal arrangement has had on the *external* assertion of the Union in the wider world. Incoherence is weakness and, taking into account the views of the various institutions, there have been agreed compromises at each step of the way for ensuring as much coherence as possible with regard to both international agreements, and wider Union policies.

International agreements take different forms in an EU context. There is a stark difference between whether a CFSP or non-CFSP legal basis is used, invariably meaning different roles for the institutions. Accordingly, the adoption of the correct legal basis for EU foreign policy matters is important, namely, because the decision-making procedures are different. The intergovernmental-like nature of CFSP matters, albeit rule-bound by the treaties, but decided upon solely within the Council, allows the Union to respond to international events using a CFSP legal instrument in a manner close to that of a nation state.[22]

The nature of international agreements conducted on a CFSP legal basis in the TEU is that they are primarily a tool of the Council, within Member State control. The discrepancies between CFSP and non-CFSP matters do not allow a clear allocation of competence between actors to develop.[23] Consequently, institutional actors other than the Council have challenged many international agreements concluded on a CFSP legal basis before the Court of Justice of the European Union (the Court),[24] claiming that the international agreements contain matters

[21] 'Coherence' stems from the French term 'cohérence', whereas in the English language version of the treaties, the word 'consistency' is used. Christophe Hillion, 'Tous Pour Un, Un Pour Tous! Coherence in the External Relations of the European Union' in Marise Cremona (ed), *Developments in EU External Relations Law* (Oxford University Press, 2008) p 13.

[22] That is despite the Union not being a state. As one Associate Justice of the US Supreme Court has noted, 'for all [the EU's] progress towards economic integration, [it] is not close' to becoming a nation state. Potter Stewart, 'Foreword' in Terrance Sandalow and Eric Stein (eds), *Courts and Free Markets: Perspectives from the United States and Europe*, vol 1 (Clarendon Press, 1982) p vii. The Court has since confirmed this: '[T]he EU is, under international law, precluded by its very nature from being considered a State.' Opinion 2/13, ECLI:EU:C:2014:2454 (*'Accession of the European Union to the European Convention for the Protection of Human Rights'*), para 156.

[23] Antonio Tizzano, 'The Foreign Relations Law of the EU between Supranationality and Intergovernmental Model' in Enzo Cannizzaro (ed), *The European Union as an Actor in International Relations* (Kluwer Law International, 2002) p 137.

[24] Such as, Case C-130/10, *Parliament v Council*, ECLI:EU:C:2012:472 ('*Smart Sanctions*'); Case C-658/11, *Parliament v Council*, ECLI:EU:C:2014:2025 ('*Mauritius*'); Case C-377/12, *Commission v Council*, ECLI:EU:C:2014:1903 ('*Philippines PCA*'); Case C-263/14, *Parliament v Council*, ECLI:EU:C:2016:435 ('*Tanzania*'). This is discussed extensively in Chapter 4 of this book.

within Union competence and, therefore, a non-CFSP legal basis should be availed of for concluding the international agreements. Accordingly, issues related to CFSP matters and international agreements will feature heavily in the following chapters.

1.1.3. A Gravitational Attraction

For EU external action, a CFSP legal basis has 'gravitational attraction' to Member States,[25] given it puts them firmly at the helm. With the Council clearly in firm control when actions or international agreements are located on a CFSP legal basis, this puts other institutions to the side. Consequently, the Parliament has been a keen litigator in constitutional questions regarding the use of a CFSP legal basis,[26] as has occasionally, to a lesser extent, the Commission. Furthermore, the Court as an institutional actor may also feel aggrieved in such circumstances,[27] not because of the legal basis of a legal act or international agreement before it, but because it is itself constrained by the treaties that have envisioned a limited role for it in CFSP matters.[28] The Court does not have full competence across all fields of Union law and, as a consequence, is not a regular court. Its limited jurisdiction in CFSP matters alters what could be a regular constitutional structure. The tip-toeing by the Court around the specified limitations gives rise to scenarios where it must, before any analysis of the relevant CFSP matters, assert jurisdiction, before proceeding with an eventual judgment.

EU external relations is an area where there are different legal instruments, and the distinction of legal bases and boundaries can seem a little artificial for practical purposes.[29] Notwithstanding the divide between CFSP and non-CFSP matters, their integration, or rather, CFSP slowly becoming more intertwined and similar to the regular EU legal order is already beginning to be seen.[30] With the continued distinct split in EU external relations between CFSP and non-CFSP legal bases, its resulting impact is the division of the policy fields. Whilst the Treaty of Lisbon attempted to bridge the gaps in EU external relations in a legal sense, it has contrastingly posed a whole new set of arguments as regards the affiliation

[25] Mauro Gatti, 'Conflict of Legal Bases and the Internal-External Security Nexus: AFSJ versus CFSP' in Eleftheria Neframi and Mauro Gatti (eds), *Constitutional Issues of EU External Relations Law* (Nomos, 2018) p 110.

[26] See Chapter 4 of this book.

[27] See Chapter 5 of this book.

[28] TEU, Articles 24(1) and 40, and TFEU, Article 275.

[29] Ingolf Pernice, 'The Treaty of Lisbon: Multilevel Constitutionalism in Action' (2009) 15 *Columbia Journal of European Law* 349 at 399.

[30] See, Panos Koutrakos, 'The Nexus between CFSP/CSDP and the Area of Freedom, Security and Justice' in Steven Blockmans and Panos Koutrakos (eds), *Research Handbook on the EU's Common Foreign and Security Policy* (Edward Elgar, 2018).

between CFSP matters and other external relations acts of the Union that are non-CFSP matters.

All actors in external relations read articles in the treaties in a certain way, often providing themselves with generous interpretations that do not always correspond with the intent of the text, or how other competing institutional actors see the same text. Equally, the issue of competence is a sensitive area of Union law, with each institution carefully scrutinising actions to ensure institutional competence is not encroached upon. When the Treaty of Lisbon came into force in 2009, the issue of competence rose in prominence and is now a major source of conflict and litigation between different institutional actors. The ensuing financial crisis meant that the European Council found intergovernmentalist zeal that ultimately weakened other institutions. As will be demonstrated by the end of the book, this instinct of Member States will have an impact on the future direction of EU foreign policy from a legal perspective.

1.2. Approach

This book adopts a legal approach, with emphasis placed on institutions and procedures. It explores the horizontal division of powers with respect to CFSP matters, as well as extensively analysing the role of two institutions in CFSP matters whose position is rather obscure – the Parliament and the Court. It does so with respect to interinstitutional battles for competence and jurisdiction, rather than scruntinising the vertical division between the Union and Member States given that interinstitutional disputes at Union level are now occurring at a growing rate. Yet, the book is also mindful of the practical necessities of legal and political engagement that are ever-present in EU external relations.

By fitting within EU external relations law as a whole, CFSP matters are analysed using an EU legal lens and their institutional dimension. By mapping out the legal dimension of CFSP matters and considering the various cases before the Court, the book analyses how this unique area of Union law has managed to remain so legally distinct for so long, and where it is likely to lead into the future. These developments raise fundamental questions about the longevity of CFSP matters as a separate legal basis for EU external action.

1.2.1. The Question of Discipline

Once upon a time, Union law was a new discipline, thus it is a relatively recent subject in law when contrasted against doctrinal heavy subjects of a more traditional legal nature. Union law was, at one stage, a sub-discipline of international law, yet, to the surprise of no one, it is now a discipline in its own right with EU sub-categories crowding in behind it. If some fields of law are overstudied and do not achieve their desired potential, then Union law has a different issue. EU external relations law more generally requires greater levels of academic scrutiny.[31] The gradual development of Union law, with practitioner routine and accomplished scholars that have analysed its in-depth usage and application over the past number of decades, has built up library catalogues with outputs that encompass what we know today of the discipline. That said, staying abreast of changes in Union law and practice is quite a challenge.[32]

Union law is not particularly sensitive towards a methodological discourse. Collectively, the study of Union law taken as a whole is a field that seeks both to widen and deepen the European integration project. It has, principally, been doctrinally focused. This assertion, evident from decades of EU legal scholarship, is an obvious conclusion. Yet, there are traces, albeit mild, of EU legal scholarship going beyond doctrinal work, for good or otherwise,[33] but that does not erase its complexity. Union law can even catch out the best of lawyers; on occasion, even specialists have got lost in its midst.[34] Furthermore, the EU legal order has not worked out a constitutional theory[35] and Union law can too be theoretically controversial given the lack of a singular guiding principle.[36] As things stand, EU external relations law makes up a growing sub-category of Union law.

External relations law, also known as foreign relations law, was developed in the United States,[37] before later gathering wider global interest. On this side of the Atlantic, interest in EU external relations law is increasing and the number of publications in the area is 'booming'.[38] As a field of study, CFSP matters and EU external relations law more generally falls somewhere between Union and international law. The divergent areas mean there are numerous complexities that are involved when the law is at work. What is most curious is that EU *external*

[31] Joris Larik, 'EU Foreign Relations Law as a Field of Scholarship' (2017) 111 *American Journal of International Law* 321 at 323.

[32] This has long been a problem. Even in the 1980s, it was said that with respect to EU treaty practice that 'it is more and more difficult to keep track of all the new developments'. Pierre Pescatore, 'Contribution to the Discussion' in Christiaan Timmermans and Edmond LM Völker (eds), *Division of Powers between the European Communities and their Member States in the Field of External Relations* (Kluwer, 1981) p 72.

[33] See, Anthony Arnull, 'The Americanization of EU Law Scholarship' in Anthony Arnull, Piet Eeckhout and Takis Tridimas (eds), *Continuity and Change in EU Law: Essays in Honour of Sir Francis Jacobs* (Oxford University Press, 2008).

[34] Michal Bobek, 'On the Application of European Law in (Not Only) the Courts of the New Member States: "Don't Do as I Say"?' in Catherine Barnard (ed), *Cambridge Yearbook of European Legal Studies 2007–2008: Volume 10* (Hart Publishing, 2008) p 24.

[35] Joseph HH Weiler, *The Constitution of Europe: 'Do the New Clothes Have an Emperor?' And Other Essays on European Integration* (Cambridge University Press, 1999) p 8.

[36] Tizzano (n 23) p 136.

[37] Curtis A Bradley, 'Foreign Relations Law as a Field of Study' (2017) 111 *American Journal of International Law* 316 at 319–20.

[38] Ramses A Wessel 'The European Court of Justice and External Relations Law: Constitutional Challenges, by Marise Cremona and Anne Thies (Oxford: Hart Publishing, 2014)'; (2015) 52 *Common Market Law Review* 1715.

relations law contains a great deal of *internal* law. This integral contradiction has given rise to the special applicability of the chosen area of law that is the subject of this book.

1.2.2. The Legal Approach

Political science does a lot of explanatory work for elucidating the vision of EU foreign policy.[39] Yet, it does little to anything on expanding on the legal dimension of this complex area of Union law. Political science long had near-exclusivity on the subject.[40] However, today, legal research can be contrasted from those offered in traditional social science research. As alluded to, in a field dominated by scholars in other disciplines, law is based on 'qualitative argument rather than… quantitative research'.[41] Likewise, research in Union law has been claimed to have its own distinct methods.[42] Therefore, the questions in law, such as those raised in this book, elucidate analysis that other disciplines would not be able to muster.

The divide between legal and political science is not as definitive as might be assumed.[43] Public policy as a concept within the Union, from a legal standpoint or otherwise, remains difficult either to categorise or pinpoint at all. In law, it can be easy to disregard other fields of research that veer away from the more traditional methods of legal research, in the same way other fields reject legal research. In EU studies, the minority that lawyers find themselves in is certainly a problem from a lawyer's perspective.[44]

Specific methodologies or conceptual frameworks are usually absent from the analysis of Union law.[45] Within EU legal studies, analysis tends to be 'reactive, event-driver and context-dependent'.[46] Union law is also inherently and

[39] For an overview, see, Ben Tonra, 'Constructing the CFSP: The Utility of a Cognitive Approach' (2003) 41 *Journal of Common Market Studies* 731.

[40] Inge Govaere, 'The External Relations of the EU. Legal Aspects' in Dieter Mahncke, Alicia Ambos and Christopher Reynolds (eds), *European Foreign Policy: From Rhetoric to Reality?* (PIE-Peter Lang, 2004) p 97.

[41] Ramses A Wessel, 'The Legal Dimension of European Foreign Policy' in Knud Erik Jørgensen and others (eds), *The SAGE Handbook of European Foreign Policy* (SAGE, 2015) p 307.

[42] Christina Eckes, 'European Union Legal Methods – Moving Away from Integration' in Ulla Neergaard and Ruth Nielsen (eds), *European Legal Method – Towards a New European Legal Realism?* (Djøf Publishing, 2013) p 174.

[43] See, Ulla Neergaard and Marlene Wind, 'Studying the EU in Legal and Political Sciences Scholarship' in Ulla Neergaard and Ruth Nielsen (eds), *European Legal Method – in a Multi-Level EU Legal Order* (Djøf Publishing, 2012).

[44] Kaarlo Tuori, 'The Relationality of European Constitution(s). Justifying a New Research Programme for European Constitutional Scholarship' in Ulla Neergaard and Ruth Nielsen (eds), *European Legal Method – Towards a New European Legal Realism?* (Djøf Publishing, 2013) p 34.

[45] Armin Von Bogdandy, 'A Bird's Eye View on the Science of European Law: Structures, Debates and Development Prospects of Basic Research on the Law of the European Union in a German Perspective' (2000) 6 *European Law Journal* 208 at 209.

[46] Neil Walker, 'Legal Theory and the European Union: A 25th Anniversary Essay' (2005) 25 *Oxford Journal of Legal Studies* 581 at 583.

uncompromisingly 'law in context'.[47] Legal concepts have become 'Europeanised' over time[48] and the cross- and interdisciplinarity in Union law is increasing,[49] despite it being artificial to suggest that interdisciplinary analysis would be able to capture the legal nuances of CFSP matters. Within the discipline of Union law, there is an inherent risk of 'herd-like' behaviour.[50] This normative standpoint, an integrationist perspective, also brings with it an ideology from the perspective of Europeanists. Whether this can be portrayed in a positive or negative light depends on a given perspective, but Union law is greatly vibrant and becoming ever a more complex polity.

Using a law-in-context approach and dealing with the thematic issue of CFSP matters, the gradual normalisation of CFSP matters and its inclinations within traditional EU external relations will become more apparent. The book frames the narrative, taking account of the law, cases and other developments before shifting the focus away from law and placing it within a broader social and political context. Firmly rooted in legal research, it delves into the intricacies of CFSP matters, with institutions pushing their separate ways to test its frontiers. Yet, it also endeavours to embrace other select literature, particularly in the field of political science, to give a broader perspective to the topic at hand. Blending the legal aspects with hints of political science provides a more rounded view of how CFSP matters manifest in practice. By combining the viewpoints from the different perspectives, a fuller picture of CFSP matters and EU external relations law will emerge.

1.2.3. The Institutional Catch

Everything in Union law is subject to a particular strand of reading. As a result, writers must be careful when approaching the issue of the role of institutions in the EU decision-making process. It is an easy task to take an institutional viewpoint and run with it. For many years, Union law and the 'writers of Europe' had institutional affiliations;[51] notwithstanding their insistence on an independent view, they often unwittingly aligned with their institutional view. Whilst it is easier to consistently approach matters that are the subject of a one-dimensional view, it does nothing to benefit legal research. Given this predicament, the book takes account

[47] Inger-Johanne Sand, 'European Legal Method: A New Teleology, Law-in-Context, a New Legal Realism or Hybrid Law?' in Ulla Neergaard and Ruth Nielsen (eds), *European Legal Method – Towards a New European Legal Realism?* (Djøf Publishing, 2013) p 232.

[48] See, Loïc Azoulai, 'The Europeanisation of Legal Concepts' in Ulla Neergaard and Ruth Nielsen (eds), *European Legal Method – in a Multi-Level EU Legal Order* (Djøf Publishing, 2012).

[49] Jo Shaw, 'The European Union: Discipline Building Meets Polity Building' in Mark Tushnet and Peter Cane (eds), *The Oxford Handbook of Legal Studies* (Oxford University Press, 2003) p 342.

[50] This is discussed at length in, Rob van Gestel and Hans-Wolfgang Micklitz, 'Why Methods Matter in European Legal Scholarship' (2014) 20 *European Law Journal* 292 at 305.

[51] Harm Schepel and Rein Wesseling, 'The Legal Community: Judges, Lawyers, Officials and Clerks in the Writing of Europe' (1997) 3 *European Law Journal* 165 at 171.

of institutional viewpoints and presents arguments from an objective standpoint, with the author not having an EU institutional interest to promote or defend.

There is no legal basis for expressing a preference for the involvement of certain institutions in external action or otherwise, as the decision-making procedures are set down by the treaties. It follows that much of the Union's law literature is sympathetic to the cause of a more unified Europe. Whilst this book mitigates for the obvious 'unity hypothesis',[52] any subjective reasoning will be brought forward only with adequate justification.

Union law cannot be understood without analysing the role and the case law of the Court.[53] Certain strands of scholarship tend to emphasise (or over-emphasise) the role that the Court has played in European integration,[54] yet there is no denying that the nature of the Court as a judicial institution has meant that its influence across the EU legal order has been considerable. However, it is equally important to consider the Court as more than just the primary developer of Union law, the 'flip-side',[55] given the multi-layered structures that are more complex in nature today. After all, the Court as a judicial body shares many similarities to that of higher courts, such as supreme or constitutional courts in Member States.

The book makes use of the relevant provisions in the treaties, cases of the Court, and other EU instruments and documents where necessary. By identifying the relative legal texts and working documents, amongst others, the history, creation, evolution, and conflict of CFSP can all be traced and analysed through a framework of Union law, leading to a normative framework for the future of the law of EU external relations.

1.2.4. Delimitation

The opening up of possibilities for avenue exploration within Union law is endless, hence the application of principled delimitation is necessary. Firstly, the book addresses the legal issues of the horizontality of CFSP matters at Union level only. It does not deal with the vertical angle of CFSP matters and its interaction with national legal orders of Member States. Secondly, it does not principally address the nuance of the Common Security and Defence Policy (CSDP). Whilst defence and security together constitute the '(cold) heart of all foreign policy'[56] and are undoubtedly interconnected with CFSP matters, it is a field of law in its own right,

[52] Bruno De Witte, 'European Law as an Academic Discipline: Unity and Fragmentation' in Mielle Bulterman and others (eds), *Views of European Law from the Mountain: Liber Amicorum Piet Jan Slot* (Kluwer Law International, 2009) p 418.

[53] Claus Gulmann, 'Methods of Interpretation of the European Court of Justice' (1980) 24 *Scandinavian Studies in Law* 187 at 189.

[54] See, Giuseppe Federico Mancini, 'The Making of A Constitution For Europe' (1989) 26 *Common Market Law Review* 595.

[55] Joakim Nergelius, *The Constitutional Dilemma of the European Union* (Europa Law Publishing, 2009) p 7.

[56] Robert Schütze, 'External Union Policies: A Substantive Overview' in Robert Schütze (ed), *Foreign Affairs and the EU Constitution: Selected Essays* (Cambridge University Press, 2014) p 443.

and has been covered elsewhere in the literature.[57] Thirdly, the use of restrictive measures (sanctions) as a policy field falls outside the scope of the book,[58] despite the legal instruments for such being located on both a CFSP and a non-CFSP legal basis. The area of counter-terrorism is a whole body of law that is disjointed from more mainstream EU external relations law.[59] Whilst sanctions are the most judicially contested element of CFSP matters, they are less stimulating for examining the CFSP puzzle from the perspective of EU constitutional law. Thus, the book will only touch upon the use of restrictive measures to the extent that it is relevant to CFSP matters for competence and institutional questions.

1.2.5. Research Questions

At the heart of this book is a legal power game. Five questions represent the challenges of setting out the law in CFSP matters and how it throws up legal conundrums in need of analysis. Firstly, to what extent are CFSP matters legally separate and distinct from other categories of Union law, particularly with respect to non-CFSP external relations? Second, what has the involvement of institutional actors beyond the Council been with respect to CFSP matters? Third, has the choice of legal basis for EU external action been central to the institutional involvement in CFSP matters? Fourth, is there institutional balance in CFSP matters, given the existence of non-CFSP external relations? Fifth and finally, what is the future of specific rules and procedures for CFSP matters within the legal framework in light of legal basis and competence developments?

For the first question, the need to probe unique specificities of CFSP matters is essential due to the specific characteristics of CFSP matters contained in the TEU, namely Articles 23 to 46. Given that the CFSP chapter in the treaties cannot be read in isolation from the other provisions located in the TFEU, the interaction between the differentiated set of external relations provisions will be probed to determine if CFSP matters are sufficiently labelled as being separate and distinct. For the second question, given the unique decision-making procedures for CFSP matters, in that they remain within the Council, it is probed to what extent this separate regime has affected actors beyond the Council within the EU legal order. More specifically, two institutions, the Parliament and the Court, are investigated to see if they are adequately equipped with the appropriate legal instruments and jurisdiction to conduct themselves as real actors in CFSP matters.

[57] For an extensive study of the Common Security and Defence Policy as a stand-alone area of Union law, see, Panos Koutrakos, *The EU Common Security and Defence Policy* (Oxford University Press, 2013).

[58] This has been covered comprehensively elsewhere. See, Christina Eckes, *EU Counter-Terrorist Policies and Fundamental Rights: The Case of Individual Sanctions* (Oxford University Press, 2009).

[59] For an initial overview of your sanctions being conducted from an EU legal standpoint, see, Tarcisio Gazzini and Ester Herlin-Karnell, 'Restrictive Measures Adopted by the EU from the Standpoint of International and EU Law' (2011) 36 *European Law Review* 798.

In answering the third question, the book explores the legal specifics of CFSP matters as to whether a particular international agreement opened, negotiated and concluded by the Union is to sit on a CFSP legal basis in the TEU, or to find an alternative non-CFSP legal basis located in the TFEU. The significance of whether a CFSP legal basis is being used simply to bypass the constitutional prerogatives of other institutions is a pertinent question, deserving of thorough analysis. Penultimately, for the fourth question, the book probes whether the Parliament, as one of the democratic legitimisers of Union action, and the Court, if it possesses adequate judicial jurisdiction, have an appropriate level of involvement in CFSP matters. In asking whether CFSP matters should remain solely at Council level or should involve a more pluralist array of actors to ensure institutional balance, the modalities of both parliamentary and judicial actions will shed light on the particular conundrums of power balance in CFSP matters. Lastly, on the fifth question, the longevity of CFSP matters, as its own specifically defined field within EU external relations is probed in light of developments that have taken place, with a particular emphasis on the post-Lisbon changes. Several happenings will expose the ongoing legal basis issues and competence disputes that have been central to CFSP matters, posing new challenges to the Union's constitutional order.

1.2.6. Outline

To answer each of the above questions in detail, the book is divided into seven chapters, each of which are set out to answer the aforementioned research questions in a manner that provides analysis, insight, and reason. This chapter has provided a brief introduction to CFSP matters and concludes with an overview of how CFSP matters are central to understanding the legal nature of EU external relations. Chapter 2, sets out the history of CFSP matters from the perspective of EU constitutional law. Without delving into the historical aspects of EU external relations and its legal regime, it would be difficult to construe an image of why and how CFSP, as a policy and legal field, came about and how it has achieved its existing status. It contextualises the history of EU external relations law and probes the constitutional framework of the CFSP provisions. In adopting a legal historical approach, it becomes apparent why CFSP matters have ended up as a legal construction.

Chapter 3 builds on the foundations of EU external relations, discussing the modern legal aspects of CFSP matters. The starting point is an analysis of the types of legal instruments that are used by the actors in CFSP matters. The post-Lisbon CFSP framework allows for simplified CFSP Decisions, as opposed to pre-Lisbon Joint Actions and Common Positions, which has ramifications for the limits for when a CFSP legal basis is permitted to be used for EU external actions. Through the understanding of the current legal forces operable in CFSP matters, the ultimate scenario when legal and political forces come together is seen and lays up the ability to discuss CFSP matters through an institutional lens.

Chapter 4 analyses the role of the Parliament in CFSP matters, given it is an interlocutor within the Union's decision-making and institutional framework. Given the non-legislative status of CFSP matters, thereby excluding the Parliament from any meaningful role on face value, the chapter identifies the different legal methods used by the Parliament in its institutitonal position to attempt to become a 'decision-maker', as opposed to a 'decision-receiver'. By examining the case law in which it has litigated, as in *Chernobyl*,[60] to the later cases such as *Mauritius* and *Tanzania*,[61] the extent to which Parliament has been indirectly changing the breadth of CFSP action is examined.

Chapter 5 leads onto the role of the Court. The involvement of the Court in CFSP matters has been deliberately condensed by the Member States to be less than that of the Court's jurisdiction with regard to other non-CFSP external relations. Despite this restriction on the Court's jurisdiction, it is nonetheless tasked with a number of duties, including attempts in individual cases to define the limit between CFSP legal bases in the TEU and non-CFSP legal bases in the TFEU. The post-Lisbon border policing duties imposed upon the Court will help to examine the true scope of its jurisdiction in CFSP matters, demonstrating the derogation on the Court's jurisdiction has been narrowly construed.

Chapter 6 examines the other factors that feed into CFSP matters. Through a normative framework, by looking at legal rules through primary and secondary law to evaluate the true democratic and accountable nature of CFSP, a picture emerges of whether it is right and proper that the institutional balance in CFSP matters accounts for how the policy field is utilised as an external relations instrument. There is a close link between legitimation in a democratic fashion and encouraging the need for supranational actors. Asking to what extent CFSP matters can be considered democratic and accountable from a supranational perspective, guided by a concern that traditional intergovernmentalism can weaken EU institutions; has an impact on the legal workings of CFSP matters. Accordingly, the chapter asks whether it is problematic if the deliberate exclusion of the Parliament and the Court in CFSP matters is justified in the 'depillarised' legal order.

In conclusion, Chapter 7 considers the durability of the legal dimension of CFSP matters as legally constructed in light of the changes seen in EU constitutional law. A *communautaire*-ian approach is adopted, projecting what the future of the law of EU foreign policy will look like, as the shape of Union law continues to evolve in practice. By veering away from the *lex lata* and refocusing on *lex ferenda*, the pressures on the 'specific rules and procedures' of CFSP matters will continue to see the legal field evolving to cater for new demands. Decisively, a comprehensive overview is recounted given the issues addressed throughout the book and offers concluding remarks to make the case for how CFSP matters, as a

[60] Case C-70/88, *Parliament v Council*, ECLI:EU:C:1990:217 and ECLI:EU:C:1991:373 ('*Chernobyl*').

[61] Case C-658/11, *Parliament v Council*, ECLI:EU:C:2014:2025 ('*Mauritius*'), and Case C-263/14, *Parliament v Council*, ECLI:EU:C:2016:435 ('*Tanzania*').

special area of Union law, should no longer exist, and should be amalgamated with the Union's other external relations policies and instruments.

1.3. Conclusion

This book is the story of power through law. Through its narrative, it will become evident that reform of the primary law with respect to CFSP matters is necessary given the developments in the field and the subsequent interpretations that the various institutions have made. Foreign policy, as a polity beyond a nation state, is still unusual internationally, making CFSP matters an exceptional area of the law. It is therefore remarkable that the EU legal order exists for foreign policy actions that now, through the Union, conduct external action under a single legal framework – the EU treaties.

Despite the Treaty of Lisbon being in effect for several years, EU external action is still on the move, with constitutional implications for actions always at stake. The essence of EU policies, whether or not it is a CFSP matter, implies that many institutions have a role to play. This inevitably presents coherence problems, both in theory, as well as in practice.[62] CFSP matters, fitting within EU external relations law and EU constitutional law more generally, means that several themes shine through. First, the substance of CFSP matters; second, the institutions in CFSP matters; and third, the procedures of CFSP matters. The law of CFSP matters, as a 'distinct sub-system' of Union law, is unique[63] striving for its objectives, representative of Europe's geopolitical interests.

Given the ever-growing complexity of global issues facing leading actors around the world, including the EU, the overlap of internal and external dimensions of policy fields for the EU will only increase. The law of EU external relations is an ever-expanding area. Its goals, aims and ultimate influence are very much evolving. Legal battles have knock-on effects in the political realm and thus turn into legal changes. What emerges is a 'recurrent degree of procedural specialisation' within the law.[64] In CFSP matters, pressures between decision-making and the functioning of institutions are put into perspective on the issues they face on legal grounds, and the effect they have on the overall legal basis for EU external action. Political actors, not legal ones, will decide the future of CFSP matters. However, law has guided and will continue to guide the process. Through the analysis in this book, the issues and challenges will be brought to light that will question the future direction of the law of EU foreign policy.

[62] Stephan Marquardt, 'The Institutional Framework, Legal Instruments and Decision-Making Procedures' in Steven Blockmans and Panos Koutrakos (eds), *Research Handbook on the EU's Common Foreign and Security Policy* (Edward Elgar, 2018) p 43.

[63] De Witte (n 13) p 61.

[64] Christophe Hillion, 'Conferral, Cooperation and Balance in the Institutional Framework of EU External Action' in Marise Cremona (ed), *Structural Principles in EU External Relations Law* (Hart Publishing, 2018) p 133.

2

The History of the Common Foreign and Security Policy

To fully account for the understanding of external relations and how each of the institutions is placed, it is both necessary and prudent to examine the history and emergence of CFSP matters all the way from the early foundations of the Union, to European Political Cooperation (EPC), and the respective Treaty developments up to the present day. This is done by giving due consideration to the difficult delineation of CFSP and non-CFSP matters in EU external relations. As shall be discussed, whilst the pillars have been abandoned formally, it is but a metaphor,[1] as special provisions still exist for CFSP matters when compared to other areas of external relations. The chapter concludes by asserting that, while the pillarisation of external relations was formally introduced in the Treaty of Maastricht and later abandoned at the Treaty of Lisbon, in practice, the separate pillars continue to be apparent on closer reading of the treaties. CFSP matters continues to be an outlier in terms of institutional involvement in external relations, in contrast with the regular functioning of decision-making in the Union today.

2.1. Introduction

EU external relations law is a multi-faceted topic. Not only is it CFSP matters, but it also encapsulates the Common Commercial Policy (CCP), development cooperation and the external dimensions of many internal policies. As such, the definition of EU external relations varies. One way, it is EU policies that 'have a dimension external to the European Union'.[2] More elaborated versions are there but, legally speaking, the law of external relations is internal Union law. The Union is constructed on an elaborate and refined system of governance based on a tiered structure of intersecting and intertwining authorities. Whilst basic legal documents can work for some entities, be they states, international organisations or

[1] Morten Broberg and Rass Holdgaard, 'EU Development Cooperation Post-Lisbon: Main Constitutional Challenges' (2015) 40 *European Law Review* 349 at 363.

[2] Marise Cremona, 'EU External Relations and the Law' in Dennis Patterson and Anna Södersten (eds), *A Companion to European Union Law and International Law* (John Wiley & Sons, 2016) p 373.

otherwise, others may need a much more detailed legal framework in which to operate, such as the Union.

Acting as the constitutional framework, the treaties of the Union are a complex legal set up. A vast amount of knowledge is required to fully grasp its contents. The treaties serve a range of purposes and bring forward legal substance to the intentions of the High Contracting Parties, but they also elucidate institutional variances within different Union policies. Designed in such a way that the separation of powers is divergent enough not concentrate too much power into singular institutional control, the actors reinforce each other to ensure they have separate and collective responsibility for the exercise and control of powers in which each is competent to act. In running through the history of EU external relations law, the constitutional nature of the field will become much more apparent.

Foreign policy and external relations in any real substantive way did not form the basis for the initial treaties that founded today's Union. This is curious, albeit not entirely surprising when it is considered that it was foreign policy issues, along with regional security concerns, that initially brought the Member States together. The Member States took it upon themselves, albeit with external influence from the United States, to come together in common spirit to develop a Union, even if it was initially to only encompass a limited number of fields. Whilst the Union is 'in many ways a fully-fledged legal system',[3] it still has several significant drawbacks.

The international legal position of the Union and its external competence is built upon its internal competence in many areas. Whereas trade has been central to the development of the Union's external relations, Member States initially had problems with the Union being involved in the fields of foreign and security policy,[4] thus giving rise to the continued issues that surround it today. In earlier days, the Union was beginning to cooperate in a limited range of fields. Starting with internal trade and the common market; it was consequently inevitable that foreign policy would, in time, make its way into the fold. In pursuing its goals, incorporating foreign policy was the first in a number of steps to help the Union achieve the goals laid down by its treaties.

Within the original treaties, there was meagreness regarding a defined competence set for the EU in external relations.[5] Before the Treaty of Lisbon, there was no singular collective view of what EU external relations were[6] and what they should look like. Even now, the external relations policies of the Union have never had a particular end-goal in mind; and instead, they have operated on an apparent

[3] Inger-Johanne Sand, 'European Legal Method: A New Teleology, Law-in-Context, a New Legal Realism or Hybrid Law?' in Ulla Neergaard and Ruth Nielsen (eds), *European Legal Method – Towards a New European Legal Realism?* (Djøf Publishing, 2013) p 214.

[4] Paul Craig, 'Democracy and Rule-Making Within the EC: An Empirical and Normative Assessment' (1997) 3 *European Law Journal* 105 at 107.

[5] Geert De Baere and Panos Koutrakos, 'The Interactions between the Legislature and the Judiciary in EU External Relations' in Philip Syrpis (ed), *The Judiciary, the Legislature and the EU Internal Market* (Cambridge University Press, 2012) p 243.

[6] Marise Cremona, 'The Union as a Global Actor: Roles, Models and Identity' (2004) 41 *Common Market Law Review* 553 at 566.

ad hoc basis. The open-ended nature of CFSP matters leaves the way clear for potential use in arising circumstances. Resultingly, what becomes evident is that EU foreign policy has been a stumbling block from an integration perspective, consistently lagging behind other policy fields in terms of its orientation towards a true single institutional framework with institutional balance.

To the untrained eye, the EU has a completely dysfunctional system of foreign policy external relations, both politically and legally. What constitutes EU foreign policy has been a deep question that was pondered during the formative years of the EU legal order. Adopted by the six original Member States, early attempts at a pan-European foreign policy sought to bring about greater political unity on issues being dealt with by their foreign ministries. In international law, 'it is conventional to think of foreign and security policy as a realm of sovereign wills and national interests *par excellence*. If law should play a role in it, it is only as an instrument for the expression and realisation of those wills and interests',[7] yet, the Union was something different.

The *ERTA* judgment from the Court in 1971 has been proclaimed as one of the most significant cases in external relations law to date,[8] acting as a major contributory factor in building the Union's external relations, allowing for the accumulation of implied external powers derived from internal competence. *ERTA* was not a Community measure and was done outside the legal order.[9] Whilst the negotiations were ongoing, the Council passed a Regulation on matters close to what Member States were doing outside the legal order. The Commission, excluded from the non-Union negotiations, felt this warranted a case being taken at the Court. Essentially, the Court found that the Community had the external authority through objectives that 'equally flow' from internal provisions in the treaties. The sheer scope of the *ERTA* doctrine caused some level of consternation and, as such, was refined by the *Kramer* judgment,[10] which was the Court demonstrating a reasonable response to pressure from Member States.[11] This acknowledged that Member States retained a 'transitional power' for international agreements entered into on their own,[12] when the Union had not yet acted.

[7] Martti Koskenniemi, 'International Law Aspects of the Common Foreign and Security Policy' in Martti Koskenniemi (ed), *International Law Aspects of the European Union* (Martinus Nijhoff Publishers, 1998) p 27.

[8] Case C-22/70, *Commission v Council*, ECLI:EU:C:1971:32 ('*European Road Transport Agreement*'), better known as '*ERTA*' or sometimes '*AETR*'. See, Piet Eeckhout, 'Bold Constitutionalism and Beyond' in Miguel Poiares Maduro and Loïc Azoulai (eds), *The Past and Future of EU Law: The Classics of EU Law Revisited on the 50th Anniversary of the Rome Treaty* (Hart Publishing, 2010) p 218.

[9] Bernard Rudden and Diarmuid Rossa Phelan, *Basic Community Cases* 2nd edition, (Oxford University Press, 1997) p 247.

[10] Cases C-3/76, 4/76 and 6/76, *Cornelis Kramer and others*, ECLI:EU:C:1976:114 ('*Kramer*'). For more, see, Derrick Wyatt, 'Competence of the Community, Internal and External' (1977) 2 *European Law Review* 41 and KR Simmonds, 'External Relations Power of the EEC: A Recent Ruling of the European Court' (1977) 26 *International and Comparative Law Quarterly* 208.

[11] Joseph HH Weiler, 'The External Legal Relations of Non-Unitary Actors: Mixity and the Federal Principle' in David O'Keeffe and Henry G Schermers (eds), *Mixed Agreements* (Kluwer Law and Taxation Publishers, 1983) p 82.

[12] Derrick Wyatt and Alan Dashwood, *The Substantive Law of the EEC* (Sweet and Maxwell, 1980) p 74.

Today, the Union operates under integrated structures, and the previous distinction between the European Community and the European Union having now been done away with.[13] However, a marked tension can be exposed in the development of the Union between organised co-operation and converging confederation. In the case of the Union's external relations, this can be broadly categorised as CFSP matters for the former and non-CFSP matters for the latter. Under existing arrangements in place since the Treaty of Lisbon, the Union's external action has attempted to be more coherent in its practice, in addition to its legal wording and structure. This integrated construction, spanning a number of policy areas, has tried to ensure a more clear-cut method for how the Union is to operate externally. What became immediately clear was that the division between the intergovernmental-esque character of CFSP matters, versus the supranational element of external relations, had still not quite fully disappeared.

2.2. Formative Days, Pillarisation, and Modern Times

In an historical tracing, an identification of the critical junctures of the integration of EU foreign policy and external relations can be made. Furthermore, the conduct of external relations by EU Member States acting unilaterally or multilaterally is premised on the notion of several obligations levied by the treaties. The first phase of soft intergovernmental coordination covered the EPC up to the 1987 Single European Act. The second phase, hard yet rule-bound intergovernmental coordination, ran from then until around the time of the Treaty of Nice. The third phase covered 'supranationalism'.[14] This may have been a premature call, since CFSP matters are not yet supranational, although, as shall be evidenced, are leaning in that direction.

The 1957 Treaty of Rome could not have foreseen a scenario where a distinct foreign policy or external relations would become any way integrated into the rule and decision-making process of the Union. External relations, never mind any form of foreign policy, were not broached in a real manner and there were no real provisions in the initial primary law of the Union regarding foreign policy. This was the custom at the time, yet still today, national constitutions of Member States only have brief foreign policy descriptions, leaving a wide margin of discretion for actors within that particular policy.

A political union has long been on the table, but the extent of such a Union's external relations is a more complex picture. Trade was, and continues to be, the mother of all policies. External policies of the then Community focused

[13] TEU, Article 1: 'The Union shall replace and succeed the European Community.'

[14] Wolfgang Wessels, 'Theoretical Perspectives. CFSP beyond the Supranational and Intergovernmental Dichotomy' in Dieter Mahncke, Alicia Ambos and Christopher Reynolds (eds), *European Foreign Policy: From Rhetoric to Reality?* (PIE-Peter Lang, 2004) p 71.

on the policies surrounding trade, leading the way on its CCP. Attempting to align cooperation between Member States on internal matters was central to this integrational effort; and any ancillary items like foreign policy were left for a later stage. The Union's focus was primarily economic, owing to its previous incarnation as the European Coal and Steel Community (ECSC).

Given that foreign policy fell into a category of 'high politics', with economics as 'low politics', it was a field that in the earlier days, was the preserve of Member States.[15] While the Union was initially concerned with fostering cooperation between European states, its focus gradually shifted onto other matters. One way of delving into policies, such as foreign policy, was to justify further reach by stating there was an economic necessity to it.[16] The establishment of a unified foreign policy in its very essence is exceptional, as it 'represent[ed] an attempt by several European states to coordinate national foreign policies, to construct a common policy in the field of foreign affairs…and to act visibly, decisively and collectively in support of this policy'.[17]

2.2.1. Earliest Days

It was not so long ago that a foreign policy of the Union would have been bitterly contested by its Member States.[18] Pre-EPC, attempts at foreign, security, and defence cooperation between European states on a multilateral level never really got off the ground. The European Defence Community (EDC), an attempt at building a pan-European existence to Soviet power to the east, failed to gather any steam in the 1950s. Planned between 1950, ending with the ratification of a Treaty in 1952,[19] defence integration failed in 1954 as France.[20] While this may have been perceived as a 'humiliating federalist failure',[21] further attempts at early integration were made.

[15] Joseph HH Weiler, *The Transnational Setting: The European Parliament and Its Foreign Affairs Committees*, vol 2 (Cedam/Oceana, 1982) p 36.

[16] FS Northedge, 'British Foreign Policy in a Community Context' in Kenneth J Twitchett (ed), *Europe and the World: The External Relations of the Common Market* (St Martin's Press, 1976) p 181.

[17] Ben Tonra, *The Europeanisation of National Foreign Policy: Dutch, Danish and Irish Foreign Policy in the European Union* (Ashgate Publishing, 2001) p 273.

[18] Joseph HH Weiler, 'The Transformation of Europe' in Joseph HH Weiler (ed), *The Constitution of Europe: 'Do the New Clothes Have an Emperor?' and Other Essays on European Integration* (Cambridge University Press, 1999) p 11.

[19] See Chapter 5, 'The EDC Treaty and its Associated Protocols, Agreements and Declarations', Edward Fursdon, *The European Defence Community: A History* (Macmillan, 1980), pp 150–90.

[20] Martin Trybus, 'The Vision of the European Defence Community and a Common Defence for the European Union' in Martin Trybus and Nigel White (eds), *European Security Law* (Oxford University Press, 2007). p. 13. See also, Martin Trybus, *European Union Law and Defence Integration* (Hart Publishing, 2005). pp. 22–23.

[21] Hjalte Rasmussen, 'After Legal Pluralism and Integration: Could Disintegration Follow?' in Peter Blume (ed), *Legal Issues at the Dawn of the New Millennium* (Djøf Publishing, 1999) p 80.

Alongside this was also a proposed European Political Community (EPC) that, whilst market-based, was to 'regulate the foreign relations of the [M]ember [S]tates'.[22] This proposal also went nowhere. It was followed some years later by the Fouchet Plan, a vision in 1961 that was also botched, but played some role in the later vision of a foreign policy for Europe. The Davignon Report, also known as the Luxembourg Report of 1970,[23] set in train the eventual development of the EPC. In a roundabout manner, by stating that the Union's economic role was pivotal, it thus indirectly linked trade and foreign policy together for the first time,[24] cementing the view that everything ancillary to internal trade between Member States had ultimately to lead back to the initial premise of Member States being in a Community together. This link between matters integral to the functioning of the Union such as trade, with an ancillary subject such as foreign policy, had the potential to spark future linkages, both practically, and legally.

The Copenhagen Report of 1973, including the newly acceded United Kingdom, Ireland, and Denmark as the first enlargement of the Union, added what had already been built upon to date. Much of this earlier window-dressing was rehashed, but at that time, no legal effects from the Copenhagen Report were in any way intended.[25] The EPC, also known as PoCo,[26] was the first time Member States began to share guarded policies. This was facilitated by COREU,[27] using telegram and fax machines. It was at this juncture that EPC began to become of greater interest to scholars.[28] It ran in parallel with the Union, but was deliberately kept apart from the legal instruments of the then Community's institutions. In addition, there were no legal limits on what could fall within EPC,[29] yet it became an 'opinion-building and decision-making system',[30] which later facilitated it finding a legal basis.

[22] Richard T Griffiths, 'Europe's First Constitution: The European Political Community, 1952–1954' in Stephen Martin (ed), *The Construction of Europe: Essays in Honour of Emile Noel* (Kluwer Academic Publishers, 1994) p 20.

[23] Report by the Foreign Ministers of the Member States on the Problems of Political Unification (Bulletin of the European Communities. November 1970, N° 11. Luxembourg) (Davignon Report).

[24] Panos Koutrakos, *Trade, Foreign Policy and Defence in EU Constitutional Law: The Legal Regulation of Sanctions, Exports of Dual-Use Goods and Armaments* (Hart Publishing, 2001) p 9.

[25] Eileen Denza, *The Intergovernmental Pillars of the European Union* (Oxford University Press, 2002) p 37.

[26] David AO Edward and Robert Lane, *Edward and Lane on European Union Law* (Edward Elgar, 2013) p 60 (section 2.47).

[27] The acronym derives from the French '*Correspondence européenne*'. See Federica Bicchi and Caterina Carta, 'The COREU Network and the Circulation of Information Within EU Foreign Policy' (2012) 34 *Journal of European Integration* 465.

[28] For example, see, Alfred Pijpers, Elfriede Regelsberger and Wolfgang Wessels (eds), *European Political Cooperation in the 1980s: A Common Foreign Policy for Western Europe?* (Martinus Nijhoff Publishers, 1988). For an excellent history of EPC from a non-legal perspective, see, Simon J Nuttall, *European Political Co-Operation* (Oxford University Press, 1992).

[29] Jürgen Schwarze, 'Towards a European Foreign Policy – Legal Aspects' in Johan K De Vree, Peter Coffey and Richard H Lauwaars (eds), *Towards a European Foreign Policy: Legal, Economic and Political Dimensions* (Martinus Nijhoff Publishers, 1987) p 75.

[30] Otto Von der Gablentz, 'Luxembourg Revisited or The Importance of European Political Cooperation' (1979) 16 *Common Market Law Review* 685 at 689.

The Parliament slated political cooperation on foreign policy matters being done outside the then Community and called for an 'end [to] the artificial distinction' between EPC and Community affairs.[31] The separateness of EPC and Community affairs is best demonstrated in an example of one 1973 incident. At the time, the 'Conference of the Foreign Affairs Ministers' discussed EPC matters once every six months. This would take place in the Member State holding the Presidency of the Council. In 1973, the Member States met in Copenhagen for EPC matters on the morning of a given day. However, when it came time to discuss Community matters, the same Ministers left Copenhagen and flew to Brussels[32] to mark the formal distinction that certain Member States insisted upon.

The 1976 Tindemans Report on the early discussion of moving from a Community to a Union cast some doubt on how a European foreign policy would work. Notably, it noted that the coordination of EU policies in the field 'would not…be adequate within the framework of the European Union'.[33] Instead, what was envisaged was a much bolder framework beyond mere coordination, and to achieve positions by majority. However, such ideas did not gather much support at the time. Continued activity outside the EU legal framework took place. This made the structure of EPC difficult to legally place, given the 'ill defined agreements or arrangements',[34] cementing its informality.

2.2.2. 1980s

Some years passed, and the 1981 London Report acknowledged what had long been already known. It stated that, the 'value that European political cooperation has steadily intensified and its scope continually broadened. This development has contributed to the ultimate objective of European Union'. Despite not a great deal of understanding of EPC at the time, with most accounts running based on the reports at their various intervals which were drafted, amended and ultimately approved unanimously by Member States, it nonetheless was intrinsically testing the early legal value of EU foreign policy. The significance of these reports and the EPC process as a whole led to its formalisation and subsequently, the establishment of CFSP matters on a legal footing.

[31] 'C 36/32. Resolution on European Political Cooperation. European Parliament. Minutes of Proceedings of the Sitting of Thursday, 19 January 1978'.

[32] Eric Stein and Louis Henkin, 'Towards a European Foreign Policy? – The European Foreign Affairs System from the Perspective of the United States Constitution' in Mauro Cappelletti, Monica Seccombe and Joseph HH Weiler (eds), *Integration Through Law: Europe and the American Federal Experience*, vols 1: Methods, Tools and Institutions. Book 3: *Forces and Potential for a European Identity* (De Gruyter, 1986) p 63.

[33] European Union. Report by Mr. Leo Tindemans, Prime Minister of Belgium, to the European Council. Bulletin of the European Communities, Supplement 1/76 (the 'Tindemans Report') (Office for Official Publications of the European Communities 1976) p 15.

[34] Jacques Steenbergen, 'Legal Instruments of External Policies of the EC' in Johan K De Vree, Peter Coffey and Richard H Lauwaars (eds), *Towards a European Foreign Policy: Legal, Economic and Political Dimensions* (Martinus Nijhoff Publishers, 1987).

The 1983 Stuttgart Declaration by the European Council was another step towards the Europeanisation of foreign policy. It promised in a Solemn Declaration on European Union to 'strengthen and develop European Political Cooperation through the elaboration and adoption of joint positions and joint action, on the basis of intensified consultations, in the area of foreign policy, including the coordination of the positions of Member States on the political and economic aspects of security, so as to promote and facilitate the progressive development of such positions and actions in a growing number of foreign policy fields'.[35] Such capacity demonstrated huge vision for the time.

Shortly after, EPC was brought into Union law through the 1987 Single European Act, albeit with unanimous voting within the Council. Separately, it expanded the place of majority voting within the Council for some policy areas that were already in the domain of EU affairs. This in itself was welcomed, as it 'greatly raise[d] the level of integration in the normative-institutional sense'.[36] However, the Single European Act did not please everyone, with it even being called 'fundamentally deceptive'.[37] Yet it brought in a permanent secretariat to support the work of the EPC, primarily to assist the rotating Presidency of the Council in formulating basic elements of a functioning policy.

Not only substantively, the very name of the Single European Act was labelled as 'rather awkward'.[38] It was there, amongst other things to 'foster a culture of cooperation',[39] between Member States and EU institutions. Title III stood as a commanding feature of the Treaty, given the strong integrative measures it took in the realm of foreign policy. That was despite some level of understanding that the integration of foreign policy into the Single European Act did not itself widen the scope of Union activity. Rather, it merely allowed the potential for it, or in other words, depended on 'what…happen[ed] elsewhere',[40] with respect to other Union policies.

Put another way, the Single European Act provided some codification of what was then an established practice. Whilst it brought about the introduction of 'Common Positions' which were utilised up to the Treaty of Lisbon in 2009, they merely served for 'a point for reference'[41] and could not be used at the time as a binding legal act.

[35] No 6/1983. Solemn Declaration on European Union, Stuttgart, June 1983 (Reproduced from the Bulletin of the European Communities).

[36] Eric Stein, 'International Integration and Democracy: No Love at First Sight' (2001) 95 *American Journal of International Law* 489 at 517.

[37] Pierre Pescatore, 'Some Critical Remarks on the "Single European Act"' (1987) 24 *Common Market Law Review* 9 at 11.

[38] Wolfgang Wessels, 'EPC after the Single European Act: Towards a European Foreign Policy via Treaty Obligations?' in Martin Holland (ed), *The Future of European Political Cooperation: Essays on Theory and Practice* (St Martin's Press, 1991) p 153.

[39] Panos Koutrakos, 'External Action: Common Commercial Policy, Common Foreign and Defence Policy, Common Security and Defence Policy' in Anthony Arnull and Damian Chalmers (eds), *The Oxford Handbook of European Union Law* (Oxford University Press, 2015) p 281.

[40] Mary T Robinson, 'Tendencies towards a European Foreign Policy' in Jürgen Schwarze and Henry G Schermers (eds), *Structure and Dimensions of European Community Policy* (Nomos, 1988) p 68.

[41] Jean-Claude Piris, *The Lisbon Treaty: A Legal and Political Analysis* (Cambridge University Press, 2010) p 240.

2.2.3. 1990s

The end of 1992, annexed to the Single European Act, was the date set for the establishment of the internal market.[42] This deadline set out when the Single European Act's replacement should have been found and came in the form of the Treaty of Maastricht. The legal framework for the formation of CFSP matters was developed, forming the basis for the three-pillar structure that lasted, formally, up until the 2009 Treaty of Lisbon. The Treaty of Maastricht brought foreign policy coordination further inside the EU legal order, albeit in a special way. In law, it was the codification of a non-EU practice to an EU practice. Whereas the Dutch Presidency of the Council in 1991 had proposed the formative manner of CFSP matters and Justice and Home Affairs (JHA) matters be integrated within the unified Union structures,[43] the proposal was not taken up. Rather, placed within the second pillar, CFSP matters were given intergovernmental character, with rules, against that of the first pillar – Community matters.

Both CFSP matters and JHA matters were extremely different to the Union at the time, so much so, that they were established away from the then 'Community Method'. The pillarisation of CFSP matters, or its separateness, did not mean it was lawless or lacked substantive basis in Union law. In fact, it was only from the Treaty of Maastricht that foreign policy became truly legal from a Union and Member State perspective. Indeed, this time period saw the EU enter a new political territory.[44] It was under the Treaty of Maastricht that the now defunct pillarised formulation of the European Community was created, ministerial meetings from EPC and the Council of the Communities (General Affairs) were merged[45] and under the new three-pillar structure of the EU, all CFSP matters came under the second pillar.

As a separate and distinct pillar dealing with all foreign policy matters, including issues pertaining to defence, CFSP matters were given intergovernmental stature, albeit rule-bound within the EU legal order, away from the involvement of most of the Union's institutions. The Treaty of Maastricht was, in effect, the 'turning point' for the establishment of the law of EU foreign policy as it integrated within the institutional framework.[46] It was also the first occasion

[42] See, Akos G Toth, 'The Legal Status of the Declarations Annexed to the Single European Act' (1986) 23 *Common Market Law Review* 803.

[43] Sandra Lavenex and William Wallace, 'Justice and Home Affairs: Towards a European Public Order?' in Helen Wallace, William Wallace and Marc Pollack (eds), *Policy-Making in the European Union* (Oxford University Press, 2005) p 461.

[44] Stephan Stetter, *EU Foreign and Interior Policies: Cross-Pillar Politics and the Social Constructions of Sovereignty* (Routledge, 2007) p 37.

[45] Simon J Nuttall, 'The Foreign and Security Policy Provisions of the Maastricht Treaty: Their Potential for the Future' in Jörg Monar, Werner Ungerer and Wolfgang Wessels (eds), *The Maastricht Treaty on European Union: Legal Complexity and Political Dynamic* (European Interuniversity Press, 1993) p 134.

[46] Jan Wouters and Hanne Cuyckens, 'Festina Lente: CFSP from Maastricht to Lisbon and Beyond' in Maartje De Visser and Anne Pieter Van Der Mei (eds), *The Treaty on European Union 1993–2013: Reflections from Maastricht* (Intersentia, 2013) p. 223.

upon which matters of security and defence were given any sort of legal recognition within the Union's legal texts.[47] The General Affairs and External Relations Council was the working forum for Foreign Ministers, with the rotating Presidency chairing the proceedings.[48] The legal provisions for CFSP matters, the new second pillar, were 'particularly detailed',[49] and maintained intergovernmental cooperation on a 'free-standing' basis,[50] albeit guided by the rules of the treaties, demonstrating its unusual legal character. Given this complexity, it has been claimed that the Treaty of Maastricht increased the institutional fragmentation already in existence.[51]

With CFSP matters as the second pillar, separated from the first pillar, the real substance of the then Community law and its separateness was felt from an early stage. It was even claimed that this signalled a 'drift away from supranational structures'.[52] The Treaty of Maastricht as a whole envisaged a lot more contestation between different institutions compared to what actually transpired. The unity goal of the Treaty of Maastricht, to the greatest extent possible by the institutions, was introduced at a time of relative harmony of common purpose. The Parliament, along with the Commission, appeared to accept their roles, despite suggested amendments.[53] There were inherent contradictions from the outset of pillarisation as, for example, the Treaty of Maastricht associated CFSP matters with the Delegations of the European Commission;[54] despite the Commission having no direct role in CFSP matters. However, the reach of the Commission did not extend any further. The pillarisation by the Treaty of Maastricht bypassed the procedures at the time for a thorough involvement of the Parliament. When the second pillar was in use for international agreements, such acts stated they were 'Acts adopted under Title V of the EU Treaty'[55] which, post-Lisbon, is the CFSP title. Whilst it has been noted that the valediction from EPC to CFSP matters as a second pillar was 'painful and problematic',[56] it was an inevitable step into the EU legal order.

[47] Shira Becker-Alon, *The Communitarian Dimension of the European Union's Common Foreign and Security Policy.* (Nomos, 2011) p 77.

[48] Christian Kaunert and Kamil Zwolski, *The EU as a Global Security Actor: A Comprehensive Analysis Beyond CFSP and JHA* (Palgrave Macmillan, 2013) p 62.

[49] David O'Keeffe, 'From Maastricht to the 1996 Intergovernmental Conference: The Challenges Facing the Union' (1994) 21 *Legal Issues of Economic Integration* 135 at 144.

[50] Paul Berman, 'The European Union – I: Development, Structure, and Decision-Making' in Sir Ivor Roberts (ed), *Satow's Diplomatic Practice* 6th edition (Oxford University Press, 2009) p 376.

[51] Bruno De Witte, 'The Decision-Making Process' in Dennis Patterson and Anna Södersten (eds), *A Companion to European Union Law and International Law* (John Wiley & Sons, 2016) p 97.

[52] Mary T Robinson, 'Constitutional Shifts in Europe and the United States: Learning From Each Other' (1996) 32 *Stanford Journal of International Law* 1 at 10.

[53] Philip Raworth, 'A Timid Step Forwards: Maastricht and the Democratisation of the European Community' (1994) 19 *European Law Review* 16 at 26.

[54] Michael Bruter, 'Diplomacy without a State: The External Delegations of the European Commission' (1999) 6 *Journal of European Public Policy* 183 at 195.

[55] Ramses A Wessel, 'Cross-Pillar Mixity: Combining Competences in the Conclusion of EU International Agreements' in Christophe Hillion and Panos Koutrakos (eds), *Mixed Agreements Revisited: The EU and its Member States in the World* (Hart Publishing, 2010) p 37.

[56] Roy H Ginsberg, 'Conceptualizing the European Union as an International Actor: Narrowing the Theoretical Capability-Expectations Gap' (1999) 37 *Journal of Common Market Studies* 429 at 431.

Yet, expectations of CFSP matters 'fixing' EPC were initially very low.[57] Once inside the treaties, CFSP matters had to progress in such a way that they did not stumble upon other areas of competence within the treaties and work in harmony with other policy fields to ensure its objectives were similarly met. Such institutional issues 'dogged' CFSP in its initial years,[58] between institutional allotment, objective setting, and investing in a whole new policy domain. The conversion of EPC to CFSP matters at the Treaty of Maastricht and the establishment of the second pillar meant foreign policy coordination was not supranationalised. However, four key differences on the transition from EPC to CFSP matters were identified:[59] a stronger emphasis on adopting Common Positions; the entering of security into the framework; the procedure for cooperation being enhanced; and the entering of EU institutions. This latter element has been the key to understanding the modern dynamics of CFSP matters.

2.2.4. Turn of the Millennium

CFSP matters were once referred to as a metaphor relating to a cathedral around the time of the Treaty of Amsterdam: the main door was the Community treaties, with CFSP matters being one of the smaller entrances.[60] Ongoing institutional deficiencies in other fields meant that enhancing the provisions relating to CFSP matters at the time of the Treaty of Amsterdam was not a real possibility. However, this is only a minor factor considering there would have been great reluctance from Member States, as few of them as there were at the time, to renounce certain national foreign policy and external relations prerogatives. One of the more significant changes to CFSP matters at the Treaty of Amsterdam was the creation of the High Representative for Foreign and Security Policy. It can be stated that, at the time, many, if not most of the Member States did not know exactly how this role would pan out in the longer term. The Treaty of Amsterdam did, however, introduce 'Common Strategies' as a new legal instrument within CFSP matters;[61] another item to be added to the 'CFSP toolbox'.[62] With 'byzantine' procedures for reaching a negotiated outcome

[57] Roy H Ginsberg, 'The EU's CFSP: The Politics of Procedure' in Martin Holland (ed), *Common Foreign and Security Policy: The Record and Reforms* (Pinter, 1997) p 12.

[58] William Wallace, 'European Foreign Policy since the Cold War: How Ambitious, How Inhibited?' (2017) 19 *British Journal of Politics and International Relations* 77 at 80.

[59] Martin R Eaton, 'Common Foreign and Security Policy' in David O'Keeffe and Patrick M Twomey (eds), *Legal Issues of the Maastricht Treaty* (Chancery 1994) pp 219–20.

[60] Laurence W Gormley, 'Reflections on the Architecture of the European Union after the Treaty of Amsterdam' in David O'Keeffe and Patrick M Twomey (eds), *Legal Issues of the Amsterdam Treaty* (Hart Publishing, 1999) p 58.

[61] Alan Dashwood, 'External Relations Provisions of the Amsterdam Treaty' (1998) 35 *Common Market Law Review* 1019 at 1030. Replicated in Alan Dashwood, 'External Relations Provisions of the Amsterdam Treaty' in David O'Keeffe and Patrick M Twomey (eds), *Legal Issues of the Amsterdam Treaty* (Hart Publishing, 1999) p 211.

[62] Hylke Dijkstra and Peter Van Elsuwege, 'Representing the EU in the Area of CFSP: Legal and Political Dunamics' in Steven Blockmans and Panos Koutrakos (eds), *Research Handbook on the EU's Common Foreign and Security Policy* (Edward Elgar, 2018) p 47.

on renegotiated treaties[63] and, despite the changes, the Treaty of Amsterdam did not revolutionise either CFSP matters or broader EU external action. There may have been disappointment, despite its slow progression being welcomed.

Shortly after, under Treaty of Nice, the then Article 47 TEU mandated that nothing in the TEU, and therefore CFSP matters, should affect the Communities, implying that CFSP matters should not venture into policies of the treaties, but policies in the treaties could encroach into CFSP. At this juncture, it was said that depillarisation 'would not affect the philosophy of the CFSP rules'.[64] Thus, the Treaty of Nice does not materially change much in CFSP matters. The journey continued with the 2001 Laeken Declaration,[65] which stated '…they [citizens] also want to see Europe more involved in foreign affairs, security and defence, in other words, greater and better coordinated action to deal with trouble spots in and around Europe and in the rest of the world'. Accordingly, less than a decade after CFSP matters had entered into the primary law of the Union as an institutional pillar, reform of CFSP matters was soon on the agenda.

The EU was once on the road to a more coherent regime of external relations through the Constitutional Treaty. CFSP matters were included as an item in the Constitutional Convention ('Convention on the Future of Europe'), the body charged with designing a constitution for Europe, for eventual presentation to the Council. This supranational forum, as opposed to an intergovernmental one, allowed for more debate about reducing the scope of the existing executives in CFSP matters.[66] Not only were the specifics of CFSP matters up for discussion, but it was also an approach to adopting overall reform of the Union's external action.[67] During the negotiations for the Constitutional Treaty, the drafters appeared to be uneasy with 'pigeon-holing' CFSP matters as an exclusive, shared or supporting competence.[68] The Constitutional Treaty intended to make one of the two areas of Union law with intergovernmental character turn more supranational in nature.[69] JHA matters were to be subsumed by the proposed structural changes after the

[63] Andrew Duff (ed), *The Treaty of Amsterdam: Text and Commentary* (Federal Trust 1997) p 124.

[64] Panos Koutrakos, 'Constitutional Idiosyncrasies and Political Realities: The Emerging Security and Defense Policy of the European Union' (2003) 10 *Columbia Journal of European Law* 69 at 73.

[65] European Council, 'Presidency Conclusions: European Council Meeting in Laeken, 14–15 December 2001, SN 300/1/01 REV 1' p 21.

[66] Erik Oddvar Eriksen, *The Unfinished Democratization of Europe* (Oxford University Press, 2009) p 111.

[67] Giovanni Grevi, 'The Institutional Framework of External Action' in Giuliano Amato, Hervé Bribosia and Bruno De Witte (eds), *Genesis and Destiny of the European Constitution: Commentary on the Treaty establishing a Constitution for Europe in the light of the travaux préparatoires and future prospects* (Bruylant, 2007) p 777.

[68] George A Bermann, 'Competences of the Union' in Takis Tridimas and Paolisa Nebbia (eds), *European Union Law for the Twenty-First Century: Rethinking the New Legal Order – Volume 1: Constitutional and Public Law, External Relations* (Hart Publishing, 2004) p 68.

[69] Paul Berman, 'From Laeken to Lisbon: The Origins and Negotiation of the Lisbon Treaty' in Andrea Biondi, Piet Eeckhout and Stefanie Ripley (eds), *EU Law after Lisbon* (Oxford University Press, 2012) p 17.

initial hesitancy located in the Treaty of Amsterdam, which inserted a five-year transition phase for moving from unanimity to QMV.[70] Despite this proposed change in JHA matters, the distinct rules for CFSP matters would have been maintained under the Constitutional Treaty.[71] Whilst enlargement has arguably been the driving force of EU external action,[72] this did not shift the framework of CFSP matters.

The Treaty of Lisbon removed the formal barriers of policies and brought everything together as one Union, viewed one way, integrating CFSP matters into the overall framework of EU external action, but still retaining its distinctiveness – a *de facto* hidden pillar. This reshaping of the treaties, recalling that the Treaty of Lisbon was once dubbed the 'Reform Treaty', had the positive effect of untangling some of the complexities in the Union's external relations, bringing some much-needed clarity and coherence to the fore. Ultimately, the merging of the EU and EC into a single legal entity, abolishing the pillars in the treaties, at least in textual terms, was 'necessary and logical'.[73] By reducing the CFSP pillar into the relative unitary legal order, becoming more streamlined, yet not fully modernised into the treaties, was a step in the right direction.

The retention of CFSP matters in Title V was a compromise for the Treaty of Lisbon,[74] which set out a more visible and distinctive external representation of the Union, particularly for issues typically seen as CFSP matters. Article 21 TEU sets out the external policy objectives of the Union, reminiscing about 'motherhood and apple pie'.[75] The Treaty of Lisbon empowered the Union to define and implement CFSP matters,[76] but despite depillarisation, the status of CFSP being separate but integrated makes it a hybrid-like entity, almost as if it had been changed to a 'horizontal pillar'.[77]

[70] Even that system itself was 'complex'. Steve Peers, 'EU Immigration and Asylum Competence and Decision-Making in the Treaty of Lisbon' (2008) 10 *European Journal of Migration and Law* 219 at 220.

[71] Paul Craig, 'Competence: Clarity, Containment and Consideration' in Ingolf Pernice and Miguel Poiares Maduro (eds), *A Constitution for the European Union: First Comments on the 2003-Draft of the European Convention* (Nomos, 2004) p 87.

[72] Thomas Christiansen, 'The European Union after the Lisbon Treaty: An Elusive "Institutional Balance"?' in Andrea Biondi, Piet Eeckhout and Stefanie Ripley (eds), *EU Law after Lisbon* (Oxford University Press, 2012) p 233.

[73] Ricardo Passos and Stephan Marquardt, 'International Agreements – Competences, Procedures And Judicial Control' In Giuliano Amato, Hervé Bribosia and Bruno De Witte (eds), *Genesis And Destiny Of The European Constitution: Commentary On The Treaty Establishing A Constitution For Europe In The Light Of The Travaux Préparatoires And Future Prospects* (Bruylant, 2007) p 886.

[74] Alan Dashwood, 'What Can Be Salvaged if the Treaty of Lisbon is Lost?' in Mielle Bulterman and others (eds), *Views of European Law from the Mountain: Liber Amicorum Piet Jan Slot* (Kluwer Law International, 2009) p 336.

[75] Alan Dashwood and others, *Wyatt and Dashwood's European Union Law* 6th edition (Hart Publishing, 2011) p 903.

[76] TEU, Article 24(2).

[77] Inge Govaere, 'To Give or To Grab: The Principle of Full, Crippled and Split Conferral of Powers Post-Lisbon' in Marise Cremona (ed), *Structural Principles in EU External Relations Law* (Hart Publishing, 2018) p 79.

2.2.5. The State of Play

The provisions in the treaties on CFSP matters have been amended and adjusted with each of the subsequent treaties after the Treaty of Maastricht. These changes at Amsterdam, Nice and Lisbon all contributed to the change; however, compared to other policies where integration has forged ahead, changes with respect to CFSP matters have taken place at a much slower pace. Member States have been resisting further integration on anything to do with CFSP matters,[78] yet the Treaty of Lisbon nonetheless made some advances in this regard.

Compared to 'a movie in slow motion',[79] the integration of CFSP into non-CFSP matters in the treaties has been deliberately and consistently foiled by Member States. The Treaty of Lisbon, formulated in the aftermath of the Constitutional Treaty project, formally entered into force in December 2009, textually dismantling the pillar structure that had defined Europe since the Treaty of Maastricht came into effect in 1993. While the third pillar measures dealing with JHA matters, including criminal law and policing measures were eventually whittled away by the Treaty of Lisbon with a five-year transitional period expiring in 2014,[80] the old second pillar, despite the fact that it is not formally in existence, is still very much alive, albeit in a shadowy sense as a hidden pillar.

The Treaty of Lisbon, in terms of completely sorting out the issues with the institutional framework of the EU, has created a framework that is much more cohesive than before. Unilateral cohesion between the Member States and the collective exertion of EU foreign policy has been to the forefront in shaping the primary law around external action. Declarations from summits,[81] albeit not hard binding instruments, have been instrumental to this.[82] The depillarisation of the Union, whilst seeking greater integration, continued to offer choices of legal bases for the Union's external action. Under formal pillarisation, there was manoeuvre for 'inter-pillar flirtation'.[83] Yet, the pillar structure is retained post-Lisbon 'in all but name'.[84] Instead, the Treaty of Lisbon, much like the Constitutional Treaty, realigned EU legal acts, making CFSP matters non-legislative and non-CFSP matters legislative.

[78] Ramses A Wessel, 'Resisting Legal Facts: Are CFSP Norms as Soft as They Seem?' (2015) 20 *European Foreign Affairs Review* 123.

[79] Wouters and Cuyckens (n 46) p 223.

[80] However, the judgments from the Court in both Case C-540/13, *Parliament v Council*, ECLI:EU:C:2015:224, and Joined Cases C-317/13 and C-679/13, *Parliament v Council*, ECLI:EU:C:2015:223, have upheld old third pillar measures after this timeframe, and allowed new measures based from them continue to be adopted.

[81] Not to be mistaken for Declarations which are annexed to the treaties.

[82] Tina Vončina, 'Speaking with One Voice: Statements and Declarations as an Instrument of the EU's Common Foreign and Security Policy' (2011) 16 *European Foreign Affairs Review* 169.

[83] Theodore Konstadinides, 'Book Review of Panos Koutrakos, The EU Common Security and Defence Policy (Oxford: Oxford University Press, 2013)' (2015) 21 *European Public Law* 395.

[84] Panos Koutrakos, 'Primary Law and Policy in EU External Relations: Moving Away from the Big Picture' (2008) 33 *European Law Review* 666 at 669.

2.3. The Divide between CFSP Matters and Non-CFSP Matters

Two competing forms of EU external relations have been in existence, with in earlier years, the distinction being whether such relations were of an economic nature, or otherwise,[85] principally when foreign policy was legally connected to the Union. The distance that was supposed to exist between the two was a necessity for national politicians and diplomats alike in earlier times. That transition of keeping the two together has eventually come down to a much more complex and unusual structure of keeping different forms of EU external action apart between CFSP and non-CFSP matters.

With the differences on a procedural level stemming from the constitutional layout from the treaties in external relations, choosing an appropriate legal basis for any given measure is important. The legal division of EU external relations between CFSP and non-CFSP matters created a clash and conflict in the execution of the Union's actions. It has always been 'bitterly contested';[86] with the divide between CFSP and non-CFSP matters being described as a 'legal firewall'[87] or, at least, an attempt at one. Whilst contestation is ripe when a physical or hypothetical border is present, one theory is that it should not matter which legal basis is chosen. This is due to the competence of the Union being assumed, in that there is at least one legal basis available. However, the legal basis selected for any measure in the EU is of constitutional significance,[88] particularly for EU institutions because of the 'distinct procedural regime' for CFSP matters as compared to non-CFSP matters.[89] With the contrast between the two being so 'stark',[90] the issue deserves further probing.

2.3.1. The Pillars

The legal dimension of EU external relations is not confined to CFSP matters and its legal basis.[91] The delineation between the two is quite fluid and the interaction

[85] Joseph HH Weiler, 'The European Parliament and Foreign Affairs: External Relations of the European Economic Community' in Antonio Cassese (ed), *Parliamentary Control Over Foreign Policy: Legal Essays* (Sijtoff and Noordhoff 1980) p 154.

[86] Dashwood and others (n 75) p 907.

[87] Steven Blockmans and Martina Spernbauer, 'Legal Obstacles to Comprehensive EU External Security Action' (2013) 18 *European Foreign Affairs Review* 7 at 15.

[88] *Opinion 2/00*, ECLI:EU:C:2001:664 ('*Cartagena Protocol*'), para 5. For all the legal issues in this case, see, Alan Dashwood, 'Opinion 2/00, Cartagena Protocol on Biosafety, 6 December 2001, Not yet Reported' (2002) 39 *Common Market Law Review* 353.

[89] Robert Schütze, *European Union Law* (Cambridge University Press, 2015) p 273.

[90] Piet Eeckhout, 'A Panorama of Two Decades of EU External Relations Law' in Anthony Arnull, Piet Eeckhout and Takis Tridimas (eds), *Continuity and Change in EU Law: Essays in Honour of Sir Francis Jacobs* (Oxford University Press, 2008) p 323.

[91] Ingolf Pernice and Daniel Thym, 'A New Institutional Balance for European Foreign Policy?' (2002) 7 *European Foreign Affairs Review* 369.

between the first pillar (non-CFSP matters) and second pillar (CFSP matters) grew steadily over time. For a long time, the lack of a specific provision as how to handle the Union's external relations between former EC competence and CFSP matters had been criticised.[92] The division (or boundary) between CFSP and non-CFSP matters has not always been easy to distinguish,[93] going back many years, even when CFSP matters, as a legal area, were in their infancy.

The Union strives to possess a framework that allows it to express to the outside world a coherent strategy, yet simultaneously allowing a role for individual Member States. It has been a long-held view by the Member States that 'foreign policy', which in Union terms is one component of external relations, would fall outside the jurisdiction of actors such as the Parliament or the Court, due to its strong intergovernmental instincts, thus remaining under the firm control of the executive. It cannot be forgotten that some Member States, particularly larger ones, continue to be active foreign policy and external relations players.[94] For an explanation as to why CFSP matters have long been located within the TEU, as opposed to the TFEU, only assumptions can be made.[95] However, the isolation that it felt in the first of the two treaties, where it was separate to that of the normal competence of the Union in the TFEU, was a deliberate act by the Member States to shield it from policy and law-making norms of supranationalism.

In the eyes of the law, it is critical within EU external action whether a CFSP or non-CFSP legal basis is adopted given that parliamentary and judicial control is different depending on the legal basis availed of. Notwithstanding the treaty-imposed division between CFSP and non-CFSP matters, there is an overlap between the two that can be difficult to reconcile. With additional emphasis placed upon the Union collectively to achieve greater coherence in its policies, this overlap can be settled in a number of ways but, primarily, by choosing the correct legal basis.

There are limitations as to what extent it is possible to combine a CFSP and a non-CFSP legal basis for international agreements.[96] This has always been a conundrum,[97] given the incompatibility, procedurally speaking. One of the main distinctions between CFSP matters contained in TEU and non-CFSP matters

[92] Jörg Monar, 'The European Union's Foreign Affairs System after the Treaty of Amsterdam: A "Strengthened Capacity for External Action"?' (1997) 2 *European Foreign Affairs Review* 413 at 434.

[93] Iain MacLeod, Ian D Hendry and Stephen Hyett, *The External Relations of the European Communities: A Manual of Law and Practice* (Clarendon Press, 1996) p 209.

[94] Thomas Ramopoulos and Jed Odermatt, 'EU Diplomacy: Measuring Success in Light of the Post-Lisbon Institutional Framework' in Astrid Boening, Jan-Frederik Kremer and Aukje van Loon (eds), *Global Power Europe – Vol. 1: Theoretical and Institutional Approaches to the EU's External Relations* (Springer, 2013) p 20.

[95] Alan Dashwood, 'Mixity in the Era of the Treaty of Lisbon' in Christophe Hillion and Panos Koutrakos (eds), *Mixed Agreements Revisited: The EU and its Member States in the World* (Hart Publishing, 2010) p 353.

[96] Broberg and Holdgaard (n 1) p 363.

[97] Enzo Cannizzaro, 'The Scope of EU Foreign Power. Is the EC Competent to Conclude Agreements with Third States Including Human Rights Clauses?' in Enzo Cannizzaro (ed), *The European Union as an Actor in International Relations* (Kluwer Law International, 2002) p 306.

contained in TFEU is the power balance between the different institutions. Therefore, the 'policing of the boundary'[98] between CFSP matters and other areas of Union competence has been one of the contemporary issues facing the Parliament and the Court, in ensuring the boundary is respected. Post-Lisbon and following on from the more consolidated Constitutional Treaty that never made it into force, the Union's array of competence in external relations is still not explicitly clear when it comes to CFSP matters.

The strong intergovernmentalist thinking, through consensus of the dominant actors,[99] makes TEU decision-making akin to classical international organisation decision-making, yet rule-bound within the EU legal order. There are also parts of the TEU that, whilst located within the CFSP articles, are not purely CFSP matters in nature. An example of this would be Article 27(3) TEU,[100] given it requires the European External Action Service (EEAS) and the High Representative to partake in non-CFSP tasks. The development of CFSP matters within Union law has been tied to the development of international legal personality of the Union,[101] which for many years, was called into question. The Community always had personality,[102] but not necessarily the Union. In CFSP matters, the Union had no personality.[103] Post-Lisbon, the Union now possesses unquestioned legal personality[104] with the ability to conclude international agreements, in collaboration with its Member States, depending on the policy area.

Procedures set out in the TEU under the CFSP title are only available when matters fall outside the limit of the formal Union competence set out in Articles 3–6 of the TFEU.[105] The exact delineation between CFSP and non-CFSP matters has no definitive limit. Given certain circumstances, the Union has a broad array of powers that can be derived from a number of legal bases to handle a variety of situations.[106] Since the Treaty of Lisbon, the Parliament's role in non-CFSP external

[98] Marise Cremona, 'The Union's External Action: Constitutional Perspectives' in Giuliano Amato, Hervé Bribosia and Bruno De Witte (eds), *Genesis and Destiny of the European Constitution: Commentary on the Treaty establishing a Constitution for Europe in the light of the travaux préparatoires and future prospects* (Bruylant, 2007) p 1200.

[99] Mark Dawson, 'The Legal and Political Accountability Structure of "Post-Crisis" EU Economic Governance' (2015) 53 *Journal of Common Market Studies* 976 at 978.

[100] Mauro Gatti, 'Diplomats at the Bar: The European External Action Service before EU Courts' (2014) 39 *European Law Review* 664 at 674.

[101] Ramses A Wessel, 'The International Legal Status of the European Union' (1997) 2 *European Foreign Affairs Review* 109 at 129.

[102] Treaty of Rome, Article 210: 'The Community shall have legal personality'.

[103] Allan Rosas, 'The European Union and Mixed Agreements' in Alan Dashwood and Christophe Hillion (eds), *The General Law of EC External Relations* (Sweet and Maxwell, 2000) p 201.

[104] TEU, Article 47: 'The Union shall have legal personality.'

[105] Joni Heliskoski, 'Adoption of Positions under Mixed Agreements (Implementation)' in Christophe Hillion and Panos Koutrakos (eds), *Mixed Agreements Revisited: The EU and its Member States in the World* (Hart Publishing, 2010) p 143.

[106] Marise Cremona, 'The EU and Global Emergencies: Competence and Instruments' in Antonis Antoniadis, Robert Schütze and Eleanor Spaventa (eds), *The European Union and Global Emergencies: A Law and Policy Analysis* (Hart Publishing, 2011) p 28.

relations, such as the ratification of an international agreement by the Union, now needs the consent of the Parliament,[107] but not with respect to international agreements concluded on a CFSP legal basis. The Treaty of Lisbon consolidated the legal instruments of the Union in the non-CFSP sphere but did not finish the job with respect to CFSP matters. With the legal acts of regulations, directives, decisions, recommendations and opinions all available to the institutions possessing the relevant competence in non-CFSP matters,[108] they are a marked distinction to CFSP matters, where regulations and directives cannot be used.

2.3.2. Beyond Economic Integration

It is difficult to say who, at the time, knew that the original form of today's Union, whether it was the ECSC or the later EEC, would go far beyond light economic integration and would eventually expand into areas such as foreign policy, given that its original external action was focused on economic affairs. The foundational blocks of CFSP matters, from a historical perspective, are political, and not legal. Furthermore, the foundations of CFSP matters were at first governed by international norms, as opposed to Union law. The concepts of Union law and the EU legal order, such as that of direct effect and primacy, did not apply. The primacy of CFSP matters over national laws, if it was ever in doubt,[109] was a proposed statement in the Constitutional Treaty,[110] but was ultimately left out of its regurgitated successor which did come into being, as the Treaty of Lisbon.

The Union's external relations, or more correctly, its foreign policy, has traditionally been on the fringes of EU policy. It is undeniable that EPC over time was reinforced, leading to CFSP as a legal field. Its alignment with EU institutions to varying degrees has institutionalised a policy that has gradually been brought closer to the Union. The intergovernmental pillars were indeed 'inherently flawed and cannot [have been] successful'.[111] The pre-Lisbon version of the current Article 40 TEU (ex-Article 47 TEU) attempted to ensure the cracks between the pillars for the Court were sealed. Whether this was a mismatch or should have been handled differently down through the years is a moot point, but nonetheless it is the existing regime that has survived to manifest itself into today's hidden pillar. There are also aspects of private international law and its place within EU external relations which must be considered in the modern era.[112] Today, CFSP matters

[107] TFEU, Article 218.

[108] TFEU, Article 288.

[109] This is discussed in Chapter 5 of this book.

[110] Article I-6, Constitutional Treaty that never entered into force: 'The Constitution and law adopted by the institutions of the Union in exercising competences conferred on it shall have primacy over the law of the Member States.' Note: This was to cover the compete sphere of activity within the EU legal order, therefore, including CFSP.

[111] Dominic McGoldrick, *International Relations Law of the European Union* (Longman, 1997) p 140.

[112] See, Alex Mills, 'Private International Law and EU External Relations: Think Local Act Global, or Think Global Act Local?' (2016) 65 *International and Comparative Law Quarterly* 541.

have moved to centre-stage and can be attributed to its legal status and practical effects. The days when EU Member States conducted foreign policy on a strictly unilateral basis are long gone. The treaties, particularly the TEU, now harbour global sights more coherently from a Union perspective. Whereas external relations, as a term in itself, is colloquially used to cover both CFSP and non-CFSP matters today, this was not always the case.

As time has progressed, Union law has devolved its way into CFSP matters that were traditionally seen as outside its realm.[113] The more procedural than substantive issues of CFSP matters in its seminal times were 'lack of power, lack of money, and lack of men'.[114] Despite these weaknesses, CFSP matters managed to build themselves into a policy that has overcome some of these problems. Instead of policies being decided on a case-by-case, state-by-state basis, they would be stronger with a unified common approach within the scope of Union law.

After the failed Constitutional Treaty, the need for a more coherent and consistent external action for the Union managed to survive and make its way into the Treaty of Lisbon. This is therefore the current operative framework for Union external action. The greater coherence of external relations policies means they have the potential to overlap,[115] despite the evident aim of the primary law. Intergovernmentalism and supranationalism 'now live together under the same roof'.[116] All the Union's different activities are catered for within the treaties, bringing together a wide variety of notions of how to bring together a Union legal order. The objective pursued, when hauled together, makes for an entire set of legal instruments that are at the disposal of a host of institutions.

2.3.3. Legal Instruments and Procedures

The external action of the Union needs the appropriate legal instruments to implement its policies. Whilst they are inherently complex in their nature, they bring forward a mix of both legal and political strands of thought that require thorough analysis, reflection and application to solve the many challenges that arise. The Union has a number of instruments at its disposal to respond to global issues through its external relations toolkit.[117] Thus, there is a consistent tension in Union law between the autonomous EU legal order, championed by institutions such as the Court, against the international organisation-like setup that Member States can

[113] An example of which is defence industries. See, Panos Koutrakos, 'The Application of EC Law to Defence Industries – Changing Interpretations of Article 296 EC' in Catherine Barnard and Okeoghene Odudu (eds), *The Outer Limits of European Union Law* (Hart Publishing, 2009).

[114] Denza (n 25) p 122.

[115] Stefan Griller, 'External Relations' in Bruno De Witte (ed), *Ten Reflections on the Constitutional Treaty for Europe* (European University Institute, 2003) p 136.

[116] Helene Sjursen, 'Not so Intergovernmental after All? On Democracy and Integration in European Foreign and Security Policy' (2011) 18 *Journal of European Public Policy* 1078 at 1084.

[117] See, Cremona, 'The EU and Global Emergencies: Competence and Instruments' (n 106).

perceive it to be at times. The Treaty of Lisbon has enhanced the constitutionalising process of non-CFSP external action to the ordinary legislative procedure but, in CFSP matters, there was limited progress, given its non-legislative status.

The foreign policy of the Union can be looked at from several angles[118] and, given that the treaties make little or no distinction between competence conferred upon the Union that is internal, external, or both, differing distinctions can be drawn. When pillarisation occurred, it could be said that only the first pillar was supranational,[119] but, there are growing supranational elements in the former second pillar. Indeed, the ghost of the pillars still exists within the post-Lisbon treaties. For better or worse, the Treaty of Lisbon did not radically redefine the process through which CFSP Decisions are arrived at. The former second and third pillars, CFSP and JHA matters, are areas where Member States expressed most hesitation in cooperating within Union structures. It could even be said that Member States were protective over their competence to the detriment of other sectoral areas where national competence has been slowly shifting away. The two external relations regimes of CFSP and non-CFSP matters were much further apart once upon a time, but have grown slowly together, implicitly and not purposefully. That being said, there has been no external relations revolution. Rather, evolution, in the Darwinian sense, has been the methodological formulation of the current state of affairs.

Following the theory that the Union's external action was connected to its internal action,[120] the parallel nature has been broken, given that the Union has a more fully fledged foreign policy today, separate from its internal design and development. Given that pillarisation occurred, it can legitimately be asked why CFSP matters were not originally put into a separate title within the treaties, as they are today, instead of being located in a separate pillar. The intergovernmental nature of CFSP matters, despite their rules, has been holding back EU foreign policy success, then,[121] and now. The political union in the making has yet to come to full fruition. This lack of political integration, and eventual political union, has meant that the vibrancy of EU foreign policy may have been dampened through the years. Instead of true reform, the Treaty of Lisbon reinforced the legal divide between CFSP matters and the other external relations of the Union, despite integrating their objectives.

External relations-wise, the treaties now reflect innovations that were once talked about as possible and are now seen reflected in legal documents, enhancing

[118] For example, see, Ernst-Ulrich Petersmann, 'The Moral Foundations of the European Union's Foreign Policy Constitution: Defining "European Identity" and "Community Interests" for the Benefit of EU Citizens' (1996) 51 *Aussenwirtschaft (Swiss Review of International Economic Relations)* 151.

[119] Peter L Lindseth, 'Democratic Legitimacy and the Administrative Character of Supranationalism: The Example of the European Community' (1999) 99 *Columbia Law Review* 628 at 652.

[120] Robert Schütze, *From Dual to Cooperative Federalism: The Changing Structure of European Law* (Oxford University Press, 2009) p 340.

[121] Youri Devuyst, 'The European Union's Constitutional Order? Between Community Method and Ad Hoc Compromise' (2000) 18 *Berkeley Journal of International Law* 1 at 3.

the Union's ability to respond to global trends and participate in international challenges across the world. Fixing the foreign policy and external relations elements has been one of the most noticeable accomplishments of the treaties on their last major revision. The constitutional structures of the Union today have been a series of compromises made over a prolonged period at different stages of the integration process. Moving forward, one step at a time, the resistance by Member States to cede powers to EU institutions was an ideological issue. Perceiving that influence from other actors could be construed as interference in Council affairs, the implementation of CFSP matters has been kept under wraps.

EU foreign policy and external relations through the decades have been problematic for constitutional reasons in some EU Member States which, in one instance, triggered a referendum.[122] The legal order derived from *Van Gend en Loos*,[123] was not applicable to the pillarised Union from the the Treaty of Maastricht through to the Treaty of Lisbon. Foreign, security, and defence affairs of the Union have always been on some level of intergovernmental 'track', with Member States always very keen on underlining the intergovernmental nature of cooperation. That, of course, has not been strictly true, given CFSP matters are governed by rules and procedures defined in the treaties, removing some of the true intergovernmentalism. Today, in non-CFSP matters, the treaties apportion rights on the main institutions, the Council, Commission, Parliament and the Court. However, with these rights also come responsibilities and probing questions that are relevant to the operation of CFSP matters.

The flexibility afforded to the areas of EU policy covering foreign, security, and defence affairs has been noteworthy,[124] allowing deviations from the general uniform nature of the EU legal order. The instincts were always against creating an EU-wide foreign policy for good reason. The demarcation lines are less visible than they were in the past, allowing the relevant actors greater scope to pursue policies on a legal basis without clear encroachment into another area. With the Treaty of Lisbon removing the formal divisions between the formal pillars of the Union, the new constitutional framework in external action allowed for greater integration of the Union's external policies. Today however, CFSP matters are part of the EU legal order, albeit with distinct features. It still resembles the founding

[122] In Ireland, see the Supreme Court decision in, *Crotty v An Taoiseach* [1987] IR 713 (Supreme Court of Ireland 1987). For more, see, David Fennelly, 'Crotty's Long Shadow: The European Union, the United Nations and the Changing Framework of Ireland's International Relations' in Eoin Carolan (ed), *The Constitution of Ireland: Perspectives and Prospects* (Bloomsbury Professional, 2012). Also, see, Renaud Dehousse and Joseph HH Weiler, 'EPC and the Single Act: From Soft Law to Hard Law?' in Martin Holland (ed), *The Future of European Political Cooperation: Essays on Theory and Practice* (St Martin's Press, 1991) p 131. Furthermore, Oran Doyle, *The Constitution of Ireland: A Contextual Analysis* (Hart Publishing, 2018) pp 37–38.

[123] Case C-26/62, *Van Gend en Loos v Administratie der Belastingen*, ECLI:EU:C:1963:1. See, Morten Rasmussen, 'Revolutionizing European Law: A History of the Van Gend En Loos Judgment' (2014) 12 *International Journal of Constitutional Law* 136.

[124] Ramses A Wessel, 'Differentiation in EU Foreign, Security, and Defence Policy: Between Coherence and Flexibility' in Martin Trybus and Nigel White (eds), *European Security Law* (Oxford University Press, 2007) p 226.

basis upon the thoughts of which it was initially adopted, with little incorporation, but room for further integration at a time when it would be politically feasible to do so.

2.4. Conclusion

Generally speaking, powers held by the Council have slowly been moving away from it and moving towards other institutional actors,[125] as well as other bodies. This diminishing power is evident when the Council is rigorously attempting to defend its interests in CFSP matters from the perceived encroachment of other institutional actors, such as the Parliament and the Court. If anything, the 1993–2009 period helped the passive observer to better understand the supranational and intergovernmental-like aspects of the Union's policies, including external relations. The subsequent depillarisation of the Union was not so much of a demolition, but rather, as will be validated by the subsequent chapters of this book, a much slower whittling away of the legal protections surrounding CFSP matters imposed by the Member States.

Not all international treaties are the same. Some create entities that 'shape the character of international society',[126] such as what came to be the EU. Taken as a whole, EU external relations still comprise large aspects of both Union and Member State involvement.[127] An independent stream of external relations policies, without the involvement of Member States at some level, has not materialised. It is hard to imagine how the authors of the original Treaty of Rome would have envisaged that foreign policy, inclusive of security and defence matters would one day become a part of the Union's external relations. Whereas the North Atlantic Treaty Organisation (NATO) and the Western European Union (WEU) took the issue of security and defence affairs of Europe at first, the role of the EU in Europe's foreign, security, and defence affairs finally came to fruition. With that progress, the legal dimension of this plays a crucial role, just as it does in Union affairs.[128]

Incrementalism has prevailed in CFSP matters, a policy area from outside the Union's structure which has slowly become a specifically designed pillar which is more integrated within the Union's legal sphere. Whilst the progressive development of the Union's treaties has crafted the external relations provisions to enable greater external action, the compromises reached by the Member States have not made for a completely clear understanding of how the law in CFSP and non-CFSP matters should operate.

[125] Deirdre Curtin, 'Democratic Accountability of EU Executive Power: A Reform Agenda for Parliaments' in Federico Fabbrini, Ernst Hirsch Ballin and Han Somsen (eds), *What Form of Government for the European Union and the Eurozone?* (Hart Publishing, 2015) p 172.

[126] Louis Henkin, *How Nations Behave: Law and Foreign Policy* (Pall Mall Press, 1968) p 20.

[127] Marise Cremona, 'Coherence Through Law: What Difference Will the Treaty of Lisbon Make?' (2008) 3 *Hamburg Review of Social Sciences* 11 at 29.

[128] See, Renaud Dehousse and Joseph HH Weiler, 'The Legal Dimension' in William Wallace (ed), *The Dynamics of European Integration* (Pinter, 1990).

3

The EU Legal Order and the Common Foreign and Security Policy

Are CFSP matters foreign policy or external relations? Long before the CFSP acronym was itself a catching term for an intergovernmental-like EU policy, this question was broached in the context of the internal market.[1] Today, the picture is more convoluted. EU foreign policy and external relations can be thought about in several ways. 'Foreign policy' as a figure of speech, has not always been a legal term.[2] CFSP matters were initially of a short-term nature, with its decision being broad within a sensitive domain.

In light of the history of how CFSP matters came about into Union law, the current state of the law with respect to CFSP matters can now be analysed. With the policy field heavily constitutionised into the EU legal order, attention can now turn to CFSP matters as they presently stand. This chapter puts into context the decision-making procedures which are applicable for CFSP matters and marks the distinction that exists for legal acts for CFSP matters, which as will become apparent, are starkly different from those resting on a non-CFSP legal basis.

3.1. Introduction

CFSP actions, as collaborative undertakings, can be much broader than this, as responses to other global issues can also come within its scope. Such matters go beyond the Union itself.[3] Whether it is diplomacy, military intervention, or even economic interest, CFSP matters are subject to public and legal interpretation in several ways. What ultimately marks foreign policy as different from other public fields is a matter of ongoing debate in many jurisdictions.

[1] See, Kenneth J Twitchett, 'External Relations or Foreign Policy?' in Kenneth J. Twitchett (ed), *Europe and the World: The External Relations of the Common Market* (St Martin's Press, 1976).

[2] Markus Krajewski, 'Foreign Policy and the European Constitution' (2003) 22 *Yearbook of European Law* 435 at 437.

[3] Eileen Denza, *The Intergovernmental Pillars of the European Union* (Oxford University Press, 2002) p 312.

Notwithstanding the pressing foreign policy concerns of a contemporary nature, CFSP matters could be said to have legal, diplomatic, and political traits. Solidarity can be said to be one of its cornerstones,[4] given the loyalty and consistency provision.[5] Nestled within the wider parameters of the EU's external relations policies that have many visions, CFSP matters are an uncharacteristic policy in EU affairs. In many ways, the existence, nature, and the scope of CFSP matters remain different from other external relations provisions. In comparison to other policy fields, it has been labelled the 'odd one out',[6] as well as having 'continuing particularity'.[7] Within its legal basis in primary law, CFSP matters can be labelled 'high politics',[8] but under strict legal conditions.

The competence of the Union as an international organisation, outside of CFSP matters, is of exceptional proportions, in that it possesses competence exclusively in certain policy fields over its Member States.[9] EU action of all kinds, including CFSP matters, operates within a single institutional framework. One of CFSP's hallmarks is its ability to be a legal instrument that is responsive to the needs of the EU's foreign policy executive, the Council, in EU external action. Thus, the question of competence arises.

3.1.1. Competence

The Union's foreign policy and external relations regime is constitutionally located in two distinct areas:[10] within Title V of the TEU, and in Part V of the TFEU. Whereas nearly all external relations matters are contained in the TFEU, CFSP matters are located in the TEU, mainly for historical reasons (as detailed in the previous chapter). CFSP matters have unique characteristics in that is 'subject to specific rules and procedures' laid out in the treaties.[11] With no comprehensive list of competence, battles have been fought on how to delineate it from other policy fields. When CFSP matters were first brought

[4] Epaminondas A Marias, 'Solidarity as an Objective of the European Union and the European Community' (1994) 21 *Legal Issues of Economic Integration* 85 at 106.

[5] TEU, Article 24(3): 'The Member States shall support the Union's external and security policy actively and unreservedly in a spirit of loyalty and mutual solidarity and shall comply with the Union's action in this area.'

[6] Bart Van Vooren and Ramses A Wessel, *EU External Relations Law: Text, Cases and Materials* (Cambridge University Press, 2014) pp 105 and 346.

[7] Alan Dashwood and others, *Wyatt and Dashwood's European Union Law* 6th edition (Hart Publishing, 2011) pp 905–7.

[8] Elfriede Regelsberger and Wolfgang Wessels, 'The CFSP Institutions and Procedures: A Third Way for the Second Pillar' (1996) 1 *European Foreign Affairs Review* 29 at 36.

[9] See, Allan Rosas, 'EU External Relations: Exclusive Competence Revisited' (2015) 38 *Fordham International Law Journal* 1073.

[10] Robert Schütze, 'External Union Powers: Competences and Procedures' in Robert Schütze (ed), *Foreign Affairs and the EU Constitution: Selected Essays* (Cambridge University Press, 2014) p 304.

[11] TEU, Article 24(1).

into the treaties, it was done on the basis that it was put on the outer edges of the Union legal order, and not as a competence *per se*. This makes it idiosyncratic as a name[12] and vis-à-vis the rest of the external relations regime. Indeed, CFSP matters, as a competence, have been given legal apprehension for a long time.

The Union's set of competence is today dispersed throughout the treaties. Articles 3 through 6 TFEU set out the categories of competence that the Union has,[13] these being exclusive,[14] shared,[15] and supporting ('support, coordinate or supplement').[16] CFSP matters do not comply with these competency groups as they have their own distinctive provisions – a special competence. As stated, CFSP matters 'shall not affect the application of the procedures and the extent of the powers of the institutions laid down by the [t]reaties'.[17]

Notwithstanding the special nature of CFSP matters, it would be wrong to assume that CFSP matters has its own legal order. Whilst the special nature conferred by the treaties includes abnormal Union decision-making, no general basis for judicial review and mostly unanimous voting procedures, it can be argued that notwithstanding such distinctions, there is only one true EU legal order.[18] The preamble of the TEU and the specific legal provisions for CFSP matters makes clear that the Union is governed on a single institutional framework. Yet this aim is a general visionary statement, and it becomes quite clear that the specifics of the treaties are not as generous to this ideal.

The EU legal order fully encompasses CFSP matters, despite its sharp differences. It can be said if it was to fit into a competence category, it would be a 'non-pre-emptive shared competence'.[19] However, labelling CFSP matters as a shared competence would be 'a poor fit'.[20] Instead, it is of a parallel nature, and Member States cannot be deterred from doing what it wishes. Despite this difficulty of putting a label on CFSP matters for competence purposes, there is no prescribed list of policy areas contained within the treaties that provide

[12] Monica Claes and Bruno De Witte, 'Competences: Codification and Contestation' in Adam Łazowski and Steven Blockmans (eds), *Research Handbook on EU Institutional Law* (Edward Elgar, 2016) p 66.

[13] Even with this list, it is not without its problems. See, Kieran St C Bradley, 'Legislating in the European Union' in Catherine Barnard and Steve Peers (eds), *European Union Law* 2nd Edition (Oxford University Press, 2017) pp 107–111.

[14] TFEU, Article 3.

[15] Ibid. Articles 4 and 5.

[16] Ibid. Article 6.

[17] TEU, Article 40.

[18] Daniel Halberstam, '"It's the Autonomy, Stupid!" A Modest Defense of Opinion 2/13 on EU Accession to the ECHR, and the Way Forward' (2015) 16 *German Law Journal* 105 at 138.

[19] Marise Cremona, 'The Union's External Action: Constitutional Perspectives' in Giuliano Amato, Hervé Bribosia and Bruno De Witte (eds), *Genesis and Destiny of the European Constitution: Commentary on the Treaty establishing a Constitution for Europe in the Light of the Travaux Préparatoires and Future Prospects* (Bruylant, 2007) p 1195.

[20] Armin Von Bogdandy and Jürgen Bast, 'The Federal Order of Competences' in Armin Von Bogdandy and Jürgen Bast (eds), *Principles of European Constitutional Law* 2nd edition (Hart Publishing, 2009) p 306.

Member States with unfettered discretion. The closest such area is 'safeguarding national security',[21] albeit that too is problematic to delineate. In practice, therefore, the doctrine of implied competence is delicate for CFSP matters, with Member States in a position to take their own measures, regardless of EU action, but must be in conformity with the duty of sincere cooperation.

Article 24 TEU sets out the potential scope of CFSP matters. This covers not only its basic institutional framework, but also the principles upon what is to guide its scope. It is linked to the Union's sincere cooperation and loyalty provision – Article 4(3) TEU – which seeks to prevent any Member State from undermining the process of policy development. With Article 24(1) TEU noting that CFSP matters have 'specific rules and procedures' *vis-à-vis* other areas of the Union decision-making architecture, it is telling that CFSP matters are no ordinary policy field that the Union is involved in. In the treaties, it is as important to read between the lines as it is to read the text itself. This broad provision has the potential to create a very comprehensive reach of competence for the conduct of EU foreign policy. However, the breath for which those provisions could apply is exaggerated.[22]

As such, CFSP matters, as a competence area, can be specified further in that it deals with powers of certain institutions to adopt decisions. Article 24(1) TEU is rigid, with little room for greater interpretation by institutional actors. Therefore, CFSP matters sit awkwardly between formative intergovernmentalism and contemporary supranationalism. Moreover, CFSP matters are in 'constitutional isolation'.[23] With the Union building its core principles in its earlier stages, and waiting later for diversity accommodation,[24] with its emergence described as a 'watershed moment',[25] CFSP matters are a representative example of being a principal victim of hotchpotch integration.

3.1.2. Retention of CFSP Matters

The treaties of Maastricht, Amsterdam, Nice, and Lisbon all had one thing in common; their forthright retention of CFSP matters in a significant way.

[21] Contained in TEU, Article 4(2). However, that must be conducted in conformity with the principle of sincere (loyal) cooperation. TEU, Article 4(3): 'Pursuant to the principle of sincere cooperation, the Union and the Member States shall, in full mutual respect, assist each other in carrying out tasks which flow from the [t]reaties. The Member States shall take any appropriate measure, general or particular, to ensure fulfilment of the obligations arising out of the [t]reaties or resulting from the acts of the institutions of the Union. The Member States shall facilitate the achievement of the Union's tasks and refrain from any measure which could jeopardise the attainment of the Union's objectives.'

[22] As contended, this would go 'far beyond what the EU Treaty intends'. Geert De Baere and Kathleen Gutman, 'Federalism and International Relations in the European Union and the United States: A Comparative Outlook' in Elke Cloots, Geert De Baere and Stefan Sottiaux (eds), *Federalism in the European Union* (Hart Publishing, 2012) p 144.

[23] Robert Schütze, *European Union Law* (Cambridge University Press, 2015) p 889.

[24] Daniel Thym, 'Foreign Affairs' in Armin Von Bogdandy and Jürgen Bast (eds), *Principles of European Constitutional Law* 2nd edition (Hart Publishing, 2009) p 317.

[25] Joris Larik, *Foreign Policy Objectives in European Constitutional Law* (Oxford University Press, 2016) p 78.

CFSP matters are an intersectional field sitting awkwardly as the foreign policy of a special enhanced international organisation,[26] which has hallmarks of international law and is collectively joined up by all EU Member States. There are conceivable arguments as to why CFSP matters might be judged from a purely international law perspective. It could even be pointed to that, in previous times, international lawyers would see CFSP matters as Union law, and EU lawyers would see the intergovernmentalism of it all, thereby seeing it as international law.[27]

CFSP matters are not intergovernmental, however, as they are within the EU legal order and thereby, governed by the rules of Union law, albeit of a special kind. By today's definition, the depillarisation has made CFSP matters less exceptional and has, in a conspicuous way, brought less of a divide between itself and non-CFSP external relations. As to what extent the policy of international law falls under CFSP matters as foreign policy against other areas of external action as non-CFSP matters is an old controversy,[28] but one that has not fully disappeared.

The purely intergovernmental aspects of CFSP matters are long gone and it is incorrect to label CFSP matters as intergovernmental.[29] Yet, altering that image that it has long possessed is difficult.[30] At the same time, however, it is not diametrically in conformity with the supranational nature of non-CFSP matters. CFSP matters are fully rooted in the constitutional framework of the Union in the treaties and, under the current treaties, CFSP and non-CFSP matters are, legally speaking, as close as they have ever been. In theory, this ought to lead to a more integrated approach to shaping the law of EU external relations.

CFSP matters have been characterised as being between 'recognised demandingness and inefficiency of the unanimity requirement'.[31] Given the potential overlap between CFSP matters and other policy areas of the Union, it is ripe for contestation. This intersectionality with other policy fields is compounded post-Lisbon; where no specific objectives for CFSP matters are explicitly defined as they were pre-Lisbon. Rather, objectives for both CFSP matters and non-CFSP matters

[26] With far easier acronyms in other languages: *Comhbheartas Eachtrach agus Slándála* (CBES) in Irish; *Politique étrangère et de sécurité commune* (PESC) in French; *Gemeinsame Außen-und Sicherheitspolitik* (GASP) in German; *Fælles udenrigs-og sikkerhedspolitik* (FUSP) in Danish; and *Gemensamma utrikes-och säkerhetspolitiken* (GUSP) in Swedish.

[27] See this view from the 1990s in, Martti Koskenniemi, 'International Law Aspects of the Common Foreign and Security Policy' in Martti Koskenniemi (ed), *International Law Aspects of the European Union* (Martinus Nijhoff Publishers, 1998).

[28] Pieter Jan Kuijper, 'Litigation on External Relations Powers after Lisbon: The Member States Reject Their Own Treaty' (2016) 43 *Legal Issues of Economic Integration* 1 at 10.

[29] Peter Van Elsuwege, 'EU External Action after the Collapse of the Pillar Structure: In Search of a New Balance between Delimitation and Consistency' (2010) 47 *Common Market Law Review* 987 at 994.

[30] Ramses A Wessel, 'Integration and Constitutionalisation in EU Foreign and Security Policy' in Robert Schütze (ed), *Globalisation and Governance: International Problems, European Solutions* (Cambridge University Press, 2018) p 340.

[31] Ben Crum and Deirdre Curtin, 'The Challenge of Making European Union Executive Power Accountable' in Simona Piattoni (ed), *The European Union: Democratic Principles and Institutional Architectures in Times of Crisis* (Oxford University Press, 2015) p 77.

are collectively apportioned to the Union as a whole, without making a distinction as to which policy field the objectives belong to. This development has been sensible for the sake of consistency.

As sources of law, general principles of Union law provide guidance to legal actors on how they can act within respect to CFSP matters. When dug deeper, however, it is apparent that many subcategories of Union law each have their own applicable general principles. EU external relations law is no different in that regard.[32] With the divide of CFSP matters and non-CFSP matters remaining after the Treaty of Lisbon and the two areas now holding a shared purpose, the overall aim of CFSP matters is less clear than it has been previously. Such a move enabling the Union's external relations to be more coherent and coordinated through a more comprehensible policy sphere is to be welcomed from a legal certainty perspective, however, it has the potential to spur conflicts surrounding institutional power that are not easy to resolve.

EU foreign policy exists to assert a European identity and has allowed the Union to promote peace, security, and progress, both in Europe and throughout the world.[33] Whilst linking identity and independence is 'remarkable',[34] it is transnational external relations that have been an essential component for Europe to be seen as a relevant global actor. In legal terms, CFSP matters are special;[35] given they are the epitome of executive power in an external fashion. It represents something very distinctive about the Union in that it represents more than an informal alignment of states for purely economic issues. Moreover, it demonstrates a partnership that delves into a deeper, meaningful understanding of what the European project has been designed to foster.

3.1.3. Rules and Content

While the former second pillar of the Union was dissolved, the legal separation between CFSP and non-CFSP matters continues to exist, with the 'hidden pillar' still visible in the textual wording of the treaties. The provisions for CFSP matters

[32] See, Anne Thies, 'General Principles in the Development of EU External Relations Law' in Marise Cremona and Anne Thies (eds), *The European Court of Justice and External Relations Law: Constitutional Challenges* (Hart Publishing, 2014).

[33] The eleventh item of the preamble to the TEU states the Union is: '[r]esolved to implement a common foreign and security policy including the progressive framing of a common defence policy, which might lead to a common defence in accordance with the provisions of Article 42, thereby reinforcing the European identity and its independence in order to promote peace, security and progress in Europe and in the world'.

[34] Robert Uerpmann-Wittzack, 'The Constitutional Role of International Law' in Armin Von Bogdandy and Jürgen Bast (eds), *Principles of European Constitutional Law* (Hart Publishng, 2009) p 160.

[35] Christina Eckes, 'The CFSP and Other EU Policies: A Difference in Nature?' (2015) 20 *European Foreign Affairs Review* 535 at 550.

in the treaties are largely procedural,[36] and the definitive boundary of competence between the Union and Member States for CFSP matters has yet to be exactly delineated. However, there are workable rules and content that govern its use.

The mechanism for the use, implementation and upholding of CFSP matters as opposed to other external relations actions is legally distinct.[37] However, like most rules, they do not exist without exceptions. CFSP matters and their execution come about through a multilateral process, albeit an unusual one,[38] with a set process within institutional structures. Substantively, it has no material content[39] and is highly contested as to its appropriate use. While Member States come from a whole host of different perspectives and priorities in foreign policy, CFSP matters can be said to be subconsciously narrowing the focus of Member States, therefore redeploying their efforts on similar outcomes. Its normative effect is that it is 'softening the sharp edges of certain [Member States'] positions'.[40]

Given that the root of EU foreign policy and external relations can be traced to historical reasoning, the legal norms prevalent in the current climate allow for a fuller explanation of CFSP matters to be exerted. Today's approach of Member States and institutions of the Union has been underpinned by a number of causal factors, including the Court's case law.[41] This codification occurs to keep the treaties in coherence with the realities of practice. However, the codification of judgments can give rise to further litigation, as codifying judgments into constitutional texts is no easy feat. Previously it could be said that CFSP matters were merely seen as something of little substantive value, with lack of flow in terms of legal output and the declaratory nature seeming as if it was of little importance to EU lawyers. This has all changed.

EU external relations law is like one body with two hands. On the one hand, are CFSP matters being controlled by one side of the brain by Member States in the Council. On the other hand, are non-CFSP matters, covering other areas of external relations, with multiple parts of the brain at work. The treaties still appear to strongly support the notion that CFSP is 'together, but apart' from the regular external relations of the Union. The procedural provisions for CFSP matters are set out in the TEU, as if the other categories of competence of the Union

[36] Christophe Hillion and Ramses A Wessel, 'Restraining External Competences of EU Member States under CFSP' in Marise Cremona and Bruno De Witte (eds), *EU Foreign Relations Law: Constitutional Fundamentals* (Hart Publishing, 2008) p 82.

[37] Panos Koutrakos, 'Current Developments: European Union External Relations' (2010) 59 *International and Comparative Law Quarterly* 481 at 487.

[38] David Long, 'Multilateralism in the CFSP' in Martin Holland (ed), *Common Foreign and Security Policy: The Record and Reforms* (Pinter, 1997) p 189.

[39] Enzo Cannizzaro, 'Unity and Pluralism in the EU's Foreign Relations Power' in Catherine Barnard (ed), *The Fundamentals of EU Law Revisited: Assessing the Impact of the Constitutional Debate*, vol XVI/2 (Oxford University Press, 2007) p 214.

[40] Ben Tonra, *The Europeanisation of National Foreign Policy: Dutch, Danish and Irish Foreign Policy in the European Union* (Ashgate Publishing, 2001) p 14.

[41] See Chapter 5 of this book.

did not exist. When articles in the treaties setting out CFSP matters are read together with general external relations provisions, such as Article 21 TEU, which sets out a non-exhaustive list of foreign policy and external action policies and actions, it can be deduced that CFSP matters, in policy terms, are difficult if not impossible to distinguish from EU external relations as a whole.

CFSP matters, as a legal field, are entrenched in the treaties that operate and function in a complex constitutional structure. Declarations 13 and 14 annexed to the treaties, inserted with the Treaty of Lisbon, were viewed as having potential for change.[42] It was even suggested that they would lead to 'a qualitative leap in the nature of EU foreign policy'.[43] Governed by consensus reached in the Council by Member States, the Decisions of the Council in CFSP matters shall be binding upon the Member States.[44] Whilst previously an instrument of the Union and Member States, the definition and implementation of CFSP matters after the Treaty of Amsterdam meant CFSP matters were for the Union only,[45] albeit with Member States in the Council still retaining decision-making abilities. The merging of the Union and the Community with the Treaty of Lisbon demonstrated that the two had grown together.[46] The Court itself, pre-Lisbon, had referred to the 'integrated but separate legal orders' of the Union and Community.[47] However, as stipulated before the entering into force of the Treaty of Lisbon, CFSP matters 'shall not prejudice the specific character of the security and defence policy of certain Member States',[48] despite the fact that the Union enters into agreements in such areas.[49]

[42] Declaration 14: 'In addition to the specific rules and procedures referred to in paragraph 1 of Article 24 of the Treaty on European Union, the Conference underlines that the provisions covering the Common Foreign and Security Policy including in relation to the High Representative of the Union for Foreign Affairs and Security Policy and the External Action Service will not affect the existing legal basis, responsibilities, and powers of each Member State in relation to the formulation and conduct of its foreign policy, its national diplomatic service, relations with third countries and participation in International organisations, including a Member State's membership of the Security Council of the United Nations. The Conference also notes that the provisions covering the Common Foreign and Security Policy do not give new powers to the Commission to initiate decisions nor do they increase the role of the European Parliament. The Conference also recalls that the provisions governing the Common Security and Defence Policy do not prejudice the specific character of the security and defence policy of the Member States.'

[43] Stephan Keukeleire and Tom Delruex, *The Foreign Policy of the European Union* 2nd edition (Palgrave Macmillan, 2014) p 157.

[44] TEU, Article 28(2): 'Decisions referred to in paragraph 1 shall commit the Member States in the positions they adopt and in the conduct of their activity.'

[45] Laurence W Gormley, 'Reflections on the Architecture of the European Union after the Treaty of Amsterdam' in David O'Keeffe and Patrick M Twomey (eds), *Legal Issues of the Amsterdam Treaty* (Hart Publishing, 1999) p 60.

[46] Ramses A Wessel, 'Reconsidering the Relationship between International and EU Law: Towards a Contents-Based Approach?' in Enzo Cannizzaro, Paolo Palchetti and Ramses A Wessel (eds), *International Law as Law of the European Union* (Martinus Nijhoff Publishers, 2012) p 17.

[47] Joined Cases C-402/05 P and C-415/05 P, *Yassin Abdullah Kadi and Al Barakaat International Foundation v Council and Commission*, ECLI:EU:C:2008:461 ('*Kadi I*'), para 125.

[48] TEU, Article 2, Treaty of Nice.

[49] See, Aurel Sari, 'The Conclusion of International Agreements by the European Union in the Context of the ESDP' (2008) 57 *International and Comparative Law Quarterly* 53.

It could be claimed that the progressive development of the treaties may have forged greater institutional cooperation in external action. This, in theory, could be to the detriment of the actual functionality of EU external action throughout the range of instruments spanning across both CFSP matters and non-CFSP matters. The cultivation of CFSP matters sits with the heads of government through the body of the European Council and the foreign ministers of Member States through the Foreign Affairs Council (FAC) and General Affairs Council (GAC). The treaties do not attempt to define what the relationship is to be between the FAC and GAC. Yet, there is a tendency for the Member State's representatives to be the same Minister – the foreign minister – sitting at both.[50]

3.1.4. Decision-making and Legal Acts

Member States have procedures in place to allow decision-making to be done through a standardised framework, usually due to a tradition of constitutionalism. Similarly, the Union is an actor that plays within a specific set of rules through both its own legal order and the global field of international law. The rules for CFSP matters have been described as *lex imperfecta*, since the Treaty of Maastricht.[51] When legal acts are used, there is a distinction to be drawn between autonomous acts – decisions; and those contractual acts – international agreements.[52] Yet, it is worth noting that for CFSP matters, the adoption of legal acts is the exception, not the rule.[53] The range of legal acts available for CFSP matters is also curtailed given the exclusion of regulations and directives. That said, implementation at national level may occur. Where powers of EU Member States are devolved in such a way that there is a division of competence between federal and sub-national entities, the two are bound by an obligation to implement Union law.[54] Therefore, CFSP Decisions must be implemented into national law, where applicable.

Article 26(2) TEU specifies that whilst the Council shall frame CFSP matters and make the necessary decisions, it is for the European Council to define

[50] Simon Duke, 'Consistency, Coherence and European Union External Action: The Path to Lisbon and Beyond' in Panos Koutrakos (ed), *European Foreign Policy: Legal and Political Perspectives* (Edward Elgar, 2011) p 40.

[51] Opinion of Advocate General Wahl, Case C-455/14 P, *H v Council*, ECLI:C:2016:212, para 38.

[52] Pieter Jan Kuijper, 'The Common Foreign and Security Policy and the Common Security and Defence Policy' in Pieter Jan Kuijper and others (eds), *The Law of the European Union* (Kluwer Law International, 2018) p 1270.

[53] Daniel Thym, 'The Intergovernmental Branch of the EU's Foreign Affairs Executive: Reflections on the Political and Security Committee' in Hermann-Josef Blanke and Stelio Mangiameli (eds), *The European Union after Lisbon: Constitutional Basis, Economic Order and External Action* (Springer, 2012) p 526.

[54] For example, in Germany, this would apply to Länder. See, Steven Blockmans, 'Between the Devil and the Deep Blue Sea? Conflicts in External Action Pursued by OCTs and the EU' in Dimitry Kochenov (ed), *EU Law of the Overseas: Outermost Regions, Associated Overseas Countries and Territories, Territories Sui Generis* (Kluwer Law International, 2011) p 316.

'general guidelines and strategic lines'. The European Council is 'the alpha and the omega'[55] when it comes to the pinnacle of powers within EU politics, where it is responsible for identifying the 'strategic interests and objectives of the Union'[56] in CFSP matters. Article 24(1) TEU, second paragraph states that CFSP Decisions are to be taken by the European Council and the Council, 'acting unanimously'. However, a number of exceptions apply, in that this is 'except where this Chapter provides otherwise'.[57] Article 31(3) TEU allows for decision-making on CFSP matters to move from unanimity to Qualified Majority Voting (QMV),[58] however, this Decision to do so would have to take place unanimously in the European Council.[59]

These methods are an expression of the retention of power for decisions by Member States, purposefully excluding other important EU institutions. This non-sharing of power with actors such as the Parliament makes it different to other areas of EU external action.[60] Legislative acts are specifically excluded from CFSP matters.[61] The main difference between legislative and non-legislative acts lies in the decision-making regime,[62] with profound implications for institutions beyond the Council. This is not helped by the fact that the treaties 'lack…any clear distinction…between legislative and non-legislative measures'.[63] To counter this, Article 32 TEU attempts to ensure that Member States consult one another within the European Council and Council to develop a common approach to decision-making. Whilst the Council ultimately acts in CFSP matters, it is the European Council that has the competence to 'identify the Union's strategic interests' and furthermore has the power to 'determine the objectives of and define general guidelines'.[64]

The legal instruments for CFSP matters previously included a mix of Joint Actions, Common Positions, and Common Strategies, but have now been collectively grouped as CFSP Decisions.[65] Joint Actions were once considered a major

[55] Deirdre Curtin, *Executive Power of the European Union: Law, Practices, and the Living Constitution* (Oxford University Press, 2009) p 70.

[56] TEU, Article 22(1).

[57] TEU, Article 31(1), first para.

[58] 'The European Council may unanimously adopt a decision stipulating that the Council shall act by a qualified majority in cases other than those referred to in paragraph 2. [Article 31(2) TEU]' For more, see, Steve Peers, 'The Future of EU Treaty Amendments' (2012) 31 *Yearbook of European Law* 17 at 65.

[59] See Chapter 7 of this book.

[60] Koen Lenaerts and Piet Van Nuffel, *European Union Law* Robert Bray and Nathan Cambien (eds) 3rd edition (Sweet and Maxwell, 2011) p 715.

[61] TEU, Article 24(1), para 2, and TEU, Article 31(1).

[62] Jan Wouters, Dominic Coppens and Bart De Meester, 'The European Union's External Relations after the Lisbon Treaty' in Stefan Griller and Jacques Ziller (eds), *The Lisbon Treaty: EU Constitutionalism without a Constitutional Treaty?*, vol 11 (Springer, 2008) p 160.

[63] Michael Dougan, 'The Convention's Draft Constitutional Treaty: Bringing Europe Closer to Its Lawyers?' (2003) 28 *European Law Review* 763 at 790.

[64] TEU, Article 26(1).

[65] Panos Koutrakos, 'Primary Law and Policy in EU External Relations: Moving Away from the Big Picture' (2008) 33 *European Law Review* 666 at 669.

parting from the consensus method,[66] but was proved not to be so. They flowed from Article 14 TEU pre-Lisbon, in the same manner that Common Positions under ex-Article 15 TEU were also absorbed. Common Positions were more ambiguous in nature, and their scope was so broad and underwhelming that they were the lowest common denominator, with leafy language, leaving it open to a variety of interpretations. This was a fear for how CFSP matters would transpire in earlier years, with anxiety that they would be reduced to 'empty phrases'.[67] The Joint Actions set out the Union's general policy in selected areas; however, they had built-in flexibility to handle an array of situations, and were also used for the designation of special representatives (EUSR).

The legal provisions for CFSP matters can be utilised for a range of Union goals, whether it is supporting the promotion of democracy in third states, or fighting the global 'war on terror',[68] amongst other goals. The first Joint Action was in regard to what was the then Yugoslavia,[69] with Joint Actions being used right up to their merger into the post-Lisbon framework, with the initiation of Operation Atalanta in the Gulf of Aden.[70] The Treaty of Lisbon abolished Joint Actions and Common Positions, with Article 25 TEU now stating the 'Union shall conduct the common foreign and security policy by…adopting decisions defining: (i) actions to be undertaken by the Union; (ii) positions to be taken by the Union'. This actions and positions distinction caters for the pre-Lisbon distinctions of Joint Actions and Common Positions that have been now streamlined into CFSP Decisions. Despite this simplification of instruments, largely terminological in nature,[71] it still must be borne in mind that the amalgamated CFSP Decisions will continue to be used for a range of different circumstances. CFSP Decisions can have vague wording,[72] but are not to be assumed as a licence to have flagrant disregard for other important aspects of Union law. For example, EU fundamental rights must

[66] Paul Craig and Gráinne De Búrca, *EC Law: Text, Cases and Materials* (Clarendon Press, 1995) p 30. On Joint Actions generally, see, Alan Dashwood, 'The Law and Practice of CFSP Joint Actions' in Cremona and De Witte (eds), *EU Foreign Relations Law: Constitutional Fundamentals* (Hart Publishing, 2008).

[67] Ramses A Wessel, 'The Inside Looking Out: Consistency and Delimitation in EU External Relations' (2000) 37 *Common Market Law Review* 1135 at 1168.

[68] See, Christophe Hillion, 'Fighting Terrorism through the Common Foreign and Security Policy' in Inge Govaere and Sara Poli (eds), *EU Management of Global Emergencies: Legal Framework for Combating Threats and Crises* (Brill 2014).

[69] L 286/1. Council Decision of 8 November 1993 Concerning the Joint Action Decided on by the Council on the Basis of Article J.3 of the Treaty on European Union on Support for the Convoying of Humanitarian Aid in Bosnia and Herzegovina (93/603/CFSP).

[70] L 301/33. Council Joint Action 2008/851/CFSP of 10 November 2008 on a European Union Military Operation to Contribute to the Deterrence, Prevention and Repression of Acts of Piracy and Armed Robbery off the Somali Coast.

[71] Bruno De Witte, 'Legal Instruments and Law-Making in the Lisbon Treaty' in Stefan Griller and Jacques Ziller (eds), *The Lisbon Treaty: EU Constitutionalism without a Constitutional Treaty?* vol 11 (Springer, 2008) p 90.

[72] See, Ramses A Wessel, 'Flipping the Question: The Reception of EU Law in the International Legal Order' (2016) 35 *Yearbook of European Law* 533.

be respected in CFSP matters.[73] There is also the ability to adopt a Decision on 'strategic interests' in the European Council in CFSP matters,[74] but post-Lisbon, this has not been utilised as a legal basis.

CFSP Decisions can attribute support to third states for specific actions. Given the foreign policy nature of CFSP matters, it is no surprise that the Council prefers to operationalise Decisions upon a CFSP legal basis, as opposed to opting for a non-CFSP legal basis for executing actions. The Council's position in the driving seat ensures that it remains in as much control as possible over the direction of EU foreign policy. Whilst Decisions are formally taken at political level, in reality, many are, in fact, taken in sub-divisions of the Council, such as the Political and Security Committee (PSC), or Committee of Permanent Representatives (COREPER). CFSP Decisions sometimes need to be taken quickly, especially if they include financial and economic matters. Swift action is therefore needed to follow-up on such commitments. Article 25 TEU permits the Union to adopt Decisions, define resulting actions, and other implementation arrangements, including positions and arrangements and the strengthening of cooperation in CFSP matters between Member States.

3.2. Non-parliamentary and Judicial Actors

Within EU foreign policy, the functional role of each of the Union's institutions differs and the typical institutional balance is not, *per se*, applicable in practice. There are 'fewer and interrelated protagonists'.[75] Union institutions, in the eyes of its judiciary, have 'broad discretion conferred…as regards the European Union's external relations'.[76] Political actors, of which the key institutions and the Member States, as a matter of course, all have differing agendas in varying Union policies. It is natural for national governments from Member States to shield as much of what they can from other actors at Union level outside of the Council. By trying to operate in a sphere free from intrusion or encroachment, CFSP matters have for many years worked through its own rules in this manner.

CFSP matters are generally seen through the eyes of the Member States who make up the Council and European Council. The strategic agenda formed by the

[73] See, Christophe Hillion, 'Decentralised Integration? Fundamental Rights Protection in the EU Common Foreign and Security Policy' (2016) 1 *European Papers* 55.

[74] TEU, Article 26(1), second para: 'If international developments so require, the President of the European Council shall convene an extraordinary meeting of the European Council in order to define the strategic lines of the Union's policy in the face of such developments.'

[75] Christophe Hillion, 'Conferral, Cooperation and Balance in the Institutional Framework of EU External Action' in Marise Cremona (ed), *Structural Principles in EU External Relations Law* (Hart Publishing, 2018) p 164.

[76] Joined Cases T-208/11 and T-508/11, *LTTE v Council*, ECLI:EU:T:2014:885 ('*Tamil Tigers*'), para 71. Institutional discretion has been discussed for some time. See, Case C-52/81, *Offene Handelsgesellschaft in Firma Werner Faust v Commission*, ECLI:EU:C:1982:369 ('*Faust*').

European Council is then left to the Council for the formulation and execution of this policy, with the assistance of Article 21 TEU. The distinction between the Council and the European Council when it comes to CFSP matters is only particularly noticeable when it comes to specific roles for invoking the passerelle clause.[77] Whilst CFSP matters at the Council are built upon consensus, this is not always reflected in the other Union institutions without such a stranglehold on CFSP matters. Tension between the European Council and other institutional actors like the Parliament can occur.[78] The European Council is today a more energetic protagonist in the origination of CFSP matters, but not on its conclusions, which are left to the Council. Nevertheless, the rise of the European Council has been predicted for some time[79] and, with many crises facing the Union since the Treaty of Lisbon, this position has been entrenched further.

3.2.1. The High Representative

The Member States in the Council are the holders of political influence in CFSP matters. The High Representative of the Union primarily fronts CFSP matters on the political stage, whom is regularly referred to informally as the 'EU foreign policy chief' but does not exercise EU foreign policy in a sole manner. The role of the High Representative was established in 1999 with the Treaty of Amsterdam and was created for CFSP matters. As a policy area, CFSP matters are under the remit of the High Representative and all other external relations policies are handled by the Commission.[80] With the European External Action Service (EEAS), the Council lost much of its executive power in CFSP matters, beyond its retained decision-making capabilities.

Elsewhere, the Commission, an 'autonomous political force',[81] has played a lesser role in CFSP matters than it would have wanted, given its extended role in non-CFSP external relations. In practice, the High Representative handles functions for EU foreign policy that would be similar to that of the Commission in other external policies. However, its multi-hatted position makes the High Representative's role most unusual, in that whilst a member of the Commission, the holders 'shall take part in its [Council's] work'.[82] This cross-cutting role is cemented,

[77] Discussed in Chapter 7 of this book.

[78] For example, see, Parliament resolution of 12 June 2013 on strengthening European democracy in the future EMU (2013/2672(RSP)), where the Parliament stated that the European Council, 'does not have any Treaty-based prerogative of legislative initiative and that it must stop instructing the Commission on the form and/or content of any further legislative initiative and bypassing the Commission's coordinating, executive and management roles as laid down in the [t]reaties'.

[79] It was called the 'real winner in the institutional battle for power that has taken place since 1999', in Joakim Nergelius, ''De-Legalize It' – On Current Tendencies in EC Constitutional Law' (2001) 21 *Yearbook of European Law* 443 at 462.

[80] Mauro Gatti, 'Diplomats at the Bar: The European External Action Service before EU Courts' (2014) 39 *European Law Review* 664 at 670.

[81] Joseph HH Weiler, *The Constitution of Europe: 'Do the New Clothes Have an Emperor?' And Other Essays on European Integration* (Cambridge University Press, 1999) p 89.

[82] TEU, Article 15(2).

with Article 27 TEU laying out the contributing and implementing aspects of the position – a coordinator in many senses of the term.

The very creation of the role of the High Representative marked an improvement in institutionalising CFSP matters. The place of the External Relations Commissioner was taken over by the High Representative. The first High Representative post-Lisbon may have been criticised for not fully developing the hat of the Vice-President of the Commission enough during the term of office, but could equally be complemented on steering the new position on a path that set the tone for how the new position across an array of areas would function.

The Constitutional Treaty had signalled this position was supposed to be a 'Union Minister for Foreign Affairs' but the Treaty never came into force. Whilst the affixation of a new title and its enhanced role were forthright and visionary, in one sense, it was seen in purely descriptive terms as 'unnecessarily provocative'.[83] Yet the mere creation of a Union Minister was not a primary reason for the Treaty's rejection. Notwithstanding the setback, the position today is largely the same post-Lisbon as it was envisaged, without the upgraded title.

3.2.2. Diplomatic and Military Actors

The Council and its sub-bodies form an extensive administrative structure to draw-up, decide, and implement CFSP matters. The Council plays a powerful role.[84] The Council Secretariat is normally responsible for legislative deliberation in non-CFSP matters. For CFSP however, it is far more controlling in this non-legislative area with executive formation, decision-making, and oversight. In this sense, it is replacing a functionary role of the Parliament and the Court by also fulfilling their traditional role, given the treaties allow for it. The Council itself could be considered an internally plural body, with working groups, sub-bodies, and preparatory compositions. Within it, discussion of EU foreign policy includes numerous stakeholders, including the European Council, the Council, the General Affairs Council, the Political and Security Committee (PSC), Committee of Permanent Representatives (COREPER), and Delegations of Member States, amongst others.

The PSC, also known as *Comité politique et de sécurité* ('COPS'), is an arm of the Council in CFSP matters. Located in Article 38 TEU with its 'political mind',[85] it is a contradiction in a sense given many of the representatives of EU Member States forming part of the PSC are career diplomats, as opposed to elected or appointed politicians. With its roots in the political directorships from national

[83] David AO Edward and Robert Lane, *Edward and Lane on European Union Law* (Edward Elgar, 2013) p 101 (Section 3.11).

[84] Philipp Dann, 'The Political Institutions' in Armin Von Bogdandy and Jürgen Bast (eds), *Principles of European Constitutional Law* 2nd edition (Hart Publishing, 2009) pp 261–66.

[85] Thym, (n 53) p 518.

foreign ministries during the days when EU foreign policy was conducted in EPC formation, it became more integrated as a permanent setup to service ESDP, later and today known as CSDP.[86] Its cementing nature as an actor within the remit of the EU legal order has meant that it is more than a mere supporting body, but rather a functional actor in the building and development of CFSP matters. It has been said that the PSC prepares with 'great care and foresight',[87] and now has a permanent chairperson. In acting in this policy sphere, the PSC acts like the Commission would in any other policy field. With light detail as regards its procedure in CFSP matters, its working arrangements are flexible,[88] but it is nonetheless a 'lynchpin' for CFSP matters.[89]

Whilst PSC plays a 'pivotal role' in determining the shape and reality of CFSP matters,[90] its setup is not a unique invention of the EU and draws strong resonance with a comparable Brussels-based actor; that of the North Atlantic Council embedded in the North Atlantic Treaty Organisation (NATO). Between the two, considerable contrasts can be drawn.[91] Below the PSC, and given that CFSP matters encompasses CSDP matters, there is also the status of the European Union Military Committee (EUMC) that encompasses all the Chiefs of Staff of the various armed forces of Member States. With the EU having multiple operational missions located in third states around the world, with each being led by an Operation Commander, the EUMC serves as the interlocutor between these operations and the political actors at EU level.[92] Homed within the Council, the PSC has no primary law relations, legally speaking, with the Parliament.

Leaving PSC to one side leads onto COREPER, which has equally compelling dimensions for CFSP matters, as it handles some overlap with the PSC. Decisions at the PSC go through to COREPER, before going onwards to the Council's political formation. The traditional role of COREPER was to secure the 'buy-in' of Member States into Union policies as it shared power with institutions that were not centred on the Member States. However, in CFSP matters, it is not other institutions it has to deal with, but rather, other sub-bodies within the Council. COREPER, officially '[a] committee consisting of the Permanent Representatives

[86] Council of the European Union, 'Presidency Report on the European Security and Defence Policy (ST 14056 2000 COR 1) (4 December 2000)'.

[87] Daniel Thym, 'Beyond Parliament's Reach? The Role of the European Parliament in the CFSP' (2006) 11 *European Foreign Affairs Review* 109 at 110.

[88] See, Ana E Juncos and Christopher Reynolds, 'The Political and Security Committee: Governing in the Shadow' (2007) 12 *European Foreign Affairs Review* 127.

[89] Stephan Marquardt, 'The Institutional Framework, Legal Instruments and Decision-Making Procedures' in Steven Blockmans and Panos Koutrakos (eds), *Research Handbook on the EU's Common Foreign and Security Policy* (Edward Elgar, 2018) p 24.

[90] Ariella Huff, 'Problems and Patterns in Parliamentary Scrutiny of the CFSP and CSDP' [2014] Observatory of Parliaments after the Lisbon Treaty 1 at 6.

[91] They are discussed at depth in, Jolyon Howorth, 'NATO and ESDP: Institutional Complexities and Political Realities' [2009] *Politique étrangère* 95.

[92] This is principally done through the Chairman. See, Mikhail Kostarakos, 'The Role of the European Union Military Committee in EU External Relations' (2018) 23 *European Foreign Affairs Review* 435.

of the Governments of the Member States',[93] is tasked with the Council's workload, 'preparing the work of the Council',[94] carrying out its tasks on a permanent basis, representing the views of the Member States. Notwithstanding COREPER's legal basis, it has strong involvement in CFSP matters given it is part-and-parcel of the Council's workload and, accordingly, is guaranteed to be at the helm of CFSP matters in conjunction with the PSC.

The EEAS, upon its establishment in 2011, encompassed the operational functions of CFSP matters.[95] The setup of the EEAS entails that the Commission, on occasion, runs parallel structures on the Union's external action outside of CFSP matters in the TFEU[96] to ensure that nothing is missed. After the establishment of the EEAS, only a small number of Directorate-Generals (DGs) moved from the Commission. Certain DGs in the field of external relations such as Humanitarian Aid and Enlargement remained in the Commission, thus continuing the dividing line between the different types of external action that the Union engages in.

The actual legal basis of the EEAS is located within the CFSP articles of the treaties under Article 27(3) TEU, which also ensured the Parliament was involved in the CFSP decision to establish the EEAS. Under the EEAS, the Delegations of the European Union can even represent the Union on CFSP matters externally.[97] despite Delegations having their legal basis set out in Article 221(1) TFEU,[98] a non-CFSP legal basis. Acts of the EEAS have been identified as not belonging exclusively to the domain of CFSP matters,[99] given its establishment was based on both a CFSP legal basis and a non-CFSP legal basis. The EEAS is, therefore, a body that has cross-treaty activities. As a result, it is apparent that institutional conflict exists between the Council, the Commission, the Parliament, and the EEAS, on matters of competence.

[93] TFEU, Article 240.

[94] TEU, Article 16(7).

[95] L 201/30. Council Decision of 26 July 2010 Establishing the Organisation and Functioning of the European External Action Service (2010/427/EU).

[96] Jan Wouters and others, 'The Organisation and Functioning of the European External Action Service: Achievements, Challenges and Opportunities' (European Parliament Directorate-General for External Policies of the Union 2013) p 46. The EEAS has been compared to being 'functionally akin to a Commission DG'. Bart Van Vooren, 'A Legal-Institutional Perspective on the European External Action Service' (2011) 48 *Common Market Law Review* 475 at 499.

[97] Edith Drieskens, 'What's in a Name? Challenges to the Creation of EU Delegations' (2012) 7 *The Hague Journal of Diplomacy* 51 at 58. It is worth noting that the Delegations are not considered as possessing legal personality in their own right. As put by the General Court, 'the legal status of the Union Delegations is characterised by a two-fold organic and functional dependence with respect to the EEAS and the Commission, which precludes their being considered a body for the purposes of Article 263 TFEU'. Case T-395/11, *Elti d.o.o. v Delegation of the European Union to Montenegro*, ECLI:EU:T:2012:274, para 46.

[98] TFEU, Article 221(1): 'Union delegations in third countries and at International organisations shall represent the Union'. Furthermore, Article 221(2) states: 'Union delegations shall be placed under the authority of the High Representative of the Union for Foreign Affairs and Security Policy. They shall act in close cooperation with Member States' diplomatic and consular missions.' That being said, Delegations are also mentioned in the CFSP Articles in the treaties, but only in passing in TEU, Article 32, third para, and TEU, Article 35, first para.

[99] Gatti (n 80) p 668.

3.2.3. The Absence of the Commission

The consistency requirement for external policies means the Commission has a similar role to that of the Council and the High Representative, ensuring overall consistency within external relations and all policies.[100] However, the European Commission has no competence to take any other actor to the Court for failing to adhere to CFSP Decisions set down in the treaties. Indeed, CFSP matters are only one of a small number of areas specified in the treaties where the Commission has no enforcement powers,[101] with its legitimacy not extending beyond the technocratic. Actions through CFSP Decisions are not based on Commission proposals; however, the ability of the Commission to have indirect influence leading to a CFSP Decision is a distinct possibility given that the Commission has a strong role to play in non-CFSP external relations. Even so, the Commission has no direct legal basis for ensuring that CFSP Decisions are implemented in conformity with the treaties.[102] This, in turn, opens up the role for Parliament to oppose the use of actions decided upon a CFSP legal basis – a right to defend its institutional prerogatives, for which it has had to litigate,[103] with a 'structural disincentive' for the Commission to have an interest in CFSP matters.[104]

Since this most recent significant overhaul, the Commission no longer has an autonomous right of initiative in CFSP matters,[105] despite it being limited in the first place.[106] On that view, and with CFSP's non-legislative legal acts, the Citizens' Initiative would appear not to apply to CFSP matters.[107] Moreover, the Treaty of Lisbon also did not provide for the Commission's full association with CFSP

[100] TEU, Article 21(3), second para: 'The Union shall ensure consistency between the different areas of its external action and between these and its other policies. The Council and the Commission, assisted by the High Representative of the Union for Foreign Affairs and Security Policy, shall ensure that consistency and shall cooperate to that effect.'

[101] Christophe Hillion, 'Overseeing the Rule of Law in the EU: Legal Mandate and Means' in Carlos Closa and Dimitry Kochenov (eds), *Reinforcing Rule of Law Oversight in the European Union* (Cambridge University Press, 2016) p 66.

[102] Jean-Claude Piris, *The Lisbon Treaty: A Legal and Political Analysis* (Cambridge University Press, 2010) p 264.

[103] See Chapter 4 of this book.

[104] Inge Govaere, 'Multi-Faceted Single Legal Personality and a Hidden Horizontal Pillar: EU External Relations Post-Lisbon' in Catherine Barnard and Okeoghene Odudu (eds), *Cambridge Yearbook of European Legal Studies 2010–2011: Volume 13* (Hart Publishing, 2011) p 108.

[105] Article 22(1) of the pre-Lisbon TEU: 'Any Member State or the Commission may refer to the Council any question relating to the common foreign policy and may submit proposals to the Council'. This provision has its roots in Article J.8(3) of the Treaty of Maastricht. See, Piris (n 102) p 262.

[106] Yet, it should be pointed out that despite the limited linking of CFSP with the Commission, its 'shaping of…CFSP [is] somewhat greater in reality than one would assume'. Henri De Waele, *Legal Dynamics of EU External Relations: Dissecting a Layered Global Player* 2nd edition (Springer, 2017) p 43.

[107] TEU, Article 11(4), the legal basis, appears directed at the Commission only. As put, 'there is no provision…for a [Citizens' Initiative] to be presented…to any of the other institutions (or bodies or agencies) of the Union for their consideration or action'. Michael Dougan, 'What Are We to Make of the Citizens' Initiative?' (2011) 48 *Common Market Law Review* 1807 at 1837.

matters, as was the case pre-Lisbon.[108] However, the Commission is the institution which could propose a change, albeit informally through a Communication, as to how CFSP matters are decided.[109] The issue of the Commission's involvement in CFSP matters remains a delicate affair.

In contrast to the Commission, the European Court of Auditors (ECA) has a role in CFSP matters. Given that all expenditures of the Union, including budgetary manners pertaining to CFSP matters fall under the jurisdiction of the ECA,[110] CFSP matters do not escape the Council's attempted institutional monopoly. The ECA undertook a special report on CFSP matters in 2001 and noted that the roles of the Council and Commission in CFSP matters made day-to-day matters for Joint Actions more complicated than they ought to have been.[111] This can partially help to explain a lesser role for the Commission today and the abolition of Joint Actions.

3.3. Choice of Legal Basis and the Centre of Gravity

Central to the issue of external relations is the choice of legal basis that is available to the empowered actors. The choice of legal basis proffers a situation where more than one legal avenue is available for pursuing a particular course of action. There are numerous cases on the choice of correct legal basis, some of more importance than others.[112]

Practical every-day politics are at the heart of both national and European governance regimes. National foreign ministries have civilised interaction with one another. Whilst they are focused on the rules of the game, they are informally bound by customary practice. Even so, every legal act of the Union must be grounded upon a legal basis as stipulated in the treaties. The choice of this legal basis is critical, particularly in external action; as it is legal basis that determines the decision-making regime that is applicable for the desired act. Hence, policy objectives may be set out to define the chosen legal basis.

[108] Article 27 of the pre-Lisbon TEU, and was originally Article J.9.

[109] See Chapter 7 of this book.

[110] TFEU, Article 287(1): 'The Court of Auditors shall examine the accounts of all revenue and expenditure of the Union. It shall also examine the accounts of all revenue and expenditure of all bodies, offices or agencies set up by the Union in so far as the relevant constituent instrument does not preclude such examination.'

[111] See, C 338/1. Court of Auditors: Special Report No 13/2001 on the Management of the Common Foreign and Security Policy (CFSP), Together with the Council's Replies and the Commission's Replies (Pursuant to Article 248(4), Second Subpara, EC) (2001/C 338/01).

[112] Case C-166/07, *Parliament v Council*, ECLI:EU:C:2009:499 ('*International Fund for Ireland*'), described as 'a positive contribution…on the choice of legal basis'. See, Koen Lenaerts, 'EU Federalism in 3-D' in Elke Cloots, Geert De Baere and Stefan Sottiaux (eds), *Federalism in the European Union* (Hart Publishing, 2012) p 29, and Tim Corthaut, 'Case C-166/07, European Parliament v. Council of the European Union, Judgment of the Court of Justice (Grand Chamber) of 3 September 2009' (2011) 48 *Common Market Law Review* 1271.

3.3.1. International Agreements

The international agreements into which the Union enters are integrally political in nature. For international agreements that the EU opens, negotiates, and concludes as part of its external relations, it is critically different from an internal point of view whether or not it includes CFSP matters. However, common features apply. International agreements for CFSP matters are entered into by the Union based on Article 37 TEU,[113] following CFSP Decisions,[114] but they are subject to other non-CFSP provisions contained within the treaties, particularly Article 218 TFEU for procedures surrounding international agreements. International agreements can be an abnormal source of Union law, but nonetheless, their uncharacteristic nature forms an 'integral part' of Union law.[115] In that vein, international agreements concluded by the Union alone on a CFSP legal basis form an integral part of the Union legal order.[116] Whereas there was some hesitation on this point, Article 216 TFEU today puts that beyond doubt,[117] as does Article 218 TFEU.[118]

The choice of legal basis, which has particular institutional implications, has seen increased litigation. From an institutional standpoint, the choice of legal basis could not be more profound. Ever since the Single European Act, the number of such cases before the Court contesting it has increased,[119] but that is not because of the treaties alone. Rather, it can also be attributed to an overall EU legal culture of litigating for change. Ascertaining whether an international agreement includes CFSP matters is an area that innately attracts controversy.[120] The choice reflects the involvement of different institutions with the decision-making procedures flowing from this choice being of critical importance. The Court only recently stated in *Ahmed Abdelaziz Ezz* that there is 'broad scope of the aims and objectives of…CFSP [matters], as expressed in Articles 3(5) TEU and 21 TEU'.[121] Thus, the language of CFSP matters and general external objectives are open to interpretation.

Every institution of the Union is guilty of interpreting the treaties to suit its own agenda. This is a necessity for survival in the complex legal web that is Union

[113] TEU, Article 37: 'The Union may conclude agreements with one or more States or International organisations in areas covered by this Chapter.

[114] TEU, Articles 28 and 29.

[115] Case C-181/73, *Haegemann v Belgium*, ECLI:EU:C:1974:41, para 5.

[116] Wessel (n 46) p 17.

[117] Allan Rosas, 'The Status in EU Law of International Agreements Concluded by EU Member States' (2011) 34 *Fordham International Law Journal* 1304 at 1343.

[118] The Court has consistently applied elements of Article 218 TFEU to the conclusion of all types of international agreements. Discussed in Chapter 4 of this book.

[119] See, Kieran St C Bradley, 'The European Court and the Legal Basis of Community Legislation' (1988) 13 *European Law Review* 379.

[120] Panos Koutrakos, 'International Agreements in the Area of the EU's Common Security and Defence Policy' in Enzo Cannizzaro, Paolo Palchetti and Ramses A Wessel (eds), *International Law as Law of the European Union* (Martinus Nijhoff Publishers, 2012) p 162.

[121] Case C-220/14 P, *Ahmed Abdelaziz Ezz and Others v Council*, ECLI:EU:C:2015:147, para 46.

law-making and competency arguments in and between Union institutions and the Member States themselves. In principle, the institutions should not use a legal basis to circumvent restrictions laid down in another legal basis. The Court has stated in earlier case law that 'the choice of legal basis for a measure may not depend simply on an institution's conviction'.[122] The choice of legal basis invariably gives rise to tensions that stoke interinstitutional conflict. Rather than institutions deliberating on whether the Union should act or not, discussion will be had on which legal bases the Union should attempt to use as a foundation for its actions. Though this is not always done, the choice of legal basis should be based on objective criteria, as stipulated time and again in the case law of the Court.

The underlying purpose of an international agreement is a core element in deciding whether a particular legal basis is appropriate. The objective of an action in deciding the legality of the legal basis is a key determinant that is used by the practitioner[123] which, for CFSP matters, is the Council. The importance of the legal basis cannot be understated. The Court itself has said, 'the choice of the appropriate legal basis has constitutional significance'.[124] This settled assertion of the Court suggests that when the treaties provide for a competence to be used for a particular measure, the action must be founded upon that basis.[125] It must be an objective test, as opposed to a subjective one, to determine the correct legal basis of a Union action or measure.

3.3.2. Objectives

The articles covering CFSP matters in the treaties, whilst on first reading would seem quite descriptive in terms of the procedures that must be followed compared to other external policies of the Union, are instead widely ambiguous. On direct reading, the choice of legal basis for external action can prove somewhat difficult given that CFSP matters 'shall cover all areas of foreign policy'.[126] Prima facie, this does not fit well with the principle of conferral set out in Article 5 TEU. This tremendously broad scope, on face value, gives the actors some flexibility in their choice of legal basis. Article 24 TEU is too broad, which therefore serves no real practicable purpose at all, and therefore, is not to be read on face value.

[122] Case C-45/86, *Commission v Council*, ECLI:EU:C:1987:163 ('*Generalised Tariff Preferences*'), para 11.

[123] Ton Van den Brink, 'Towards an Ever Clearer Division of Authority Between the European Union and the Member States?' in Ton Van den Brink, Michiel Luchtman and Miraslava Scholten (eds), *Sovereignty in the Shared Legal Order of the EU: Core Values of Regulation and Enforcement* (Intersentia, 2015) p 222.

[124] *Opinion 2/00*, ECLI:EU:C:2001:664 ('*Cartagena Protocol*'), para 5.

[125] Case C-155/07, *Parliament v Council*, ECLI:EU:C:2008:605 ('*European Investment Bank*'), para 34. This is supported by Case C-338/01, *Commission v Council*, ECLI:EU:C:2004:253, para 60, and Case C-533/03, *Commission v Council*, ECLI:EU:C:2006:64, para 45.

[126] TEU, Article 24(1).

Such far-reaching possibilities are different to other Union policies, which usually have a particular objective in mind. With EU foreign policy, there is no definitive end goal; with aims and objectives arising at various times, which the Council may pursue if it so decides. If one were to read Article 24 TEU in isolation from the rest of the treaties, it could be understood that CFSP matters refer to all areas of the Union's external relations. This, of course, is not the case, as specific competence laid out in the treaties should be read alongside the general competence like the broad-stroke policy claims that CFSP matters make.[127] With Article 1 TEU requiring that the TEU and TFEU be given 'the same legal value', it does not indicate what legal basis would be most appropriate.

With Article 40 TEU stating that CFSP matters 'shall not affect the application of the procedures and the extent of the powers of the institutions laid down by the treaties for the exercise of the Union competences referred to in Articles 3 to 6 TFEU', there is no preference given to either a CFSP legal basis or a non-CFSP legal basis. The TFEU recognises CFSP matters in Article 2(4) TFEU, stating 'the Union shall have competence, in accordance with the provisions of the Treaty on European Union, to define and implement a common foreign and security policy, including the progressive framing of a common defence policy'. Article 40 TEU therefore can be said to be 'protection against mutual encroachment'[128] and allowing such a legal basis dispute to be fought at the Court. Article 40 TEU's legitimate aim, however, is to protect the rules-based intergovernmental decision-making of CFSP matters.

There are conflicting viewpoints on whether EU foreign policy is too enshrined in EU constitutional law, or whether it should be given more flexibility. Thus, it can be questioned if there is too much constitutional law in the external relations.[129] Inevitability, the limits of a CFSP legal basis are tested and disputed between actors, before eventually ending up in front of the EU judiciary. The Court itself, whilst somewhat restricted in CFSP matters,[130] is not as curtailed as it once was.[131] When action is taken before the Court, it is usually because an actor with an interest in the choice of legal basis believes the incorrect basis has been selected over an alternative.

Under the arrangements before the Treaty of Lisbon, Article 2 TEU stated the Union should 'maintain in full the *acquis communautaire* and build on it with a view to considering to what extent the policies and forms of cooperation introduced by this [t]reaty may need to be revised with the aim of ensuring

[127] This is covered in full by, Cremona (n 19) pp 1201–02.

[128] Dashwood and others (n 7) p 908.

[129] See, Bruno De Witte, 'Too Much Constitutional Law in the European Union's Foreign Relations?' in Cremona and De Witte (eds), *EU Foreign Relations Law: Constitutional Fundamentals* (Hart Publishing, 2008).

[130] Discussed extensively in Chapter 5 of this book.

[131] See, Christophe Hillion, 'A Powerless Court? The European Court of Justice and the Common Foreign and Security Policy' in Marise Cremona and Anne Thies (eds), *The European Court of Justice and External Relations Law: Constitutional Challenges* (Hart Publishing, 2014).

the effectiveness of the mechanisms and the institutions'. This statement could have been interpreted as stating that, where it is necessary, a Union competence should be used. This wording is no longer present in the treaties post-Lisbon and has been deleted, with its meaning and historic term that will disappear into EU legal history. With Article 1 TEU now stating both the TEU and TFEU 'shall have the same legal value', this equal basis between the two treaties poses a problem for saying categorically which legal basis for external action measures should be used. Pre-Lisbon, whilst priority was given to an EC legal basis, now TFEU,[132] the present Article 40 TEU now provides equality between the TEU and TFEU competence, reinforced by Article 1 TFEU.[133] This, in turn, means that the pre-Lisbon era of the first pillar always winning no longer applies.

Objectives of EU legal acts are not an easy issue to trace, especially when pre-Lisbon, the Court said objectives in the TEU against those in the TFEU, cannot necessarily be linked.[134] Deciphering the ultimate aim of EU international agreements, versus other ancillary measures contained within an agreement is a futile exercise, and one that may not be justiciable.[135] To give an example, international agreements on a CFSP legal basis do not have to be purely CFSP matters, but rather, have to be primarily CFSP matters, and can incorporate CCP elements.[136] When choosing an appropriate legal basis, an EU legal act must rest on objective factors that are amenable to judicial review, with due respect to the aim and content of that measure. This is settled case law of the Court and continues to be recited time and again,[137] with the Court even updating that test to not only include the aims and content, but also 'the context…at issue'.[138] Yet, this can be difficult to determine, and the predictability of finding such factors can be uncertain.

[132] The former pre-Lisbon TEU, Article 47 stated, 'nothing in this Treaty shall affect the [t]reaties establishing the European Communities', hence gave primacy to the EC Treaty (now TFEU).

[133] TEU, Article 1, para 2: 'This Treaty and the Treaty on European Union constitute the [t]reaties on which the Union is founded. These two [t]reaties, which have the same legal value, shall be referred to as 'the [t]reaties.'

[134] Opinion 2/94, ECLI:EU:C:1996:140 ('*Accession by the Community to the European Convention for the Protection of Human Rights and Fundamental Freedoms*'), para 30. This was reaffirmed in, Joined Cases C-402/05 P and C-415/05 P, *Yassin Abdullah Kadi and Al Barakaat International Foundation v Council and Commission*, ECLI:EU:C:2008:461 ('*Kadi I*'), para 126.

[135] This is discussed in the context of the CCP in, Marise Cremona, 'Balancing Union and Member State Interests: Opinion 1/2008, Choice of Legal Base and the Common Commercial Policy under the Treaty of Lisbon' (2010) 35 *European Law Review* 678.

[136] Inge Govaere, 'EU Common Commercial Policy Throwing Off the Shackles of "Mixity"' in Inge Govaere, Reinhard Quick and Marco Bronckers (eds), *Trade and Competition Law in the EU and Beyond* (Edward Elgar, 2011) p 148. For more on the intersection of CFSP matters and CCP matters, see, Andrea Ott and Guillaume Van der Loo, 'The Nexus between the CCP and the CFSP: Achieving Foreign Policy Goals through Trade Restrictions and Market Access' in Steven Blockmans and Panos Koutrakos (eds), *Research Handbook on the EU's Common Foreign and Security Policy* (Edward Elgar, 2018).

[137] Recently, see, Case C-363/14, *Parliament v Council*, ECLI:EU:C:2015:579, para 41; Case C-43/12, *Commission v Parliament and Council*, ECLI:EU:C:2014:298, para 29; Case C-411/06, *Commission v Parliament and Council*, EU:C:2009:518 ('*Basel Convention*'), para 45; Case C-130/10, *Parliament v Council*, EU:C:2012:472 ('*Smart Sanctions*'), para 42.

[138] Joined Cases C-626/15 and C-659/16, *Commission v Council (AMP Antarctique)*, ECLI:EU:C:2018:925, para 76. Previously, the context was only something the Court alluded to, such as

3.3.3. The Legal Basis

Upon the Council deciding that it wishes for the Union to enter into negotiations with a third party with the aim of concluding an international agreement, it nominates a negotiator.[139] Given that international agreements concluded on a CFSP legal basis embrace some elements of policies that could otherwise be concluded on a non-CFSP legal basis, the potential right of the Commission to be included in such agreements can be threatened. An established practice has emerged where the executive actor of a contested action, such as an internal legal act, or an international agreement will include a preamble. This, in turn, can be used purely for litigation purposes if the legal act were to be questioned on legal basis grounds before the Court,[140] to determine its centre of gravity. How the centre of gravity is specifically defined, however, by the key actors such as the Court is an intriguing question that needs to be probed much further.

It is not just the Parliament which has contested the legal basis of actions when it comes to matters of CFSP matters.[141] In the *Kazakhstan* case,[142] the Commission had contended that the Council had included an incorrect legal basis for the position of the Union within a Cooperation Council of Enhanced Partnership and Cooperation Agreement (EPCA) between the Union and its Member States, and Kazakhstan.[143] The position used both a CFSP legal basis and a non-CFSP legal basis. Given that the EPCA had very little to do with CFSP matters,[144] the Commission was dissatisfied with the additional CFSP legal basis added onto the non-CFSP legal basis, as this meant circumventing the decision-making procedures set down in the treaties. The Court agreed with the Commission, in that the Council had erred in including a CFSP provision, Article 31(1) TEU;[145]

'[t]he context of the measure in question may be relevant to the choice of its legal basis'. Case C-81/13, *United Kingdom of Great Britain and Northern Ireland v Council of the European Union*, ECLI:EU:C:2014:2449, para 38.

[139] TFEU, Article 218(3).

[140] Nicholas Emiliou, 'Opening Pandora's Box: The Legal Basis of Community Measures before the Court of Justice' (1994) 19 *European Law Review* 488 at 499.

[141] For the Parliament and its institutional rights, see Chapter 4 of this book.

[142] Case C-244/17, *Commission v Council (Accord avec le Kazakhstan)*, ECLI:EU:C:2018:662.

[143] The contested decision was, L 73/15. Council Decision (EU) 2017/477 of 3 March 2017 on the Position to Be Adopted on Behalf of the European Union within the Cooperation Council Established under the Enhanced Partnership and Cooperation Agreement between the European Union and Its Member States, of the One Part, and the Republic of Kazakhstan, of the Other Part as Regards the Working Arrangements of the Cooperation Council, the Cooperation Committee, Specialised Subcommittees or Any Other Bodies. The EPCA is L 29/1. Council Decision (EU) 2016/123 of 26 October 2015 on the Signing, on Behalf of the European Union, and Provisional Application of the Enhanced Partnership and Cooperation Agreement between the European Union and Its Member States, of the One Part, and the Republic of Kazakhstan, of the Other Part.

[144] Title II of the EPCA covered 'Political Dialogue; Cooperation in the field of Foreign and Security Policy', but by and large, the EPCA covered non-CFSP policies. L 29/3. Enhanced Partnership and Cooperation Agreement between the European Union and Its Member States, of the One Part, and the Republic of Kazakhstan, of the Other Part.

[145] 'It is clear that…links between the Partnership Agreement and the CFSP are not sufficient for it to be held that the legal basis of the decision on the signing of that agreement'. Case C-244/17, *Commission v Council (Accord avec le Kazakhstan)*, ECLI:EU:C:2018:662, para 42.

in addition to non-CFSP provisions, Article 91 TFEU, Article 100(2) TFEU, Article 207 TFEU and Article 209 TFEU. This centre of gravity approach, along the lines of primary objectives and ancillary objectives have been broached in other areas[146] and has not been confined to CFSP matters. The centre of gravity test, also known as a primary objective test, can be said to be a poor method of dealing with cases where there are multiple choices for a legal basis.[147] As such, it could even be said it is not an effective appliance for the field of external relations as a whole.[148]

Article 40 TEU has been described as the 'non-mutual contamination clause',[149] also known as a scheme of 'monitoring compliance'. Like many Articles in the treaties, it has its history. Prior to the Treaty of Lisbon coming into force, it was positioned as the then Article 47 TEU, stated that 'nothing in this [t]reaty shall affect the treaties establishing the European Communities'. Pre-Lisbon, a preference was given to an EC legal basis to prevent competence creep in CFSP matters. The way in which Union acted at this time could be challenged on this compliance article under the then Article 46(f) TEU on the limited jurisdiction of the Court, with examples being the *Ship-Source Pollution*, *Environmental Criminal Penalties*, and *Airport Transit Visas* cases.[150] The present Article 40 TEU attempts to ensure a level playing field between the TEU and TFEU, that is, a constitutional constraint on actions on a CFSP legal basis taking place within competence elsewhere in the treaties, but also *vice versa*. This division, arguably, makes it an opulent ground for legal basis disputes. It is hardly surprising that some Member States initially opposed the border-policing role now vested upon the Court during the Intergovernmental Conference leading to the Treaty of Lisbon. However, Article 40 TEU was cleverly worded for furthering the rules-based intergovernmental operation of CFSP matters.

[146] See, eg, in Case C-137/12, *Commission v Council*, ECLI:EU:C:2013:675 ('*Conditional Access Convention*'), para 76.

[147] The test being used in Case C-211/01, *Commission v Council* ('*Road Transport Agreement*'), ECLI:EU:C:2003:452. See, Christoph Herrmann, 'Gripping Global Governance: The External Relations of the EU Between the Treaty of Nice and the Convention on the Future of Europe' in Takis Tridimas and Paolisa Nebbia (eds), *European Union Law for the Twenty-First Century: Rethinking the New Legal Order – Volume 1: Constitutional and Public Law, External Relations* (Hart Publishing, 2004) p 297.

[148] Geert De Baere, 'From "Don't Mention the Titanium Dioxide Judgment" to "I Mentioned It Once, But I Think I Got Away with It All Right": Reflections on the Choice of Legal Basis in EU External Relations after the Legal Basis for Restrictive Measures Judgment' in Catherine Barnard and others (eds), *Cambridge Yearbook of European Legal Studies 2012–2013: Volume 15* (Hart Publishing, 2013) p 557.

[149] TEU, Article 40: 'The implementation of the common foreign and security policy shall not affect the application of the procedures and the extent of the powers of the institutions laid down by the [t]reaties for the exercise of the Union competences referred to in Articles 3 to 6 of the Treaty on the Functioning of the European Union. Similarly, the implementation of the policies listed in those Articles shall not affect the application of the procedures and the extent of the powers of the institutions laid down by the [t]reaties for the exercise of the Union competences under this Chapter.'

[150] Case C-440/05, *Commission v Council*, ECLI:EU:C:2007:625 ('*Ship-Source Pollution*'), para 74; Case C-176/03, *Commission v Council*, ECLI:EU:C:2005:542 ('*Environmental Criminal Penalties*'), para 53; and again under even older treaties, see, Case C-170/96, *Commission v Council*, ECLI:EU:C:1998:219 ('*Airport Transit Visas*').

With having universal external objectives for CFSP matters and non-CFSP matters being an asset for improving the coherence and effectiveness of EU external action, that political choice would not be without consequence. As such, without specific objectives for CFSP matters, the use of Article 40 TEU on border policing makes it a task that is intrinsically difficult. Furthermore, when the Council chooses a CFSP legal basis for an international agreement, that option can be difficult to challenge before the Court.[151] With no possibility for a TFEU legal basis preference, strictly speaking, it has potentially made the operation of external action more complex.

3.3.4. International Agreements

International agreements that the Union enters into can be divided into two parts: the substantive, and the procedural. Both are equally important for EU institutions, as treaty-making has produced some of the Court's most noteworthy case law going back many years.[152] The importance attached to the EU being in a position to conclude international agreements alone in particular fields cannot be underestimated. The general basis for these agreements stems from Article 216(1) TFEU, which specifies that the Union 'may conclude an agreement with one or more third countries or international organisations where the [t]reaties so provide or where the conclusion of an agreement is necessary in order to achieve, within the framework of the Union's policies, one of the objectives referred to in the [t]reaties, or is provided for in a legally binding Union act or is likely to affect common rules or alter their scope'.

International agreements are different to internal legal instruments availed of by the Union. Whereas internal Union instruments may be construed narrowly to reach a very particular short-medium term goal, international agreements are much broader in nature, and tend to foresee their applicability for a longer period of time. An assortment of sectoral areas can be included within an international agreement, with some fields being of more prominence than others, depending on whom the proposed international agreement is going to be with. Understanding why international agreements are so critical to the functioning of the Union can help to explain the (over-)reliance upon them.

In the earlier days of the then Community, the Member States had significant and long-established bilateral relations with third states and, with CCP as an exclusive competence of the Union, it was its primary instrument for

[151] Marise Cremona, 'External Competences and the Principle of Conferral' in Robert Schütze and Takis Tridimas (eds), *Oxford Principles of European Union Law, vol 1: The European Union Legal Order* (Oxford University Press, 2018) p 1125.

[152] Marise Cremona, 'The Doctrine of Exclusivity and the Position of Mixed Agreements in the External Relations of the European Community' (1982) 2 *Oxford Journal of Legal Studies* 393 at 393.

engaging externally. In external relations, mixed agreements are extensively used. Their nature has captured the attention of many scholars.[153] Since the Treaty of Maastricht, international agreements of a mixed nature have evolved further.[154] With CFSP matters not having specific objectives of its own since 2009, international agreements based on a CFSP legal basis are thus more likely to be subject to contestation by EU institutions beyond the Council, compared to other international agreements. Furthermore, there is a distinction to be drawn between the legal actions of signing of an international agreement, in contrast to its formal conclusion.

The Union was setup as a regular international organisation as opposed to the one of cooperative federalised structure that we see today. With the slow and natural transition to the Union in the way it acts,[155] it has an implicit effect on the nature of the international agreements it concludes. International agreements can be concluded in many areas covered by the treaties, covering both CFSP matters and non-CFSP matters. International agreements on CFSP matters in the pre-Lisbon times had their own procedure,[156] but have since come under the general Article 218 TFEU provisions. It is the Council in non-CFSP matters who issues the negotiating mandates of the Union for international agreements.[157] However, for CFSP matters, no mandate needs to be issued given the Council does everything internally, subject to their notification requirements under Article 218 TFEU. In non-CFSP matters, consent is required by the Parliament for international agreements, which come through the ordinary legislative procedure,[158] whereas for CFSP matters, no consent is necessary. International agreements concluded on a CFSP legal basis are almost always done by the Union alone, without Member States. Therefore, 'mixity' is not a predominant feature in CFSP matters in the same way it is for non-CFSP matters.

3.4. Contestation

EU external action is institutionally disjointed, yet, it operates within the EU legal framework. Had history taken a different course, EU external relations instruments

[153] See, David O'Keeffe and Henry G Schermers (eds), *Mixed Agreements* (Kluwer Law and Taxation Publishers, 1983) and, Christophe Hillion and Panos Koutrakos (eds), *Mixed Agreements Revisited: The EU and Its Member States in the World* (Hart Publishing, 2010).

[154] Frank Hoffmeister, 'Curse or Blessing? Mixed Agreements in the Recent Practice of the European Union and Its Member States' in Christophe Hillion and Panos Koutrakos (eds), *Mixed Agreements Revisited: The EU and its Member States in the World* (Hart Publishing, 2010) p 250.

[155] Robert Schütze, 'Federalism and Foreign Affairs: Mixity as a (Inter)national Phenomenon' in Christophe Hillion and Panos Koutrakos (eds), *Mixed Agreements Revisited: The EU and its Member States in the World* (Hart Publishing, 2010) p 72.

[156] See, Stephan Marquardt, 'The Conclusion of International Agreements Under Article 24 of the Treaty on European Union' in Vincent Kronenberger (ed), *The European Union and the International Legal Order: Discord or Harmony?* (TMC Asser Press, 2001).

[157] The negotiating mandate is sometimes also called a negotiating directive.

[158] TFEU, Article 218(6)(a)(v).

would have looked much different than they do today. Arguably, there is room for greater external action optimisation, yet the primary law framework dividing CFSP and non-CFSP matters has remained relatively stable. CFSP matters are not merely just one small part of Union law, but rather, a heavily significant feature of EU external relations law in its own right. Despite the often-leafy textual nature of CFSP matters, it is no small matter. As it is part of the constitutional framework of the Union, the legal provisions providing for CFSP matters have operative features that are utilised regularly for the implementation of Union legal acts.

The distinctive nature and features of CFSP matters have remained intact through several treaty revisions. Indeed, the legal architecture of external relations is difficult without a good understanding of the treaty development.[159] The apparent legal 'unity' of the Union,[160] may have been spoken about too soon, but nonetheless has been debated.[161] Given what is known of CFSP and non-CFSP matters working under one banner of the Union, it can be questioned whether actual Union coherence is really no more than a façade. Having EPC matters merged into the Union ended the 'artificial seclusion' of the two regimes,[162] with EPC matters being outside the Union, but other external policies with overlapping effect being inside.

In setting out CFSP matters, the treaties are not there to preserve national independence, or safeguard prerogatives.[163] Rather, they ensure codifying the practice of external action as developed. CFSP matters can be seen as the ultimate meeting of legal and political actors. What continues to mark them out are their key defining characteristics – decision-making procedures, stemming from its intergovernmental roots, maintaining strong executive power for Member States. The notion of executive power in the original design of the Union was never supposed to lie with Union actors beyond the Commission.[164] Yet Member States had a strong interest in keeping certain Union policies within the Council domain. Accordingly, from an integration perspective, the separation of CFSP matters from other areas of external action by the Union has been subject to entrenched criticism.

The existence of CFSP matters does not mean that the EU and its Member States have a single foreign policy, in fact, it is quite the opposite. EU Member States continue to have the ability to pursue their own agenda in the field, as long

[159] Marise Cremona, 'The Draft Constitutional Treaty: External Relations and External Action' (2003) 40 *Common Market Law Review* 1347 at 1366.

[160] See, Armin Von Bogdandy, 'The Legal Case for Unity: The European Union as a Single Organization with a Single Legal System' (1999) 36 *Common Market Law Review* 887.

[161] See, Nadia Klein and Wolfgang Wessels, 'CFSP Progress or Decline after Lisbon?' (2013) 18 *European Foreign Affairs Review* 449.

[162] Edmund Wellenstein, 'Twenty-Five Years of European Community External Relations' (1979) 16 *Common Market Law Review* 407 at 421.

[163] Eileen Denza, 'Lines in the Sand: Between Common Foreign Policy and Single Foreign Policy' in Takis Tridimas and Paolisa Nebbia (eds), *European Union Law for the Twenty-First Century: Rethinking the New Legal Order – Volume 1: Constitutional and Public Law, External Relations* (Hart Publishing, 2004) p 264.

[164] Deirdre Curtin, 'Democratic Accountability of EU Executive Power: A Reform Agenda for Parliaments' in Federico Fabbrini, Ernst Hirsch Ballin and Han Somsen (eds), *What Form of Government for the European Union and the Eurozone?* (Hart Publishing, 2015) p 178.

as this does not come into direct conflict with an agreed course of action. The foundational elements of the Union's external relations have remained static for some time and show no signs of being unearthed in the foreseeable future. The structure of CFSP matters remains a legal choice of the High Contracting Parties to the treaties; with a desire by EU Member States to retain as much autonomy as possible over the law of EU foreign policy. With a high level of control, Member States are of the opinion that they are adequately able to defend national interests and exert control over EU foreign policy. For example, in the United Kingdom's 2016 balance of competences review, it stated that for CFSP matters, 'the balance of competence lies squarely with the Member States'.[165]

The preamble to the TEU expresses the desire to have an 'efficient functioning of the institutions…to enable them better to carry out, within a single institutional framework the tasks entrusted to them'. It is clear that external relations and the existence of CFSP matters in no way fulfil this desired goal just yet. Large to near-absolute consensus is still needed in CFSP matters from a political perspective, and certainly from a legal standpoint. Occasional proposals are floated suggesting radical reform to decision-making procedures for CFSP matters, such as a veto only for the five large EU Member States[166] or more realistic proposals.[167] Leading up to the Constitutional Treaty, proposals were considered to allow QMV within the Council on a range of policy areas instead of unanimity, including for CFSP matters. However, with 'deeply entrenched views' held by several Member States,[168] CFSP matters in overall form did not make it into a package of QMV issues. Instead, the unanimity clauses for CFSP matters were maintained,[169] which has continued post-Lisbon.

3.4.1. The Flexibility Clause

External policies of the Union can vary, and at times, they can be 'ruthlessly cross-cutting'.[170] Article 352 TFEU today serves as the basis for the entry of EU

[165] HM Government, 'Review of the Balance of Competences between the United Kingdom and the European Union: Foreign Policy' (HM Government 2013) p 5.

[166] Geoffrey Howe, 'Towards a Common Foreign Policy' in Tom Heukels, Niels Blokker and Marcel Brus (eds), *The European Union after Amsterdam: A Legal Analysis* (Kluwer Law International, 1998) p 200.

[167] See Chapter 7 of this book.

[168] Bobby McDonagh, 'The Intergovernmental Conference: How the Deal Was Done' in Giuliano Amato, Hervé Bribosia and Bruno De Witte (eds), *Genesis and Destiny of the European Constitution* (Brussels, Bruylant, 2007) p 123.

[169] Ricardo Passos and Stephan Marquardt, 'International Agreements – Competences, Procedures and Judicial Control' in Giuliano Amato, Hervé Bribosia and Bruno De Witte (eds), *Genesis and Destiny of the European Constitution* (Brussels, Bruylant, 2007) p 898.

[170] Hans Merket, 'The EU, Human Security and the Insulation of the CFSP: Comparing Recent Policy and Judicial Tendencies', in Aaron Matta and Tamara Takács (eds), *Human Security as a Tool for Comprehensive Approach for Human Rights and Security Linkages in EU Foreign Policy* (TMC Asser Institute, 2014) p 25.

competence into areas that are not covered by the treaties, beyond the defined conferral of competence. Whilst this may appear to allow a possible basis for EU external action, Declaration 41 of the treaties, which addresses Article 352 TFEU, specifies that actions can be confined to specific legal bases.[171] Whilst this flexibility clause pre-Lisbon was incarnated as Article 308 EC and Article 235 EC before that again,[172] its potential to be interpreted expansively would clearly need to be curtailed in two instances, by both the Court and the treaties themselves.

As will be seen in the next chapter, the Parliament has consistently been attempting to get a greater foothold in CFSP matters. One of the ways in which it has done so is for the flexibility clause – Article 352 TFEU – to be utilised as a legal basis, as it requires its consent. Following the Paris Summit, the Heads of State and government undertook to 'make the widest possible use of all the dispositions of the [t]reaties, including [the flexibility clause]'.[173] Whilst of limited use before then (it was even considered a 'dead letter')[174], it was used rigorously between *Massey-Ferguson* and *Generalised Tariff Preferences*.[175] Given that its use developed from being a purely internal market measure to being reincarnated as a tool for all potential areas of Union competence, it could be a legal basis for measures not specifically envisaged by the drafters. Yet Declaration 42 annexed to the treaties is unequivocal in that Article 352 TFEU 'cannot serve as a basis for widening the scope of Union powers beyond the general framework created by the provisions of the [t]reaties as a whole and, in particular, by those that define the tasks and the activities of the Union'.

As controversial as Article 352 TFEU may be, it has been deployed, notwithstanding its limitations, on a regular basis[176] but, rightly or wrongly, it cannot be used for the evasion of the CFSP matters of the treaties.[177] This has been made clear with the Treaty of Lisbon. Article 352(4) TFEU stated that the clause 'cannot serve as a basis for attaining objectives pertaining to…[CFSP] and any acts

[171] The reading of the Declaration would appear to be less than clear. See, Damian Chalmers, Gareth Davies and Giorgio Monti, *European Union Law: Text and Materials* 3rd edition (Cambridge University Press, 2014) p 216.

[172] See, Robert Schütze, 'Organized Change towards an "Ever Closer Union": Article 308 EC and the Limits to the Community's Legislative Competence' (2003) 22 *Yearbook of European Law* 79.

[173] 'Communiqué Issued by the Heads of State or Government of the Nine after Their Summit Conference in Paris'. 'Statement from the Paris Summit (19 to 21 October 1972)'.

[174] Pierre Pescatore, *The Law of Integration: Emergence of a New Phenomenon in International Relations, Based on the Experience of the European Communities* (A W Sijthoff, 1974) p 41.

[175] Case C-8/73, *Hauptzollamt Bremerhaven v Massey-Ferguson GmbH*, ECLI:EU:C:1973:90, and, Case C-45/86 *Commission v Council*, ECLI:EU:C:1987:163 ('*Generalised Tariff Preferences*') For more on the flexibility clause and its journey over time in the EU legal order, see, Graham Butler, 'The EU Flexibility Clause Is Dead, Long Live the EU Flexibility Clause' in Antonina Bakardjieva Engelbrekt and Xavier Groussot (eds), *The Future of Europe: Political and Legal Integration Beyond Brexit* (Hart Publishing, 2019).

[176] See, Gráinne De Búrca and Bruno De Witte, 'The Delimitation of Powers between the EU and Its Member States' in Anthony Arnull and Daniel Wincott (eds), *Accountability and Legitimacy in the European Union* (Oxford University Press, 2003).

[177] Alan Dashwood, 'Article 308 EC as the Outer Limit of Expressly Conferred Community Competence' in Catherine Barnard and Okeoghene Odudu (eds), *The Outer Limits of European Union Law* (Hart Publishing, 2009) p 43.

adopted pursuant to this Article shall respect the limits set out in Article 40, second paragraph, [TEU]'. Now clear, although not explicitly stated to begin with, CFSP matters have never been utilised by the flexibility clause, which is hardly surprising, given that the scope of CFSP matters has always been sufficiently flexible in its own right.

Despite the fact that objectives cannot, in themselves, serve as a legal basis for extending the powers of the Union,[178] it nonetheless demonstrates the continued distinction between the former second and third pillars – that JHA matters may be utilised by the flexibility clause, but not CFSP matters. It could even be said the breadth of this restriction on Article 352 TFEU could have effects beyond CFSP matters;[179] ensuring overexpansion is kept to a minimum.

3.4.2. The Legal Nature of CFSP Matters

The legal nature of CFSP matters entails that there is no legislation, a lack of adequate judicial review, dubious institutional balance, and questionable primacy and direct effect. The Union has constitutionalised policy goals[180] and this is welded into the very fabric of the treaties. Yet, despite being centric to Union law, actions based on a CFSP legal basis must be implemented into the national legal orders when applicable. One of the explanatory factors for its lack of primacy and direct effect can be attributed to a limited array of cases asking such questions to the Court.[181]

CFSP matters have a peculiar non-existent balance between the different institutions of the Union. Even so, it is there primarily to serve as a legal instrument for 'reinforcing the European identity and its independence in order to promote peace, security and progress in Europe and in the world'.[182] Its legal nature is the consequence of integration and has produced effects within the wider legal order. The foreign policy sphere and other areas of external competence characteristically overlap, and the dividing line between them has been politically sensitive. Absolute separation of them is unrealistic, and attempting to divide them so categorically would create unworkable scenarios. Diversity must be accommodated within the Union's external relations,[183] the same way it is

[178] As argued, if they could, there would be no need for a 'safeguard' excluding CFSP from the flexibility clause. Furthermore, there might not be a need for the flexibility clause at all. Joris Larik, From Speciality to a Constitutional Sense of Purpose: On the Changing Role of the Objectives of the European Union (2014) 63 *International and Comparative Law Quarterly* 935 at 957.

[179] Gavin Barrett, 'Creation's Final Laws: The Impact of the Treaty of Lisbon on the "Final Provisions" of Earlier Treaties' (2008) 27 *Yearbook of European Law* 3 at 44.

[180] Gareth Davies, 'The European Union Legislature as an Agent of the European Court of Justice' (2016) 54 *Journal of Common Market Studies* 846.

[181] Wessel, (n 46) p 17. For more on this, see Chapter 5 of this book.

[182] Preamble to the TEU.

[183] See, Panos Koutrakos, 'The Elusive Question for Uniformity in EC External Relations' in Alan Dashwood and others (eds), *Cambridge Yearbook of European Legal Studies 2001: Volume 4* (Hart Publishing, 2002)

accommodated internally. Any discussion of CFSP and intergovernmentalism of any description often 'conceals the fact that CFSP [D]ecisions are taken by the Union'.[184] Instead, elements of supranationalism are beginning to be woven into the fabric. EU foreign policy accordingly shows 'significant cooperative federal substance'.[185] CFSP matters have yet to be fully communitarised however,[186] so the ghosts of the Treaty of Maastricht still linger.

The former Joint Actions and Common Positions, terminologically ambiguous terms, are no more. By having several different instruments for CFSP matters in the past, it arguably exposed the Union's own weaknesses.[187] CFSP matters run in parallel with the foreign policy and external relations of Member States. With the broad interpretation of the goals of CFSP matters, the legal parameters can be understood as setting out the framework for how EU external relations as a whole should be carried out. CFSP matters can be said to be much more normalised now than they have ever been, and the consolidation of different instruments for CFSP matters into one – Decisions – was long overdue, and is one issue that has been appropriately rectified.

3.4.3. Longevity

The Treaty of Lisbon only made 'limited progress' on CFSP matters.[188] It attempted to ensure the competing interests of the different institutions and the Member States struck the right balance, but little changed. The additional subsidiarity checks brought in by the Treaty of Lisbon play no part in CFSP matters.[189] One of the more striking elements of CFSP matters is that Decisions are largely adopted at the Council without any debate.[190] This fact in and of itself demonstrates the importance of the role that the Council's sub-bodies play in preparing the substance of the Decisions that are ultimately waved through at political level. Political dialogue is crucial to the functioning of any Union policy, which regrettably, is absent.

[184] Wessel (n 30) p 349.

[185] Robert Schütze, *From Dual to Cooperative Federalism: The Changing Structure of European Law* (Oxford University Press, 2009) p 343.

[186] Opinion of Advocate General Wahl, Case C-455/14 P, *H v Council*, ECLI:EU:C:2016:212, para 1.

[187] Roy H Ginsberg, 'The EU's CFSP: The Politics of Procedure' in Martin Holland (ed), *Common Foreign and Security Policy: The Record and Reforms* (Pinter, 1997) p 22.

[188] Piet Eeckhout, 'The EU's Common Foreign and Security Policy after Lisbon: From Pillar Talk to Constitutionalism' in Andrea Biondi, Piet Eeckhout and Stefanie Ripley (eds), *EU Law after Lisbon* (Oxford University Press, 2012) p 290.

[189] However, given CFSP matters are not an exclusive competence of the Union, it is assumed that subsidiarity, as per TEU, Article 5(3), is meant to apply to CFSP matters. Geert De Baere, 'Subsidiarity as a Structural Principle Governing the Use of EU External Competences' in Marise Cremona (ed), *Structural Principles in EU External Relations Law* (Hart Publishing, 2018) p 107.

[190] Ramses A Wessel, 'Common Foreign, Security, and Defense Policy' in Dennis Patterson and Anna Södersten (eds), *A Companion to European Union Law and International Law* (John Wiley & Sons, 2016) p 373.

A smaller number of institutional actors makes it easier to navigate for the institutional actor that commands the power which, for CFSP matters, is the Council. Whilst the level of expertise available within the Council on CFSP matters may indeed be high, the lack of other involved institutions is out-of-kilter with how other Union policies are formulated, debated, and executed. The marginal role of the Commission in CFSP matters is quite remarkable when contrasted with other policy fields. Whereas its enforcement role is relatively powerful when it comes to ordinary EU policy matters, its wings have been unilaterally clipped in CFSP matters. Whilst it has the competence to issue reasoned opinions in normal policy areas, as well as other formal and informal instruments, it cannot do this for CFSP matters.[191]

When a Member State deviates from agreed positions and courses of action within CFSP matters, it would be for the Council itself to resolve. A sizeable Council operation exists for CFSP matters with multiple sub-actors at play. The intergovernmentalism in CFSP is so strong that it competes with ordinary fields of decision-making in terms of administrative capability. If the PSC is an overseer, but also a decision-maker, this can be problematic from a governance perspective, given the irreconcilable duties expected of it. Ideally, an executive body should not just be overseeing its own executive. Accordingly, some other body ought to have a say in such processes.

3.5. Conclusion

CFSP matters have been used as a propeller for greater Union outreach in the wider world. However, where an action on a CFSP legal basis has inflated the scope of EU power, it may be to the detriment of other Union policies that have taken place under more plural decision-making arrangements. CFSP legal bases are actively used, adapting to the changing priorities of EU foreign policy. The potential overlap of CFSP matters and non-CFSP matters provide much of the fruit in the legal basis arguments that will continue to give shape to how the legal regime governing CFSP matters will end up becoming.

The rule of thumb is that unanimity remains central to decision-making for CFSP matters. CFSP matters are still 'political foreign policy'[192] with a healthy dose of law. Supranational foreign policy is not a phenomenon to which the world's actors are accustomed. Accordingly, the procedural aspects of the law of EU foreign policy, as one arm of the Union's external relations, is a puzzling feature to those outside the Union itself. The treaties, even now, do not provide the observer or

[191] Ramses A Wessel, 'The Legal Dimension of European Foreign Policy' in Knud Erik Jørgensen and others (eds), *The SAGE Handbook of European Foreign Policy* (SAGE, 2015) p 309.

[192] Pieter Jan Kuijper, 'An Introduction to Union External Action, Its Scope, Its Institutions and Its Instruments' in Pieter Jan Kuijper and others (eds), *The Law of the European Union* (Kluwer Law International, 2018) p 1232.

practitioner with a full picture of the operability of the provisions covering CFSP. As a policy area, these matters were previously 'ill-defined' in terms of substance and content[193] and it remains much the same today. From the outside, it looks as intergovernmental in its orientation as it was when it was inserted into treaties, although now within the EU legal framework, EU foreign policy through law allows the Union to better exert itself through a variety of ways.

With differentiated legal bases in EU external action, several ambiguities have remained, and what legal basis should be utilised for achieving a particular Union goal externally remains the subject of legal debate. Control of CFSP matters has principally lain with the Council. Through revision of the treaties, CFSP matters could move towards more EU-centred decision-making, away from decision-making merely within the Council. Over recent decades, there have been ample opportunities to iron out such issues through amendments to the treaties. CFSP matters, in the meantime, have continued to escape other institutions such as the Parliament and the Court. These two institutions will form the basis of the next two chapters.

[193] Piet Eeckhout, *Does Europe's Constitution Stop at the Water's Edge? Law and Policy in the EU's External Relations* (Europa Law Publishing, 2005) p 3.

4

The European Parliament and the Common Foreign and Security Policy

In fitting with the major themes of the constitutional law of CFSP matters, namely, executive prerogative and the exceptionalism of foreign policy, this chapter moves focus onto the long plight of parliamentarism in EU foreign policy. What precisely constitutes foreign policy may be nothing more than words by some interpretations in political terms, never mind binding law, but is of crucial importance for EU institutional actors. Whilst the institutions bring forward legal substance of the intentions of the High Contracting Parties, they also allow for institutional variances with regard to different Union policies. Through analysis of EU foreign policy as a legal concept, and an understanding of fitting the European Parliament within the institutional architecture of EU decision-making, this chapter looks at the extent of the Parliament's involvement as a legally significant actor in CFSP matters, determining the nuances that distinguish the policy from other Union policies. It comes to comprehend that the Parliament's stake in the processes surrounding CFSP matters – both formally and informally through law – has increased over time.

The chapter is structured as follows. Firstly, Section 2 discusses the history of Parliament in the EU institutional architecture, in addition to touching upon the delicacies of the Parliament's right as a legal actor before the Court. Section 3 commences discussion of the legal powers the Parliament possesses in CFSP matters that are of a softer nature. Subsequently, Section 4 then analyses the more formal powers the Parliament is in the possession of, and how it utilises them to its own advantage. This sets up Section 5 where the Court's litigation strategy for its own institutional ends is unfolded, and its involvement in CFSP matters is scrutinised – opening debate on the pleadings it has taken to justify its institutional standing. After uncovering the legal strategy of the Parliament's litigation at the Court, Section 6 then puts the Parliament's institutional standing in context by investigating how CFSP legal bases and non-CFSP legal bases have become entangled and how legal acts may be adopted upon dual legal bases – highlighting the compatibility issues and decision-making anomalies that presently exist. Penultimately, the chapter contemplates the future of the Parliament's role in EU foreign policy through its designation and practice in CFSP matters. Finally, Section 8 draws concluding observations, leading on to determine the jurisdiction of the Court of Justice in respect of CFSP matters in the following chapter. Through the analysis, it will become evident how the constitutional law of CFSP matters has evolved and how such a policy has been handled institutionally by the Parliament.

4.1. Introduction

Just like there are limits to the EU legal order,[1] there are also limits on the Parliament within that legal order. The distinction between executive powers and a parliamentary assembly in foreign policy has been a running debate in the United States for decades.[2] As a parliamentary actor, the United States Congress has 'an elaborate institutional machinery devoted to foreign relations'[3] and thus, institutional progression in recent times has waned, with a balance being found between executive and congressional readings. Yet in the EU, the parliamentary actor in foreign policy is continuing to evolve as is the historical dominance of executive powers in the field. The Parliament is a politically strong voice, but contrastingly is not necessarily a strong legal actor in CFSP matters, making it a paradox worth exploring. The Parliament is an 'it' and not a 'they'; given that for legal purposes, it is of one institutional mind.

Parliamentary involvement in public policy is an essential procedural requirement for any functioning democratic entity, just as the Union claims to be.[4] In this vein, the Parliament sets down the constitutional element of democratic representation and, as an institution, it is 'central to the constitutional debate' of the Union.[5] However, the Parliament does not have the same prerogatives in EU foreign policy in comparison to the way national parliaments in national foreign policy do, as the two are fundamentally different entities, operating in different realms on vertical levels. In EU Member States, the national parliaments hold executive powers to account through their own involvement in domestic foreign policy. Thus, analogised at EU level, it is the Parliament, on a normative level, that should theoretically hold EU foreign policy to account. One theory for the Parliament's lack

[1] See, Riccardo Monaco, 'The Limits of the European Community Order' (1976) 1 *European Law Review* 269.

[2] See, 'Congressional v. Executive Powers' in Chapter 5, Thomas M Franck, *Political Questions Judicial Answers: Does the Rule of Law Apply to Foreign Affairs?* (Princeton University Press, 1992) pp 90–96. Furthermore, see Chapter 10, 'Legislative Power in Foreign Affairs' in Michael D Ramsey, *The Constitution's Text in Foreign Affairs* (Harvard University Press, 2007).

[3] Curtis A Bradley and Jack L Goldsmith, *Foreign Relations Law: Cases and Materials* 4th edition (Wolters Kluwer Law and Business 2011) p 150.

[4] TEU, Preamble; TEU, Article 2; and Title II: Provisions on Democratic Principles (TEU, Articles 9–12).

[5] Simon Hix, Tapio Raunio and Roger Scully, 'Fifty Years on: Research on the European Parliament' (2003) 41 *Journal of Common Market Studies* 191 at 192.

of involvement in CFSP matters is the particularities of CFSP in international law, and its origins explaining a lack of involvement, called a 'parliamentary deficit'.[6] This can be attributed to the reality that there is little political connexion linking the Parliament and the Council. An assumption is therefore made that in actively involving a legislature in EU foreign policy and external relations more generally, the Parliament is seeking to make the most of its expanding constitutional powers. Like any self-regarding actor, the Parliament has substantial interest when the treaties are being reformed.[7] Despite progressive moves by the Parliament to enhance its oversight in policies of the Union and subsequently be rewarded with such endeavours in treaty reforms, its role in CFSP matters has been slow to develop. Theories of institutional actions without their interests being considered is not a completed theory, but one that this chapter wishes to build upon, adding to an understanding of the Parliament from a legal standpoint.

It is often the case in foreign policy that decisions, either at national or EU level, 'need to be taken speedily'.[8] Parliamentary involvement is therefore seen at a later stage, when decisions have already been taken and subsequent follow-up does little to change anything. The Parliament can make political claims for inclusion that do not necessarily stack up in law. It is a non-sovereign body and by its very nature, co-exists with other parliamentary settings such as national and regional parliaments. The Treaty of Lisbon gently enhanced the powers of the Parliament generally, namely, as a co-legislator. It was afforded full co-legislator status with regard to legislative acts; a significant capability in considering legislative authority in a range of fields. This made it 'almost a normal parliament'.[9] Prior to the Treaty of Lisbon, the terms of legislation, legislative procedure, and legislative instruments were not to be found in the treaties.[10] Yet today, CFSP matters are non-legislative, and thus, marginalisation was retained. Therefore, what exactly did the Treaty of Lisbon do for the Parliament in CFSP matters?

The narrative of the Parliament's powers can vary. The Parliament can run the risk of being a 'pet object'[11] rather than the serious institution which it sees itself as. When the Treaty of Maastricht came into effect, the Parliament's role was

[6] Daniel Thym, 'Foreign Affairs' in Armin Von Bogdandy and Jürgen Bast (eds), *Principles of European Constitutional Law* 2nd edition (Hart Publishing, 2009) p 323.

[7] Kieran St C Bradley, 'The European Parliament and Treaty Reform: Building Blocks and Stumbling Blocks' in David O'Keeffe and Patrick M Twomey (eds), *Legal Issues of the Amsterdam Treaty* (Hart Publishing, 1999) p 124.

[8] Christopher Lord, 'The Political Theory and Practice of Parliamentary Participation in the Common Security and Defence Policy' (2011) 18 *Journal of European Public Policy* 1133 at 1140.

[9] Pieter Jan Kuijper, 'Recent Tendencies in the Separation of Powers in EU Foreign Relations: An Essay' in Eleftheria Neframi and Mauro Gatti (eds), *Constitutional Issues of EU External Relations Law* (Nomos, 2018) p 210.

[10] Ton Van den Brink, 'The Relationship between the European and the National Legislatures from the Perspective of Constitutional Integrity' in Fabian Amtenbrink and Peter AJ Van den Berg (eds), *The Constitutional Integrity of the European Union* (TMC Asser Press, 2010) p 117.

[11] Philipp Dann, 'The Political Institutions' in Armin Von Bogdandy and Jürgen Bast (eds), *Principles of European Constitutional Law* 2nd edition (Hart Publishing, 2009) pp 241–242.

considered to be 'little more than marginal'.[12] Saying that, the Parliament was still rather keen on having CFSP matters, in some way, brought within the law.[13] The Parliament's limited influence that has historically been afforded to it, in the formative years of the Union, has partially triggered today's position where it acts in CFSP matters as if it was attempting to make up for lost time. Speaking presently, its powers flow from Article 14 TEU, which states '[t]he European Parliament shall, jointly with the Council, exercise legislative and budgetary functions. It shall exercise functions of political control and consultation as laid down in the [t]reaties'. From that, a number of powers flow, including legislative, budgetary, and supervisory functions. Therefore, barring exceptions, the Parliament is an actor in the external action of the Union, regardless of the legal basis in the TEU or TFEU. However, for CFSP matters, with it being of exceptional status in legal terms, the Parliament is, by the treaties, given a different role. In the treaties, it states the 'specific role of the European Parliament and of the Commission in this area is defined by the [t]reaties',[14] which is a derogation from Article 14 TEU. This, in turn, means that the Parliament has been profoundly constrained in terms of its role in CFSP matters.[15]

The boundary for determining where CFSP matters end and begin *vis-à-vis* non-CFSP matters is a difficult task, but is of critical import for the Parliament and its operational nature. The Parliament has acted as a pro-integration institution but tends to be a preference-outlier.[16] It is the weakest of the main institutions when it comes to general powers across the treaties, in contrast to the Council, the European Council, the Commission, and the Court. In addition to the Parliament, other relevant bodies and agencies are also excluded from CFSP matters.[17] In non-CFSP matters, the Parliament has slowly seen progression through the different revisions of the treaties. Not all actions resulting from other institutional actors require its approval.[18] The ordinary legislative procedure is in use in

[12] Eric Stein, 'Foreign Policy at Maastricht: "Non in Commotione Dominus"' (1992) 29 *Common Market Law Review* 663. Repeated in, Eric Stein, *Thoughts from a Bridge: A Retrospective of Writings on New Europe and American Federalism* (University of Michigan Press, 2000) p 304.

[13] Simon J Nuttall, *European Foreign Policy* (Oxford University Press, 2000) p 271.

[14] TEU, Article 24(1), para 2. The current Article 24 TEU can be traced back to Article 11 TEU pre-Lisbon, under the Treaty of Nice.

[15] Richard Whitman and Ana Juncos, 'The Lisbon Treaty and the Foreign, Security and Defence Policy: Reforms, Implementation and the Consequences of (Non-)Ratification' (2009) 14 *European Foreign Affairs Review* 25 at 30.

[16] Simon Hix, 'Neither a Preference-Outlier nor a Unitary Actor: Institutional Reform Preferences of the European Parliament' (2005) 3 *Comparative European Politics* 131 at 132.

[17] For example, the role of the EU's Fundamental Rights Agency (FRA) in CFSP matters has been curtailed. Any involvement of the FRA in CFSP matters could be said to affect the 'smooth functioning of institutional executive arrangements'. Damian Chalmers, 'The Politics of European Reason and New Reasons for European Politics: The European Union Fundamental Rights Agency' in Andrea Ott and Ellen Vos (eds), *Fifty Years of European Integration: Foundations and Perspectives* (TMC Asser Press, 2009) p 89.

[18] Armin Von Bogdandy, 'Founding Principles' in Armin Von Bogdandy and Jürgen Bast (eds), *Principles of European Constitutional Law* 2nd edition (Hart Publishing, 2009) p 50.

non-CFSP matters through co-decision and QMV where there are extensive powers for the Parliament.

The involvement of an actor like the Parliament in CFSP matters is based on the balance of actors on both horizontal and vertical plains, within the overall institutional and governance field. Yet, the notion of institutional balance is not unique to the Union. The results of meaningful checks and balances have long been a feature of US-style government from the foundation of its constitutional doctrines.[19] The Parliament possesses many rights in the field of external relations, such as in trade. In many non-CFSP matters, these rights are as extensive as those of national parliaments in Member States.[20] As a result, one of the questions facing the Parliament is whether the rules of CFSP matters specified by the treaties correspond with how they may actually be applied in an operational setting. A legislature overseeing an executive is a difficult and strenuous task, with actors possessing a wide range of interests – repeatedly delicate – meaning that parliamentary involvement is all the more challenging.

In this chapter, the position of the Parliament in CFSP matters is to be explored, with a view to charting the legal position and technicalities that have been crafted over the decades. As put, CFSP matters are akin to 'crippled conferral',[21] in that its democratic and judicial control in the EU legal order does not match the existence of CFSP competence within that legal order. It will become evident that the Parliament, in an ideal world, would prefer to have all external action by the Union conducted on a non-CFSP legal basis, thereby ensuring its involvement. The chapter also delves into the Parliament's willingness to hold a more commanding influence over CFSP matters, which could be incompatible with the structural make-up of the EU, given the diluted nature of the policy.

4.2. A Tale of History

In a range of policy fields, historically, the Parliament's input into Union decision-making has been poor.[22] In the earlier days of academic discussion on the external relations of the Union, it was just the Commission and the Council taking up centre-stage, with the Parliament nowhere in sight.[23] When the later debate took

[19] See, James Madison, 'Federalist No. 51: The Structure of the Government Must Furnish the Proper Checks and Balances Between the Different Departments', *New York Packet* (1788).

[20] Alan Dashwood, 'EC External Relations and the CFSP (Position Paper)' in Alan Dashwood (ed), *Reviewing Maastricht: Issues for the 1996 IGC* (Sweet and Maxwell, 1996) p 231.

[21] Inge Govaere, 'To Give or To Grab: The Principle of Full, Crippled and Split Conferral of Powers Post-Lisbon' in Marise Cremona (ed), *Structural Principles in EU External Relations Law* (Hart Publishing, 2018) p 72.

[22] Jan Wouters, 'Institutional and Constitutional Challenges for the European Union – Some Reflections in the Light of the Treaty of Nice' in Alfred E Kellermann, Jaap W de Zwaan and Jenö Czuczai (eds), *EU Enlargement: The Constitutional Impact at EU and National Level* (TMC Asser Press, 2001) p 48.

[23] For example, see, Dale S Collinson, 'Foreign Relations Powers of the European Communities: A Comment on Commission v. Council' (1971) 23 *Stanford Law Review* 956.

place, however, discussion continued on how representation through an elected assembly would function.[24] Long before there was the Parliament as we know it today, it was perceived that foreign policy was not to be a matter for parliaments.[25]

Along this line of thinking, the Parliament never traditionally had a role in international agreements that the Union opened, negotiated, and eventually concluded. The mere involvement of representatives in a democratically elected forum in EU foreign policy was a notion that elder generations of European leaders may have balked at. This was given that executives traditionally enjoyed relative independence from parliaments, who would inevitably try to exert control themselves, narrowing the executive's scope for action in a particular policy domain. This historical feature of how parliaments in nation states operated is reminiscent of how the Union, as the then Assembly, when it came to the external affairs of the then Community.

4.2.1. The Parliament as an Institution

From the outside looking in, the Parliament was 'in no sense a legislature'.[26] When foreign policy coordination commenced in Europe, the thought of including an institution or body of the Union was completely disregarded and not entertained. Early objections to this long-held view came at the behest of the political institutions – the Commission and the Parliament. Puzzlingly, it was the Commission which was the verbal objector to this,[27] not the Parliament. The Common Assembly, the early predecessor of the Parliament, had a restrained role in the limited external relations of the pioneering Union – the European Coal and Steel Community (ECSC), the European Economic Community (EEC) and the more marginal European Atomic Energy Community (EURATOM). The ECSC, created by the Treaty of Paris in 1951, had envisaged that an Assembly, the predecessor to the Parliament, 'shall exercise the supervisory powers which are granted to it'.[28]

[24] See, Piet Dankert, 'What Parliament for Europe?' in Tom Heukels, Niels Blokker and Marcel Brus (eds), *The European Union after Amsterdam: A Legal Analysis* (Kluwer Law International, 1998).

[25] Michael Ameller, *Parliaments: A Comparative Study on the Structure and Functioning of Representative Institutions in Fifty-Five Countries* 2nd edition (Inter-Parliamentary Union by Cassell 1966) p 310.

[26] Eric Stein, 'The New Institutions' in Eric Stein and Thomas L Nicholson (eds), *American Enterprise in the European Common Market: A Legal Profile*, vol 1 (University of Michigan Press, 1960) p 52.

[27] Giorgio Gaja, 'European Parliament and Foreign Affairs: (1) Political Cooperation among the Nine' in Antonio Cassese (ed), *Parliamentary Control Over Foreign Policy: Legal Essays* (Sijtoff and Noordhoff, 1980) p 191. In fact, with the enactment of the Treaty of Lisbon, the Commission lost power in CFSP matters, with the exception of the implementation of the EU budget. Ricardo Gosalbo-Bono and Frederik Naert, 'The Reluctant (Lisbon) Treaty and Its Implementation in the Practice of the Council' in Piet Eeckhout and Manuel López-Escudero (eds), *The European Union's External Action in Times of Crisis* (Hart Publishing, 2016) p 27.

[28] Article 20, Treaty of Paris, 1951. European Coal and Steel Community (ECSC) Treaty.

These supervisory powers were just the starting point for the Parliament's influence. At the Treaty of Rome, these supervisory powers were upgraded further to 'advisory and supervisory' powers,[29] further entrenching the Parliament's position. Recent work on uncovering the truth behind why the Parliament, then Assembly, was left out of the relevant provisions for it to bring an action for annulment before the Court in the final text of the Treaty of Rome appears to have been a result of a political compromise.[30] The 'passive onlooker' status was not enough for the Parliament.[31] The mere fact of a parliament in existence for a federal entity would mean that such a notion would want 'to speak in terms of federal legislative powers'.[32] The Parliament, once established, always wanted more, and got it, but ever so gradually.

From the outset, the Parliament as an institution had autonomy to organise itself internally,[33] as long nothing was in violation of the treaties. The Parliament has always been an active institution in protecting what it sees as its own prerogatives, based on the text of the treaties, as well as an unwritten set of principles of where it sees itself ought to have such powers. It has never seen itself as a completed institution, but one in need of constant transformation.[34] It even colloquially used the name 'Parliament' (its official name was Assembly) long before its name was officially changed by the Single European Act 1986. Thus, it has had a long journey to get to the point where it achieved greater institutional powers, and it is no accident that its powers saw a steady increase. Whilst the Parliament was active in acquiring new powers in Union affairs, it was far from an uneasy journey. The *Luns* and *Westerterp* reforms of 1964 and 1973 allowed the then indirectly elected Assembly to debate the opening of negotiations for international agreements of association and trade nature with third countries.[35] In the EPC years, the *Copenhagen* Report of 1973 expressed signs that the intensification of EPC would entail meeting with members of the 'political committee' of the Parliament. In 1978, the Parliament adopted a resolution stating substantively that it was not being properly informed and called for it to be 'fully informed concerning all joint foreign policy decisions taken by the Nine [Member States]'.[36]

[29] Article 137, Treaty of Rome, 1957, European Economic Community (EEC) Treaty.

[30] Anne Boerger and Bill Davies, 'Imaging the Course of European Law? Parti Ecologiste "Les Verts" v. Parliament as a Constitutional Milestone in EU Law' in Bill Davies and Fernanda Nicola (eds), *EU Law Stories: Contextual and Critical Histories of European Jurisprudence* (Cambridge University Press, 2017) pp. 84–85.

[31] Robert Schütze, *European Constitutional Law* 2nd edition (Cambridge University Press, 2015) p 164.

[32] Ernst B Haas, *The Unity of Europe: Political, Social and Economic Forces 1950–1957* (Stevens and Sons, 1958) p 391.

[33] Eric Stein, Peter Hay and Michel Waelbroeck, *European Community Law and Institutions in Perspective: Text, Cases and Readings* (The Michie Company, 1976) p 43.

[34] Richard Corbett, Francis Jacobs and Michael Shackleton, 'The European Parliament at Fifty: A View from the Inside' (2003) 41 *Journal of Common Market Studies* 353 at 355.

[35] The *Luns* and *Westerterp* reforms are discussed in Donatella M Viola, *European Foreign Policy and the European Parliament in the 1990s: An Investigation into the Role and Voting Behaviour of the European Parliament's Political Groups* (Ashgate Publishing, 2000) p 29.

[36] C 36/32. Resolution on European Political Cooperation. European Parliament. Minutes of Proceedings of the Sitting of Thursday, 19 January 1978.

4.2.2. Direct Elections and its Impact

Differing levels of involvement of the Parliament in CFSP matters were envisaged. These ranged from the Parliament having no role whatsoever, to assistance in defining priorities and objectives.[37] Even in the 1970s before direct elections to the Parliament, its outlook on external relations was diverse.[38] Pre-1979, the Parliament could have been seen as a transnational assembly rather than a functional parliament. Despite this innate position, it always sought to be a co-decider or co-legislator, on either par or at a superior level to other institution bodies. Direct elections gave the Parliament new impetus in external relations, given its continued importance.[39] After 1979's first direct elections, the Parliament began to assert its new position, wherever possible. The *London* Report of 1981, collated and adopted by Foreign Ministers of the Member States at the time, paved the way for more contact between EPC and the Parliament, with lobbying from the Parliament to ensure this occurred. The *Dooge* Report in 1985 acknowledged the role of the Parliament and the Court in the Union's architecture.[40] Prior to the enactment of the Single European Act (SEA) in 1986, the Parliament had a distant impact on the Union's general external relations. With the SEA, assent was required by the Parliament for particular categories of international agreements.[41] Article 30(4) allowed for a practice to be established by the Parliament to have some level of involvement in EPC.[42] When revising the treaties at this juncture, Member States favoured adopting a smoother functioning Union in a manner that, in their view, was in its best interests, as opposed to finding an increased role for Parliament.[43]

The early instances of the Parliament's litigation provide a healthy vision of the judicial strategy that the institution deployed. The Parliament's collection of actions across the entire spectrum of Union law can subsequently be followed.[44] It made its first appearance before the Court in 1964 on the trivial matter of

[37] Alan Dashwood, 'What Can Be Salvaged If the Treaty of Lisbon Is Lost?' in Mielle Bulterman and others (eds), *Views of European Law from the Mountain: Liber Amicorum Piet Jan Slot* (Kluwer Law International, 2009) p 339.

[38] Patricia M Leopold, 'External Relations Power of EEC in Theory and in Practice' (1977) 26 *International and Comparative Law Quarterly* 54 at 69.

[39] Joseph HH Weiler, 'The European Parliament and Foreign Affairs: External Relations of the European Economic Community' in Antonio Cassese (ed), *Parliamentary Control Over Foreign Policy: Legal Essays* (Sijtoff and Noordhoff, 1980) p 183.

[40] 'Report of the Ad Hoc Committee for Institutional Affairs to the European Council (Brussels, 29–30 March 1985) (the' Dooge Report')' (ECSC-EEC-EAEC 1985) pp 30–31.

[41] Koen Lenaerts and Piet Van Nuffel, *Constitutional Law of the European Union* (Robert Bray ed., Sweet and Maxwell, 1999) p 294.

[42] Article 30, para 4, Single European Act. See, Roman Schmidt-Radefeldt, 'Article 36 [The Parliamentary Dimension of CFSP]' in Hermann-Josef Blanke and Stelio Mangiameli (eds), *The Treaty on European Union (TEU): A Commentary* (Springer 2013) p 1120.

[43] Bradley (n 7) p 127.

[44] For a non-legal overview, see, Margaret McCown, 'The European Parliament before the Bench: ECJ Precedent and EP Litigation Strategies' (2003) 10 *Journal of European Public Policy* 974.

parliamentary immunity,[45] long before the dual mandate of persons sitting in both national parliaments and the Parliament was abolished. Substantively, on institutional powers, the Parliament supported an action in *Roquette Frères*,[46] to ensure its right as an institution was upheld and that it was consulted where appropriate. On the same day as the judgment was provided in *Roquette Frères*, the Court also delivered a judgment in the *Maizena* case,[47] in which the Court upheld, in both judgments, the Parliament's status as interveners. The Council, in opposing the Parliament's intervention, said the power of the Parliament to intervene had to be provided for expressly in primary law, which it was not under the then Article 173 EEC.[48] The Court said in *Roquette Frères* that, 'although [there is] limited [institutional balance], it reflects...the fundamental democratic principle that the peoples should take part in the exercise of power through the intermediary of a representative assembly'.[49] This phrase, later recited in other cases including *Titanium Dioxide*,[50] was 'music to the ears' of the actors seeking greater input,[51] including the Parliament. Notable, however, is that neither the judgments in *Roquette Frères* nor *Maizena* made reference to the Court's earliest case, the well-known *Meroni* case, on institutional balance, which stated 'there can be seen in the balance of powers which is characteristic of the institutional structure of the [Union] a fundamental guarantee granted by the [treaties]'.[52]

4.2.3. The Right to Sue and be Sued

The Parliament's right to bring actions before the Court under the treaties was once considered to be only of theoretical interest.[53] Much has happened since. What followed was *Les Verts*, a landmark judgment for the Parliament as an institution,[54] as it became a triggering sign that its institutional power could be strengthened through litigation before the Court. In extremely clever pleadings

[45] Case C-101/63, *Albert Wagner v Jean Fohrmann and Antoine Krier*, ECLI:EU:C:1964:28 ('*Wagner*').

[46] Case C-138/79, *Roquette Frères v Council*, ECLI:EU:C:1980:249.

[47] Case C-139/79, *Maizena v Council*, ECLI:EU:C:1980:250. See, Trevor C Hartley, 'Consulting the European Parliament' (1981) 6 *European Law Review* 181.

[48] Patricia M Leopold, 'Community Law-Making: Opinions of the European Parliament' (1982) 2 *Oxford Journal of Legal Studies* 454 at 456.

[49] Case C-138/79, *Roquette Frères v Council*, ECLI:EU:C:1980:249, para 33.

[50] Case C-300/89, *Commission v Council*, ECLI:EU:C:1991:244 ('*Titanium Dioxide*'), para 20. In *Titanium Dioxide*, the Court annulled a directive because of the additional legal basis. For critical remarks, including the fact that the directive was, in fact, adopted through the correct procedure, see Trevor C Hartley, *European Union Law in a Global Context: Text, Cases and Materials* (Cambridge University Press, 2004) p 60.

[51] Catherine Barnard, 'Where Politicians Fear to Tread?' (1992) 17 *European Law Review* 127 at 130.

[52] Case C-9/56, *Meroni & Co., Industrie Metallurgiche, SpA v High Authority of the European Coal and Steel Community*, ECLI:EU:C:1958:7, p. 152.

[53] Stein (n 26) p 65.

[54] Case C-294/83, *Parti écologiste 'Les Verts' v Parliament*, ECLI:EU:C:1986:166. See, Graham Butler, 'Implementing a Complete System of Legal Remedies in EU Foreign Affairs Law' (2018) 24 *Columbia Journal of European Law* 637.

on admissibility,[55] it forced the Court to acknowledge that the Parliament had the legal standing to be sued.[56] This led to a defining period of competence for the Parliament through its discovery of new-found powers. While the case might be noted for many other things,[57] including the use of the law of the Member States,[58] it was a seminal point for the integration-minded institutions, given that the negotiations leading to the Single European Act had recently concluded. It has even been suggested that the *Les Verts* judgment could not have been decided in any other way.[59] According to the current President, 'it would have been unimaginable for the [Court] to deny legal protection', particularly given that the Union was 'explicitly founded on a representative democracy'.[60] Following *Les Verts*, in that the Parliament as an institution could be sued as a defendant, it thus developed into the Parliament's right to sue – as a litigant – to lodge actions for annulment.

The Parliament's right to bring an action for annulment was initially denied by the Court in *Comitology*,[61] a case that was quickly a blemish on the Court's jurisprudence. Here, the Court decided to explicitly disregard the Opinion of Advocate General Darmon on the point of the Parliament's *locus standi*. He had suggested the Court allow the Parliament to possess 'the capacity to bring an action for annulment…where rights or powers of its own are adversely affected'.[62] The Court disagreed. However, it was not long changing its mind. With the Parliament's argument of institutional equality, it may have been 'barking up the wrong tree',[63] and the judgment was quickly reversed in *Radioactive Contamination of*

[55] As detailed by one of the agents for Parliament, Jean Paul Jacqué, 'Les Verts v The European Parliament' in Miguel Poiares Maduro and Loïc Azoulai (eds), *The Past and Future of EU Law: The Classics of EU Law Revisited on the 50th Anniversary of the Rome Treaty* (Hart Publishing, 2010) p 317.

[56] The *juge rapporteur* in *Les Verts* recalled that a colleague on the bench said to him that the admissibility of a party to bring an action for annulment against Parliament would receive the greatest attention. Recounted in, René Joliet, 'Le remboursement des frais electoraux: un contentieux oublié' in Manuel Pérez González (ed), *Hacia un nuevo orden internacional y europeo: estudios en homenaje al profesor don Manuel Díez de Velasco* (Tecnos 1993) Reproduced in English as, David T Keeling and René Joliet, 'The Reimbursement of Election Expenses: A Forgotten Dispute' (1994) 19 *European Law Review* 243.

[57] Four chapters in one book have been dedicated to the importance of *Les Verts*. See, Koen Lenaerts, 'The Basic Constitutional Charter of a Community Based on the Rule of Law' in Miguel Poiares Maduro and Loïc Azoulai (eds), *The Past and Future of EU Law: The Classics of EU Law Revisited on the 50th Anniversary of the Rome Treaty* (Hart Publishing, 2010); Jacqué (n 55); Alberto Alemanno, 'What Has Been and What Could Be, Thirty Years after Les Verts/European Parliament' in Miguel Poiares Maduro and Loïc Azoulai (eds), *The Past and Future of EU Law: The Classics of EU Law Revisited on the 50th Anniversary of the Rome Treaty* (Hart Publishing, 2010); Neil Walker, 'Opening or Closure? The Constitutional Intimations of the ECJ' in Miguel Poiares Maduro and Loïc Azoulai (eds), *The Past and Future of EU Law: The Classics of EU Law Revisited on the 50th Anniversary of the Rome Treaty* (Hart Publishing, 2010). Also, Butler (n 54).

[58] Nial Fennelly, 'Legal Interpretation at the European Court of Justice' (1997) 20 *Fordham International Law Journal* 656 at 677.

[59] Koen Lenaerts, 'Some Thoughts about the Interaction between Judges and Politicians' (1992) *University of Chicago Legal Forum* 93 at 113.

[60] ibid. p 113.

[61] Case C-302/87, *Parliament v Council*, ECLI:EU:C:1988:461 ('*Comitology*').

[62] Opinion of Advocate General Darmon, Case C-302/87, *Parliament v Council*, ECLI:EU:C:1988:263 ('*Comitology*').

[63] Joseph HH Weiler, 'Pride and Prejudice: Parliament v. Council' (1989) 14 *European Law Review* 334 at 338.

Foodstuffs, otherwise known as the *Chernobyl* case, in the first of two judgments. Prior to *Chernobyl*,[64] the Parliament had taken an active stance in seeking for its standing under the then Article 173 EC to be recognised, but had to wait for the correct opportunity to arise. *Chernobyl* tested whether the legal order was subject to judicial checks on authority where the Treaty was silent. The contestation principally centred on Council Regulation 3954/87,[65] but the Court's position on the Parliament's *locus standi* changed, despite the fact that the treaties did not provide it with the ability to challenge encroachment upon its own prerogatives. *Chernobyl* allowed the Parliament to participate in Court action, despite there being no basis in the treaties and led to the *verbatim* transposition of a segment of the judgment into the Treaty of Maastricht.[66]

Chernobyl was a landmark judgment for the Parliament, described as a chapter in a chain novel akin to Dworkanism,[67] that is now codified in the treaties. The Court's judgment in *Chernobyl* might have been outside the specific wording of the article, yet, that is not the same as reading-in the Parliament into the treaties more generally.[68] The Opinion of the Advocate General in *Chernobyl*[69] was said to have played a large role in convincing the Court to change its mind *vis-à-vis* its prior judgment in *Comitology*.[70] Furthermore, the Parliament appears to have demonstrated 'remarkable determination' in its pursuit.[71] Undeniably, debate continued to rumble over the precise scope of the Parliament's powers when the treaties make provision for it.[72] Looking back in time, the dispute settled at the Court would never have occurred if the Intergovernmental Conference leading to the Single European Act had adopted a passage in the Treaty leading to a right of legal standing for Parliament. Furthermore, the landmark judgments for Parliament in both *Les Verts* and *Chernobyl* occurred in a very short space of time, and they have not escaped controversy and dissent. A noted critic has pointed to the fact that both

[64] Case C-70/88, *Parliament v Council*, ECLI:EU:C:1990:217 and ECLI:EU:C:1991:373 ('*Chernobyl*').

[65] L 371/11. Council Regulation (EURATOM) No. 3954/87 of 22 December 1987 Laying down Maximum Permitted Levels of Radioactive Contamination of Foodstuffs and of Feedingstuffs Following a Nuclear Accident or Any Other Case of Radiological Emergency.

[66] Agnieszka Piekutowska, 'Towards the Democratization of the EU? Strengthening Prerogatives of the European Parliament in the Case Law of the Court of Justice of the European Union' in Elzbieta Kuzelewska and others (eds), *European Judicial Systems as a Challenge for Democracy*, vol 3 (Intersentia, 2015) p 62.

[67] Joxerramon Bengoetxea, *The Legal Reasoning of the European Court of Justice* (Clarendon Press, 1993) p 105.

[68] David T Keeling, 'In Praise of Judicial Activism. But What Does It Mean? And Has the European Court of Justice Ever Practiced It?' in Antonino Giuffrè (ed), *Scritti in onore di Giuseppe Federico Mancini: Volume 2* (Dott A Giuffrè Editore 1998) p 520.

[69] Opinion of Advocate General Van Gerven, Case C-70/88, *Parliament v Council*, ECLI:EU:C:1991:270 ('*Chernobyl*').

[70] Nial Fennelly, 'Reflections of an Irish Advocate General' (1996) 5 *Irish Journal of European Law* 5 at 18. Also, Takis Tridimas, *The General Principles of EU Law* 2nd edition (Oxford University Press, 2006) p 13.

[71] Giuseppe Federico Mancini and David T Keeling, 'Democracy and the European Court of Justice' (1994) 57 *Modern Law Review* 175 at 180.

[72] For example, see, Nicholas Emiliou, 'Protecting Parliamentary Prerogatives' (1993) 18 *European Law Review* 56.

the *Les Verts* and *Chernobyl* judgments were contrary to the treaties, explicitly and implicitly,[73] which is why the treaties were amended to copy parts of the judgments into the revised treaties. Notwithstanding this, these developments, largely positive for the Parliament, came at a time when questions were being asked about the Court's own expansive interpretation of matters coming before it, which partly explains the *Comitology* judgment, from which it quickly reversed. The line of cases, including *Chernobyl*, was a huge development for Parliament, given that previously, it could only participate in preliminary reference cases on the Court's invitation[74] and in its position as an employer in staff cases when it, as an institution, was defending itself in litigation.[75]

Developments stemming from the Single European Act continued and were enhanced when CFSP matters came about in the subsequent Treaty revision that became the Treaty of Maastricht through Article J7 TEU.[76] Providing the Parliament with new powers through the Treaty of Maastricht, amongst others, was noted as being hardly surprising.[77] During the Intergovernmental Conference negotiating the Treaty of Maastricht, the Parliament sought co-decision powers for itself,[78] but not any specific powers regarding the unique provisions that were going to become CFSP matters. Overall, the Treaty of Maastricht proved to be a seismic shift in how the Parliament's legal powers were governed, with a number of legal developments paving the way for it to become more effective in CFSP matters and other policy areas. Following this was the Treaty of Amsterdam, which formally did nothing for the Parliament in CFSP matters[79] and was recognised as a defect at that juncture. However, in other fields, the Parliament had a number of successes.[80] The limited scope of the Parliament's formal viewpoint in CFSP matters at the time allowed for mere informal influence on a practical level as it sought involvement in the Union's external relations.

[73] Trevor C Hartley, *Constitutional Problems of the European Union* (Hart Publishing, 1999) p 53.

[74] Kieran St C Bradley, 'The Variable Evolution of the Standing of the European Parliament in Proceedings Before the Court of Justice' (1988) 8 *Yearbook of European Law* 27 at 29.

[75] Francis G Jacobs, 'Isoglucose Resurgent: Two Powers of the European Parliament Upheld by the Court' (1981) 18 *Common Market Law Review* 219 at 220. The Assembly, as the Parliament's predecessor, was defending itself in civil service (staff) cases, even in the early cases where the Court had 'full review powers'. Werner Feld, *The Court of the European Communities: New Dimension in International Adjudication* (Martinus Nijhoff Publishers 1964) p 81.

[76] Ramses A Wessel, *The European Union's Foreign and Security Policy: A Legal Institutional Perspective*, vol. 33 (Kluwer Law International 1999) p 94.

[77] Robert Lane, 'New Community Competences under the Maastricht Treaty' (1993) 30 *Common Market Law Review* 939 at 976.

[78] C 324/219. European Parliament. Intergovernmental Conferences – Budgetary Control – Financing of the Communities. Resolution on the Intergovernmental Conferences in the Context of the European Parliament's Strategy for European Union (A3-270/90) 22 November 1990.

[79] Laurence W Gormley, 'Reflections on the Architecture of the European Union after the Treaty of Amsterdam' in David O'Keeffe and Patrick M Twomey (eds), *Legal Issues of the Amsterdam Treaty* (Hart Publishing, 1999) p 62.

[80] See, Simon Hix, 'Constitutional Agenda-Setting Through Discretion in Rule Interpretation: Why the European Parliament Won at Amsterdam' (2002) 32 *British Journal of Political Science* 259.

4.2.4. Towards the Modern Era

The Parliament's intent has long been to increase its role in EU foreign policy and external relations,[81] which is evident given its record of accomplishment in accumulating competence. Yet, the Legal Service of the Parliament, where expertise was accumulated for legal actions, was late to the game in comparison to the two major institutional Legal Services of the Council and the Commission. The Parliament in the past had been refused a number of answers to questions in the field of foreign policy,[82] and a debate on CFSP matters used to occur only once per year.[83] Whilst the trend of empowerment for the Parliament from treaty-to-treaty is clear, the reforms were not always as deep as Parliament itself would have preferred.[84] There were dissenters that even objected to the Parliament even being labelled a 'parliament' today. A parliament has connotations of a body that is comparable to an entity seen in nation states. Arguers of this proposition in an EU setting would be more inclined to give it its former title of an 'assembly', given that it is just one interlocutor in the EU decision-making process. The more cynical view of the establishment of the Assembly was to 'make things look brighter than they were'.[85]

Whereas the Parliament's role in the EPC, the predecessor to CFSP, was limited and underwhelming, its dissatisfaction was well known. Yet, in the present era, it sits in a depillarised Union with limited access to CFSP Decisions and related actions, including international agreements. The decision-making procedures within the Parliament have previously been much more complex, and simplification had long been on the agenda.[86] The frustration that was vented has contributed to its long-strident attempts to achieve institutional justification for its cause. Today's treaties present a slightly different picture of engagement between the Parliament and CFSP matters. The Parliament for many years had to use its limited place within the treaties, given it saw itself as being in a position to give its view on the shape and direction of Europe. This is particularly given the fact that there are no constitutional or procedural preclusions from the Parliament expressing its viewpoint on any particular matter. Parliaments are often given the leisurely ability of being in a position to conduct their deliberative abilities in a manner that

[81] Roland Bieber, 'Democratic Control of European Foreign Policy' (1990) 1 *European Journal of International Law* 148.

[82] See, Case T-14/98, *Hautala v Council*, ECLI:EU:T:1999:157, and Kieran St C Bradley, 'The Institutional Law of the European Union in 1999' (1999) 19 *Yearbook of European Law* 547 at 575.

[83] Jean-Claude Piris, *The Lisbon Treaty: A Legal and Political Analysis* (Cambridge University Press, 2010) p 262.

[84] Giacomo Benedetto and Simon Hix, 'Explaining the European Parliament's Gains in the EU Constitution' (2007) 2 *Review of International Organization* 115 at 116.

[85] Hjalte Rasmussen, 'After Legal Pluralism and Integration: Could Disintegration Follow?' in Peter Blume (ed), *Legal Issues at the Dawn of the New Millennium* (Djøf Publishing, 1999) p 84.

[86] See, Ricardo Gosalbo-Bono, 'Co-Decision: An Appraisal of the Experience of the European Parliament as Co-Legislator' (1994) 14 *Yearbook of European Law* 21.

is within their competence. At present, the Parliament sits between being a political actor and a specialised institution.[87] It can be said that internationally, its role in external affairs is an example of a parliament's 'modern role'.[88] The Parliament's actions are set down in Article 231 TFEU stating that '[s]ave as otherwise provided in the treaties, the European Parliament shall act by a majority of the votes cast. The Rules of Procedure shall determine the quorum'. This basic reading means that the Parliament appears to operate under a simple majoritarian system, given that the quorum is just one third of all members.[89] Its evolutionary status, gradually edging its way into more realms of Union policy, can be called the *parliamentary push*. The detailed list of Resolutions from when CFSP matters was introduced in 1992 demonstrates this.[90]

The Parliament has expanded, both in terms of the number of members and its ability to scrutinise EU policies. It has developed mechanisms and working methods of obtaining competence and jurisdiction in areas that the treaties have not decided to confer upon it. As the treaties have been redesigned to include the expanding field of policy goals for the Union, the Parliament has been an active player in shoring up its own interests. It has taken initiatives to extend its influence on a gradual basis on CFSP matters.[91] For international agreements based on a CFSP legal basis, no approval of the Parliament is required and 'no official political nexus' is evident.[92] This compares to non-CFSP matters where the strengthened role of Parliament means the ordinary legislative procedure applies for the ratification of international agreements on a non-CFSP legal basis. Parliamentary involvement in international agreements on a non-CFSP legal basis is now the rule rather than the exception. The Court has recognised that institutional powers, 'particularly as regards the involvement of the European Parliament, are not always

[87] See discussion in, Andreas Maurer, 'The Legislative Powers and Impact of the European Parliament' (2003) 41 *Journal of Common Market Studies* 227 at 236.

[88] Davor Jančić, 'Globalizing Representative Democracy: The Emergence of Multilayered International Parliamentarism' (2015) 38 *Hastings International and Comparative Law Review* 197 at 211.

[89] See, Article 168(2), European Parliament, 'Rules of Procedure – 8th Parliamentary Term (July 2014)'.

[90] Some are listed in, Ramses A Wessel, 'Good Governance and EU Foreign, Security and Defence Policy' in Deirdre Curtin and Ramses A Wessel (eds), *Good Governance and the European Union: Reflections on Concepts, Institutions and Substance* (Intersentia, 2005) p 222. See, 'Report of the Committee on Institutional Affairs on the Structure and Strategy for the European Union with Regard to Its Enlargement and the Creation of a Europe-Wide Order (A3-0189/92) (Rapporteur: Mr Klaus Hänsch)' (European Parliament 1992) A3-0189/92; 'Report of the Committee on Foreign Affairs and Security on Shaping the European Community's Common Foreign Policy (A3-0322/92) (Rapporteur: Mr Josep Verde I Aldea)' (European Parliament 1992) A3-0322/92; 'Report of the Committee on Institutional Affairs on the Future Relations between the European Union, WEU and the Atlantic Alliance (A3-0041/94) (Rapporteur: Mr Karel De Gucht)' (European Parliament 1994) A3-0041/94; 'Report on Improving the Impact of Joint Actions Committee on Foreign Affairs, Security and Defence Policy (A4-0133/97) (Rapporteur: Mr Enrique Barón Crespo)' (European Parliament 1997) A4-0133/97.

[91] Helene Sjursen, 'Not so Intergovernmental after All? On Democracy and Integration in European Foreign and Security Policy' (2011) 18 *Journal of European Public Policy* 1078 at 1090.

[92] Henri De Waele, *Layered Global Player: Legal Dynamics of EU External Relations* (Springer, 2011) p 34.

based on consistent criteria',[93] adding further impulses to the Parliament's actions. The Treaty of Maastricht paved the way for a larger Legal Service of the Parliament, which today has an array of lawyers to functionally handle and construe added benefit for the institution.

The Parliament is now operating under the ordinary legislative procedure in areas other than CFSP matters, and is actively involved in nearly all parts of EU policy. The Constitutional Treaty was the first EU treaty that included provisions to allow the Parliament to participate in the conclusion phase of the Union's international agreements,[94] but that Treaty's fate is well known.[95] Despite this, the Parliament's influence in legislative areas can be measured,[96] but given that CFSP matters are non-legislative in nature, it is much more difficult to quantify accurately. One view is that the Parliament's role in CFSP matters is still 'extremely limited'.[97] Nevertheless, steps towards becoming a more important actor can be traced through legal developments. Article 24(1) TEU specifies '[t]he specific role of the European Parliament and of the Commission in this area is defined by the [t]reaties',[98] and furthermore, 'the adoption of legislative acts shall be excluded'.[99] Whilst the former statement by the treaties may be criticised for barely bothering to further define what it meant,[100] the latter has meant that as non-legislative instruments, CFSP matters would continue to be excluded from the general scope of where the Parliament could formally act as it would in any other area of policy.

4.3. Soft Legal Powers in CFSP Matters

The Parliament noted in a 1999 report that a confirmation hearing should be held for the High Representative, 'as a precondition for developing a close and constructive relationship between Parliament and the High Representative'.[101] No formal power currently exists for approving or rejecting individual members of the Commission, including the High Representative. However, a meeting with the proposed High Representative takes place, with a legal basis stemming from

[93] Case C-242/87, *Commission v Council*, ECLI:EU:C:1989:217 ('*Erasmus*'), para 13.

[94] Ricardo Passos and Stephan Marquardt, 'International Agreements – Competences, Procedures and Judicial Control' in Giuliano Amato, Hervé Bribosia and Bruno De Witte (eds), *Genesis and Destiny of the European Constitution: Commentary on the Treaty establishing a Constitution for Europe in the light of the travaux préparatoires and Future Prospects* (Bruylant, 2007) p 898.

[95] See Chapter 2 of this book.

[96] See, Amie Kreppel, 'Moving Beyond Procedure An Empirical Analysis of European Parliament Legislative Influence' (2002) 35 *Comparative Political Studies* 784.

[97] Panos Koutrakos, 'Judicial Review in the EU's Common Foreign and Security Policy' (2018) 67 *International and Comparative Law Quarterly* 1 at 4.

[98] TEU, Article 24(1) from Section 1 'Common Provisions' from Chapter 2 'Specific Provisions on the Common Foreign and Security Policy'.

[99] The current Article 24 TEU can be traced back to Article 11 TEU pre-Lisbon, under the Treaty of Nice.

[100] David AO Edward and Robert Lane, *Edward and Lane on European Union Law* (Edward Elgar, 2013) p 139 (section 3.75).

[101] 'Report on the Role of the Union in the World: Implementation of the Common Foreign and Security Policy for 1998 (A4-0242/99)' (European Parliament 1999) A4-0242/99.

Article 17(7) TEU, holding power over the approval of the High Representative, in conjunction with the other Commission as an entire body.[102] Even so, the Parliament can make what it wishes of a confirmation hearing. Just because the Parliament may not have legalised capabilities in certain fields, does not mean it does not have the power of debate. The Parliament possesses the right to initiate its own reports, including on CFSP matters.[103]

4.3.1. Parliamentary Committees

One of the methods employed by the Parliament to exercise greater involvement in Union affairs was the establishment of Committees. In external action, they have proven to be an effective forum within the Parliament's own structures for attempting to exercise scrutiny powers, going beyond mere involvement. Committees, such as the Committee on Foreign Affairs (AFET, derived from *Affaires Étrangères*), are utilised in the face of the Parliament's growing external activities.[104] It is worth recalling that the Parliament, whilst legally seen as one actor, is not unified from a political perspective. Parliamentary disunity can occur between Committees with rivalries that go beyond legal competence and jurisdiction and veer into the political arena. A typical example of where a jurisdictional conflict could arise would be between AFET and the Committee on Budgets (BUDG). Given the budget for CFSP matters is one of the few areas of involvement for the Parliament, the claiming of the area by AFET, successfully, may be warranted from AFET's perspective.

The lack of unity within the Parliament can result in minority opinions of members to reports occurring[105] and thus be detrimental to the institution's overall goal of greater institutional balance. However, at the very least, the Parliament has a coherent internal committee structure for dealing with CFSP matters and has learnt from the experiences of some Member States in the past that had multiple committee forums within a single national parliament.[106]

[102] TEU, Article 17(7), para 3: 'The President, the High Representative of the Union for Foreign Affairs and Security Policy and the other members of the Commission shall be subject as a body to a vote of consent by the European Parliament. On the basis of this consent, the Commission shall be appointed by the European Council, acting by a qualified majority.'

[103] Nathaniel Lalone, 'Accountability in the EU's Common Foreign and Security Policy: Lessons from the Common Commercial Policy' in Esther Barbé and Anna Herranz (eds), *The Role of Parliaments in European Foreign Policy: Debating on Accountability and Legitimacy* (Office of the European Parliament, 2005) p 3.

[104] See, Fabio Longo, Cristina Fasone and Sarah Delputte, 'The Diplomatic Role of the European Parliament's Standing Committees, Delegations and Assemblies: Insights from ACP–EU Inter-Parliamentary Cooperation' (2016) 11 *The Hague Journal of Diplomacy* 161.

[105] For example, see 'Report on the Annual Report from the Council to the European Parliament on the Common Foreign and Security Policy (12562/2011 -2012/2050(INI)) – 29 August 2012)' (European Parliament 2012) A7-0252/2012 p 33.

[106] Denmark in the past had three parliamentary committees dealing with foreign policy. See, Isi Foighel and Claus Gulmann, 'Parliamentary Foreign Affairs Committees in Denmark' in Antonio Cassese (ed), *Parliamentary Foreign Affairs Committees: The National Setting*, vol 1 (Cedam/Oceana, 1982).

There is minimal reference to the President of the Parliament within the treaties.[107] Article 235(2) TFEU allows the President of the Parliament to interact with the Council, but only on the Council's assent. This provision does not mean that the President is a full participant in the Council debate, but simply that s/he may be heard. However, the President of the Parliament has an increased presence now more than ever before,[108] thanks, in part, to particular personalities and their preferences, even though the role is non-existent in foreign policy decision-making from a legal perspective. Despite the role's democratic credentials and the political clout which the President might hold externally, it is just one of a number of figures in a crowded field, with more authoritative and executive actors competing for attention in foreign policy issues.

4.3.2. Report Writing

Another method of parliamentary involvement in CFSP matters is producing reports, where several matters can be highlighted and analysed. With the Parliament examining a report after CFSP Decisions are taken and actions followed, retrospectively, they provide little meaning for actual involvement of the Parliament in CFSP Decisions, thereby continuing the practice of the Parliament's involvement in CFSP matters being minimal. While retrospective reports are excellent tools for researchers to analyse CFSP actions, decision-making and other factors, in practice, they serve as little more than records that may one day end up in books on the external action of the Union addressing a particular point in time. In the same way that the Commission can issue non-binding recommendations,[109] the Parliament is competent to issue non-binding actions in the form of resolutions to supplement its reports. Rapporteurs functioning within the Parliament who produce reports have some impact on the actions of the Union.[110]

The Parliament must also be conscious of the fact that where it has an obligation to act under the treaties, the Council may do so without its specific consent if

[107] TEU, Article 14(4) on the election of the President of the Parliament; TFEU, Article 235(2) on the President of the Parliament being heard by the Council on invitation; TFEU, Article 294(8)(b) on the procedures for the adoption of acts and other provisions; TFEU, Article 297(1) on the signature of legislative acts adopted under the ordinary legislative procedure; TFEU, Article 314(4)(c) TFEU on the special legislative procedure; TFEU, Article 314(9) on the declaration of the budget; TFEU, Article 324 on regular meetings between the Presidents of the Commission, Council and Parliament; Article 3 of Protocol 1 on the role of national parliaments; Article 6 of Protocol 2 on the application of the principles of subsidiarity and proportionality; and Article 6 of Protocol 3 on the statute of the Court of Justice.

[108] Luigi Gianniti and Nicola Lupo, 'The Role of the European Parliament President in Parliamentary Diplomacy' (2016) 11 *The Hague Journal of Diplomacy* 144 at 147.

[109] TFEU, Article 288.

[110] Outside of CFSP matters, see, Giacomo Benedetto, 'Rapporteurs as Legislative Entrepreneurs: The Dynamics of the Codecision Procedure in Europe's Parliament' (2005) 12 *Journal of European Public Policy* 67.

they do not perform their obligations on time.[111] Yet, post-Lisbon, the Parliament has been active in ensuring that its view is heard, and put into the establishment of the new body that will largely be involved with CFSP matters in the Union, the new European External Action Service (EEAS).[112] The Council established the EEAS through a CFSP Decision, in which the Parliament was closely involved during the establishment process,[113] where it acted as one of the four parties as prescribed by Article 27(3) TEU.[114] The Council Decision to establish the EEAS noted it shall 'extend appropriate support and cooperation to the other institutions and bodies of the Union, in particular to the Parliament'.[115] Yet, beyond the involvement of the Parliament in the establishment of the EEAS, the treaties appear not to have given the Parliament a close role regarding the EEAS and the High Representative post-establishment.[116] With the EEAS so heavily involved in the preparatory work of the Foreign Affairs Council (FAC)[117] meetings that are chaired by the High Representative – and tasked with some of the responsibility for implementing CFSP Decisions – it represented a strong effort on the Council's part to bring the Parliament closer to CFSP matters, but on an imprecise footing. Such implementing actions would normally fall to the Commission. However, Article 291(2) TFEU vests the implementing powers in the Council covering Articles 24–26 TEU,[118] which are CFSP legal bases.

Each year, the Council is required to submit an Annual Report to the Parliament on CFSP matters.[119] Previously, these have been used to vent institutional

[111] Case C-65/93, *Parliament v Council*, ECLI:EU:C:1995:91 ('*Generalised Tariff Preferences*') See, Ton Heukels, 'Case C-65/93, European Parliament v Council of the European Union, Judgment of 30 March 1995, (Full Court): Article 43 of the EEC Treaty – Obligation to Consult the Parliament' (1995) 32 *Common Market Law Review* 1407; Piet Van Nuffel, 'Case Law: Case C-65/93, European Parliament v Council of the European Union, 1995 ECR 1-643 (Extension of System of Generalized Tariff Preferences)' (1995) 1 *Columbia Journal of European Law* 504.

[112] For an overview of this process, see, Bart Van Vooren, 'A Legal-Institutional Perspective on the European External Action Service' (2011) 48 *Common Market Law Review* 475 at 478.

[113] See, Elisabeth Wisniewski, 'The Influence of the European Parliament on the European External Action Service' (2013) 18 *European Foreign Affairs Review* 81.

[114] TEU, Article 27(3): 'The Council shall act on a proposal from the High Representative after consulting the European Parliament and after obtaining the consent of the Commission.'

[115] EEAS Decision, Article 3(4): L 201/30. Council Decision of 26 July 2010 Establishing the Organisation and Functioning of the European External Action Service (2010/427/EU).

[116] Mauro Gatti, *European External Action Service: Promoting Coherence through Autonomy and Coordination* (Brill 2016) p 185.

[117] The meeting of foreign ministers used to occur in the General Council and along with the Agricultural Council were seen as the two most important formations of the Council. Wolfgang Wessels, 'The EC Council: The Community's Decisionmaking Center' in Robert O Keohane and Stanley Hoffmann (eds), *The New European Community: Decisionmaking and Institutional Change* (Westview Press, 1991) p 134. For more on the FAC/GAC distinction, see Chapter 3 of this book.

[118] Kieran St C Bradley, 'Delegation of Powers in the European Union: Political Problems, Legal Solutions?' in Carl Fredrik Bergström and Dominique Ritleng (eds), *Rulemaking by the European Commission: The New System for Delegation of Powers* (Oxford University Press, 2016) p 72.

[119] For recent years reports, see, Council of the European Union, 'CFSP Annual Report 2014. Main Aspects and Basic Choices of the CFSP (Part II, Point E, Paragraph 25 of the Interinstitutional Agreement of 2 December 2013) – 2014 – Draft Annual Report from the High Representative of the European Union for Foreign Affairs and Security Policy to the European Parliament (11083/15)' (Council of the

frustration; recently, however, they have been much more focused on the substance of CFSP matters.[120] In the past, there was no legal basis for decision-making adopted by the Council on a CFSP legal basis to be accountable for measures taken.[121] The legal basis for this is formalised through interinstitutional agreements, flowing from the primary law.

4.3.3. Parliamentary Debate

The involvement of the Parliament in the legal instruments with third states was not always guaranteed before the Treaty of Lisbon. An anomaly lay in the fact that Article 179 EC was a facilitation of co-decision for the Parliament on development cooperation, but Article 181(a) EC was used by the Union for cooperation instruments with third states. This was not co-decision, meaning there was no involvement of the Parliament.[122] Today, co-decision for the Parliament is the result of a huge amount of energy ploughed into smoother interinstitutional relations.[123] One of the stock mechanisms of the Parliament in CFSP matters is today's Article 36 TEU,[124] the most prominent reference to the Parliament when

European Union 2015) 11083/15; Council of the European Union, 'CFSP Annual Report 2013. Main Aspects and Basic Choices of the CFSP (Part II, Point E, Paragraph 25 of the Interinstitutional Agreement of 2 December 2013) – 2013 – Annual Report from the High Representative of the European Union for Foreign Affairs and Security Policy to the European Parliament (12094/14)' (Council of the European Union 2014) 12094/14; Council of the European Union, 'CFSP Annual Report 2012. Main Aspects and Basis Choices of the CFSP (Point G, Paragraph 43 of the Interinstitutional Agreement of 17 May 2006) – 2012 – Annual Report from the High Representative of the European Union for Foreign Affairs and Security Policy to the European Parliament (14924/13)' (Council of the European Union 2013) 14924/13; Council of the European Union, 'CFSP Annual Report 2011. Main Aspects and Basis Choices of the CFSP (Point G, Paragraph 43 of the Interinstitutional Agreement of 17 May 2006) – 2011 – Annual Report from the High Representative of the European Union for Foreign Affairs and Security Policy to the European Parliament (14605/1/12)' (Council of the European Union 2012) 14605/1/12; Council of the European Union, 'CFSP Annual Report 2010. Main Aspects and Basis Choices of the CFSP (Point G, Paragraph 43 of the Interinstitutional Agreement of 17 May 2006) – 2010 – Annual Report from the High Representative of the European Union for Foreign Affairs and Security Policy to the European Parliament (12562/11)' (Council of the European Union 2011) 12562/11.

[120] For example, a report recently said that the High Representative had a 'cooperative attitude towards Parliament, aimed at strengthening her accountability to the institution'. See, 'Report on the Annual Report from the High Representative of the European Union for Foreign Affairs and Security Policy to the European Parliament (2014/2219(INI))' (European Parliament 2015) A8-0039/2015. p 9 (para 27).

[121] Gormley (n 79) p 62.

[122] Daniela Gauci, 'The European Parliament and EU External Aid: Measures of Response to Emergency Situations' in Antonis Antoniadis, Robert Schütze and Eleanor Spaventa (eds), *The European Union and Global Emergencies: A Law and Policy Analysis* (Hart Publishing, 2011) p 291. For a more thorough insight into the pre-Lisbon situation, see, Ricardo Passos and Daniela Gauci, 'European Parliament and Development Cooperation: Shaping Legislation and the New Democratic Scrutiny Dialogue' in Sandra Bartelt and Philipp Dann (eds), *Entwicklungszusammenarbeit im Recht der Europäischen Union – The Law of EU Development Cooperation* (Nomos, 2008).

[123] Katrin Huber and Michael Shackleton, 'Codecision: A Practitioner's View from inside the Parliament' (2013) 20 *Journal of European Public Policy* 1040 at 1042.

[124] TEU, Article 36: 'The High Representative of the Union for Foreign Affairs and Security Policy shall regularly consult the European Parliament on the main aspects and the basic choices of the

it comes to CFSP matters within the treaties. It is vastly similar to its predecessor, Article 21 TEU pre-Lisbon, with the wording having evolved through the revisions of treaties.[125]

Certain features can be drawn from the current wording of Article 36 TEU. Firstly, strictly speaking, it does not provide the Parliament any formal powers in the decision-making processes. Rather, it entitles the Parliament to a 'triad of information, consultation and debate'.[126] In its earlier days, parliamentarians had a marginal position regarding the hearings held with the High Representative and struggled to grasp any real emphasis from hearing-to-hearing, demonstrating a weakness in not only the compellability of the Parliament, but also its effectiveness as a parliamentary actor. The language used in Article 36 TEU such as 'regularly', 'main aspects' and 'basic choices' which is extremely light terminology, does not bode well. The precision, or the lack of it, with such phraseology has meant that inevitably, the institution is distant from the heart of actual decision-making. It could even be stated that such terminology is 'not encouraging' for the Parliament and its perspective.[127] Such terms are in no way further defined or elaborated on by the treaties. Furthermore, the Parliament does not possess the possibility to be consulted on 'individual foreign policy measures', which 'erodes the obligation imposed on the High Representative' in the first place.[128] With vague and little legal significance lies large discretion for institutional interpretation. Accordingly, the intricate framing of actions with a wide array of policy choices within the breadth of CFSP matters is beyond the Parliament's true grasp. Any potential for real decision-making has not been on the table from the get-go, and Article 36 TEU reduces it to merely an echo-chamber of political debate that lacks rigour.

The creation of the office of the High Representative was initially opposed by the Parliament, which instead favoured the duties and functions being handled by the now defunct Commission for External Action.[129] Nevertheless, 1998 was the first year in which the debate on 'main aspects and basic choices' took place.[130] The first permanent High Representative demonstrated keenness to engage constantly with

common foreign and security policy and the common security and defence policy and inform it of how those policies evolve. He shall ensure that the views of the European Parliament are duly taken into consideration. Special representatives may be involved in briefing the European Parliament. The European Parliament may address questions or make recommendations to the Council or the High Representative. Twice a year it shall hold a debate on progress in implementing the common foreign and security policy, including the common security and defence policy.'

[125] This evolution started with Article 30(4) of the Single European Act, followed by Article J7 TEU, succeeded by Article J11 TEU after Amsterdam, Article 21 TEU after Nice, up to today's Article 36 TEU post-Lisbon.

[126] Schmidt-Radefeldt (n 42) p 1120.

[127] Geert De Baere, 'EU External Action' in Catherine Barnard and Steve Peers (eds), *European Union Law* 2nd edition (Oxford University Press, 2017) p 734.

[128] Robert Schütze, 'Parliamentary Democracy and International Treaties' (2017) 8 *Global Policy* 7 at 10.

[129] Ben Crum, 'Parliamentarization of the CFSP through Informal Institution-Making? The Fifth European Parliament and the EU High Representative' (2006) 13 *Journal of European Public Policy* 383 at 392.

[130] Steve Peers, 'Common Foreign and Security Policy 1998' (1998) 18 *Yearbook of European Law* 659 at 660.

AFET, which in turn has been the basis for today's current primary law arrangement. The High Representative engaging with the Parliament, labelled 'a habit',[131] was an involved interaction of civility and willingness rather than of necessity or legal mandate. It was questioned for many years whether this arrangement applied prospectively,[132] until an interinstitutional agreement on budgetary discipline and sound financial management stated consultation with the Parliament by the Council would be 'forward-looking'[133] and supported the legitimacy of the High Representative's role. The Article 36 TEU debates now occur approximately once every six months and take place in the AFET Committee, as opposed to the full plenary of the Parliament. Whilst the Article 36 TEU meetings were formal and held in the public domain, the High Representative then, as now, conducted informal meetings with MEPs away from the eyes of the public.

The growing role for the Parliament in general Union affairs, in particular through its budgetary powers, ensures the High Representative, the EEAS and the Commission will take the Article 36 TEU procedure more seriously. The same Article 36 TEU is also the basis to occasionally hear from special representatives of the Union in appearances before the Parliament.[134] Whilst there is little evidence to support or deny the Parliament's persuasion of the High Representative's approach to CFSP matters as a direct result of these Article 36 TEU engagements, they continue to occur. Instances where the High Representative is being deputised can be a delicate issue due to the multi-hatted role that it pertains. Seen from a Council perspective, the High Representative holds the position *intuitu personae*, with that officeholder alone,[135] therefore it is not deputable. In practice, however, there are options. Another member of the Commission may take the High Representative's place when appearing before the Parliament to discuss non-CFSP matters, whilst another member of the FAC would fill in on CFSP matters – likely the Foreign Minister of the Member State holding the rotating Presidency of the Council.

Beyond these debates, Article 36 TEU could also be interpreted as having a much broader meaning. Viewed another way, it could be plausible that the

[131] Ramses A Wessel, 'The Dynamics of the European Union Legal Order: An Increasingly Coherent Framework of Action and Interpretation' (2009) 5 *European Constitutional Law Review* 117 at 127.

[132] Robert Schütze, 'The "Treaty Power" and Parliamentary Democracy: Comparative Perspectives' in Robert Schütze (ed), *Foreign Affairs and the EU Constitution: Selected Essays* (Cambridge University Press, 2014) p 390.

[133] C 139/1. Interinstitutional Agreement of 17 May 2006 between the European Parliament, the Council and the Commission on Budgetary Discipline and Sound Financial Management (2006/C 139/01), para 43.

[134] The Union has representatives for thematic issues and regional areas. For example, on human rights, see, L 200/21. Council Decision 2012/440/CFSP of 25 July 2012 Appointing the European Union Special Representative for Human Rights, most recently extended by, L 43/29. Council Decision (CFSP) 2015/260 of 17 February 2015 Extending the Mandate of the European Union Special Representative for Human Rights and for Afghanistan, see, L 326/1. Council Joint Action of 10 December 2001 Concerning the Appointment of the Special Representative of the European Union (2001/875/CFSP), mostly recently extended by L 294/53. Council Decision (CFSP) 2015/2005 of 10 November 2015 Extending the Mandate of the European Union Special Representative in Afghanistan.

[135] Gosalbo-Bono and Naert (n 27) p 33.

Parliament could be put as close to CFSP Decisions as possible – a view that would clearly not be shared by the Council. Article 36 TEU is an inherently rigid instrument and an overly structured dialogue may not serve the greater interests of the Parliament. Consistently through its reports, the Parliament has said it 'does not consider itself adequately consulted as provided for by Article 21 [now Article 36 TEU] of the Treaty on European Union through the Council's current practice'.[136] While the Article 36 TEU criteria may eventually lead to a possibility for AFET to become a forum where the High Representative is interrogated by the Parliament, it presently has nothing more than a 'mere advisory function'.[137] Notwithstanding the cynicism that prevails from many quarters, debate in the Parliament does have the indirect means of providing the Council with some level of direction in CFSP matters. Article 36 TEU is not and arguably should not be, the only avenue for dialogue between the High Representative and the Parliament. The second High Representative, during the confirmation hearings with the Parliament in 2014, stated the dialogue would be within 'forward-looking documents setting out the main features and basic choices',[138] thereby sticking to the intentions of the treaties. This followed from the declaration on political accountability by the first post-Lisbon High Representative,[139] who provided a litany of scenarios where the Parliament could be involved and how the EEAS in CFSP matters would operate. However, the terminology used was 'couched in vague language based on complex arrangements'.[140] This proves that political commitments by actors charged with executing CFSP matters do not necessarily mean that intentions go anywhere beyond the specific obligations of the treaties.

4.4. Stronger Legal Powers in CFSP Matters

In addition to the provisions in the treaties covering CFSP matters, other articles could serve the purpose of empowering the Parliament. The Parliament has formal powers in the Union's external relations, including the assent/consent procedure,

[136] 'Report on the Annual Report from the Council to the European Parliament on the Main Aspects and Basic Choices of CFSP, Including the Financial Implications for the General Budget of the European Communities – 2003 (8412/2004 – 2004/2172(INI))' (European Parliament 2005) A6-0062/2005.

[137] Donatella M Viola, 'The Genesis of the European Parliament: From Appointed Consultative Assembly to Directly Elected Legislative Body' in Donatella M Viola (ed), *Routledge Handbook of European Elections* (Routledge 2016) p 11.

[138] 'Answers to the European Parliament: Questionnaire to the Commissioner-Designate, Federica Mogherini, High Representative of the Union for Foreign Affairs and Security Policy, Vice-President of the Commission' (European Parliament, October 2014) p 3.

[139] C 201/1. Adoption of a Council Decision Establishing the Organisation and Functioning of the European External Action Service (2010/C 210/01) Draft Declaration by the High Representative on Political Accountability'.

[140] Panos Koutrakos, 'The European Union's Common Foreign and Security Policy after the Treaty of Lisbon' (Swedish Institute for European Policy Studies (SIEPS) 2017) 2017:3 p 46.

the powers of forging interinstitutional and framework agreements and budgetary authority. The Constitutional Treaty, as did the Treaty of Lisbon, maintained certain specificities for concluding international agreements in CFSP matters.[141] Pre-Lisbon, the Parliament had no involvement in the concluding stage of an international agreement. However, the text of the Treaty of Lisbon brought about some minor changes with huge ramifications, and has been the subject of much case law in recent years.[142]

Tucked away in the TFEU is an important substantive article – Article 218 TFEU – on the arrangements of the Union concerning international agreements. Substantiated by the Treaty of Lisbon, it is one of the most important aspects of institutional development of the Parliament in external relations. The Parliament, as a co-legislator with the Council, acknowledges that CFSP matters are not considered as legislative acts, despite being legal acts. Accordingly, it is the prerogative of the Parliament to challenge actions of other EU institutions that it believes may be acting contrary to the treaties. As an example, for the conclusion of international agreements, Article 218 TFEU is applicable and therefore, on a formal basis, the role of the Parliament comes in.[143] As the Court has held for the conclusion of international agreements, Article 218 TFEU is 'an autonomous and general provision of constitutional scope, in that it confers specific powers on the EU institutions…[w]ith a view to establishing a balance between those institutions'.[144] The involvement of the Parliament in the conclusion of Council agreements pre-Lisbon was not as prominent.[145] In fact, they were contained in a mere four scenarios.[146] Accordingly, the rule for agreements was that the Parliament was excluded and its inclusion was on a specified, exceptional basis.

[141] Passos and Marquardt (n 94) p 887. For a look into the political dynamics of CFSP matters and the Constitutional Treaty, see, Udo Diedrichs and Funda Tekin, 'CFSP after the Constitutional Treaty: The Stakes for the Future' in Sergio Carrera and Thierry Balzacq (eds), *Security Versus Freedom? A Challenge for Europe's Future* (Routledge, 2006) p 246.

[142] See, Allan Rosas, 'Recent Case Law of the European Court of Justice Relating to Article 218 TFEU' in Jenö Czuczai and Frederik Naert (eds), *The EU as a Global Actor – Bridging Legal Theory and Practice: Liber Amicorum in Honour of Ricardo Gosalbo Bono* (Brill, 2016).

[143] TFEU, Article 218(6). From a Council perspective, the increased role of the Parliament is with respect to international agreements. Gosalbo-Bono and Naert (n 27) p 15.

[144] Case C-425/13, *Commission v Council*, ECLI:EU:C:2015:483 ('*Australia ETS*'), para 62. The Parliament intervened in support of the Commission, for otherwise, 'the position of the Parliament and its margin of influence on the negotiations would be completely jeopardized'. Ricardo Passos, 'The External Powers of the European Parliament' in Piet Eeckhout and Manuel López-Escudero (eds), *The European Union's External Action in Times of Crisis* (Hart Publishing, 2016) p 109.

[145] See, Aline De Walsche, 'La procédure de conclusion des accords internationaux' in Jean-Victor Louis and Marianne Dony (eds), *Relations extérieures* (Editions de l'Université de Bruxelles, 2005).

[146] EC, Article 300(3), para 2, provided for 'agreements referred to in Article 310 [association agreements], other agreements establishing a specific institutional framework by organising cooperation procedures, agreements having important budgetary implications for the Community and agreements entailing amendment of an act adopted under the procedure referred to in Article 251 [co-decision] shall be concluded after the assent of the European Parliament has been obtained'. Passos (n 144) p 86.

4.4.1. Consent and Information Powers

At the institutional apex of international agreements in all its forms is the Council. This is stressed by Article 218 TFEU, sub-section 2, which states '[t]he Council shall authorise the opening of negotiations, adopt negotiating directives, authorise the signing of agreements and conclude them'. Therefore, Article 218 TFEU appears to leave out a role for the Parliament in the opening of negotiations leading to an international agreement, applicable regardless of whether such an international agreement has a CFSP legal basis or a non-CFSP legal basis. Yet, Article 218 TFEU plays a strong role on the principle of institutional balance and the separation of powers within the Union. In the words of one Advocate General, Article 218 TFEU sets down the basis for 'the Commission (which initiates the process and represents the EU externally), the Council (which is responsible for deciding that the EU is to be bound by international law) and the Parliament (which must at all times be informed and may be asked either to consent or to give an opinion)'.[147] Strictly speaking, Article 218(6) TFEU deliberately excludes the Parliament from the conclusion of all CFSP agreements.[148] It provides that the Council is not obliged to seek the involvement of the Parliament to conclude international agreements based upon a CFSP legal basis. Another important feature of Article 218 TFEU introduced in the Treaty of Lisbon is that it allows for mixing CFSP legal bases and non-CFSP legal bases. This mixing was explicitly disallowed by the Court pre-Lisbon in *ECOWAS*, discussed later in this chapter. While Article 218 TFEU notes the Parliament's legislative involvement on non-CFSP matters, the difficulty arises in that the treaties do not elaborate on the Parliament's role in areas where an agreement may contain a mixture of CFSP matters and other external elements of the Union where the Parliament does have the competence.

Article 218 TFEU provides two different powers to the Parliament for the making of international agreements – that of the right to consent, and the right to information. It partially makes up for the divide between CFSP legal bases and non-CFSP legal bases divided between the TEU and TFEU. Depending on whether it is an international agreement for CFSP matters or an international agreement for non-CFSP matters, the role of the Parliament may vary. As a general premise, it has been highlighted how the Article is actually poorly worded,[149] as it does not mandate for definite that the negotiator for international agreements be the Council itself (through the High Representative) for CFSP matters; or for non-CFSP matters, the Commission. On the right to consent, the Parliament does

[147] Opinion of Advocate General Sharpston, Joined Cases C-103/12 and C-165/12, *Parliament and Commission v Council*, ECLI:EU:C:2014:334 ('*French Guiana*'), para 116.

[148] TFEU, Article 218(6): '...except where agreements relate exclusively to the common foreign and security policy...' Schütze, 'The "Treaty Power" and Parliamentary Democracy: Comparative Perspectives' (n 132) p 390.

[149] Piet Eeckhout, *EU External Relations Law* 2nd edition (Oxford University Press, 2011) p 196.

not have the right of consent to international agreements that are concluded solely on a CFSP legal basis. On the right to information, Article 218 TFEU on the right of the Parliament to information is applicable through the negotiation process for international agreements for CFSP matters and non-CFSP matters. Article 218 TFEU's predecessor, Article 300 EC, as it was pre-Lisbon, detailed similar informational rights. However, this was only when it concerned provisional application of an agreement,[150] or the suspension of an agreement, in addition to the establishment of a 'Community' position in a body stemming from an international agreement.[151] Today, the working method for the Parliament's right to information for international agreements is that it is applicable regardless of whether it is a CFSP legal basis or non-CFSP legal basis.[152]

Article 218(10) TFEU is an important procedural aspect of EU external relations that greatly favours the Parliament compared to previous positions. It states that the Parliament must be 'immediately and fully informed at all stages' of the international agreement. This is a new, far-reaching right of the Parliament, with a legal guarantee in place to ensure its role. Compared to the pre-Lisbon scenario where the Parliament was a mere adviser to the Council,[153] or provided with a consultative opportunity, this is a substantive provision. An unusual feature, it links the rights of the Parliament to be informed on an international agreement concluded on a CFSP legal basis, but not on the right to consent to an international agreement on a CFSP legal basis. Yet, when being drafted, the provision could have made a distinction between the information rights afforded to the Parliament dependent upon the subject matter. Instead, Article 218(10) TFEU applied information rights to the Parliament for all types of international agreements. This provision in itself significantly enhanced the Parliament in asserting new powers and bringing it closer to CFSP matters. The Court has unconstrained jurisdiction as regards Article 218 TFEU, which is used as the legal basis for the conclusion of international agreements to which the Union is a party. This is applicable to both international agreements for CFSP matters and non-CFSP matters – the jurisprudence of which is detailed later in this chapter.

The Opinion procedure that the Court is occasionally asked to deploy, based on Article 218(11) TFEU, specifies that certain bodies can ask for a binding Opinion

[150] Notably, the Treaty of Lisbon did not extend an explicit reach of Parliament's prerogatives with respect to provisional application of international agreements. Passos (n 144) p 119. However, TFEU, Article 218(10) could be interpreted as such an extension.

[151] EC, Article 300(2), para 3: 'The European Parliament shall be immediately and fully informed of any decision under this paragraph concerning the provisional application or the suspension of agreements, or the establishment of the Community position in a body set up by an agreement.'

[152] A discussion on this from a national Member State perspective can be seen in, Ivo Van Der Steen, 'Mixity in Practice–A View from The Netherlands' in Christophe Hillion and Panos Koutrakos (eds), *Mixed Agreements Revisited: The EU and its Member States in the World* (Hart Publishing, 2010) p 302.

[153] Deirdre Curtin, 'Official Secrets and the Negotiation of International Agreements: Is the EU Executive Unbound?' (2013) 50 *Common Market Law Review* 423 at 444. See, Daniel Thym, 'Beyond Parliament's Reach? The Role of the European Parliament in the CFSP' (2006) 11 *European Foreign Affairs Review* 109.

of the Court on draft international agreements before they are concluded.[154] The bodies under the current treaties that can ask for such an Opinion are the Council, the Commission, Member States, and the Parliament. Accordingly, it can be said that this binding Opinion allows the Court to directly thread through the political choices made by the other institutions. This grouping of bodies with *locus standi* to request an Opinion was narrower previously, as it did not include the Parliament. Its early predecessor had it restricted to the Council, the Commission and Member States, despite the Parliament asking to be included.[155] Today, Article 218(11) TFEU permits the Parliament to bring the Court into answering questions with profound political implications.[156] An Opinion could be on deciphering the limits of CFSP matters, 'border policing' as per Article 40 TEU, instead of Article 218(11) TFEU. However, the use of Article 218(11) TFEU by the Parliament in respect of international agreements on a CFSP legal basis may be extremely limited, given the procedure can only be invoked in an *ex ante* fashion. Once an international agreement is concluded, it is no longer an 'agreement envisaged' and instead no longer comes under the scope of Article 218(11) TFEU. Furthermore, given the Court's curtailed jurisdiction in CFSP matters,[157] it is not fully clear how Article 218 TFEU would apply to the Parliament's institutional advantage. Nevertheless, it can be anticipated that the Court would apply the Opinion procedure to a draft international agreement on a CFSP legal basis[158] if it was requested. This is supported by the fact that in *Opinion 2/13*,[159] the Court examined the draft agreement with a keen eye towards the structural position of CFSP matters in the treaties.

Article 218 TFEU has had other effects beyond CFSP matters and, in practice, has extended the practice of the Parliament's involvement in internal Union measures.[160] For example, for JHA matters, which were once upon a time the third pillar, are with the involvement of the Parliament. To avoid the Parliament exercising its veto in non-CFSP matters, the Parliament is brought closer to

[154] See, Graham Butler, 'Pre-Ratification Judicial Review of International Agreements to Be Concluded by the European Union' in Mattias Derlén and Johan Lindholm (eds), *The Court of Justice of the European Union: Multidisciplinary Perspectives* (Hart Publishing, 2018) For a more detailed analysis, see, Stanislas Adam, *La procédure d'avis devant la Court de justice de l'Union européenne* (Bruylant 2011).

[155] C 324/219 (n 78) at p 237.

[156] Notably, as opposed to the Commission which is the usual institution requesting Opinions of the Court, the Parliament was requesting an Opinion on the draft Agreement between Canada and the European Union on the transfer and processing of Passenger Name Record data. *Opinion 1/15*, ECLI:EU:C:2017:592 ('*EU-Canada Passenger Name Records*').

[157] Considered further in Chapter 5 of this book. Furthermore, see, Graham Butler, 'The Coming of Age of the Court's Jurisdiction in the Common Foreign and Security Policy' (2017) 13 *European Constitutional Law Review* 673.

[158] Govaere (n 21) p 84.

[159] Opinion 2/13, ECLI:EU:C:2014:2454 ('*Accession of the European Union to the European Convention for the Protection of Human Rights*'), paras 249–257.

[160] Bjorn Kleizen, 'Mapping the Involvement of the European Parliament in EU External Relations – a Legal and Empirical Analysis' *Centre for the Law of EU External Relations* (TMC Asser Institute, 2016) p 8.

negotiations of international agreements at earlier stages by the Council. The collapse of the pillars contributed to consolidating Article 218 TFEU as a procedural basis for international agreements. Taken as a whole, Article 218 TFEU granting the right for Parliament to be included in some manner in all international agreements that the Union concludes can be seen as a 'major extension of the Parliament's powers in the sphere of EU external relations'[161] and cements the Parliament's future role in such agreements. At the same time, however, for the purposes of the Parliament's involvement, the depillarisation of the Union did not in itself lead to increased influence, due to the realignment of EU legal acts.[162]

4.4.2. Interinstitutional and Framework Agreements

On top of the treaties, shaping the formation of how institutions operate and the competence conferred upon them, there are interinstitutional agreements permissible to flesh out and expand on the basic requirements of primary law. Interinstitutional agreements are a manifestation of informal practices taking hold,[163] having strong ramifications for the operational practice of EU institutions and have been labelled as a process of 'sub-constitutional engineering'.[164] These agreements, stemming from Article 295 TFEU,[165] play an important role for the Parliament when participating in Union affairs.[166] In addition, the Parliament's right to information is also derived from 'constitutional practice and influenced by interinstitutional agreements'.[167] These interinstitutional agreements 'may be of a binding nature', meaning their actual binding nature is uncertain, except for where the parties explicitly state so. This potential of interinstitutional agreements

[161] Jörg Monar, 'The Rejection of the EU-US SWIFT Interim Agreement by the European Parliament: A Historic Vote and Its Implications' (2010) 15 *European Foreign Affairs Review* 143 at 145.

[162] 'The much-publicised abolition of the pillar structure…is of a lesser importance to public and parliamentary scrutiny as the new division of legal instruments into "legislative" and "non-legislative" in fact rather cements it.' Heidi Hautala, 'The Role of Parliaments in the EU Constitutional Framework: A Partnership or Rivalry?' in Deirdre Curtin, Alfred E Kellermann and Steven Blockmans (eds), *The EU Constitution: The Best Way Forward?* (TMC Asser Press, 2005) p 228.

[163] Steven Van Hecke and Wouter Wolfs, 'The European Parliament and European Foreign Policy' in Knud Erik Jørgensen and others (eds), *The SAGE Handbook of European Foreign Policy* (SAGE 2015) p 294.

[164] Isabella Eiselt and Peter Slominski, 'Sub-Constitutional Engineering: Negotiation, Content and Legal Value of Interinstitutional Agreements in the EU' (2006) 12 *European Law Journal* 209.

[165] TFEU, Article 295: 'The European Parliament, the Council and the Commission shall consult each other and by common agreement make arrangements for their cooperation. To that end, they may, in compliance with the [t]reaties, conclude interinstitutional agreements which may be of a binding nature.' It is worth noting that they are also mentioned with regard, specifically, to the Commission in TEU, Article 17.

[166] See, Daniela Kietz and Andreas Maurer, 'The European Parliament in Treaty Reform: Predefining IGCs through Interinstitutional Agreements' (2007) 13 *European Law Journal* 20.

[167] Andrea Ott, 'The European Parliament's Role in EU Treaty-Making' (2016) 23 *Maastricht Journal of European and Comparative Law* 1009 at 1017.

was only permissible post-Lisbon;[168] before they were not sufficiently precise, notwithstanding their existence, to fill the gaps where binding primary law was silent. Nonetheless, the Court recognised in *FAO* that internal arrangements, as opposed to interinstitutional agreements between EU institutions, could have a binding effect.[169] The potential binding nature of the interinstitutional agreements has been a positive development; otherwise, there would be the potential for institutions to deviate from them at times that they wished, without the possibility of other institutions holding them to account. The Parliament has been particularly successful as an institutional actor in negotiating interinstitutional agreements;[170] in as far as it is for its own benefit.

The internal workings and agreements that are achieved have a profound impact on the EU's external relations. Despite the fractured nature of institutional divisions when it comes to CFSP matters, both the Parliament and the Council have demonstrated a clear willingness to work with one another when common ground is established. For example, sensitive information that the Council may possess can be accessed by the Parliament in limited fields, defined by an interinstitutional agreement.[171] That initiative has been the Parliament's work[172] and has led to it eventually being better informed. However, negative reactions by certain institutions to interinstitutional agreements by *other* institutions can be provocative.[173] Beyond the Council in CFSP matters, given that the Commission has extensive powers in EU external relations in non-CFSP matters, it is unsurprising that the Parliament seeks a close working relationship with the Commission. In view of this reality, shortly after the entry into force of the Treaty of Lisbon, the two institutions concluded a 'framework agreement'.[174] Article 10 states that the Commission shall take into account the Parliament's view in CFSP matters 'within its competence[]' although the Commission is also limited, as specified in the CFSP chapter of the treaties. Furthermore, Article 25 of the agreement envisaged that the Commission will 'systematically inform' the Parliament of negotiation outcomes.

[168] Michelle Cini, 'EU Decision-Making on Inter-Institutional Agreements: Defining (Common) Rules of Conduct for European Lobbyists and Public Servants' (2013) 36 *West European Politics* 1143.

[169] Case C-25/94, *Commission v Council*, ECLI:EU:C:1996:114 ('*FAO*'). See, Judith Hippler Bello and Beate Rudolf, 'Commission of the European Communities v Council of the European Union' (1997) 91 *American Journal of International Law* 349; Noreen Burrows, 'COREPER, Competence and Conservation' (1997) 22 *European Law Review* 64.

[170] Curtin (n 153) p 443.

[171] C 298/1. Interinstitutional Agreement of 20 November 2002 between the European Parliament and the Council Concerning Access by the European Parliament to Sensitive Information of the Council in the Field of Security and Defence Policy (2002/C 298/01).

[172] Jörg Monar, 'Interinstitutional Agreements: The Phenomenon and Its New Dynamics after Maastricht' (1994) 31 *Common Market Law Review* 693 at 716.

[173] Andrea Ott, 'The Legal Bases for International Agreements Post-Lisbon: Of Pirates and the Philippines' (2014) 21 *Maastricht Journal of European and Comparative Law* 739 at 752.

[174] L 304/47. Interinstitutional Agreements: Framework Agreement on Relations between the European Parliament and the European Commission.

The Council was particularly aggrieved with the framework agreement. It noted that 'several provisions of the [f]ramework [a]greement have the effect of modifying the institutional balance set out in the [t]reaties', in which it extended the Parliament's prerogatives 'that are not provided for in the [t]reaties'.[175] Furthermore, it noted it was 'particularly concerned by the provisions on international agreements, infringement proceedings against Member States and transmission of classified information to the European Parliament' and thus, such a framework agreement 'cannot be applied to the Council'. It even went as far as threatening to refer the actions of the Parliament to the Court if the Council's prerogatives under the treaties were to be questioned.[176]

The most recent interinstitutional agreement with the Council with regard to CFSP matters relating to the Parliament was concluded in 2014.[177] Such agreements ensure practices surrounding CFSP matters are legalised and, thus, act as a mechanism for avoiding litigation between institutions. Given the EEAS is within the domain of CFSP matters in addition to the Council and the High Representative, there could be merit in the Parliament exploring interinstitutional agreements with the EEAS; however, there would appear to be no legal basis for allowing the EEAS to enter into such an agreement.[178] Whilst the application of the 2014 interinstitutional agreement continues, consistent development of CFSP practices is necessary for the effective functioning of CFSP matters.

4.4.3. Budgetary Matters

Without a budget, nothing can be achieved. For many years during the pre-Lisbon era, the only substantial appliance that was available to the Parliament in terms of its actual influence on CFSP matters was through its budget provision. The powers of the Parliament in general budgetary matters were confined to non-compulsory expenditure. Given that the setup provided by the Treaty of Maastricht was a feeble compromise, some Member States were keen to have national budgets utilised, to limit the influence of the Parliament. Today, post-Lisbon, the budgetary nature of the Union means that every item, across the entirety of the Union must be agreed

[175] 'Press Release: 3039th Council Meeting, 21 October 2010, 15172/10 – Relations between the European Parliament and the Commission – Council Statement' p 17.

[176] For more, see, 'Framework Agreement on the Relations between the European Parliament and the Commission (15018/10)'.

[177] C 95/1. Interinstitutional Agreement of 12 March 2014 between the European Parliament and the Council Concerning the Forwarding to and Handling by the European Parliament of Classified Information Held by the Council on Matters Other than Those in the Area of the Common Foreign and Security Policy (2014/C 95/01).

[178] Mauro Gatti, 'Diplomats at the Bar: The European External Action Service before EU Courts' (2014) 39 *European Law Review* 664 at 679.

by the Parliament,[179] including CFSP matters. Whatever gripe the Member States in the Council had about the supranational-focused Parliament, the budgetary field is one of the Parliament's few key powers in CFSP matters. Simply put, the Parliament cannot be 'bypassed'.[180] The budgetary process amounts to a direct influence on CFSP matters, and budgets can be amended, merely for the purpose of exerting influence.

The underlying basis for a portion of the annual EU budget is to support the decision-making process in CFSP matters, that is, the Decisions of the Member States in the Council. Pre-Maastricht, when CFSP matters were EPC matters, the costs were outside of the EU legal order and accordingly, well beyond the Parliament's remit. When CFSP matters were brought inside the primary law of the Union, dividing who was charged with what was never going to be an easy operational process. Ultimately, expenditure would lie with Member States or would fall within the Union's budget if Member States agreed.[181] At the early stage of formulation for CFSP matters, the Parliament, with its particular role, sought to impose its involvement on expenditure for CFSP matters. This drive would have come from MEPs, political groupings, the Legal Service of the Parliament, and the institution as a whole – attempting to use its powers as a steering instrument. The only additional power for the Parliament in CFSP matters in the Treaty of Amsterdam was the then Article 28(3) TEU, which allowed operational expenditure on CFSP matters under the budget of the Community.[182] However, this excluded defence operations where the Council had unanimously decided so. Administrative costs would automatically fall within the Community budget, but as per the Treaty of Amsterdam, operational costs were assumed within the Community budget, unless stated otherwise – a 'flipping' exercise from the previously negotiated position as set out in the Treaty of Maastricht. The present practice is that all expenditure arising from CFSP actions are charged to the EU budget, with the exception of EU military operations.[183]

Operational expenditure today for CSDP missions under a CFSP decision-making regime, however, can come from national budgets of Members States. Yet, CSDP missions of civilian nature have long been the main expenditure item when it came to the spending of the budget for CFSP

[179] Richard Corbett, 'The Evolving Roles of the European Parliament and of National Parliaments' in Andrea Biondi, Piet Eeckhout and Stefanie Ripley (eds), *EU Law after Lisbon* (Oxford University Press, 2012) p 256.

[180] Henri De Waele, *Legal Dynamics of EU External Relations: Dissecting a Layered Global Player* 2nd edition (Springer 2017) p 42.

[181] In the spirit of CFSP decision-making, this decision would have to be unanimous.

[182] Gormley (n 79) p 62.

[183] Stephan Marquardt, 'The Institutional Framework, Legal Instruments and Decision-Making Procedures' in Steven Blockmans and Panos Koutrakos (eds), *Research Handbook on the EU's Common Foreign and Security Policy* (Edward Elgar, 2018) p 35.

matters. An interinstitutional agreement covering financing CFSP matters was first reached in 1997 between the Council, the Commission and the Parliament,[184] which has since been replaced with a subsequent 2006 agreement on general budgetary discipline and sound financial management.[185] The most recent interinstitutional agreement on budgetary matters was concluded in 2013,[186] which specifically discusses the financing of CFSP matters. A major concession to the Parliament in that interinstitutional agreement was that when the Council makes a CFSP Decision that entails expenditure, it must be communicated to the Parliament by 'no later than five working days', with a detailed costs breakdown. This action greatly enhances the Parliament's ability to be involved at an early stage of CFSP matters and CSDP matters, but does not yet entitle it to advance information.

The budgetary situation for CFSP matters today makes no legal distinction for operational or administrative expenditure,[187] as it did previously. The Parliament is competent to refuse certain budgetary provisions regarding CFSP matters.[188] The Parliament has on occasion refused to approve parts of the budget,[189] and such action strongly demonstrates its intention to become an even stronger performer in CFSP matters. The Parliament is not the only institution that sees the possibilities for enhancing its own standing in the budgetary field, as the Commission also has ambition in this regard. In earlier times, with respect to the budgetary procedure of the Union, the Parliament and the Commission found each other to be the 'best ally'.[190]

There is no accompanying Regulation for how the budget for CFSP matters is to be used. A gentleman's agreement was once present between the Parliament

[184] European Commission, C/97/243. Signing of the Interinstitutional Agreement on Financing of the CFSP.

[185] See, Section G, C 139/1. Interinstitutional Agreement of 17 May 2006 between the European Parliament, the Council and the Commission on Budgetary Discipline and Sound Financial Management (2006/C 139/01) (n 133).

[186] C 373/1. Interinstitutional Agreement of 2 December 2013 between the European Parliament, the Council and the Commission on Budgetary Discipline, on Cooperation in Budgetary Matters and on Sound Financial Management (2013/C 373/01).

[187] That is, unless military or defence matters are at stake, or when the Council decides otherwise. See, Roman Schmidt-Radefeldt, 'Article 41 [Financing the CFSP]' in Hermann-Josef Blanke and Stelio Mangiameli (eds), *The Treaty on European Union (TEU)* (Springer 2013); Günter Sautter, 'The Financing of Common Foreign and Security Policy – on Continuity and Change' in Hermann-Josef Blanke and Stelio Mangiameli (eds), *The European Union after Lisbon: Constitutional Basis, Economic Order and External Action* (Springer 2012); Fabien Terpan, 'Financing Common Security and Defence Policy Operations: Explaining Change and Inertia in a Fragmented and Flexible Structure' (2015) 24 *European Security* 221.

[188] Koen Lenaerts and Piet Van Nuffel, *European Union Law* Robert Bray and Nathan Cambien (eds) 3rd edition (Sweet and Maxwell, 2011) p 720.

[189] Kieran St C Bradley, 'The Institutional Law of the European Union in 1998 (Incorporating Legal Developments in the European Parliament)' (1998) 18 *Yearbook of European Law* 577 at 505.

[190] Ole Due, 'Legal Remedies for the Failure of European Community Institutions to Act in Conformity with EEC Treaty Provisions' (1990) 14 *Fordham International Law Journal* 341 at 353.

and the Council regarding the budgetary provisions for CFSP matters.[191] The Multiannual Financial Framework (MFF) of the Union for the 2014–2020 period set aside over €2.3 billion for CFSP matters – a total of 0.22 per cent of the overall EU budget – approximately €320 million per annum over the period,[192] which was adopted as a Regulation.[193] For the Parliament, there is the discharge procedure under Article 319 TFEU, which underlines its powerful budgetary position, which it can use at will. However, Article 312(5) TFEU is applicable during the adoption of the MFF,[194] with a sense of cooperation of the political institutions necessary in order to achieve its eventual adoption. This can be equated roughly to the process for concluding international agreements – the practice under Article 218 TFEU – ensuring some level of institutional balance in the Union's decision-making.

The Council admittedly stated that given the nature of CFSP matters, it means 'it is impossible to predict' what the budget for CFSP matters will be from year-to-year.[195] However, one major factor to consider for the budget for CFSP matters is that a sizeable proportion of it is provided for existing commitments. With this budgetary competence that the Parliament preserves on each occasion when the Council adopts a CFSP Decision, the costing of such a decision is made known to the Parliament through a *fiche financière* (financial statement), which first appeared in a Parliament proposal for an interinstitutional agreement on financing CFSP matters.[196] This was later incorporated into an interinstitutional agreement on budgetary discipline.[197] Such a statement can include costing breakdowns regarding timescale, deployments, property, transport, and other related items, which would all be managed by the Council.

The Commission, supported by the Parliament, once challenged this, claiming that monies had to be implemented by the Commission and not the Council.[198]

[191] Jörg Monar, 'The Financial Dimension of the CFSP' in Martin Holland (ed), *Common Foreign and Security Policy: The Record and Reforms* (Pinter, 1997) p 38.

[192] 'European Commission, Budget, Multiannual Financial Framework, Figures and Documents. Financial Framework 2014–2020 as Established by Council Regulation No. 1311/2013 (Excluding Adjustments)'.

[193] For the most recent adopted MFF, see, L 347/884. Council Regulation (EU, EURATOM) No 1311/2013 of 2 December 2013 Laying down the Multiannual Financial Framework for the Years 2014–2020.

[194] TFEU, Article 312(5): 'Throughout the procedure leading to the adoption of the financial framework, the European Parliament, the Council and the Commission shall take any measure necessary to facilitate its adoption.'

[195] Council of the European Union, 'CFSP Budget Orientations for 2016 and 2017 (6383/16)', p 2.

[196] C 286/80. European Parliament. Financing CFSP. Resolution on the Proposal for an Interinstitutional Agreement between the European Parliament, the Council and the European Commission on Provisions Regarding Financing of the Common Foreign and Security Policy (A4-0249/97) (16 July 1997), p 81.

[197] C 172/1. Interinstitutional Agreement of 6 May 1999 between the European Parliament, the Council and the Commission on Budgetary Discipline and Improvement of the Budgetary Procedure (1999/C 172/01).

[198] Case C-16/88, *Commission v Council*, ECLI:EU:C:1989:397.

The Court rejected the Commission's pleadings, stating that 'the Commission is wrong to maintain that the Council cannot confer upon it…the power to adopt individual measures when such measures have financial implications'.[199] Notwithstanding the budgetary powers of the Parliament, parliamentarians may not view the budgetary process as an effective method of exerting parliamentary influence on CFSP matters. The value of the Parliament's 'purse power'[200] is therefore varied. The jurisdiction of the Court in a budgetary commitment for CFSP matters has been affirmed,[201] but may fall outside its scope if of military nature.[202] The Court has recognised the involvement of the Parliament in shaping the Union's budget.[203] It is somewhere where the Parliament is recognised as having greater interaction with the Council given its powers here.[204] The budgetary competence of the Parliament is thus a powerful instrument. Whilst litigation on the budgetary aspects of CFSP matters has not flourished to date, it may very well be an area that is litigated before the Court at a future juncture.

4.5. Taking CFSP Matters to the Court

Litigation on legal basis arguments may seem 'slightly obscure to the outside world',[205] but within the sphere of Union law, it is of constitutional importance. Taking court cases has been a tool for the Parliament, and the Court has had a sizeable role in ensuring the Parliament's role in institutional affairs.[206] Whereas cases on CFSP matters are taken by the Parliament as a whole, they further the interests of and benefit the AFET Committee more than anyone else. Whilst the early days of the Court's judgment saw the Commission and the Court engage in prodding exercises,[207] almost alliance-like, in CFSP matters by contrast, the Parliament has few alliances in its litigation strategy.[208]

[199] Ibid. para 18. For more on this case, see, John Forman, 'Case 16/88, Commission, Supported by Parliament v Council, Judgment of 24 October 1989' (1990) 27 *Common Market Law Review* 872.

[200] Originally, 'the power of the purse' from, Richard F Fenno Jr., *The Power of the Purse: Appropriations Politics in Congress* (Little, Brown and Company 1966).

[201] Case C-439/13 P, *Elitaliana SpA v Eulex Kosovo*, ECLI:EU:C:2015:753.

[202] As noted in Opinion of Advocate General Jääskinen [Second of Two] of 21 May 2015, Case C-439/13 P, *Elitaliana SpA v Eulex Kosovo*, ECLI:EU:C:2015:341, para 60.

[203] See, Case C-189/97, *Parliament v Council*, ECLI:EU:C:1999:366 ('*Mauritania Fisheries Agreement*').

[204] Panos Koutrakos, *EU International Relations Law* (Hart Publishing, 2006) p 393. See, David Scannell, 'Financing ESDP Military Operations' (2004) 9 *European Foreign Affairs Review* 529.

[205] Ricardo Gosalbo-Bono and Sonja Boelaert, 'The European Union's Comprehensive Approach to Combating Piracy at Sea: Legal Aspects' in Panos Koutrakos and Achilles Skordas (eds), *The Law and Practice of Piracy at Sea: European and International Perspectives* (Hart Publishing, 2014) p 159.

[206] See, Kieran St C Bradley, 'Maintaining the Balance: The Role of the Court of Justice in Defining the Institutional Position of the European Parliament' (1987) 24 *Common Market Law Review* 41.

[207] Joseph HH Weiler, 'Community Member States and European Integration: Is the Law Relevant?' in Loukas Tsoukalis (ed), *The European Community: Past, Present and Future* (Basil Blackwell, 1983) p 46.

[208] The Commission has an interest in siding with the Parliament in pushing for a non-CFSP legal basis. Monica Claes and Bruno De Witte, 'Competences: Codification and Contestation' in Adam Łazowski and Steven Blockmans (eds), *Research Handbook on EU Institutional Law* (Edward Elgar, 2016) p 66.

The treaties guarantee the independence of the Parliament, and its status today as an 'autonomous self-organisation'[209] has allowed it to pursue its institutional desires to a greater extent than ever before. Article 232 TFEU specifies '[t]he European Parliament shall adopt its Rules of Procedure, acting by a majority of its Members' and this can be interpreted as the institution being free of administrative control by any other EU institution. That is not to say that such internal management of the Parliament is not subject to adequate oversight. The General Court in the *Martinez* case asserted that a pleading on the internal rules and administrative procedures of the Parliament may come before the EU courts.[210] As will be demonstrated, litigation before the Court has been a prime avenue for the Parliament to empower itself as an institution.

4.5.1. Explaining Litigation

Before resorting to litigation on CFSP matters, the Parliament had availed of creative means for involvement in Union policies. The democratic impulse for how the Parliament performs is notable, yet it cannot go without questioning. The underlying struggle for powers and involvement of the Parliament in areas formally beyond its reach according to primary law is well known, yet it can be questioned whether Parliament should have the right to strive for enhanced positions for itself.[211] The self-initiated quest, driven by lawyers and political figures alike, has demonstrated the flexibility and scope within the existing treaties for institutional furtherance. In order to get influence in CFSP matters, the Parliament had to first establish over a long series of legal battles the right to be involved in other non-CFSP fields, which it progressively managed to do with cases such as *Roquette Frères* and *Chernobyl*, amongst others.[212] The focus on gaining institutional rights in the legislative field meant, in time, focus shifted to attaining involvement rights in the non-legislative field of CFSP matters. Despite this battle of standing,[213] the Parliament continued forward with its agenda.

The Parliament is a master at advancing its own agenda *vis-à-vis* other institutions. With CFSP matters falling mainly to the executive, the Parliament has striven for influence in Decisions adopted by the Council in CFSP matters. Furthermore, with the Court's position as the institution charged with policing the boundary

[209] Hauke Brunkhorst, 'Democracy under Siege: The Decay of Constitutionalization and the Crisis of Public Law and Public Opinion' in Poul F Kjaer and Niklas Olsen (eds), *Critical Theories of Crisis in Europe: From Weimar to the Euro* (Rowman & Littlefield, 2016) p 183.

[210] Joined Cases T-222/99, T-327/99 and T-329/99, *Jean-Claude Martinez, Charles de Gaulle, Front national and Emma Bonino and Others v Parliament*, ECLI:EU:T:2001:242 ('*Martinez*'), para 62.

[211] Joseph HH Weiler, *The Transnational Setting: The European Parliament and Its Foreign Affairs Committees*, vol. 2 (Cedam/Oceana, 1982) p 70.

[212] Case C-138/79, *Roquette Frères v Council*, ECLI:EU:C:1980:249 and, Case C-70/88, *Parliament v Council*, ECLI:EU:C:1990:217 [First of Two] ECLI:EU:C:1991:373 [Second of Two], ('*Chernobyl*').

[213] For an overview, see, Bradley (n 74).

between CFSP matters and non-CFSP matters,[214] and taking from a much earlier declaration to 'exploit to the very limit the possibility offered' by the treaties,[215] the Parliament has sought increased use of the Court's services to rule on the extent of this indistinct boundary. Litigation has previously been used by the Parliament as a strategy for exerting greater power in various situations it finds itself in as an institution.[216] Given that the treaties at various points are vague, giving open-ended meanings to many provisions, this policing function bestowed upon the Court has been no straightforward task, which the Parliament has skilfully exposed as much as possible. Yet, whilst the Parliament acts, its advances are not unique. In fact, other institutions are equally adamant at protecting and advancing their own array of competence[217] and are equally able to defend themselves against the intrigues of the Parliament. Many areas of Union law have been considered by the Parliament post-Lisbon in an effort to ascertain the scope of its powers under the new revised set of treaties. As shall be seen when discussing cases pre- and post-Lisbon, it will be demonstrated that even CFSP matters, which are in many instances beyond the scope of its prerogatives, is not invulnerable to the spread of the Parliament's endeavours.

Like the Parliament, the Court, too, is significantly constrained by the treaties when it comes to CFSP matters. In a general expression, the Court has claimed the Parliament acts in a manner that 'reflects a fundamental democratic principle that the peoples should take part in the exercise of power through the intermediary of a representative assembly',[218] boding well with the Parliament's Legal Service. The general jurisdiction of the Court is set out in Article 19 TEU. However, Article 24(1) TEU and Article 275 TFEU allow for derogation from this general jurisdiction.[219] The jurisprudence from the Court states that when competence of the Union is an issue in a case, the Court cannot be excluded entirely.[220] Rather than the Court finding itself at the centre of conflicts between EU institutions and Member States, it is between the EU institutions themselves, adjudicating upon interinstitutional disputes in respect of EU external action. The encounters before the Court begin, not because EU institutions disagree with one another on the

[214] TEU, Article 40. See, Marise Cremona, 'The Union's External Action: Constitutional Perspectives' in Giuliano Amato, Hervé Bribosia and Bruno De Witte (eds), *Genesis and Destiny of the European Constitution: Commentary on the Treaty establishing a Constitution for Europe in the Light of the travaux préparatoires and Future Prospects* (Bruylant, 2007) p 1200.

[215] Bradley (n 7) p 127.

[216] Holly Cullen and Andrew Charlesworth, 'Diplomacy by Other Means: The Use of Legal Basis Litigation as a Political Strategy by the European Parliament and Member States' (1999) 36 *Common Market Law Review* 1243.

[217] For more, see, Federico Fabbrini, 'Austerity, the European Council and the Institutional Future of the European Union: A Proposal to Strengthen the Presidency of the European Council' (2015) 22 *Indiana Journal of Global Legal Studies* 29 at 72.

[218] Case C-300/89, *Commission v Council*, ECLI:EU:C:1991:244 ('*Titanium Dioxide*'), para 20.

[219] See Chapter 5 of this book.

[220] Case C-124/95, *The Queen, ex parte Centro-Com Srl v HM Treasury and Bank of England*, ECLI:EU:C:1997:8, para 30.

substance of particular CFSP matters, but usually on the legal basis upon which the action has been made. Potential infringements of the Parliament's powers by other institutions have been actively fought in many ways. An early reading of the cases stemming from the Court on issues when choices are available to institutional actors regarding two (or more) legal bases for actions being pursued would lead a reader to see a tendency for the Court to favour the inclusion of the Parliament.[221]

4.5.2. Pre-Lisbon Litigation on CFSP Matters

Given the Parliament's limited role in CFSP matters, one of the key tools it has at its disposal is the ability to bring actions against other institutions before the Court to determine the legality of EU acts. Over the past decade, a number of important cases have been lodged by the Parliament against both the Commission and the Council relating to CFSP matters as the Parliament attempted to acquire greater powers in EU foreign policy. Unsurprisingly, the 'who decides?' dilemma was at the fore of the legal debate. One of the seminal cases in CFSP matters pre-Lisbon was *ECOWAS*,[222] also known as *Small Arms and Light Weapons*. Other boundary-policing cases up to *ECOWAS* were between first (Community) and third (JHA) pillars.[223] However, *ECOWAS* presented the Court with a prime opportunity to border police the first and second pillars, clarifying the relationship.

The pre-Lisbon case, operating under the treaties as amended by the Treaty of Nice, had some intriguing facts. The Union had adopted legal acts as a Council Decision,[224] implementing a Joint Action,[225] to prevent the dispersal of small arms and light weapons with another international organisation, the Economic Community of West African States ('ECOWAS'). The Commission, with the support of the Parliament, sought an annulment of the Council Decision, as, in their view, the incorrect legal basis had been chosen. The Council adopted a CFSP Joint Action,[226] taken exclusively on a CFSP legal basis, whereas the Commission contended that this was the incorrect legal basis for the matter. This was the

[221] Such instances, according to Advocate General Maduro, 'reveal a preference' [of the Court]. Case C-411/06, *Commission v Parliament and Council*, ECLI:EU:C:2009:189 ('*Basel Convention*'), para 5.

[222] Case C-91/05, *Commission v Council*, ECLI:EU:C:2008:288 ('*ECOWAS*').

[223] For example, Case C-170/96, *Commission v Council*, ECLI:EU:C:1998:219 ('*Airport Transit Visas*').

[224] L 359/65. Council Decision 2004/833/CFSP of 2 December 2004 Implementing Joint Action 2002/589/CFSP with a View to a European Union Contribution to ECOWAS in the Framework of the Moratorium on Small Arms and Light Weapons.

[225] L 191/1. Council Joint Action of 12 July 2002 on the European Union's Contribution to Combating the Destabilising Accumulation and Spread of Small Arms and Light Weapons and Repealing Joint Action 1999/34/CFSP (2002/589/CFSP).

[226] The treaties at first did not define what a 'Joint Action' exactly was. See, Simon J Nuttall, 'The Foreign and Security Policy Provisions of the Maastricht Treaty: Their Potential for the Future' in Jörg Monar, Werner Ungerer and Wolfgang Wessels (eds), *The Maastricht Treaty on European Union: Legal Complexity and Political Dynamic* (European Interuniversity Press, 1993) p 135.

Commission's perspective given that the Cotonou Agreement, signed five years earlier,[227] had in Article 11 ('Peace-building policies, conflict prevention and resolution') measures provided for ensuring that the distribution of small arms and light weapons would be prevented. At issue in *ECOWAS*, therefore, was whether the external objectives of the Union in pursuing external action fell under a CFSP legal basis, or whether it fell under development cooperation on a non-CFSP legal basis. As a policy field in and of itself, development cooperation has been a broadening area of competence[228] and has included cohorts of aid agreements over the decades. Even with poverty eradication as part of the policy, there remains considerable scope for other measures to be included within development cooperation.[229] There continues to be a limited role for the Parliament in the European Development Fund (EDF), even though it is managed by the Commission. This is due to the fund being separated from the general Commission budget as a result of pooling by Member States, which in turn provides the Parliament a much more limited role in the process.

The Court in *ECOWAS* demonstrated under the treaties at the time that no Union measure should be adopted under the second (CFSP) or third (JHA) pillar where it was possible to adopt such a measure under a Union competence in the first pillar. What the Court did in the *ECOWAS* judgment was annul the CFSP Decision of the Council, whilst at the same time leaving the original Joint Action as it was. It has been said that the judgment may have been avoided if the objectives of CFSP matters and development cooperation had not been made simultaneously.[230] *ECOWAS* meant that 'normal' Union policies, non-CFSP matters, were given priority over those of CFSP matters,[231] in that a CFSP legal basis cannot be used where relevant competence is conferred upon the Union. The Court thus held that putting CFSP matters and development cooperation onto a dual legal basis was impossible. Then the Article 47 TEU (now Article 40 TEU) precluded the use of a dual legal basis[232] where a number of legal bases could attempt to be founded

[227] L 317/3. Partnership Agreement between the Members of the African, Caribbean and Pacific Group of States of the One Part and the European Community and Its Member States, of the Other Part, Signed in Cotonou on 23 June 2000.

[228] See, Morten Broberg and Rass Holdgaard, 'Demarcating the Union's Development Cooperation Policy after Lisbon: Commission v Council (Philippines PCFA)' (2015) 52 *Common Market Law Review* 547; Morten Broberg and Rass Holdgaard, 'EU Development Cooperation Post-Lisbon: Main Constitutional Challenges' (2015) 40 *European Law Review* 349; Morten Broberg, 'What Is the Direction for the EU's Development Cooperation after Lisbon? A Legal Examination' (2011) 16 *European Foreign Affairs Review* 539.

[229] See, Robert Schütze, 'EU Development Policy: Constitutional and Legislative Foundation(s)' in Catherine Barnard and others (eds), *Cambridge Yearbook of European Legal Studies 2012–2013: Volume 15* (Hart Publishing, 2013).

[230] Alan Dashwood, 'Article 47 TEU and the Relationship between First and Second Pillar Competences' in Alan Dashwood and Marc Maresceau (eds), *Law and Practice of EU External Relations: Salient Features of a Changing Landscape* (Cambridge University Press, 2008) p 99.

[231] Maja Brkan, 'The Role of the European Court of Justice from Maastricht to Lisbon: Putting Together the Scattered Pieces of Patchwork' in Maartje De Visser and Anne Pieter Van Der Mei (eds), *The Treaty on European Union 1993–2013: Reflections from Maastricht* (Intersentia, 2013) p 86.

[232] Eeckhout (n 149) p 180.

on both the first and second pillars. With multiple legal bases thus excluded, a single legal basis had to be found to carry out the particular external actions, be it a CFSP legal basis or a non-CFSP legal basis, grounded upon objective criteria. This impossibility of a dual legal basis, however, did not mean a measure could not be split. 'Splitting' would involve the separation of a Union legal act into two, with each being concluded on separated legal bases to cater for the different decision-making regimes.

The *ECOWAS* judgment pre-Lisbon was clear – it was the establishment of the centre of gravity test in external relations and contributed towards a better understanding of the mutual non-encroachment clause. The centre of gravity test was around before *ECOWAS* and was used in previous cases such as *Environmental Criminal Penalties*.[233] Following the *Portugal v Council* case from earlier times, the Court stated that an objective 'must be determined having regard to its essential object…provided that those clauses do not impose such extensive obligations'.[234] Legal bases from both the TEU and TFEU that bring forward different procedures of Union decision-making had to be avoided as much as possible. The Court specified that a CFSP legal basis was incorrectly chosen and the judgment gave superiority to the non-CFSP basis. It found that where multiple objectives were attempted to be reached, the first pillar should be preferred. *ECOWAS* was an attempt by the Court to find the main purpose of an international agreement, which is an impossible task. However, as shall be seen, this was revisited at a later juncture.

The judgment in *ECOWAS* has been criticised as the Court trying to 'have the cake and eat it too'.[235] In what could be said to be a short judgment given the issues at hand,[236] the relevance of *ECOWAS* can be called into question considering that judgment was delivered prior to the entry into force of the Treaty of Lisbon. *ECOWAS* turned out to be one of a small number of cases in which a preference for a first pillar (non-CFSP) legal basis was permissible, following the entering of the equality of the TEU and TFEU with the Treaty of Lisbon. Such a judgment would unlikely occur under the post-Lisbon version of the treaties. Whilst Lisbon's depillarisation has technically set aside some of the relevance of the *ECOWAS* judgment, given that TFEU preferences can no longer trump those of the TEU, it is nonetheless still an important constitutional milestone for CFSP matters and serves as historical guidance for future cases on CFSP matters that arise in interinstitutional litigation on disputes over legal bases.

[233] For example, testing for the 'centre of gravity' had been conducted to delineate not just CFSP matters from non-CFSP matters, but also the then first pillar from the then third pillar (JHA) See, Case C-176/03, *Commission v Council*, ECLI:EU:C:2005:542 ('*Environmental Criminal Penalties*').

[234] Case C-268/94, *Portugal v Council*, ECLI:EU:C:1996:461, para 39.

[235] Bart Van Vooren, 'The Small Arms Judgment in an Age of Constitutional Turmoil' (2009) 14 *European Foreign Affairs Review* 231 at 232. Also, see, Bart Van Vooren, 'EU–EC External Competences after the Small Arms Judgment' (2009) 14 *European Foreign Affairs Review* 7.

[236] Ester Herlin-Karnell, '"Light Weapons" and the Dynamics of Art 47 EU – The EC's Armoury of Ever-expanding Competences' (2008) 71 *Modern Law Review* 998 at 1002.

Different policies of the Union have the inherent capacity of drowning out others. Shortly after the *ECOWAS* case was lodged at the Court by the Commission (supported by the Parliament) against the Council, the Parliament launched its own action for annulment against the Commission in separate proceedings in another border-policing dispute between CFSP matters and non-CFSP matters, which has come to be known as the *Philippines Border Management* case.[237] Much as in *ECOWAS*, the apparent overlap of policy objectives came to the fore. The *Philippines Border Management* case presented questions of whether development cooperation policy was being over-encroached by security matters. The first time that the Union declared that peace and security were essential for sustainable development was in the European Security Strategy in 2003.[238] The issue of security often gets tied up in a legal dilemma, whether it should be dealt with on a CFSP legal basis or a non-CFSP legal basis. With the security-development nexus a critical component of this framework for operating,[239] the *Philippines Border Management* case was again testing the centre of gravity.

The Commission had adopted a decision, not published in the *Official Journal*, to approve projects to be funded by the then Communities,[240] based on the implementing powers that it believed it had stemming from Council Regulation (EEC) No. 443/92.[241] Given the number of legal bases that such a measure could have, be it a CFSP legal basis or a development cooperation (non-CFSP) legal basis, the Court again took a centre of gravity approach – a 'predominant purpose test' – as opposed to looking at a secondary or ancillary purpose. Whilst the concern of the Parliament when intervening was to ensure that its position in the institutional framework was not circumvented by another institution,[242] the case was ultimately decided in favour of both the Commission and the Parliament. The case was said to have been 'a very uncompromising view',[243] regarding the bond connecting CFSP matters and another policy in the treaties pre-Lisbon.

4.5.3. Post-Lisbon Litigation on CFSP Matters

After the Treaty of Lisbon, the nature of the boundary between CFSP matters and non-CFSP matters was changed, with a more developed textual reading of the new

[237] Case C-403/05, *Parliament v Commission*, ECLI:EU:C:2007:624 ('*Philippines Border Management*').

[238] See, European Council, 'European Security Strategy – A Secure Europe in a Better World', 2003.

[239] For analysis on further legal issues at work here, see, Hans Merket, 'The EU and the Security-Development Nexus: Bridging the Legal Divide' (2013) 18 *European Foreign Affairs Review* 83.

[240] Philippines Border Management Project, No ASIA/2004/016-924.

[241] L 52/ 1. Council Regulation (EEC) No 443/92 of 25 February 1992 on Financial and Technical Assistance to and Economic Cooperation with, the Developing Countries in Asia and Latin America, as amended.

[242] Marise Cremona, 'Case C-403/05, European Parliament v Commission (Philippines Border Management Project), Judgment of the Grand Chamber of 23 October 2007, [2007] ECR I-9045' (2008) 45 *Common Market Law Review* 1727 at 1737.

[243] Marcus Klamert, 'Conflicts of Legal Basis: No Legality and No Basis but a Bright Future under the Lisbon Treaty?' (2010) 35 *European Law Review* 497.

Article 40 TEU. It was argued before the entry into force of the new Article 40 TEU (ex-Article 47 TEU), that it would not necessarily lead to prioritising a non-CFSP legal basis. Rather, it was advocated that measures could be split into both a CFSP legal basis and non-CFSP legal basis.[244] The Court had to deal with the issues differently and *ECOWAS* was no longer to be the default case for what defined relations between CFSP matters and non-CFSP matters. Accordingly, the significance of *ECOWAS* was not destined to last very long. After the entry into force of the Treaty of Lisbon, the Court was swiftly called upon to enact and interpret the new treaties. *Smart Sanctions*, otherwise known as the *Legal Basis for Restrictive Measures* judgment,[245] was the first post-Lisbon case dealing with the delimitation of CFSP matters *vis-à-vis* non-CFSP matters. The Parliament asked the Court to annul Council Regulation (EU) No 1286/2009,[246] amending Regulation (EC) No 881/2002.[247] For the Parliament, there was a procedural difference, and it wanted to ensure greater democratic involvement in its own eyes by seeking inclusion of itself. The Council, unsurprisingly, pointed to the preamble of the Regulation, which it had carefully drafted in the event of the legal act being challenged. Whilst the insertion of a preamble may be a prudent exercise, it immediately points to a potential lack of confidence in a chosen legal basis by the drafter. The Council claimed that 'it is not procedures that define the legal basis of a measure[,] but the legal basis of a measure that determines the procedures to be followed in adopting that measure',[248] borrowing the Court's own terminology.

The Parliament in *Smart Sanctions* pleaded that Article 75 TFEU, combating terrorism, would have been a more appropriate legal basis for the action than Article 215 TFEU, thereby including the Parliament. In Grand Chamber formation, the Court rejected the Parliament's argument that it would be contravention of Union law to bring forward measures having a direct impact on fundamental rights of individuals without the involvement of the Parliament.[249] Furthermore, it also rejected the view put forward by the Parliament that the measure ought to have been adopted under Article 75 TFEU, thereby guaranteeing parliamentary participation through the ordinary legislative procedure. The Court held that the Council's adoption of the contested Regulation on an Article 215(2) TFEU legal basis, as opposed to Article 75 TFEU, was correct, dismissing the Parliament's

[244] Joni Heliskoski, 'Small Arms and Light Weapons within the Union's Pillar Structure: An Analysis of Article 47 of the EU Treaty' (2008) 33 *European Law Review* 898 at 911.

[245] Case C-130/10, *Parliament v Council*, ECLI:EU:C:2012:472 ('*Smart Sanctions*').

[246] L 346/42. Council Regulation (EU) No. 1286/2009 of 22 December 2009 Amending Regulation (EC) No. 881/2002 Imposing Certain Specific Restrictive Measures Directed against Certain Persons and Entities Associated with Usama Bin Laden, the Al-Qaida Network and the Taliban.

[247] L 139/9. Council Regulation (EC) No. 881/2002 of 27 May 2002 Imposing Certain Specific Restrictive Measures Directed against Certain Persons and Entities Associated with Usama Bin Laden, the Al-Qaida Network and the Taliban and Repealing Council Regulation (EC) No 467/2001 Prohibiting the Export of Certain Goods and Services to Afghanistan, Strengthening the Flight Ban and Extending the Freeze of Funds and Other Financial Resources in Respect of the Taliban of Afghanistan.

[248] Case C-130/10, *Parliament v Council*, ECLI:EU:C:2012:472 ('*Smart Sanctions*'), para 80.

[249] Ibid. para 83.

action in its entirety. Article 75 TFEU on face value does not have external value;[250] but rather, it is internally focused on JHA; whereas, by contrast, Article 215 TFEU is explicitly for restrictive measures. Thus, it found that the restrictive measures were the centre of gravity, a CFSP legal basis; as opposed to a JHA legal basis. The case featured elements of the earlier case law, particularly in connection with the ordinary legislative procedure,[251] and the judgment can be said to have altered the hierarchy of policies concerning the choice of correct legal basis.[252] The Court questioned this and stated that 'it is not possible for the two provisions to be cumulated, one with the other, in order to serve as a twofold legal basis for a measure such as the contested regulation',[253] implying a dual legal basis would not have been possible, reciting its old case law stemming from *Titanium Dioxide*,[254] which was 'resurrected'.[255]

An eye-catching conundrum arose in the Opinion of the Advocate General in *Smart Sanctions*, which was not taken up by the Court. The Advocate General considered the pre-Lisbon objectives for CFSP matters, despite the fact that post-Lisbon, specific objectives for CFSP matters were abolished. The Advocate General stated that the provisions of Article 21(2)(a), (b) and (c) TFEU of the treaties, post-Lisbon, were the same as those assigned to CFSP matters under the treaties pre-Lisbon, as per the then Article 11(1) TEU.[256] The Opinion was thus backwards looking – a retrograde viewpoint in fully embracing the nature of CFSP matters as it was when the case was litigated. If anything, it is a proven scenario that it may be possible to use older versions of the treaties to interpret current provisions within the treaties. Given the Court did not follow the Advocate General on this specific point – attaching objectives to different parts of the EU external provisions either to CFSP matters or non-CFSP matters – the overall picture of the legal basis of particular external actions is less clear. How the Court arrives at its conclusion as to the primary objective of a particular international agreement can remain a mystery. Therefore, the 'who decides?' challenge issue remained centre-stage. The fluidity of CFSP matters and external relations legal bases meant that CFSP matters were by no means settled case law, and that this would be the first in a series of cases to follow.

[250] Marise Cremona, 'External Competences and the Principle of Conferral' in Robert Schütze and Takis Tridimas (eds), *Oxford Principles of European Union Law, vol 1: The European Union Legal Order* (Oxford University Press, 2018) p 1118.

[251] Kathleen Gutman, *The Constitutional Foundations of European Contract Law: A Comparative Analysis* (Oxford University Press, 2014) p 291.

[252] Brkan (n 231) p 86.

[253] Case C-130/10, *Parliament v Council*, ECLI:EU:C:2012:472 ('*Smart Sanctions*'), para 49.

[254] Case C-300/89, *Commission v Council*, ECLI:EU:C:1991:244 ('*Titanium Dioxide*').

[255] Geert De Baere, 'From "Don't Mention the Titanium Dioxide Judgment" to "I Mentioned It Once, But I Think I Got Away with It All Right": Reflections on the Choice of Legal Basis in EU External Relations after the Legal Basis for Restrictive Measures Judgment' in Catherine Barnard and others (eds), *Cambridge Yearbook of European Legal Studies 2012–2013: Volume 15* (Hart Publishing, 2013) p 561.

[256] Opinion of Advocate General Bot, Case C-130/10, *Parliament v Council*, ECLI:EU:C:2012:50 ('*Smart Sanctions*'), para 63.

Piracy has been a prevalent theme in the Union's external action in recent years. Whereas piracy is a major cause of concern for the EU in the Gulf of Aden and the Indian Ocean, it has led to international agreements being concluded between the EU and third states. The Union thus concluded a number of them with Mauritius and Tanzania, amongst others. The legal basis for such international agreements was undertaken on a CFSP legal basis, Article 37 TEU, thus meaning that the Parliament ought to be informed of developments as per Article 218(10) TFEU. However, this did not always occur. Thus, the next attempt by the Parliament to gather further involvement in external relations through litigation was in *Mauritius*,[257] another case broaching the question of whether particular external Union measures are CFSP matters or non-CFSP matters. Again, where the legal basis for an external measure is disputed, the action of the Court has been to look to the content of the action, when its purpose is multifaceted, to identify the central or primary purpose, and equally, finding what the complimentary or secondary purpose, distinguishing what the correct legal basis for external action is.

Launched in 2008,[258] an EU naval force (EUNAVFOR or Operation Atalanta), acting as a joint naval operation under the command of the Union, commenced an action to counter piracy and armed robbery at sea in the West Indian Ocean off the coast of the horn of Africa. It has been re-authorised on several occasions since, last extended to December 2020 by a CFSP Decision in 2018.[259] With this, the Union entered into a number of international agreements with states in the region, namely Mauritius,[260] amongst others. In essence, the international agreement arranged for the transfer of individuals from naval vessels under the command of the Union to Mauritian authorities during the operation of the Union's CSDP anti-piracy mission, Operation Atalanta, off the coast of Somalia,[261] so that those suspected persons could be put on trial in that state. Given the Operation's existence, a debate arose about the full scope and extent of EUNAVFOR. Was it purely maritime security – CFSP matters/CSDP matters – or a more encompassing exercise taking a more integrated approach with the region as a whole? Given that a CFSP Decision established Operation Atalanta, the question was whether an international agreement with third states could be concluded based on the provisions

[257] Case C-658/11, *Parliament v Council*, ECLI:EU:C:2014:2025 ('*Mauritius*').

[258] L 301/33. Council Joint Action 2008/851/CFSP of 10 November 2008 on a European Union Military Operation to Contribute to the Deterrence, Prevention and Repression of Acts of Piracy and Armed Robbery off the Somali Coast.

[259] L 194/142. Council Decision (CFSP) 2018/1083 of 30 July 2018 Amending Joint Action 2008/851/CFSP on a European Union Military Operation to Contribute to the Deterrence, Prevention and Repression of Acts of Piracy and Armed Robbery off the Somali Coast.

[260] L 254/1. Council Decision 2011/640/CFSP of 12 July 2011 on the Signing and Conclusion of the Agreement between the European Union and the Republic of Mauritius on the Conditions of Transfer of Suspected Pirates and Associated Seized Property from the European Union-Led Naval Force to the Republic of Mauritius and on the Conditions of Suspected Pirates after Transfer.

[261] See, Marianne Riddervold, 'Finally Flexing Its Muscles? Atalanta – The European Union's Naval Military Operation against Piracy' (2011) 20 *European Security* 385.

under Article 37 TEU (CFSP legal basis)[262] or rather, on another legal basis in the TFEU (a non-CFSP legal basis). It could even have been considered whether a dual legal basis would have been permissible. However, the problem with a dual legal basis, emanating from both the TEU and TFEU, was that this dual nature brings with it procedural aspects of institutional decision-making that are not in conformity with each other.

The international agreement led to a case being brought to the Court, by the Parliament, raising a number of questions. Firstly, on substantial grounds, the Parliament was of the view that with Operation Atalanta allowing the transfer of individuals to the state of Mauritius who were suspected of engaging in acts of piracy and, given their conditions after their transfer, the international agreement should not be concluded on a CFSP legal basis. Its view was that the international agreement was not exclusively dealing with CFSP matters. With development cooperation flowing from the old first pillar, and with police cooperation and criminal law matters flowing from the former third pillar, a non-CFSP legal basis in the TFEU would have been more appropriate in the Parliament's view. Accordingly, the Parliament said it should have been included in the conclusion of the international agreement – providing consent – as per Article 218(6)(a)(v) TFEU. Thus, it was a CFSP legal basis versus JHA (non-CFSP) legal basis dispute. Secondly, on procedural grounds, the Parliament also argued that its notification rights stemming from Article 218(10) TFEU were not respected.

In *Mauritius*,[263] the Court once again did not provide any guidance to actors on how the delimitation between CFSP matters and other policy areas should be determined more precisely beyond what it had already stated in other cases. The Court had to interpret the Article 218(6) TFEU phrase 'agreements [that] relate exclusively to the Common Foreign and Security Policy'. The Parliament had proposed a particular legal argument that attempted to set apart the reasoning for a substantive legal basis, over a procedural legal basis,[264] which the Court did not address in its judgment – an essentially minimalist element of its judgment, avoiding the institutional discussion of substantive legal basis for the international agreement. The Parliament's push for a stricter reading of the term 'exclusively' was not effective. Given that the Parliament admitted during the case that the predominant object of the international agreement was related to CFSP matters,[265] but had nonetheless included non-CFSP matters, it is unsurprising that the Court rejected its argument on this particular pleading. The Court concluded that the Parliament did not possess the right to be formally consulted prior to the

[262] TEU, Article 37: 'The Union may conclude agreements with one or more States or international organisations in areas covered by this Chapter.'

[263] Case C-658/11, *Parliament v Council*, ECLI:EU:C:2014:2025 ('*Mauritius*').

[264] Geert De Baere and Tina Van den Sanden, 'Interinstitutional Gravity and Pirates of the Parliament on Stranger Tides: The Continued Constitutional Significance of the Choice of Legal Basis in Post-Lisbon External Action' (2016) 12 *European Constitutional Law Review* 85 at 91.

[265] Pieter Jan Kuijper, 'Litigation on External Relations Powers after Lisbon: The Member States Reject Their Own Treaty' (2016) 43 *Legal Issues of Economic Integration* 1 at 6.

conclusion of international agreements when they are done on a CFSP legal basis.[266] The Court found that the Parliament agreed that another policy area – a non-CFSP legal basis – was incidental. This was not enough to make it an international agreement which could be concluded on a non-CFSP legal basis. If the Court had accepted the Parliament's arguments – that it should have been founded upon a non-CFSP basis – it would have blown open the legal barrier between CFSP legal bases and non-CFSP legal bases. With the Court opting to uphold the distinction, it defended the legal nature of CFSP matters.

However, that was just the first of the two pleadings the Parliament put forward. The Court also had to address the procedural aspects – the right for the Parliament to be informed stemming from Article 218(10) TFEU.[267] *Mauritius* was the first case where the Court was asked to interpret Article 218 TFEU post-Lisbon and thus apply it to a scenario concerning CFSP matters in light of the post-Lisbon framework.[268] Accordingly, the Court interpreted Article 218(10) TFEU as meaning there is no differentiation between international agreements when it comes to a CFSP legal basis or non-CFSP legal basis. The Council's argument of informing the Parliament through the *Official Journal* has been labelled 'staggering'.[269] Instead, the obligation to notify under Article 218(10) TFEU remains with the Council. Regardless of what the parties took away from the case, the judgment from the Court has clarified the nature of Article 218(10) TFEU, in that it is all-encompassing. As stated in earlier case law, 'a mere practice cannot override the provisions of the Treaty'.[270] *Mauritius*, therefore, has been a procedural victory for the Parliament, but not one on substance, and can be interpreted as broadening its standing in its information rights from the Council.[271] The earlier the notifications of international agreements are sent to the Parliament by the Council and the sooner they are posted in the Union's *Official Journal*, will lessen the likelihood of inter-institutional conflict and litigation.

It has been put forward that Article 40 TEU, although not applied in this *Mauritius* judgment, could be used to bring the legal bases of CFSP and non-CFSP together.[272] A dual legal basis may have been considered if the EU foreign

[266] This is premised, however, on the basis that the international agreement relates primarily to CFSP matters.

[267] TFEU, Article 218(10): 'The European Parliament shall be immediately and fully informed at all stages of the procedure.'

[268] It should also be noted that it is not just the Parliament as an institution that has litigated before the Court which TFEU, Article 218 has come into play. See, Case C-660/13, *Council v Commission*, ECLI:EU:C:2016:616 ('*Swiss Financial Contribution*'). Valerie Demedts and Merijn Chamon, 'The Commission Back on the Leash: No Autonomy to Sign Non-Binding Agreements on Behalf of the EU: Council v. Commission' (2017) 54 *Common Market Law Review* 245.

[269] Panos Koutrakos, 'Inter-Institutional Disputes and Treaty-Making' (2014) 39 *European Law Review* 599 at 600.

[270] Case C-327/91, *France v Commission*, ECLI:EU:C:1994:305, para 36.

[271] Graham Butler, 'Pinpointing the Appropriate Legal Basis for External Action' (2015) 6 *European Journal of Risk Regulation* 323 at 327.

[272] Annegret Engel, 'Delimiting Competences in the EU: CFSP versus AFSJ Legal Bases' (2015) 21 *European Public Law* 47 at 59.

policy action had been crafted in a separate manner.[273] The Advocate General in *Mauritius* appeared to suggest that, whilst the agreement was correctly founded upon a CFSP legal basis, he did not appear to adopt an *ECOWAS* approach by excluding dual legal bases. Nor was *ECOWAS* approached in any substantial way by the Court. What is furthermore notable in *Mauritius* was the Court's silence on Article 40 TEU. Despite this obfuscation by the Court, the judgment has been a major contribution to the understanding of the conclusion of international agreements,[274] particularly the Parliament's role in CFSP matters. *Mauritius* expanded the role and involvement of the Parliament in international agreements for CFSP matters on procedural grounds, much to the Parliament's satisfaction and the Council's displeasure. Yet, the Council will also be able to see this as a reassurance of the CFSP legal basis on substantive grounds, as the Court saw a CFSP legal basis as the correct way to execute the external action. It has been argued that the Pirate Transfer Agreement (PTA) should have been adopted under two separate legal acts to cater for the legal basis dispute.[275] How the judgment affected the future and long-term case law concerning CFSP matters was to follow.

Whilst Operation Atalanta demonstrates CSDP in action, the direct impact of CFSP Decisions has been increasing.[276] A second EU naval operation, Operation Sophia (EUNAVFOR Med), was launched in 2015 on a CFSP legal basis in the treaties,[277] yet no cases dealing with the substance or the decision-making process on procedural grounds have reached the Court. The Council Decision for Operation Sophia was inspired by that of Operation Atalanta and was founded on a CFSP legal basis. Whilst military matters do come under the wing of CSDP and, therefore, a CFSP legal basis, this alone may not justify such a legal basis. Operation Sophia tackles matters of migration and is more in fitting with the EU's comprehensive approach to migration,[278] which makes its CFSP legal basis less justifiable. Put more clearly, the naval mission 'provides a snapshot of the intensity with which [JHA matters]…have penetrated CSDP [matters]'.[279] It could therefore

[273] Leendert H Erkelens, *Institutional and Legal Aspects of EU's Judicial Policy to Fighting Piracy off the Coast of Somalia* (TMC Asser Institute, 2014) p 51.

[274] Peter Van Elsuwege, 'Securing the Institutional Balance in the Procedure for Concluding International Agreements: European Parliament v. Council (Pirate Transfer Agreement with Mauritius)' (2015) 52 *Common Market Law Review* 1379.

[275] Claudio Matera and Ramses A Wessel, 'Context or Content? A CFSP or AFSJ Legal Basis for EU International Agreements' [2014] *Revista de Derecho Comunitario Europeo* 1047 at 1059.

[276] See, Christina Eckes, 'Common Foreign and Security Policy: The Consequences of the Court's Extended Jurisdiction' (2016) 22 *European Law Journal* 492.

[277] L 157/51. Council Decision (CFSP) 2015/972 of 22 June 2015 Launching the European Union Military Operation in the Southern Central Mediterranean (EUNAVFOR Med). See, Graham Butler and Martin Ratcovich, 'Operation Sophia in Uncharted Waters: European and International Law Challenges for the EU Naval Mission in the Mediterranean Sea' (2016) 85 *Nordic Journal of International Law* 235.

[278] On this, see, Graham Butler, 'EU Foreign Policy and Other EU External Relations in Times of Crisis: Forcing the Law to Overlap?' in Elżbieta Kużelewska, Amy Weatherburn and Dariusz Kloza (eds), *Irregular Migration as a Challenge for Democracy* (Intersentia, 2018).

[279] Panos Koutrakos, 'The Nexus between CFSP/CSDP and the Area of Freedom, Security and Justice' in Steven Blockmans and Panos Koutrakos (eds), *Research Handbook on the EU's Common Foreign and Security Policy* (Edward Elgar, 2018) p 307.

be argued that Operation Sophia ought to be have been split, ensuring a non-CFSP legal basis, likely to come from JHA measures where migration legal bases are detailed, in addition to its CFSP legal basis.

Following *Mauritius*, there was the *Philippines PCA* case.[280] Though neither brought nor supported by the Parliament, it had ramifications for delimiting CFSP matters from other external policies of the Union. In *Philippines PCA*, the non-CFSP matter of development cooperation was the subject of a dispute. It surrounded a Council Decision,[281] which was taken upon a Commission Decision on a Framework Agreement on Partnership and Cooperation between the EU, its Member States and the Philippines.[282] The legal basis for the international agreement in the eyes of the Commission was in Articles 207 and 209 TFEU, which concerns the Common Commercial Policy (CCP) and the Development Cooperation respectively. The Commission also proposed the use of Article 218(5) TFEU as the procedural basis for authorising the signing of the agreement. The Council Decision accepted this – to authorise the conclusion of the international agreement – but added legal bases to the Commission's by inserting Articles 79(3), 91,100 and 191(4) TFEU, concerning the readmission of non-nationals, transport and environmental provisions, respectively. The Council believed that this was the necessary legal bases. The Commission was not satisfied with the Council adding the additional legal bases, as it believed the grounds for the Partnership and Cooperation Agreement (PCA) with the Philippines came within the ambit of Articles 207 and 209 TFEU alone. The Commission, conscious of other PCAs with neighbouring states to the Philippines that would be negotiated at a later juncture, knew that the Council would also try to add legal bases to other PCAs and, as such, sought clarification from the Court to attempt to prevent the Council's initiatives from going forward.

With the growth and expansive nature of development policy cooperation, the Court has the ability to use a test derived from *Natural Rubber*,[283] and confirmed by the *Portugal v Council* judgment,[284] called an 'absorption doctrine'.[285] Effectively, this is utilised by the Court to determine if the foremost objective takes over other legal bases 'which are pursuing objectives of a subsidiary or ancillary nature'.[286] The Court thus held in *Philippines PCA* that the added legal bases to the

[280] Case C-377/12, *Commission v Council*, ECLI:EU:C:2014:1903 ('*Philippines PCA*').

[281] L 134/3. Council Decision of 14 May 2012 on the Signing, on Behalf of the Union, of the Framework Agreement on Partnership and Cooperation between the European Union and Its Member States, of the One Part and the Republic of the Philippines, of the Other Part (2012/272/EU).

[282] Proposal for a Council Decision on the signing of the Framework Agreement on Partnership and Cooperation between the European Union and its Member States, of the one part and the Republic of the Philippines, of the other part (COM(2010) 460 final).

[283] Opinion 1/78, ECLI:EU:C:1979:224 ('*Natural Rubber*').

[284] Case C-268/94, *Portugal v Council*, ECLI:EU:C:1996:461.

[285] For more on this doctrine, see, Stanislas Adam, 'The Legal Basis of International Agreements of the European Union in the Post-Lisbon Era' in Inge Govaere and others (eds), *The European Union in the World: Essays in Honour of Marc Maresceau* (Martinus Nijhoff Publishers 2014) p 80.

[286] Peter Van Elsuwege, 'The Potential for Inter-Institutional Conflicts before the Court of Justice: Impact of the Lisbon Treaty' in Marise Cremona and Anne Thies (eds), *The European Court of Justice and External Relations Law: Constitutional Challenges* (Hart Publishing, 2014) p 117.

agreement by the Council were too extensive and not distinct enough from the existing legal bases that the Commission had set down.[287] Thus, in agreeing with the Commission and the Advocate General,[288] the Court annulled the Council Decision. In its reasoning, citing the *Smart Sanctions* judgment,[289] the Court stated that only if 'several objectives which are inseparably linked without one being secondary and indirect in relation to the other, [then] the measure must be founded on the various corresponding legal bases'.[290] This was conditioned, however, on the legal bases being procedurally compatible. The judgment can therefore be said to have restricted the practice of additional legal bases that are not strictly necessary,[291] moving away from the *Swedish Match* judgment,[292] which allowed additional legal bases if they are procedurally compatible. Furthermore, it can be said that the *Philippines PCA* judgment is a strong attempt to overcome a competence demarcation.[293] However, what is notable about *Philippines PCA* is that it fuels the practice to go for a fewer number of legal bases, which may be at the behest of its prior case law.[294]

Subsequently, the *Tanzania* judgment,[295] delivered in 2016, was a rekindling of the *Mauritius* case taken by the Parliament. The main pleadings were the same as those in *Mauritius*,[296] which saw the international agreement reached between the Union and Tanzania being concluded on a CFSP legal basis only. The Council Decision,[297] on the signing and conclusion of an agreement with Tanzania, was in line with ongoing anti-piracy operations in the region.[298] The *Tanzania* application was lodged by the Parliament at the Court one month before the *Mauritius* judgment was delivered, but with the Opinion of the Advocate General in

[287] Case C-377/12, *Commission v Council*, ECLI:EU:C:2014:1903 ('*Philippines PCA*'), para 59.

[288] Opinion of Advocate General Mengozzi, Case C-377/12, *Commission v Council*, ECLI:EU:C:2014:29 ('*Philippines PCA*').

[289] Discussed earlier in this section. Case C-130/10, *Parliament v Council*, ECLI:EU:C:2012:472 ('*Smart Sanctions*').

[290] Case C-377/12, *Commission v Council*, ECLI:EU:C:2014:1903 ('*Philippines PCA*'), para 34.

[291] Ott, (n 173) p 748.

[292] Case C-210/03, *The Queen, on the application of: Swedish Match AB and Swedish Match UK Ltd v Secretary of State for Health*, ECLI:EU:C:2004:802 ('*Swedish Match*').

[293] Broberg and Holdgaard, (n 228) p 560.

[294] Opinion 1/94, *Competence of the Community to conclude international agreements concerning services and the protection of intellectual property*, ECLI:EU:C:1994:384 (*WTO*) See, Gosalbo-Bono and Naert (n 27) p 51.

[295] Case C-263/14, *Parliament v Council*, ECLI:EU:C:2016:435 ('*Tanzania*').

[296] Discussed earlier in this section. Case C-658/11, *Parliament v Council*, ECLI:EU:C:2014:2025 ('*Mauritius*').

[297] L 108/1. Council Decision 2014/198/CFSP of 10 March 2014 on the Signing and Conclusion of the Agreement between the European Union and the United Republic of Tanzania on the Conditions of Transfer of Suspected Pirates and Associated Seized Property from the European Union-Led Naval Force to the United Republic of Tanzania.

[298] See, Daniel Thym, 'Transfer Agreements for Pirates Concluded by the EU – a Case Study on the Human Rights Accountability of the Common Security and Defence Policy' in Panos Koutrakos and Achilles Skordas (eds), *The Law and Practice of Piracy at Sea: European and International Perspectives* (Hart Publishing, 2014).

Mauritius to hand.[299] The Parliament may have pre-empted the *Mauritius* judgment, thereby hoping for a second attempt in *Tanzania* for a full fleshing out of the Article 40 TEU parameters. Following the failure and silence of the Court in the *Mauritius* judgment to touch substantially upon Article 40 TEU, the Parliament in *Tanzania* again sought a definition of Article 40 TEU. A dual legal basis could have been used according to the Parliament as its pleading stressed the substantive legal basis being Article 37 TEU – a CFSP legal basis; and Articles 82 and 87 TFEU – a non-CFSP legal basis. *Tanzania* brought back the ongoing discussion as to whether a dual legal basis be possible for the conclusion of future international agreements that encompass both CFSP and non-CFSP matters. The Opinion of the Advocate General in *Tanzania* found the Parliament's first pleading contesting the legal basis issue to be unfounded[300] and stated that the Council was correct in selecting a CFSP legal basis. Nonetheless, on the second pleading, the Advocate General agreed that the Council had infringed Article 218(10) TFEU by failing to keep the Parliament 'immediately' informed. The Court's judgment reflected both these assertions of the Advocate General thus annulling the Council's CFSP Decision. Interestingly, the judgment made no mention of the EEAS, who actually negotiated the PTA with Mauritius on the Union's behalf,[301] reinforcing the unusual status of the EEAS as a non-institution in the governing framework of the Union's apparatus.

Taken in isolation, the successful procedural pleadings of the Parliament in *Mauritius* and *Tanzania* are noteworthy. The Council's flagrant breaches of Article 218(10) TFEU on notification grounds constituted violations, demonstrating the importance of procedural requirements. However, the Council cannot be solely to blame as Article 218 TFEU can be equated to a 'battlefield',[302] with other institutions equally willing to extract their own institutional ends from it. Yet, the Court's conclusions in *Mauritius* and *Tanzania* are fully justified for they provide strength in the argument that '[e]ach institution shall act…in conformity with the procedures, conditions and objectives set out in them'.[303] If international agreements founded on a CFSP legal basis were to continue under such questionable practices, it 'would be counterproductive and detrimental to the smooth interactions between the institutions in other fields of external relations'.[304] Accordingly, the Court's judgments demonstrate considerable strength in ensuring a functioning

[299] Opinion of Advocate General Bot, Case C-658/11, *Parliament v Council*, ECLI:EU:C:2014:41 ('*Mauritius*'). The Advocate General did not address TEU, Article 40 in substance in *Mauritius*.

[300] Opinion of Advocate General Kokott, Case C-263/14, *Parliament v Council*, ECLI:EU:C:2015:729 ('*Tanzania*)', para 73. She did, however, find in favour of the Parliament's argument regarding notification. See para 103.

[301] Kuijper (n 9) p 229.

[302] See, Anne Pieter Van Der Mei, 'EU External Relations and Internal Inter-Institutional Conflicts: The Battlefield of Article 218 TFEU' (2016) 23 *Maastricht Journal of European and Comparative Law* 1051.

[303] TEU, Article 13(2).

[304] Panos Koutrakos, 'Institutional Balance and Sincere Cooperation in Treaty-Making under EU Law' (2019) 68 *International and Comparative Law Quarterly* 1 at 18.

democratic process. Given the imprecise scope of Article 218 TFEU as a whole, leaving the Court to clean up the poorly drafted article, it leaves it open to a variety of institutional interpretations.

4.6. The Parliament in Context

Whilst the Union can be understood as a system of government in a unique supranational sense, its separation of powers is much more distinct than what is seen in Member States, with the principle of institutional balance. An 'organic understanding' of the separation of powers[305] does not fit the Union model of institutions or the power that balances them between one another. The confrontations between the Parliament and the Council, whilst cordial, are still chief opponents to each other in legal disputes on CFSP matters of an institutional nature. The demarcation line between a CFSP legal basis and a non-CFSP legal basis has been contested by the Parliament for the furthering of its own institutional strength, but this is not solely confined to institutions. The *Kadi I* case is an explicit example of this.[306] This proves that the 'abolished' second pillar of the EU legal order has left a lasting legacy, with pillar-like provisions remaining intact. Whilst it may seem that there is a craving for litigation to achieve institutional ends, it appears that the Parliament only litigates when it sees itself succeeding in its pleadings, as opposed to appealing every potential opportunity.

The Parliament's actions, through litigation or otherwise, could be seen as not being within the spirit and intended meaning of the TEU.[307] This has not prevented numerous attempts to seek greater involvement and the adherence to the treaties by the Council. The Parliament's rigour of defending its interests and on occasion winning at the Court, either symbolically or substantially, have permitted it to become an established player in the external action of the Union. From the Parliament's perspective, it would clearly like to have a lot more influence but, from the Council's perspective, it is clearly content with the current level of involvement, and shows no intention of budging any further beyond a strict interpretation of the treaties.

4.6.1. Institutional Prerogatives

It has never been in the Council's interests to advocate that CFSP matters are anything more than a Council entitlement. Any swaying on its prerogatives in

[305] Koen Lenaerts, 'Some Reflections on the Separation of Powers in the European Community' (1991) 28 *Common Market Law Review* 11 at 12.

[306] Joined Cases C-402/05 P and C-415/05 P, *Yassin Abdullah Kadi and Al Barakaat International Foundation v Council and Commission*, ECLI:EU:C:2008:461 ('*Kadi I*').

[307] Florika Fink-Hooijer, 'The Common Foreign and Security Policy of the European Union' (1994) 5 *European Journal of International Law* 173 at 185.

CFSP matters would ultimately be against its own institutional interests, thereby granting more rights to other institutions like the Parliament. One of the more prominent instances was an issue of comitology, albeit under a legislative procedure.[308] The Court's case law in bringing the Parliament into the legal system of the Union has been likened to 'a stool with two and a half legs'.[309] The earlier case law – *Les Verts*, *Roquette Frères* and *Chernobyl*, amongst others – opened up legal means to the Parliament that were available to other institutions. The Court's judgments from this period may serve as an informal source of inspiration for the current line of case law, exposing the Parliament to CFSP matters on a limited basis on procedural grounds.

With that in mind, however, full transposition of pre-Lisbon case law, such as *ECOWAS*, to post-Lisbon cases has not followed through. Litigation on CFSP matters has been the Parliament trying to curb the Council's power. The Council has, in the past, litigated against the Parliament exercising powers on non-compulsory budgetary matters[310] and its competence regarding budget revenues.[311] In cases on CFSP matters, the Court as a whole has not overly frustrated the attempts by the Parliament to seek protection of its prerogatives defined by the treaties. The Parliament has, arguably, done well for itself, despite having fewer powers than it believes it should have. The cases demonstrate the Court's ability to embrace the Parliament, but only when it finds it has the genuine right of involvement in Union affairs as strictly in accordance with the treaties, which to date has meant through the procedural provisions. However, whereas the Council Decisions contested in the *Mauritius* and *Tanzania* judgments were annulled, it points to examples of the regard the Court has for its own role in CFSP matters, particularly when it intersects with areas that go beyond its normal type of case.[312]

There is reason to believe that the Court has used vagueness in the treaties as a mechanism to further European integration.[313] Therefore, distinctions can be drawn between the Court engaging in the practice of furthering integration or rather – merely and sometimes reluctantly – filling in the gaps that the Intergovernmental Conferences failed to account for in the text of the treaties. Between the

[308] Robert Schütze, '"Delegated" Legislation in the (New) European Union: A Constitutional Analysis' (2011) 74 *Modern Law Review* 661 at 678. For a detailed account, see, Kieran St C Bradley, 'The European Parliament and Comitology: On the Road to Nowhere?' (1997) 3 *European Law Journal* 230.

[309] Bradley, (n 74) p 55.

[310] Case C-34/86, *Council v Parliament*, ECLI:EU:C:1986:291 ('*Budget*').

[311] Case C-284/90, *Council v Parliament*, ECLI:EU:C:1992:154 ('*Budgetary Revenues*') For more cases on non-CFSP matters between the Parliament and the Council, see, Francis G Jacobs, 'Is the Court of Justice of the European Communities a Constitutional Court?' in Deirdre Curtin and David O'Keeffe (eds), *Constitutional Adjudication in European Community and National Law: Essays for the Hon Mr Justice T F O'Higgins* (Butterworths, 1992).

[312] For more, Gunnar Beck, *The Legal Reasoning of the Court of Justice of the EU* (Hart Publishing, 2013) p 361.

[313] Takis Tridimas, 'Bifurcated Justice: The Dual Character of Judicial Protection in EU Law' in Allan Rosas, Egils Levits and Yves Bot (eds), *The Court of Justice and the Construction of Europe: Analyses and Perspectives on Sixty Years of Case-law – La Cour de Justice et la Construction de l'Europe: Analyses et Perspectives de Soixante Ans de Jurisprudence* (TMC Asser Press, 2013) p 14.

long-winded judgments, that can occasionally give an insight into the long-term thinking of the Court, particular weight can be given to judgments of the Grand Chamber, the '*crème de la crème*' of judgments.[314] Accordingly, with a majority of judges sitting in such instances, Grand Chamber judgments in the area of CFSP matters can give future direction to various Chambers of the Court as to when and how to handle such scenarios.

The Parliament has been taking the Court's temperature over its pleas that non-CFSP legal bases would be more appropriate for the particular actions that the Council is taking. The case law demonstrates the clear contradiction in the eyes of the Council between what it sees as concepts of policy-making and the representation of particular institutions in CFSP matters. At times, the levelling of the institutional power between the Parliament and the Council, whilst potentially warranted for governance reasons,[315] could be in clear contradiction with the treaties and its drafter's intentions. The Council has recognised the role that the treaties give to the Parliament[316] albeit with some disquiet, but has fended off the Parliament's calls for alternative legal bases. For example, in *Smart Sanctions*, the Court said that an argument for democratic involvement of the Parliament is not enough to warrant the winning of a case.[317] There has been other informal discussion of the Parliament's role in international agreements. In the *International Organisation for Vine and Wine* case,[318] the Advocate General stated that the application of Article 218(9) TFEU would diminish the position of the Parliament when the Union is concluding international agreements,[319] but the Court did not follow up this particular point.[320]

This distant position that the Parliament finds itself in within the primary law does not deprive it of its information rights afforded to it by the treaties under Article 218 TFEU. The Court can be said to have followed other case law, particularly the theoretical line stemming from the *Opinion 2/00*, in that 'practical difficulties...cannot be accepted as relevant when selecting the legal basis'.[321]

[314] Adam Łazowski, 'Advocates General and Grand Chamber Cases: Assistance with the Touch of Substitution' (2012) 14 *Cambridge Yearbook of European Legal Studies* 635 at 632.

[315] See Chapter 6 of this book.

[316] Jenö Czuczai, 'Mixity in Practice: Some Problems and Their (Real or Possible) Solution' in Christophe Hillion and Panos Koutrakos (eds), *Mixed Agreements Revisited: The EU and its Member States in the World* (Hart Publishing, 2010) p 239.

[317] Case C-130/10, *Parliament v Council*, ECLI:EU:C:2012:472 ('*Smart Sanctions*'), para 82.

[318] Case C-399/12, *Germany v Council*, ECLI:EU:C:2014:2258 ('*International Organisation of Vine and Wine*').

[319] Opinion of Advocate General Cruz Villalón, Case C-399/12, *Germany v Council*, ECLI:EU:C:2014:289 ('*International Organisation of Vine and Wine*'), para 113. Theodore Konstadinides, 'In the Union of Wine: Loose Ends in the Relationship between the European Union and the Member States in the Field of External Representation – Case C-399/12 Germany v. Council, Judgment of the Court of Justice of 7 October 2014' (2015) 21 *European Public Law* 679 at 683.

[320] Case C-399/12, *Germany v Council*, ECLI:EU:C:2014:2258 ('*International Organisation of Vine and Wine*').

[321] Opinion 2/00, ECLI:EU:C:2001:664 ('*Cartagena Protocol*'), para 41.

This encirclement of the Parliament, with the helpful support of the Commission,[322] has meant the impact of the annulment of the Council acts, such as in *Mauritius* and *Tanzania*, has had an impact on how the Council will have to act in future scenarios. To a certain extent, the Parliament has had to be an alliance-builder in this exercise. Bringing in the Commission to support its pleadings in the *Mauritius* and *Tanzania* cases has been important for demonstrating that Council actions, using CFSP legal instruments, have ramifications far beyond those of the Parliament itself. The Court has previously said, 'to proceed on an incorrect legal basis is therefore liable to invalidate the act concluding the agreement'[323] and in CFSP matters, it has stuck to this principle of invalidating the agreements when the Council has erred.

4.6.2. Scope of EU External Action

It can theoretically be argued that it is impossible to determine what the exact scope of EU external action may be. The lack of distinct objectives for both CFSP matters and non-CFSP matters can raise concerns about the appropriateness, relevance and preciseness of a centre of gravity test, for there needs to be a definitive anchorage point. It can also be noted that the greater number of powers being transferred to institutional actors by the Member States inherently decreases the scope for action within the understanding of CFSP matters and increases the potential scope for action on a non-CFSP legal basis. Thus, with CFSP matters becoming an even narrower field of powers and competence, its use will continue to be limited if other institutions, particularly the Parliament, refuse to give it any latitude in how it operates. Consequently, the tests, such as the centre of gravity test that the Court applies, may be a futile exercise in the future. The Court can be said to be elusive on the precise scope of the test and, given that it is open to abuse, and that its unsuitability has been highlighted.[324] When drafting international agreements for CFSP matters, the Council can see them as the heart of the agreement, but use it as a disguise for including items that would, or should, find their legal basis elsewhere in the treaties. Such strategic placing by the Council, given the Treaty of Lisbon reforms removing the preference for a TFEU legal basis, means the legal basis can shift back and be set upon a CFSP legal basis. Whether this irony was intended, is a pertinent question.

In light of this increasingly difficult challenge, the Court may have to invent a new doctrine for applying legal bases tests when 'border policing' the divide between CFSP and non-CFSP matters. Such an approach may give recourse to greater emphasis on institutional balance of powers. The means of interpreting

[322] Kieran St C Bradley, 'Sense and Sensibility: Parliament v. Council Continued' (1991) 16 *European Law Review* 245 at 248.

[323] Opinion 2/00, ECLI:EU:C:2001:664 ('*Cartagena Protocol*'), para 5.

[324] See, De Baere and Van den Sanden (n 264) p 86.

the treaties in this regard, however, will leave open charges against it, depending on what form of new doctrine it may apply. The Court has relied upon policy documents in coming to its determinations in both *ECOWAS* and *Philippines Border Management*.[325] This demonstrates that beyond the primary law in CFSP matters, other factors can help the Court in determining the legal basis of measures. Furthermore, the judgments of *Smart Sanctions* and *Mauritius* are affirmative decisions by the Court to secure its mandate and influence in CFSP matters. Yet, the Court has not ruled on the precise boundary of CFSP matters against non-CFSP matters. Whilst it claims it has not had the opportunity to do so, among other matters,[326] it is unlikely that the Court is willing to say either and is willingly ignoring an opportunity to state the limit, which it may possess through Article 40 TEU. Rule 141 of the Parliament's Rules of Procedure sets out the inner-institutional process upon which it may decide to file an action at the Court on the compatibility of an international agreement with the treaties through the Opinion procedure.[327] This is the Parliament's prerogative set down in the treaties under Article 218(11) TFEU.[328] The catch with the Parliament's Rules of Procedure is, however, that they are written by the Parliament, for the Parliament. Hence, it is important not to read too much into them or see them as a reliable source of law as Parliament's idealism can get caught up in its own self-proclaimed text.

4.6.3. Legal Basis

It is natural that institutions seeking greater and more extensive powers, will prefer legal bases that enhance their aspirations. By contrast, those with a less integrative agenda would prefer the retention of prerogatives derived from legal bases to the contrary. The choice of legal basis is not solely confined to external relations matters or the division of CFSP legal bases and non-CFSP legal bases. It also extends to areas such as criminal law[329] and other JHA matters. The choice of a legal basis for an external act can be made with the intention of deliberately avoiding the inclusion of the Parliament.[330] In *ECOWAS*, pre-Lisbon, a dual legal basis was contested, given that an EC

[325] Ibid. p 95.
[326] The Court '...has not yet had the opportunity to define the extent to which its jurisdiction is limited in CFSP matters.' Opinion 2/13, ECLI:EU:C:2014:2454 ('*Accession of the European Union to the European Convention for the Protection of Human Rights*'), para 251.
[327] European Parliament, 'Rules of Procedure – 8th Parliamentary Term (January 2017)'. pp. 87–88.
[328] Rule 141: Proceedings before the Court of Justice of the European Union in, European Parliament (n 89).
[329] See, Samuli Miettinen, 'Criminal Competence and the Choice of Legal Basis: Space in the Margins?' (2015) 5 *European Criminal Law Review* 222.
[330] Philippe de Schoutheete de Tervarent, 'EC External Relations and the CFSP (Summing Up)' in Alan Dashwood (ed), *Reviewing Maastricht: Issues for the 1996 IGC* (Sweet and Maxwell, 1996) p 272.

(non-CFSP) legal basis would take precedence over a CFSP legal basis.[331] The adoption of a dual legal basis between pillars was possible pre-Lisbon.[332] Under these arrangements, if an international agreement was to encompass elements from the first pillar (non-CFSP) and third pillar (JHA), a mixed agreement would be resorted to, entailing a role for both the Union and the Member States together.

With different legal bases needed for different actions, the impact on the Parliament's prerogatives has been central to the legal basis argument. The Parliament's view before the entering into force of the Treaty of Lisbon was that 'any future mixed agreement combining non-CFSP and CFSP elements must normally be dealt with under a single legal basis, which should be the one directly related to the main subject-matter of the agreement'.[333] Saying that, recent practice has demonstrated that international agreements primarily related to non-CFSP matters, but having an element of CFSP matter about them, have been adopted upon a non-CFSP legal basis. For example, in the Stabilisation and Association Agreement with Serbia, it noted that 'at the request of the Parties, political dialogue may also take place' in respect of CFSP matters.[334] Similarly, in the Partnership and Cooperation Agreement with Iraq, Title I covers 'Political dialogue and cooperation in the field of foreign and security policy'.[335] Both these agreements highlight the incidental nature of CFSP matters.

4.6.4. Dual Legal Bases

With improved coherence of the legal order with the Treaty of Lisbon, a legal basis for a Union act stretching across both the TEU and TFEU, encompassing a CFSP legal basis and a non-CFSP legal basis is possible, albeit with distinctions. From a Commission perspective, it may be seen that Article 218 TFEU allows for international agreements to be concluded with both a CFSP legal basis and a

[331] Alan Dashwood, 'The Continuing Bipolarity of EU External Action' in Inge Govaere and others (eds), *The European Union in the World: Essays in Honour of Marc Maresceau* (Martinus Nijhoff Publishers, 2014) p 10.

[332] For example, in, Case C-355/04 P, *Segi, Arait, Zubimendi Izaga and Aritza Galarraga v Council*, ECLI:EU:C:2007:116 ('*Segi*'), between the second (CFSP) and third (JHA) pillars. See, Christina Eckes, 'How Not Being Sanctioned by a Community Instrument Infringes a Person's Fundamental Rights: The Case of Segi' (2006) 17 *King's Law Journal* 144.

[333] C 212 E/37. Parliament's New Role and Responsibilities in Implementing the Lisbon Treaty (P6_TA(2009)0373) European Parliament Resolution of 7 May 2009 on Parliament's New Role and Responsibilities in Implementing the Treaty of Lisbon (2008/2063(INI)) (2010/C 212 E/08), para 47.

[334] Article 11(2), L 278/16. Stabilisation and Association Agreement between the European Communities and Their Member States of the One Part and the Republic of Serbia, of the Other Part. For the conclusion of the Stabilisation and Association Agreement with Serbia, see, ibid.

[335] L 204/20. Partnership and Cooperation Agreement between the European Union and Its Member States, of the One Part and the Republic of Iraq, of the Other Part. For the conclusion of this international agreement, see, L 204/18. Council Decision of 21 December 2011 on the Signing, on Behalf of the European Union and Provisional Application of Certain Provisions of the Partnership and Cooperation Agreement between the European Union and Its Member States, of the One Part and the Republic of Iraq, of the Other Part (2012/418/EU).

non-CFSP legal basis.[336] The Court has left open the possibility of accepting a dual legal basis to be used in the future, stating in *Mauritius* that certain measures 'will have to be founded, exceptionally, on the various corresponding legal bases'[337] – a claim it has made before in a number of instances, including in *Basel Convention*.[338] In *Tanzania*,[339] the Court 'appears to avoid a clear response' as to whether Article 218 TFEU permits a dual legal basis.[340] Yet, it is apparent that Article 218 TFEU now allows for dual legal basis international agreements to be concluded, not as a mixed agreement, but rather as one integrated agreement, respecting the procedural aspects of both CFSP and non-CFSP matters. Therefore, the issue of splitting the *conclusion* of international agreements between a CFSP legal basis and a non-CFSP legal basis is not a viable option but yet, the adoption of legal acts using both a CFSP and a non-CFSP legal basis may be possible. This was attempted in the EPCA with Kazakhstan, notwithstanding the fact that it took over three months for the legal act to be published.[341] However, the Court annulled a subsequent decision of the Cooperation Council within the confines of the international agreement adopted on both a CFSP legal basis and a non-CFSP legal basis, given the Decision unnecessarily contained a CFSP legal basis.[342] The Court appears to have done this without any particular reliance upon Article 40 TEU – the border-policing provision. Importantly, however, it did not rule out the inclusion of both a CFSP legal basis and a non-CFSP legal basis in the future.

Furthermore, for the accession of the Union to the Treaty of Amity and Cooperation in Southeast Asia,[343] the Council adopted a Decision based upon both a CFSP legal basis and a non-CFSP legal basis – that of development cooperation.[344] This has given rise to 'mutual encroachment' of policy area.[345]

[336] Fernando Castillo de la Torre, 'The Court of Justice and External Competences After Lisbon: Some Reflections on the Latest Case Law' in Piet Eeckhout and Manuel López-Escudero (eds), *The European Union's External Action in Times of Crisis* (Hart Publishing, 2016).

[337] Case C-658/11, *Parliament v Council*, ECLI:EU:C:2014:2025 ('*Mauritius*'), para 43.

[338] Case C-411/06, *Commission v Parliament and Council*, EU:C:2009:518 ('*Basel Convention*'), also known as the '*Shipment of Waste*' case.

[339] Case C-263/14, *Parliament v Council*, ECLI:EU:C:2016:435 ('*Tanzania*').

[340] Soledad R Sánchez-Tabernero, 'The Choice of Legal Basis and the Principle of Consistency in the Procedure for Conclusion of International Agreements in CFSP Contexts: Parliament v. Council (Pirate-Transfer Agreement with Tanzania)' (2017) 54 *Common Market Law Review* 899 at 905.

[341] L 29/1. Council Decision (EU) 2016/123 of 26 October 2015 on the Signing, on Behalf of the European Union and Provisional Application of the Enhanced Partnership and Cooperation Agreement between the European Union and Its Member States, of the One Part and the Republic of Kazakhstan, of the Other Part.

[342] '[T]he Council was wrong to include Article 31(1) TEU in the legal basis of the contested decision and that decision was wrongly adopted under the voting rule requiring unanimity'. Case C-244/17, *Commission v Council (Accord avec le Kazakhstan)*, ECLI:EU:C:2018:662, para 47.

[343] L 154/1. Council Decision 2012/308/CFSP of 26 April 2012 on the Accession of the European Union to the Treaty of Amity and Cooperation in Southeast Asia.

[344] TEU, Articles 31(1) and 37; and TFEU, Articles 209, 212, 218(6)(a) and 218(8).

[345] Morten Broberg, 'EU Development Cooperation and the CFSP: Mutual Encroachment?' in Steven Blockmans and Panos Koutrakos (eds), *Research Handbook on the EU's Common Foreign and Security Policy* (Edward Elgar, 2018) p 274.

Importantly however, the Council has opted for Member States to conclude the international agreement themselves, and not on a CFSP legal basis.[346] Therefore, it appears to be a case of optional mixity. The reliance on both a CFSP legal basis and non-CFSP legal basis has also been opted for in other instances in recent times.[347]

A definitive position of the institutional actors is beginning to emerge, in that an act based upon a dual or an array of legal bases is possible and utilised. However, some level of caution is to be noted. In *Air Transport Agreement*,[348] the Advocate General stated that the adopting of a hybrid act is 'not provided for by the [t]reaties',[349] a point which the Court agreed with.[350] The Advocate General furthermore stated that the future of international agreements adopted upon a legal basis with different decision-making procedures 'constitute[s] a dangerous precedent of contamination of the autonomous decision-making process of the EU institutions that is liable, therefore, to cause damage to the autonomy of the EU as a specific legal system'.[351] The Court, on the dual legal basis at issue in *Air Transport Agreement*, said Article 218 TFEU 'does not enable the voting rules applicable within the Council to be determined'.[352] This would imply a note of caution, in that the Court is able and willing to annul EU legal acts when adopted on a dual legal basis. However, it is unclear whether this could be analogised to an international agreement containing CFSP matters.

The treaties have a long-established principle of balance between the institutions.[353] If adopting a CFSP legal basis for an international agreement, in conjunction with a non-CFSP legal basis, it is a conundrum how the two procedures are reconciled. Mixing a CFSP legal basis with a non-CFSP legal basis through the ordinary legislative procedure means the procedures are effectively incompatible with one another. The issue is that this scenario would *de facto* lead to a non-CFSP legal basis and its procedures being used, thereby undermining the Treaty objectives for institutional balance. Moving all actions related to CFSP matters to a non-CFSP legal basis disregards and infringes the competence of the

[346] Gosalbo-Bono and Naert (n 27) p 28.

[347] For example, L 321/1. Council Decision (EU) 2016/2079 of 29 September 2016 on the Signing, on Behalf of the European Union and Provisional Application of the Partnership Agreement on Relations and Cooperation between the European Union and Its Member States, of the One Part and New Zealand, of the Other Part.

[348] Opinion of Advocate General Mengozzi, Case C-28/12, *Commission v Council*, ECLI:EU:C:2015:43 ('*Air Transport Agreement*').

[349] Ibid. para 75.

[350] 'The adoption of a joint decision is not provided for by that article [Article 218 TFEU]'. Case C-28/12, *Commission v Council*, ECLI:EU:C:2015:282 ('*Air Transport Agreement*'), para 23.

[351] Opinion of Advocate General Mengozzi, Case C-28/12, *Commission v Council*, ECLI:EU:C:2015:43 ('*Air Transport Agreement*'), para 80.

[352] Case C-28/12, *Commission v Council*, ECLI:EU:C:2015:282 ('*Air Transport Agreement*'), para 30.

[353] Case C-327/91, *France v Commission*, ECLI:EU:C:1994:305, para 28, which has recently been cited in Opinion of Advocate General Wathelet, Case C-425/13, *Commission v Council*, ECLI:EU:C:2015:174 ('*Australia ETS*'), para 84. See, Youri Devuyst, 'The European Union's Institutional Balance after the Treaty of Lisbon: Community Method and Democratic Deficit Reassessed' (2008) 39 *Georgetown Journal of International Law* 247; Paul Craig, 'Institutions, Power and Institutional Balance' in Paul Craig and Gráinne De Búrca (eds), *The Evolution of EU Law* 2nd edition (Oxford University Press, 2011).

Council as the treaties presently stand. This action would appear to be contrary to the institutional balance that the treaties have provided for to date. By combining legal bases, it stands that the Parliament could possibly gain by granting it a wider scope for inclusion in particular actions.

The Court has been debating the issue of dual legal bases for some time with regard to CFSP matters and, from the case law, it seems that it has not yet come to a position that it has been able to stand fully behind. Mixing legal bases has received the blessing of the Court before in a different policy area. For example, in *International Fund for Ireland*,[354] the Court, pre-Lisbon, found that even though the procedural requirements under two different articles in the treaties were qualified majority and unanimity, a dual legal basis was workable.[355]

4.6.5. Formality and Informality

Beyond the legal questions that the Parliament has put before the Court, a huge amount of resources are needed so that the Parliament is in a position to handle every issue in EU external action. Due to the volume of EU external action, it is picking its battles carefully, with litigation based on arguments that it believes it can win. The formality of Union law has for long dominated the legal scene, with little focus on informal practice that has developed over a period of time. It has, therefore, adopted a more sophisticated approach to analyse these underlying currents that do not always see the limelight in the same manner as legal texts.[356]

The Parliament plays an active role in non-CFSP external action of the Union. Where it is not formally an active participant, it does perform as an active observer in various processes. Informal practices have been critical for the Parliament in CFSP matters. However, the drawbacks of informally influencing CFSP matters invariably leads to the Parliament's efforts having no hard binding effect in the short term. All interested actors in EU external action can appreciate that courteous arrangements between institutions of all persuasions are for the best of the Union. Facilitating their respective roles within the governance framework has enhanced the preparation and execution of external action. This was recognised in the lead-in to establishing the Constitutional Treaty.[357]

[354] Case C-166/07, *Parliament v Council*, ECLI:EU:C:2009:499 ('*International Fund for Ireland*').

[355] Piet Eeckhout, 'The EU's Common Foreign and Security Policy after Lisbon: From Pillar Talk to Constitutionalism' in Andrea Biondi, Piet Eeckhout and Stefanie Ripley (eds), *EU Law after Lisbon* (Oxford University Press, 2012) p 276.

[356] Deirdre Curtin, 'The Sedimentary European Constitution – The Future of "Constitutionalisation" without a Constitution' in Ingolf Pernice and Evgeni Tanchev (eds), *Ceci n'est pas une Constitution – Constitutionalisation without a Constitution?* vol. 7 (Nomos, 2009) p 77.

[357] 'The European Convention: The Secretariat: Final Report of Working Group VII on External Action. From Working Group VII – "External Action" to Members of the Convention (CONV 459/02)', para 22.

Law-making on an informal basis is usually not preserved for international organisations,[358] but informal practice *within* an international organisation is how the Parliament initially obtained its formal powers. Its involvement in any EU foreign policy issues in the early days of the EPC would have been considered premature before direct elections to the Parliament were introduced in 1979.[359] The earlier days of political cooperation saw the Parliament acquire additional involvement without formalised legal arrangements in the treaties. Rather, declarations by Member States to involve the Parliament in a limited way were utilised.[360] The informal practices that have been developed to date have been steadily in favour of the Parliament in terms of competence building. The Parliament has successfully managed to convince other actors within the EU to 'concede certain informal powers'.[361] An example of this is the fact that, over time, the Parliament has been an effective institution builder by seeking for its practices to become established and later formalised by means of the treaties or otherwise. Whilst categorised as interinstitutional bargaining,[362] it is not just other EU bodies the Parliament has had to contend with. It has also had to compete with the Parliamentary Assembly of the Western European Union (WEU PA) as a formal body charged with overseeing and legitimising foreign, security, and defence matters.

One of the inherent identified limitations of parliamentary actors in the involvement of external actions, particularly matters such as foreign policy in a theoretical sense, is that unfolding events alter policies on a rapid basis.[363] In practice, the Parliament makes use of its non-binding resolutions to make its position on certain international affairs known to the Council on topical external matters. The overall escalation of the Parliament's breadth of activities internally within the Union has had huge ramifications for the institution's role on the global stage. This transition to captivating itself on the world stage has meant its role in the Union's foreign policy can be treated more seriously.

The buried Constitutional Treaty contained a modest proposal to allow for the Commission and the to-be-established Union Minister for Foreign Affairs to make a joint recommendation for the opening of negotiations for international agreements.[364] This would have allowed legal basis issues to be ironed out at earlier stages in the process of developing an international agreement. However, as the

[358] In fact, they normally occur in 'a loosely organised network or forum'. Sanderijn Duquet and others, 'Upholding the Rule of Law in Informal International Lawmaking Processes' (2014) 6 *Hague Journal on the Rule of Law* 75 at 82.

[359] Bradley (n 7) p 125.

[360] Gaja (n 27) p 191.

[361] Crum (n 129) p 384.

[362] Berthold Rittberger, 'Institutionalizing Representative Democracy in the European Union: The Case of the European Parliament' (2012) 50 *Journal of Common Market Studies* 18 at 33.

[363] Eileen Denza, *The Intergovernmental Pillars of the European Union* (Oxford University Press, 2002) p 324.

[364] The European Convention: The Secretariat: Draft Articles on External Action in the Constitutional Treaty. From the Praesidium to the Convention (CONV 685/03) 03.

Constitutional Treaty's potential for coming into force diminished, so did this proposal, which did not find its way into the Treaty of Lisbon. What manifested was that for international agreements on CFSP matters, it is the High Representative who makes the recommendation to the Council for opening negotiations,[365] marking another distinction between external action on a CFSP and a non-CFSP legal basis.[366] How this would be reconciled for adopting international agreements on a dual legal basis as the default position for the Union is not yet fully clear. Notwithstanding the cleavages of involvement of different political party groups,[367] the Parliament has through its MEPs, informally expanded the High Representative's role with the institution in CFSP matters.

4.7. The Future of the Parliament in CFSP Matters

A parliament can act as a guardian of a constitution,[368] and 'the Parliament's role in the sphere of…CFSP [matters] is by no means negligible' is how the Court has viewed the matter.[369] The credibility concept is fundamental for exerting influence and power across the EU decision-making regime. It is accepted that parliaments have limits on their powers and influence and so it can be questioned what type of powers parliaments should have. Electing a government may be one, ratifying international treaties another, and another again approving budgetary matters are typical characteristics of a parliament. At national level, parliaments have been losing their power to the executives due to necessary prompt decision-making and increased complexities.[370] An increased presence of the Parliament in Union affairs has long been coming and overtly predicted.[371] It is clear that there is a

[365] TFEU, Article 218(3): 'The Commission, or the High Representative of the Union for Foreign Affairs and Security Policy where the agreement envisaged relates exclusively or principally to the common foreign and security policy, shall submit recommendations to the Council, which shall adopt a decision authorising the opening of negotiations and, depending on the subject of the agreement envisaged, nominating the Union negotiator or the head of the Union's negotiating team.'

[366] Geert De Baere, 'The Basics of EU External Relations Law: An Overview of the Post-Lisbon Constitutional Framework for Developing the External Dimensions of EU Asylum and Migration Policy' in Marleen Maes, Marie-Claire Foblets and Philippe De Bruycker (eds), *External Dimensions of European Migration and Asylum Law and Policy/Dimensions Externes du Droit et de la Politque d'Immigration et d'Asile de l'UE* (Bruylant, 2011) p 142.

[367] For an earlier discussion of this, see, Viola (n 35).

[368] Juliane Kokott and Martin Kaspar, 'Ensuring Constitutional Efficacy' in Michael Rosenfeld and András Sajó (eds), *The Oxford Handbook of Comparative Constitutional Law* (Oxford University Press, 2012) p 800. From another viewpoint, courts and judges can also do likewise. See, Helle Krunke, 'Courts as Protectors of the People: Constitutional Identity, Popular Legitimacy and Human Rights' in Martin Scheinin, Helle Krunke and Marina Aksenova (eds), *Judges as Guardians of Constitutionalism and Human Rights* (Edward Elgar, 2016).

[369] Case C-130/10, *Parliament v Council*, ECLI:EU:C:2012:50 ('*Smart Sanctions*'), para 71.

[370] Antonio Cassese, 'Preface' in Antonio Cassese (ed), *Parliamentary Control Over Foreign Policy: Legal Essays* (Sijtoff and Noordhoff, 1980) p vii.

[371] Gerhard Bebr, *Development of Judicial Control of the European Communities* (Martinus Nijhoff Publishers, 1981) p 466.

parliamentary deficit when it comes to CFSP matters. The Parliament is provided with 'continuous special treatment',[372] but not, from its own institutional perspective, in a positive sense.

The transformation of the Assembly into the directly elected Parliament offered much hope for parliamentary involvement in EU foreign policy. These expectations, largely from within the Parliament, have not lived up to the expected reality. The Parliament and its powers are explained through its increased role in the legislative process, which, arguably,[373] leads to an indirect push for ensuring Parliament's involvement in the non-legislative field of CFSP matters. The Parliament possesses more power than the treaties actually prescribe and even more than the drafters had intended. This is something it may choose to highlight and a fact that the Council may find difficult to deny. Nonetheless, the Parliament remains a secondary institution in CFSP matters. Just as was the case in the 1990s when EU foreign policy was introduced, any influence that the Parliament has in CFSP matters is not fully supported in the treaties.

4.7.1. The Role of the Court

The treaties are never going to provide a definitive outcome or remedy for the institution that feels aggrieved that another institution has not followed procedures. Instead, there is an intermediator in the form of the Court to resolve an immediate conflict. The Court is not blind to disputes of an institutional nature and it has consistently recognised the role that each institution plays according to the treaties in its own view.[374] The Court has been indispensable for the functioning of CFSP matters, balancing the protection of CFSP matters for the Council, whilst simultaneously furthering the Parliament's prerogatives. However, saying the Court has 'parliamentarised' CFSP matters may be premature. Since *Roquette Frères*,[375] the involvement of the Parliament has been significantly enhanced in Union decision-making. Yet, a conscious effort has been made by the drafters of the treaties to continuously keep the Parliament at arm's length when it comes to CFSP matters.

The Court, in cases involving the Parliament, can descend into a forum for inter-institutional debate.[376] In earlier cases, the Court has 'risen to the challenge',[377]

[372] Daniel Thym, 'Parliamentary Involvement in European International Relations' in Marise Cremona and Bruno De Witte (eds), *EU Foreign Relations Law: Constitutional Fundamentals* (Hart Publishing, 2008) p 219.

[373] Simon Hix and Bjørn Høyland, 'Empowerment of the European Parliament' (2013) 16 *Annual Review of Political Science* 171 at 185.

[374] The Court is said to recognise the role of the Parliament and Court in the role of European integration. See, Pierre Pescatore, 'Reconnaissance et contrôle judiciaire des actes du Parlement européen' (1978) 14 *Revue trimestrielle de droit européen* 581.

[375] Case C-138/79, *Roquette Frères v Council*, ECLI:EU:C:1980:249.

[376] Harm Schepel and Erhard Blankenburg, 'Mobilizing the European Court of Justice' in Gráinne De Búrca and Joseph HH Weiler (eds), *The European Court of Justice* (Oxford University Press, 2001) p 18.

[377] Jukka Snell, 'Free Movement of Capital: Evolution as a Non-Linear Process' in Paul Craig and Gráinne De Búrca (eds), *The Evolution of EU Law* 2nd edition (Oxford University Press, 2011) p 105.

not to favour it in terms of institutional preference, but to adjudicate within strict confines. When the Court got it wrong on the involvement of the Parliament in *Comitology*,[378] it quickly reversed its decision in *Chernobyl* within a very short timeframe.[379] The 'flood' of cases claiming abuse did not happen[380] and the *Chernobyl* judgment held that some involvement for the Parliament was a minimum standard for consistency with the treaties as they then stood.[381]

Post-*Chernobyl*, the Council continued to challenge the basis for the Parliament to bring actions for annulment, such as in the *National Road Haulage* case.[382] Nonetheless, the Court has stood firm behind its *Chernobyl* decision. What is so striking about the Parliament's ability to litigate, is that it appears to have initially occurred by a meeting of the Court in private as an administrative decision resulting in an Order of the Court when considering allowing the Parliament to intervene in *Roquette Frères*. This Order was not published[383] and was only mentioned in the judgment.[384] This in itself meant the Parliament in subsequent years could avail of litigation to resolve some of its other grievances, involving itself in other disputes and defend itself when actioned against.[385]

The Parliament, whilst achieving its legal right to protect its prerogatives, did campaign post-Maastricht for its standing to be increased, with the possibility to intervene, without the explicit restriction of merely protecting its prerogatives.[386] As the only institution of the Union that is subject to a popular vote of the European citizenry, the legitimacy of the Parliament can often be an unseen benefit of its pleadings. In conformity with this notion, the pleadings of the Parliament have certainly earned a sympathetic ear in the Court. However, the demarcation lines for CFSP matters are not ultimately determined by the Parliament, but rather by the Court. The Court has been charged with too easily favouring the Parliament's viewpoints over those of the drafters of the treaties and their implicit intentions in the past.[387] It has been actively expressed with a level

[378] Case C-302/87, *Parliament v Council*, ECLI:EU:C:1988:461 ('*Comitology*').

[379] Case C-70/88, *Parliament v Council*, ECLI:EU:C:1990:217 and ECLI:EU:C:1991:373 ('*Chernobyl*').

[380] Kieran St C Bradley, '"Better Rusty than Missin"?: Institutional Reforms of the Maastricht Treaty and the European Parliament' in David O'Keeffe and Patrick M Twomey (eds), *Legal Issues of the Maastricht Treaty* (Chancery 1994) p 202. Some potentially envisaged a flood of 'political abuse'. For example, see, Weiler, 'Pride and Prejudice: Parliament v. Council' (n 63), which turned out to be incorrect.

[381] Bradley (n 380) p 201.

[382] Case C-65/90, *Parliament v Council*, ECLI:EU:C:1992:325 ('*National Road Haulage*'), para 12.

[383] Jacobs (n 75) p 223.

[384] Case C-138/79, *Roquette Frères v Council*, ECLI:EU:C:1980:249, para 3. See, Emil Kirchner and Karen Williams, 'The Legal, Political and Institutional Implications of the Isoglucose Judgments 1980' (1983) 22 *Journal of Common Market Studies* 173.

[385] For example, see, Case C-48/81, *Germany v Commission* [withdrawn]; Case C-230/81, *Luxembourg v Parliament*, ECLI:EU:C:1983:32 ('*Seat of Parliament*'); Case C-72/82, *Council v Parliament* [withdrawn]; and Case C-13/83, *Parliament v Council*, ECLI:EU:C:1985:220 ('*Common Transport Policy*').

[386] Ole Due, 'The Judicial System of the European Union in the Perspective of the 1996 Intergovernmental Conference' in Göran Melander (ed), *Modern Issues in European Law: Nordic Perspectives: Essays in Honour of Lennart Pålsson* (Kluwer Law International, 1997) p 28.

[387] Hjalte Rasmussen, *European Court of Justice* (GadJura, 1998) pp 200–201.

of concern that adopting measures on a legal basis that allow for a preference of the Parliament may be without any legal basis.[388] Thus, case law confirming the involvement of the Parliament, where prompted by the treaties, should be genuine and sincere. Furthermore, given the Parliament's status as a majoritarian institution, increasing its significance by whatever means, can lead to raising 'other democratic problems'.[389] Despite the Court's role in the Parliament's litigation proceedings, the Court has based its adjudications on frameworks surrounding the governance regime as envisaged by the treaties to the greatest extent possible. Thus, the Court has not necessarily encroached into the political sphere in the same way in which the Parliament is trying to enter.

4.7.2. The Push of Parliament and Resistance of the Council

Why is the Parliament so keen to get involved in the Union's foreign policy? The Council's artillery in CFSP matters are a force to be reckoned with. If past performance is a good indicator of future performance, how the Parliament has acted with its powers in non-CFSP matters post-Lisbon provides the framework for how it would operate its external powers, albeit still curtailed, with respect to CFSP matters. That is, if specific powers in that regard were conferred. The Parliament is still in no way equal to the Council in CFSP matters and the power to formulate CFSP Decisions is not within its grasp. Parliamentary debates do not amount to legal text and do not generate legal effect. Given its involvement in non-CFSP matters post-Lisbon as a co-legislator, it is not short of tasks to undertake. Acquiring more involvement in foreign policy issues such as CFSP matters would increase its workload. Reinforcing the powers of Parliament by any means can have the indirect effect of creating deadlocks,[390] an issue that would result in the measurable impact of EU external action disappearing as a result of its absence.

The design of the treaties with respect to CFSP matters may not have suited the Parliament's interests, yet may not necessarily have been designed to shield the Parliament. Rather, combined organisational development and legalisation were the priority,[391] which inherently omitted the Parliament. The Parliament's evolutionary framework is demonstrative of the incremental nature of the Union's

[388] Opinion of Advocate General Maduro, Case C-411/06, *Commission v Parliament and Council*, ECLI:EU:C:2009:189 ('*Basel Convention*') para 6, and accompanying footnotes. Furthermore, it has been argued the Member States 'choices could have been different' with respect to institutional structure. See, Paul Craig, 'The EU, Democracy and Institutional Structure: Past, Present and Future' in Antonina Bakardjieva Engelbrekt and Xavier Groussot (eds), *The Future of Europe: Political and Legal Integration Beyond Brexit* (Hart Publishing, 2019).

[389] Miguel Poiares Maduro, *We the Court: The European Court of Justice and the European Economic Constitution: A Critical Reading of Article 30 the EC Treaty* (Hart Publishing, 1998) p 114.

[390] Ibid. p 115.

[391] Aurel Sari, 'Between Legalisation and Organisational Development: Explaining the Evolution of EU Competence in the Field of Foreign Policy' in Paul James Cardwell (ed), *EU External Relations Law and Policy in the Post-Lisbon Era* (TMC Asser Press, 2012) p 87.

primary law and its perils. In a cross-cutting manner, the Parliament can be said to be the 'formal institutional manifestation' of the Union.[392] The Parliament, today, in most Union policies, has strong powers, including those for future revisions to primary law. For example, Article 48(2) and (6) TEU inserted a new power for the Parliament to propose amendments to the treaties. The Parliament has been aggressive in getting ahead of the treaties; however, the Council has in recent times acted recklessly,[393] making it look like an irresponsible institutional actor.

With the Parliament's continued accumulation of power and involvement, it jealously protects its rights. Article 27(3) TEU explicitly permitted the Parliament to be consulted on one CFSP Decision, to allow the establishment of the EEAS. Not only does this prove that the Parliament has the potential for a greater level of involvement in CFSP matters, but the establishment of the EEAS in 2011 following the EEAS Decision in 2010 showed how the Parliament had acted in a responsible fashion towards the outer edges of involvement in the law of EU foreign policy. The overarching problem remains that the Council does not have to answer to the Parliament. The closer the EEAS gets to the Commission, the more the Parliament gains in respect of its influence in CFSP matters. Articles 223–234 TFEU set down the institutional provisions that the Parliament can utilise. During the period leading up to the establishment of the EEAS, the Parliament stated: 'it is of the utmost importance to ensure that community policies are not intergovernamentalised',[394] demonstrating its consent to the EEAS's creation that it was more in line with Commission activities. The Parliament was innovative in its attempts, post-Lisbon, to shape the EEAS,[395] attempting to strengthen its abilities in EU external action. The experience of using legal mechanisms for its own institutional gain will not be lessons easily forgotten in its institutional memory.

The tendency of the Parliament to grasp more power through the Court has not just been solely as advancing that of the Parliament, but also, the Court itself. The results of the Court's judgments in cases on CFSP matters taken by the Parliament is 'not a one-way street solely protecting the rights of the Parliament',[396] but instead and equally so, ensuring that the role of the other key actors, the Commission, the Council and of course the Court, are also observed. The Parliament and the Commission have both worked together to ensure that 'creeping intergovernmentalisation' does not occur in supranational policies.[397] Whilst they have

[392] Christina Eckes, 'How the European Parliament's Participation in International Relations Affects the Deep Tissue of the EU's Power Structures' (2014) 12 *International Journal of Constitutional Law* 904 at 928.

[393] For example, such as in *Mauritius* and *Tanzania*, by not fully informing Parliament as per its TFEU, Article 218(10) obligation.

[394] 'Press Release: The Conference of Presidents on the External Action Service', 10 June 2010.

[395] Kolja Raube, 'The European External Action Service and the European Parliament' (2012) 7 *The Hague Journal of Diplomacy* 65 at 79.

[396] Klamert (n 243) p 513.

[397] Andrea Ott, 'Between Pillars and Policies: The Quest for Consistency in EU External Relations Law' in Maartje De Visser and Anne Pieter Van Der Mei (eds), *The Treaty on European Union 1993–2013: Reflections from Maastricht* (Intersentia, 2013) p 262.

both been watching the Council's actions closely, they have not always done so in harmony with one another. It may have been logical to see it as a foregone conclusion that CFSP matters would be absorbed by regular Union decision-making with QMV in the Council, and the conversion to the ordinary legislative procedure to transform CFSP matters into legislative acts. This has not happened to date.[398]

The treaties have maintained the intergovernmental-like method of involvement for the Parliament,[399] thus meaning it stays at a distance. However, even if such scrutinising powers did exist, '[t]he effective exercise of Parliament's power of scrutiny does not require the use of powers of compulsion in every case'.[400] The Parliament and its advances encapsulate the will of 'parliamentising' all policies as an integral part of the development of Union law and its legal order. The constitutionally weak Parliament initiated many proposals for alleviating its own plight with varied levels of success. Its direct and indirect means of penetration into CFSP matters will continue, regardless of whether formal furtherance will be on the table for discussion in future Treaty revisions. The Parliament's approval of a new treaty at a future Intergovernmental Conference would be inherently conditional on it acquiring even more involvement.

Parliamentary behaviour through legal instruments has been instrumental. What started as a mere budgetary competence in CFSP matters has provided the Parliament with a much larger appetite. Garnering enthusiasm for the Parliament's positions amongst other institutional actors has been a futile exercise however. The strategy deployed by the Parliament to close the parliamentary hollow with respect to CFSP matters may be too rigorous and forthcoming for intergovernmentally minded actors to handle. It could be argued by even the most ardent integrationists that the Parliament's rough-and-ready approach – perceived power-grabbing – may be difficult to stomach at times. The wider inclusion of other institutions like the Parliament in CFSP matters may not be desirable, but at the same time, the Parliament only represents the views of European citizens and plays a role in shaping policies of all kinds from a European perspective. Despite the Parliament's quibbles and regular annoyances at its legal position, it still has a much stronger role to play in the Union's external relations than before.

One hypothesis of how CFSP matters could be improved whilst retaining their differentiation from other Union policies would be to ensure the policy was accountable to the Parliament,[401] thus providing for greater parliamentary involvement. The fear that the Parliament could become obstructionist in CFSP matters might once have been legitimate. However, recourse to law to see if this manifested itself appears to have been unfounded. The Parliament's consent powers in international agreements located in Article 218 TFEU may be read in conjunction with the sincere

[398] See Chapter 7 of this book.

[399] Ariella Huff, 'Executive Privilege Reaffirmed? Parliamentary Scrutiny of the CFSP and CSDP' (2015) 38 *West European Politics* 396 at 397.

[400] Campbell McLachlan, *Foreign Relations Law* (Cambridge University Press, 2014) p 190.

[401] Vernon Bogdanor, 'EC External Relations and the CFSP (Discussant's Remarks)' in Alan Dashwood (ed), *Reviewing Maastricht: Issues for the 1996 IGC* (Sweet and Maxwell, 1996) p 240.

cooperation (loyalty) provisions of the treaties more generally. Article 4(3) TEU provides that '[p]ursuant to the principle of sincere cooperation, the Union and the Member States shall, in full mutual respect, assist each other in carrying out tasks which flow from the [t]reaties'. With CFSP matters left outside of the Union structure for many years to 'avoid stricter Community discipline',[402] it was foreseen for many years that the Parliament would seek to actively curtail the use of CFSP legal bases. Yet, the Parliament's practice can be interpreted as a player rather than as an obstructer. This implies institutional cooperation with respect to international agreement making, meaning the Parliament cannot be an absolute obstructionist even if it wanted to.

What does the Council have to fear with respect to the Parliament? In the run-up the entering into force of the Treaty of Lisbon, the Council undertook rapid activity to conclude an international agreement before 1 December 2009 when the decision-making procedure for international agreements for non-CFSP matters was to change. Whilst it cannot be said with any level of certainty, one of the plausible reasons for wanting to rush through the international agreement pre-Lisbon, as opposed to post-Lisbon, might have been to deliberately obfuscate the Parliament's involvement. The strength of the Council in both CFSP matters and non-CFSP matters as a policy-making is still dominant.

4.7.3. Growing Parliamentary Powers

It is undeniable that the growth of powers of the Parliament over a prolonged period has inevitably led to more complicated administrative arrangements that are hidden from plain sight. In the *Mauritius* judgment, where the substance had not gone the Parliament's way, the notification grounds under Article 218(10) TFEU have cleverly been the trump card. Furthermore, Article 218(6)(a)(v) TFEU can be said to have been a 'small revolution' for EU external action.[403] Coupled with *Tanzania*, this line of case law from the Court has cautiously allowed the Parliament to delve further into CFSP matters when the Parliament has found sufficient reason when the Council has erred.

Even in the 1980s, it was said there needed to be an appropriate protection system in place to protect the Parliament's legal competence.[404] The Court's position as an adjudicator has been central to ensuring that the Parliament's competence has been upheld, but only as far as when the Parliament contests that other institutions have ignored its powers. The Parliament is institutionally becoming

[402] Renaud Dehousse and Joseph HH Weiler, 'The Legal Dimension' in William Wallace (ed), *The Dynamics of European Integration* (Pinter, 1990) p 257.

[403] De Baere, 'EU External Action' (n 127) p 743.

[404] Gerhard Bebr, 'Case C-70/88, European Parliament v. Council, Judgment of the Court of Justice of 22 May 1990' (1991) 28 *Common Market Law Review* 663 at 679.

more normal but, even so, it retains its 'federalist voice'[405] in its continuous and never-ending strife for importance. The will for the Parliament to exercise its power in CFSP matters – the former second pillar – has not diminished. With the change in EU external action infrastructure after the implementation of the Treaty of Lisbon, the parliamentary mechanisms must also keep up with transformation at the same pace.

Despite the Treaty of Lisbon changes, the powers of the Parliament in CFSP matters remain largely the same.[406] The competence of the Parliament primarily lies in policies situated in the TFEU and not to the same extent in the TEU where CFSP matters are located. The Parliament only has the capability to initiate real influence when it comes to the work of the Commission. The articles in the treaties providing for CFSP matters, whilst creating a special position in Union law *vis-à-vis* decision-making, do not allow actors to proceed alone. The provisions for CFSP matters are dependent on the articles for non-CFSP matters for particular actions, such as Article 218 TFEU for the conclusion of international agreements. Notwithstanding the case for the inclusion of the Parliament in more international agreements, it may not necessarily be the 'panacea' for law making.[407]

The Parliament's position in CFSP matters can be contrasted starkly with non-CFSP matters. To take just one example, Article 207 TFEU sets down the framework for the CCP, in which Article 207(2) TFEU is clear in defining the role of the Parliament. Moreover, there is an additional section, Article 207(3) TFEU, to ensure that the Parliament is kept fully up-to-date concerning matters falling within this legal basis. Through external relations, there has been a strengthening of the Parliament, but there is an inherent threat that the weakening of the Parliament and the strengthening of the Council in economic matters due to the ongoing financial difficulties in the Eurozone could spill over into other fields. The Parliament, in areas of its competence, can and will veto proposed legislation.[408] Its role in international agreements for non-CFSP matters like SWIFT and ACTA[409] is continuing to be a political game played out, with the institution experimenting with its competence. The Parliament would not be litigating the internal legal dimension of EU external action if it did not perceive there to be a violation of its institutional prerogatives.

There are many reasons for the Council strongly defending the nature of CFSP matters in cases such as *Mauritius* and *Tanzania*, amongst others. Whilst yielding

[405] Peter D Sutherland, 'Joining the Threads: The Influences Creating a European Union' in Deirdre Curtin and David O'Keeffe (eds), *Constitutional Adjudication in European Community and National Law: Essays for the Hon. Mr. Justice T. F. O'Higgins* (Butterworths, 1992) p 13.

[406] Piris (n 83) p 262.

[407] This claim was in reference to the flaws of international law-making. See, Mario Mendez, 'The Enforcement of EU Agreements: Bolstering the Effectiveness of Treaty Law?' (2010) 47 *Common Market Law Review* 1719 at 1726.

[408] For the first instance of where this occurred in the post-Lisbon context, see, Monar (n 161).

[409] SWIFT (Terrorist Finance Tracking Program) and ACTA (Anti-Counterfeiting Trade Agreement), See, Katharina Meissner, 'Democratizing EU External Relations: The European Parliament's Informal Role in SWIFT, ACTA and TTIP' (2016) 21 *European Foreign Affairs Review* 269.

small elements of involvement to the Parliament through revisions to the treaties in redefining the institutional balance, there is also a greater risk from the Council's perspective. Not only could the cases taken by Parliament favour greater involvement, but there is also the possibility of external EU acts being opened up to private litigants.[410] This is despite the *Sogelma* judgment from the General Court reiterating that entities subject to legal effects that have an impact on their legal position are entitled to bring actions.[411]

For the Parliament, CFSP matters are its Achilles heel, with its formal rights in CFSP matters reserved to a form of observation, information and comment.[412] National parliaments, too, have difficulty in acquiring sufficient parliamentary involvement in EU foreign policy on a national level,[413] which cannot compensate sufficiently for the Parliament's deficient position in CFSP matters. This status of the Parliament makes it more of a spectator rather than a player. Greater involvement for Parliament in the framework governing CFSP matters could be good,[414] but the treaties make no specification for this. The treaties do, however, make provision under Article 295 TFEU for an interinstitutional agreement to bring together the Council, the Commission and the Parliament to determine a greater role for the Parliament in CFSP matters, thus avoiding any forms of hard-fought litigation in front of the Court. The feasibility of an interinstitutional agreement reaching the breadth of the Parliament's anticipated aims might be far-fetched, but it would further be a step in the Parliament's aim of being treated as more of an equal player.[415] That would certainly be better than the present state of international agreements based upon a CFSP legal basis that are notified to the Parliament as a *fait accompli*.

4.7.4. Further Contestation

There is also the added quandary that it is contested whether the Parliament is, in fact, a true democratic forum for the Union's agenda. Too much Parliament

[410] For this concern in counter-piracy operations, see, Gosalbo-Bono and Boelaert (n 205) p 159.

[411] Case T-411/06, *Sogelma – Societá generale lavori manutenzioni appalti Srl v European Agency for Reconstruction*, ECLI:EU:T:2008:419, para 85. This is supported by Case C-164/02, *Netherlands v Commission*, ECLI:EU:C:2004:54, para 13 and, Case C-147/96, *Netherlands v Commission*, ECLI:EU:C:2000:335, para 25.

[412] Schmidt-Radefeldt (n 42) p 1119.

[413] For example, see, Helle Krunke, 'Development in National Parliaments' Involvement in Ordinary Foreign Policy and European Policy – Denmark' (2007) 13 *European Public Law* 335. Furthermore, see, Graham Butler, 'The Interparliamentary Conference on the CFSP/CSDP: A New Forum for the Oireachtas in Irish and EU Foreign Policy?' (2015) 26 *Irish Studies in International Affairs* 163.

[414] As advocated in, De Baere, (n 255) p 549.

[415] The European Court of Auditors noted in 2001 that the role of the Commission in CFSP matters should be clarified. To do this, it recommended an interinstitutional agreement be concluded, which should also include the Parliament. C 338/1. Court of Auditors: Special Report No 13/2001 on the Management of the Common Foreign and Security Policy (CFSP), Together with the Council's Replies and the Commission's Replies (Pursuant to Article 248(4), Second Subparagraph, EC) (2001/C 338/01). p 14. Thus, secondary law mechanisms can also assist the Parliament.

can have its downsides: too much involvement could run contrary to the effective implementation of external action. The EU's mode of government is clear in that the commanding underwriters of the treaties wish to obfuscate the Parliament wherever possible. For the Parliament, it still sees the institutional imbalance with respect to CFSP matters as a severe problem that it will continue to strive to correct. With the Parliament's practice of lunging for power, it can be labelled a 'distortion of the [t]reaties'.[416] With all the will in the world, there is no legal basis within the treaties for expanding the role of the Parliament in the decision-making procedure for CFSP matters. What is really at stake when the Parliament litigates in CFSP matters is a proxy war being fought between greater integration versus the maintenance of the *status quo*. A clear attempt to master the art of seduction has been undertaken by the Parliament at the Court, which it has not fell for, for fear of upsetting a settling institutional balance. Case law on CFSP matters shows that it is not the international agreements themselves that are being challenged, but rather that they are being used in an indirect fashion for institutional compliance with the treaties. This is similar to the litigation on international law within the Union legal order on GATT.[417]

The Parliament, whilst active, 'doesn't have a political system'.[418] On the EU stage, the Parliament's involvement consists of a limited set of formal powers as the Council remains in the firm control of the decision-making in CFSP matters. It can be concluded decisively that the Parliament has a limited role in CFSP matters, but nonetheless attempts to pursue the Council through the Court. The Parliament's future role as an 'onlooker' may continue for some time to come,[419] despite changes in the way the Parliament has cleverly litigated to grasp a better role for itself. It is important to recall that the Parliament is not alone in finding itself situated outside the usual ordinary legislative procedure for CFSP matters as the Court is a companion in feeling the wrath of the treaties regarding its own jurisdiction.

Whilst a parliament may be 'nothing less than a big meeting of more or less idle people',[420] the Parliament of the Union for now is primarily in a position for citizens to be heard. The Parliament has come a long way since the indirectly elected Assembly, whose legal powers were few and far between. In its earlier days, the strongest legal power it had was to dismiss the Commission.[421] For a long time, the EU's executive meeting in the Council commanded powers that went unchecked with no involvement whatsoever of an elected parliamentary institution. This has

[416] Jean-Claude Piris, *The Future of Europe: Towards a Two-Speed EU?* (Cambridge University Press, 2012) p 31.

[417] Robert Schütze, 'The Morphology of Legislative Power in the European Community: Legal Instruments and the Federal Division of Powers' (2006) 25 *Yearbook of European Law* 91 at 140.

[418] Philip Allott, 'Democracy, Accountability and Transparency (Discussant's Remarks)' in Alan Dashwood (ed), *Reviewing Maastricht: Issues for the 1996 IGC* (Sweet and Maxwell, 1996) p 103.

[419] Schmidt-Radefeldt (n 42) p 1120.

[420] See, Walter Bagehot, *The English Constitution* (Miles Taylor ed, Oxford University Press, 2001) p 130. Originally published in 1867.

[421] John Temple Lang, *The Common Market and Common Law* (University of Chicago Press, 1966) p 12.

been reigned in and the Council is certainly more cautious in its approach. To be substantially relevant, more involvement for the Parliament backed up by solid and binding legal provisions in primary law may be needed. While some may portray the Court as having an onus on supporting 'weaker' institutions,[422] that is by no means a consensus view. If the Parliament wants to take a formal grip on CFSP matters, beyond litigating at the Court as is its present strategy, it should seek the appropriate Treaty amendment in order for that desire to be fulfilled. If the Council wants to retain its powers in CFSP matters as it is currently, it will have to come up with justifications for this retention, despite Member States being the parties controlling the text of the treaties.

4.8. Conclusion

This chapter has exposed the legal challenge that the Parliament faces in its attempted involvement in CFSP matters, thus exposing the limiting nature on institutions that CFSP can have. Understanding the Parliament's institutional status in CFSP matters, a non-legislative area of Union law, is key to developing and building upon understanding CFSP matters as a special area of Union law, flowing from its 'specific rules and procedures'.[423] The progressive rebalancing of the treaties in favour of the Parliament is undeniable,[424] but this has had relatively slow impact upon CFSP matters. As far back as the late 1950s and early 1960s, the Parliament has 'not been happy about its relationship with the Council'.[425] It is apparent that the status of the Parliament from the outset by the High Contracting Parties was deliberate rather than an omission. Its weakening, which in the Treaty of Rome remains partly unexplained,[426] but from there, the Parliament knew it was considered for stronger institutional standing and so fought for it. It subsequently went from the 'fringes' of the EU legal order[427] to one closer to the Union's political life more generally. In CFSP matters, therefore, when the Parliament was again excluded, all it has sought to do is to have its status in CFSP matters equated to the status it has in non-CFSP matters. The logic of rules-based intergovernmentalism, the increased role of the Parliament in non-CFSP matters, and the steady nature of the law for CFSP matters was bound to continue to reach a breaking point at some juncture. Yet, that point has still not been reached.

[422] Stein (n 12) p 155.
[423] TEU, Article 24(1).
[424] Laurent Godmer and Guillaume Marrell, 'The Creation of Institutional Expertise at the European Parliament: Legal and Political Resources of the Members of the Constitutional Affairs Committee' in Antoine Vauchez and Bruno De Witte (eds), *Lawyering Europe: European Law as a Transnational Social Field* (Hart Publishing, 2013) p 154.
[425] Stein (n 26) p 64.
[426] Boerger and Davies (n 30) p 85.
[427] Paul Joan George Kapteyn and Pieter VerLoren van Themaat, *Introduction to the Law of the European Communities: After the Coming into Force of the Single European Act* (Laurence W Gormley ed., Kluwer Law and Taxation Publishers, 1989) p 145.

The Parliament is keeping account of wider trends with respect to the EU's international agreements in non-CFSP matters. In could even be said it has 'put itself on the map of international relations',[428] at least in respect of international agreements on non-CFSP matters. For example, the Parliament intervened in support of the Commission in *Australia ETS*,[429] to ensure that institutional balance in the negotiations was protected.[430] Whilst the Court did not fully address the intervention of the Parliament on its institutional role in the negotiation process,[431] it is clearly Parliament's intention to raise this point again at the correct moment. Furthermore, in *Broadcasting Organisations*,[432] the Parliament again intervened in support of the Commission in seeking an annulment of a Council Decision to open negotiations on an international agreement. The Parliament, despite pleading there was an Article 218 TFEU issue at stake, did not see this point addressed in the Court's judgment, given that the other plea was well-founded and thus, 'the contested decision must be annulled and it is unnecessary to examine the other pleas raised by the Commission in support of its action'.[433] These cases point to a wider trend that the Parliament takes an interest in all fields with an external dimension. It has tried this in previous cases, such as the in *Lomé Convention* where it was unsuccessful,[434] which proves it must carefully select the instances where it believes it has a valid plea. Saying that, from a Council perspective, it has viewed the Parliament as adhering to its 'well-known method of seizing any opportunity to increase its powers beyond the scope of the provisions in the [t]reaties'.[435]

International agreements are complex instruments where information is key to understanding their context and content. With this, adequate information being provided to decision makers is a prerequisite before informed consent can be given. Given the Council and the Parliament must decide and make informed decisions with respect to international agreements for non-CFSP matters, the Parliament could argue at future intergovernmental conferences that the time has come for it to be included in the conclusion of international agreements in CFSP matters.

[428] Christina Eckes, *EU Powers Under External Press,ure: How the EU's External Actions Alter Its Internal Structures* (Oxford University Press, 2019) p 170.

[429] Case C-425/13, *Commission v Council*, ECLI:EU:C:2015:483 ('*Australia ETS*').

[430] The Parliament had argued that the TFEU 'does not authorise the Council to adopt unilaterally new negotiation arrangements that would be imposed on the negotiator. If that were so, both the powers of the Commission, in its function as negotiator and those of the Parliament would be affected'. Case C-425/13, *Commission v Council*, ECLI:EU:C:2015:483 ('*Australia ETS*'), para 42.

[431] Passos (n 144) p 111.

[432] Case C-114/12, *Commission v Council*, ECLI:EU:C:2014:2151 ('*Broadcasting Organisations*').

[433] Ibid. para 104.

[434] Case C-316/91, *Parliament v Council*, ECLI:EU:C:1994:76 ('*Lomé Convention*') According to one perspective, 'a violation of...prerogatives is a matter of substance and not a condition for the admissibility of the action' and thus, 'if the Parliament states that the legal basis of the act in question is wrong and under the condition that the provision which in its view would have constituted the correct legal basis, contains a prerogative'. René Barents, 'Case C-316/91, Parliament v. Council, Judgment of 2 March 1994 (Full Court), [1994] ECR 1-653' (1995) 32 *Common Market Law Review* 249 at 254.

[435] Gosalbo-Bono and Naert (n 27) p 82.

The argument could even be made by the Parliament that its role is essential for the downward flow of information from the legislature to citizens. Following *Mauritius* and *Tanzania*, it could furthermore be argued that an inter-institutional agreement could be reached between the Parliament and the Council to have the 'transmission of information relating to CFSP matters' made more fluid.[436]

The Parliament in external relations is still a minor institution in comparison to its role in internal Union policies.[437] However, its powers under Article 218 TFEU have certainly been promoted for both CFSP and non-CFSP matters and the Parliament will continue to push through litigation to find the outer limits of its prerogatives under Article 218 TFEU. In fact, in non-CFSP matters, it has gone from minimal consent to formal consent. For example, when the Commission is negotiating international agreements, it would be wise to note the views of the Parliament, given its power to withhold consent. The consequences and ramifications of withholding consent are huge. Yet, post-Lisbon practice has demonstrated, some could argue, that the Parliament has used its newfound powers with 'a high sense of responsibility, fully aware of the consequences of its decisions [of] withholding consent'.[438] This is the same way it has acted in the past with respect to budgetary responsibility, whereby 'the Parliament's record demonstrates that its determination to reach compromises and to avoid deadlocked situations'.[439] By ensuring consultation with the relevant committee of the Parliament, ensuring 'avoid[ing] accepting solutions which risk becoming unacceptable' to the Parliament as well as the Council.[440] Advocates of the Parliament's involvement in the EU's external relations may still not be satisfied with Article 218 TFEU given its silence on particular aspects of the formulation of international agreements. Article 218(10) TFEU only speaks of its role in the conclusion of an international agreement and leaves out any reference to the Parliament in the opening of international negotiations, choosing the appropriate negotiator and having a say in the negotiation directives. Until this is achieved, it is unlikely that such decision-making prerogatives will reach the Parliament for CFSP matters.

The days of the Court making clear strides forward in the name of ensuring that the 'law is observed',[441] as it did in *Chernobyl*, have largely stayed in the past, but are beginning to re-emerge, for example in *Rosneft*.[442] Whilst the Court emerged 'unscathed' following *Chernobyl*,[443] grand steps forward in the future through

[436] Passos (n 144) p 128.
[437] De Baere (n 366) p 141.
[438] Passos (n 144) p 86.
[439] Paul Joan George Kapteyn, 'The European Parliament, the Budget and Legislation in the Community' (1972) 9 *Common Market Law Review* 386 at 401.
[440] Rosas (n 142) p 377.
[441] Currently manifested in the treaties through TEU, Article 19(1).
[442] Case C-72/15, *Rosneft Oil Company OJSC v Her Majesty's Treasury, The Secretary of State for Business, Innovation and Skills, The Financial Conduct Authority*, ECLI:EU:C:2017:236. Butler, 'The Coming of Age of the Court's Jurisdiction in the Common Foreign and Security Policy' (n 157). Also, see Chapter 5 of this book.
[443] Mancini and Keeling (n 71) p 185.

jurisprudence may be less likely, with judicial minimalism at work. For the Parliament to progress its institutional status as a body with a greater say in the agenda of the Union may appear to be a 'reasonable way for democratic institutions to move along.'[444] However, a greater say in the conclusion of international agreements for non-CFSP matters such as trade, cannot be equated with a greater say in the conduct of day-to-day foreign policy. With the Council having an approach where a CFSP legal basis is to be used as widely as it possibly can, the reactionary effect to this is that other institutions – like the Parliament – have attempted to narrow it through practice and litigation. It is in the Parliament's interest to get the Court to apply its reasoning – that a CFSP legal basis in TEU and a non-CFSP legal basis in TFEU should be used for international agreement. The case-by-case approach to the development of Parliament's involvement in CFSP matters appears to be the most clear-cut way forward for the Parliament, just as the Court adopts the same approach when its own jurisdiction is questioned, as will be discussed in the next chapter.

[444] James H Mathis, 'How Much Democracy Can Economic Integration Bear?' (2017) 44 *Legal Issues of Economic* Integration 1 at 2.

5

The Court of Justice and the Common Foreign and Security Policy

Beyond the place of Parliament in CFSP matters, as discussed in the previous chapter, regarding whether it should be more involved in the policy, it can be noted that the relationship that CFSP matters have with other EU institutions in the field of foreign policy has been lacking.[1] Jurisdictionally, the Court is not fully granted the same jurisdiction on CFSP matters, in textual terms, vis-à-vis other non-CFSP matters in the EU legal order. Therefore, this makes CFSP matters an unusual part of the EU legal order. Where the treaties fall short on providing a particular level of institutional guidance, the Court, when asked, ensures that the treaties and the Court's own jurisprudence on the EU legal order as a whole is adhered to. As an institution, the Court has demonstrated a healthy willingness to question the authority of other EU institutions when it believes it has overstepped the boundaries of their given authority. This is particularly evident in the constitutional law of CFSP matters. Given the lack of involvement of the Parliament in CFSP matters, it can now be assessed if a lack of parliamentary involvement in CFSP matters has been supplemented by a role for judicial involvement.

When the Union wishes to act internationally, such as, for example, when concluding international agreements, there are choices to be made regarding the agreement's legal basis, depending on the policy area. This external action creates an internal dilemma for the Union as there are choices to be made regarding the choice of legal basis for such agreements. Depending on the policy field, there can be a range of which to choose from, with the choice between a CFSP legal basis; a non-CFSP legal basis; or as of late, both. From an institutional point of view, different legal bases have consequential outcomes for a variety of EU actors. International agreements to which the Union is a party have presented particular challenges for the Court as it goes about defending the EU legal order that it itself champions.

The debate on an appropriate role for the Court as the Union's judicial body, against the powers of other institutional bodies in CFSP matters, has not yet come to full fruition. As a policy area, an eager attempt has been made by Member States

[1] Gráinne De Búrca, 'International Law Before the Courts: The EU and the US Compared' (2015) 55 *Virginia Journal of International Law* 685 at 695.

to shield CFSP matters from judicial review. This chapter proposes to understand the role of the Court in CFSP matters with regard to its constitutional status, as well as its contributory development towards EU external relations law more generally. In doing so, the chapter discusses whether there is a definitive role for the Court in CFSP matters, taking into account the specific impositions of the treaties.

The chapter begins by providing an overview of the unique circumstances of the Court's jurisdiction in CFSP matters as set down in the treaties, as well as the rationale for the limitation placed upon it. Subsequently, the nature of the Court's jurisdiction is analysed, followed by how the Court has understood such derogations on its jurisdiction. With this understanding elucidated in its judgments, it emerges that the Court has taken a rather generous institutional position towards itself, notwithstanding the explicit intent of how the treaties have attempted to construe its role.

With the treaties still entailing limited jurisdiction of the Court in CFSP matters, and the case law in no way settled, there remain outstanding questions regarding the full scope of the Court's jurisdiction. These open questions are considered in line with whether the Court ought to adopt a political question doctrine when cases are framed as legal questions, but in fact, are based upon political and policy choices. In light of the analysis, the chapter considers what the future holds for the jurisdiction of the Court in CFSP matters and argues that the direction of its case law indicates that, at a future juncture, full jurisdiction will have to be conferred upon it.

5.1. Introduction

The Court has been instrumental in the consistent development of the external relations of the EU.[2] As a constitutional system, the Union is based on the rule of law.[3] Such a conception exists because of the institutional balance the Union has developed through the numerous institutions, bodies, and agencies that form its collective being. These tasks mandated by the treaties outline the way each should operate, mostly specifying what they are bound or allowed to do; but rarely what they are not permitted to do. The role of the Court is still essential for the functioning of the Union in external relations, because the treaties are, for their users and readers, at times unclear, non-specific, and even blatantly inconsistent. This chapter addresses the jurisdictional issues and affords an opportunity

[2] Panos Koutrakos, *Trade, Foreign Policy and Defence in EU Constitutional Law: The Legal Regulation of Sanctions, Exports of Dual-Use Goods and Armaments* (Hart Publishing, 2001) p 2.

[3] It is referenced twice in the preamble to the TEU, as well as TEU, Article 2, and within external action chapter of the treaties in TEU, Article 21. See, Case C-294/83, *Parti écologiste 'Les Verts' v Parliament*, ECLI:EU:C:1986:166, and Alberto Alemanno, 'What Has Been, and What Could Be, Thirty Years after Les Verts/European Parliament' in Miguel Poiares Maduro and Loïc Azoulai (eds), *The Past and Future of EU Law: The Classics of EU Law Revisited on the 50th Anniversary of the Rome Treaty* (Hart Publishing, 2010).

to examine the state of play for the Court in CFSP matters in the post-Lisbon environment.[4] This is particularly necessary given that the Treaty of Lisbon, effective since 2009, has gone some way to strengthening the Court in CFSP matters.

The Court, in the same way as the other institutions and bodies of the Union, is responsible for the development of the Union's legal framework. It has the jurisdiction provided to it by the treaties, when requested, based on a preliminary reference or direct action, to review areas of EU external relations competence, including but not limited to, the Common Commercial Policy (CCP), development cooperation, humanitarian aid, and so forth. However, this does not cover CFSP matters which, as outlined earlier in this book, is due to the differentiated status and nature of CFSP matters as a policy field. The limitations imposed by the treaties on the Court's role in CFSP matters pose an array of challenges. Therefore, it can be asked to what extent the Court has made efforts to respect the nature of its jurisdiction in CFSP matters, whilst simultaneously upholding the EU legal order.

The manner in which the Court has jurisdiction with regard to CFSP legal acts is no straightforward issue. How it distinguishes between the legal framework for CFSP matters, and that of ordinary or normal EU external relations law, has been essential for shaping the institutional design of EU external action. However, this task is premised on sufficient jurisdiction existing for the Court to make a determination. Debate on the jurisdiction of the Court has been taking place since its inception,[5] particularly given the occasional ambiguity of its role. In the Court's earlier years, it was conscious of its own jurisdiction and the issues pertaining to it. At times, the Court has undoubtedly engaged, for one reason or another, in 'conspicuous exercises [of] gap-filling'.[6] The framework of CFSP matters is notable given the special position of the Court. Yet at the same time, there is the possibility that it can 'define the external contours of its jurisdiction'.[7] The jurisdiction of the Court is assumed competent in the substantial form, but CFSP matters appear as an exception to the rule.

With the treaties now guaranteeing TEU and TFEU harmony, it can be reasonably claimed that the choice of legal basis has become more difficult to delineate, thus increasing the potential role for the Court to define a CFSP matter. Yet, if constrained, this increased need for the Court is confounded by the treaties' attempt to continue to hold it back. As put, it is possible to 'sympathi[s]e with

[4] For example, see, Stefan Griller, 'The Court of Justice and the Common Foreign and Security Policy' in Allan Rosas, Egils Levits and Yves Bot (eds), *The Court of Justice and the Construction of Europe: Analyses and Perspectives on Sixty Years of Case-law – La Cour de Justice et la Construction de l'Europe: Analyses et Perspectives de Soixante Ans de Jurisprudence* (TMC Asser Press, 2013).

[5] For one of its earliest commentaries, see, DG Valentine, 'The Jurisdiction of the Court of Justice of the European Communities to Annul Executive Action' (1960) 36 *British Yearbook of International Law* 174.

[6] Anthony Arnull, 'Me and My Shadow: The European Court of Justice and the Disintegration of European Union Law' (2007) 31 *Fordham International Law Journal* 1174 at 1182.

[7] Koen Lenaerts, 'Direct Applicability and Direct Effect of International Law in the EU Legal Order' in Inge Govaere and others (eds), *The European Union in the World: Essays in Honour of Marc Maresceau* (Martinus Nijhoff Publishers, 2014) p 47.

[the Court] over the failure of the Member States to entrust it with judicial review of CFSP action'.[8] Yet small changes have been afoot. The wording of the treaties with regard to the Court in CFSP matters changed with the implementation of the Treaty of Lisbon. This is consistent with history given that each treaty revision has seen, with the Member States' consent, the jurisdiction of the Court expand.[9] The Treaty of Lisbon permitted the Court to make 'authoritative pronouncements' in a limited range of CFSP instruments,[10] and provided it with general jurisdiction, save for where the treaties determine otherwise, with one such area being CFSP matters.

The merging of external relations objectives by the Treaty of Lisbon should have spurred on institutional cooperation, theoretically speaking, without institutions needing to resort to the Court for adjudication. The act of finding institutional balance is made delicate given there is no Treaty-mandated guidance on what determines or shapes institutional balance. However, institutional balance is normatively understood as eliminating centralised power-holding and favouring the de-concentration of powers. As will be demonstrated, the case law has allowed the complexity and jurisdiction of the Court in CFSP matters to be played out in full before it, whilst providing lawyers with a firmer understanding of CFSP matters and how these should be maintained according to the treaties.

5.2. Situating CFSP Matters

Despite the Court being one of the main drivers behind European integration since its inception, its role in CFSP matters is obscure. As a policy, CFSP matters are at the forefront of the Union's external relations on both legal and political levels. CFSP matters has its own chapter in the TEU, nestled in Title V,[11] whereas non-CFSP matters are located elsewhere in the treaties, primarily in the TFEU. With the formal pillars no longer in existence since the Treaty of Lisbon,[12] cases coming before the Court having elements of CFSP are generally cross-policy in nature; giving rise to inherent difficulties as the treaties impose limitations on its jurisdiction. Thus, it was always going to be inevitable that the Court would be placed in positions where it is to rule on where the border between the former pillars are within the current treaties. Moreover, with the treaties not completely clear on exactly what constitutes CFSP matters, it is inevitable that it would be left to the Court to decide the extent of this boundary.

[8] Eileen Denza, 'Forging Links between Legal Orders' (2016) 35 *Yearbook of European Law* 589 at 601.

[9] R Daniel Kelemen, 'The Court of Justice of the European Union in the Twenty-First Century' (2016) 79 *Law and Contemporary Problems* 117 at 129.

[10] Geert De Baere, *Constitutional Principles of EU External Relations* (Oxford University Press, 2008) p 212.

[11] TEU, Articles 23–46.

[12] Albeit, CFSP matters are still a *de facto* hidden pillar. See Chapters 2 and 3 of this book.

The primary law of the Union restricts the jurisdiction of the Court in CFSP matters.[13] Accordingly, the boundary between CFSP matters and non-CFSP matters is difficult to place. The treaties, creating a constitutional order with cavities, somewhat vaguely delineate the limited jurisdiction of the Court in CFSP matters. Courts of law, especially those of a supreme or constitutional nature are entrusted with delimiting various actors, be they institutional or the Member States, in a constitutional order. It was not envisaged, at first, that the Court would progress in such a comprehensive way towards the development of Union law. Yet today, the Court is obliged to fill in the cavities of the treaties, ensuring a consistent interpretation of Union law through mechanisms such as direct action, preliminary references, opinions, and other types of cases.

5.2.1. The Judiciary and Foreign Policy

The issue of the judiciary and foreign policy can be a complicated one for different types of actors, be they centralised or federal states.[14] As a piecemeal structure, the EU legal order actively discriminates against certain institutions. Just as the role of the Parliament is curtailed in CFSP matters,[15] the Court is also beleaguered by constitutional hurdles. This exclusion of the Court in CFSP matters has 'puzzled some' over time.[16] It has even been said that an apparent lack of judicial supervision could make CFSP matters weak and ineffective.[17] Yet, it is too simplistic to say that the Court is excluded absolutely from CFSP matters. There are three articles in both the TEU and TFEU, which state the role of the Court when dealing with CFSP matters, namely; Article 24(1) TEU,[18] Article 40 TEU,[19] and

[13] Title V (General Provisions on the Union's External Action and Specific Provisions on the Common Foreign and Security Policy), Articles 23–46 TEU for CFSP matters, while separately, TFEU, Article 275.

[14] See, Lawrence Collins, 'Foreign Relations and the Judiciary' (2002) 51 *International and Comparative Law Quarterly* 485, and Louis Henkin, *Foreign Affairs and the United States Constitution* 2nd edition (Clarendon Press, 1996).

[15] See Chapter 4 of this book.

[16] Marise Cremona, 'The Union's External Action: Constitutional Perspectives' in Giuliano Amato, Hervé Bribosia and Bruno De Witte (eds), *Genesis and Destiny of the European Constitution: Commentary on the Treaty establishing a Constitution for Europe in the light of the travaux préparatoires and future prospects* (Bruylant, 2007) p 1198.

[17] Piet Eeckhout, *EU External Relations Law* 2nd edition (Oxford University Press, 2011) p 172.

[18] TEU, Article 24(1), para 2: '…The Court of Justice of the European Union shall not have jurisdiction with respect to these provisions [the Common Foreign and Security Policy], with the exception of its jurisdiction to monitor compliance with Article 40 of this Treaty and to review the legality of certain decisions as provided for by the second paragraph of Article 275 of the Treaty on the Functioning of the European Union.'

[19] TEU, Article 40: 'The implementation of the common foreign and security policy shall not affect the application of the procedures and the extent of the powers of the institutions laid down by the [t]reaties for the exercise of the Union competence[] referred to in Articles 3 to 6 of the Treaty on the Functioning of the European Union. Similarly, the implementation of the policies listed in those Articles shall not affect the application of the procedures and the extent of the powers of the institutions laid down by the [t]reaties for the exercise of the Union competence[] under this Chapter [Specific Provision on the Common Foreign and Security Policy].'

Article 275 TFEU.[20] Whilst the three articles are there to exclude the Court in CFSP matters, it does not necessarily mean that CFSP matters are entirely immune from oversight of the judiciary at Union level. The general jurisdiction conferred upon the Court grants it some discretion to weigh in on certain CFSP matters, which has allowed it to tread carefully in a guarded legal minefield. As such, therefore, the jurisdiction of the Court is often understated.

By looking at what the judiciary of the Union does in CFSP matters, we can view this in contrast with its role in non-CFSP external relations in an effort to examine how the Court manages judicial review in CFSP matters. With the wording of Article 24(1) TEU stating that the Court does 'not have jurisdiction with respect to [CFSP matters]', it has been suggested that the Court should not find itself in a position to ignore the provisions of the treaties on CFSP matters in their entirety. Rather, it should be read that it must consider them when interpreting and applying provisions from elsewhere in the treaties.[21]

Assessments of what a court of law's role should be ranges from a norm elaborator to an enforcer. Yet, with respect to one of its primary functions, judicial review, the Court has a recognised 'monopoly' on the activities of EU institutions.[22] Despite the Union being depillarised by the Treaty of Lisbon, the ring-fenced nature of CFSP matters remained.[23] Actions on a CFSP legal basis are non-legislative, therefore, not subject to the ordinary legislative procedure that governs nearly every other part of Union decision-making. With Article 19(1) TEU stating the Court 'shall ensure that in the interpretation and application of the [t]reaties the law is observed', it implicitly means that it can, to a certain degree, have jurisdiction in CFSP matters. This must be reconciled by the Court ensuring that Union law is observed, despite it being partially excluded from so doing. Article 19 TEU says that the Court 'shall' ensure that the interpretation and application of the treaties are observed, and likewise, that EU Member States 'shall' make remedies sufficient for effective legal protection in Union law. Consequently, the most audacious reading suggests that it must mean that the breadth of Article 19 TEU alone could override the attempted exclusion of the Court in CFSP matters. As will become apparent when the case law is analysed, the Court is certainly veering in this direction.

[20] TFEU, Article 275: 'The Court of Justice of the European Union shall not have jurisdiction with respect to the provisions relating to the common foreign and security policy nor with respect to acts adopted on the basis of those provisions. However, the Court shall have jurisdiction to monitor compliance with Article 40 of the Treaty on European Union and to rule on proceedings, brought in accordance with the conditions laid down in the fourth para of Article 263 of this Treaty, reviewing the legality of decisions providing for restrictive measures against natural or legal persons adopted by the Council on the basis of Chapter 2 of Title V of the Treaty on European Union.'

[21] Cremona (n 16) p 1199.

[22] View of Advocate General Kokott, Opinion 2/13, ECLI:EU:C:2014:2475 ('*Accession of the European Union to the European Convention for the Protection of Human Rights*'), para 101.

[23] For more on this, see, Paul James Cardwell, 'On "Ring-Fencing" the Common Foreign and Security Policy in the Legal Order of the European Union' (2013) 64 *Northern Ireland Legal Quarterly* 443.

5.2.2. Judicial Exclusion

It must be queried why the Court would have such a restrictive role in CFSP matters to begin with. The reasons for the Court's exclusion are numerous, ranging from the idea that foreign policy actions are at the height of political sensitivity to the short-term nature of some CFSP matters. The reasons why the Union's judiciary might not be legally gifted when it comes to some aspects of EU external action has been eloquently put by a former member of the Court: '[f]oreign policy decisions have a different kind of complexity, however: the relevant facts, the evaluation of risks, the necessary contacts, the responsibility for the consequences, they are all beyond the area of judicial investigation'.[24] Another reason is that CFSP matters are a mix of political and legal thinking[25] and that acts of foreign policy are not always hard legislative instruments. Rather, CFSP matters tend to be legal decisions that cannot be subjugated to intense scrutiny compared to other acts of public policy. From that perspective, foreign policy on a CFSP legal basis may be much more legal than foreign policy instruments, if any, in Member States. However, the most curious theory for deliberate continued judicial exclusion would be that judges would come with a background where they had elaborated on the doctrine of EU external relations law; and that such integrationist thinking would not necessarily be in conformity with the views of other more traditional international lawyers, who naturally could be much closer to assuming more state sovereignty.[26]

The Court, in the same way as the other institutional and non-international actors of the Union, is responsible for the development of the Union's legal framework. With the exception of restrictive measures and the delimitation of CFSP matters and non-CFSP matters, an Advocate General has said that the role of the Court in CFSP matters is 'highly regrettable from the aspect of integration policy'.[27] It can be said that the Member States were reluctant to see judicial aspects of their foreign, security, and defence affairs to a judiciary beyond the state,[28] as it could be perceived as a renunciation of sovereign rights. This hesitance of the Member States can be traced to a level of suspicion of the Court when it comes to judicial involvement; for fear the Court would attempt to assert itself as the ultimate decisive arbiter and depart from existing in a purely judicial domain. It was the belief of Member States that issues such as that should be disjointed from what

[24] Thijmen Koopmans, *Courts and Political Institutions: A Comparative View* (Cambridge University Press, 2003) p 101.

[25] David AO Edward, 'Is Art L of the Maastricht Treaty Workable?' in Georg Ress, Jürgen Schwarze and Torsten Stein (eds), *Die Organe der Europäischen Union im Spannungsfeld zwischen Gemeinschaft und Zusammenarbeit* (Nomos, 1995) p 23.

[26] Eileen Denza, *The Intergovernmental Pillars of the European Union* (Oxford University Press, 2002) p 312.

[27] View of Advocate General Kokott, Opinion 2/13, ECLI:EU:C:2014:2475 ('*Accession of the European Union to the European Convention for the Protection of Human Rights*'), para 101.

[28] Maria-Gisella Garbagnati Ketvel, 'The Jurisdiction of the European Court of Justice in Respect of the Common Foreign and Security Policy' (2006) 55 *International and Comparative Law Quarterly* 77 at 79.

they feared to be an overly eager Court to engage in 'judicial activism'.[29] Qualms against activism and integrationalism may be perceived, but this does not justify a position without taking an objective viewpoint. Whilst this crusading charge is nothing new to the debate, the Court has, more generally, defended itself against such charges.[30]

Member States of the Union did not waste much time disenfranchising the Court in CFSP matters when it was first being incorporated into the treaties.[31] Following the Treaty of Maastricht, the Treaty of Amsterdam was the first occasion on which the Court was given jurisdiction within the TEU.[32] Even the Constitutional Treaty, which arguably went further than the Treaty of Lisbon on integration, had not proposed absolute jurisdiction for the Court in CFSP matters. For the Constitutional Treaty, the jurisdictional concerns for the Court in CFSP matters were again highlighted, being described as 'potentially damaging'.[33] However, during these deliberations on the Constitutional Treaty, judicial control of CFSP matters or non-CFSP external relations as a whole was not in any way central to the discussion.[34] There were some notable exceptions in the discussion about the exclusion of the Court's jurisdiction in CFSP matters.[35] It nonetheless continued to exclude the jurisdiction of the Court,[36] but provided it with a monitoring

[29] Ramses A Wessel, 'Resisting Legal Facts: Are CFSP Norms as Soft as They Seem?' (2015) 20 *European Foreign Affairs Review* 123 at 137.

[30] Michael Dougan, 'Judicial Activism or Constitutional Interaction? Policymaking by the ECJ in the Field of Union Citizenship' in Hans-Wolfgang Micklitz and Bruno De Witte (eds), *The European Court of Justice and the Autonomy of the Member States* (Intersentia, 2012) p 114.

[31] Joseph HH Weiler, 'The Autonomy of the Community Legal Order: Through the Looking Glass' in Joseph HH Weiler (ed), *The Constitution of Europe: 'Do the New Clothes Have an Emperor?' and Other Essays on European Integration* (Cambridge University Press, 1999) p 313.

[32] See, Albertina Albors-Llorens, 'Changes in the Jurisdiction of the European Court of Justice under the Treaty of Amsterdam' (1998) 35 *Common Market Law Review* 1273. Furthermore, Nial Fennelly, 'Jurisdiction of the Court of Justice Following the Entry into Force of the Treaty of Amsterdam' [1999] European Parliament: Liberty, Security, Justice: An Agenda for Europe, Working Document, Civil Liberties Series, LIBE 106 EN 19. p 24.

[33] See, 'Editorial: The CFSP under the EU Constitutional Treaty? Issues of Depillarisation' (2005) 42 *Common Market Law Review* 325.

[34] Bruno De Witte, 'The Constitutional Law of External Relations' in Ingolf Pernice and Miguel Poiares Maduro (eds), *A Constitution for the European Union: First Comments on the 2003 Draft of the European Convention* (Nomos, 2004) p 105.

[35] Koen Lenaerts and Damien Gerard, 'The Structure of the Union According to the Constitution for Europe: The Emperor Is Getting Dressed' (2004) 29 *European Law Review* 289 at 303.

[36] Article III-376: 'The Court of Justice of the European Union shall not have jurisdiction with respect to Articles I-40 and I-41 and the provisions of Chapter II of Title V concerning the common foreign and security policy and Article III-293 insofar as it concerns the common foreign and security policy. However, the Court shall have jurisdiction to monitor compliance with Article III-308 and to rule on proceedings, brought in accordance with the conditions laid down in Article III-365(4), reviewing the legality of European decisions providing for restrictive measures against natural or legal persons adopted by the Council on the basis of Chapter II of Title V.' For discussion on this point, Takis Tridimas, 'The European Court of Justice and the Draft Constitution: A Supreme Court for the Union?' in Takis Tridimas and Paolisa Nebbia (eds), *European Union Law for the Twenty-First Century: Rethinking the New Legal Order – Volume 1: Constitutional and Public Law, External Relations* (Hart Publishing, 2004) p 128.

compliance role.[37] When the Constitutional Treaty keeled over, and the time came to bring forward the Treaty of Lisbon, the wording of the treaties with regard to the Court in CFSP matters changed, to provide what is today Article 24 TEU, Articles 40 TEU and 275 TFEU. To comprehend the provisions properly, they should be read together, despite being separated in the treaties.

5.2.3. The (Limited) Judicial Inclusion

The Court has previously been of the opinion that when the competence of the Union is at issue, prior to the existence of what is now Article 40 TEU, the Court could not be excluded entirely.[38] Accordingly, the Court must ensure that institutions, in whatever form, maintain the appropriate relationship in CFSP matters according to the respective roles that are prescribed for them in the treaties. The absence of an efficient legal mechanism to establish the consistency between CFSP matters and non-CFSP matters has been an issue that has been highlighted for some time.[39] Article 40 TEU provides the Court with a competence to scrutinise acts on a CFSP legal basis to the extent that it does not encroach upon the competence entrusted upon other EU institutions. Article 40 TEU can also be used by the Court to prevent the legislature from using implied powers conferred on the Union from expanding further,[40] ensuring that the 'ring-fenced' nature of CFSP matters continues. Its intent has been to protect institutions favouring one legal basis over another.[41] Under pre-Lisbon rules, Article 40 TEU (then Article 47 TEU) mandated that nothing in the TEU, and therefore CFSP matters, could affect the European Communities, implying that CFSP matters should not venture into policies of the treaties, but policies in the treaties might encroach into CFSP matters. However, post-Lisbon, this was changed to ensure mutual non-encroachment. The exclusionary ideal of the Member States intending to leave the Court out of CFSP matters has faded given this limited judicial inclusion.

The treaties specify that the Court's jurisdiction in CFSP matters can be split into general categories. The first category is the power to decide whether to accept jurisdiction in CFSP matters at all; and secondly, to examine the limits of CFSP matters as a legally distinct field, ensuring it does not encroach upon the other

[37] Articles III-308 and III-365. Ricardo Passos and Stephan Marquardt, 'International Agreements – Competences, Procedures and Judicial Control' in Amato, Bribosia and De Witte (n 16) p 911.

[38] This principle was evident in Case C-124/95 *The Queen, ex parte Centro-Com Srl v HM Treasury and Bank of England*, ECLI:EU:C:1997:8.

[39] Jörg Monar, 'The European Union's Foreign Affairs System after the Treaty of Amsterdam: A "Strengthened Capacity for External Action"?' (1997) 2 *European Foreign Affairs Review* 413 at 434.

[40] Theodore Konstadinides, 'EU Foreign Policy under the Doctrine of Implied Powers: Codification Drawbacks and Constitutional Limitations' (2014) 39 *European Law Review* 511 at 523.

[41] Marise Cremona, 'Defining Competence in EU External Relations: Lessons from the Treaty Reform Process' in Alan Dashwood and Marc Maresceau (eds), *Law and Practice of EU External Relations: Salient Features of a Changing Landscape* (Cambridge University Press, 2008) p 45.

matters vested in other Treaty provisions. The first scenario for Article 275 TFEU, which was newly inserted in the Treaty of Lisbon, is when the legality of acts on a CFSP legal basis are challenged on the grounds of an act going beyond CFSP matters and encroach upon other areas of Union competence.[42] However, the second scenario covers the legality of restrictive measures adopted on a CFSP legal basis. The Court has confirmed, following the General Court,[43] that it does not have jurisdiction 'to take cognisance of an action seeking to assess the lawfulness',[44] showing there is a limit to how generously the Court construes its jurisdiction given the limitations. Whilst the absolute specificity of CFSP matters has started to wane,[45] a number of judgments suggest that any extension of the Court's jurisdiction through interpretation can be both accepted and rejected,[46] demonstrating that it can interpret both the breadth and limits of its jurisdiction in a manner that is in compliance against and with the intentions of the drafters.

5.3. A Constrained Court?

With this unusual place of the Court with respect to CFSP matters, as a policy area, it is said to have incomplete judicial 'coverage',[47] and that the 'precise contours' of the Court's jurisdiction in CFSP matters is not a fully painted picture.[48] Member States have attempted to shelter CFSP matters from other prevailing integrationist forces that is dominant in other policy fields. Aside from the initial moves to marginalise it, the jurisdiction of the Court has been expanding throughout Treaty revision over the decades. Pre-Lisbon, the Court had little jurisdiction in the TEU

[42] Pieter Jan Kuijper, Jan Wouters, Frank Hoffmeister, Geert De Baere and Thomas Ramopoulos, *The Law of EU External Relations: Cases, Materials, and Commentary on the EU as an International Legal Actor* (Oxford: Oxford University Press, 2013) p 863. TFEU, Article 275 has been labelled as being 'deeply regrettable', for it 'effectively replace[s] the "rule of law" with the rule of the executive'. Robert Schütze, *European Union Law* 2nd edition (Cambridge University Press, 2018) p 353.

[43] Case T-509/10, *Manufacturing Support & Procurement Kala Naft Co, Tehran v Council*, ECLI:EU:T:2012:201.

[44] Case C-348/12 P, *Council v Manufacturing Support & Procurement Kala Naft Co, Tehran*, ECLI:EU:C:2013:776, para 99. In that case, L 195/39. Council Decision of 26 July 2010 Concerning Restrictive Measures against Iran and Repealing Common Position 2007/140/CFSP.

[45] Christophe Hillion, 'A Powerless Court? The European Court of Justice and the Common Foreign and Security Policy' in Marise Cremona and Anne Thies (eds), *The European Court of Justice and External Relations Law: Constitutional Challenges* (Hart Publishing, 2014) and also 'The Protection of Fundamental Rights in the EU Common Foreign and Security Policy – "A Half Measure"?' (2016) 19 *Europarättslig Tidskrift* 45 at 46.

[46] Compare, for instance, to the standing issue outside of CFSP matters in, for example, Case C-583/11 P, *Inuit Tapiriit Kanatami and Others v Parliament and Council*, ECLI:EU:C:2013:625.

[47] Ricardo Gosalbo-Bono and Sonja Boelaert, 'The European Union's Comprehensive Approach to Combating Piracy at Sea: Legal Aspects' in Panos Koutrakos and Achilles Skordas (eds), *The Law and Practice of Piracy at Sea: European and International Perspectives* (Hart Publishing, 2014) p 158.

[48] Opinion of Advocate General Wahl, Case C-455/14 P, *H v Council*, ECLI:EU:C:2016:212, para 2.

more generally,[49] and the default position was that it was not entitled to rule in non-Community fields, unless so provided.[50] As a result, CFSP matters were not the only area where judicial control was subject to restrictions in the past.

The Court's role was restricted in third pillar matters too, with its own set of restrictions; the Court's authority in Police and Judicial Cooperation (PJC) was also circumscribed.[51] Both second (CFSP matters) and third pillars (JHA matters) were perceived as being at the heart of the competence of Member States. Today, the Court is assumed to have jurisdiction in all areas of the treaties, unless otherwise specified, such as its attempted exclusion in CFSP matters. Article 276 TFEU also prohibits the Court from having jurisdiction in matters of internal security or proportionality by law enforcement.[52] With the treaties not completely clear on the exact limits of CFSP matters, it is inevitable that it will be left to the Court, with its limited remit, to decide the extent of this perceived boundary.

5.3.1. Handling Exclusion

Ever since CFSP matters have been contained within the treaties, the Court's jurisdiction has not significantly altered from the explicit mandate it was given by the Member States at the Intergovernmental Conferences. However, when they have been altered, it has been to a narrow degree to ensure individual rights are protected. This exclusion of the Court in CFSP matters has extended right through from the Treaty of Maastricht in the then Article L[53] to the present post-Lisbon environment. Despite the Court's expansion into new areas, particularly after the Treaty of Maastricht,[54] its jurisdiction in CFSP matters has not been significantly increased. Saying that, other developments over a longer period of time have effected the Court's jurisprudence. Given that the Single European Act (SEA) moved some policy fields from unanimity to qualified majority voting, this could

[49] David AO Edward and Robert Lane, *Edward and Lane on European Union Law* (Edward Elgar, 2013) p 176 (S 5.27).

[50] TEU, Article 46, pre-Lisbon.

[51] Steve Peers, 'Who's Judging the Watchmen? The Judicial System of the "Area of Freedom Security and Justice"' (1998) 18 *Yearbook of European Law* 337. Furthermore, John A Usher, 'Variable Geometry or Concentric Circles: Patterns for the European Union' (1997) 46 *International and Comparative Law Quarterly* 243 at 252, and Passos and Marquardt (n 37) p 991.

[52] The precise wording reads '...the Court of Justice of the European Union shall have no jurisdiction to review the validity or proportionality of operations carried out by the police or other law-enforcement services of a Member State or the exercise of the responsibilities incumbent upon Member States with regard to the maintenance of law and order and the safeguarding of internal security'. For more on TFEU, Article 276, see, Alicia Hinarejos, *Judicial Control in the European Union: Reforming Jurisdiction in the Intergovernmental Pillars* (Oxford University Press, 2009) pp 109–111.

[53] For more on Article L at the Treaty of Maastricht, see, Denis J Edwards, 'Fearing Federalism's Failure: Subsidiarity in the European Union' (1996) 44 *American Journal of Comparative Law* 537 at 533.

[54] Maja Brkan, 'The Role of the European Court of Justice from Maastricht to Lisbon: Putting Together the Scattered Pieces of Patchwork' in Maartje De Visser and Anne Pieter Van Der Mei (eds), *The Treaty on European Union 1993–2013: Reflections from Maastricht* (Intersentia, 2013) p 77.

have been a licence for the Court to act in a more 'aggressive' manner in instilling certain virtues,[55] such as institutional balance, rights of individuals and its own jurisdiction.

The pillarised Union, introduced at the Treaty of Maastricht, in a circumventive fashion put a limit on the powers of EU institutions. This ultimately meant delineation between different policies and difficulties in linking different areas of the treaties.[56] With the Court as a self-imposed proponent of the Union's external competence, it has engaged in bringing forward the concept of parallelism.[57] Where competence of the Union is held, this could allow it to engage externally, thereby preventing Member States from encroaching into the same sphere. This *ERTA* doctrine permitted external powers deriving from internal competence.[58] The Court, whilst possessing strength in shaping the Union legal order as a whole, has not played a strong role in shaping policy choices in external relations.[59] In non-CFSP matters, for example, the Court has only ever found that the external powers of the Union were misused.[60] On CFSP matters, as will be demonstrated, it has correspondingly stuck to jurisdiction, legal basis and other related matters, without pondering questions of wider significance.

The basis for judicial exclusion at Union level from CFSP matters may have been a precautionary measure. The Court ruled in *Pupino*,[61] pre-Lisbon, that indirect effect was to be read across from the third pillar (JHA matters).[62] However, it had other implications. Concern may have focused on how the then first pillar of the legal order would fall into the third pillar. The temptation was that Member States would use a third pillar legal basis; the question might have arisen as to what extent third pillar measures would prevent the use of a first pillar legal basis. Cases such as this led to 'legal ad-hocery',[63] as debate seethed over Court jurisdiction in the area.

[55] Koen Lenaerts, 'Some Thoughts About the Interaction Between Judges and Politicians in the European Community' (1992) 12 *Yearbook of European Law* 1 at pp 24–25.

[56] José Luís da Cruz Vilaça, *EU Law and Integration: Twenty Years of Judicial Application of EU Law* (Hart Publishing, 2014) p 95.

[57] Gerard Conway, *The Limits of Legal Reasoning and the European Court of Justice* (Cambridge University Press, 2012) p 241.

[58] Case C-22/70, *Commission v Council*, ECLI:EU:C:1971:32 ('*European Road Transport Agreement*'), better known as '*ERTA*'. See, Paolo Mengozzi, 'The EC External Competencies: From the ERTA Case to the Opinion in the Lugano Convention' in Miguel Poiares Maduro and Loïc Azoulai (eds), *The Past and Future of EU Law: The Classics of EU Law Revisited on the 50th Anniversary of the Rome Treaty* (Hart Publishing, 2010).

[59] See, Graham Butler, 'In Search of the Political Question Doctrine in EU Law' (2018) 45 *Legal Issues of Economic Integration* 329. Also, Marise Cremona, 'A Reticent Court? Policy Objectives and the Court of Justice' in Cremona and Thies (n 45).

[60] As noted in, Marise Cremona, 'Structural Principles and Their Role in EU External Relations Law' in Marise Cremona (ed), *Structural Principles in EU External Relations Law* (Hart Publishing, 2018) p 4.

[61] Case C-105/03, *Criminal Proceedings against Maria Pupino*, ECLI:EU:C:2005:386 ('*Pupino*').

[62] See, Maria Fletcher, 'Extending "Indirect Effect" to the Third Pillar: The Significance of Pupino?' (2005) 30 *European Law Review* 862.

[63] Bruno De Witte, 'Chameleonic Member States: Differentiation by Means of Partial and Parallel International Agreements' in Bruno De Witte, Dominik Hanf and Ellen Vos (eds), *The Many Faces of Differentiation in EU Law* (Intersentia, 2001) p 261.

5.3.2. Finding a Balance

On a number of occasions, the Court has used its judicial role to underscore the primacy of the treaties over international obligations.[64] When it came to defining the scope of competence for various external measures when the Union possess external competence, the Court has little issue in defining where the balance lies.[65] Much of the balance is 'ultimately in the hands of the Court',[66] putting it in an extremely powerful position. Consistent case law from the Court suggests that when selecting a legal basis for a particular measure, an objective test should be applied by the legal service of the institution, agency or body in question to ensure that the legal basis is correct and subject to judicial review.

One of the gripping issues in CFSP matters has been the question of the legal basis of certain international agreements that the Union wishes to enter into. There are often a number of choices that are available for the EU negotiating party when looking towards the conclusion and ratification of an international agreement. If an international agreement is proposed and it relates principally to CFSP matters, the Court does not have the competence to examine the legality of the Council's CFSP Decision regarding the conclusion of the agreement. However, problems arise when the Court is asked to decide whether a particular agreement is 'principally' a CFSP matter. This results in Article 40 TEU being deployed to determine where the balance of a particular external measure lies, as will be subsequently evident.

5.3.3. National Courts

Turning to national courts, there is in nothing, in theory, to prevent national courts in EU Member States from ruling on CFSP matters, but only as regards the effects of CFSP matters within their respective national legal orders. This thereby makes CFSP matters subject to mixed judicial control in a multilevel judicial field. It is not customary for the national courts of most Member States to have much association or involvement with the foreign policy of the Member State in which a national court exercises jurisdiction. However, this can principally be asserted because national governments have inherent competence to conduct foreign policy matters,[67] which are usually of a political and policy nature, as opposed being legally binding in the same manner of national legislation.

[64] Daniel Thym, 'Foreign Affairs' in Armin Von Bogdandy and Jürgen Bast (eds), *Principles of European Constitutional Law* 2nd edition (Hart Publishing, 2009) p 327.

[65] For example, Case C-467/98, *Commission v Denmark*, ECLI:EU:C:2002:625 ('*Open Skies*').

[66] Pieter Jan Kuijper, 'Recent Tendencies in the Separation of Powers in EU Foreign Relations: An Essay' in Eleftheria Neframi and Mauro Gatti (eds), *Constitutional Issues of EU External Relations Law* (Nomos, 2018) pp 214–215.

[67] That national foreign policy must be in accordance with decided EU foreign policy, for which Member States are bound by the duty and obligation of sincere cooperation.

For national courts, *Foto-Frost* is a judgment of the Court worth reiterating.[68] It firmly stated that a national court cannot invalidate a legal act of the EU. Instead, that role is squarely a prerogative of the Court. However, the difficulty arises when a discrepancy arises between Union acts conducted on a CFSP legal basis and this comes into conflict with the domestic laws of a particular Member State.

Whilst a national court cannot annul a legal act on a CFSP legal basis (or any EU legal act for that matter), it can invalidate the implementing acts taken within that national context stemming from a legal act on a CFSP legal basis, subject to its own national restrictions. As part of Operation Atalanta (EUNAVFOR), to which the *Mauritius* judgment is linked, a national court in Germany was faced with a question of German involvement on fundamental rights grounds.[69] The applicant failed to have the national measures as part of the CSDP operation within the legal framework invalidated. In such instance, a preliminary reference to the Court may not be possible because of its exemptions, as will be later discussed in the *Rosneft* case.[70] Therefore, whilst the Court has a constrained role in CFSP matters; it is nonetheless provided with the power to define the limit of this external competence on all external action, including on CFSP matters,[71] even though national courts cannot invalidate CFSP legal acts.

5.3.4. Judicial Engagement

Cases heard by the Court have challenged acts on a CFSP legal basis on the grounds that an action goes beyond what is understood as a CFSP matter and extends into other areas of Union competence.[72] The Court is obliged to balance the autonomy of the Union's own legal order against its own position in CFSP matters, as the judiciary of the Union, against a potentially non-judicially reviewable policy field. Given the general jurisdiction of the Court provided by Article 19 TEU, the derogation stemming from Article 275 TFEU can be interpreted either broadly or narrowly.

[68] Case C-314/85, *Foto-Frost v Hauptzollamt Lübeck-Ost*, ECLI:EU:C:1987:452. See, Michael Dougan, *National Remedies Before the Court of Justice: Issues of Harmonisation and Differentiation* (Hart Publishing, 2004) p 320.

[69] *Feststellung der Rechtswidrigkeit der Festnahme eines somalischen Staatsangehörigen im Golf von Aden von der deutschen Bundesmarine wegen des Verdachts eines (versuchten) seeräuberischen Angriffs (hier: Militäroperation Atalanta)* (Determination of the illegality of the arrest of a Somali national in the Gulf of Aden by the German Federal Navy on suspicion of a (attempted) piracy attack (Operation Atalanta), Oberverwaltungsgericht (OVG) (Administrative High Court) North Rhine-Westphalia (NRW), 4 A 2948/11, Germany, 18 September 2014. This case is referenced in, Hillion, (n 45) p 55.

[70] Case C-72/15, *Rosneft Oil Company OJSC v Her Majesty's Treasury, The Secretary of State for Business, Innovation and Skills, The Financial Conduct Authority*, ECLI:EU:C:2016:381.

[71] Piet Eeckhout, *External Relations of the European Union: Legal and Constitutional Foundations* (Oxford University Press, 2004) p 163.

[72] For example, see, Case C-91/05, *Commission v Council*, ECLI:EU:C:2008:288 ('*ECOWAS*'); Case C-403/05, *Parliament v Commission*, ECLI:EU:C:2007:624 ('*Philippines Border Management*'); Case C-658/11, *Parliament v Council*, ECLI:EU:C:2014:2025 ('*Mauritius*'); and Case C-263/14, *Parliament v Council*, ECLI:EU:C:2016:435 ('*Tanzania*').

The Court has not in any way attempted to shy away from CFSP matters, in fact, quite the opposite.[73] This has long been a dreaded scenario for the High Contracting Parties. In the Treaty of Maastricht, the restriction of the Court in CFSP matters may not have been as rigid as Member States wanted it to be.[74] As will be seen, the levering open of jurisdiction to the Court has happened incrementally. The use of the flexibility clause to bring new areas into Union law has also opened up those areas to the jurisdiction of the Court,[75] despite the flexibility clause having an external limit;[76] and in its present form, it cannot be used for CFSP matters.[77]

The Court has itself stated that, pre-Lisbon, its position with respect to CFSP matters was less extensive than the TEU as a whole.[78] The General Court said that a budgetary element of CFSP matters in the then second pillar meant the Court had the jurisdiction to hear a case, even though it centred on CFSP matters.[79] On appeal, this was an interpretation recommended to be upheld by the Advocate General,[80] and was later affirmed by the Court.[81] There is no equivalent of the former Article 46 TEU in the treaties post-Lisbon, but this small change from limited jurisdiction to assumed jurisdiction, albeit significant,[82] meant derogations on the Court's jurisdiction had to be imposed in specific areas. Yet, this has not meant that CFSP legal acts escape the jurisdiction of the Court entirely. Both the *Gestoras* and *Segi* cases implied that the exceptions applied to the jurisdiction of the Court should be read in a narrow manner,[83] and supervision by the Court can be conducted.

With international agreements having their position based within international law, the jurisdiction of the Court could be said to be limited to annulling internal Union acts. This limits the Court to annulling a Council Decision internally within

[73] In fact, it recently said it 'cannot, for want of jurisdiction'. See, Opinion 2/13, ECLI:EU:C:2014:2454 ('*Accession of the European Union to the European Convention for the Protection of Human Rights*'), para 253.

[74] See, Nanette Neuwahl, 'Foreign and Security Policy and the Implementation of the Requirement of "Consistency" under the Treaty on European Union' in David O'Keeffe and Patrick M Twomey (eds), *Legal Issues of the Maastricht Treaty* (Chancery, 1994).

[75] See, Graham Butler, 'The EU Flexibility Clause Is Dead, Long Live the EU Flexibility Clause' in Antonina Bakardjieva Engelbrekt and Xavier Groussot (eds), *The Future of Europe: Political and Legal Integration Beyond Brexit* (Hart Publishing, 2019).

[76] Robert Schütze, 'From Rome to Lisbon: "Executive Federalism" in the (New) European Union' (2010) 47 *Common Market Law Review* 1385 at 1410.

[77] See Chapter 3 of this book.

[78] Case C-355/04 P, *Segi, Arait, Zubimendi Izaga, and Aritza Galarraga v Council*, ECLI:EU:C:2007:116 ('*Segi*'), para 50.

[79] Case T-231/04, *Hellenic Republic (Greece) v Commission*, ECLI:EU:T:2007:9, para 74.

[80] Opinion of Advocate General Mazák, Case C-203/07 P, *Hellenic Republic (Greece) v Commission*, ECLI:EU:C:2008:270, para 54.

[81] Case C-203/07 P, *Hellenic Republic (Greece) v Commission*, ECLI:EU:C:2008:606, para 40.

[82] Gavin Barrett, 'Creation's Final Laws: The Impact of the Treaty of Lisbon on the "Final Provisions" of Earlier Treaties' (2008) 27 *Yearbook of European Law* 3 at 37.

[83] Case C-354/04 P, *Gestoras Pro Amnistía, Juan Mari Olano Olano, Julen Zelarain Errasti v Council*, ECLI:EU:C:2007:115, para 53, and Case C-355/04 P, *Segi, Arait, Zubimendi Izaga, and Aritza Galarraga v Council*, ECLI:EU:C:2007:116 ('*Segi*'), para 53. As noted, certain parts of the two judgments were 'practically identical'. Koen Lenaerts, 'The Rule of Law and the Coherence of the Judicial System of the European Union' (2007) 44 *Common Market Law Review* 1625 at 1630.

Union law, whilst maintaining the external effects to be consistent with the international legal principle of *pacta sunt seventa*.[84] With restrictive measures, which are partly grounded on a CFSP legal basis through a CFSP Decision on Article 29 TEU, and a non-CFSP Regulation on Article 215 TFEU, the Court does have the jurisdiction to examine if such measures impose on other Union competence.[85] With this array of cases where it has explicit jurisdiction for individuals, a high number of cases are appealed to the General Court,[86] and on occasion appealed up to the Court. Thus, where the Court is not specifically prevented from ruling on the legality of restrictive measures against persons, groups, or bodies, it may be construed that allowing the Court to have a limited amount of judicial insight in CFSP matters, in essence, allows for the gradual opening of CFSP matters to full judicial review.

5.4. Questioning Jurisdiction

Judicial review is characteristically a power struggle between an applicant and a respondent. As much as it may seem that it does not want to embattle itself in such situations, the Court adopts an objective, as opposed to a subjective, test to assist in its judgments with respect to external relations.[87] By taking an objective approach to the cases before it, the Court looks to both the purpose of the act and its overarching aim in each cases, before reaching a decision. In CFSP matters, it is clear that the Court, first and foremost, has to answer questions about its own jurisdiction to rule, if such jurisdiction is disputed. The Court has been requested on many occasions to rule on complex cases relating to CFSP matters. To resolve inter-institutional conflict and decipher the exact position of the Court concerning review of CFSP matters, it is necessary to outline the positions it has previously taken on this issue.

Adjudication by the Court has increased rapidly in the past fifteen years,[88] It has always been subconsciously examining itself to ensure its efficiency and prudence in dealing with the matters that have come before it. With EU foreign policy being contested on a legal basis and other technical intricacies, battle lines have been drawn between different legal actors. With the EU formerly a pillar

[84] See, Samuli Miettinen, 'Annulment in Action: How Does the Court of Justice of the European Union Explain Maintaining the Legal Effects of Annulled Instruments?' in Jarna Petman (ed), *Finnish Yearbook of International Law 2012–2013: Volume 23* (Hart Publishing, 2016).

[85] TEU, Article 40 and TFEU, Article 275.

[86] See, Christina Eckes, 'EU Restrictive Measures against Natural and Legal Persons: From Counterterrorist to Third Country Sanctions' (2014) 51 *Common Market Law Review* 869.

[87] Bart Van Vooren and Ramses A Wessel, *EU External Relations Law: Text, Cases and Materials* (Cambridge University Press, 2014) p 142.

[88] See, Dorte Sindbjerg Martinsen, *An Ever More Powerful Court? The Political Constraints of Legal Integration in the European Union* (Oxford University Press, 2015). Figure 1: Data Court Jurisprudence 1961–2014.

project built upon a 'highly convoluted structure',[89] inter-pillar disputes before the Court continue to exist and be a regular feature of competence disputes between the institutions in CFSP matters. By putting CFSP matters through the Court's jurisdictional questions, it can be seen how the Court has shaped it as a constitutionalised, legal field. The judgments before the Court dealing with CFSP matters have, as of late, been seeking the Court's assistance with watering down the solidity in which CFSP matters, as a policy field, have been managed and controlled by the Council. With other institutions and legal actors seeking to challenge the actions taken by the Council in CFSP matters, pursuing such actions in the Court can be seen as an attractive option to dilute the Council's institutional power.

5.4.1. A Question of Jurisdiction

It was once claimed that '[t]he Court…cannot have control of its own jurisdiction. The ground rules must be clearly defined in a [Union] governed by the rule of law'.[90] As normative as that may be, it is quite distant from the reality where the Court defines its own jurisdiction. Cases like *National Road Haulage* have cemented the role of the Court in the jurisdictional issues of actors in their right to bring an action for annulment.[91] With the pillarisation of the Union, it was first acknowledged by the Court in *Grau Gomis* that it had 'no jurisdiction to interpret' certain matters that were carved out from judicial review by the treaties.[92] Around the same time, however, in *Airport Transit Visas*,[93] the Court demonstrated its ability to conduct border policing between the first and third pillars. The admissibility of the case demonstrated the Court's protection of Union competence against those pushed by the Member States.[94] By accepting that the Court itself could examine jurisdiction on the matter, it effectively confirmed it looks into the content of the measure to access compliance with the competence of the Union as set out in the treaties. The case clearly demonstrated that the Court could review pillar activity, at least with respect to the first and third pillars.

[89] Deirdre Curtin, 'The Constitutional Structure of the Union: A Europe of Bits and Pieces' (1993) 30 *Common Market Law Review* 17 at 23.

[90] Opinion of Advocate General Ruiz-Jarabo Colomer, Case C-17/00, *François De Coster v Collège des bourgmestre et échevins de Watermael-Boitsfort*, ECLI:EU:C:2001:366, para 61.

[91] Case C-65/90, *Parliament v Council*, ECLI:EU:C:1992:325 ('*National Road Haulage*') See, Henry G Schermers and Piet Jan Slot, 'Case C-65/90, European Parliament v Council of the European Communities, Judgment of 16 July 1992' (1993) 30 *Common Market Law Review* 1067 at 1069.

[92] Case C-167/94, *Criminal proceedings against Juan Carlos Grau Gomis and others*, ECLI:EU:C:1995:113, para 6.

[93] Case C-170/96, *Commission v Council*, ECLI:EU:C:1998:219 ('*Airport Transit Visas*'). As noted by the Advocate General, the 'limitations on the Court's jurisdiction, however, do not deprive it of power to consider the content of the contested act for the purpose of the present action' [compared to *Grau Gomis*]. Opinion of Advocate General Fennelly, Case C-170/96, *Commission v Council*, ECLI:EU:C:1998:43 ('*Airport Transit Visas*'), para 11.

[94] Nial Fennelly, 'The Area of "Freedom, Security and Justice" and the European Court of Justice – a Personal View' (2000) 49 *International and Comparative Law Quarterly* 1 at 13.

When it came to the then second pillar, however, it had been argued previously that given the position of CFSP matters before the Union Courts, national courts in Member States should have jurisdiction when it comes to judicial review.[95] This, as often highlighted, was far from ideal.[96] Whilst *Haegemann* is known for asserting that international agreements form an integral part of the legal order,[97] it was also a case where the Court asserted jurisdiction through a preliminary reference on an external relations case, meaning that even when not specifically envisaged, the Court has ways to assert its jurisdiction. Similarly, in *Svenska Journalistförbundet*,[98] the General Court asserted that merely because the documents sought came under the CFSP provisions of the treaties, this did not in itself exclude the Court having jurisdiction. The General Court drew a distinction that it was not reviewing the legality of the measure under the then Article L, but rather, public access to such measures.[99] It furthermore justified its expansive interpretation on jurisdiction in a comparative perspective, in that it had jurisdiction to review certain JHA measures based on the third pillar just, like CFSP matters, another policy field, that is formulated based on rules-based cooperation. This *Svenska Journalistförbundet* judgment has been labelled one of the General Court's boldest,[100] as it made the step of asserting itself against the will of the Council.

The Court had previously expressed the view that when the competence of the Union is at issue in a case, pre-Article 40 TEU, it cannot be excluded entirely,[101] in contrast to how other interpreters of the treaties might see it. The Court, in attempting to provide a remedy in the *UPA* judgment, said it may not widen its own jurisdiction beyond the treaties themselves.[102] In the *ECOWAS* case,[103] arguably one of the most prominent cases on delineating CFSP and non-CFSP matters just prior to the entry into force of the Treaty of Lisbon, the basis for the action to determine the Article 40 TEU border policing role that the Court plays was not questioned. However, the jurisdiction of the Court to determine the legality of the Joint Action under Article 277 TFEU, then Article 230 EC, was contested.

[95] This position is supported in the Opinion of Advocate General Mengozzi, Cases C-354/04 P, *Gestoras Pro Amnistía, Juan Mari Olano Olano, and Julen Zelarain Errasti v Council of the European Union ('Gestoras')*, and Case C-355/04 P, *Segi, Arait, Zubimendi Izaga, and Aritza Galarraga v Council*, ECLI:EU:C:2006:667 ('*Segi*'), para 99.

[96] For example, Alicia Hinarejos, 'Judicial Control of CFSP in the Constitutional Treaty: A Cherry Worth Picking?' (2006) 25 *Yearbook of European Law* 363 at 392.

[97] Case C-181/73, *Haegemann v Belgium*, ECLI:EU:C:1974:41.

[98] Case T-174/95, *Svenska Journalistförbundet v Council*, ECLI:EU:T:1998:127. This judgment is analysed further in Chapter 6 of this book.

[99] Case T-174/95, *Svenska Journalistförbundet v Council*, ECLI:EU:T:1998:127, para 85.

[100] Peter Dyrberg, 'Current Issues in the Debate on Public Access to Documents' (1999) 24 *European Law Review* 157 at 161.

[101] This principle was evident in, Case C-124/95, *The Queen, ex parte Centro-Com Srl v HM Treasury and Bank of England*, ECLI:EU:C:1997:8.

[102] Case C-50/00 P, *Unión de Pequeños Agricultores v Council*, ECLI:EU:C:2002:462.

[103] Case C-91/05, *Commission v Council*, ECLI:EU:C:2008:288 ('*ECOWAS*').

The latter was not dealt with in full by the Court, yet it nonetheless appeared to suggest it had jurisdiction, given its connectedness to its border policing role.[104]

5.4.2. Post-Lisbon

Contestation within EU external relations law and finding the dividing line between CFSP and non-CFSP matters can be considered an inherently good exercise. The playing out of such arguments elucidate better validations and force institutions and legal actors to justify their stances. Given that jurisdictional matters for the Court underwent a flipping exercise in the Treaty of Lisbon, it is most prudent to look at the litigation on CFSP matters after this development. In *Smart Sanctions*,[105] the jurisdiction of the Court was not at issue, yet in *Mauritius*, the Court said that given Article 19 TEU gave general jurisdiction to the Court, it must be interpreted that the derogations imposed by Article 24 TEU and Article 275 TFEU must 'be interpreted narrowly'.[106] This, in itself, is not surprising; the Court interprets exceptions in a narrow manner, as otherwise, they would inevitably be exploited by the Council, further skewing any sense of institutional balance. It is thus construed that allowing the Court to have a limited amount of judicial control in CFSP matters – competence delimitation through Article 40 TEU and sanctions through Article 275 TFEU – in essence allows for the opening up of judicial control on a wider range of CFSP matters.

When the Court affirms jurisdiction in a case, it does not stop there. By patrolling the border between CFSP and non-CFSP matters, it looks to substance. Whilst the Court in *Mauritius* may have upheld the CFSP legal basis, it nonetheless accepted jurisdiction in the case. In *Eulex Kosovo*,[107] the General Court said the defendant lacked legal capacity.[108] Due to this technicality, it was not required to cast judgment on the 'alleged lack of jurisdiction of the General Court concerning acts adopted on the basis of the provisions of the [T]FEU…relating to…CFSP [matters]'.[109] On appeal to the Court, the Advocate General in his initial Opinion

[104] Ibid. para 34. See, Christophe Hillion and Ramses A Wessel, 'Competence Distribution in EU External Relations after Ecowas: Clarification or Continued Fuzziness?' (2009) 46 *Common Market Law Review* 551 at 569.

[105] Case C-130/10, *Parliament v Council*, ECLI:EU:C:2012:472 ('*Smart Sanctions*').

[106] Case C-658/11, *Parliament v Council*, ECLI:EU:C:2014:2025 ('*Mauritius*'), para 70. Also, see, Louise Halleskov Storgaard, 'EU Law Autonomy versus European Fundamental Rights Protection – On Opinion 2/13 on EU Accession to the ECHR' (2015) 15 *Human Rights Law Review* 485 at 498.

[107] Case T-213/12, *Elitaliana SpA v Eulex Kosovo*, ECLI:EU:T:2013:292.

[108] It has been noted that the CFSP Decision giving effect to Eulex Kosovo has been amended following the judgment, giving it different legal capacities. L 174/42. Council Decision 2014/349/CFSP of 12 June 2014 Amending Joint Action 2008/124/CFSP on the European Union Rule of Law Mission in Kosovo, Eulex Kosovo. As noted, Pieter Jan Kuijper, 'The Common Foreign and Security Policy and the Common Security and Defence Policy' in Pieter Jan Kuijper and others (eds), *The Law of the European Union* (Kluwer Law International, 2018) pp 1281–1282.

[109] Case T-213/12, *Elitaliana SpA v Eulex Kosovo*, ECLI:EU:T:2013:292, para 45.

did not broach the issue of jurisdiction.[110] Following another oral hearing on the specific issue of jurisdiction, upon which the Court raised the question of its own motion,[111] a second Opinion was delivered,[112] recommending the jurisdiction of the Court. The Opinion stated that even though a measure may be adopted under Title V, the provisions relating to CFSP matters of the treaties, the Court had jurisdiction in the matter given that it fell within the budgetary constraints of the Union.

The Court emphatically stated that '[h]aving regard to the specific circumstances of the present case, the scope of the limitation, by way of derogation, on the Court's jurisdiction, which is provided for in the final sentence of the second subparagraph of Article 24(1) TEU and in Article 275 TFEU, cannot be considered to be so extensive as to exclude the Court's jurisdiction to interpret and apply the provisions of the Financial Regulation with regard to public procurement'.[113] Ultimately, therefore, the *Eulex Kosovo* judgment is demonstrative of the Court delving into CFSP matters, which was something the General Court had restrained itself from doing. The case also reveals different views from within the EU judiciary as regards the true scope of the Court's jurisdiction in CFSP matters.

5.4.3. The Hurdle to ECHR Accession

Accession of the Union to the European Convention on Human Rights (ECHR) would have resolved some of the issues surrounding the judicial gap in CFSP matters. Given that actions on a CFSP legal basis may not always be compatible with human rights,[114] it has been recognised that the Union being a party to the ECHR would resolve some deficiencies. The accession of the Union to the ECHR was always going to be difficult, for the Union's 'competence to legislate on the subject-matters dealt with in the Convention has not been…transferred from the Member States to the [Union]'.[115] In this vein, an earlier attempt at accession was shot down by the Court in *Opinion 2/94*,[116] which 'implicitly reject[ed] the notion of external control by the Strasbourg machinery'.[117] Even with the

[110] Opinion of Advocate General Jääskinen [First of Two] of 4 December 2014, Case C-439/13 P, *Elitaliana SpA v Eulex Kosovo*, ECLI:EU:C:2014:2416.

[111] Caroline Naômé, *Appeals before the Court of Justice of the European Union* (Oxford University Press, 2018) p 114.

[112] Opinion of Advocate General Jääskinen [Second of Two] of 21 May 2015, Case C-439/13 P, *Elitaliana SpA v Eulex Kosovo*, ECLI:EU:C:2015:341.

[113] Case C-439/13 P, *Elitaliana SpA v Eulex Kosovo*, ECLI:EU:C:2015:753, para 49.

[114] Brkan (n 54) p 113.

[115] Max Sørensen, 'The Enlargement of the European Communities and the Protection of Human Rights' in Bartholomeus Landheer (ed), *European Yearbook, Vol. XIX* (Martinus Nijhoff Publishers 1973) p 7.

[116] Opinion 2/94, ECLI:EU:C:1996:140 ('*Accession by the Community to the European Convention for the Protection of Human Rights and Fundamental Freedoms*').

[117] John L Murray, 'The Influence of the European Convention on Fundamental Rights on Community Law' (2010) 33 *Fordham International Law Journal* 1388 at 1397.

first failed attempt, the then second pillar of CFSP matters alongside the other third pillar of JHA matters was of concern for accession,[118] given the method of decision-making was different from mainstream supranational activity.

Following the amendments to EU primary law by the Treaty of Lisbon, Article 6(2) TEU stipulated that the Union 'shall accede to the European Convention for the Protection of Human Rights and Fundamental Freedoms', supported by Protocol 8 and Declaration 2 of the treaties. Between 2010 and 2013, a Draft Accession Agreement (DAA) was negotiated during intense rounds of discussion between the relevant parties.[119] With the importance of the matter for the Union, the Commission referred the DAA under the Article 218(11) TFEU Opinion procedure to the Court to ensure its compatibility with the treaties.[120] The Opinion of the Court was set to be highly contentious given it had rejected becoming a party to the ECHR once before under the same procedure.

Central to the Court's dilemma was that the proposed DAA would cover the entirety of the Union's undertakings. The question, therefore, was whether it would have regard for the specific nature of particular areas of Union law that are special in the Union's legal order. The prestige that the Court prides itself on came into play when it wasted no time in grasping an opportunity to use the jurisdictional derogation imposed on it to prevent an international agreement from proceeding. In a wide-ranging Opinion, the Court in *Opinion 2/13* detailed a number of incompatibilities with the proposed DAA and ultimately found it not to comply with the primary law of the Union. It found fundamental problems with the agreement, stating it undermined the autonomy of Union law and its entire legal order. CFSP matters were just one of a number of issues the Court identified with the agreement for the Union to accede to the ECHR.

The most striking element of the Opinion is that the Court exercised jurisdiction over the DAA that covered CFSP matters. It did this, without any reluctance, or apparent opposition from the parties before the Court. In its interpretation, allowing a non-Union body, the ECtHR, to have jurisdiction over an EU policy domain such as CFSP matters, where the Court itself does not have full jurisdiction was a bold proposal. In the eyes of the Court, with the agreement failing to have regard for the setup of CFSP matters by not giving appropriate jurisdictional safeguards, and the possibility for Union law to be deciphered in a way that is uncontrollable by itself, was a step beyond acceptable. This train of thought is not

[118] Síofra O'Leary, 'Accession by the European Community to the European Convention on Human Rights – The Opinion of the ECJ' [1996] *European Human Rights Law Review* 362 at 366.

[119] Council of Europe and European Commission, 'Fifth Negotiation Meeting between the CDDH Ad Hoc Negotiation Group and the European Commission on the Accession of the European Union to the European Convention on Human Rights' (Council of Europe 2013) 47+1(2013)008rev2.

[120] The Opinion procedure affords the Court, as an institution, strong influence upon the foreign relations matters of EU, particularly regarding competence internally within the Union, and the constitutional nature of the Union externally. See, Graham Butler, 'Pre-Ratification Judicial Review of International Agreements to Be Concluded by the European Union' in Mattias Derlén and Johan Lindholm (eds), *The Court of Justice of the European Union: Multidisciplinary Perspectives* (Hart Publishing, 2018).

altogether surprising given the Court's past performance. One of the ways in which the Court exercises its 'legal agenda' is through 'selective input…[on]…the determination of the boundaries of its jurisdiction'.[121] In *Opinion 2/13*, the Court stated that putting a hypothetical limit on the scope of its powers in CFSP matters was premature, as it has not had the opportunity previously to state the exact boundary of its jurisdiction in CFSP matters.[122] Neither was it likely to be willing to define that limit. The Court said that given the structures of the treaties to exclude certain acts in CFSP matters from the Court, Union law alone could only explain this given that, under the DAA, the ECtHR would be in a position to judicially review acts in all areas of Union law, including CFSP matters. The Court said this enabled the transfer of Union law exclusively to a non-EU body[123] and referred to a previous Opinion which stated that these said acts could not be exclusively conferred to a non-EU body,[124] even though it would only be on areas covered by the ECHR.

One reading of *Opinion 2/13* shows that the Court wished to see an amendment to the DAA so that the jurisdiction of the ECtHR in legal acts on a CFSP legal basis would be curtailed.[125] The other solution that the Court might also settle for, despite not setting it out itself, would be to open up jurisdiction of CFSP matters to the Court. It could be argued that the Court was compelled to ensure basic rights were appropriately protected by finding the DAA incompatible with the treaties, for fear of what national courts would do if EU accession occurred and left a vacuum with respect to CFSP matters that the Court was legally unable to fulfil. In line with the potential conflict between national courts and the Court in the *Solange* line of thinking, with particular regard to the Federal Constitutional Court in Germany,[126] the Court's foresight has demonstrated how seriously it viewed a potential threat, and thus fended it off with rigour.

The Court, in effect, said that this threatened the very nature of the EU legal order given its limited jurisdiction in CFSP matters, and with no similar derogation placed on the ECtHR. The Court appeared to be very willing to use CFSP matters as one of many reasons to protect not only the EU legal order, but also its own interests. It could be argued that the handling of CFSP matters by the Court is not as clear-cut as it suggests in *Opinion 2/13*. It has even been suggested that

[121] Miguel Poiares Maduro, *We the Court: The European Court of Justice and the European Economic Constitution: A Critical Reading of Article 30 the EC Treaty* (Hart Publishing, 1998) p 19.

[122] Opinion 2/13, ECLI:EU:C:2014:2454 ('*Accession of the European Union to the European Convention for the Protection of Human Rights*'), para 251.

[123] It has been claimed that the Court got its 'exclusive' claim wrong, given the national legal space for national courts to act. See, Christophe Hillion, 'Decentralised Integration? Fundamental Rights Protection in the EU Common Foreign and Security Policy' (2016) 1 European Papers 55.

[124] Opinion 1/09, ECLI:EU:C:2011:123 ('*Creation of a Unified Patent Litigation System*'), paras 78, 80, and 89.

[125] Jörg Polakiewicz, 'Accession to the European Convention on Human Rights (ECHR) – An Insider's View Addressing One by One the CJEU's Objections in Opinion 2/13' (2016) 36 *Human Rights Law Journal* 10 at 19.

[126] See, Mattias Kumm, 'Who Is the Final Arbiter of Constitutionality in Europe?: Three Conceptions of the Relationship Between the German Federal Constitutional Court and the European Court of Justice' (1999) 36 *Common Market Law Review* 351.

Opinion 2/13 puts a limit on the role that national courts play in CFSP matters, saying that the Court believes all judicial authorities dealing with Union legal matters ought to be excluded, except for itself.[127] Whilst this may or may not be the case, it still raises questions as to how far the Court could go, if it so wishes, to set out its own jurisdiction in CFSP matters, which it has not done to date. However, it is clear that the Court will never fully define the extent of the limitations posed on it, as it would effectively be pigeonholing itself for future cases.

The issue of CFSP matters in *Opinion 2/13* goes further. If the drafters of the DAA were willing to give jurisdiction over CFSP matters to the ECtHR, what is to say jurisdiction over CFSP matters could, as it presently stands, end up in front of the International Court of Justice (ICJ). Moreover, the same could be said for other international courts and tribunals such as the the International Tribunal for the Law of the Sea (ITLOS),[128] with respect to the EU's martime operations. The *Mox Plant* case would seem to serve as a rebuttal to this view.[129] In addition, Article 344 TFEU specifies that disputes concerning the treaties should not go elsewhere,[130] other than the Court itself.[131] This reading of Article 344 TFEU in *Opinion 2/13* is thought to be strict,[132] in line with previous cases in which the Court has taken a 'straight and narrow' approach.[133] EU Member States accordingly have no discretion for where they can settle judicial disputes that are of a particular nature. This would imply that no forum shopping in the international arena for CFSP matters is allowed. Article 344 TFEU's predecessor, Article 292 EC, was not applicable to CFSP matters, given the provision did not extend from the Community to the Union, when a clear distinction was made. A potential case at the ICJ would be a moot point, given the possibility for initiating a case would be limited to Member States, where the admissibility of the case itself would be a point of contention. Furthermore, the Statute of the ICJ in Article 34(1) specifies that, '[o]nly states may be parties in cases before the Court'.[134] Accordingly, *Opinion 2/13* has been criticised for first stating that the ECtHR would be judicially reviewing CFSP

[127] This claim by the Court is outlined in, Hillion (n 45) p 53.

[128] Christophe Hillion and Ramses A Wessel, '"The Good, the Bad and the Ugly": Three Levels of Judicial Control over the CFSP' in Steven Blockmans and Panos Koutrakos (eds), *Research Handbook on the EU's Common Foreign and Security Policy* (Edward Elgar, 2018) p 75.

[129] Case C-459/03, *Commission v Ireland*, ECLI:EU:C:2006:345 ('*Mox Plant*') See, Nikolaos Lavranos, *Jurisdictional Competition: Selected Cases in International and European Law* (Europa Law Publishing, 2009) p 28, and Nico Schrijver, 'Case C-459/03, Commission of the European Communities v Ireland, Judgment of the Court (Grand Chamber) of 30 May 2006, [2006] ECR I-4635' (2010) 47 *Common Market Law Review* 863.

[130] TFEU, Article 344: 'Member States undertake not to submit a dispute concerning the interpretation or application of the [t]reaties to any method of settlement other than those provided for therein.'

[131] This view is supported in De Baere (n 10) p 177.

[132] Opinion of Advocate General Wahl, Case C-455/14 P, *H v Council*, ECLI:EU:C:2016:212, para 47.

[133] Pieter Jan Kuijper, 'The Case Law of the Court of Justice of the EU and the Allocation of External Relations Powers: Whither the Traditional Role of the Executive in EU Foreign Relations?' in Cremona and Thies (n 45) p 112.

[134] 'Charter of the United Nations and the Statute of the International Court of Justice'. Article 34(1), Statute of the International Court of Justice.

matters,[135] and secondly for claiming 'exclusivity' on the judicial scene,[136] appearing to ignore national courts.

The legal nature of *Opinion 2/13* can be questioned for its own institutional motives and whether the Opinion was a political act dressed in the cloak of legal argumentation. How accession of the Union to the ECHR may be overcome is a matter that will remain the subject of intense debate. One consideration will be whether the Court's objections to how CFSP matters will manifest in the future and whether the development of further case law will straighten out the issues raised by the Court, or if the setup of CFSP matters in the treaties will have to be altered. The issues related to CFSP matters raised by the Court in *Opinion 2/13* will be the most difficult to overcome within the current framework of the treaties. In the event neither occurs, it is likely, politically speaking, that the further negotiations that will attempt to overcome *Opinion 2/13* will result in the next DAA again being subject to an Opinion of the Court through the Article 218(11) TFEU opinion procedure.

5.4.4. Further Litigation

The *H v Council* judgment has been another case of the Court prising open its jurisdiction.[137] A Grand Chamber judgment, it was an appeal of an Order of the General Court.[138] Initially, upon receipt of the case, the General Court said it had no jurisdiction on the matter given the CFSP matters, thereby interpreting the treaties' provisions on lack of jurisdiction – Article 24(1) TEU and Article 275 TFEU – in a broad manner. The applicant appealed the case to the Court as it was of the view that the staffing issue was an administrative act and could not be construed as to entail non-jurisdiction of the Court, notwithstanding the fact that the European Union Police Mission (EUPM) in Bosnia and Herzegovina (BiH) was formed on a CFSP legal basis.[139] The case presented itself as an opportunity for the Court to refine the extent of its jurisdiction in CFSP matters. In the General Court, both the Council and the Commission said the matter was a CFSP matter and, therefore, pursuant to the second paragraph of Article 24(1) and the first paragraph of Article 275 TFEU, the General Court did not possess any jurisdiction over it. The General Court agreed.

On appeal, the Advocate General said the General Court was correct in saying it had no jurisdiction.[140] However, the Court took a contrasting outlook and, whilst

[135] Piet Eeckhout, 'Opinion 2/13 on EU Accession to the ECHR and Judicial Dialogue: Autonomy or Autarky?' (2015) 38 *Fordham International Law Journal* 955 at 988.

[136] See, Hillion, (n 45).

[137] Case C-455/14 P, *H v Council*, ECLI:EU:C:2016:569.

[138] Case T-271/10, *H v Council*, ECLI:EU:T:2014:702.

[139] L 322/22. Council Decision 2009/906/CFSP of 8 December 2009 on the European Union Police Mission (EUPM) in Bosnia and Herzegovina (BiH).

[140] Opinion of Advocate General Wahl, Case C-455/14 P, *H v Council*, ECLI:EU:C:2016:212, paras 30–94.

acknowledging that, principally, it can be assumed that its jurisdiction does not extend to the provisions related to CFSP matters in the treaties, known as Title V, or Articles 23–46 TEU, it stated that the general exclusion of the Court cannot extend to all aspects of CFSP matters. Based on this assertion, it can be assumed that acts adopted on a CFSP legal basis may potentially come within the Court's jurisdiction. Despite the EUPM being formed on a CFSP legal basis through Articles 28 and 43(2) TEU, the issue, was whether administrative decisions falling within the 'day-to-day' sphere of operations on the ground in the EUPM constitute non-jurisdiction of the Court. The CFSP Decision establishing the EUPM, amongst other things, set out the staffing arrangements for the mission. What was clear from the Decision is that EUPM staff are all subject to the rules and direction of the Civilian Operation Commander. This is sensical, given that the idea of senior officials not being in central control of all staff would be an operational and logistical nightmare.

On closer inspection of the CFSP Decision, however, the legal positions are in fact distinct, in that some staff are seconded from national public bodies, while others are seconded from various EU institutions, agencies, and bodies. Despite this difference, the CFSP Decision allows for the coordination of day-to-day operations to cover all staff. The Court used this tool to prise open jurisdiction for the matter at hand. Given that acts of staff management occurs in all EU public bodies, the Court noted that the CFSP Decision on staff arrangements within the EUPM is similar to those exercised in EU institutions.[141] As a result, the Court believed that the derogations imposed on its jurisdiction in both Article 24(1) TEU and Article 275 TFEU cannot prevent it from exercising review over staff management in the EUPM, notwithstanding the fact that an EUPM is situated on a CFSP legal basis.

This interpretation by the Court was not without further justification. Reliance was also placed upon a CFSP Decision governing the statute, seat and operational rules of the European Defence Agency (EDA),[142] which conferred jurisdiction upon the Court to adjudicate on matters relating to seconded national experts. Furthermore, the Court said, 'the very existence of effective judicial review [is] designed to ensure compliance with provisions of [Union] law'.[143] This was not the first time that the Court had used rule of law considerations in justifying judicial review, originally stemming from *Les Verts*.[144] In addition, the Court stated that the issue in this particular case was redeployment, and not secondment itself, which it says the General Court mistook.

The Court's *H v Council* judgment can be commended for trying to exclude perceived meddling by national authorities of Member States in what are essential

[141] Case C-455/14 P, *H v Council*, ECLI:EU:C:2016:569, para 54.

[142] L 266/55. Council Decision (CFSP) 2015/1835 of 12 October 2015 Defining the Statute, Seat and Operational Rules of the European Defence Agency.

[143] Case C-455/14 P, *H v Council*, ECLI:EU:C:2016:569, para 41.

[144] Case C-294/83, *Parti écologiste 'Les Verts' v Parliament*, ECLI:EU:C:1986:166. See, Koen Lenaerts, 'The Basic Constitutional Charter of a Community Based on the Rule of Law' in Miguel Poiares

EU external missions,[145] which is well beyond the remit of Member State's domestic legal orders. Yet the *H v Council* judgment can be criticised for making a false comparison in which it looked at a CFSP Decision related to the EDA and applied it, by analogy, to a CSDP mission also established by a CFSP Decision. Comparing a permanent fixture such as the EDA with a legal basis in primary law,[146] with a temporary fixture such as a CSDP mission whose comparability is not as straightforward as the Court reasoned, given they are characteristically different creatures. However, notwithstanding the contested reasoning of the Court in *H v Council*, the treaties attempting to exclude it from CFSP matters cannot be interpreted as being that everything to do with CFSP matters is beyond the Court's reach.

To interpret all things relating to CFSP matters, including administrative, procedural and operational issues, as being actions on a CFSP legal basis to escape judicial oversight of the EU judicial body would have been over-interpretation of the restrictions on the Court that have been set down by the treaties. However, what is construed as an act on a CFSP legal basis has become smaller as a result, as the Court took a narrow construal of what an act is, and the derogations imposed on the restrictive judicial review arrangements. The treaties distinguish between acts of foreign policy and implementing acts, with Article 40 TEU stating '[t]he implementation of…[CFSP matters] shall not affect the application of the procedures and the extent of the powers of the institutions laid down by the [t]reaties for the exercise of the Union competence'. Even through implementing acts of foreign policy, in the Court's interpretation, it would be erroneous to construe all decisions of various importance on a CFSP legal basis as to exclude judicial review.

Notwithstanding the environment in which missions like the EUPM operate, the Council's argument in *H v Council* – that an operational issue in the context of security and defence should fall outside the EU judicature – is not particularly strong. The CFSP Decision by the Council on the EDA, the year prior to *H v Council*, mean it, in a way, flatly contradicted itself. Perhaps without realising the full ramifications of that Council Decision,[147] it had a spillover effect. The Council trampled over its own arguments by granting the Court jurisdiction within a previous CFSP Decision, but then tried to claim that it did not have the same adjudication powers within a different CFSP Decision on an EUPM. As a result, *H v Council* is another case in a series of breakthroughs for the Court in CFSP matters, and its result can be interpreted as meaning that a measure concluded

Maduro and Loïc Azoulai (eds), *The Past and Future of EU Law: The Classics of EU Law Revisited on the 50th Anniversary of the Rome Treaty* (Hart Publishing, 2010) p 303. Furthermore, Graham Butler, 'Implementing a Complete System of Legal Remedies in EU Foreign Affairs Law' (2018) 24 *Columbia Journal of European Law* 637.

[145] Kuijper (n 108) p 1282.

[146] TEU, Article 42(3), second para, and TEU, Article 45. It also has secondary law provisions. L 183/16. Council Decision 2011/411/CFSP of 12 July 2011 Defining the Statute, Seat and Operational Rules of the European Defence Agency and Repealing Joint Action 2004/551/CFSP.

[147] L 266/55. Council Decision (CFSP) 2015/1835 of 12 October 2015 Defining the Statute, Seat and Operational Rules of the European Defence Agency (n 142).

on a CFSP legal basis does not, de facto, exclude the Court. Whilst *H v Council* extended the jurisdiction of the Court in CFSP matters, it did not, as should be remembered, completely set down the case for judicial review of acts on a CFSP legal basis in themselves. It was, rather, another marked exception to the limitations placed on the Court's jurisdiction.

Whilst the Court's *Mauritius* and *Tanzania* judgments, as discussed in the previous chapter, have demonstrated that it has been strong on institutional procedures, ensuring that CFSP decision-making also respects non-CFSP articles that are applicable, such as Article 218 TFEU; another matter is notable. The Court in *H v Council* opened up its jurisdiction in CFSP matters without making use of Article 40 TEU, its border-policing role between CFSP and non-CFSP matters. In addition, traces of the General Court's *Svenska Journalistförbundet* judgment can be spotted in the Court's judgment.[148]

In an unusual scenario, it would appear that the General Court has become much more reserved in its jurisdiction in CFSP matters than twenty years ago, and it is the Court which has been much more courageous. The outcome of *H v Council* meant the General Court's order finding of no jurisdiction has been set aside. Article 61 of the Statute of the Court permitted it to send back cases to the General Court,[149] for which it will be bound now on points of law that have been issued by the Court. Hence, the Court bounced the issue back to the General Court to decide the case on matters of substance, now that its jurisdiction had been affirmed.[150]

5.4.5. A Preliminary Reference

Whilst *H v Council* has implicitly affirmed that 'CFSP [matters are] fully integrated in the EU legal order',[151] it is not as fully as may be anticipated, for the jurisprudence has not been exhausted. The *Rosneft* case came to the Court from a British court via the preliminary reference procedure, which, amongst other things, dealt with the Court's jurisdiction in CFSP matters.[152] With narrow legal standing for the rights of individuals taking direct actions, as an alternative, preliminary references have functioned as an indirect filtering mechanism for individuals using national courts to seek access to the Court.

[148] Case T-174/95, *Svenska Journalistförbundet v Council*, ECLI:EU:T:1998:127.

[149] C 83/210. Protocol (No 3) on the Statute of the Court of Justice of the European Union.

[150] Case T-271/10 RENV, *H v Council*, ECLI:EU:T:2018:180. On procedural grounds, the case that returned to the General Court has been appealed again to the Court. Case C-413/18 P, *H v Council*, pending.

[151] Peter Van Elsuwege, 'Upholding the Rule of Law in the Common Foreign and Security Policy: H v Council' (2017) 54 *Common Market Law Review* 841 at 858.

[152] Case C-72/15, *Rosneft Oil Company OJSC v Her Majesty's Treasury, The Secretary of State for Business, Innovation and Skills, The Financial Conduct Authority*, ECLI:EU:C:2016:381.

Individuals are in a peculiar position when it comes to legal standing before the EU courts. This is no different in CFSP matters, albeit with its own legal specifics. The wording of the second paragraph of Article 275 TFEU specifies that the jurisdiction of the Court is confined to restrictive measures cases,[153] which are direct actions taken to the General Court. Article 275 TFEU appears not to provide for cases that arise as a result of preliminary references. It has been argued that the Court 'may afford possibilities' to handle preliminary references in this field,[154] whilst acknowledging the case law is not complete in the area. The *Rosneft* case afforded the Court the possibility to clarify the parameters of its potential judicial review powers over CFSP matters that do not relate to restrictive measures through the preliminary reference procedure.

It was argued nearly a decade prior to *Rosneft* that concerns over the rule of law and the uniformity of Union law could be used as a justification for the Court to open up the preliminary reference procedure to CFSP matters.[155] The *Rosneft* scenario, therefore, had been a long time coming. Cases on CFSP matters coming to the Court as preliminary references provide new challenges. Whereas the landmark cases on CFSP matters to date have been direct actions, many of which have been inter-institutional litigation, the preliminary reference cases on CFSP matters ultimately go back to the appropriate national court for application.

The judgment in *Rosneft* has, to date, provided the 'rich[est] conception of the Court's role in CFSP matters'.[156] The High Court of England and Wales in the United Kingdom asked a number of questions of the Court, including whether it had jurisdiction under a preliminary reference to rule on questions relating to a CFSP Decision[157] (which was subsequently amended by two other CFSP Decisions)[158] and a Council Regulation[159] (subsequently amended by

[153] TFEU, Article 275, second para: '…the Court shall have jurisdiction to monitor compliance with Article 40 of the Treaty on European Union and to rule on proceedings, brought in accordance with the conditions laid down in the fourth paragraph of Article 263 of this Treaty, reviewing the legality of decisions providing for restrictive measures against natural or legal persons adopted by the Council on the basis of Chapter 2 of Title V of the Treaty on European Union.'

[154] See the case for this being set out in, Koen Lenaerts, Ignace Maselis and Kathleen Gutman, *EU Procedural Law* (ed Janek Tomasz Nowak) 3rd edition (Oxford University Press, 2014) p 458 (para 10.04).

[155] De Baere (n 10) p 186.

[156] Panos Koutrakos, 'Judicial Review in the EU's Common Foreign and Security Policy' (2018) 67 *International and Comparative Law Quarterly* 1. p 23.

[157] L 229/13. Council Decision 2014/512/CFSP of 31 July 2014 Concerning Restrictive Measures in View of Russia's Actions Destabilising the Situation in Ukraine.

[158] L 271/54. Council Decision 2014/659/CFSP of 8 September 2014 Amending Decision 2014/512/CFSP Concerning Restrictive Measures in View of Russia's Actions Destabilising the Situation in Ukraine; L 349/58. Council Decision 2014/872/CFSP of 4 December 2014 Amending Decision 2014/512/CFSP Concerning Restrictive Measures in View of Russia's Actions Destabilising the Situation in Ukraine, and Decision 2014/659/CFSP Amending Decision 2014/512/CFSP.

[159] L 229/1. Council Regulation (EU) No 833/2014 of 31 July 2014 Concerning Restrictive Measures in View of Russia's Actions Destabilising the Situation in Ukraine.

two other Regulations).[160] By asking questions of this nature, it brought forward the issue of whether the Court even had the jurisdiction to hear the case to begin with, having regard to Articles 19(1), 24, and 40 TEU, Article 275 TFEU, and Article 47 CFR.

The *Gestoras* and *Segi* cases,[161] whilst former third pillar judgments, presented a similar, albeit different conundrum, that would help guide the Court in *Rosneft*, allowing it to exercise jurisdiction in CFSP matters, subject to Article 267 TFEU. The former Article 35(1) TEU, in which Article 267 TEU has its roots, would have to be interpreted broadly for the Court to be in a position to find jurisdiction. In both *Gestoras* and *Segi*, the Court found that 'preliminary [references] [are] designed to guarantee observance of the law in the interpretation and application of the Treaty, [and] it would run counter to that objective to interpret Article 35(1)… narrowly'. Given the recent *H v Council* judgment as discussed above, it was highly likely the Court would find jurisdiction for itself in *Rosneft*, if it was to apply the former third pillar rules to the former second pillar.

To put the *Rosneft* case in context, a two-step process was put in place for restrictive measures to be legally crafted with two differing legal instruments at work to give full effect in the EU legal order. For the first step, the Council, as per Article 29 TEU, made a CFSP Decision based on the CFSP chapter of the treaties. A follow-up Council Regulation under Article 215 TFEU subsequently follows this. The relationship between the CFSP Decision and non-CFSP Regulation is the key to unlocking the puzzle. The legal basis of Article 215 TFEU permits Union actors to allow the relationship between a CFSP and a non-CFSP legal basis to flourish. The *Kadi I* case emphasised that where a bridge is extended between the TEU and the TFEU, such as the objectives of the TEU against those of Article 75 TFEU (ex-Article 60 EC) and Article 215 TFEU (ex-Article 301 EC), such a bridge only exists where a link has been made 'explicitly'.[162] Article 215 TFEU is an exceptional fusion facilitation method in the treaties whereby a non-CFSP provision can only be utilised on foot of another legal act on a CFSP legal basis.

In the Opinion of the Advocate General in *Rosneft*, he noted that the Court's jurisdiction in the sphere of CFSP matters is limited by Article 24(1) TEU and Article 275 TFEU 'at first sight'.[163] Article 263 TFEU states that the Court has

[160] L 271/3. Council Regulation (EU) No 960/2014 of 8 September 2014 Amending Regulation (EU) No 833/2014 Concerning Restrictive Measures in View of Russia's Actions Destabilising the Situation in Ukraine; L 349/20. Council Regulation (EU) No 129/2014 of 4 December 2014 Amending Regulation (EU) No 833/2014 Concerning Restrictive Measures in View of Russia's Actions Destabilising the Situation in Ukraine and Amending Regulation (EU) No 960/2014 Amending Regulation (EU) No 833/2014.

[161] Case C-354/04 P, *Gestoras Pro Amnistía, Juan Mari Olano Olano, Julen Zelarain Errasti v Council*, ECLI:EU:C:2007:115, and Case C-355/04 P, *Segi, Arait, Zubimendi Izaga, and Aritza Galarraga v Council*, ECLI:EU:C:2007:116 ('*Segi*').

[162] Joined Cases C-402/05 P and C-415/05 P, *Yassin Abdullah Kadi and Al Barakaat International Foundation v Council and Commission*, ECLI:EU:C:2008:461 ('*Kadi I*'), para 202.

[163] Opinion of Advocate General Wathelet, Case C-72/15, *Rosneft Oil Company OJSC v Her Majesty's Treasury, The Secretary of State for Business, Innovation and Skills, The Financial Conduct Authority*, ECLI:EU:C:2016:381, para 39.

jurisdiction to answer actions brought by the Parliament on the grounds of essential procedural requirements, misuse of institutional powers, and infringements of the Treaties more generally. Article 263 TFEU, fourth paragraph, states that '[a]ny natural or legal person may, under the conditions laid down in the first and second paragraphs, institute proceedings against an act addressed to that person or which is of direct and individual concern to them, and against a regulatory act which is of direct concern to them and does not entail implementing measures'. If interpreted narrowly, this could mean that preliminary references for CFSP matters could be excluded. The Advocate General skirted this interpretation by noting the inconsistency in the drafting of particular parts of the treaties,[164] stating that Article 24(1) TEU allows the Court to 'review the legality of certain decisions'. Furthermore, the Advocate General stated the Court does have jurisdiction to hear the preliminary reference, stating that 'in accordance with the last sentence of the second subparagraph of Article 24(1) TEU and Article 275 TFEU, the Court has jurisdiction to give a preliminary [reference], under Article 267 TFEU'.[165]

On the substance of the jurisdictional question in *Rosneft*, and in line with previous case law on the limitations on its jurisdiction, the Court argued that these limitations had to be narrowly interpreted. It said 'the principle of effective judicial protection…implies that the exclusion of the Court's jurisdiction in [CFSP matters] should be interpreted strictly'.[166] The Court went so far as to say that 'neither the [TEU] nor the [TFEU] indicates that an action for annulment brought before the General Court, pursuant to the combined provisions of Articles 256 and 263 TFEU, constitutes the sole means for reviewing the legality of decisions providing for restrictive measures against natural or legal persons, to the exclusion, in particular, of a [preliminary reference] on validity'.[167] It used a number of different articles in EU primary law to claim jurisdiction – Articles 19, 24, and 40 TEU, Article 275 TFEU, and Article 47 CFR.

Article 24 TEU can be seen as insufficiently precise. In just one sentence it states that the role of the Parliament and Commission 'is defined by the [t]reaties' in CFSP matters, but 'hardly bother[s]' to elaborate the details.[168] The text of Article 24(1) TEU, with respect to the derogations in the Court's jurisdiction, appears to be open to greater interpretation than other carve-outs. Article 24 TEU and Article 275 TFEU appear to possess similar features. However, on closer inspection, the wording is slightly different. Taken together, Article 24 TEU and Article 275 TFEU allow the Court 'a comfortable margin of interpretation'[169] and allows significant discretion upon the Court to determine if a particular matter is amenable to judicial review or not.

[164] Ibid. para 60.
[165] Ibid. para 92.
[166] Case C-72/15, *Rosneft Oil Company OJSC v Her Majesty's Treasury, The Secretary of State for Business, Innovation and Skills, The Financial Conduct Authority*, ECLI:EU:C:2016:381, para 74.
[167] Ibid. para 70.
[168] Edward and Lane (n 49) p 139.
[169] Sara Poli, 'The Common Foreign Security Policy after Rosneft: Still Imperfect but Gradually Subject to the Rule of Law' (2017) 54 *Common Market Law Review* 1799 at 1810.

In the Court's judgment in *Rosneft*, it placed greater emphasis on Article 24 TEU than on Article 275 TFEU. This focus on Article 24 TEU allowed the Court to read around Article 263 TFEU, or, to put it more bluntly, to avoid it altogether. Moreover, the language of Article 275 TFEU made many suggestions. Firstly, post-Lisbon, it provided an explicit legal basis for entities to challenge CFSP legal acts targeting them. Second, in keeping with the Court's overall narrow approach to allowing direct challenges to EU legal acts, it has interpreted the kinds of applicants allowed to use Article 275 TFEU.[170] In *Eulex Kosovo*, as recalled, the Court determined that Article 24 TEU and Article 275 TFEU together could 'not be considered to be so extensive as to exclude the Court's jurisdiction to interpret and apply the provisions of the Financial Regulation with regard to public procurement'.[171]

By analogy, the Advocate General in *Rosneft* said 'there is a difference in wording between the second subparagraph of Article 24(1) TEU and the first paragraph of Article 275 TFEU', potentially leaving the reader with the 'false impression that the [EU] [c]ourts have no jurisdiction'.[172] The Court, approvingly, stated that Article 24 TEU refers to Article 275 TFEU 'in order to determine not the type of procedure under which the Court may review the legality of certain decisions, but rather the type of decisions whose legality may be reviewed by the Court, within any procedure that has as its aim such a review of legality'.[173] This interpretative understanding has precedent. Prior to the entry into force of the Treaty of Lisbon, applicants could circumnavigate the narrow grounds for *locus standi*, a tactic that the Court allowed. For example, in *OMPI*,[174] the General Court annulled a Common Position founded upon a CFSP legal basis,[175] the first time it ever did so.[176]

Article 263 TFEU focuses on the question of legality,[177] as it incorporates many legal concepts, each with a different interpretation of what legality entails. Legality is a broad term and questions often arise about its scope. Textually, Article 263 TFEU is uncomfortable reading for the Court and does not sit

[170] As noted, '[t]he Court has never adopted such a broad interpretation of the first paragraph of Article 275 TFEU'. Opinion of Advocate General Wathelet, Case C-72/15, *Rosneft Oil Company OJSC v Her Majesty's Treasury, The Secretary of State for Business, Innovation and Skills, The Financial Conduct Authority*, ECLI:EU:C:2016:381, para 45.

[171] Case C-439/13 P, *Elitaliana SpA v Eulex Kosovo*, ECLI:EU:C:2015:753, para 49.

[172] Opinion of Advocate General Wathelet, Case C-72/15, *Rosneft Oil Company OJSC v Her Majesty's Treasury, The Secretary of State for Business, Innovation and Skills, The Financial Conduct Authority*, ECLI:EU:C:2016:381, para 44.

[173] Case C-72/15, *Rosneft Oil Company OJSC v Her Majesty's Treasury, The Secretary of State for Business, Innovation and Skills, The Financial Conduct Authority*, ECLI:EU:C:2016:381, para 70.

[174] Case T-228/02, *Organisation des Modjahedines du peuple d'Iran v Council*, ECLI:EU:T:2006:384 ('*Modjahedin I*').

[175] Note that Common Positions are no longer CFSP legal acts and instead have been consolidated into a CFSP Decision. See Chapter 3 of this book.

[176] See, Christina Eckes, 'Case T-228/02, Organisation Des Modjahedines Du Peuple d'Iran v Council and UK (OMPI)' (2007) 44 *Common Market Law Review* 1117.

[177] For an overview of this extensive area, see, Laurence W Gormley, 'Judicial Review – a New Dawn after Lisbon?' in Henning Koch and others (eds), *Europe. The New Legal Realism: Essays in Honour of Hjalte Rasmussen* (Djøf Publishing, 2010).

well with its 'desire for jurisdiction'.[178] Accordingly, it is unclear how 'a complete system of legal remedies and procedures' à la *Les Vert*[179] could be measured against the legality of Article 263 TFEU. Explicitly, Article 275 TFEU refers to Article 263 TFEU, as the Court acknowledged, but that reference 'was not considered relevant'.[180] By contrast, it has been argued that if the drafters wanted to include the Article 267 TFEU preliminary reference procedure within EU restrictive measures law, then it would have specifically said so in Article 275 TFEU.[181]

Article 19(1) TEU served as another cornerstone of the *Rosneft* judgment. It states that 'Member States shall provide remedies sufficient to ensure effective legal protection in the fields covered by Union law'. Therefore, the scope of the provision has increased dramatically to include Union measures of any description within the scope of the Court's judicial review. At best, Article 19 TEU is flexible enough to accommodate the variety of circumstances that may be presented for adjudication. At worst, it is a potential license for the Court to do as it pleases. Prior to Article 19 TEU, when no such precise specification for judicial protection existed in Union law, the Court had held in *UPA* that it was for the national courts of the Member States to put procedures in place to ensure effective judicial review and protection.[182] This can be linked with Article 40 TEU and the Court's border policing role. Although the treaties do not explain the precise meaning of Article 40 TEU, the Court can consider questions regarding its application no matter what type of case is before the Court.

In *Rosneft*, the Court asserted that Article 40 TEU was not specific enough to find that it did not have jurisdiction and could therefore be construed as conferring jurisdiction. It explained that while it had jurisdiction to monitor compliance under Article 40 TEU, the primary law of the Union 'd[id] not make provision for any particular means by which such judicial monitoring is to be carried out'.[183] Moreover, Article 19 TEU served as a basis for the Court to claim that the monitoring provision of Article 40 TEU fell 'within the scope of the general jurisdiction that Article 19 TEU confers on the Court to ensure that in the interpretation and application of the [t]reaties the law is observed'.[184] Thus, deriving powers under Article 19 TEU, the Court determined that it had jurisdiction to examine the CFSP Decision and its compliance with Article 40 TEU. Yet, the monitoring provision is not itself an effective tool for challenging restrictive measures, thus, the

[178] Graham Butler, 'The Coming of Age of the Court's Jurisdiction in the Common Foreign and Security Policy' (2017) 13 *European Constitutional Law Review* 673 at 688.

[179] Case C-294/83, *Parti écologiste 'Les Verts' v Parliament*, ECLI:EU:C:1986:166, para 23.

[180] Koutrakos, 'Judicial Review in the EU's Common Foreign and Security Policy' (n 156) p 22.

[181] Poli (n 169) p 1821.

[182] It is 'for the Member States to establish a system of legal remedies and procedures which ensure respect for the right to effective judicial protection'. Case C-50/00 P, *Unión de Pequeños Agricultores v Council*, ECLI:EU:C:2002:462, para 41.

[183] Case C-72/15, *Rosneft Oil Company OJSC v Her Majesty's Treasury, The Secretary of State for Business, Innovation and Skills, The Financial Conduct Authority*, ECLI:EU:C:2016:381, para 62.

[184] Ibid. para 62.

Rosneft judgment can be viewed as a continued license for political institutions to issue detailed CFSP Decisions for restrictive measures. Given that Article 19 TEU is by no means the sole treaty article describing the contours of the Court's functions and jurisdiction, reading too much into Article 19 TEU may prove to be a flaw in its reasoning.

In *Rosneft*, the Court also drew in the rule of law and the CFR. One Advocate General has said that '[t]he ground rules [for the Court's jurisdiction] must be clearly defined in a [Union] governed by the rule of law'.[185] The formative case of *Van Duyn* came about after much debate within EU legal circles[186] and is known for a number of reasons.[187] However, a lesser-known view is that *Van Duyn* was 'essentially concerned with assuring respect for the rule of law'.[188] Today, the rule of law is built into the structural framework of the Union and is inherent in most of its policies. This includes CFSP matters, despite the limitations on the Court's jurisdiction.[189] Over time, the Court has gradually become more dependent on the rule of law, ensuring 'democracy, human rights and constitutions enforced by independent judiciaries'.[190] Thus, its eagerness to use the rule of law where appropriate is not entirely surprising. The *Rosneft* judgment referred to the rule of law, taking a broad view, noting that the 'very existence of effective judicial review designed to ensure compliance with provisions of [Union] law is of the essence of the rule of law'.[191] The Court did not have to use the rule of law alone to justify its judgment; rather, it invoked the principle as an additional ground to support its declaration of jurisdiction. The rule of law is an important value in Union law, and the Court could deliver more value-laden judgments in the future, given how easily it invoked rule of law in *Rosneft*.

Rosneft also centred on whether acts on a CFSP legal basis can be challenged on the basis of fundamental rights, a question of Article 47 CFR and whether a right to an effective remedy applies. The incorporation of the CFR into EU primary law was a long process, characterised by a complicated debate regarding how to incorporate human rights into the EU legal order. This road led to concessions on the scope of the CFR. For example, in the pre-Lisbon era, primary law was shaped so that it 'clearly implie[d] a lack of competence for the Court…to review both acts

185 Opinion of Advocate General Ruiz-Jarabo Colomer, Case C-17/00, *François De Coster v Collège des bourgmestre et échevins de Watermael-Boitsfort*, ECLI:EU:C:2001:366, para 61.

186 Case C-41/74, *Yvonne van Duyn v Home Office*, ECLI:EU:C:1974:133.

187 It was the first case finding the direct effect of directives; it determined some of the scope given to public policy exemptions for restricting free movement of workers; it was the first preliminary reference from the newly acceded United Kingdom; and the case, given the subject matter, the Church of Scientology, generated quite the media interest in the Court's work.

188 Giuseppe Federico Mancini, *Democracy and Constitutionalism in the European Union: Collected Essays* (Hart Publishing, 2000) p 6.

189 Ricardo Gosalbo-Bono, 'Some Reflections on the CFSP Legal Order' (2006) 43 *Common Market Law Review* 337 at 347.

190 'Judges as Diplomats in Advancing the Rule of Law: A Conversation with President Koen Lenaerts and Justice Stephen Breyer' (2017) 66 *American University Law Review* 1159 at 1165.

191 Case C-72/15, *Rosneft Oil Company OJSC v Her Majesty's Treasury, The Secretary of State for Business, Innovation and Skills, The Financial Conduct Authority*, ECLI:EU:C:2016:381, para 73.

of the institutions of the Union and implementing measures taken by EU Member States for their compatibility with any standard of fundamental rights'.[192] The Treaty of Lisbon changed this, giving the CFR's additional relevance, but limited applicability. The initial scope of the CFR was addressed in *Åkerberg Fransson*,[193] but its applicability to CFSP matters had yet to be fully and authoritatively determined by the Court. Article 47 CFR corresponds closely to Article 6(1) ECHR. Questions have lingered about whether the preliminary reference procedure can be made fully compatible with the guarantees of the Convention, such as that of effective legal remedies.[194] Article 47 CFR could be construed to mean that any court or tribunal may provide 'effective remedies'. A national court's refusal to make a reference to the Court 'should thus be analysed in the light of Article 47 [CFR]',[195] which would cover all questions of Union law, including CFSP matters. However, a direct action before the General Court may suffice to meet the Union's fundamental rights obligations under the CFR. In addition to the CFR's text, the Court has used the 'Explanations Relating to the [CFR]' to help it to interpret the true meaning of the CFR's terms,[196] a practice it began in *DEB*.[197]

The *Rosneft* case was the first time the Court invoked the CFR in its reasoning in a case on CFSP matters.[198] At the time of *Les Verts*, the Court had no CFR to refer to and had to be creative in finding a legal justification for its judgment. The right of access to a process overseen by a judicial body was established later in *Johnston*, which held that 'all persons have the right to obtain an effective remedy in a competent court',[199] thereby meaning an 'effective judicial remedy'.[200] The *Johnston* principles were subsequently incorporated into EU primary law.[201] Accordingly, the Court's lack of jurisdiction in CFSP matters since the Treaty of Lisbon was 'susceptible for challenge by reference to Article 47 [CFR]'[202] and the

[192] Koen Lenaerts and Eddy De Smijter, 'The Charter and the Role of the European Courts' (2001) 8 *Maastricht Journal of European and Comparative Law* 90 at 94.

[193] Case C-617/10, *Åklagaren v Hans Åkerberg Fransson*, ECLI:EU:C:2013:105.

[194] Takis Tridimas, 'Knocking on Heaven's Door: Fragmentation, Efficiency and Defiance in the Preliminary Reference Procedure' (2003) 40 *Common Market Law Review* 9 at 31.

[195] Clelia Lacchi, 'Multilevel Judicial Protection in the EU and Preliminary References' (2016) 53 *Common Market Law Review* 679 at 688.

[196] Koen Lenaerts and José Antonio Gutiérrez-Fons, 'To Say What the Law of the EU Is: Methods of Interpretation and the European Court of Justice' (2014) 20 *Columbia Journal of European Law* 3 at 52.

[197] Case C-279/09, *DEB Deutsche Energiehandels- und Beratungsgesellschaft mbH v Bundesrepublik Deutschland*, ECLI:EU:C:2010:811, paras 31–40.

[198] Case C-72/15, *Rosneft Oil Company OJSC v Her Majesty's Treasury, The Secretary of State for Business, Innovation and Skills, The Financial Conduct Authority*, ECLI:EU:C:2016:381, paras 73, 74, and 81.

[199] Case C-222/84, *Marguerite Johnston v Chief Constable of the Royal Ulster Constabulary*, ECLI:EU:C:1986:206, para 19.

[200] Ibid. para 58.

[201] Michael Dougan, 'The Vicissitudes of Life at the Coalface: Remedies and Procedures for Enforcing Union Law before the National Courts' in Paul Craig and Gráinne De Búrca (eds), *The Evolution of EU Law* (Oxford University Press, 2011) p 431.

[202] Laurent Pech and Angela Ward, 'Article 47 – Right to an Effect Remedy and to a Fair Trial (Effective Judicial Remedies before the Court of Justice)' in Steve Peers and others (eds), *The EU Charter of Fundamental Rights: A Commentary* (Hart Publishing, 2014) p 1248.

Court finally reviewed such a challenge in *Rosneft*. This may appear to be contrary to the understanding that the Court 'may not rely on the [CFR] so as to expand its jurisdiction over areas that the authors of the [t]reaties expressly sought to insulate from judicial scrutiny'.[203] However, CFSP matters are a field where '[f]undamental rights may now be relied upon as grounds of review' more generally.[204] Therefore, in *Rosneft*, the Court tied CFSP matters more closely to the CFR; and so, this connection is likely to persist in all future cases on CFSP matters.

If the Court had adopted an approach in *Rosneft* which did not allow for indirect access for individuals aggrieved by acts on a CFSP legal basis, supplementing restricted direct access, it would have contributed towards supporting an area of Union law where there would be a judicial vacuum. Framed in this line of thought, the Court rejecting jurisdiction in *Rosneft* due to it being a preliminary reference as opposed to a direct action would be unusual. If the Court cannot answer a case on CFSP matters through the preliminary reference procedure, this would undermine the whole system of judicial remedies. It could even be said that without widespread use and the capabilities of the preliminary reference procedure, to use an old description, 'the roof would collapse'.[205] An Advocate General has previously alluded to how national courts should continue to send cases on CFSP matters to the Court, despite the boundaries to its jurisdiction in the area.[206] The question of whether the doctrine of primacy extends to CFSP matters has not been directly broached,[207] but finding a lack of jurisdiction of the Court to give a judgment from a preliminary reference case could mean the issue of primacy and direct effect may never make it onto the table.[208]

5.4.6. Continued Questioning

The Court's role in external relations expanded when adjudication extended beyond international agreements and focused on other factors such as legal basis and validity.[209] The delimitation of CFSP matters and the recent case law has long

[203] Koen Lenaerts and José Antonio Gutiérrez-Fons, 'The Place of the Charter in the EU Constitutional Edifice' in Steve Peers and others (eds), *The EU Charter of Fundamental Rights: A Commentary* (Hart Publishing, 2014) p 1572.

[204] Ibid.

[205] Giuseppe Federico Mancini and David T Keeling, 'From CILFIT to ERT: The Constitutional Challenge Facing the European Court' (1991) 11 *Yearbook of European Law* 1 at 2–3.

[206] Opinion of Advocate General Wahl, Case C-455/14 P, *H v Council*, ECLI:EU:C:2016:212, para 91.

[207] Discussed later in this Chapter. Also, Bruno De Witte, 'Direct Effect, Primacy, and the Nature of the Legal Order' in Paul Craig and Gráinne De Búrca (eds), *The Evolution of EU Law* 2nd edition (Oxford University Press, 2011) p 346.

[208] Bruno De Witte, 'The European Union as an International Legal Experiment' in Gráinne De Búrca and Joseph HH Weiler (eds), *The Worlds of European Constitutionalism* (Cambridge University Press, 2011) p 47.

[209] Antonio Tizzano, 'The Foreign Relations Law of the EU between Supranationality and Intergovernmental Model' in Enzo Cannizzaro (ed), *The European Union as an Actor in International Relations* (Kluwer Law International, 2002) p 141.

been predicted.[210] Just after the Treaty of Lisbon came into force, it was predicted that the use of CFSP legal bases alongside that of other Union competence, non-CFSP matters, would raise a number of issues.[211] This is notwithstanding the relatively small number of cases of constitutional nature on CFSP matters; within which there are opportunities for the Court to express itself on CFSP matters.

As is evident, the Court has been requested on a number of occasion to rule on 'sensitive and very complex' cases relating to CFSP matters.[212] It is evident that litigation in CFSP matters before the Court falls mainly to quarrels over jurisdiction and competence. The Court's decisions have had, or at least attempt to find, the middle ground. With national courts in Member States being competent to examine CFSP matters guaranteed by Article 274 TFEU,[213] preliminary reference cases have inevitably arisen. The difficulty arises when a discrepancy would arise between Union acts conducted on a CFSP legal basis that come into conflict with the domestic laws of Member States. The Court has demonstrated a particular level of pragmatism that suits the institutional actors as well as its own interests. The broadening of its jurisdiction in CFSP matters is only occurring where it has been essential as the least-worst option from a legal order and uniformity perspective.

The continued limitation of the Court's jurisdiction in CFSP matters has been said to be 'unnecessary and undesirable'.[214] Nevertheless, the Court has adopted a narrow, 'even retrograde' view of new provisions in view of some,[215] particularly with regard to respecting the CFSP legal basis in both *Mauritius* and *Tanzania* judgments. Despite this charge put against the Court, the overall body of case law reveals that it is not constrained as to what it may include within their judgments. For example, in *H v Council*, the Court brought in a Council Decision, unrelated to the facts before it, to justify its reasoned outcome. The various cases ascribed above can point to anomalies that may not necessarily have occurred in the earlier days of case law from the Court.

Progressively, the Court has seen the number of its cases rise quite considerably, alongside the breadth of issues that are before it on a consistent basis. In *Les Verts*, the Court said that 'neither [Member States or institutions] can avoid a review of the question whether the measures adopted by them are in conformity with the basic constitutional charter, the Treaty'.[216] On a strict reading of *Les Verts*,

[210] Tim Corthaut, 'An Effective Remedy for All? Paradoxes and Controversies in Respect of Judicial Protection in the Field of the CFSP under the European Constitution' (2005) 12 *Tilburg Foreign Law Review* 110 at 144.

[211] Alan Dashwood, 'Mixity in the Era of the Treaty of Lisbon' in Christophe Hillion and Panos Koutrakos (eds), *Mixed Agreements Revisited: The EU and its Member States in the World* (Hart Publishing, 2010) p 354.

[212] Andrea Biondi and Silvia Bartolini, 'Recent Developments in Luxembourg: The Courts' Activities in 2013' (2014) 20 *European Public Law* 611 at 630.

[213] TFEU, Article 274: 'Save where jurisdiction is conferred on the Court of Justice of the European Union by the [t]reaties, disputes to which the Union is a party shall not on that ground be excluded from the jurisdiction of the courts or tribunals of the Member States.'

[214] Cremona (n 16) p 1194.

[215] Kuijper (n 42) p 14.

[216] Case C-294/83, *Parti écologiste 'Les Verts' v Parliament*, ECLI:EU:C:1986:166, para 23.

it can be implied that nothing can escape judicial review in Union law – not even CFSP matters.

5.5. Lingering Questions

It is inevitable that some cases come before the Court that do not have CFSP matters as their focus, but nonetheless have elements of CFSP matters attached to them.[217] In such scenarios, it is thus obliged to interpret the element touching upon CFSP matters.[218] In *Rosneft*, the Court had to declare jurisdiction to prevent national courts from invoking the *acte clair* doctrine in cases where, as the Court saw it, there may have been no recourse to the Court if they incorrectly applied such a doctrine. For otherwise, a consequentialist line of thinking, would allow for varying interpretations to evolve at different national courts, without the possibility for the Court to clarify the law. In this line of thinking, there are a number of outstanding issues with respect to CFSP matters that overlap with the jurisdiction of the Court that have yet to be fully addressed. Each will be discussed in turn.

5.5.1. Primacy

Primacy exists to ensure that EU legal actions are applicable in national law. It dictates that it is national courts and other related national bodies that disapply national laws of Member States when they are in conflict with Union law. Primacy, as a constitutional principle, never formally made it into the Union's primary law as a specific textual element,[219] despite being contained in a specific Declaration annexed to the treaties.[220] It can even be said that the formal absence of primacy in the treaties is meant to preserve some level of national constitutional identity for the superior courts of Member States.[221]

Despite no primacy clause in the treaties, there continues to be lingering questions over the true scope of primacy over CFSP matters, despite the doctrine

[217] For example, see, Case C-550/09, *E and F*, ECLI:EU:C:2010:382.

[218] Morten Broberg and Niels Fenger, *Preliminary References to the European Court of Justice* (Oxford University Press, 2010) p 113.

[219] Although, it was located in the Constitutional Treaty that never made it into force. See, Per Cramér, 'Does the Codification of the Principle of Supremacy Matter?' in John Bell and Claire Kilpatrick (eds), *Cambridge Yearbook of European Legal Studies 2004–2005: Volume 7* (Hart Publishing, 2006).

[220] Declaration 17 of the treaties (Declaration concerning primacy): 'The Conference recalls that, in accordance with well settled case law of the Court of Justice of the European Union, the [t]reaties and the law adopted by the Union on the basis of the [t]reaties have primacy over the law of Member States, under the conditions laid down by the said case law. The Conference has also decided to attach as an Annex to this Final Act the Opinion of the Council Legal Service on the primacy of EC law as set out in 11197/07 (JUR 260).'

[221] Joris Larik, *Foreign Policy Objectives in European Constitutional Law* (Oxford University Press, 2016) p 186.

being one of the early emanating canons of Union law. The European constitutional system has been careful when declaring which principles do or do not apply to selective areas. More generally, however, the treaties have still not handled or attempted to address the issue of primacy of CFSP matters.[222] When the Treaty of Lisbon put an end to the pillar structure, it might have been assumed that the principle of primacy of Union law would stretch beyond the former first pillar areas and begin to cover what were formerly the second and third pillars. Yet, such an assertion is false. Although the pillar structure was formally abandoned, CFSP matters remained an area with special decision-making rules.[223]

As pronounced by the Court as far back as *Costa v ENEL*, in that 'the [t]reaty…could not…be overridden by domestic legal provisions',[224] the application of primacy to CFSP matters is nonetheless not entirely clear. This is given there is no case law to look to,[225] despite the very concept of primacy being re-stated by the Court repeatedly.[226] Primacy functions well due to the existence of the preliminary reference procedure. In CFSP matters, however, prior to *Rosneft*, was a perilous situation. Having national courts disapply national law – the implementation of CFSP matters in a domestic legal order – without any level of certainty whether the national law actually is in conflict with Union law, was an unjustifiable situation.[227] Primacy may not have applied to all CFSP Decisions because questions on CFSP matters could previously not be sent to the Court through a preliminary reference.[228] The Court confirmed in *Rosneft* that the right of a national court to have its questions answered eclipses the incongruities of the treaties on the Court not having full jurisdiction. The opportunity was thus given to the Court, and it swiftly made full use of the circumstances to rectify one such ambiguity, whilst leaving aside the issue of primacy.

This is an important matter that hinges on a question of competence. Article 2(4) TFEU states '[t]he Union shall have competence, in accordance with the provisions of the [TEU], to define and implement a common foreign and security policy', but does not strictly apportion it the exclusive, shared, or supporting competence defined in Articles 3–6 TFEU. Although it is difficult to pin a label on CFSP matters, it has to fit somewhere in the spectrum of competence.

[222] Cremona (n 16) p 1194.
[223] See Chapter 3 of this book.
[224] Case C-6/64, *Flaminio Costa v ENEL*, ECLI:EU:C:1964:66, p 594.
[225] Peter Van Elsuwege, 'EU External Action after the Collapse of the Pillar Structure: In Search of a New Balance between Delimitation and Consistency' (2010) 47 *Common Market Law Review* 987 at 989.
[226] Case C-106/77, *Amministrazione delle Finanze dello Stato v Simmenthal SpA*, ECLI:EU:C:1978:49, and as of late, Case C-378/17, *The Minister for Justice and Equality and The Commissioner of the Garda Síochána v Workplace Relations Commission*, ECLI:EU:C:2018:979. See, John A Usher, 'The Primacy of Community Law' (1978) 3 *European Law Review* 214.
[227] Cramér (n 219) p 72.
[228] Marise Cremona, 'The Two (or Three) Treaty Solution: The New Treaty Structure of the EU' in Andrea Biondi, Piet Eeckhout and Stefanie Ripley (eds), *EU Law after Lisbon* (Oxford University Press, 2012) p 53.

For CFSP matters, competence is non-pre-emptive,[229] in a shared manner. Thus, while Member State actions implementing their own foreign policy can run concurrently to Union actions,[230] the principle of sincere cooperation applies, covering both CFSP matters and non-CFSP matters within external relations.[231] Article 24(3) TEU obliges Members States to act in their individual capacities in such a manner that they 'shall support the Union's external and security policy actively and unreservedly in a spirit of loyalty and mutual solidarity and shall comply with the Union's action in this area'.[232] However, that is not substitute for a clear assertion of the primacy of CFSP matters.

Before the Court's judgment in *Rosneft*, it would be left to national courts to deal with the primacy of CFSP legal acts and national law, with no possibility for the Court to clarify. The consequence of this would be that national courts could interpret primacy the same way they interpret international law generally,[233] differing from the way the Court might interpret it. If the various national courts adjudicate differently on whether to apply the doctrine of primacy, this would not bode well for a coherent EU legal order. With *Rosneft*, the Court now has jurisdiction to declare the primacy of CFSP Decisions over national law, if so asked. Both the Declaration annexed to the treaties, and the Opinion of the Council Legal Service cited within it,[234] do not contain any reservation in respect of CFSP matters.[235] Thus, it is possible to draw the understanding that given the absence of such qualification, the primacy of CFSP matters over national law is understood to exist.

It remains to be seen how far the Court will go in extending the primacy of an act on a CFSP legal basis over national law, although recent jurisprudence gives

[229] Declaration (No 13) concerning the common foreign and security policy, and Declaration (No 14) concerning the common foreign and security policy.

[230] Other such external policies of a parallel nature, outside of CFSP matters, include development cooperation and humanitarian aid. Andrés Delgado Casteleiro, *The International Responsibility of the European Union: From Competence to Normative Control* (Cambridge University Press, 2016) p 29.

[231] Eleftheria Neframi, 'The Duty of Loyalty: Rethinking Its Scope through Its Application in the Field of EU External Relations' (2010) 47 *Common Market Law Review* 323. Moreover, see, Christophe Hillion, 'Mixity and the Coherence in EU External Relations: The Significance of the "Duty of Cooperation"' in Hillion and Koutrakos (eds), (n 211). Albeit, the duty was originally considered more flexible in practice. See, Stephen Hyett, 'The Duty of Co-Operation: A Flexible Concept' in Alan Dashwood and Christophe Hillion (eds), *The General Law of EC External Relations* (Sweet and Maxwell, 2000).

[232] TEU, Article 24(3) furthermore states: '...The Member States shall work together to enhance and develop their mutual political solidarity. They shall refrain from any action which is contrary to the interests of the Union or likely to impair its effectiveness as a cohesive force in international relations.'

[233] De Baere (n 10) p 203.

[234] 'It results from the case law of the Court of Justice that primacy of EC law is a cornerstone principle of Community law. According to the Court, this principle is inherent to the specific nature of the European Community. At the time of the first judgment of this established case law (Costa/ENEL, 15 July 1964, Case 6/64) there was no mention of primacy in the treaty. It is still the case today. The fact that the principle of primacy will not be included in the future treaty shall not in any way change the existence of the principle and the existing case-law of the Court of Justice.' Opinion of the Legal Service (Subject: Primacy of EC Law) (11197/07) (JUR 260).

[235] Allan Rosas and Lorna Armati, *EU Constitutional Law: An Introduction* 3rd edition (Hart Publishing, 2018) p 66.

some indication. For example, in *Opinion 2/13*, the Court said that primacy is one of the 'essential characteristics [that] have given rise to a structured network of principles, rules and mutually interdependent legal relations'.[236] Yet such a proclamation of primacy of CFSP matters over national acts would be a 'significant shift in the balance of power'.[237] However, with such a view, a contrary argument can be made. Given the treaties are otherwise rather descriptive with regard to CFSP matters, and that they contain no text or language on the non-applicability of primacy in CFSP matters, it is therefore perfectly conceivable that primacy of CFSP legal acts over national law is the most logical outline. Primacy is not expressly excluded, and therefore, could be found to apply.

5.5.2. Scope of the Opinion Procedure

Elsewhere, the (attempted) accession of the Union to the ECHR has stirred up questions about the Court's jurisdiction in CFSP matters. The Court has previously stated that the Opinion procedure contained within Article 218(11) TFEU has its limits. In *obiter dicta*, it has asked 'whether it would be appropriate to remove to the judicial arena disputes which could just as satisfactorily be settled at a political level'.[238] Given that CFSP matters were still new to the EU legal order at the time of the first attempt to accede to the ECHR, they featured little in the discussion.[239] When an Opinion was requested, the Court in *Opinion 2/94* dealt accession a swift blow by finding the EU had no competence to accede,[240] therefore there was no need to address issues related to CFSP matters.

It was not until many years later that accession was attempted again, this time with the support of Article 6(2) TEU and discussions leading to a DAA.[241] Again, an Opinion of the Court was requested under Article 218(11) TFEU.[242] The Court in *Opinion 2/13* claimed it had 'not yet had the opportunity to define the extent to which its jurisdiction is limited in CFSP matters'.[243] Yet for the purposes of EU accession to the ECHR, it said 'it is sufficient to declare that, as [Union] law

[236] Opinion 2/13, ECLI:EU:C:2014:2454 ('*Accession of the European Union to the European Convention for the Protection of Human Rights*'), para 167.

[237] Eileen Denza, 'Lines in the Sand: Between Common Foreign Policy and Single Foreign Policy' in Takis Tridimas and Paolisa Nebbia (eds), *European Union Law for the Twenty-First Century: Rethinking the New Legal Order – Volume 1: Constitutional and Public Law, External Relations* (Hart Publishing, 2004) p 269.

[238] 'Report of the Court of Justice on Certain Aspects of the Application of the Treaty on European Union' (Court of Justice of the European Communities 1995).

[239] Barring an honourable exception. O'Leary (n 118) p 366.

[240] Opinion 2/94, ECLI:EU:C:1996:140 ('*Accession by the Community to the European Convention for the Protection of Human Rights and Fundamental Freedoms*').

[241] Council of Europe and European Commission (n 119).

[242] For a fuller account of the Opinion procedure before the Court, see, Butler, 'Pre-Ratification Judicial Review of International Agreements to Be Concluded by the European Union' (n 120).

[243] Opinion 2/13, ECLI:EU:C:2014:2454 ('*Accession of the European Union to the European Convention for the Protection of Human Rights*'), para 251.

now stands, certain acts adopted in the context of the CFSP fall outside the ambit of judicial review by the Court of Justice'.[244] One of the charges the Court opened itself up to on CFSP matters was that it interpreted its own jurisdiction over them rather rigidly. Remarkably, its narrow and unspecific proclamation over its jurisdiction in *Opinion 2/13* can be seen against the backdrop that it examined the DAA anyway.[245]

Yet, whilst *Opinion 2/13* dealt with CFSP matters, which were important grounds for why the Court ultimately found the DAA incompatible with the treaties, that opens up wider questions about relevant legal actors requesting an Opinion when an international agreement, based upon a CFSP legal basis, could be brought before the Court for questions of its compatibility. Article 218 TFEU as a whole encompasses the procedure for the conclusion of international agreements more generally, be it based on a CFSP legal basis or a non-CFSP legal basis. Therefore, it must be assumed the Opinion procedure covers an international agreement proposed to be concluded on a CFSP legal basis. However, the issue here is a practical one, given that when a CFSP legal basis is used for an international agreement, it is usually only the Council that is involved in the opening, negotiation, and conclusion of such an agreement. The Council only has to notify other institutions after an international agreement has entered into force. The clearest examples of this reality were in both the *Mauritius* and *Tanzania* cases.[246] In such circumstances, the other legal actors with sufficient legal standing, such as the Commission and the Parliament, did not even have the possibility to refer such a draft international agreement to the Court for an Opinion in an *ex ante* fashion. Rather, therefore, as a matter of practice, only *ex post* cases appear to be possible for draft international agreements to be concluded on a CFSP legal basis.

5.5.3. Damages

The very existence of damages as a legal remedy within the sphere of Union law has had immense effect. Yet, the issue of damages in CFSP matters is not clear. By their very nature, damages affect actors' behaviour with respect to obligations that stem from Union law. CFSP matters and its constitutional structure set the requirements and threshold to be met before damages apply which, in practice, is very high. The Court has shown restraint by shying away from pronouncements on how the lawfulness of Union actions is compatible with international law.[247]

[244] Ibid. para 252.

[245] Christina Eckes, 'Common Foreign and Security Policy: The Consequences of the Court's Extended Jurisdiction' (2016) 22 *European Law Journal* 492 at 493.

[246] Case C-658/11, *Parliament v Council*, ECLI:EU:C:2014:2025 ('*Mauritius*'); Case C-263/14, *Parliament v Council*, ECLI:EU:C:2016:435 ('*Tanzania*').

[247] Anne Thies, *International Trade Disputes and EU Liability* (Cambridge University Press, 2013) p 76.

However, there is much more scope for actions for damages when the Union has not followed its own internal law.

Article 268 TFEU and Article 340 TFEU govern damages and the contractual liability of the Union.[248] It could be interpreted that allowances for damages brought against the Union exist for whatever kind of action.[249] However, the extent to which this applies to CFSP matters is unclear given the limited jurisdiction of the Court. This reveals a void in the system of judicial protection provided by the treaties. Given how CFSP matters are implemented in practice, the role that Member States play, given their potential involvement in actions on a CFSP legal basis, must be considered. Liability for unlawful actions can be shared between the Union and Member States,[250] but the role of the Court is starkly different from the role played by national courts, as national authorities could only apportion damages attributed by Member State actions.

The General Court has to date taken a narrow view as regards the potential for damages in CFSP matters.[251] Whilst being awarded damages may be possible, applicants have not had much success to date.[252] In *Georgias and Others*,[253] the General Court in a case on CFSP matters linked the settled case law on damages. It stated that if any of the settled condition for damages is not met,[254] then 'the action must be dismissed in its entirety', and thus, other matters do not need to be considered by the General Court. Furthermore, in *Jannatian*, the General Court

[248] TFEU, Article 268: 'The Court of Justice of the European Union shall have jurisdiction in disputes relating to compensation for damage provided for in the second and third paragraphs of Article 340', and Article 340 TFEU: 'The contractual liability of the Union shall be governed by the law applicable to the contract in question. In the case of non-contractual liability, the Union shall, in accordance with the general principles common to the laws of the Member States, make good any damage caused by its institutions or by its servants in the performance of their duties. Notwithstanding the second para, the European Central Bank shall, in accordance with the general principles common to the laws of the Member States, make good any damage caused by it or by its servants in the performance of their duties. The personal liability of its servants towards the Union shall be governed by the provisions laid down in their Staff Regulations or in the Conditions of Employment applicable to them.'

[249] Kathleen Gutman, 'Liability for Breach of EU Law by the Union, Member States and Individuals: Damages, Enforcement and Effective Judicial Protection' in Adam Łazowski and Steven Blockmans (eds), *Research Handbook on EU Institutional Law* (Edward Elgar, 2016) p 445.

[250] See generally, Wouter Wils, 'Concurrent Liability of the Community and a Member State' (1992) 17 *European Law Review* 191. Furthermore, Paul Craig, *EU Administrative Law* 2nd edition (Oxford University Press, 2012) pp 698–702.

[251] For example, see, Case T-338/02, *Segi and Others v Council of the European Union*, ECLI:EU:T:2004:171; Case T-187/11, *Mohamed Trabelsi and Others v Council of the European Union*, ECLI:EU:T:2013:273, para 48, where the Court said the claim for damages was 'manifestly inadmissible'; and Case T-218/11, *Habib Roland Dagher v Council of the European Union*, ECLI:EU:T:2012:82.

[252] Hillion (n 45) p 51.

[253] Case T-168/12, *Aguy Clement Georgias and Others v Council of the European Union and European Commission*, ECLI:EU:T:2014:781.

[254] The conditions being: (1) Conduct of the institutions, alleged by the applicant, being unlawful; (2) Damage must be suffered; and (3) The existence of a causal link between the conduct alleged and damage suffered. The Court in *Georgias* drew two cases for this support. Firstly, from the Court, Case C-26/81, *SA Oleifici Mediterranei v European Economic Community*, ECLI:EU:C:1982:318, para 16; and secondly, from the General Court, Case T-175/94, *International Procurement Services SA v Commission of the European Communities*, ECLI:EU:T:1996:102, para 44.

held that, in light of the provisions on CFSP matters in the treaties, 'a claim seeking compensation for the damage allegedly suffered as a result of the adoption of an act relating to [CFSP matters] falls outside the jurisdiction of the Court'.[255] This is due to Article 275 TFEU, second paragraph, stating the treaties 'do[] not give the Court…jurisdiction to hear or determine any kind of claim for compensation'.[256]

However, the question of how damages might be applicable because of acts on a CFSP legal basis, besides restrictive measures, for example, as a result of CSDP missions and so forth, remains open, but will eventually need to be addressed. There is an understanding in some quarters that the Court could not adjudicate on damages for CSDP missions.[257] This is particularly troubling, given that military missions, one type of CSDP missions, is where violations of human rights can occur. The entire realm of CFSP matters is an area where 'the most serious infractions of values are liable to occur'.[258] In such a scenario, it is likely that jurisdiction to rule will have to be settled before the Court addresses the substance of a question of damages.

Damages can be tied to fundamental rights, which are also protected by the primary law of the Union. Actions for damages have not always been found admissible, particularly if they have been disguised as an action for annulment.[259] Individuals could be affected by EU activity of an operational capacity by actions that are formulated upon a CFSP legal basis,[260] for instance, if errors in CFSP Decisions are copied into EU measures, such as non-CFSP legal acts. The Union may be sued in damages actions on the basis of a non-CFSP Regulation, adopted on an Article 215 TFEU legal basis. Bringing such an action based on Article 340 TFEU to the non-CFSP Regulation may mean, in turn, that the CFSP Decision directed at an addressee does not need to be determined at length.

The unimplemented Constitutional Treaty would have led to the further development of the law on CFSP matters, yet it still would not have resolved the issue of damages.[261] The foreseen lack of damages available in CFSP matters is comparable to how, in the old pillar system, it stood alongside the third pillar, another area in which damages did not apply. It was not for a lack of trying however, as the Court affirmed in both *Gestoras* and *Segi* that it lacked this jurisdiction.[262]

[255] Case T-328/14, *Mahmoud Jannatian v Council of the European Union*, ECLI:EU:T:2016:86, para 31.

[256] Ibid. para 30.

[257] Frederik Naert, 'European Union Common Security and Defence Policy Operations' in André Nollkaemper and Ilias Plakokefalos (eds), *The Practice of Shared Responsibility in International Law* (Cambridge University Press, 2017) p 692.

[258] Stephen Weatherill, *Law and Values in the European Union* (Oxford University Press, 2016) p 406.

[259] Walter Van Gerven, 'The Legal Protection of Private Parties in the Law of the European Economic Community' in Francis G Jacobs (ed), *European Law and the Individual* (North Holland, 1976) p 14.

[260] Anne Thies, 'General Principles in the Development of EU External Relations Law' in Cremona and Thies (n 45) p 150.

[261] Koen Lenaerts and Tim Corthaut, 'Of Birds and Hedges: The Role of Primacy in Invoking Norms of EU Law' (2006) 31 *European Law Review* 287 at 314.

[262] Case C-354/04 P, *Gestoras Pro Amnistía, Juan Mari Olano Olano, Julen Zelarain Errasti v Council*, ECLI:EU:C:2007:115; and Case C-355/04 P, *Segi, Arait, Zubimendi Izaga, and Aritza Galarraga v Council*, ECLI:EU:C:2007:116 ('*Segi*').

However, the Treaty of Lisbon changed this and was seen as a 'great step forward',[263] with the third pillar fully absorbed into the Union's system of judicial protection. Yet the manner in which damages are applicable to CFSP matters, the former second pillar, remains unclear.

Despite the exercise of jurisdiction by the Court in cases like *Rosneft*, it appears that actions for damages coming within the remit of the Court on purely CFSP matters is not going to be entertained by the Court. A more formative manner would be a formal amendment of the treaties would be needed for such an extension, if desired. The Court could have addressed damages in *Opinion 2/13*, given that one of the intervening Member States claimed that, by their reading of the treaties, the Court did not have the applied jurisdiction 'to rule on claims in non-contractual liability in which compensation is sought for damage resulting from a CFSP act or measure'.[264] Yet the Court chose not to address the matter, and it thus remains to be settled.

5.5.4. Staffing

The issue of staffing in CSDP missions, or in other bodies established on a CFSP legal basis, is another area where the extent of the Court's jurisdiction has yet to be fully clarified. The jurisdiction of the Court in staff-related questions and its relationship with CFSP matters may appear to be trivial, but they are immensely important for the overall special character of CFSP matters. *H v Council* concerned the Court's ability to render judgment in a staffing case with respect to a CSDP mission. Such discussion feeds into a broader determination of how the Court can be involved in the operation of the EEAS.[265] At its very basis, it could be asked whether staffing matters escape the Court's protection given a CFSP legal basis, and thus, fall into the jurisdictional carve-out; or whether staffing matters merely constitute a normal matter falling within the scope of judicial review.

What the Court did in *H v Council* was to equate the staffing arrangements in the EDA,[266] in which it was specifically conferred staffing jurisdiction by a CFSP Decision to a CSDP mission founded upon a CFSP legal basis. The implications of the judgment appear to have escaped the attention of the General Court when it gave an order in *Jenkinson* shortly after.[267] However, beyond *H v Council*, there has

[263] Kathleen Gutman, 'The Evolution of the Action for Damages against the European Union and Its Place in the System of Judicial Protection' (2011) 48 *Common Market Law Review* 695 at 701.

[264] Opinion 2/13, ECLI:EU:C:2014:2454 ('*Accession of the European Union to the European Convention for the Protection of Human Rights*'), para 133.

[265] Mauro Gatti, *European External Action Service: Promoting Coherence through Autonomy and Coordination* (Brill 2016) p 188.

[266] L 245/17. Council Joint Action 2004/551/CFSP of 12 July 2004 on the Establishment of the European Defence Agency.

[267] Case T-602/15, *Liam Jenkinson v Council of the European Union and Others*, ECLI:EU:T:2016:660. Appealed on procedural grounds, which succeeded at the Court: Case C-43/17 P, *Liam Jenkinson v Council of the European Union and Others*, ECLI:EU:C:2018:531. The case is currently back, pending again at the General Court: Case T-602/15 RENV, *Jenkinson v Council and Others*, pending.

also been the *KF v SatCen* case involving a challenge to an internal staffing action by the European Union Satellite Centre (SatCen),[268] which was founded upon a CFSP legal basis.[269] As an EU agency, with a legacy of being incorporated within the WEU, its tasks have been to support the Union and its Member States in 'products and services based on exploiting space assets and collateral data, including satellite imagery and aerial imagery, and related services'.

The applicant in their pleading drew a distinction between matters of foreign policy that comes under a CFSP legal basis and, within that same legal basis, matters that are 'purely administrative and relate to staff management'.[270] Thus, the applicant's argument was that the curtailment of the EU judiciary's jurisdiction with respect to CFSP matters only concerned political and strategic matters. Moreover, given that the applicant had no means of alleviation before a national court of any description,[271] failing to assert jurisdiction would deprive the applicant of judicial protection. By contrast, SatCen as the defendant claimed that the treaties did not contain any explicit provisions giving jurisdiction to the EU judiciary over staff disputes between it and its staff. In absence of this, Article 263(5) TFEU[272] allows alternative means of dispute settlement; SatCen claimed that its own Appeal Board was competent to rule on disputes, as per Article 28(6) of its Staff Regulations,[273] and thus possess exclusive jurisdiction,[274] therefore, excluding the General Court.

At first glance, the issue dealt with by the Court previously in *H v Council* appeared relevant to *KF v SatCen*. However, the factual circumstances differed, as did the law. Whilst Article 11(6) of the CFSP Decision on the EDA specifically granted the Court jurisdiction, as utilised in *H v Council* over EDA staffing disputes,[275] no such jurisdiction was explicitly conferred upon the Court in the SatCen staffing arrangements,[276] or by its predecessors.[277] The facts of *H v Council* concerned a seconded expert to the mission established on a CFSP legal basis.

[268] Case T-286/15, *KF v European Union Satellite Centre (SatCen)*, ECLI:EU:T:2018:718. Note, this judgment is pending appeal in Case C-14/19 P, *European Union Satellite Centre (SatCen) v KF*, pending.

[269] L 200/5. Council Joint Action of 20 July 2001 on the Establishment of a European Union Satellite Centre (2001/555/CFSP). For the sake of legal clarity and to consolidate previous changes to the establishing Joint Action of SatCen, a new Decision was adopted in 2014. L 188/73. Council Decision 2014/401/CFSP of 26 June 2014 on the European Union Satellite Centre and Repealing Joint Action 2001/555/CFSP on the Establishment of a European Union Satellite Centre.

[270] Case T-286/15, *KF v European Union Satellite Centre (SatCen)*, ECLI:EU:T:2018:718, para 60.

[271] Ibid. para 63.

[272] TFEU, Article 263, fifth para: 'Acts setting up bodies, offices and agencies of the Union may lay down specific conditions and arrangements concerning actions brought by natural or legal persons against acts of these bodies, offices or agencies intended to produce legal effects in relation to them.'

[273] L 276/1. Council Decision 2009/747/CFSP of 14 September 2009 Concerning the Staff Regulations of the European Union Satellite Centre. Note, there is now an updated Staff Regulation. See, L 123/7. Council Decision (CFSP) 2017/824 of 15 May 2017 Concerning the Staff Regulations of the European Union Satellite Centre.

[274] Case T-286/15, *KF v European Union Satellite Centre (SatCen)*, ECLI:EU:T:2018:718, paras 65–68.

[275] L 266/55. Council Decision (CFSP) 2015/1835 of 12 October 2015 Defining the Statute, Seat and Operational Rules of the European Defence Agency (n 142).

[276] L 276/1. Council Decision 2009/747/CFSP of 14 September 2009 (n 273).

[277] L 39/44. Staff Regulations of the European Union Satellite Centre, 9 February 2002.

By contrast, the matter in *KF v SatCen* was an individual employed as contract staff, albeit in the position of Head of the Administrative Division of the agency. Accordingly, direct transposition was not possible;[278] however, it would be highly influential in determining jurisdiction.

Despite the distinction, the General Court launched a full-throated defence of the Court's *H v Council* judgment,[279] noting that 'the fact that the contested decisions fall within the framework of the function of a body operating in the field of…CFSP [matters] cannot, in itself, mean that the EU judicature lacks jurisdiction to rule on this dispute'.[280] Moreover, given how Article 24(1) TEU and Article 275 TFEU derogations are to be interpreted narrowly and that Article 47 CFR supports this view.[281] the General Court determined the actions in question were those 'purely acts of staff management',[282] so the dispute was 'comparable to disputes between an institution, body, office of agency of the [EU] which are not covered by…CFSP [matters]…which may be brought before the EU judicature under Article 270 TFEU'.[283] The General Court justified including contract staff within the scope of its jurisdiction to exercise judicial review because of an anomaly in the existing establishing decision of SatCen.[284] Namely, Article 8(3) provided for seconded officials to be within the jurisdiction of the EU judiciary,[285] but not contract staff.

In a consequentialist reading, if the General Court had found otherwise, it would have left staff in different Union offshoots falling with the scope of CFSP matters treated differently, leading to divergent and inconsistent case law, which would ultimately have to be rectified. Given the General Court had prior jurisdiction with respect to staff of EU institutions and equal treatment,[286] it saw no distinction here, and thus, exercised jurisdiction accordingly, despite the absence of an affirmative legal basis to do so. In light of the increasing size and capabilities of CSDP missions, staffing issues are likely to continue to arise, as will the

[278] Case T-286/15, *KF v European Union Satellite Centre (SatCen)*, ECLI:EU:T:2018:718, para 78.

[279] Case C-455/14 P, *H v Council*, ECLI:EU:C:2016:569.

[280] Case T-286/15, *KF v European Union Satellite Centre (SatCen)*, ECLI:EU:T:2018:718, para 83.

[281] The General Court here invoked, as support, Case C-72/15, *Rosneft Oil Company OJSC v. Her Majesty's Treasury, The Secretary of State for Business, Innovation and Skills, The Financial Conduct Authority*, ECLI:EU:C:2017:236.

[282] Case T-286/15, *KF v European Union Satellite Centre (SatCen)*, ECLI:EU:T:2018:718, para 91.

[283] Ibid. para 95. The General Court invoked an analogous situation with respect to the European Investment Bank (EIB), implying bodies of all kinds with CFSP matters are not unique. Case T-192/99, *Roderick Dunnett, Thomas Hackett and Mateo Turró Calvet v European Investment Bank*, ECLI:EU:T:2001:72, para 54.

[284] L 188/73. Council Decision 2014/401/CFSP of 26 June 2014 (n 269).

[285] Article 8(3): 'The need for secondment of staff to SATCEN shall be determined by the Board in consultation with the Director of SATCEN. In agreement with the Director, experts from Member States and officials from the EEAS, Union institutions agencies or bodies may be seconded to SATCEN for an agreed period, either to posts within SATCEN's organisational structure and/or for specific tasks and projects.'

[286] To cite one illustration of the General Court and the European Central Bank (ECB), Case T-333/99, *X v European Central Bank*, ECLI:EU:T:2001:251, para 40.

legal complexity of the jurisdiction of the Court. In response to piracy off the east African coast, the Union launched Operation Atalanta (EUNAVFOR) in 2008 to combat such activity[287] and to protect core European interests and support third states in such endeavours. It subsequently launched its second naval mission, Operation Sophia (EUNAVFOR Med) in 2015,[288] in response to irregular migrants crossing the Mediterranean. Such large-scale CSDP missions reveal staffing issues that may in turn end up before the Union's judiciary where its jurisdiction to rule will be questioned once again.

5.5.5. Infringements

Infringement actions by Member States for failure to comply with CFSP legal acts do not lie within the ambit of the Court's jurisdiction.[289] Generally speaking, infringements of Union law may be initiated at both the Union level[290] and by other Member States,[291] but the Commission has a specific role in CFSP matters that is 'defined by the [t]reaties', as per Article 24 TEU.[292] Therefore, implementation of CFSP matters at national level cannot be brought before the Court through an infringement action by the Commission.

The lack of infringement proceedings in CFSP matters is also underlined with regard to the duty of sincere cooperation that is applicable with Article 24(3) TEU, third paragraph, stating that '[t]he Council and the High Representative shall ensure compliance with these principles' and not the Commission or the Court. Moreover, Article 260(3) TFEU implies that infringements brought to the Court are to be of a legislative nature. Accordingly, given CFSP legal acts are non-legislative, which underlines that CFSP matters are exempt from infringement actions by the Commission. By contrast, a Member State failing to fulfil its obligations flowing from a CFSP Decision would be rare, given that the vast majority of decisions must be taken unanimously. That, however, does not rule out the possibility for inter-state litigation in CFSP matters taken upon Article 259 TFEU, for this refers to obligations arising under Union law, and not merely EU legislation.[293]

[287] L 301/33. Council Joint Action 2008/851/CFSP of 10 November 2008 on a European Union Military Operation to Contribute to the Deterrence, Prevention and Rerression of Acts of Piracy and Armed Robbery off the Somali Coast. See, Graham Butler and Martin Ratcovich, 'Operation Sophia in Uncharted Waters: European and International Law Challenges for the EU Naval Mission in the Mediterranean Sea' (2016) 85 *Nordic Journal of International Law* 235.

[288] L 122/31. Council Decision (CFSP) 2015/778 of 18 May 2015 on a European Union Military Operation in the Southern Central Mediterranean (EUNAVFOR Med).

[289] Geert De Baere, 'European Integration and the Rule of Law in Foreign Policy' in Julie Dickson and Pavlos Eleftheriadis (eds), *Philosophical Foundations of European Union Law* (Oxford University Press, 2012) p 369.

[290] By the Commission, as per Article 258 TFEU.

[291] TFEU, Article 259. For more, see, Graham Butler, 'The Court of Justice as an Inter-State Court' (2017) 36 *Yearbook of European Law* 179.

[292] TEU, Article 24(1), second para.

[293] Butler (n 291).

5.5.6. Forum Non Conveniens

Forum shopping, in legal terms, can be classified as selecting the best avenue for seeking adjudication with the intent being that it would reach a desired result favourable to the applicant. It is akin to cherry picking, and could be a new development in CFSP matters because of the *Rosneft* judgment and the Court's assertion of jurisdiction for challenges of a CFSP Decision through a preliminary reference. Whilst *Rosneft* has had the effect that cases on CFSP matters can reach the EU judiciary two ways – both through direct actions and preliminary references – there are still distinctions to draw.

As put by the General Court, 'the legal basis of the action for annulment, namely Article 263 TFEU, differ[s] from those of a [preliminary reference] introduced by Article 267 TFEU' with respect to CFSP matters,[294] principally due to the fact-finding work that the General Court does. Furthermore, 'the conditions relating to the cause of action and subject matter of the [current] dispute cannot be regarded as being fulfilled…for the purpose of a finding that the authority of *res judicata* attaches to the [*Rosneft*] judgment'.[295] This, in effect, is the General Court trying to ensure that the potential ramification of *Rosneft*, that cases on CFSP matters would be more speedily heard through the preliminary reference procedure, is offset by ensuring the General Court has a continued role in restrictive measures cases.[296]

Restrictive measures, given their CFSP legal basis, take up a substantial portion of its docket, with parties traditionally bringing actions to the General Court under Article 263 TFEU.[297] The litigant in *Rosneft* brought a case to the General Court,[298] in conjunction with a case before a national court. Nothing in primary law or the Court's own internal rules of procedure prevents or even discourages this from occurring. An issue therefore arises as to how judicial review of

[294] Case T-715/14, *PAO Rosneft Oil Company, formerly NK Rosneft OAO and Others v Council of the European Union*, ECLI:EU:T:2018:544, para 98.

[295] Ibid. para 99.

[296] It should be noted that this *PAO Rosneft* judgment of the General Court is currently pending appeal before the Court. Case C-732/18 P, *Rosneft e.a v Council*, pending.

[297] TFEU, Article 263, fourth para: 'Any natural or legal person may, under the conditions laid down in the first and second paras, institute proceedings against an act addressed to that person or which is of direct and individual concern to them, and against a regulatory act which is of direct concern to them and does not entail implementing measures.'

[298] Case T-715/14, *PAO Rosneft Oil Company, formerly NK Rosneft OAO and Others v Council of the European Union*, ECLI:EU:T:2018:544. Once the case was also on the docket of the Court, the General Court case was stayed by an Order of the President of the Council Court pending the judgment of the Court in Case C-72/15. This was in accordance with Article 54, third para of the Statute of the Court: 'Where the Court of Justice and the General Court are seised of cases in which the same relief is sought, the same issue of interpretation is raised or the validity of the same act is called in question, the General Court may, after hearing the parties, stay the proceedings before it until such time as the Court of Justice has delivered judgment or, where the action is one brought pursuant to Article 263 of the Treaty on the Functioning of the European Union, may decline jurisdiction so as to allow the Court of Justice to rule on such actions. In the same circumstances, the Court of Justice may also decide to stay the proceedings before it; in that event, the proceedings before the General Court shall continue.'

CFSP matters works when a preliminary reference is made under Article 267 TFEU by a national court to the Court of Justice while a direct action on the same matter is before the General Court under Article 263 TFEU. Both procedures, preliminary references and direct actions, accomplish similar objectives, ensuring effective judicial protection. However, for judicial protection to work effectively, only one route to a judicial remedy is needed.

In *Brahim Samba Diouf*, the Court stated that '[t]he principle of effective judicial protection affords an individual a right of access to a court or tribunal but not to a number of levels of jurisdiction'.[299] The *forum non conveniens* doctrine, a 'judge-made concept'[300] according to which a judicial body may decide it will not exercise jurisdiction over a matter, means that another judicial forum may be the more appropriate venue for answering certain questions. The Court in *Rosneft* might have wanted to invoke the *forum non conveniens* principle whereby the General Court would be designated the better court for dealing with the substance of the challenged restrictive measure. Yet, it did not do so. The Court had previously addressed the *forum non conveniens* issue head on, albeit in a different context. In *Owusu*,[301] the Court held that Member States must accept jurisdiction in certain cases to ensure legal uniformity across the Member States.[302] However, given that the questions in *Rosneft* arrived at the Court from a national court through the preliminary reference procedure, an invocation of the *forum non conveniens* doctrine would have been unsuitable. This finding is in stark contrast to a prior case on CFSP matters, *H v Council*,[303] an appeal from the General Court in which, once the Court had established the jurisdiction of the EU courts, it sent the case back to the General Court for adjudication on the merits.[304] *H v Council* therefore confirms that the EU courts are the proper forum for judicial review in CFSP matters, and not national courts.

The fact that the *Rosneft* judgment favoured a preliminary reference over a direct action is consequential because it may relieve the General Court of some of its caseload. This is particularly remarkable because there are 'good arguments supporting the view that the preliminary [reference] procedure does not offer an equivalent alternative to a direct action before the EU courts'.[305] These arguments

[299] Case C-69/10, *Brahim Samba Diouf v Ministre du Travail, de l'Emploi et de l'Immigration*, ECLI:EU:C:2011:524, para 69.
[300] Trevor C Hartley, 'The European Union and the Systematic Dismantling of the Common Law of Conflict of Laws' (2005) 54 *International and Comparative Law Quarterly* 813.
[301] Case C-281/02, *Andrew Owusu v NB Jackson, trading as "Villa Holidays Bal-Inn Villas" and Others*, ECLI:EU:C:2005:120. For commentary, see, Adrian Briggs, 'The Death of Harrods: Forum Non Conveniens and the European Court' (2005) 121 *Law Quarterly Review* 535.
[302] Ibid. paras 43–46.
[303] Case C-455/14 P, *H v Council*, ECLI:EU:C:2016:569. Appeal of Case T-271/10, *H v Council*, ECLI:EU:T:2014:702. For analysis, see, Van Elsuwege (n 151).
[304] Case T-271/10 RENV, *H v Council*, ECLI:EU:T:2018:180. On procedural grounds, the case that returned to the General Court has been appealed again to the Court. Case C-413/18 P, *H v Council*, pending.
[305] Christina Eckes, *EU Counter-Terrorist Policies and Fundamental Rights: The Case of Individual Sanctions* (Oxford University Press, 2009) p 349.

include the fact that an entity subject to restrictive measures goes on an indirect path to the Court via a national court; and the preliminary reference follows a longer (albeit faster) procedural road to a legal remedy than a direct action. Given the very nature of the preliminary reference procedure, it has been argued that preliminary references may never come before the General Court because the procedure 'cannot logically operate with a hierarchical [Union] judicial system tuned to eventually produce two such authoritative pronouncements'.[306] Thus, *Rosneft* may prompt targets of EU restrictive measures to forum-shop, in that firstly, they may bring a direct action to the General Court; and, secondly, for speedier results, simultaneously lodge a complaint before a national court and seek a referral to the Court.

Such forum shopping could lead to circumvention of time limits for bringing cases. While the validity of Union law measures can be challenged through any means that a question reaches the Court, procedural distinctions apply. For example, direct actions for annulment under Article 263 TFEU must be brought within two months[307] while preliminary references under Article 267 TFEU have no prescribed time limit. Theoretically, the unlimited period provided to applicants under the preliminary reference procedure may threaten the limitation that applies under the direct action procedure. One month after the applicant in *Rosneft* filed a direct action with the General Court, it separately brought a lawsuit before a national court.[308] This could be seen as an attempt to *de facto* extend the time limit applicants face under the *TWD* doctrine,[309] which prevents cases coming under a preliminary reference after the specified period that is set down for actors with sufficient *locus standi* to bring a direct action. As the Court explained, this would 'in effect enable the person concerned to overcome the definitive nature which the decision assumes as against that person once the time-limit for bringing an action has expired'.[310] The *TWD* doctrine was not directly addressed in *Rosneft*, but the Court did affirm that the applicant had standing to challenge the measure before the General Court.[311] In another recent restrictive measures case, however, in

[306] Hjalte Rasmussen, 'Docket Control Mechanisms, the EC Court and the Preliminary References Procedure' in Mads Andenas (ed), *Article 177 References to the European Court: Policy and Practice* (Butterworths 1994) p 93. That is assuming that if the General Court gave judgments in preliminary reference cases, they would be appealable to the Court.

[307] TFEU, Article 263, sixth para: 'The proceedings provided for in this Article shall be instituted within two months of the publication of the measure, or of its notification to the plaintiff, or, in the absence thereof, of the day on which it came to the knowledge of the latter, as the case may be.'

[308] Poli (n 169) p 1802.

[309] Case C-188/92, *TWD Textilwerke Deggendorf GmbH v Bundesrepublik Deutschland*, ECLI:EU:C:1994:90.

[310] Ibid. para 18.

[311] 'It is inherent in that complete system of legal remedies and procedures that persons bringing proceedings must, when an action is brought before a national court or tribunal, have the right to challenge the legality of provisions contained in European Union acts on which a decision or national measure adopted in respect of them is based, pleading the invalidity of that decision or measure, in order that the national court or tribunal, having itself no jurisdiction to declare such invalidity, consults the Court on that matter by means of a [preliminary reference], unless those persons unquestionably

A and Others, the Court confirmed that the *TWD* doctrine should not be abused when there are multiple ways to challenge a legal act.[312]

With the jurisdiction in cases on CFSP matters through the preliminary reference procedure and the possibility of forum shopping between the Court and the General Court, there is the possibility that forum shopping in restrictive measures cases could emerge, and therein lies the potential for the role of the General Court in direct actions in restrictive measures cases to be undermined. Forum shopping is not new in Union law in a horizontal sense as the issue potentially arose as a result of the *Masterfoods* case.[313] However, forum shopping between different national courts in Member States never materialised.[314] Forum shopping on a vertical level because of *Rosneft* is much more problematic. Litigants, if they have the option, choose their battleground based on a number of factors, including the ability to plead a case in their favour, but also the timeframe that a court or tribunal needs to render a decision. This is not to say that the litigant in *Rosneft* was necessarily forum shopping, but rather that the judgment has potentially set the stage for future cases. Going forward, an individual chamber of the General Court handling a case can take a decision to stay proceedings, allowing the Court to deal with a preliminary reference case on its docket first. Therefore, a scenario could develop in which the Court, in a future *Rosneft*-esque case, might prefer to dismiss it or, alternatively, encourage parties to take a direct action to the General Court.

Pre-Lisbon, the avenues for challenging the Union's restrictive measures through a preliminary reference were also dealt with in *Segi*,[315] challenging a Common Position. After that judgment, similar concerns about forum shopping arose. There the question was whether national courts should hear cases brought by legal entities subject of restrictive measures determined by their residence or by their citizenship,[316] if they were even Union citizens at all. However, this issue never arose given the abolition of Common Positions by the Treaty of Lisbon

had the right to bring an action against those provisions on the basis of Article 263 TFEU and failed to exercise that right within the period prescribed.' Case C-72/15, *Rosneft Oil Company OJSC v Her Majesty's Treasury, The Secretary of State for Business, Innovation and Skills, The Financial Conduct Authority*, ECLI:EU:C:2017:236, para 67.

[312] 'It follows that a request for a preliminary [reference] concerning the validity of an act of the European Union can be dismissed only in the event that, although the action for annulment of an act of the European Union would unquestionably have been admissible, the natural or legal person capable of bringing such an action abstained from doing so within the prescribed period and is pleading the unlawfulness of that act in national proceedings in order to encourage the national court to submit a request for a preliminary [reference] to the Court of Justice concerning the validity of that act, thereby circumventing the fact that that act is final as against him once the time limit for his bringing an action has expired.' Case C-158/14, *A and Others v Minister van Buitenlandse Zaken*, ECLI:EU:C:2017:202, para 70. It is worth noting that *A and Others* and *Rosneft* had the same *juge rapporteur* and were delivered in the same month – March 2017.

[313] Case C-344/98, *Masterfoods Ltd v HB Ice Cream Ltd*, ECLI:EU:C:2000:689.

[314] Imelda Maher, 'Competition Law Modernization: An Evolutionary Tale?' in Paul Craig and Gráinne De Búrca (eds), *The Evolution of EU Law* 2nd edition (Oxford University Press, 2011) p 733.

[315] Case C-355/04 P, *Segi, Arait, Zubimendi Izaga, and Aritza Galarraga v Council*, ECLI:EU:C:2007:116 ('*Segi*').

[316] Christina Eckes, 'Sanctions against Individuals: Fighting Terrorism within the European Legal Order' (2008) 4 *European Constitutional Law Review* 205 at 212.

shortly thereafter. The possibility of forum shopping has the potential to deprive the General Court of a sizeable portion of its docket. It remains to be seen if and how forum shopping will manifest itself in future cases on CFSP matters, including restrictive measures.

5.5.7. The Role of National Courts

There is a broad understanding that judicial power within the Union is to encompass not just the EU courts, but also the national courts within EU Member States.[317] The monopolistic reading of the Court's continued assertion of ultimate interpretation has been claimed to have little textual support.[318] However, that is what has happened. It has long been held, since *Foto-Frost*,[319] that only the Court itself, and not national courts, can invalidate Union law. In light of the *Rosneft* judgment, it has been advocated that *Foto-Frost* be revisited, and adjusted, to take into account the curtailed jurisdiction of the Court.[320] This would be an abnormal route for the Court to follow, given that when *Foto-Frost* was decided, the Court had less jurisdiction than it does in the post-Lisbon world. The *Foto-Frost* doctrine has worked well up to now, and the Court has not seen fit for it to be revisited. Arguably, chipping away at the *Foto-Frost* doctrine would have the potential for it to be undermined altogether.

Although national courts are crucial to the effective functioning of the EU legal order, they are largely invisible in the text of the treaties. The *Les Verts* doctrine[321] of a *complete* system of legal remedies and procedures in the EU legal order can be interpreted to mean that a single entity, the Court, cannot be single-handedly responsible for judicial remedies. A *complete* system, instead, comes from the notion that multiple actors can provide legal remedies, guaranteeing a role for national courts. The EU's judicial architecture is decentralised, generating dialogue between the courts of all kinds, at both appellate and first-instance levels in the Member States. The decentralisation of the EU judicial system imposes widespread obligations. For example, national courts' failure to comply with 'the mandate of [Article 267 TFEU – the preliminary reference procedure] is of course itself a treaty violation'[322] and thus, they too fit into the *Les Verts* doctrine. National courts

[317] Koen Lenaerts, 'Some Reflections on the Separation of Powers in the European Community' (1991) 28 *Common Market Law Review* 11 at 18.

[318] Gareth Davies, 'Does the Court of Justice Own the Treaties? Interpretative Pluralism as a Solution to over-Constitutionalisation' (2018) 24 *European Law Journal* 358 at 365.

[319] Case C-314/85, *Foto-Frost v Hauptzollamt Lübeck-Ost*, ECLI:EU:C:1987:452.

[320] Koutrakos (n 156) p 32.

[321] Case C-294/83, *Parti écologiste 'Les Verts' v Parliament*, ECLI:EU:C:1986:166, para 23. See Butler (n 144).

[322] Eric Stein, Peter Hay and Michel Waelbroeck, *European Community Law and Institutions in Perspective: Text, Cases and Readings* (The Michie Company, 1976) p 262. As demonstrated recently, Case C-416/17, *Commission v France*, ECLI:EU:C:2018:811, for the failure of the French *Conseil d'État* to make a reference to the Court.

are already strongholds when it comes to providing effective remedies. Colloquially put, 'the torch...has been passed on to them'[323] and they too give effect to Union law and are therefore jointly responsible for ensuring judicial protection. If, hypothetically, the Court did not undertake judicial review of CFSP legal acts, what forum would there be for judicial review of CFSP matters? The apparent answer would be the national courts. Within the EU legal order, national courts retain certain powers, and the enforcement of Union law is 'in principle [left] to the national courts'.[324] Yet, national courts cannot do what the Court does, namely, authoritatively interpret or invalidate Union law.

The retention of power by the national courts poses inherent problems for the EU legal order. In *Busseni*,[325] the Court declared that '[i]t would...be contrary to the objectives and the coherence of the [t]reaties' if some Union treaties had the Court as their ultimate arbiter,[326] but the European Coal and Steel Community Treaty (ECSC) had no such arbiter. Such a division would result in a situation in which powers 'were to be retained exclusively by the various national courts, whose interpretations might differ',[327] preventing the uniform interpretation of Union law. In addition, the practical result of the *Segi* judgment was that if a national court was unsure about the validity of an EU legal act with respect to restrictive measures, it could make a preliminary reference,[328] even though the text of the treaties at the time did not provide for preliminary references explicitly.

Given that *Segi* was resolved a decade before *Rosneft*, it is puzzling why it took so long for the jurisdictional questions in cases on CFSP matters based on a preliminary reference to be answered. One possible answer is the fact that CFSP legal acts have not always been 'sufficiently clear and precise',[329] in comparison to other EU legal acts. Notwithstanding the prominence of national courts in ensuring that Union law functions effectively, one could read *Rosneft* to mean that national courts were 'dismissed' from the task of providing sufficient judicial protection.[330] The Court labelled national courts as '"ordinary" courts within the [EU] legal order'.[331] This status in turn begs the question of whether national courts are servants of Union law, with the Court as the master of Union law. The role of

[323] Theodore Konstadinides, *The Rule of Law in the European Union: The Internal Dimension* (Hart Publishing, 2017) p 136.

[324] Koen Lenaerts and Piet Van Nuffel, *European Union Law* Robert Bray and Nathan Cambien (eds) 3rd edition (Sweet and Maxwell, 2011) p 524.

[325] Case C-221/88, *European Coal and Steel Community v Acciaierie e Ferriere Busseni SpA (in liquidation)*, ECLI:EU:C:1990:84.

[326] Such as the European Economic Community treaty and the Euratom treaty.

[327] Case C-221/88, *European Coal and Steel Community v Acciaierie e Ferriere Busseni SpA (in liquidation)*, ECLI:EU:C:1990:84, para 16.

[328] De Baere (n 10) p 185.

[329] Cramér (n 219) p 72. This is supported in, Ramses A Wessel, 'Good Governance and EU Foreign, Security and Defence Policy' in Deirdre Curtin and Ramses A Wessel (eds), *Good Governance and the European Union: Reflections on Concepts, Institutions and Substance* (Intersentia, 2005) p 241.

[330] Koutrakos (n 156) p 23.

[331] Opinion 1/09, ECLI:EU:C:2011:123 ('*Creation of a Unified Patent Litigation System*'), para 80.

national courts has been fixed since *Foto-Frost*,[332] when national courts, whatever their stature, were duly informed that their powers did not extend to invalidating Union law. Even as early as the 1960s, before *Foto-Frost* confirmed the situation, it was understood that '[t]he Court alone can invalidate illegal acts' of the Union.[333] Given that the contemporary Article 344 TFEU provides that 'Member States undertake not to submit a dispute concerning the interpretation or application of the [t]reaties to any method of settlement other than those provided for therein', it could be read that the Court is the only body to resolve CFSP matters.

National courts could be seen as mere supporters of the EU legal order, without any meaningful role in decision-making once a preliminary reference has returned to them. That is not to say the Court had or has abandoned national courts; indeed, quite the opposite. The Court championed the role of national courts in *Opinion 1/09* when it stated that 'the tasks attributed to the national courts and to the Court of Justice respectively are indispensable to the preservation of the very nature of the law established by the [t]reaties'.[334] Furthermore, it stated that the preliminary reference procedure is 'essential for the preservation of the [Union] character of the law established by the [t]reaties'.[335] Whatever the implications stemming from *Rosneft*, they ultimately came at the cost of preserving the functioning and effectiveness of Article 267 TFEU.

The uniformity of Union law can 'be frustrated' by national courts,[336] particularly if they act in a manner that undermines Union law. In addition, there are limits to the effectiveness of national courts under Union law, and it may be preferable in many instances to have issues solved by an EU court. As one well-cited Advocate General Opinion noted, 'proceedings before national courts are not, however, capable of guaranteeing that individuals seeking to challenge the validity of [Union] measures are granted fully effective judicial protection'.[337] To prevent any lack of judicial cooperation from hindering the effective functioning of the EU legal order, dialogue, cooperation, and respect for the courts' differing judicial roles is essential.

In the early days, the Court had to secure the cooperation and goodwill of national courts,[338] not only for referring cases, but also for enforcing them. Legally, national courts are bound to observe the principle of sincere cooperation

[332] Case C-314/85, *Foto-Frost v Hauptzollamt Lübeck-Ost*, ECLI:EU:C:1987:452.

[333] John Temple Lang, *The Common Market and Common Law* (University of Chicago Press, 1966) p 15.

[334] Opinion 1/09, ECLI:EU:C:2011:123 ('*Creation of a Unified Patent Litigation System*'), para 85.

[335] Ibid. para 83.

[336] Jeffrey C Cohen, 'The European Preliminary Reference and US Supreme Court Review of State Court Judgments: A Study in Comparative Judicial Federalism' (1996) 44 *American Journal of Comparative Law* 421 at 443.

[337] Opinion of Advocate General Jacobs, Case C-50/00 P, *Unión de Pequeños Agricultores v Council of the European Union*, ECLI:EU:C:2002:197, para 40.

[338] Giuseppe Federico Mancini, 'The Making of A Constitution For Europe' (1989) 26 *Common Market Law Review* 595 at 605. See also, Mauro Cappelletti, *The Judicial Process in Comparative Perspective* (Clarendon Press, 1989) p 367.

under Article 4(3) TEU,[339] which is applicable to CFSP matters.[340] Extensive cooperation now takes place, and on the same day the Court delivered its judgment in *Rosneft*, a forum of judges from the EU courts and the superior national courts of the Member States noted that '[t]he Court of Justice, in close cooperation with the national courts, will continue to fulfil the duty entrusted to it by the [t]reaties of ensuring respect for the law by all and for all, thereby safeguarding the values common to the citizens of the EU and the Member States'.[341] Yet, the *Rosneft* judgment's rejection of a meaningful role for national courts in CFSP matters could strain the otherwise cooperative relationship shared by the national and European courts. The Court's repudiation of a role for national courts in filling the legal gaps that remain with respect to CFSP matters has been strongly criticised,[342] and calls could be made, given such developments, for allowing national courts a greater role in the judicial review of CFSP matters.

The separation of powers between the Union judiciary and the national judiciary has long been clear. Before *Foto-Frost* was decided, it was argued that 'it is a matter for the [Union] Court to interpret [Union] law and to determine the validity of acts of the institutions', and, accordingly, 'it is for the national judge to apply this law, thus interpreted and evaluated, in resolving the case before [themselves]'.[343] This uncompromising approach appears to mark a clear hierarchy. The *Foto-Frost* doctrine has been directly linked with CFSP matters[344] and there is no reason to suggest that just because these are different from other Union policies, *Foto-Frost* would not apply. There is one EU legal order, of which CFSP matters are an element, maintaining its 'specific rules of procedures'.[345] *Rosneft* did not alter the *Foto-Frost* doctrine,[346] but rather, it firmly supported it.

Calls have been made for a greater role for national courts in the EU legal order more generally,[347] but as evidenced in *Rosneft*, the Court is not willing to

[339] TEU, Article 4(3): 'Pursuant to the principle of sincere cooperation, the Union and the Member States shall, in full mutual respect, assist each other in carrying out tasks which flow from the [t]reaties. The Member States shall take any appropriate measure, general or particular, to ensure fulfilment of the obligations arising out of the [t]reaties or resulting from the acts of the institutions of the Union. The Member States shall facilitate the achievement of the Union's tasks and refrain from any measure which could jeopardise the attainment of the Union's objectives.'

[340] See Andrés Delgado Casteleiro and Joris Larik, 'The Duty to Remain Silent: Limitless Loyalty in EU External Relations?' (2011) 36 *European Law Review* 524.

[341] Press, Release: Judges' Forum: Celebration of the 60th Anniversary of the Signing of the Rome Treaties – March 2017.

[342] See, Koutrakos (n 156).

[343] Pierre Pescatore, *The Law of Integration: Emergence of a New Phenomenon in International Relations, Based on the Experience of the European Communities* (A W Sijthoff, 1974) p 99.

[344] Opinion of Advocate General Wahl, Case C-455/14 P, *H v Council*, ECLI:EU:C:2016:212, para 102.

[345] TFEU, Article 24(1).

[346] It ought to be noted that in *Segi*, it was proposed by the Advocate General that the *Foto-Frost* doctrine would not apply to the then pillars – CFSP matters and JHA matters – thus finding a strong role of national courts. Opinion of Advocate General Mengozzi, Cases C-354/04 P, *Gestoras Pro Amnistía, Juan Mari Olano Olano, and Julen Zelarain Errasti v Council of the European Union ('Gestoras')*, and Case C-355/04 P, *Segi, Arait, Zubimendi Izaga, and Aritza Galarraga v Council*, ECLI:EU:C:2006:667 ('*Segi*'), para 121. However, that was a point that the Court did not follow.

[347] See, Jan Komárek, '"In the Court(s) We Trust?" On the Need for Hierarchy and Differentiation in the Preliminary Ruling Procedure' (2007) 32 *European Law Review* 467.

seriously entertain this idea. If national courts are empowered to adjudicate on CFSP matters, their competence would only extend to the disapplication of legal measures on a CFSP legal basis in the national context. This would not only prove wildly insufficient for ensuring proper remedies for subjects and objects of the EU's restrictive measures regime but would also be unsatisfactory from a legal certainty perspective, potentially leading to divergences among the different national courts. Granting powers to national courts in CFSP matters as an indirect way for the Member States to retain some level of control simply tiptoes around the critical flaws in EU primary law. Such a position would be unsustainable in the long-term and would inevitably cause fractures in the EU legal order. Setting aside the national courts' role in CFSP matters is not the same as abandoning them, however. As the Advocate General noted in *H v Council*, granting national courts the power to annul EU legal acts, such as CFSP legal acts, would lead to 'potential[ly] grave repercussions on the Union's and Member States' security and foreign policy'.[348] Thus, it is perfectly legitimate to ensure that judicial review is maintained at EU level for the functioning of the EU legal order.

The number of cases on CFSP matters of constitutional importance to reach the Court is always going to be limited, given that access to it is quite restricted. However, if national courts are to be left to deal with CFSP matters, notwithstanding the *Foto-Frost* judgment,[349] this may potentially lead to different interpretations emerging, lacking any form of coherence. With a Court not having the ability to rule in CFSP matters, authority would then appear to revert to the national courts. Given that Member States may never have wished to transfer the competence,[350] it is the natural fallback. Despite national adjudication on CFSP matters being limited and thus confined to the national jurisdiction, alternative versions of case law without clear guidance from the Court on matters of Union law can only be detrimental. The hesitation to allow the Court full jurisdiction in some aspects of the treaties demonstrates distrust. The intended isolation of CFSP matters in the treaties, according to the British Foreign Secretary prior to the amendments of the Treaty of Lisbon, was to 'ensure the "ring-fencing" of CFSP [matters] as a distinct, equal area of action'.[351] By contrast, what the revision actually did was to empower the Court to get a better foothold in CFSP matters.

Most recently, CFSP matters arose between a national court in the United Kingdom in 2018 dealing with whether, in absence of jurisdiction of the Court,

[348] Opinion of Advocate General Wahl, Case C-455/14 P, *H v Council*, ECLI:EU:C:2016:212, para 102.

[349] Case C-314/85, *Foto-Frost v Hauptzollamt Lübeck-Ost*, ECLI:EU:C:1987:452. See, Gerhard Bebr, 'The Reinforcement of the Constitutional Review of Community Acts Under Article 177 EEC Treaty (Case 314/85 and 133 to 136/85)' (1988) 25 *Common Market Law Review* 667.

[350] This argument is made in another relatable context in, Joni Heliskoski, 'The Jurisdiction of the European Court of Justice to Give Preliminary Rulings on the Interpretation of Mixed Agreements' (2000) 69 *Nordic Journal of International Law* 395.

[351] House of Commons Foreign Affairs Committee, 'Foreign Policy Aspects of the Lisbon Treaty' (House of Commons 2008) HC120-II, Third Report of Session 2007–08, Volume II. p 70.

that national courts should exercise jurisdiction. In *Tomanović v European Union*,[352] the Commission, repesentating the Union as a whole,[353] argued that it not to be inferred from Article 19(1) TEU that national courts have jurisdiction on CFSP matters just because the Court itself does not on the basis of other articles in the treaties. In the Commission's support was a line of case law that supported the notion that not every action that has its initial foundation on a CFSP legal basis means that the jurisdiction of the Court is absolutely curtailed. On this basis, in the specific circumstance of the case, it could be inferred that the Court may have jurisdiction, and thus, means the national court does not have jurisdiction.

The national court in *Tomanović v European Union* was of the view that the principle of *Foto-Frost* and the right of the individual under Article 47 CFR were difficult to square.[354] However, the national court ultimately affirmed and embraced the post-Lisbon jurisprudence of the Court on CFSP matters, namely *Eulex Kosovo*, *H v Council*, *KF v SatCen*, in that not all actions on a CFSP legal basis fall into a judicial vacuum. Moreover, given the Court's assertion in *Opinion 2/13* that it has 'not yet had the opportunity to define the extent to which its jurisdiction is limited in CFSP matters'[355] weighed particularly heavily on the national court.

The national court acknowledged that there is a judicial vacuum with respect to CFSP matters. However, it was not willing to 'go first' with respect to asserting jurisdiction. It chose not to make a preliminary reference, despite the urging of the Commission, concluding that the more suitable place for judicial review was at the Court. Therefore, the role that national courts play in CFSP matters, for now, will remain an unanswered legal question. The implications of this judgment are that EU bodies may find it more difficult to plead before the Court in that future, arguing that it lacks jurisdiction in CFSP matters.

Unquestionably, the Court sees itself as the proper forum for determining the validity of EU legal acts, reiterating the rationale of *Foto-Frost*.[356] Yet, this assertion

[352] *Verica Tomanović and Others v The European Union, the Council of the European Union, the High Representative of the Union for Foreign Affairs and Security Policy, and the European Union Rule of Law Mission in Kosovo (Eulex Kosovo)*, High Court of Justice, Queen's Bench Division, Royal Courts of Justice, London, United Kingdom, Case No HQ18X02173, 13 February 2019. The author is grateful to Becket Bedford for calling this case to attention.

[353] TFEU, Article 335: 'In each of the Member States, the Union shall enjoy the most extensive legal capacity accorded to legal persons under their laws; it may, in particular, acquire or dispose of movable and immovable property and may be a party to legal proceedings. To this end, the Union shall be represented by the Commission. However, the Union shall be represented by each of the institutions, by virtue of their administrative autonomy, in matters relating to their respective operation.'

[354] *Verica Tomanović and Others v The European Union, the Council of the European Union, the High Representative of the Union for Foreign Affairs and Security Policy, and the European Union Rule of Law Mission in Kosovo (Eulex Kosovo)*, High Court of Justice, Queen's Bench Division, Royal Courts of Justice, London, United Kingdom, Case No HQ18X02173, 13 February 2019, Mr. Justice Murray, para 76.

[355] Opinion 2/13, ECLI:EU:C:2014:2454 ('*Accession of the European Union to the European Convention for the Protection of Human Rights*'), para 251.

[356] The Court has said that it is 'best placed to give a ruling on the validity of acts of the Union'. Case C-72/15, *Rosneft Oil Company OJSC v Her Majesty's Treasury, The Secretary of State for Business, Innovation and Skills, The Financial Conduct Authority*, ECLI:EU:C:2017:236, para 79.

of the application of the *Foto-Frost* doctrine on CFSP matters is dependent upon the existence of jurisdiction. The Court has mechanisms in place 'to obtain the observations of Member States and the institutions of the Union'[357] and it implied that national courts would not be in a position to do likewise – a correct observation on the inherent structural deficiencies in national courts' abilities. A system of 'decentrali[s]ed judicial control of CFSP [matters]' would be quite a problem.[358] With centralisation preferred over decentralisation, the future of the Court's judicial review remains strong.

5.6. Political Questions

Taking into account the nature of the execution of foreign policy, CFSP matters may seem unfit for judicial review. International events require swift and decisive action. CFSP matters may once have been viewed as reactionary, short-term, dealing with matters with limited cooperation between Member States. The reality in the contemporary era is much different, with a strategic vision for a long-term EU foreign policy and the wide-ranging and deep commitment of Member States in strides towards common goals, regulated by law. Ultimately, the fact that CFSP matters bring about more political questions before the Court has implications for the political question doctrine across the EU legal order. Even with the Court possessing jurisdiction, which, as demonstrated, is 'coming of age',[359] that is not to say the Court would ever have much to say in terms of substance on CFSP matters. As things stand, there are no determinable factors for what makes CFSP legal acts not subject to judicial review, beyond the attempted exclusion of the Court's jurisdiction, which, as demonstrated, is read narrowly.

Doctrines in law can often overlap with one another, and such overlaps and the invocation of the political question doctrine can become conflated, such as a question before a court failing a 'ripeness' test,[360] but the political question doctrine is different. The political question doctrine prohibits courts from adjudicating on particular matters. Simply put, a court of law invokes this doctrine when it believes it lacks the jurisdiction to rule upon legal actions or actions having legal effects that are more attached to political activity. Political questions are strongly tied to allocations of power and can concern different branches of government, including the judiciary. Formally speaking, the political question doctrine provides 'a technical legal basis for courts to refuse to consider the lawfulness of an action' taken pursuant to foreign policy.[361]

[357] Ibid. para 79.

[358] Hillion and Wessel (n 131) p 85.

[359] See, Butler (n 178).

[360] Alexander M Bickel, *The Least Dangerous Branch: The Supreme Court at the Bar of Politics* 2nd edition (Yale University Press, 1986) p 118.

[361] With regard to the political question doctrine in the United States. Stephen Breyer, *The Court and the World: American Law and the New Global Realities* (Alfred A Knopf, 2015) p 19.

There is no ideal or easy approach to defining political questions. Thus, there is a problem in Union law in that there is no explicit doctrine on what constitutes a political question.[362] The Court has to answer questions of political relevance,[363] but is more cautious with political questions. Defining political questions can be unappealing because they require analysis on a case-by-case basis. Courts can 'try to exert the force of reason on what are basically technical rules aimed at technocratic ends'[364] with mixed results. Each legal order must formulate its own test or doctrine in order to accommodate these inevitable concerns and questions as they arise. The political question doctrine does not assert that judgments never have a political dimension as there are many political elements of judgments evident in the Court's case law. Rather, a political question implies a choice between two or more alternatives, the outcomes of which are not solutions to given legal problems. The presence of choices raise questions about who makes them; be they executive, political, administrative, or judicial decisions.

The intensity of judicial review is subject to different standards. Intertwining the judiciary in fields of political questions is a matter that any constitutional entity views with a great deal of caution. Judicial review by the Court in Union law ought to differ in its latitude and intensity, depending on the issue that has been brought before it. It is claimed that in national settings, it 'would require something extraordinary for a court to intervene in relation to the manner of exercise [of foreign policy]'.[365] By contrast at Union level, it could be contended that the very existence of the Court in the Union's framework meant that limitations upon the Court's jurisdiction 'have been disposed of',[366] given the tasks which have been assigned to the Court, and thus, there has been no need for a political question doctrine. The Court has the possibility to interfere in the political and policy choices of the Union's political institutions. Some methods of review are more endearing than others,[367] yet the Court has, to date, not elaborated on what amounts to a political question.

The interpretation of certain foreign policy questions, such as the Court's jurisdiction, hinges upon many matters, such as, *inter alia*, the objectives of EU foreign policy[368] or the need to resolve constitutional disputes. The dividing line between law and politics is an eternal question, but actions taken in the context of foreign policy can be described as political, in the sense that 'in democracies

[362] See, Butler (n 59).

[363] Miguel Poiares Maduro, 'Interpreting European Law – On Why and How Law and Policy Meet at the European Court of Justice' in Henning Koch and others (eds), *Europe. The New Legal Realism: Essays in Honour of Hjalte Rasmussen* (Djøf Publishing, 2010) p 467.

[364] Again, with respect to the United States. Stephen Breyer, 'Judicial Review of Question of Law and Policy' (1986) 38 *Administrative Law Review* 363 at 395.

[365] See, Paul Craig, 'Engagement and Disengagement with International Institutions: The UK Perspective' in Curtis A Bradley (ed), *Oxford Handbook of Comparative Foreign Relations Law* (Oxford University Press, 2019).

[366] Pescatore (n 343) p 84.

[367] As put, the ability of the Court in its Opinions, through Article 218(11) TFEU, means it offers the Court a more likely interference, than say, a preliminary reference case. Eckes (n 245) p 501.

[368] Larik (n 221) p 18.

[the dividing line is] part of the process of political debate'.[369] It has long been held that the Court must pay heed to considerations of a legal nature versus those of a political nature.[370] As the Court has acknowledged, the Union's political institutions are 'allowed…broad discretion in areas which involve political, economic and social choices'.[371] Yet, despite this claim, it 'seems apparent that currently there is no such thing as an explicit justiciability or political question doctrine in [Union] law per se'.[372] Whatever view one takes of interpreting foreign policy matters, the Court's judgment in *Rosneft* brushed aside active policy choices made by the drafters of the treaties, an act in itself inherently political.

It is routine for the Court to adjudicate on competency disputes between different institutions or to rule on the correct interpretation of the treaties regarding allocations of power between EU institutions in the name of institutional balance. Such disputes are central to the Court's role as the Union's judiciary. Yet, the Court might find that it lacks jurisdiction over a policy area without defined legal standards, such as in CFSP matters. The Court is not the institution to decide the non-legal questions that arise in such contexts. It has long been aware of the dangers of diverting political disputes to the judicial arena unnecessarily. During the 1995 Intergovernmental Conference, the Court considered 'whether it would be appropriate to remove to the judicial arena disputes which could just as satisfactorily be settled at a political level',[373] and there is no doubt that the Court would be very reluctant to delve into CFSP matters that could significantly hamper the political side of the Union's external action.

Conflicts of Union law cannot always be resolved within the political institutions of the Union, but the Court can decide them when there is a legal issue at stake.[374] However, '[a] true…[Union] will not be forged merely by judgments of the Court…[as] [t]hat will above all require lucid and courageous political decisions'.[375] Therefore, the Court is regularly asked to address 'politically charged

[369] Wolfgang Friedmann, *The Changing Structure of International Law* (Columbia University Press, 1964) p 7.

[370] DG Valentine, *The Court of Justice of the European Communities: Volume One: Jurisdiction and Procedure* (Stevens and Sons, 1965) p 388.

[371] Case C-440/14 P, *National Iranian Oil Company v Council of the European Union*, ECLI:EU:C:2016:128, para 77.

[372] Elaine Fahey, 'Challenging EU-US PNR and SWIFT Law before the Court of Justice of the European Union' in Patryk Pawlak (ed), *The EU-US Security and Justice Agenda in Action* (European Union Institute for Security Studies, 2011) p 56.

[373] 'Report of the Court of Justice on Certain Aspects of the Application of the Treaty on European Union' (n 238) As discussed in, Ole Due, 'The Judicial System of the European Union in the Perspective of the 1996 Intergovernmental Conference' in Göran Melander (ed), *Modern Issues in European Law: Nordic Perspectives: Essays in Honour of Lennart Pålsson* (Kluwer Law International, 1997) p 28.

[374] For example, when a Member State violates Union law. Koen Lenaerts, 'Constitutionalism and the Many Faces of Federalism' (1990) 38 *American Journal of Comparative Law* 205 at 252.

[375] Josse Mertens de Wilmars and Jacques Steenbergen, 'The Court of Justice of the European Communities and Governance in an Economic Crisis' (1984) 82 *Michigan Law Review* 1377 at 1398. Replicated in, Josse Mertens de Wilmars and Jacques Steenbergen, 'The Court of Justice of the European Communities and Governance in an Economic Crisis', *The Art of Governance: Festschrift zu Ehren von Eric Stein* (Nomos, Verlagsgesellschaft mbH & Co KG 1987) p 260.

questions left unsolved by the political process'[376] and examine them on the merits. This occasionally results in the outsourcing of fractious political issues and questions to a judicial body that only decides questions of law. The treaties provide some guidance, but the ambiguity leaves considerable room for judicial interpretation and discretion, and some would criticise the exercise of such discretion. Allowing the Court to unilaterally decide what constitutes a political question could mean that 'many articles of the [treaties]…would never be reviewed'.[377] Yet, an overly cautious Court would also have its opponents; while the Court may exceed its jurisdiction, it may also underuse it.

Just how far the Court should delve into political matters has arisen before in non-CFSP matters. In the *Fediol* judgment, the Court granted the political institutions deference to make political decisions in the Union's interests.[378] An Advocate General elaborated on this decision a little later, in another case called *Maclaine Watson*,[379] saying that the 'existence of legal criteria of assessment constitutes one of the determinant factors as regards the court's jurisdiction'.[380] In *Commission v Greece*, another Advocate General briefly discussed how to distinguish the political dimension of a legal act.[381] More recently in *Kadi I*, another Advocate General acknowledged that it is 'never an easy task' for the Court to determine when it was 'reaffirming the limits that the law imposes on certain political decisions' compared to 'trespassing into the domain of politics'.[382] Furthermore, the Advocate General stated that 'the claim that a measure is necessary for the maintenance of international peace and security cannot operate so as to silence the general principles of [Union] law and deprive individuals of their fundamental rights'. However, the Court did not make any such reference to any form of doctrine, either affirming it may exist or determining that a political question did not apply in that specific case. Another Advocate General has said '[t]here are simply no juridical tools of analysis for approaching such problems' in regard to a 'political assessment of an eminently political question'.[383] This has been described as the closest the Court, albeit an Opinion of an Advocate General,

[376] Koen Lenaerts and José Antonio Gutiérrez-Fons, 'The Constitutional Allocation of Powers and General Principles of EU Law' (2010) 47 *Common Market Law Review* 1629 at 1668.

[377] Edwards (n 53) p 555.

[378] Case C-191/82, *EEC Seed Crushers' and Oil Processors' Federation (FEDIOL) v Commission*, ECLI:EU:C:1983:259, para 26.

[379] Case C-241/87, *Maclaine Watson & Company Limited v Council and Commission of the European Communities*, ECLI:EU:C:1990:189.

[380] Opinion of Advocate General Darmon, Case C-241/87, *Maclaine Watson & Company Limited v Council and Commission of the European Communities*, ECLI:EU:C:1989:229, para 78.

[381] Opinion of Advocate General Jacobs, Case C-120/94, *Commission of the European Communities v Hellenic Republic*, ECLI:EU:C:1995:109, para 48.

[382] Opinion of Advocate General Maduro, Case C-402/05 P and C-415/05 P, *Yassin Abdullah Kadi and Al Barakaat International Foundation v Council and Commission*, ECLI:EU:C:2008:11 ('*Kadi I*'), para 45.

[383] Opinion of Advocate General Jacobs, Case C-120/94, *Commission of the European Communities v Hellenic Republic*, ECLI:EU:C:1995:109, para 59.

has come to addressing the political question doctrine.[384] Delving a little deeper allows an examination of how political questions arise in CFSP matters.

5.6.1. Political Questions and CFSP Matters

The Court has widened the scope for judicial review of Union actions conducted under a CFSP legal basis, and thus the Court risks straying into political territory. If it had a well-founded fear that it was getting 'too close to the political arena and having it decide on political "hot potatoes"',[385] the Court could invoke the political question doctrine. From the earliest days of considering European defence cooperation through the failed EDC formulated in the 1950s,[386] matters of military and defence matters had 'deeply political underpinnings'.[387] Thus, contemporary CSDP matters would be an area that is ripe for the use of the doctrine, as would matters of national security and the formation of national armed forces. CSDP missions, be they civilian or military, are a vast applied undertaking. As put, '[t]he planning and execution…must meet so many legal, political and practical challenges'.[388] In *H v Council*,[389] the Court provided an understanding that staffing of a CSDP mission can be equated with that of a permanent EU agency such as the EDA. This has been criticised given that CSDP missions are 'specific initiatives undertaken ad hoc pursuant to the political will of the Council'.[390] Equating them with permanent bodies could be read as extending the Court into political territory where the doctrine might have been suitable. However, the Court avoided invoking the doctrine and sent the case back to the General Court once jurisdiction was affirmed.[391]

The *Rosneft* case may have brought the Court close to a political question given it was a case involving restrictive measures imposed on a Russian oil and gas firm, which was partly owned by the Russian State. The Commission in the oral hearing attempted to sway the Court into invoking the doctrine, ultimately

[384] Eeckhout, *External Relations of the European Union: Legal and Constitutional Foundations* (n 71) p 452.

[385] Gil Carlos Rodríguez Iglesias, 'The Court of Justice, Principles of EC Law, Court Reform and Constitutional Adjudication' (2004) 15 *European Business Law Review* 1115 at 1117.

[386] See Chapter 2 of this book.

[387] Panos Koutrakos, *The EU Common Security and Defence Policy* (Oxford University Press, 2013) p 8.

[388] Panos Koutrakos, 'International Agreements in the Area of the EU's Common Security and Defence Policy' in Enzo Cannizzaro, Paolo Palchetti and Ramses A Wessel (eds), *International Law as Law of the European Union* (Martinus Nijhoff Publishers 2012) p 177.

[389] Case C-455/14 P, *H v Council*, ECLI:EU:C:2016:569. An appeal of Case T-271/10, *H v Council*, ECLI:EU:T:2014:702.

[390] Koutrakos (n 156) p 12.

[391] Case T-271/10 RENV, *H v Council*, ECLI:EU:T:2018:180. On procedural grounds, the case that returned to the General Court has been appealed again to the Court. Case C-413/18 P, *H v Council*, pending.

trying to prevent it from exercising jurisdiction over the Decision adopted upon a CFSP legal basis through the preliminary reference procedure, attempting to prevent the Court from getting into what the Commission saw as a policy choice behind actions on a CFSP legal basis. Captivatingly, the Commission had made the opposite argument in *Eulex Kosovo*, claiming that public procurement law was a 'legislative factor extraneous to…CFSP [matters]'.[392] In *Rosneft*, the Advocate General reasoned that 'the reason for the limitation of the Court's jurisdiction in CFSP matters…is that CFSP acts are, in principle, solely intended to translate decisions of a purely political nature connected with implementation of…CFSP [matters]'.[393] He further stated that 'it is difficult to reconcile judicial review with the separation of powers'.[394] He saw no need to define or delineate which actions or objectives required a CFSP legal basis, as opposed to those needing a non-CFSP legal basis, which was an undertaking conducted in a previous case by one of his colleagues.[395]

The Court's conclusion that it did have jurisdiction in this case on CFSP matters coming from an Article 267 TFEU preliminary reference is at odds with a view recently expressed in *Opinion 2/13*. The Advocate General said the 'clear wording' of Article 275 TFEU, second paragraph, 'refers only to jurisdiction for actions for annulment brought by individuals in accordance with the fourth paragraph of Article 263 TFEU against restrictive measures, but not to any other subject-matter of an action or type of action, and certainly not to references from national courts or tribunals as provided for in Article 267 TFEU'.[396]

This points to sharp differences that can be made in arguments about how jurisdiction in CFSP matters is structured and interpreted. With such contrasting viewpoints, it may well be asked whether such jurisdictional questions would ever hinge upon political questions. It is not apparent from *Rosneft* whether the Court's extension of jurisdiction applies only to restrictive measures or also to other types of CFSP legal acts. Yet, the political question doctrine as applied to other acts on a CFSP legal basis could hinge upon a foreign policy decision, in contrast to restrictive measures, which have a specific treaty mandate for judicial review. Such a choice might consist of whom to sanction or what type of CSDP mission to launch. However, the circumstances in *Rosneft* did not meet the threshold for constituting a political question. With that in mind, however, the broad potential of actions on

[392] Opinion of Advocate General Jääskinen [Second of Two] of 21 May 2015, Case C-439/13 P, *Elitaliana SpA v Eulex Kosovo*, ECLI:EU:C:2015:341, para 43.

[393] Opinion of Advocate General Wathelet, Case C-72/15, *Rosneft Oil Company OJSC v Her Majesty's Treasury, The Secretary of State for Business, Innovation and Skills, The Financial Conduct Authority*, ECLI:EU:C:2016:381, para 52.

[394] Ibid.

[395] Opinion of Advocate General Bot, Case C-130/10, *Parliament v Council*, ECLI:EU:C:2012:50 ('*Smart Sanctions*'), para 63. This interpretation has come in for criticism however. Geert De Baere and Tina Van den Sanden, 'Interinstitutional Gravity and Pirates of the Parliament on Stranger Tides: The Continued Constitutional Significance of the Choice of Legal Basis in Post-Lisbon External Action' (2016) 12 *European Constitutional Law Review* 85 at 105.

[396] View of Advocate General Kokott, Opinion 2/13, ECLI:EU:C:2014:2475 ('*Accession of the European Union to the European Convention for the Protection of Human Rights*'), para 252.

a CFSP legal basis means that such cases are more likely to raise political questions than actions on a non-CFSP legal basis. Nonetheless, the Court can take, as it took, a teleological approach, toning-down the active policy choice, a political choice by the drafters of the treaties in excluding restrictive measures from the scope of questions that can be sent to the Court through the preliminary reference procedure. The Court thus rejected invoking the doctrine, but it did not define what the doctrine might have been since the circumstances of the case did not warrant it.

The treaties specify how CFSP matters should be handled, namely by excluding institutional actors. However, the articles in the treaties that govern how Union law flows more generally, 'including procedural provisions', are 'not covered by the exclusion of jurisdiction'.[397] The unitary nature of the procedural provisions demonstrates the Court's respect for its conferred jurisdiction, while simultaneously preventing the Court from veering into fields where it ought not to go, such as substantive policy proclamations. The Court may adopt other interpretative methods in order to ensure that CFSP matters never reach a stage where the Court specifically invokes the political question doctrine.

In *Kala Naft*,[398] an appeal of a General Court judgment,[399] the Court began to shape the primitive contours and outline the silhouette of the political question doctrine in CFSP matters. In agreement with the General Court, it found that 'the Court…does not have jurisdiction to take cognisance of an action seeking to assess the lawfulness of Article 4 of Decision 2010/413'.[400] Given that Article 4 of Decision 2010/413[401] was 'of a general nature' and did not refer to identifiable natural or legal persons, it did not constitute a restrictive measure.[402] This interpretative method approach is rather reverential to the Council, and thus, is a *de facto* recognition that there is some form of political question doctrine in restrictive measures imposed on a CFSP legal basis. However, the criteria that the Court used were not clear or prescribed.

5.6.2. Dividing the Legal and the Political

The Court may yet find itself in a situation where it is asked to interpret a matter verging upon a political question, leading it to 'act under the premise

[397] Marise Cremona, '"Effective Judicial Review Is of the Essence of the Rule of Law": Challenging Common Foreign and Security Policy Measures Before the Court of Justice' (2017) 2 *European Papers* 671 at 682.

[398] Case C-348/12 P, *Council v Manufacturing Support & Procurement Kala Naft Co., Tehran*, ECLI:EU:C:2013:776.

[399] Case T-509/10, *Manufacturing Support & Procurement Kala Naft Co, Tehran v Council of the European Union*, ECLI:EU:T:2012:201.

[400] Case C-348/12 P, *Council v Manufacturing Support & Procurement Kala Naft Co, Tehran*, ECLI:EU:C:2013:776, para 99.

[401] L 195/39. Council Decision of 26 July 2010 (n 44).

[402] Case T-509/10, *Manufacturing Support & Procurement Kala Naft Co, Tehran v Council of the European Union*, ECLI:EU:T:2012:201, para 37.

of judicial restraint'.[403] This point has still not yet been reached, but it cannot be far into the future. It is perfectly conceivable that a case on CFSP matters may force the Court to write a future judgment elaborating on the political question doctrine in the not-so-distant future. The considerable deference granted by the Court to the political institutions to conduct political affairs has worked to the EU institutions advantage, namely the Council, as long as there is compliance with primary law. Critically, the political question doctrine does not mean that the political institutions can do whatever they want. Leaving entire areas of the treaties outside of the scope of judicial review merely to satisfy skeptical concerns about an over-active court would not serve justice for anyone, including the Member States themselves.

Whereas the doctrine may be considered for multiple strands of Union law, some fields stand out, in that it is 'most obvious in the cases touching upon foreign relations'.[404] Judiciaries usually show a significant amount of restraint when faced with acts of government relating to foreign policy matters, particularly when there are dynamics that represent political choice. Foreign policy of any description is normally formulated and executed by political actors, be they executives or, to a lesser extent, legislators. Yet, foreign policy matters also come before judicial actors. Applying the doctrine might allow a court of law the discretion to 'sit out major foreign [policy] cases'[405] and it has been argued extensively that courts are constrained in foreign policy cases more than they are in other types of cases. To date, the Court has discounted an explicit doctrine in CFSP matters, much as it has in other fields, but CFSP matters are a field where it is more implicit. Notwithstanding the attempted exclusion of CFSP matters from judicial review, *prima facie*, the Court has been delivering judgments on the margins of its jurisdiction, with the treaties catering for an explicit circumstance where the doctrine be adopted – that of the question of jurisdiction itself.

Foreign policy matters are a formative part of the contemporary EU constitution and lend themselves to a particularly special position in the EU constitutional order. CFSP matters allow the Union to act 'in world affairs, without overstraining the system beyond its capacities'.[406] A number of opportunities have arisen post-Lisbon where the doctrine could have been developed for CFSP matters,[407] and it therefore appears to be a field of law where the doctrine may appear because it can be seen as being more political than legal in nature. Such a hypothesis could render CFSP matters, as a policy field, unsuitable for judicial review to take place.

[403] Hinarejos (n 96) p 393.

[404] Fritz W Scharpf, 'Judicial Review and the Political Question: A Functional Analysis' (1966) 75 *Yale Law Journal* 517 at 567.

[405] Louis Henkin, *Foreign Affairs and the Constitution* (Foundation Press, 1972) p 215.

[406] Achilles Skordas, 'Is Europe an Aging Power with Global Vision – A Tale on Constitutionalism and Restoration' (2005) 12 *Columbia Journal of European Law* 241 at 286.

[407] Case C-658/11, *Parliament v Council*, ECLI:EU:C:2014:2025 ('*Mauritius*'), Case C-263/14, *Parliament v Council*, ECLI:EU:C:2016:435 ('*Tanzania*'). See, Luigi Lonardo, 'The Political Question Doctrine as Applied to Common Foreign and Security Policy' (2017) 22 *European Foreign Affairs Review* 571.

Thus, the use of the doctrine in CFSP matters may be easier to see compared to other fields of Union law, due to the fact that there is 'no question of any measures to enforce compliance'[408] through the political process or Court direction.

CFSP matters, as a name, can be an 'umbrella term',[409] given that it covers a variety of actions, and its scope of 'all areas of foreign policy',[410] and is entirely dependent on the political will of Member States as to choices of what actions should be on a CFSP legal basis. In *Opinion 2/13*, the Court acknowledged that 'certain [CFSP] acts fall outside the ambit of judicial review by the Court',[411] but despite the extensive judgment, the Court did not define what it meant by 'certain acts' falling outside of judicial review. This could mean that the Court viewed its jurisdiction in CFSP matters not being conferred upon it explicitly, or, by contrast, that if its jurisdiction was not curtailed, some matters would call for the need of the doctrine. Judicial actors casting review over foreign policy decisions have long been a point of contention in national frameworks, which have been transposed upwards to an equally applicable question at Union level. However, while executive and judicial actors might be hesitant in situating specific circumstances for courts in foreign policy, it is rare to find scenarios where there is prescribed jurisdiction for courts in foreign policy from within state systems. This makes the EU and its own judicial system an anomaly. In practice, the embedded nature of the Court's tendency to grant itself jurisdiction,[412] even in tenuous cases, sits uncomfortably with the eventuality that it may decline to provide judgment in a field where it has been active in expanding its own jurisdiction.

EU foreign policy is established 'through…political and legal procedures'[413] and traditional views of foreign policy see it as an 'expression and realisation of…wills and interests'.[414] Given the legal nature of CFSP matters, the legal instruments that give effect to foreign policy wishes do much more than merely express wills and interests as they are legal acts with legal effect. CFSP matters are '[not] vague political guideline[s]'.[415] Rather, they are guided by foreign policy objectives, which can feed into how the Court conducts its review. The scope of specific

[408] Denza (n 26) p 312.

[409] Deirdre Curtin, 'Legal Acts and the Challenges of Democratic Accountability' in Marise Cremona and Claire Kilpatrick (eds), *EU Legal Acts: Challenges and Transformations* (Oxford University Press, 2018) p 13.

[410] TEU, Article 24(1).

[411] Opinion 2/13, ECLI:EU:C:2014:2454 ('*Accession of the European Union to the European Convention for the Protection of Human Rights*'), para 252.

[412] For example, Case C-455/14 P, *H v Council*, ECLI:EU:C:2016:569, and Case C-72/15, *Rosneft Oil Company OJSC v Her Majesty's Treasury, The Secretary of State for Business, Innovation and Skills, The Financial Conduct Authority*, ECLI:EU:C:2017:236.

[413] Panos Koutrakos, 'Constitutional Idiosyncrasies and Political Realities: The Emerging Security and Defense Policy of the European Union' (2003) 10 *Columbia Journal of European Law* 69 at 79.

[414] Martti Koskenniemi, 'International Law Aspects of the Common Foreign and Security Policy' in Martti Koskenniemi (ed), *International Law Aspects of the European Union* (Martinus Nijhoff Publishers, 1998) p 27.

[415] Mireia Estrada Cañamares, '"Building Coherent EU Responses": Coherence as a Structural Principle in EU External Relations' in Marise Cremona (ed), *Structural Principles in EU External Relations Law* (Hart Publishing, 2018) p 249.

objectives set down in the treaties may be perceived as political questions,[416] Article 21 TEU, with its scope stretching across both CFSP matters and other external relations.

How the EU reacts to international events varies depending on the prevailing political winds. Certain foreign policy actions require decisive action in a prompt fashion, with prevailing political situations potentially warranting swift action. Judicial review of CFSP matters is a mixture of both substantive and procedural law. Conducting extensive review in substantive CFSP matters is certainly more difficult than in procedural matters. The former, being challenging at best, would extend the Court into a domain where policy choices exist and, thus, circumstances may warrant the invocation of the doctrine. The procedural grounds review, on the other hand, is much less likely to encounter the same conundrums of the divisions of legal and political questions. Yet, the trickiest matter that the Court might face is determining whether a question before it is either substantive or procedural. It is conceivably possible that separating a substantive from a procedural issue would be an insurmountable challenge.

A straightforward reading of the treaties would leave the reader with the impression that the drafters wished to exclude the Court's role in certain aspects of Union law. However, as elucidated in this chapter, that has not lived up to that expectation. Whilst actions taken on a CFSP legal basis are within 'the scope of political discretion',[417] it has been articulated that the Court determining its jurisdiction in post-Lisbon cases on CFSP matters has so far found itself going beyond its mandate to answer questions,[418] but as contended, without interfering in substantive policy matters. Article 40 TEU provides for a non-encroachment clause, or in other words, an explicit monitoring role for the Court when it is called upon. One interpretation is that Article 40 TEU implies that the doctrine is provided for in CFSP matters through EU primary law,[419] detailing the drafters' understanding of areas of EU policy that are off-limits to the Court. Having CFSP matters *de facto* outside the remit of judicial review, barring the limited exceptions, may make it easy for the Court to decline jurisdiction in cases on CFSP matters on the mere basis of Article 24 TEU and Article 275 TFEU. Yet it has not done so.

Restrictive measures are partly concluded on a CFSP legal basis and are subject to intense judicial review by the Court. Like other fields, no explicit doctrine has been seen to date in this field, yet there appears to be traces. In *OMPI*,[420] the Court annulled a Common Position founded upon a CFSP legal basis when Common

[416] Eleftheria Neframi, 'Vertical Division of Competences and the Objectives of the European Union's External Action' in Marise Cremona and Anne Thies (eds), *The European Court of Justice and External Relations Law: Constitutional Challenges* (Hart Publishing, 2014) p 25.

[417] Eckes (n 245) p 499.

[418] See, Koutrakos (n 156).

[419] Kuijper (n 133) p 99.

[420] Case T-228/02, *Organisation des Modjahedines du peuple d'Iran v Council*, ECLI:EU:T:2006:384 ('*Modjahedin I*').

Positions might have been considered political in nature. Subsequently in *Kadi I*,[421] the Commission and the Council contended the Court could not determine the validity of the implementing measures in Union law flowing from a UN Security Council Resolution.[422]

5.6.3. A Need for a Political Question Doctrine

The line between law and politics is thin, and the Court could be clearer in providing general guidelines for itself. There is no docket control system at the Court, so it must deal with, in some form, every case that arrives on its docket. Without any level of docket control, the Court may have to invoke the political question doctrine sooner rather than later. A test to determine what constitutes a political question, firmly grounded on specific criteria, is long overdue, but it is not clear when it will be forthcoming. This requires the Court to have finely tuned insight, wisdom, and acumen.

Other matters in Union law have been labelled as political questions. For example, one late former President of the Court labelled the principle of subsidiarity as a 'political assessment',[423] but the Court has not yet made an authoritative determination in this regard. A grounded test, firmly based on specific criteria for the Court to determine what touches upon a political question, is long overdue, given that the Court is slowly adapting to acknowledging the doctrine, but is doing so in an unsatisfactory manner. Elaborating on the doctrine would ensure some level of legal certainty across an array of different legal contexts. Not doing so causes difficulties for understanding whether the political question doctrine is to apply or not apply. Without properly defined standards, the invocation of the doctrine in Union law can give rise to added legal uncertainty.

It is put that it is only a matter of time, given the Court's expanding jurisdiction in CFSP matters, before questions will be asked of the Court that will go well beyond legal questions. Political questions are for the political process, yet courts of law should not be afraid of answering delicate questions of law with political significance. The days when courts may have been 'overzealous' and got 'too far out in front' of acceptable judicial review have been left behind.[424] The justifiability of cases that the Court answers as part of its routine is important for retention of

[421] Joined Cases C-402/05 P and C-415/05 P, *Yassin Abdullah Kadi and Al Barakaat International Foundation v Council and Commission*, ECLI:EU:C:2008:461 ('*Kadi I*').

[422] Paolo Palchetti, 'Judicial Review of the International Validity of UN Security Council Resolutions by the European Court of Justice' in Enzo Cannizzaro, Paolo Palchetti and Ramses A Wessel (eds), *International Law as Law of the European Union* (Martinus Nijhoff Publishers, 2012) p 387.

[423] Rodríguez Iglesias (n 385) p 1117.

[424] With respect to the United States at least. Michael J Glennon, 'Foreign Affairs and the Political Question Doctrine' (1989) 83 *American Journal of International Law* 814 at 816.

the Court's legitimacy. Future questions asked of the Court may begin to veer into policy and political questions. The inherent weakness of future cases, particularly those with political choices, is that the Court may be asked to make value judgments. For justiciable questions in EU, there ought to be 'judicially discoverable criteria'.[425] Without set standards of judicial review, the Court is not in a position to answer questions before it. As a result, the Court may need to create and invoke an explicit doctrine to refuse to answer unsuitable questions that lack a specific connection to the law.

Most cases that become before the Court are run-of-the-mill. The Court has 'succeeded in rendering the most far-reaching rulings in relatively trivial controversies'.[426] Yet the Court needs to remain sensitive to the manner in which it conducts judicial review, and that means knowing which cases to and which not to adjudicate in. Some matters are so contentious in the EU, however (eg, long-drawn-out inter-state disputes that are devoid of legal issues) that a judicial ruling through a court of law of any description should not be made, barring exceptional circumstances. Since *Les Verts*,[427] when the Court first declared that the Union was based on the rule of law, the essence of judicial review was relaunched with new vigour. If the ideas of *Les Verts* are to be truly applied, it demands judicial review in nearly all circumstances where questions of Union law arise. Creating a distinctive test for the correct application of the doctrine is the way forward in the EU. Highly contested cases without legal questions can arise; thus, a political question doctrine in Union law must be given serious consideration.

5.7. A Changing Border

The slow convergence of CFSP and non-CFSP matters, at least procedurally within the EU external action framework, is evident. This process, albeit incrementally, is occurring, with nothing but time allowing progression to evolve in a way that occurs naturally, or alternatively, treaty revision, slowing down the process. With rules and principles from Union law more generally applying to CFSP matters, the Union-wide application of rules and principles means that CFSP matters, as a policy field, are becoming more akin to other areas of non-CFSP external relations. It can be contemplated whether the boundary between CFSP legal bases and non-CFSP legal bases is fixed or moving,[428] thus being contrary to the principle of legal certainty.

[425] Pieter Jan Kuyper and Karel Wellens, 'Deployment of Cruise Missiles in Europe: The Legal Battles in the Netherlands, the Federal Republic of Germany and Belgium' (1987) 18 *Netherlands Yearbook of International Law* 145 at 187.

[426] Eric Stein, *Thoughts from a Bridge: A Retrospective of Writings on New Europe and American Federalism* (University of Michigan Press, 2000) p 155.

[427] Case C-294/83, *Parti écologiste 'Les Verts' v Parliament*, ECLI:EU:C:1986:166, para 23.

[428] Ronald Van Ooik, 'Cross-Pillar Litigation Before the ECJ: Demarcation of Community and Union Competences' (2008) 4 *European Constitutional Law Review* 399 at 412.

Where constitutional dictum specifies, the Union should act in a predicable fashion.[429] Whilst the Court is in no position to dictate what legal bases ought to be used for EU external action, questions relating to such choice of legal basis continue to exist.

As seen in the post-Lisbon jurisprudence, it is apparent that the Court is happy to review elements of cases on CFSP matters, despite the apparent restrictions imposed on its jurisdiction by the treaties. By doing so, the Court is broadening the remit of certain actors within EU external relations by ruling on the limit for what is permissible for actions situated on a CFSP legal basis. Therefore, the continued exclusion of the Court, textually, is but an anomaly. It has been argued that the traditional exclusionary ideal of the Member States of the Court from CFSP matters has already waned,[430] and certainly, the wording of the restrictions on the Court is not as tight as it may seem. Thus, the divide between CFSP matters and non-CFSP matters may naturally erode over time. Notably, the Court has even moved on, in some cases, to not even addressing the question of jurisdiction, such as in *Kazakhstan*.[431] With Article 40 TEU empowering the Court with the responsibility for patrolling the border to ensure the implementation of CFSP matters does not materially affect the Union's other competence, and *vice-versa*, this mutual non-encroachment could mean there is scope for the Court to have not only jurisdiction, but to penetrate powers into CFSP matters too.

The recurring theme between the case law in CFSP matters has clearly been the maintenance of balance between the institutional actors. It has been suggested that if the Court was to exercise jurisdiction over CFSP matters, it would do so on matters of substance that would be 'very, very light touch'.[432] Assuming the Court would not go wild with newfound powers, in the meantime, its position in CFSP matters has been how the rule of law has been advanced outside the normal Union processes.[433] The Council should not be afraid of the Court, given that the Court has proceeded with procedural review as opposed to a substantive review.[434] Even though the Court continues to be formally excluded from CFSP matters, there is a constitutional role for it in that policy.[435] An argument for enhancing the Court's

[429] Alec Stone Sweet and Thomas Brunell, 'Constructing a Supranational Constitutions' in Alec Stone Sweet (ed), *The Judicial Construction of Europe* (Oxford University Press, 2004) p 93, when discussing, Case C-314/85, *Foto-Frost v Hauptzollamt Lübeck-Ost*, ECLI:EU:C:1987:452.

[430] See, Hillion (n 45).

[431] Case C-244/17, *Commission v Council (Accord avec le Kazakhstan)*, ECLI:EU:C:2018:662. However, in the same case, the Advocate General did discuss whether the Court even had jurisdiction, which, in her Opinion, it did. Opinion of Advocate General Kokott, Case C-244/17, *Commission v Council (Accord avec le Kazakhstan)*, ECLI:EU:C:2018:364, paras 28–31.

[432] See, Paul Craig in United Kingdom's House of Lords, 'House of Lords European Union Committee, 6th Report of Session 2003–04, The Future Role of the European Court of Justice: Report with Evidence (HL Paper 47)' para 97, p 31.

[433] De Baere (n 289) p 356.

[434] For example, long before CFSP matters were a legal policy domain, see, Case C-191/82, *EEC Seed Crushers' and Oil Processors' Federation (FEDIOL) v Commission*, ECLI:EU:C:1983:259, para 30.

[435] Ramses A Wessel, 'The Constitutional Unity of the European Union: The Increasing Irrelevance of the Pillar Structure?' in Jan Wouters, Luc Verheij and Philipp Kiiver (eds), *European Constitutionalism beyond Lisbon* (Intersentia, 2009) p 298.

jurisdiction in CFSP matters would be that the correct interpretation of acts on a CFSP legal basis could be applied in a clear and precise manner, especially given that the validity of acts on a CFSP legal basis is not always clear. Yet, answering questions of validity has been avoided.[436] A pattern has emerged when the Court is interpreting the limits of its competence as defined by primary law. Whilst the Court is restricted in its approach to external action, one Advocate General has stated that '[EU] [c]ourts will in the future be unable to avoid addressing the issue of the inadequacy of the protection of individuals' rights in the context of external action'.[437] This statement can be interpreted as seeing that CFSP matters should be fair game for the Court in terms of jurisdiction, just like any other policy field.

There is seen a certain level of dynamic interpretation that insinuates that the treaties are not as clear-cut when it comes to institutional involvement in CFSP matters. Therein lies an inherent problem for the Court: should it interpret provisions in the treaties from the drafter's perspective, or, find an alternative approach which fulfils a legally sound conclusion to satisfy the legal conundrum before it? The Court is not an apolitical actor. It is cognisant of the operational environment in which it carries out its functions. Keenly aware of its own limits, the Court has not been shy in interpreting the boundary of different acts in the past. For example, the former third pillar measures had to be delimited from those of the then Community as the Court had limitations in JHA matters. The Court has previously been willing to test the exclusion of its jurisdiction in given circumstances and will likely continue to do so in the future. Such a scenario may be involving a military mission under a CSDP legal basis when an individual's human rights standard may not be compliant with Union law.[438] The ramifications for such a judgment at a given opportunity would be unmatched, compared to the Court's approach to its jurisdiction in CFSP matters to date. The administration of justice and upholding the treaties is the primary function for which it exists, so any new lines being drawn will be keenly observed.

5.7.1. A Time for Reflection

Using the best of sporting metaphors,[439] the Court is the umpire of its own game. It views itself as *the* guarantor of the treaties, ensuring that other institutions follow

[436] For example, see, Stian Øby Johansen, 'Accountability Mechanisms for Human Rights Violations by CSDP Missions: Available and Sufficient?' (2017) 66 *International and Comparative Law Quarterly* 181.

[437] Opinion of Advocate General Jääskinen [Second of Two] of 21 May 2015, Case C-439/13 P, *Elitaliana SpA v Eulex Kosovo*, ECLI:EU:C:2015:341, para 66.

[438] Daniel Thym, 'Transfer Agreements for Pirates Concluded by the EU – a Case Study on the Human Rights Accountability of the Common Security and Defence Policy' in Panos Koutrakos and Achilles Skordas (eds), *The Law and Practice of Piracy at Sea: European and International Perspectives* (Hart Publishing, 2014) p 181.

[439] The sporting metaphor belongs to Chief Justice of the United States, John Roberts, who, during his confirmation hearing before the Judiciary Committee of the United States Senate in 2005, said a judge's role is to 'to call balls and strikes[,] and not to pitch or bat'.

it and the flowing legal order. CFSP matters bind the Union's institutions and its Member States, with norms arising as a result.[440] Why the principal exclusion of the Court continues to be problematic is the uncertainty that it may generate. The Court's role has been crucial in developing, more broadly, the demeanour of EU external relations, both legally and politically. Whether it should continue to adopt a pragmatic approach, an integrationist approach, or rather one that is in favour of the drafters of the treaties, is a speculative question, but with consequential effects.

Continuing that train of thought, whether it pursues an agenda of expanding Union competence under the pretext of interpretation, or otherwise, the Court's overall record in all policy domains of managing the limits of Union competence has been varied, with no clear methodological path being followed. Changes to the Court's jurisdiction in CFSP matters have come about as a result of both formal textual changes to the treaties and the case law that it itself has been responsible for. The *Rosneft* judgment might have been the opportunity for the Court to pre-empt the next Intergovernmental Conference by allowing preliminary references to it in cases on CFSP matters. The amendments to the jurisdiction of the Court made by the Treaty of Lisbon gifted opportunities for further expansion into new realms, which it has exploited. This was the inevitable result as the growing jurisdiction of the Court is not surprising when its origins are considered. As noted in its infancy, the Court's extensive jurisdiction was greater than that of other international adjudication bodies of its time,[441] to reflect the specificity of the Union.

Every court is given the difficult task of deciding matters before it in one way or another. For the Court's handling of CFSP matters, this means satisfying the academic inquiry of pushing CFSP matters to its treaty limits on the one hand and satisfying the practical issue in the case to hand that has real implications on the other. The potential powers of the Court are strong enough to retain the power to define the nature and scope of EU external relations law, refining the legal effect of Union law instruments and developing new doctrines leading to its development. With its widening jurisdictional space on a general and explicit basis, its marginal jurisdiction in CFSP matters looks more misplaced than ever. Thus, the Court itself appears not to view any contradiction of widening its jurisdiction within politically acceptable limits.

The Due Report in 2000 made a number of recommendations regarding the future of the EU courts.[442] At the time, it was praised for its willingness to consult,[443] by looking at a number of options for the structure of the EU's

[440] Jan Willem Van Rossem, 'The EU at Crossroads: A Constitutional Inquiry into the Way International Law Is Received within the EU Legal Order' in Enzo Cannizzaro, Paolo Palchetti and Ramses A Wessel (eds), *International Law as Law of the European Union* (Martinus Nijhoff Publishers, 2012) p 84.

[441] Werner Feld, *The Court of the European Communities: New Dimension in International Adjudication* (Martinus Nijhoff Publishers, 1964) p 34.

[442] Ole Due and others, 'Report by the Working Party on the Future of the European Communities' Court System (the 'Due Report')' (European Commission 2000).

[443] Paul Craig, 'The Jurisdiction of the Community Courts Reconsidered' in Gráinne De Búrca and Joseph HH Weiler (eds), *The European Court of Justice* (Oxford University Press, 2001) p 213.

judiciary, and how jurisdiction would be managed between the Court and the General Court. What it did not do, however, was to consider the actual jurisdiction the EU judicial system. Thus, potential utterances on CFSP matters and other areas at the time were not included. A huge change in the Court's approach to CFSP matters has evolved over the past 20 years, going initially from *Grau Gomis*,[444] right through to *Opinion 2/13*, starting with an absolute hands-off approach, to using its curtailment of jurisdiction for justifying the scuppering of Union accession to an international agreement.

5.7.2. The Reasoning in Cases on CFSP Matters

Whilst the Court has knocked down some bricks from the wall holding up CFSP matters, it has been careful not to chip it away altogether for fear of itself losing the legitimacy of its actions by going too far. There is the appearance coming from the Court that it is using opportunities provided to it to slowly chip away at the provisions on CFSP matters in the treaties, eventually tearing down the wall that separates it from non-CFSP external action. Like any other court of law, the Court plays a role in ensuring order and 'unity in diversity'.[445] In light of its judgments, however, it can be asked if the Court has had it both ways with respect to CFSP matters. Resorting to less significant issues on the political spectrum, such as the focus on legal bases, transparency, procedures, and general principles, has been the Court's preferred method. Thus far, once jurisdiction has been asserted, it has not made policy decisions. It has not turned to declaring EU acts in CFSP matters unlawful themselves just yet, but that is not to say it may never be contemplated in the future. Instead, the Court has attempted to bring about a system of reasoning that is within politically acceptable means.

It can be argued that given ambiguity in cases before it, the Court is left with little other choice. As a fallback, it also uses more general understandings to justify the limits grounds upon which it may acceptably adjudicate. In *Mauritius*, the Court said that with Article 19 TEU providing general jurisdiction to the Court, derogations must be construed in a narrow sense.[446] This was also done in *Rosneft*, thus, using Article 19 TEU, the Court sees itself as exercising a constitutional role. The Court may continue to chisel away at the limits of its jurisdiction in CFSP matters, or it may adopt a more cautious approach to accepting too wide

[444] Case C-167/94, *Criminal proceedings against Juan Carlos Grau Gomis and others*, ECLI:EU:C:1995:113 ('*Grau Gomis*').

[445] Joxerramon Bengoetxea, 'Rethinking EU Law in the Light of Pluralism and Practical Reason' in Miguel Poiares Maduro, Kaarlo Tuori and Suvi Sankari (eds), *Transnational Law: Rethinking European Law and Legal Thinking* (Cambridge University Press, 2014) p 167.

[446] Case C-658/11, *Parliament v Council*, ECLI:EU:C:2014:2025 ('*Mauritius*'), para 70.

a jurisdiction without sufficient indicators from the legislature that this is permissible. *Opinon 2/13* in itself may be indirectly attempting to extend the scope of judicial review of CFSP matters by identifying its unique nature and using it for its own institutional interests.[447] Notwithstanding this perception, the case demonstrated that the Court can defend the provisions on CFSP matters in the treaties.

Part of the Court's issue with defining its own jurisdiction is that it can often disregard the text of the treaties at times, in favour of what *ought* to be there. There is a legitimacy and accountability problem with this, never mind a democratic one, if the Court's actions stretch creative interpretations a little too far. The Court's previous actions may have caused and thus triggered its exclusion from CFSP matters at the Treaty of Maastricht. The approach of the Court from its inception in 1952 up to the early 1990s may have spooked the Member States into transferring 'sovereign' foreign, security, and defence matters under its jurisdiction. Yet, it was not just Member States who were initially concerned about the Court in CFSP matters. The Commission also had reservations.

The Court is not the possessor of unconditional wisdom, as it is just and reasonable that its decisions to expand its jurisdiction are appropriately questioned and critiqued. The Court has to ask itself some questions, such as, for example, what role it wishes to have. It has found itself to be a 'competent constitutional adjudicator'[448] rather than being a blind actor, subject to policy considerations.[449] For a long time, it has been a constitutional court in the making, despite the EU legal system potentially being unsuited for one.[450] The Court finds itself in a predicament: it does not possess the necessary jurisdiction it desires; yet is willing to defend the nature of the jurisdiction that it has been granted. With this, the Court puts the higher objective of itself as the supreme arbiter of Union law to ensure the EU legal order that it has fought for decades to build and consequently uphold.

To accuse the Court of activism in CFSP matters would be untrue. The evidence suggests that if the Court had full jurisdiction in CFSP matters, it would act in a responsible fashion. The substance of CFSP matters is not delved into, but procedural review can occur, which the Court had duly handled. However, the cases that

[447] See, Graham Butler, 'The Ultimate Stumbling Block? The Common Foreign and Security Policy, and Accession of the European Union to the European Convention on Human Rights' (2016) 39 *Dublin University Law Journal* 229.

[448] Eleanor Sharpston and Geert De Baere, 'The Court of Justice as a Constitutional Adjudicator' in Anthony Arnull and others (eds), *A Constitutional Order of States? Essays in EU Law in Honour of Alan Dashwood* (Hart Publishing, 2011) p 149.

[449] Alan Dashwood, 'The Limits of European Community Powers' (1996) 21 *European Law Review* 113 at 128.

[450] Ole Due, 'A Constitutional Court for the European Communities' in Deirdre Curtin and David O'Keeffe (eds), *Constitutional Adjudication in European Community and National Law: Essays for the Hon Mr Justice T F O'Higgins* (Butterworths, 1992) p 10.

have led to the Court ruling in cases on CFSP matters give rise to the question of the applicability of the political question doctrine. Officially, the Court does not have the doctrine as part of its judicial framework, but it does raise questions about justiciability. The legitimate question that can be asked is whether the questions before the Court in some cases are of a *political* nature. If the decision-making process for CFSP matters was more integrated like broader decision-making in the Union, such as in non-CFSP matters, the inter-institutional disputes would not be arising before the Court.

5.7.3. The Existence of the Border

The border between CFSP and non-CFSP matters was around long before the current incarnation of the treaties.[451] The Court's border policing has been resolute and has not been afraid of annulling measures where encroachment has occurred. Given that CFSP and JHA matters made up the former second and third pillars, with distinct procedural and decision-making regimes applicable for each, there is consistency from the Court in that it can apply jurisdictional principles from one to the other. This was most evident, and a direct link was made in the *Svenska Journalistförbundet* judgment.[452] Like the jurisdiction issue to police the border in *Airport Transit Visas*,[453] the links between CFSP matters and JHA matters when it comes to the role of the Court are evident. Similarities in the Court's position on CFSP matters can be traced to the former third pillar pre-Lisbon.[454] New developments in the law and practice of external relations for CFSP legal acts and non-CFSP legal acts could necessitate the Court to revisit and further consider the jurisdictional aspects of CFSP matters.

The General Court, as seen in *H v Council*,[455] has been much more cautious in declaring jurisdiction in cases on CFSP matters, and instead has waited for the direction of the Court. However at the same time, the General Court continues to assert jurisdiction in CFSP matters with regard to restrictive measures. In *Bank Mellat*,[456] the General Court stated that 'the exception to the jurisdiction of the Courts of the European Union provided for in Article 275 TFEU cannot be interpreted as going so far as to preclude review of the legality of a measure adopted under Article 215 TFEU' when applied to restrictive measures.

[451] Allan Rosas and Lorna Armati, *EU Constitutional Law: An Introduction* (Hart Publishing, 2012) p 243.

[452] Case T-174/95, *Svenska Journalistförbundet v Council*, ECLI:EU:T:1998:127.

[453] Case C-170/96, *Commission v Council*, ECLI:EU:C:1998:219 ('*Airport Transit Visas*').

[454] See, Steve Peers, 'Finally "Fit for Purpose"? The Treaty of Lisbon and the End of the Third Pillar Legal Order' (2008) 27 *Yearbook of European Law* 47.

[455] For the General Court case on initially declining jurisdiction, see, Case T-271/10, *H v Council*, ECLI:EU:T:2014:702, and on appeal on points of jurisdiction, see, Case C-455/14 P, *H v Council*, ECLI:EU:C:2016:569.

[456] Case T-160/13, *Bank Mellat v Council*, ECLI:EU:T:2016:331.

5.7.4. Jurisdiction in Perspective

Debate on the Court's role in CFSP matters has not yet gathered full steam, maybe because the constitutional framework is relatively clear regarding its intended role.[457] But yet, with a singular set of external objectives for the Union, it is difficult, for example, to determine whether or not an agreement is related to CFSP matters in principle[458] and the treaties require the Court to have a role. The importance of the Court in this area going forward cannot be underestimated. Through no fault of its own, perfect or near-perfect occasions can arise when it can rule on CFSP matters, should it feel the need to do so, to uphold Union law. It can thus be argued that with the continuing choice of legal bases on potential CFSP matters, alongside other issues that previously came under different pillars of the treaties, litigation is likely to continue before the Court which will continue to find itself in the position of adjudicator-in-chief as EU institutions continue to keep battling over contentious issues relating to CFSP matters.

The underlying problematic aspects of European integration is that there is no judicial control, and thus constitutional principles and procedure are ripe for being undermined and circumvented. This adds to a hypothesis that the Court ought to hold 'inherent jurisdiction' to make a stronger 'contribution to the administration of justice in the [Union]'.[459] The exclusion of the Court in CFSP matters has been disappointing according to some[460] and has demonstrated Member States' 'aversion to any "judicialisation" of the diplomatic processes'.[461] With the rule of law a core component of the Union and its legal regime, the lack of judicial jurisdiction continues to be problematic from a legal certainty perspective.[462] The Court's silence on its limits in CFSP matters as seen in *Opinion 2/13*[463] is *de facto* shaping the nature of EU external relations policies, leaving it to the political institutions to resolve. Beyond such jurisdictional matters, however, there are some bigger questions at play. The Court is facing a challenge on whether it is to follow an integrationist route, that of 'more Europe' or to appease the Council members by allowing 'constitutional mediation'.[464] Acting in its role of border

[457] De Búrca (n 1) p 695.

[458] Passos and Marquardt (n 37) p 899.

[459] Anthony Arnull, 'Does the Court of Justice Have Inherent Jurisdiction?' (1990) 27 *Common Market Law Review* 683 at 706.

[460] See, Marise Cremona, 'The Union as a Global Actor: Roles, Models and Identity' (2004) 41 *Common Market Law Review* 553 at 571.

[461] Eric Stein, 'European Foreign Affairs System and the Single European Act of 1986' (1989) 23 *The International Lawyer* 977 at 987.

[462] That is despite there being 'some amount of fuzziness in the way the Court uses its past rule of law case law in justifying its findings' in the *Rosneft* case. Mirka Kuisma, 'Jurisdiction, Rule of Law, and Unity of EU Law in Rosneft' (2018) 37 *Yearbook of European Law* 3 at 18.

[463] Opinion 2/13, ECLI:EU:C:2014:2454 ('*Accession of the European Union to the European Convention for the Protection of Human Rights*'), para 251.

[464] See, Marie-Pierre F Granger, 'The Court of Justice's Dilemma: Between "More Europe" and "Constitutional Mediation"' in Christopher J Bickerton, Dermot Hodson and Uwe Puetter (eds), *The New Intergovernmentalism: States and Supranational Actors in the Post-Maastricht Era* (Oxford University Press, 2015).

policing between the CFSP and non-CFSP legal bases, it has tried to refrain from demonstrating a pro-*communautaire* bias towards a supranational legal order. If the Court is consistently annulling Union acts because of substantive or procedural matters or is delivering rulings finding incompatibility with the treaties, it can become an issue of whether legal actors like the Council and the Parliament will retain an interest in exhausting their institutional battles against one another at the Court.

The Union could have a fully fledged Court to deal with the complex matters before it and adjudicate accordingly. Instead, it is left with a Court with one of its hands permanently tied behind its back. The jurisdictional position of the Court remains as uncertain as it ever has, and for now, more cases will determine the way forward for its jurisdiction on CFSP matters. For a lack of judicial control by the Court, CFSP matters have been subject to political control internally within the Council. Yet, the Court dragging its feet in political questioning is inherently a dangerous move.[465] Not only is that not the intention of the treaties, but it would also risk losing its basis to answer legal questions.

The adoption of relevant amendments to the treaties to empower the Court to have greater judicial oversight of CFSP matters is possible. This would provide some liberation to the Court which finds itself in a stranglehold. However, the question needs to be asked whether the accompanying responsibility of the Court would be a suitable forum. The adjudication of the Court could give rise to future foreign policy and external relations actions being conducted on bilateral or multilateral levels outside Union law. This push factor would, from a Union perspective, be detrimental to the overall coherence and consistency its legal order, which incrementally has seen CFSP matters edge towards its natural and eventual home – forming a normal part of the EU decision-making framework, with no curtailments on the Court's jurisdiction.

5.8. Conclusion

If CFSP matters as a regime of specific rules and procedures were to be attempted today, the current institutions would not tolerate it as an acceptable means of decision-making within the EU. As it stands, full judicial protection by the Court might not be achievable,[466] despite the 'complete' system of remedies and procedures that the treaties and case law it has built up. It has been contended that the Court's

[465] See, Butler (n 59).

[466] See the section titled 'Is the assumption correct that the preliminary [reference] procedure provides full and effective judicial protection against general Community measures?' in, Opinion of Advocate General Jacobs, Case C-50/00 P, *Unión de Pequeños Agricultores v Council*, ECLI:EU:C:2002:197, paras 36–49.

jurisdiction has been extended by the Treaty of Lisbon, but on a 'hidden' basis.[467] This does not just apply to CFSP matters, but extends across all matters of EU external action. The Court's institutional role as the arbitrator for legal disputes means it is a critical cog in the wheel of elaborating on the external effect of Union law. Its 'laboratory'[468] status means that its role in shaping external relations law is always going to be followed closely. With the former pillars no longer formally in existence since the Treaty of Lisbon, the cross-policy cases coming before the Court will give rise to inherent difficulties. Whilst it has been said that omitting the Court from having jurisdiction from CFSP matters was a mistake,[469] one positive view of CFSP matters as a policy domain could be that it is a 'sector-specific adaptation',[470] catering for preferences of the Member States.

The purported Chinese wall between CFSP matters and other Union policies may have been much more distinct in the past, but CFSP matters still remain in diluted form from the perspective of the Court's jurisdiction. The EU cannot be a real constitutional order if it lacks basic characteristics such as full judicial review on legal matters. If the Union is to live up to the Court's *Les Verts* expectation of establishing 'a complete system of legal remedies and procedures designed to permit the Court of Justice to review the legality of measures adopted by the institutions',[471] major constitutional change of the Union will be needed. The future of cavities in the EU judicial order depends, largely, on the Court's own interpretation of its jurisdiction to rule. This responsibility to police itself is a task that will have to be threaded on with immense care and precision.

Once, 'tucked away in the fairyland Duchy of Luxembourg',[472] the Court is tasked by the treaties to adjudicate in important cases, with parties arguing before it on both legal basis and other grounds. What the future holds is inevitable. There is the slow and gradual shift, continuing with the Treaty of Lisbon, towards a supranational policy that will one day entail full Court competence in all areas of Union policy. As time goes on, the two differing legal regimes of CFSP and non-CFSP matters in EU external action will slowly intertwine and merge. Until such time as these issues of EU constitutional law are ironed out, the Court will continue to be asked detailed questions about its jurisdiction in CFSP matters.

[467] Christina Eckes, 'The CFSP and Other EU Policies: A Difference in Nature?' (2015) 20 *European Foreign Affairs Review* 535.

[468] Piet Eeckhout, 'A Panorama of Two Decades of EU External Relations Law' in Anthony Arnull, Piet Eeckhout and Takis Tridimas (eds), *Continuity and Change in EU Law: Essays in Honour of Sir Francis Jacobs* (Oxford University Press, 2008) p 337.

[469] Cremona (n 16) p 1203.

[470] Daniel Thym, 'Parliamentary Involvement in European International Relations' in Marise Cremona and Bruno De Witte (eds), *EU Foreign Relations Law: Constitutional Fundamentals* (Hart Publishing, 2008) p 220.

[471] Case C-294/83, *Parti écologiste 'Les Verts' v Parliament*, ECLI:EU:C:1986:166, para 23. See also, Butler (n 144).

[472] Eric Stein, 'Lawyers, Judges, and the Making of a Transnational Constitution' (1981) 75 *American Journal of International Law* 1.

6

Other Issues and the Common Foreign and Security Policy

Whilst the positions of the Parliament and the Court in CFSP matters have been strengthened through institutional practice and litigation, this raises questions about the multifaceted nature of CFSP matters. Governance, democracy, legitimacy, and accountability all have assumptions built into them. The treaties attribute powers to actors and marginal actors in CFSP matters, but remains primarily in the hands of the Council, as is evident from the previous chapters. The interconnected nature of governance, democracy, legitimacy, and accountability has been developed over a prolonged period, so unbundling them may upset their intertwined nature. By focusing on governance from a Union viewpoint; democracy from a parliamentary perspective; legitimacy from a citizen's angle; and that of accountability from a Court standpoint, a picture will emerge of governance, democracy, legitimacy, and accountability within CFSP matters. The four, taken together, are important elements of public administration.

A primary concern underlining CFSP matters and its overall decision-making and execution arrangements is the issue of narrow institutional involvement. Developing CFSP Decisions is not rule-making,[1] but rather, is executive power by its very nature. Within this executive arrangement are diplomatic elements of CFSP matters, which are involved in the actual decision-making to be made below ministerial level. It is undeniable that the most recent significant overhaul of EU primary law by the Treaty of Lisbon strengthened a number of issues within the Union's decision-making process; namely, governance, democracy, legitimacy, and accountability. However, a lack of relevant involvement mechanisms does not just relate to CFSP matters, but also the former third pillar, JHA.[2] The mere discussions of the four elements together demonstrate the additional issues with the Union's legal framework for CFSP matters.

The law-making powers of the Union, governed by the competence conferred upon the relevant institutions, are inherently complex. Governance, democracy, legitimacy, and accountability may at first glance be considered attractive features

[1] Daniel Thym, 'The Intergovernmental Constitution of the EU's Foreign, Security and Defence Executive' (2011) 7 *European Constitutional Law Review* 453 at 463.

[2] See, Juan Santos Vara, 'The External Activities of AFSJ Agencies: The Weakness of Democratic and Judicial Controls' (2015) 20 *European Foreign Affairs Review* 118.

of any given entity. Yet a serious question can be asked; why do CFSP matters need to have their governance, democracy, legitimacy, and accountability traits analysed? Foreign policies of Member States within the Union have never truly been subject to any form of genuine involvement of national parliaments or been exposed to weighty judicial review. Therefore, why should that be expected of the Union? This chapter questions whether it is appropriate to begin the shift from assuming that a true EU foreign policy by way of a regime for CFSP matters can be held to the same standards as those in Member States, or whether such standards should be addressed from a Union perspective, given its particular status. By attempting to craft some answers to these questions, the chapter underlines the normative framework of the Union,[3] whilst simultaneously questioning the very essence of the structure upon which the Union and, more particularly for CFSP matters, is based. By using a framework of political accountability,[4] the chapter carves out a model for the governance, democracy, legitimacy, and accountability in the legal nature of CFSP matters.

6.1. Introduction

The legal regime for CFSP matters is purposefully convoluted. The complexity in which it operates should not distract from the awareness that must observe the political aspects of the policy.[5] As demonstrated in the previous chapters, control, in terms of executive actions in CFSP matters, is held by the Council. This has pushed the Parliament and the Court to the margins of influence and involvement, but not without a fight. COREPER and the PSC are important Council-centric bodies in CFSP matters operate within and through national officials under a mandate from their national government, with the support of the Council Secretariat. The Council, therefore, is not internally controlled by supranational mechanisms. With the balance of power in CFSP matters shifted away from many EU institutions, how CFSP matters are governed, democratised, legitimised, and ultimately accountable is important for the existence of the Union's foreign policy. There is no perfect legal model or framework for how governance, democracy, legitimacy, and accountability should work in an EU setting. It can, however, be embraced or rejected according to the ideals that the entity holds. As actions on a CFSP legal basis continue to evolve as an anomaly within the EU legal order, so will the governance, democracy, legitimacy, and accountability issues that accompany them.

[3] This is elaborated in, Armin Von Bogdandy, 'Founding Principles of EU Law: A Theoretical and Doctrinal Sketch' (2010) 16 *European Law Journal* 95.

[4] See, Paul Craig, 'Accountability' in Anthony Arnull and Damian Chalmers (eds), *The Oxford Handbook of European Union Law* (Oxford University Press, 2015) p 432.

[5] Paul Craig, *The Lisbon Treaty: Law, Politics, and Treaty Reform* (Oxford University Press, 2011) p 418.

By blending the components together, it is possible to formulate a prism in which an executive ought to function.[6]

Those with an interest, active or passive, must absorb a significant amount of reasoning to comprehend the scale of the procedures required to pass a particular measure in both CFSP and non-CFSP matters in EU external relations law. Rights of the executive are crucial, as are those of a parliamentary entity when a polity is governed on the principles of democracy. It is beyond doubt that democratic credentials are now sown into the constitutional framework of the Union, sitting solidly in the treaties, but the particular type of democracy that works for the Union is not comparable to Member States' respective arrangements. This essence of democratic values, by being centrally located in the underpinning treaties, speaks to the length at which the institutional actors and that of its crafters are willing to demonstrate the legitimacy and accountability of its actions. This does not mean that democratic input providing this legitimacy and accountability should be invested into one actor however. The Union interest that is normally pushed in non-CFSP matters by the Commission is absent in CFSP matters, and the citizens' interests by the Parliament is limited. This goes against a traditional view of EU constitutionalism.[7]

This chapter looks at the features of CFSP matters through a number of lenses. On the parliamentary spectrum, the first question is whether the Parliament is even a suitable institution to be involved in CFSP matters. Given that CFSP matters are still decided upon by Member States through the Council, it can be contemplated, from a governance and democratic perspective, whether the Parliament's position is adequate. On the judicial side, with growing competence on general matters of EU public policy being transferred to EU institutions, the case law seen in the previous two chapters may give rise to suspicions that the Court has a policy of favourably interpreting the needs of the Parliament on procedural grounds. Whereas this is debated, it can also be argued that the line of case law has been within the scope of what the treaties have provided for. With the balance of powers in CFSP matters not embedded in the EU institutions except for the Council, how CFSP matters are managed, legitimised, and ultimately accountable, are important for its existence as a policy field. As CFSP matters continue to evolve, this chapter captures the current state of its essence.

6.2. Governance, Values, and the Rule of Law

The treaties embody the general constitutional landscape of Member States that flow into the governing arrangements of the Union. Governance, tied with

[6] As per, Deirdre Curtin, Peter Mair and Yannis Papadopoulos, 'Positioning Accountability in European Governance: An Introduction' (2010) 33 *West European Politics* 929.

[7] Gráinne De Búrca, 'The Constitutional Challenge of New Governance in the European Union' (2003) 28 *European Law Review* 814 at 817.

regulation, is consistently talked about in a reform sense. In a relatable sense, foreign policy discussions have now descended from the great and the good, and instead, are discussed by mere 'products of the modern meritocracy'.[8] In Union law terms beyond CFSP matters, governance is primarily, if not exclusively shaped around the legislative area.[9] In discussing the nature of CFSP matters, however, given the non-legislative nature of CFSP matters, little if anything is ever said of governance in CFSP matters. The focus of the treaties in the provisions on CFSP matters sets out a very specified set of governance arrangements. This is by contrast to the absence of detailed inter-institutional arrangements in other policy fields. Coupled with this constitutional manifestation in the exercise of this effort, it is seen that CFSP Decisions have the capacity to be overtly detailed, and as such, their non-legislative nature has the ability for their legal nature to be examined from a governance perspective.

6.2.1. Governance

The term in itself, governance, can be difficult to define. One prominent EU legal scholar has said, '[o]h dear! You know that the word "governance" makes me reach for my revolver'.[10] The statement in itself might summarise how lawyers can tend to feel about bringing matters of governance into the legal field. Global governance regimes are a conundrum for scholars as they seek increased accountability, which has proven challenging and provocative.[11] Governance is not a fully developed concept in Union law as its definition is vague at best,[12] and no matter how it is framed, it is subject to differing interpretations of what it means in a legal context. The practice of good governance is included in the primary law of the Union, noting that '[i]n order to promote good governance and ensure the participation of civil society, the Union's institutions, bodies, offices and agencies shall conduct their work as openly as possible'.[13] For example, use of an appropriate legal basis can be down to the practice of good governance. Many actors drive governance in

[8] Pieter Jan Kuijper, 'Recent Tendencies in the Separation of Powers in EU Foreign Relations: An Essay' in Eleftheria Neframi and Mauro Gatti (eds), *Constitutional Issues of EU External Relations Law* (Nomos, 2018) p 204.

[9] See, Mark Dawson, 'New Modes of Governance' in Dennis Patterson and Anna Södersten (eds), *A Companion to European Union Law and International Law* (John Wiley & Sons, 2016).

[10] Words attributed to Alan Dashwood. See, Alison McDonnell, "Farewell and Thanks to Alan" in A Constitutional Order of States? Essays in EU Law in Honour of Alan Dashwood (Oxford: Hart Publishing, 2011), ix–xi at p x.

[11] Michael Goodhart, 'Accountable International Relations' in Mark Bovens, Robert E Goodin and Thomas Schillemans (eds), *The Oxford Handbook of Public Accountability* (Oxford University Press, 2014) p 293.

[12] Christian Joerges, 'The Commission's White Paper on Governance in the EU – A Symptom of Crisis?' (2002) 39 *Common Market Law Review* 441 at 443.

[13] TFEU, Article 15(1).

a European context, but the Commission has positioned itself in a leading role,[14] outside of the framework for CFSP matters.

The principle of institutional balance is tied to the democratic values emanating from the Union's own constitutional design. Governance, therefore, is meant to be applied to international organisations like the Union, just as it would for Member States. The manner in which EU foreign policy has traditionally been carried out has been crafted, decided, and executed by executive authority alone. Yet, for a system of governance to work, certain attributes must be present. These can include measures for introducing proposals, scrutinising such planned courses of action, ideally between a diversity of actors. CFSP matters fail this criterion, given a lack of institutional diversity in its processes. Similarly, judicial review of EU actions have been fundamental for the efficacy of Union measures in all its forms. A useful riddle to recall is that 'there is no accountable governance without accountability arrangements'[15] and given such a deficit in CFSP matters, this is the nub of the problem in CFSP matters as the area continues to evolve.

Global governance is not without its problems. Governance can be accused of structural bias,[16] putting narrow interests over general interests. The merging concepts of 'new governance' and law are much more correlated than is usually expected.[17] Governance for the Union is particular; after all, it was the Union which invented a 'Community Method' for how to handle its legislative affairs. Whereas this method was said to be 'ill-equipped to sustain the European integration project',[18] it was by far a better arrangement than the existing arrangements set down in the treaties for CFSP matters. Notwithstanding the internal issues of institutional arrangements of EU external action, a concept of a 'governance mode of foreign policy' can be said to have opened up.[19] Legal instruments and their guiding force demonstrate the approach that the EU has taken towards shaping the outside world through actions on a CFSP legal basis.

[14] For its 2011 leading document, see, C 287/1. 'European Governance: A White Paper' (COM(2001) 428) July 2001 (2001/C 287/01).

[15] Mark Bovens, 'Two Concepts of Accountability: Accountability as a Virtue and as a Mechanism' (2010) 33 *West European Politics* 946 at 963.

[16] Miguel Poiares Maduro, 'Legal Travels and the Risk of Legal Jet-Lag: The Judicial and Constitutional Challenges of Legal Globalisation' in Mario Monti and others (eds), *Economic Law and Justice in Times of Globalisation – Wirtschaftsrecht und Justiz in Zeiten der Globalisierung: Festschrift for Carl Baudenbacher* (Nomos, 2007) p 184.

[17] Neil Walker and Gráinne De Búrca, 'Reconceiving Law and New Governance Narrowing the Gap: Law and New Approaches to Governance in the European Union' (2007) 13 *Columbia Journal of European Law* 519 at 536.

[18] Kenneth A Armstrong, 'New Governance and the European Union: An Empirical Conceptual Critique' in Gráinne De Búrca, Claire Kilpatrick and Joanne Scott (eds), *Critical Legal Perspectives on Global Governance* (Hart Publishing, 2014) p 270.

[19] See, Gráinne De Búrca, 'EU External Relations: The Governance Mode of Foreign Policy' in Bart Van Vooren, Steven Blockmans and Jan Wouters (eds), *The EU's Role in Global Governance: The Legal Dimension* (Oxford University Press, 2013).

Broadly speaking, CFSP Decisions are political actions, however, administratively, they are implemented by diplomats and bureaucrats – actions contributing to administrative governance[20] and have binding legal effect. The EEAS, in part responsible for the coordination of CFSP matters through the High Representative, has 'a strand' of accountability to the Parliament[21] but that, in itself, does not mean it has an important governance role. During the EEAS's creation, the Parliament was able to extract concessions,[22] enhancing its own involvement in its subsequent operations. Yet, the Parliament does not hear from high-level appointments in the EEAS who discharge large parts of actions on a CFSP legal basis. The High Representative is politically accountable for CFSP matters to the Parliament in a relatively mild-mannered fashion through Article 36 TEU, but having officials from the EEAS attend the Parliament through AFET removes this political accountability, and instead moves towards a system of delegated accountability.

The underlying hypothesis on how decision-making in CFSP matters is conducted follows an intergovernmental, rule-bound approach. Every CFSP Decision is taken in the Council. The breadth of bodies consulted in the formation of Decisions, formally or informally, is deliberately narrow. However, CFSP matters, as a policy field, much like any other, is pan-European, and therefore it is not for any single national parliament or national court in any Member State to have the authority over CFSP matters as a whole. As CFSP matters are situated within the Council for sole decision-making, it is not possible for each national parliament to hold national implementation of CFSP Decisions to account.

6.2.2. Values

The Union is grounded on core principles and values originating from its Member States. Furthermore, its identity, culture, and legal order are an ongoing exchange of traditions. CFSP matters are reflective of these central principles and values that attempt to bind the Member States together as one Union. The European Council sets the strategic interests and objectives of CFSP matters[23] which the Council subsequently executes through Decisions. This broad scope is qualified in the same Article by ensuring their consistency with Article 21 TEU on the external values of the Union. The treaties, when speaking of the character and formulation of the Union's values, does so when speaking about its policies as a whole.

[20] Simon Duke and Sophie Vanhoonacker, 'Administrative Governance in the CFSP: Development and Practice' (2006) 11 *European Foreign Affairs Review* 163 at 164.

[21] Bart Van Vooren, 'A Legal-Institutional Perspective on the European External Action Service' (2011) 48 *Common Market Law Review* 475 at 492.

[22] Kolja Raube, 'Democratic Accountability and EU Governance: The EEAS and the Role of the European Parliament' in David Spence and Jozef Bátora (eds), *The European External Action Service: European Diplomacy Post-Westphalia* (Palgrave Macmillan, 2015) p 145.

[23] TEU, Article 22(1): '[T]he European Council shall identify the strategic interests and objectives of the Union. Decisions of the European Council on the strategic interests and objectives of the Union shall relate to the common and security policy and to other areas of the external action of the Union…'.

It does not attempt to siphon off CFSP matters as a separate policy with different value-orientation.

With the role that the EU has on the world stage, it is capable of influencing normative thinking on the global political scene, which in turn shapes international norms. The treaties state '[t]he Union's action on the international scene shall be guided by the principles which have inspired its own creation, development and enlargement, and which it seeks to advance in the wider world'.[24] By incorporating the norms of its Member States and transplanting them across the EU legal order, it has sought to build valued-based norms in its laws. Similarly, the Union has taken international law norms and inserted them into the EU system of norms,[25] which have strengthened its legal framework.

The convolution of *ad hoc* democratic and accountable inclinations has resulted in an unclear demonstration of inherent EU values. Democratic values can be expressed through determining a legal basis for external action. For example, the selection of a non-CFSP legal basis could be interpreted as being more democratic in the eyes of the Parliament, whereas the option of a CFSP legal basis would be more democratic from the viewpoint of the Council. What this demonstrates is that values in EU external relations are completely dependent on the institutional perspective. The Council has previously argued, correctly, that, 'it is not procedures that define the legal basis of a measure but the legal basis of a measure that determines the procedures to be followed in adopting that measure',[26] as supported by the Court.[27]

6.2.3. Rule of Law

It is to be expected that the Union respects its own primary law, with the treaties specifying that 'the Union shall act only within the limits of the competence[] conferred upon it'.[28] There is no concrete and unified definition of what fits the notion of the rule of law.[29] Yet, without it, the success of the EU would suffer, and the institutional elements of the polity would lack the necessary powers to give effect to their desired actions. Given this wide variety of interpretative means of deciphering what the rule of law is, and what it is not, the Union has attempted, through the primary law, to define its external competence.

[24] TEU, Article 21.

[25] Marise Cremona, 'Values in EU Foreign Policy' in Malcolm Evans and Panos Koutrakos (eds), *Beyond the Established Legal Orders: Policy Interconnections between the EU and the Rest of the World* (Hart Publishing, 2011) p 313.

[26] Case C-130/10, *Parliament v Council*, ECLI:EU:C:2012:472, ('*Smart Sanctions*') para 80.

[27] Case C-658/11, *Parliament v Council*, ECLI:EU:C:2014:2025, ('*Mauritius*') para 57; Case C-540/13, *Parliament v Council*, ECLI:EU:C:2015:224, para 12.

[28] TEU, Article 5(2).

[29] See, Paul Craig, 'Formal and Substantive Conceptions of the Rule of Law: An Analytical Framework' [1997] *Public Law* 467.

The treaties resolutely state that the Union is based upon the rule of law.[30] This was not a given at first. As it stands, Article 2 TEU states that the Union 'is founded on the values of respect for…the rule of law'. This emanated from *Les Verts*, in which the Court stated the Union is 'based on the rule of law'.[31] The *Gestoras* and *Segi* judgments have affirmed that applicants before the Court cannot argue that actions grounded upon certain legal bases are without adequate judicial protection.[32] In more recent times, the Court has become 'more and more dependent on a rule of law', based on an understanding that 'encompasses democracy, human rights and constitutions enforced by independent judiciaries'.[33] With rising internal threats within the Union, its eagerness to use the principle, where appropriate, is not entirely surprising. When it comes to general objectives of the Union, CFSP matters are no different from other aspects of EU external action. For example, the General Court said 'it cannot be acceptable, in a [Union] based on the rule of law, that such acts [of non-institutions] escape judicial review'.[34] Each revision of the treaties has reinforced these underlying principles as the Union has closely aligned itself to the international legal order. If a polity such as the EU, which bases itself on the rule of law, prevents full judicial review of certain legal acts, then that polity has a number of outstanding issues from a governance perspective.

In the European Security Strategy of 2003, amidst internal conflict amongst Member States about how to respond to global concerns on the 'war on terror', the Union stood for '[t]he development of a stronger international society, well-functioning international institutions and a rule-based international order'.[35] Notwithstanding unified external objectives of a general nature that feed into all Union policies, the rule of law in EU external action can be differentiated from the *promotion* of the rule of law by third parties.[36] Whilst adequate rule of law norms through international judicial bodies have the potential to be a 'troublesome threat' if not adequately constructed,[37] internally within the Union, the Court's institutional position is sufficiently robust to withstand such challenges.

[30] See, the preamble to the TEU, Articles 2 and 21.

[31] The Union is 'based on the rule of law'. Case C-294/83, *Parti écologiste 'Les Verts' v Parliament*, ECLI:EU:C:1986:166, para 23.

[32] Case C-354/04 P, *Gestoras Pro Amnistía, Juan Mari Olano Olano, Julen Zelarain Errasti v Council*, ECLI:EU:C:2007:115 ('*Gestoras*'), para 57 and, Case C-355/04 P, *Segi, Arait, Zubimendi Izaga, and Aritza Galarraga v. Council*, ECLI:EU:C:2007:116 ('*Segi*'), para 57.

[33] 'Judges as Diplomats in Advancing the Rule of Law: A Conversation with President Koen Lenaerts and Justice Stephen Breyer' (2017) 66 *American University Law Review* 1159 at 1165.

[34] Case T-411/06, *Sogelma – Societá generale lavori manutenzioni appalti Srl v European Agency for Reconstruction (AER)*, ECLI:EU:T:2008:419, para 37.

[35] European Council, 'European Security Strategy – A Secure Europe in a Better World', 2003, p 36.

[36] Ricardo Gosalbo-Bono, 'The Significance of the Rule of Law and Its Implications for the European Union and the United States' (2010) 72 *University of Pittsburgh Law Review* 229 at 326.

[37] Brian Z Tamanaha, *On the Rule of Law: History, Politics, Theory* (Cambridge University Press, 2004) p 134.

The rule of law is a contemporary issue that is being grappled with in the Union. The Copenhagen Criteria must be followed for new states acceding to the Union,[38] but yet, once acceded, holding the entrance standards is more difficult for the EU institutions to manage. As well highlighted in the past, some Member States have been eroding the criteria of democracy and human rights. This has caught the attention of the Commission, which has yet to fully deploy the Article 7 TEU mechanism for responding to such threats. Yet, while it is important for such powers internally, they also have implications for the Union's powers externally. The European Union Rule of Law Mission in Kosovo, Eulex Kosovo,[39] is a prime example of the EU externally being able to bring about changes and improvements to rule of law frameworks beyond its own borders.[40] This was undertaken upon a CFSP legal basis, as was the EU Rule of Law Mission to Georgia (EUJUST THEMIS)[41] and the European Union Integrated Rule of Law Mission for Iraq (EUJUST LEX-Iraq).[42] Such well-intentioned external missions, however, are now immune from institutional interests. The Council, unsurprisingly, prefers rule of law missions to be based on a CFSP legal basis, whereas the Commission and the Parliament would prefer a scenario where a non-CFSP legal basis would be availed of, if even possible.

6.3. Democracy and Participatory Parliaments

There is already an acknowledged critical democratic issue with the foreign policy of the EU, at least according to political science.[43] From a legal perspective, this is also evident. However, far from a negative outlook, the development of the EU can be said to have made foreign policy a domain that has undergone 'a wave of democratisation'.[44] The EU has its own select view of democracy, and the nation-state style of democracy and accountability cannot be transplanted onto the Union. They are different monsters who need alternative solutions. Democratic ideals

[38] For more on this, see, Christophe Hillion, 'The Copenhagen Criteria and Their Progeny' in Christophe Hillion (ed), *EU Enlargement: A Legal Approach* (Hart Publishing, 2004).

[39] L 42/92. Council Joint Action 2008/1247CFSP of 4 February 2008 on the European Union Rule of Law Mission in Kosovo, Eulex Kosovo.

[40] Notably, one Member State, Cyprus, availed of the possibility of constructive absention, based on what is now Article 31(1) TEU, second para. See, Council of the European Union, 'CM 448/08'. For further elaboration, see, Martina Spernbauer, *EU Peacebuilding in Kosovo and Afghanistan* (Brill, 2014) p 197.

[41] L 228/21. Council Joint Action 2004/523/CFSP of 28 June 2004 on the European Union Rule of Law Mission in Georgia, EUJUST THEMIS.

[42] L 62/37. Council Joint Action 2005/190/CFSP of 7 March 2005 on the European Union Integrated Rule of Law Mission for Iraq, EUJUST LEX.

[43] Helene Sjursen, 'The EU's Common Foreign and Security Policy: The Quest for Democracy' (2011) 18 *Journal of European Public Policy* 1069.

[44] Pieter Jan Kuijper, 'The Case Law of the Court of Justice of the EU and the Allocation of External Relations Powers: Whither the Traditional Role of the Executive in EU Foreign Relations?' in Marise Cremona and Anne Thies (eds), *The European Court of Justice and External Relations Law: Constitutional Challenges* (Hart Publishing, 2014) p 113.

and principles are sown solidly into the constitutional framework of the Union through the treaties. This has been, in part, thanks to the efforts undertaken by the Court with respect to its democracy-promotion judgments.[45] Yet, democracy has an inherent problem, in that its furtherance is seen as a good development. Depending on a given persuasion, this might not necessarily be a problem in and of itself, but it demonstrates that 'more democracy' cannot be directly correlated with a stronger, more coherent and better-governed foreign policy.

Just like governance, democracy has no straightforward definition, but it extends beyond active electoral participation through a balloting process at regular intervals. A common conception of what defines democracy is intermittent elections, free of irregularities, where the people choose their representatives. While this is the case for Member States of the EU, where citizens of their respective states go to the polls for parliamentary elections every few years to select their representatives or executives, this is not the case, strictly speaking, for the EU. The expectations of democracy within the Union are 'state-inspired',[46] but democracy can take a number of different formulations, in that it is not identical to the versions of democracy that are seen within the Member States themselves. Colloquially put, sovereignty and democracy are 'not natural bedfellows',[47] but, nonetheless, are in perpetual coexistence. Consistent involvement is needed beyond campaigns and procedural public democratic exercises to democratise and legitimise executive powers. Therefore, in an EU context, democracy is understood through institutions and accompanying procedures.[48] Such features of democracy provide decisions, legal development, and an operative framework for how decisions are arrived at.

A number of special provisions in the treaties guarantee democratic legitimacy of the Union, ensuring tight control by Member States. In light of the sovereign debt crisis that arose around the time of the ratification of the Treaty of Lisbon and, given its imperfectness, many improvements, particularly within economic governance, had to be fought for.[49] This included subsequent amendment of the treaties, such as the insertion of Article 136(3) TFEU and the establishment of the European Stability Mechanism (ESM) outside of the EU legal order, amongst others. Article 31 TEU sets out rules of the voting procedure for CFSP matters within the Council, which guarantees unanimity as the general rule,

[45] See, Giuseppe Federico Mancini and David T Keeling, 'Democracy and the European Court of Justice' (1994) 57 *Modern Law Review* 175.

[46] Stephen Weatherill, 'Competence and Legitimacy' in Catherine Barnard and Okeoghene Odudu (eds), *The Outer Limits of European Union Law* (Hart Publishing, 2009) p 26.

[47] Francis G Jacobs, *The Sovereignty of Law: The European Way* (Cambridge University Press, 2007) p 138.

[48] Roland Bieber, 'Democratic Control of International Relations of the European Union' in Enzo Cannizzaro (ed), *The European Union as an Actor in International Relations* (Kluwer Law International, 2002) p 105.

[49] As put, 'a great deal remains to be done in respect of most aspects of economic and monetary union'. Gavin Barrett, 'European Economic Governance: Deficient in Democratic Legitimacy?' (2018) 40 *Journal of European Integration* 249 at 259. See also, Diane Fromage, 'The European Parliament in the Post-Crisis Era: An Institution Empowered on Paper Only?' (2018) 40 *Journal of European Integration* 281.

barring limited exceptions.[50] This strong guarantee of consent to all CFSP Decisions for a range of external acts, from adopting positions to international agreements, provides strong national democratic involvement, but not any form of supranational democracy.

Member States can have different understandings when it comes to linking democracy and constitutionalisation. The Federal Constitutional Court of Germany has said that the Union 'still lacks a democratically legitimated Parliament… fully responsible on a political level'.[51] However, comparisons of national and EU framework systems fail to observe their respective regimes. The Court has previously rejected the ideas that an analogy can be explicitly made between the scope of powers of the Parliament and those of Member States' national parliaments.[52] As such, it is assumed that electoral power means more at national level than in the European field.[53] Furthermore, certain legal bases in the treaties tend to have a greater democratic character than others (eg, actions in EU external relations on a non-CFSP legal basis demand parliamentary participation through the Parliament through the ordinary legislative procedure). Alternatively, a CFSP legal basis does not have the democratic credentials from a supranational point of view, given the lack of parliamentary participation stemming from the EU's constitutional design. Yet, contrastingly, a CFSP legal basis is democratic from a national perspective.

6.3.1. Democratic Credentials

Democracy is closely interwoven with the institutional balance within the Union and, in principle, applies to both CFSP and non-CFSP matters. Yet, integrating the Union comes at a political price. In the striven attempt of the treaties to exclude the Parliament and the Courts in CFSP matters, the democratic nature of CFSP matters can be called into question. The TEU, introduced by the Treaty of Maastricht, brought the issue of democracy within the Union to the fore and had to be dealt with, but nonetheless discriminated between first, second and third pillar matters.[54] In respect of non-CFSP matters, the case law from the Court

[50] TEU, Article 31(1): 'Decisions under this Chapter shall be taken by the European Council and the Council acting unanimously, except where this Chapter provides otherwise.' For more, see the following concluding Chapter of this book.

[51] Decision of the Federal Constitutional Court in Germany, 29 May 1974 ('*Solange I*'), 2 BvL 52/71 (37, 271). This was in the context of the treaties then not having a 'codified catalogue of fundamental rights'. See, Norbert Reich, 'Judge-Made "Europe a La Carte": Some Remarks on Recent Conflicts between European and German Constitutional Law Provoked by the Banana Litigation' (1996) 7 *European Journal of International Law* 103 at 104.

[52] Case C-189/97, *Parliament v Council*, ECLI:EU:C:1999:366 ('*Mauritania Fisheries Agreement*'), para 34.

[53] Joseph HH Weiler, Ulrich Haltern and Franz C Mayer, 'European Democracy and Its Critique' (1995) 18 *West European Politics* 4 at 8.

[54] With the Treaty of Maastricht and the incorporation of the Schengen Agreement provisions, when the Parliament and Court were excluded. See, Deirdre Curtin and Herman Meijers, 'The Principle

has said that 'legislative process reflects…the fundamental democratic principle that the people must share in the exercise of power through a representative assembly'.[55] Democracy readily accepts the notion of the ability of democratic institutions to withhold influence on executive actors. EU democracy, however, particularly for CFSP matters, is very different.

As demonstrated in previous chapters, the Parliament's role in Union decision-making, particularly in CFSP matters, has historically been curtailed. Thus, the democratic process of CFSP matters is in the hands of the very few. It largely escapes intense scrutiny at the Parliament beyond a select few procedures that have been ingrained to ensure some level of democratic accountability. The Parliament has long called for complete democratisation of CFSP matters, as far back as the Treaty of Maastricht.[56] The lack of an adequate role for the Parliament is clearly a persistent problem from a democratic perspective. The Parliament, in its capacity as a democratic institution, must provide a 'democratic foundation' of the Union in its external relations.[57] As an institution, it can be confident of its 'democratic credentials'[58] and the Union has 'democracy-affirming qualities without which it would be unambiguously undemocratic'.[59] The Parliament has never made any secret of its desired ambition of more involvement in CFSP matters, for it 'seek[s]…democratic supervision over measures which are not subject to parliamentary supervision at the national level'.[60] Direct elections commenced in 1979 and undoubtedly added more weight to the Parliament's claim of having more legitimacy than other institutional actors.

There are two common methods of parliamentary democracy in the national political spheres in Member States: representative democracy and parliamentary government. Yet, democracy beyond the nation state in Europe is well and truly alive.[61] At Union level, Article 10(1) TEU specifies '[t]he functioning of the Union

of Open Government in Schengen and the European Union: Democratic Retrogression?' (1995) 32 *Common Market Law Review* 391.

[55] Case T-135/96, *Union Européenne de l'artisanat et des petites et moyennes entreprises (UEAPME) v Council*, ECLI:EU:T:1998:128, para 88. In doing so, the General Court cited an earlier Court of Justice judgment, Case C-139/79, *Maizena v Council*, ECLI:EU:C:1980:250, para 34.

[56] See 'Report of the Committee on Foreign Affairs and Security on Shaping the European Community's Common Foreign Policy (A3-0322/92) (Rapporteur: Mr Josep Verde i Aldea)' (European Parliament 1992) A3-0322/92.

[57] Joseph HH Weiler, 'The European Parliament and Foreign Affairs: External Relations of the European Economic Community' in Antonio Cassese (ed), *Parliamentary Control Over Foreign Policy: Legal Essays* (Sijtoff and Noordhoff, 1980) p 158.

[58] Daniel Thym, 'Beyond Parliament's Reach? The Role of the European Parliament in the CFSP' (2006) 11 *European Foreign Affairs Review* 109.

[59] Damian Chalmers, 'The Democratic Ambiguity of EU Law Making and Its Enemies' in Anthony Arnull and Damian Chalmers (eds), *The Oxford Handbook of European Union Law* (Oxford University Press, 2015) p 304.

[60] Kieran St C Bradley, 'Halfway House: The 2006 Comitology Reforms and the European Parliament' (2008) 31 *West European Politics* 837 at 852.

[61] See, Deirdre Curtin, *Postnational Democracy: The European Union in Search of a Political Philosophy* (Kluwer Law International 1997).

shall be founded on representative democracy'. Accordingly, the phrase excludes the Parliament from being the sole control or accountability mechanism for any form of EU governance arrangements. The place of the citizen for democratic purposes is shared between national and EU institutions, representing a disconnection that can be difficult to grasp. Furthermore, there is the view that an elected Parliament should be equally able to participate in the formulation of policies that stretch across all Member States.[62]

Presumption is placed upon there being an inherent incongruity between reaching a democratic ideal and the process of constitutionalisation within the Union.[63] With CFSP matters being a constitutionalised process, this must be structured in a manner consistent with the democratic principles upon which the Union is built. Textually, Article 10(2) TEU recognises that the Union has democratic legitimacy by having two institutions central to its system, the Parliament and the Council,[64] in that order. From the Parliament's perspective, the Union's external relations must be legitimate, with control from a democratic standpoint being vital.[65] The Parliament, on occasion, has cited itself as 'a source of democratic legitimacy for…CFSP [matters]…over which it exercises political scrutiny',[66] which is quite a claim given the actual legal arrangements.

For CFSP matters, intricate discussions do not involve national parliaments nor the Parliament. Democratic accountability for strands of intergovernmentalism is of 'little relevance'.[67] The Council, to keep parliamentary involvement at bay, has used phrases such as 'closely associated', 'regularly inform' and 'take into consideration',[68] and has consistently sought to keep any democratic involvement away from Union-level forums. The Council's institutional viewpoint, therefore, is that the Parliament's democratic principles are of little concern. The Parliament is not the only provider of democracy, however, notwithstanding its level of representativeness. Allowing the Parliament to have a more

[62] Jürgen Habermas, 'The Crisis of the European Union in the Light of a Constitutionalization of International Law' (2012) 23 *European Journal of International Law* 335 at 346.

[63] Helle Krunke, 'European Law as a Process between Constitutionalization and Democratization' in Hanne Petersen and others (eds), *Paradoxes of European Legal Integration* (Ashgate Publishing, 2008) p 12.

[64] TEU, Article 10(2): 'Citizens are directly represented at Union level in the European Parliament. Member States are represented in the European Council by their Heads of State or Government and in the Council by their governments, themselves democratically accountable either to their national Parliaments, or to their citizens.'

[65] Ricardo Passos, 'Mixed Agreements from the Perspective of the European Parliament' in Christophe Hillion and Panos Koutrakos (eds), *Mixed Agreements Revisited: The EU and its Member States in the World* (Hart Publishing, 2010) p 270.

[66] See, European Parliament, European Parliament's approach to implementing Articles 9 and 10 of Protocol 1 to the Lisbon Treaty as regards parliamentary cooperation in the field of CFSP/CSDP 2011 [B7-0388/2011].

[67] András Sajó, 'Constitution without the Constitutional Moment: A View from the New Member States' (2005) 3 *International Journal of Constitutional Law* 243 at 260.

[68] Ramses A Wessel, *The European Union's Foreign and Security Policy: A Legal Institutional Perspective*, vol 33 (Kluwer Law International, 1999) p 214.

active role in CFSP matters could be construed as democratic multiplicity, but the current democratic arrangements for CFSP matters are far from adequate. Yet democracy is an end in and of itself.[69] The fact that EU external action can have stronger accountability and democratic credentials is not reason enough to base foreign policy acts on a non-CFSP legal basis.

6.3.2. Bringing about Democracy

Theorising the various ways for the Parliament to act in EU external action can be done in three ways: firstly, as controllers and scrutinisers; secondly, as decision-makers and legislators; and thirdly, as parliamentary diplomats.[70] Around the time when EPC was gathering pace,[71] the make-up of the Union was far smaller in terms of the number of Member States compared to the modern era. There was no High Representative, the Parliament had just had its first ever direct elections and the EU's own distinctive foreign policy was more-or-less non-existent. When CFSP matters as a new policy domain was brought into the treaties, the system of checks and balances was less than adequate. What has prevailed from this era is that CFSP matters, within the Council under the auspices of the Union, but having much of the implementing measures instituted at Member State level, constitutes dual levels of implementation. Given the continued existence of the hidden pillar for CFSP matters, the responsibility for democracy falls predominantly on national parliaments, not the Parliament.

To ensure democracy in CFSP and non-CFSP matters, making use of the Parliament's few powers and the Court's limited jurisdiction, procedural powers must be taken seriously. This can include involvement for the Parliament in the negotiation of international agreements.[72] The Treaty of Lisbon had a strong democratising element to it, enhancing the position of the Parliament in the treaties, which provided for it as a co-decider in legislative (non-CFSP) areas. This has included expanding the areas of exclusive competence in its Common Commercial Policy (CCP). Approval of national parliaments has since been needed for the conclusion of mixed agreements, but not for CFSP matters. Such mixed agreements concluded by the Union are subject to 'double parliamentary control'.[73]

[69] It is 'a means, even if an indispensable means'. See, Joseph HH Weiler, 'Europe: The Case Against the Case for Statehood' (1998) 4 *European Law Journal* 43 at 60.

[70] Kolja Raube, 'Parliamentarisation Approach: Parliamentary Control in EU Foreign Policy' in Maciej Wilga and Ireneusz Pawel Karolewski (eds), *New Approaches to EU Foreign Policy* (Routledge, 2014) p 130.

[71] See Chapter 2 of this book.

[72] Christina Eckes, 'How the European Parliament's Participation in International Relations Affects the Deep Tissue of the EU's Power Structures' (2014) 12 *International Journal of Constitutional Law* 904 at 908.

[73] Passos (n 65) p 290.

The Court has hinted at the possibility that the role of Parliament should, from a democratic perspective, be allowed information in some form, as per the treaties. After all, information is power. Article 218 TFEU on international agreements has many democratic features. The Court has, appropriately, approved of the Parliament's claims of entitlement to information under Article 218 TFEU, as seen the in the *Mauritius* and *Tanzania* cases,[74] which in effect, made information-sharing obligations higher upon the Council. It represents a clear view of the Court that the exercise of power through the institutions has to be underlined by the fundamental principles of democracy. In *Svenska Journalistförbundet*, in an old judgment, the General Court said a Council Decision on public access to documents was intended 'with a view to strengthening the democratic character of the institutions and the trust of the public in the administration'.[75] In even earlier case law, the Court said 'the fundamental democratic principle that the peoples should take part in the exercise of power through the intermediary of a representative assembly',[76] that is, the Parliament.

Having fewer institutions in any policy, national or European, makes it easier for the empowered actors to exert influence without interrogation. Whilst the smaller number of actors in CFSP matters makes the task of the Council more straightforward from an institutional perspective, it does not make it any more democratic, but rather, less democratic compared to other Union policies that are subjected to regular decision-making procedures. The participation rights of the Parliament to be involved in 'political choices' has been upheld by the Court[77] and so a participatory role for institutions beyond the Council may be warranted. This is particularly so, given that CFSP Decisions within the Council are generally decided without any debate at political level,[78] and are mainly handled diplomatically and administratively. COREPER and the PSC are important bodies in CFSP matters,[79] but are handled by national officials under a mandate from national governments of Member States.

The relationship between the Union and national parliaments is direct, but 'unmediated',[80] thus allowing significant flexibility from actors on both playing fields. Decision-making for CFSP matters traditionally lay with national governments and, as a result, it has been national parliaments who have been

[74] Case C-658/11, *Parliament v Council*, ECLI:EU:C:2014:2025 ('*Mauritius*'); and Case C-263/14, *Parliament v Council*, ECLI:EU:C:2016:435 ('*Tanzania*').

[75] 'L 340/43. Council Decision of 20 December 1993 on Public Access to Council Documents (93/731/EC)'. Case T-174/95, *Svenska Journalistförbundet v Council*, ECLI:EU:T:1998:127, para 66.

[76] Case C-138/79, *Roquette Frères v Council*, ECLI:EU:C:1980:249, para 4.

[77] Case C-355/10, *Parliament v Council*, ECLI:EU:C:2012:516 ('*Border Surveillance*'), para 76. See, Graham Butler, 'In Search of the Political Question Doctrine in EU Law' (2018) 45 *Legal Issues of Economic Integration* 329.

[78] Ramses A Wessel, 'Common Foreign, Security, and Defense Policy' in Dennis Patterson and Anna Södersten (eds), *A Companion to European Union Law and International Law* (John Wiley & Sons, 2016) p 397.

[79] See Chapter 3 of this book.

[80] Leonard FM Besselink, 'The Place of National Parliaments within the European Constitutional Order' in Nicola Lupo and Cristina Fasone (eds), *Interparliamentary Cooperation in the Composite European Constitution* (Hart Publishing, 2016).

permitted to 'ensure democratic control of...CFSP [matters]'.[81] Therefore, the Parliament has competition for parliamentary involvement in CFSP matters. While the Parliament and national parliaments are not directly comparable, they do attempt to operate within the same sphere of influence. With it not being possible to adequately control the Council by individual national parliaments, the insufficient methods of parliamentary involvement mean that reform of checks and balances is needed to bring about a democratic regime that is suitable for the framework of CFSP matters. If actions on a CFSP legal basis are to be truly accountable, the executive actors would have to engage with the Parliament in a more constructive manner to ensure its inputs are facilitated.

6.3.3. Subsidiarity

The treaties have progressively gone the extra mile to increase the potential applicability of subsidiarity in the Union. In particular, Article 5(3) TEU says that for 'areas which do not fall within its exclusive competence, the Union shall act only if and in so far as the objectives of the proposed action cannot be sufficiently achieved by the Member States...but can rather, by reason of the scale or effects of the proposed action, be better achieved at Union level'. Subsidiarity can be considered a principle that applies right throughout the treaties, including for CFSP matters. Whereas it might be discussed in the context of restraining encroaching federalism,[82] it is rarely discussed in the context of CFSP matters. The preamble of the treaties states 'decisions are taken as closely as possible to the citizen in accordance with the principle of subsidiarity', with Article 5 TEU placing particular emphasis on it lying within the grasp of national parliaments. This reversion of subsidiarity to national parliaments was not included in the original Treaty of Rome, and was only included in the Single European Act with regard to environmental policy.[83]

The justiciability of subsidiarity has been discussed in cases before the Court on a substantive level,[84] and has been affirmed by cases taken at the Court.[85] Whereas the initial subsidiarity review was limited and confined to narrow procedural matters,[86] the present treaties cater for the Court to broaden this scope,

[81] Ben Crum, 'Parliamentarization of the CFSP through Informal Institution-Making? The Fifth European Parliament and the EU High Representative' (2006) 13 *Journal of European Public Policy* 383 at 389.

[82] See, Xavier Groussot and Sanja Bogojevic, 'Subsidiarity as a Procedural Safeguard of Federalism' in Loïc Azoulai (ed), *The Question of Competence in the European Union* (Oxford University Press, 2014).

[83] Article 130R(4), inserted by the Single European Act.

[84] Alexander Mackenzie Stuart, 'Subsidiarity – A Busted Flush?' in Deirdre Curtin and David O'Keeffe (eds), *Constitutional Adjudication in European Community and National Law: Essays for the Hon Mr Justice T F O'Higgins* (Butterworths 1992) p 22.

[85] See, Gráinne De Búrca, 'The Principle of Subsidiarity and the Court of Justice as an Institutional Actor' (1998) 36 *Journal of Common Market Studies* 217.

[86] Ton Van den Brink, 'The Substance of Subsidiarity: The Interpretation and Meaning of the Principle after Lisbon' in Martin Trybus and Luca Rubini (eds), *The Treaty of Lisbon and the Future of European Law and Policy* (Edward Elgar, 2012) p 163.

if it so desires. In addition, Protocols 1 and 2 annexed to the treaties outline the role of national parliaments in the EU along with the application of the principles of subsidiarity and proportionality. Protocol 2 applies the early warning mechanism. Whilst it is a democratising feature of the treaties, it only applies to draft legislative acts adopted by the Commission in a range of fields.[87] Since CFSP matters are non-legislative and the Commission is not a central actor in CFSP matters, it is of no importance for the provisions of the treaties on CFSP matters.

The foreign policy competence of national governments is undoubtedly shrinking as more external relations matters are decided at Union level in the Council. Furthermore, globalisation is a contributory factor for how decision-making in national contexts is becoming, in some cases, obsolete. This loss of freedom to choose appropriate external action for their Member States inescapably tests the role that national parliaments have over their national governments in CFSP matters. It is known that activity by national parliaments and its committees can in no way compare to the ability and powers of the Parliament as an institution of the Union. The Court has rejected any level of tolerance towards accepting such comparison between the Parliament and national parliaments.[88] Ultimately, national parliaments of individual Member States 'only have individual control over Council members and not collective control over the Council'.[89] Therefore, national parliaments are not suitable actors for overseeing CFSP matters entirely.

Nonetheless, given the legal framework of CFSP matters, as well as the principle of subsidiarity is within the treaties, there must be some form of link between the policy domain and the constitutional principle. With CFSP matters not having any specific objectives that deviate from the general external objectives of the Union as a whole, it is discernible that actions on a CFSP legal basis are only to be used when Union interests are at stake and not those of individual Member States. This is consistent with the premise that Member States retain their competence to act on the international stage in their own right when there is no defined EU position through the CFSP decision-making process, and are not acting contrary to stated EU positions that have previously been agreed.

6.3.4. Interparliamentary Democracy

The legal basis for interparliamentary contacts varies, as it can range from subsidiarity provisions in the treaties for engagement with national parliaments, to provisions from partnership agreements with third states.[90] With national

[87] Philipp Kiiver, 'The Early-Warning System for the Principle of Subsidiarity: The National Parliament as a Conseil d'Etat for Europe' (2011) 36 *European Law Review* 98 at 100.

[88] Case C-189/97, *Parliament v Council*, ECLI:EU:C:1999:366 ('*Mauritania Fisheries Agreement*'), para 34.

[89] Christopher Lord, 'The Political Theory and Practice of Parliamentary Participation in the Common Security and Defence Policy' (2011) 18 *Journal of European Public Policy* 1133 at 1142.

[90] For example, Article 17 on the Joint Parliamentary Assembly, titled, 'ACP-EU Joint Parliamentary Assembly' as a consultative body. See, L 317/3. Partnership Agreement between the Members of the

parliaments seeking to cast some form of involvement in EU foreign policy, it is conceivable that a collaborative effort would be undertaken, with all seemingly attempting to execute similar levels of involvement, and would come together for the purposes of achieving common goals. It was for these purposes that the Conference of Community and European Affairs Committees of Parliaments of the European Union (COSAC) was founded.

The legal basis for interparliamentary conferences is derived from Protocol 1 of the treaties, specifying '[t]he European Parliament and national Parliaments shall together determine the organisation and promotion of effective and regular interparliamentary cooperation within the Union'.[91] Following this, the more recently founded Interparliamentary Conference on the CFSP/CSDP has been an actor in the field. Yet, the Parliament is not always so eager to engage with national parliaments, given their potential as competitive actors in the policy domain. While both the Parliament and national parliaments have built interparliamentary cooperation in CFSP matters,[92] the forum did not receive much positive reaction.[93] It is therefore questionable as to what extent a more ingrained Interparliamentary Conference on CFSP/CSDP would have in increasing overall cooperation on substantive CFSP matters between the Parliament and national parliaments.

It can be argued that national parliaments have greater potential for powers in CFSP matters than does the Parliament in terms of political involvement. Coupled with this, there is a divide between Member States who wish to continue with a strong international presence on the world stage unilaterally, and those seeking a more integrated, unified, and coherent external dimension of EU foreign policy. Moreover, some Member States, particularly those smaller in nature, may have difficulty separating their foreign policies entirely from the Union's, given the limited impact they can have unilaterally on a whole host of world affairs.

6.4. Legitimacy

Within the Union, legitimacy for its actions comes from a number of sources, both practicably and legally. The Union balances on a two-tier federal structure,[94] ensuring a certain level of checks and balances. In this line of thinking and, through a legal lens, questions turn on the democratic legitimacy of the Union.

African, Caribbean and Pacific Group of States of the One Part, and the European Community and Its Member States, of the Other Part, Signed in Cotonou on 23 June 2000.

[91] Protocol 1, Article 9.

[92] Jan Wouters and Kolja Raube, 'The Interparliamentary Conference on Common Foreign and Security Policy: A Quest for Democratic Accountability in EU Security Governance' in Nicola Lupo and Cristina Fasone (eds), *Interparliamentary Cooperation in the Composite European Constitution* (Hart Publishing, 2016) p 245.

[93] For an early assessment, see, Graham Butler, 'The Interparliamentary Conference on the CFSP/CSDP: A New Forum for the Oireachtas in Irish and EU Foreign Policy?' (2015) 26 *Irish Studies in International Affairs* 163.

[94] For the arguments in this regard on EU federalism, see, Robert Schütze, 'On "Federal" Ground; The European Union as an (Inter)national Phenomenon' (2009) 46 *Common Market Law Review* 1069.

On the practical side is the institutional setup, which is supported by two alternative views of democratic representation. First is the Council, where the Member States are directly represented by their national governments including, to a lesser extent, the national parliaments; and second, by the European peoples directly through the Parliament, the directly and, arguably, most representative institution of them all.

Questions need to be answered to ensure that the external action of the EU has democratic legitimacy. Throughout its history, the EU has intentionally sought to legitimise its practices using a variety of different methods. One way has been to acknowledge that the Parliament and national parliaments play important roles in 'providing authorisation, representation and accountability in the Union'.[95] The Treaty of Lisbon reiterated that the Union is grounded on its principles of a representative democracy. Such notions would lead one to believe that these principles would encompass the Parliament within the complete institutional framework of decisions. Changes in the balance of powers on an institutional level has tended to favour the Parliament through interpretation, persistence, and litigation. This raises questions about the legitimacy of such developments. Yet, the Parliament has had no major breakthrough on CFSP matters, and has instead seen mere incremental developments.

6.4.1. Institutional Legitimacy

Each institution of the Union is always in search of greater legitimacy amongst whomever it views as its audience. This is not a new strain, but rather an ongoing quest. The two diminished actors in CFSP matters, the Parliament and the Court, source their legitimacy from different beings. It is the parliamentary actor, as opposed to the judicial actor, who provides the appropriate legitimacy to the Union's policies. Thus, it can be argued that parliaments, in whatever form, will be held higher in democratic legitimacy terms than courts. The legitimacy of the Court is consistently subject to additional questioning as a result. Given the innovative role of the Court in the constitutional structures of the Union,[96] the changes resulting from its judgments occur through its own internal direction, rather than by consensus from a plurality of actors. The legitimacy of the Court can be undermined when it delivers judgments that are contrary to the views of the parties before it, contributing to rising tensions. Whereas the Parliament can source legitimacy directly from the citizens of the Union, the Court has a much more difficult time in finding an underlying authority. Therefore, given that national parliaments are better functioning creatures at providing legitimacy, it can be considered here

[95] David Judge and David Earnshaw, *The European Parliament* 2nd edition (Palgrave Macmillan, 2008) p 273.

[96] For example, see, Case C-294/83, *Parti écologiste 'Les Verts' v Parliament*, ECLI:EU:C:1986:166. See, Graham Butler, 'Implementing a Complete System of Legal Remedies in EU Foreign Affairs Law' (2018) 24 *Columbia Journal of European Law* 637.

whether the Parliament should be the main foundation of legitimacy for CFSP matters.

The Parliament sees itself as the main supplier of this supposed legitimacy and its credentials in this regard are quite strong. However, to view the Parliament as an all-encompassing body, with equal say on all Union measures, would be mistaken. The Parliament is only involved during ordinary legislative procedures, to which CFSP matters do not belong because of their non-legislative nature. It can be said that the Parliament is on the margins of supplying legitimacy to Union policies as it is the Council which can claim a 'strong indirect legitimation' made up of national governments of Member States with 'considerable extraconstitutional powers'.[97]

The Parliament derives its legitimacy directly from European citizens instead of national governments. Its legitimacy is important, but that is not to say the European governance structures ought to turn into a parliamentary system.[98] The Treaty of Lisbon proved significant for the Parliament, but not substantial enough. Despite its democratic credentials, as an institution, the Parliament has failed to make a true connection with the citizenry of the EU Member States. Its early transformation into a directly elected body has not proved sufficient to meet the Union's needs.[99] Whilst it actively engages in non-CFSP areas of EU external action, it has, on the whole, not captured the imagination of democratic idealism. Presently, CFSP matters are legitimised by Member States devising tight control, which to them, entails unanimity prevailing in the Council.

6.4.2. Constitutional Location

The treaties, at different junctures, had additional measures included to improve the legitimacy of the Union. Yet, much of this development has not had direct legitimacy ramifications for all areas of Union law. One such example is the office of the European Ombudsman. Whilst the Treaty of Maastricht created the position in 1992, the European Ombudsman's powers did not initially cover CFSP matters.[100] Its remit was only extended to cover CFSP matters through Article 228 TFEU.[101] The Ombudsman's status has been described as something

[97] Habermas (n 62) p 345.

[98] Philipp Dann, 'The Political Institutions' in Armin Von Bogdandy and Jürgen Bast (eds), *Principles of European Constitutional Law* 2nd edition (Hart Publishing, 2009) p 269.

[99] See, Yves Mény, 'De la démocratie en Europe: Old Concepts and New Challenges' (2003) 41 *Journal of Common Market Studies* 1 at 8.

[100] Steve Peers, 'The New Regulation on Access to Documents: A Critical Analysis' (2001) 21 *Yearbook of European Law* 385 at 439.

[101] See, European Ombudsman, 'Decision of the European Ombudsman Closing His Own-Initiative Inquiry OI/12/2010/(BEH)MMN Concerning the Council of the European Union, the European Commission and the High Representative / European External Action Service'; European Ombudsman, 'Decision of the European Ombudsman Closing the Own-Initiative Inquiry OI/15/2014/PMC into the Way in Which the European External Action Service (EEAS) Handles Allegations of Serious Irregularities Involving the EU Rule of Law Mission (Eulex) in Kosovo'.

between the functions of the Parliament and the Court and even a 'surrogate court'.[102] Yet, its foundations can be seen to be reacting to the need to protect the rights of individuals with large amounts of administrative activity and high levels of regulation.[103] Yet, some of its functions overlap with the tasks of other actors in the EU legal framework.[104]

Looking at legitimacy alone however, is not enough. Nor is turning to a judiciary to enforce any such notions. No court of any persuasion is on firm ground when it declares that actions of the political actors are legitimate. Rather, legitimacy as a political notion cannot be broached on legal arguments alone. Similarly, no executive wants interference from legislators in what they perceive to be executive prerogatives. Thus, imposing decision-making capabilities or even involving institutions ill-equipped to handle such decision-making capacity can itself be an unaccountable transfer of competence. The Parliament's feeble position in CFSP matters could be counterbalanced, from a legitimacy viewpoint, by looking to the position of national parliaments who could oversee and control such a policy. Whereas enhanced legitimacy for the Union has long been required,[105] along with the strengthening of its supranational institutions, the Parliament has been a consistent victor in successive reforms of the treaties.[106] Such developments have demonstrated an attempt to strengthen the Union's legitimacy, but not on CFSP matters in itself.

6.5. Accountability

It is true to say that constitutional thought on EU institutions has focused on balance, as opposed to any meaningful sense of accountability. The EU treaties do not explicitly prescribe a form of accountability. Therefore, it has to be implicitly present elsewhere. The closest the treaties come to doing this with respect to the institutions is Article 13(2) TEU.[107] As a transnational entity, accountability for transnational actors such as the EU can be problematic. The issues with formulating

[102] Adam Tomkins, 'Transparency and the Emergence of a European Administrative Law' (1999) 19 *Yearbook of European Law* 217 at 242.

[103] Anne Peters, 'The European Ombudsman and the European Constitution' (2005) 42 *Common Market Law Review* 697.

[104] Katja Heede, 'Enhancing the Accountability of Community Institutions and Bodies: The Role of the European Ombudsman' (1997) 3 *European Public Law* 587.

[105] Alan Dashwood, 'Democracy, Accountability and Transparency (Position Paper)' in Alan Dashwood (ed), *Reviewing Maastricht: Issues for the 1996 IGC* (Sweet and Maxwell, 1996) pp 84–85.

[106] See, Paul Craig, 'The Role of the European Parliament under the Lisbon Treaty' in Stefan Griller and Jacques Ziller (eds), *The Lisbon Treaty: EU Constitutionalism without a Constitutional Treaty?*, vol 11 (Springer, 2008).

[107] TEU, Article 13(2): 'Each institution shall act within the limits of the powers conferred on it in the [t]reaties, and in conformity with the procedures, conditions and objectives set out in them. The institutions shall practice mutual sincere cooperation.'

an accountability structure are well known.[108] Perspectives on accountability are divided between scholars within the same disciplines. As a legal concept, it is not entirely captivating, but similarly, it cannot be overlooked. At different hierarchical levels on the political spectrum, accountability has a varying range of interpretations and meanings. There is even the 'transatlantic divide' that adds to the debate.[109] Thus, there is the need to differentiate between appropriate forms of accountability for the ultimate purpose of achieving a suitable accountable framework for CFSP matters.

Within constitutional systems or systems operating under a democratic regime accountability has two meanings.[110] Firstly, an executive accountable *to* a legislative body for future action; and second, an executive accountable *by* a legislative body for past action. The problem with this framework, however, is that it does not fit CFSP matters, for once decisions have been adopted, in theory, the accountability system reverts back to the national legislatures of Member States, rather than a centralised legislature at EU level. With this in mind, and with the EU being driven and even characterised by a centralising trend,[111] it can be questioned whether the Union ought to be subjected to alternative types of accountability for CFSP matters. Being examined as on a normative basis, the framework of putting CFSP matters through an accountability inquiry elucidates key issues at the heart of the debate. Executive control in CFSP matters is firmly in the hands of the Council, without a decisive shift to a more plural form of decision-making, taking into account other institutional actors.

There is no perfect model or framework for how accountability should work in the EU. Traditionally, classical systems of accountability 'render actors accountable to parliament and the courts'.[112] Whether accountability is in *ex ante* or *ex post* form is crucial for the functions of a particular Union policy. If there was an institution which could be singled out for expressing deep interest in accountability, it would be the Parliament; for it has long expressed concern about Council activity that is typically shielded from public view.[113] It is not alone in this endeavour, as the Court has also had a critical role in ensuring that the accountability of the Union is maintained.

[108] Giandomenico Majone, 'Europe's "Democratic Deficit": The Question of Standards' (1998) 4 *European Law Journal* 5 at 25.

[109] Mark Bovens, Thomas Schillemans and Paul 't Hart, 'Does Public Accountability Work? An Assessment Tool' (2008) 86 *Public Administration* 225 at 226.

[110] Walter Van Gerven, 'Two Twin-Principles of EU Law: Democracy and Accountability, Consistency and Convergence' in Ulf Bernitz and others (eds), *General Principles of EC Law in a Process of Development* (Kluwer Law International, 2008) p 32.

[111] Juliane Kokott and Martin Kaspar, 'Ensuring Constitutional Efficacy' in Michael Rosenfeld and András Sajó (eds), *The Oxford Handbook of Comparative Constitutional Law* (Oxford University Press, 2012) p 802.

[112] Imelda Maher, 'Economic Governance: Hybridity, Accountability and Control' (2007) 13 *Columbia Journal of European Law* 679 at 694.

[113] Päivi Leino, 'The Principle of Transparency in EU External Relations Law: Does Diplomatic Secrecy Stand a Chance of Surviving the Age of Twitter?' in Marise Cremona (ed), *Structural Principles in EU External Relations Law* (Hart Publishing, 2018) p 207.

There is a built-in assumption which resonates widely when speaking of the Union; that its institutions and accompanying actions fail to meet sufficient accountability standards that would be expected of institutions who wield such power. Just as EU Member States must democratically legitimise its policies to a democratically elected parliament, it might be expected that the Union do the same, or at the very least, cater for substantially improved arrangements. The challenge of accountability in CFSP matters centres on two aspects. First, it is unlikely there is a universal belief amongst Council members as to what role other institutional actors should have in CFSP matters, as they would see the existing regime as being sufficient. This would be followed in the second instance by how an alternative accountability regime would work in practice. Accordingly, it is important to detach normative accountability standards to the type seen in an EU setting.

Institutionally, there is the pitfall that the Parliament falls out of the normal accountability loop because of how the treaties provide for it as an institution. Aesthetically, the legal distinction between CFSP and non-CFSP matters in the Union's external relations does not matter beyond the legal level. Yet, for CFSP matters, the Council cannot be held accountable at Union level,[114] which is still true, notwithstanding reforms brought by the Treaty of Lisbon. Thus, it is claimed that accountability within the articles on CFSP matters in the TEU are deficient in contrast to those in the TFEU. For accountability purposes, achieving accountability levels for CFSP matters is of equal importance for non-CFSP matters, given the equality of the two treaties.

There is little doubt that acts adopted on a CFSP legal basis do have an accountability problem. Even during the major discussion about changing the primary law, its mechanisms have remained opaque. With differing interpretations of accountability and no consensus on how it should be practiced in EU governance arrangements, it cannot automatically be expected that an accountability framework is applied to CFSP matters or any other Union policy. Typically, accountability has been conducted through informing activities, which was precisely one of the issues in the *Mauritius* case,[115] where the Council did not live up to its obligation to inform the Parliament of the conclusion of an international agreement as specified by Article 218(10) TFEU.

The Parliament often makes its best effort in attempting to hold Union institutions, be it the Council or the Commission depending on the policy field, accountable for its actions. Despite holding public hearings and engagements at relevant junctures with the appropriate actors, such as just before the establishment of the EEAS,[116] its meaningful impact for cementing concrete legal

[114] Ramses A Wessel, 'Good Governance and EU Foreign, Security and Defence Policy' in Deirdre Curtin and Ramses A Wessel (eds), *Good Governance and the European Union: Reflections on Concepts, Institutions and Substance* (Intersentia, 2005) p 250.

[115] Case C-658/11, *Parliament v Council*, ECLI:EU:C:2014:2025, ('*Mauritius*').

[116] As stipulated by TEU, Article 27(3).

accountability structures remains lacking. In order to bring about accountability to Parliament, it would have to undergo a transformative phase of renewal and further empowerment.

6.5.1. Transparency

The close link between the Union's governance arrangements and those of transparency sets a constitutional tone for the Union's external action. A lack of transparency is a marked trait of activity which principally sits within a single institution. It is closely interwoven with accountability, and cannot ultimately be achieved in a meaningful manner without it. There are preconceived notions of what transparency means in the EU legal system. Transparency, as a principle or doctrine, allows for entities beyond the EU institutions and Member State governments to be better informed of decision-making and governance arrangements. It can even allow citizens to be more active in shaping the future direction of the Union.

Five transparency values have been identified in an EU context:[117] access to documents, knowledge, comprehensibility and accessibility, consultation, and duty to give reasons. In a confident manner, it has been claimed that the accession of two Nordic states has seen increased interest in transparency issues within the Union.[118] Some Union policies operate in secret and access to documents can often be an issue.[119] CFSP matters are not the EU's showcase for transparency, but neither are the political institutions. The Council, the main body charged with nearly all aspects of CFSP matters, is only transparent on legislative matters,[120] which CFSP matters are not. That said, the principle of transparency set out in Article 15(1) TFEU is understood to apply to CFSP matters.

The right of access to information is fundamental to a functioning democracy. With transparency therefore bundled with democracy, it is not a surprise that right of access to information was included in Article 42 CFR.[121] Access to Council documents in CFSP matters, however, is much tighter than those in non-CFSP matters. The Parliament has had to fight for renewed inter-institutional agreements to get

[117] Damian Chalmers and Adam Tomkins, *European Union Public Law: Text and Materials* (Cambridge University Press, 2007) p 317.

[118] See, Virpi Tiili, 'Transparency – An Everlasting Challenge for the European Union' in Pascal Cardonnel, Allan Rosas and Nils Wahl (eds), *Constitutionalising the EU Judicial System: Essays in Honour of Pernilla Lindh* (Hart Publishing, 2012).

[119] See, Deirdre Curtin, 'Overseeing Secrets in the EU: A Democratic Perspective' (2014) 52 *Journal of Common Market Studies* 684.

[120] TFEU, Article 15(2): 'The European Parliament shall meet in public, as shall the Council when considering and voting on a draft legislative act.'

[121] See, Deirdre Curtin and Joana Mendes, 'Article 42 – Right of Access to Documents' in Steve Peers and others (eds), *The EU Charter of Fundamental Rights: A Commentary* (Hart Publishing, 2014).

access to limited documents on CFSP matters.[122] This goes hand-in-hand with its institutional 'quest' for more transparency in the EU legal system.[123] That, in turn, raises questions about the implications of inter-institutional agreements,[124] where information and power is annexed for select actors coming within the scope of an agreement.

A noticeable trait in the treaties has been the shift towards making the EU more transparent in its law-making activities. Since the Treaty of Lisbon, the Parliament has been pushing for greater transparency in areas of trade,[125] given its explicit consent powers within the CCP. Indeed, the cultural tradition of the Member States as regards the open or closed nature of public institutions varies widely.[126] It had been highlighted in earlier times that the framework of EPC, and later the framework of CFSP matters, raised a number of transparency issues.[127] Thus, it was the Treaty of Maastricht that began to change attitudes towards transparency.[128]

6.5.2. Access to Information and Documents

Notwithstanding that access to documents is only a limited element of available information in CFSP matters,[129] it is a critical element of the legal dimension of EU external actions. As stated, if 'government secrecy…[is] carried far enough, such secrecy will destroy the political process'.[130] The EU courts play a central role in access to documents. This may even be so if there was an absence of legislation,[131] meaning the Court could assert rights for access to documents. Cases before

[122] See, C 95/1. Interinstitutional Agreement of 12 March 2014 between the European Parliament and the Council Concerning the Forwarding to and Handling by the European Parliament of Classified Information Held by the Council on Matters Other than Those in the Area of the Common Foreign and Security Policy (2014/C 95/01).

[123] Luca Prete, *Infringement Proceedings in EU Law* (Kluwer Law International 2017) p 337.

[124] See, Sonja Puntscher Riekmann, 'The Cocoon of Power: Democratic Implications of Interinstitutional Agreements' (2007) 13 *European Law Journal* 4.

[125] Guri Rosén, 'Contestation and Co-Optation: Why Secrecy in EU External Relations Varies' (2018) 41 *West European Politics* 933 at 951.

[126] See, Ulf Öberg, 'EU Citizens' Right to Know: The Improbable Adoption of a European Freedom of Information Act' in Alan Dashwood and Angela Ward (eds), *Cambridge Yearbook of European Legal Studies 1999: Volume 2* (Hart Publishing, 2000).

[127] Nanette Neuwahl, "Foreign and Security Policy and the Implementation of the Requirement of 'Consistency' under the Treaty on European Union," in *Legal Issues of the Maastricht Treaty* (Chancery, 1994), 227–46 at 234.

[128] Peter Dyrberg, 'Accountability and Legitimacy: What Is the Contribution of Transparency?' in Anthony Arnull and Daniel Wincott (eds), *Accountability and Legitimacy in the European Union* (Oxford University Press, 2002) p 86.

[129] As put, from a political science perspective, '[m]uch of the [CFSP] process involves meetings, deliberations, and informal communications' that are outside the role of documents. Mai'a K Davis Cross, 'Secrecy and the Making of CFSP' (2018) 41 *West European Politics* 914 at 917.

[130] Alexander M Bickel, *The Morality of Consent* (Yale University Press, 1975) p 81.

[131] Hans Ragnemalm, 'The Community Courts and Openness within the European Union' in Alan Dashwood and Angela Ward (eds), *Cambridge Yearbook of European Legal Studies 1999: Volume 2* (Hart Publishing, 2000) p 29.

the EU judiciary dealing with access to documents first arrived in *Carvel* before the General Court,[132] in which it took a limited view of a claimed right[133] and declined the opportunity afforded to it. This initial guarded approach, possessing a non-expansive vision, demonstrated a large amount of caution. Similarly, in *Netherlands v Council*,[134] the caution which the Court took towards transparency was notable and comparable.

Even documents that are not legal in nature can still contain vital operational information which feeds into the EU decision-making process. Thus, it is natural such items are sought to be actors on the sidelines of formal decision-making. A general interest lies in giving the public access to documents and, more broadly, relevant information, wherever possible. With EU primary law only going so far, secondary legislation had to be formulated. Thus, Regulation 1049/2001 became the underlining basis for public access to documents;[135] it made no distinction between CFSP and non-CFSP matters, other than institutional respect for security. It was thereby accepted that restrictions on access to documentation and information had to be justified.

Information has been the key to the Parliament's involvement in the external relations of the Union. During the Treaty of Nice negotiations, the Parliament focused on foreign policy and constitutional law matters during negotiations.[136] Following this, the Council and Parliament attempted to improve transparency in foreign, security, and defence policies;[137] yet, this has only extended to themselves. Over time, the Council has altered its position when it comes to the Parliament and access to sensitive documents.[138] Starting with an absolutist approach of non-inclusion, it has gradually softened its position. The Parliament's own report on addressing classified information held by the Council in CFSP matters has said '[t]ransparency and access to all relevant documents and information is the very basis of and a compulsory precondition for democracy, and especially for the [institution] to be capable to do its work'.[139] In turn, classified information

[132] Case T-194/94, *John Carvel and Guardian Newspapers Ltd v Council*, ECLI:EU:T:1995:183 ('*Carvel*').

[133] Kenneth A Armstrong, 'Citizenship of the Union? Lessons from Carvel and The Guardian' (1996) 59 *Modern Law Review* 582 at 584.

[134] Case C-58/94, *Netherlands v Council*, ECLI:EU:C:1996:171.

[135] L 145/43. Regulation (EC) No 1049/2001 of the European Parliament and of the Council of 30 May 2001 Regarding Public Access to European Parliament, Council and Commission Documents.

[136] Guri Rosén, 'A Match Made in Heaven? Explaining Patterns of Cooperation between the Commission and the European Parliament' (2016) 38 *Journal of European Integration* 409 at 415.

[137] For example, see, C 298/1. Interinstitutional Agreement of 20 November 2002 between the European Parliament and the Council Concerning Access by the European Parliament to Sensitive Information of the Council in the Field of Security and Defence Policy (2002/C 298/01).

[138] Guri Rosén, 'EU Confidential: The European Parliament's Involvement in EU Security and Defence Policy' (2015) 53 *Journal of Common Market Studies* 383 at 394.

[139] European Parliament, 'Report on the Conclusion of an Interinstitutional Agreement between the European Parliament and the Council Concerning the Forwarding to and Handling by the European Parliament of Classified Information Held by the Council on Matters Other than Those in the Area of the Common Foreign and Security Policy (2012/2069(ACI))' (European Parliament 2012) A7-0245/2012 at p 28.

can be passed between the EU and third states through international agreements, concluded on a CFSP legal basis, including with Russia,[140] Liechtenstein,[141] Montenegro[142] and the Organisation for Joint Armament Cooperation (OCCAR).[143] This sharing of information by the Council with non-Union entities, has thus meant the Parliament's claim to such information ought also to increase. Post-Lisbon, security arrangements between the Council and the Parliament since 2011 have improved.[144] Even so, the information flow is often incomplete,[145] and there remains much room for improvement.

6.5.3. Individual Challenges

In the *Svenska Journalistförbundet* case before the General Court, it was stated that '[t]he fact that the [EU courts]…by virtue of [the treaties have] no jurisdiction to review the legality of measures adopted…does not curtail its jurisdiction in the matter of public access to those measures'.[146] This was swiftly followed by *Hautala*,[147] which confirmed that the EU courts do have jurisdiction to hear public access to documents cases. The applicant was a Finnish member of the Parliament and had asked to see a report of the CFSP Working Group of Conventional Arms Exports, which sat within the Council. Stemming from *Hautala*, it was confirmed that the EU courts could assert themselves in the pillar structure on access to documents cases. The General Court said that 'the fact that under [the treaties that]…the [General Court] does not have jurisdiction to assess the lawfulness of [such CFSP] acts…does not exclude its jurisdiction to rule on public

[140] L 155/56. Council Decision of 17 November 2009 Concerning the Conclusion of the Agreement between the Government of the Russian Federation and the European Union on the Protection of Classified Information (2010/348/EC).

[141] L 187/1. Council Decision 2010/404/CFSP of 14 June 2010 Concerning the Signing and Conclusion of the Agreement between the European Union and the Principality of Liechtenstein on Security Procedures for Exchanging Classified Information.

[142] L 260/1. Council Decision 2010/587/CFSP of 14 June 2010 Concerning the Signing and Conclusion of the Agreement between the European Union and Montenegro on Security Procedures for Exchanging and Protecting Classified Information.

[143] L 229/1. Council Decision 2012/486/CFSP of 23 July 2012 Concerning the Signing and Conclusion of the Agreement between the Organisation for Joint Armament Cooperation and the European Union on the Protection of Classified Information.

[144] C 190/2. Decision of the Bureau of the European Parliament of 6 June 2011 Concerning the Rules Governing the Treatment of Confidential Information by the European Parliament (2011/C 190/02).

[145] Ricardo Passos, 'The External Powers of the European Parliament' in Piet Eeckhout and Manuel López-Escudero (eds), *The European Union's External Action in Times of Crisis* (Hart Publishing, 2016) p 101.

[146] Case T-174/95, *Svenska Journalistförbundet v Council*, ECLI:EU:T:1998:127, para 85.

[147] Case T-14/98, *Hautala v Council*, ECLI:EU:T:1999:157. This General Court was subsequently appealed to the Court of Justice, which upheld the General Court's judgment. See, Case C-353/99 P, *Council v Hautala*, ECLI:EU:C:2001:661. See, Päivi Leino, 'Case C-353/99 P, Council v Heidi Hautala, Judgment of the Full Court of 6 December 2001, Nyr, Appeal Against the Judgment of the Court of First Instance of 19 July 1999 in Case T-14/98, Hautala v Council [1999] II-2489' (2002) 39 *Common Market Law Review* 621.

access to those acts'.[148] In such cases, when the jurisdiction is affirmed, the EU judiciary has to balance the interests of the Council against those of the applicant in question.

The Finnish MEP had pleaded that there would be 'no harm to the public interest concerning international relations would flow from disclosure'.[149] However, the General Court said that 'review by the [General Court] must be limited to verifying whether the procedural rules have been complied with, [and that] the contested decision is properly reasoned, and the facts have been accurately stated, and whether there has been a manifest error of assessment of the facts or a misuse of powers'.[150] Notably, the General Court 'ma[de] no distinction between document[ation] and information',[151] and did not separate them theoretically and practically. However, the broader question of the substance of documents themselves was left for another time. That took a number of years to be elaborated on, culminating in *Kuijer*.[152]

With *Hautala*, there was enough to suggest that, judicially, it had begun to be recognised that there was a broad right of access to information. Furthermore, the General Court also hinted in *Svenska Journalistförbundet* that there was an implicit assumption that a new general principle was emerging in the EU legal order, that of access to information. Therefore, the jurisprudence regarding transparency, across both CFSP and non-CFSP matters, was not to provide any exemptions *en masse*. Today, Article 17(3) of the Council's Rules of Procedure states: '[t]he Council or Coreper shall decide unanimously, on a case-by-case basis, whether there should be publication in the Official Journal by the Secretary-General of the decisions referred to in Article 25…TEU'.[153] This cements the *ex post* nature of access to information in CFSP matters, notwithstanding the fact that, in reality, most CFSP Decisions are published.[154]

Whilst *Hautala* dealt with jurisdiction head-on, the *Svenska Journalistförbundet* case was via the back door,[155] with the intervening Member States, not the Council, raising the issue. *Hautala* represented a marked move to a more assertive position from the initial *Carvel* and *Netherlands v Council* judgments, recognising the potential of transparency. Likewise, in *Mattila*,[156] the public interest in

[148] Case T-14/98, *Hautala v Council*, ECLI:EU:T:1999:157, para 42.

[149] Noel Travers, 'Access to Documents in Community Law: On the Road to a European Participatory Democracy' (2000) 35 *Irish Jurist* 164 at 202.

[150] Case T-14/98, *Hautala v Council*, ECLI:EU:T:1999:157, para 72.

[151] Leonor Rossi and Patricia Vinagre e Silva, *Public Access to Documents in the EU* (Hart Publishing, 2017) p 108.

[152] Case T-211/00, *Kuijer v Council*, ECLI:EU:T:2002:30.

[153] See, L 325/35. Council Decision of 1 December 2009 Adopting the Council's Rules of Procedure (2009/937/EU).

[154] Geert De Baere, *Constitutional Principles of EU External Relations* (Oxford University Press, 2008) p 171.

[155] Tomkins (n 102) p 232.

[156] Case C-353/01 P, *Olli Mattila v Council and Commission*, ECLI:EU:C:2004:42 ('*Mattila*'), an appeal of Case T-204/99, *Olli Mattila v. Council and Commission*, ECLI:EU:T:2001:190 ('*Mattila*').

non-CFSP matters showed the Court further asserting its position in transparency matters.

6.5.4. Ongoing Debate

The transparency debate within the EU has been lengthy and remains a salient topic, with many cases concerning access to documents still appearing before the General Court. Links between transparency, access to information and documents, and democracy itself is evident in case law such as in *Turco* and *Access Info Europe*.[157] Direct actions taken against EU institutions form a sizeable portion of the General Court's caseload.[158] In *Turco*, where the Council was rebuffing access to information, the Court said 'it is for the Council to balance the particular interest to be protected by non-disclosure…the public interest in the document being made accessible in the light of the advantages stemming…from increased openness, in that this enables citizens to participate more closely in the decision-making process and guarantees that the administration enjoys greater legitimacy and is more effective and more accountable to the citizen in a democratic system'.[159]

Given that the Council operates in a non-legislative capacity in CFSP matters, the breath of the application of this judgment to CFSP matters is up for discussion. In another case, another member of the Parliament took a case in the General Court against the Council on access to documents,[160] which amusingly, the Parliament did not support. Yet when the Member of Parliament won, the Council appealed to the Court,[161] with the Parliament intervening along with the Commission. This demonstrates the Parliament's lack of willingness to use litigation alone to achieve institutional ends, as it is aware that inter-institutional agreements and other forms of secondary law also have a part to play.

In ensuring openness and transparency, the Court will continue to be a principal actor in guiding the development of access to information as part of an accountability drive. The sheer quantity of requests that institutions receive regarding access to documents means that the Council is only likely to refuse access to documents on CFSP matters where it believes it can legitimately do so,

[157] Joined Cases C-39/05 P and C-52/05 P, *Sweden and Turco v Council*, ECLI:EU:C:2008:374 ('*Turco*') Case C-280/11 P, *Council v Access Info Europe*, ECLI:EU:C:2013:671, on appeal from Case T-233/09, *Access Info Europe v Council*, ECLI:EU:T:2011:105. See, Vigjilenca Abazi and Maarten Hillebrandt, 'The Legal Limits to Confidential Negotiations: Recent Case Law Developments in Council Transparency: Access Info Europe and In 't Veld' (2015) 52 *Common Market Law Review* 825.

[158] Given these access to documents cases are being handled by the General Court, its case law is subject to later rectification by the Court. See, Joni Heliskoski and Päivi Leino, 'Darkness at the Break of Noon: The Case Law on Regulation No 1049/2001 on Access to Documents' (2006) 43 *Common Market Law Review* 735 at 779.

[159] Joined Cases C-39/05 P and C-52/05 P, *Sweden and Maurizio Turco v Council*, EULI:EU:C:2008:374 ('*Turco*'), para 45.

[160] Case T-529/09, *Sophie in 't Veld v Council*, ECLI:EU:T:2012:215.

[161] Case C-350/12 P, *Council v in 't Veld*, ECLI:EU:C:2014:2039.

and will defend its position before the EU courts. Therefore, whilst some information is flowing, there are lingering problems.

6.6. Conclusion

By blending governance, democracy, legitimacy, and accountability conundrums together, it is possible to formulate a prism in which CFSP matters can also involve a parliamentary body and a judicial organ. In light of the unique characteristics of CFSP matters, it is clear, given the defective governance, democracy, legitimacy, and accountability arrangements, that greater reach for democratic and judicial actors in CFSP matters is both warranted and necessary, and that 'foreign [policy], too…need[s] checks and balances.'[162]

A debate rumbles on about which institution should represent the Union on an external basis. For example, the Council and the Commission continue to battle over the true external agent who should conduct the Union's legal affairs.[163] As a whole, the Union's commitment to governance, democracy, legitimacy, and accountability is unwavering, but it is not as easy to demonstrate applicability. The Union, far from being a parliamentary government with a fusion of powers, has an expectation deficit that is not easy to overcome.

Inter-institutional agreements and other softer forms of communication have strengthened the Parliament, but can be seen as greater steps towards the inevitable. There is a normative vision put forward for why EU decision-making has to accommodate 'more democracy'.[164] The treaties in the eyes of integrationists see the Union as an incomplete contract for the full unification of Europe. The melding of governance, democracy, legitimacy, and accountability might arguably lead to a federal vision for EU external actions through a unification of CFSP and non-CFSP matters. Such an approach, as it stands, goes against the premise upon which the treaties exist.

It can be contended that the Union 'is doomed never to be truly democratic',[165] for as long as intergovernmental instincts, albeit rule-bound, prevail in favour of supranationalism, without greater inclusion of the Parliament and the Court. It will be a political decision for where democracy is going to lie in the Union; be it at Member State or Union level. Parliamentary democracy may be the norm throughout Europe, and therefore, it is the natural fallback model. The national and EU systems of governance still operate in tandem and whilst this will continue, they will still be incorrectly contrasted against one another.

[162] Louis Henkin, *Constitutionalism, Democracy, and Foreign Affairs* (Columbia University Press, 1990) p 38.

[163] For example, see, Case C-73/14, *Council v Commission*, ECLI: EU:C:2015:663 ('*ITLOS*').

[164] Koen Lenaerts, 'The Principle of Democracy in the Case Law of the European Court of Justice' (2013) 62 *International and Comparative Law Quarterly* 271 at 312.

[165] Giuseppe Federico Mancini, 'Europe: The Case for Statehood' (1998) 4 *European Law Journal* 29 at 41.

Member States continue to have significant amounts of constitutional responsibility for CFSP matters through their own domestic legal orders. There remains a level of concern that adding further legitimacy to CFSP matters within the current framework may actually be harmful to how the policy works in practice. The Parliament would argue that they still do not have enough democratic control over CFSP matters, despite pushing for many years to develop new involvement. There is an argument that a more rigorous role for the Parliament within the treaties will not immediately solve all the problems related to CFSP matters. But providing new powers to the Parliament to cure the ill of a democracy problem is simply not going to solve the issue.

The strong intergovernmental sway of the Council in CFSP as compared to non-CFSP matters continues to be a challenge. Opportunities to adopt meaningful transparent means of conducting policy-making in CFSP matters are few and far between. With no real desire amongst the Council to broaden the level of input into CFSP matters, the procedures will remain stagnant, and will continue as they always have. Foreign policy within the legal order faces major choices, political in nature, for the development of parliamentary and judicial involvement. Notwithstanding the benefits of having a broader selection of actors involved in CFSP matters beyond the Council, the selection of a legal basis that broadens the number of actors, to include the Parliament, and the Court, is undeniably modifying the balance of powers set down in the treaties. The future of CFSP matters as a policy domain with 'specific rules and procedures'[166] will be contemplated in the concluding chapter.

[166] TEU, Article 24(1), second para.

7

The Future of the Common Foreign and Security Policy

This chapter addresses the *lex ferenda*, or the law as it ought to be. Conclusively, it argues that the legal distinction that exists in EU external relations law – between CFSP matters and non-CFSP matters – needs to be abolished. The Union method ought to prevail in the future with the 'specific rules and procedures' for CFSP no longer being necessary for the Union to be an effective global legal actor in the decades to come. There has been increased integration between CFSP matters and non-CFSP matters over time, so the merging of the two on the basis of the Union's objectives ought to be realised.

There is no crystal ball to look into and guide the future of EU foreign policy and its legal regime. Instead, reasonable assumptions can be made. The normative approach of this chapter has been threaded carefully. Law not only helps to shape the institutional framework of the Union, but also the practices of these institutional actors within the defined architecture, which in turn, shapes the law through practice. The temptation to propose changes or reforms to an area has to strike a fine balance between different institutional actors' perspectives.

Thus far, the book has carefully documented and analysed the way CFSP matters actually are, whereas this chapter takes a new turn, looking at how EU foreign policy, as a legal field, could be. It is by no means a complete offering for what the future may hold for the law of EU foreign policy, but a reasonable path forward will be considered. Behind the proposition of this chapter is the *Les Verts* doctrine, that there ought to be a 'complete system of legal remedies and procedures',[1] which, is best achieved through one set of laws that govern EU external relations, rather than the two as it currently stands. CFSP matters have a 'heavy procedurali[s]ed framework',[2] and coupled with its legal clunkiness and differentiation with non-CFSP matters, it is no longer fit for the current age.

[1] Case C-294/83, *Parti écologiste 'Les Verts' v Parliament*, ECLI:EU:C:1986:166, para 23. See, Graham Butler, 'Implementing a Complete System of Legal Remedies in EU Foreign Affairs Law' (2018) 24 *Columbia Journal of European Law* 637.

[2] Panos Koutrakos, 'Foreign Policy between Opt-Outs and Closer Cooperation' in Andrea Ott, Bruno De Witte and Ellen Vos (eds), *Between Flexibility and Disintegration: The Trajectory of Differentiation in EU Law* (Edward Elgar, 2017) p 423.

7.1. Introduction

CFSP matters are a highly constitutionalised field of Union law. The EU legal order has progressively grown and reached an 'all time high' with the Treaty of Lisbon[3] allowing the Union's full potential to be realised. The integration of external objectives for both CFSP matters and non-CFSP matters by the Treaty of Lisbon in what is currently Article 21 TEU had to mean something. Before the full effects of the integration of the external objectives was implemented, it was predicted that the CFSP provisions of the treaties would 'most likely…tilt the balance in favour of [a] CFSP' legal basis,[4] as opposed to a non-CFSP legal basis. Whilst the Court has played a critical role here,[5] the lack of specific objectives for CFSP matters has meant that as a policy field, it has become more difficult to defend. The long-term effect of this change has yet to be fully revealed, but in time, will stand as progress towards fully constitutionalising all EU external relations matters under a non-CFSP legal basis.

The treaties remain massively ambitious. One root of the legal issues arising in EU external action from the perspective of the Parliament and the Court has been the delineation between CFSP and non-CFSP matters. Realising its true motivation will take time, effort, and, likely, more political deliberation and legal litigation to understand the breadth of actions that may be taken. As the Union has developed, accumulating more competence, bringing about more sophisticated decision-making processes, other factors have changed with it. 'Pie-sharing' continues in EU external relations law,[6] as battles over competence between EU institutions, and between the EU and its Member States arise. Even with the Treaty of Lisbon reforms, the external relations of the EU continue to suffer from unnecessary complexity. It could even be said the Union, to date, has been a 'political and legal settlement',[7] and one that will continue to define its existence.

The workability, as against the desirability of a CFSP legal basis, versus a non-CFSP legal basis for EU external action, is quite a legal conundrum from an institutional perspective. Calls for the ordinary legislative procedure to be expanded

[3] Ramses A Wessel, 'Reconsidering the Relationship between International and EU Law: Towards a Contents-Based Approach?' in Enzo Cannizzaro, Paolo Palchetti and Ramses A Wessel (eds), *International Law as Law of the European Union* (Martinus Nijhoff Publishers, 2012) p 17.

[4] Inge Govaere, 'Multi-Faceted Single Legal Personality and a Hidden Horizontal Pillar: EU External Relations Post-Lisbon' in Catherine Barnard and Okeoghene Odudu (eds), *Cambridge Yearbook of European Legal Studies 2010–2011: Volume 13* (Hart Publishing, 2011) p 106.

[5] See Chapter 5 of this book.

[6] Poignantly been coined in, Theodore Konstadinides, 'In the Union of Wine: Loose Ends in the Relationship between the European Union and the Member States in the Field of External Representation – Case C-399/12 Germany v Council, Judgment of the Court of Justice of 7 October 2014' (2015) 21 *European Public Law* 679 at 688.

[7] Damian Chalmers, 'The Democratic Ambiguity of EU Law Making and Its Enemies' in Anthony Arnull and Damian Chalmers (eds), *The Oxford Handbook of European Union Law* (Oxford University Press, 2015) p 325.

have been proposed academically,[8] and equally spirited attempts at overall institutional reform have been offered.[9] These considerations are particularly relevant to the law of EU foreign policy. Yet in the meantime, to ensure an appropriate balance of powers between Union institutions, as defined by the Member States, the limits of existing competence have to be respected.

There are significant dangers of having a very wide legal basis for external action, yet this will ensure that legal measures are sufficiently broad to conduct a chosen measure with a policy objective in mind. Firstly, it has to be ensured that a wide legal basis does not encompass other legal bases contained within the EU legal order, so as to make them irrelevant. A wide legal basis invariably leads to absolute gravitational pull. Secondly and contrastingly, a narrow legal basis may operationally be a nuisance, as requiring numerous legal bases for every single EU competence that is within its sphere may be an equally arduous task. Accordingly, striking the correct balance between a CFSP legal basis and a non-CFSP legal basis should be treated with delicacy, and in practice, must be undertaken with utmost precision.

Reform of CFSP matters as a policy field has been a long-running debate,[10] with various developments throughout the years highlighting the various modifications that may be needed. To date, any reform has been half-hearted, with compromise between actors leaving fudged outcomes. Certainly, the EU's absorption of the Community at the Treaty of Lisbon has been beneficial for EU external action, but there remains scope for greater institutional involvement in CFSP matters, which will continue to grow louder and stronger as the existing CFSP decision-making regime appears increasingly out-of-kilter with other areas of EU policy. If the objectives of EU external action can merge, then so can the two respective sets of legal bases.

Whilst the effectiveness of the law of EU external action may be difficult to measure in a precise manner, CFSP matters have contributed immensely to resolving issues that EU Member States have felt necessary to tackle on a pan-European basis. Yet it is unequivocal that CFSP matters sit legally where they do because of political considerations. Under previous generations of political leaders and civil servants of Permanent Representations of Member States to the Union, there would have been hostility towards overarching involvement of EU institutional actors in foreign policy matters. This historical sensitivity is not as closely held today. Instead, the sensitive areas now surround issues of taxation, national budgetary control, and economic issues.[11]

[8] See, Jürgen Habermas, 'Democracy in Europe: Why the Development of the EU into a Transnational Democracy Is Necessary and How It Is Possible' (2015) 21 *European Law Journal* 546.

[9] See, Federico Fabbrini, 'The Relationship Between the European Council and the Council: Institutional Arguments in Favour of an EU Senate' (2016) 22 *European Public Law* 485.

[10] See, Daniel Thym, 'Reforming Europe's Common Foreign and Security Policy' (2004) 10 *European Law Journal* 5.

[11] Deirdre Curtin, 'Democratic Accountability of EU Executive Power: A Reform Agenda for Parliaments' in Federico Fabbrini, Ernst Hirsch Ballin and Han Somsen (eds), *What Form of Government for the European Union and the Eurozone?* (Hart Publishing, 2015) p 175.

It has been demonstrated that CFSP and non-CFSP matters in external relations have their similarities.[12] Yet, it has long been recognised that it has been extremely difficult to separate EU foreign policy from other external policies of the Union.[13] Even more forcefully, this separation of CFSP from non-CFSP matters has been called an 'original sin'.[14] This chapter reflects on the future prospects the law of EU foreign policy has within the EU legal order. Mundane crisis-addressing days in EU affairs around the time of the Treaty of Lisbon are soon to be a distant memory. The deep freeze of constitutional inaction will eventually be re-examined, beginning a discussion about what could change in the future. Without knowing the exact course that Member States with institutional pressure will follow will depending on the deliberations, but external relations issues must and will be addressed.

7.2. Reform of EU Foreign Policy Law

There is significant internal pressure for reform in the EU legal order. Discussion on the reform has had longstanding presence in the Union's administration, political and legal circles. The jurisprudence of the Court has alleviated some of this pressure for reform,[15] for good or for bad. For the EU's foreign policy, this sense of reform is with respect to decision-making. The promotion of the Union method of decision-making has long been 'a legal technique for the structuring of interrelations'.[16] The push for reform is not *per se* at the need to involve institutions like the Parliament or the Court. Rather, the need for reform in CFSP decision-making procedures lies on the need for a more reliable foreign policy for Europe as a whole, with changing power structures in the global sphere.

7.2.1. Moving Towards QMV

In the absence of abolishing a distinct legal basis for CFSP matters, there has been discussion about whether, within CFSP matters, more decisions could be adopted

[12] See, Paul James Cardwell, 'The Legalisation of European Union Foreign Policy and the Use of Sanctions' (2015) 17 *Cambridge Yearbook of European Legal Studies* 287.

[13] Martti Koskenniemi, 'International Law Aspects of the Common Foreign and Security Policy' in Martti Koskenniemi (ed), *International Law Aspects of the European Union* (Martinus Nijhoff Publishers, 1998) p 36.

[14] Piet Eeckhout, *External Relations of the European Union: Legal and Constitutional Foundations* (Oxford University Press, 2004) p 145.

[15] Considerably, the *Rosneft* judgment. See Chapter 5 of this book. Moreover, see, Inge Govaere, 'Interconnecting Legal Systems and the Autonomous EU Legal Order: A Balloon Dynamic' in Inge Govaere and Sacha Garben (eds), *The Interface Between EU and International Law: Contemporary Reflections* (Hart Publishing, 2019).

[16] Peter Hay, *Federalism and Supranational Organizations: Patterns or New Legal Structures* (University of Illinois Press, 1966) p 301.

through QMV, as opposed to unanimity. In fact, the political discussion around the consideration has never been absolutely ignored,[17] but instead, has been a lingering background consideration. It has long been doubted that unanimous decision-making would ever be able to achieve significant progress. For example, unanimity of Member States has made it 'hard to believe that the aim of a real E[U] foreign policy can ever be reached'.[18] However, unanimity has prevailed, despite the understandable worry that was prevalent when EPC was in its latter stages of existence, before being transformed into what is today included within CFSP matters.

Preservation of the *status quo* regarding the delineation between a CFSP legal basis and a non-CFSP legal basis is a real consideration. Whereas this may be a conservative choice,[19] it may also be the only option where political agreement for going forward cannot be found. CFSP matters are not the last bastion of unanimity in the treaties as a whole. Unanimity in the Council is still required with respect to the accession of new Member States,[20] use of the flexibility clause,[21] and harmonisation of taxation,[22] amongst others. However, none of these is *per se* directly related to the external relations of the Union.

Despite their relative success on the political spectrum, CFSP matters have been labelled as a mere 'appetizer' for a true EU foreign policy.[23] Unanimity removes some of the Union's global potential that has, to date, not been tapped. After all, the greatest challenge for CFSP matters was, and continues to be, reconciling all Member States under united positions. Enthusiasm for change generated by the Member States has been slow. That is despite certain world events. For example, the break-up of Yugoslavia around the same time that CFSP matters were brought within the treaties[24] exposed the deficiencies in the unanimity approach to decision-making.

With the SEA, decision-making by QMV was first introduced into the Union, and later accepted to be the standard norm across most areas of the treaties. Presently, Article 238 TFEU sets down the usual decision-making procedures that are applicable within the Council. In particular, it is Article 238(3) TFEU, coupled with Article 16 TEU, that governs the current rules on QMV. By contrast,

[17] Ramses A Wessel, 'Initiative and Voting in Common Foreign and Security Policy: The New Lisbon Rules in Historical Perspective' in Hermann-Josef Blanke and Stelio Mangiameli (eds), *The European Union after Lisbon: Constitutional Basis, Economic Order and External Action* (Springer, 2012) p 506.

[18] Christiaan Timmermans, 'The (In)Adequacy of Legal Instruments for a European Foreign Policy, a Co-Report' in Johan K De Vree, Peter Coffey and Richard H Lauwaars (eds), *Towards a European Foreign Policy: Legal, Economic and Political Dimensions* (Martinus Nijhoff Publishers, 1987) p 136.

[19] Ingolf Pernice and Daniel Thym, 'A New Institutional Balance for European Foreign Policy?' (2002) 7 *European Foreign Affairs Review* 369 at 373.

[20] TEU, Article 49.

[21] TFEU, Article 352.

[22] TFEU, Article 113.

[23] Loukas Tsoukalis, *In Defence of Europe: Can the European Project Be Saved?* (Oxford University Press, 2016) p 44.

[24] Steven Blockmans, 'The EU's Modular Approach to Defence Integration: An Inclusive, Ambitious and Legally Binding PESCO?' (2018) 55 *Common Market Law Review* 1785 at 1805.

Article 24(1) TEU and Article 31(1) TEU state that unanimity is the rule for CFSP decision-making. The increasing disparity between CFSP decision-making and non-CFSP decision-making within the EU legal order suggests the regime for CFSP matters is increasingly out-of-kilter with the normal method of Union decision-making through QMV. Questions thus arise about how reform, if pursued, could be executed.

7.2.2. Political or Judicial Reform

There are two ways to reform the law. Firstly, legislatively through the political process, or through treaty amendment. Secondly, and alternatively, through judgments of the Court through the judicial process. EU legal scholars are most guilty of seeking reform of Union law through the Court alone. Naturally, there is an alluring temptation for them to believe in the Court,[25] for often judicial reform is institutionally easier and swifter than political reform.

In certain fields, it might be more beneficial for one form of reform over another. This has been recognised in the Court's own internal workings. According to one former President, 'problems will not wait for a legislative solution. If they arise in an action, the judge must solve them. It is a well-known fact that the inactivity of the legislature compels the courts to decide questions and to solve problems the settlement of which properly belongs to the province of the legislature'.[26] If political decision-making is absent, then naturally, judicial adjudication has to fill some of the void.

The Court's line of case law with regard to EU external relations cases has been seen as ending with an 'internal/external parallelism'.[27] Later, the Court's entry into adjudication on CFSP matters has meant that when the interpretation of CFSP decisions is necessary, intergovernmental diplomacy in the Council is not the sole means of resolving such matters, as the Court is able and willing to interpret the provisions when required. As a result of judicial developments, the Court itself could offer one avenue of slowly diminishing and dissuading the use of CFSP legal bases, and begin to nudging the Council into finding the centre of gravity of external action on non-CFSP legal bases. This avenue of reform, whilst possible,

[25] This is true across many areas of Union law. This has also been pointed to in, Panos Koutrakos, 'Public Security Exceptions and EU Free Movement Law' in Panos Koutrakos, Niamh Nic Shuibhne and Philip Syrpis (eds), *Exceptions from EU Free Movement Law: Derogation, Justification and Proportionality* (Hart Publishing, 2016) p 216.

[26] Hans Kutscher, 'Methods of Interpretation as Seen by a Judge at the Court of Justice', *Judicial and Academic Conference 27–28 September 1976* (Court of Justice of the European Communities 1976) p 35.

[27] Eric Stein and Louis Henkin, 'Towards a European Foreign Policy?–The European Foreign Affairs System from the Perspective of the United States Constitution' in Mauro Cappelletti, Monica Seccombe and Joseph HH Weiler (eds), *Integration Through Law: Europe and the American Federal Experience*, vols 1: Methods, Tools and Institutions. Book 3: Forces and Potential for a European Identity (De Gruyter, 1986) p 22.

would run into severe criticism of the Court, however, for interfering in policy choices made with respect to the formation of primary law and the adoption of secondary law. In the words of one of the Court's strongest critics, 'it should not come as a surprise if the federalist tribe at the Court considers propping up a continued activist course'.[28]

Judicial reform has its own limits. For judgments of the Court are only ever one aspect of disputed matters within Union law, and are only legal developments in the sunshine. They do not necessarily take account of disputes settled diplomatically or those upon which there is large consensus. Moreover, judgments only offer a limited view. It is the Court that usually has to face the specific legal conundrums, but it is primarily left to democratic actors to frame the law in the first place. Admittedly, the treaties do not themselves establish a 'complete system of remedies and procedures' as the Court once claimed.[29] However, that has not stopped the Court from trying to complete its own doctrine. Incremental change in the law of EU foreign policy should not be left to the judiciary alone as there is also a large role for the political process.

Political reform of Union law may take longer and is more cumbersome, but arguably, it is the best way. As put by a former President of the Court, a true Union will 'not be forged merely by judgments of the Court'. Rather, it 'will above all require lucid and courageous political decisions'.[30] Either way, differences will need to be resolved on matters of EU external action with solutions that are effective and workable, and capable of managing the continued interests of the Union and its Member States.

7.2.3. The Difficulty of Reform

Making EU external action more effective is, in all respects, in the interests of both the Union and the Member States. Notwithstanding questions of political or judicial reform, it would be plausible for reform of the law of CFSP matters to include stronger institutional arrangements for institutions like the Parliament and the Court. Yet, changes from the *status quo* are never easy to bring about. Moving CFSP matters to QMV and away from unanimity is not all that different from the process that occured more generally in the 1980s, when there was consensus that something had to be done to overcome Member State vetoes.[31]

[28] Hjalte Rasmussen, 'Present and Future European Judicial Problems after Enlargement and the Post-2005 Ideological Revolt' (2007) 44 *Common Market Law Review* 1661 at 1685.

[29] Case C-294/83, *Parti écologiste 'Les Verts' v Parliament*, ECLI:EU:C:1986:166, para 23. See, Butler (n 1).

[30] Josse Mertens de Wilmars and Jacques Steenbergen, 'The Court of Justice of the European Communities and Governance in an Economic Crisis' (1984) 82 *Michigan Law Review* 1377 at 1398.

[31] As recounted in, Alan Dashwood, 'Editorial: April 1985: The Dooge Committee and Majority Voting on the Council' (1985) 10 *European Law Review* 85.

Toil and trouble is an inevitable part of the political process. It is easy to chastise legal regimes such as the legal setup for CFSP matters, but it is more difficult to convince others of the need for change. Not only is there hesitancy about reforming the treaties by the Member States, but there is also hesitation within the framework of the existing treaties to exercise reforms. Despite the treaties having passerelle clauses more generally beyond explicit CFSP matters,[32] they has not been used in any field since the enactment of the Treaty of Lisbon.

In *Opinion 2/13*,[33] the Court plainly had misgivings about areas of Union law which it did not have explicit jurisdiction over, being subject to the law of another international court – the ECtHR. Saying that, it could and has been argued that it is not that the Court mistrusts the ECtHR, but rather, it does not place enough trust in its own Member States,[34] who might attempt to undermine the influence of the Court in the EU legal order. That said, normalising CFSP matters so that they become more akin to other areas of EU external action would allow a truer EU foreign policy to emerge, representative of a plurality of world events.

A complete overhaul of treaties, amalgamating CFSP and non-CFSP decision-making to result in a Union method is unlikely in the short term. For major steps in an integrationist direction have scarcely been taken in the history of the Union's existence. Rather, incrementalism has prevailed.

7.2.4. The Commission's Push

Given that Union has not had the ability to adopt positions through unanimity on several of its self-identified values, goals, and priorities, this setback ultimately means the *status quo* must be questioned. Some of these examples include being unable to pronounce the Union's view on human rights in China at the UNHRC in June 2017; delayed targeted restrictive measures in Venezuela given internal changes to their democratic governance regime; deferred agreement on human rights and civil society priorities with Egypt through its partnership priorities; one Member State insisting on amending the arms embargo against Belarus when it was up for renewal; delaying the extension to civilian CSDP missions in the Sahel region and Iraq, respectively; watering down EU statements on issues related to Israel, despite long-standing EU positions on the issue of Jerusalem; and being unable to exert the Union's views on the outcome of the Permanent Court of Arbitration (PCA) ruling with respect to the Philippines/China dispute over islands in the South China Sea. All contain different aspects of political bargaining, but have not necessarily been related. Thus, reform would inevitably be pushed up the political agenda.

[32] Analysed later in this Chapter.

[33] Opinion 2/13, ECLI:EU:C:2014:2454 ('*Accession of the European Union to the European Convention for the Protection of Human Rights*').

[34] Julio Baquero Cruz, *What's Left of the Law of Integration? Decay and Resistance in European Union Law* (Oxford University Press, 2018) p 165.

Politically, changing CFSP decision-making to QMV has long been discussed at political level between Member States,[35] but with few concrete developments to show for such deliberation. The passerelle clause in Article 31(3) TEU would signal a sign of future development in the absence of treaty revision. Such debate is now moving into the public sphere. In the State of the Union speech by the President of the European Commission in 2018, he stated that '[w]e should move to qualified majority voting not in all but in specific areas'.[36]

It was not out of nowhere in 2018 that this became a priority. In the previous year's State of the Union speech, the President said '[i]n order to have more weight in the world, we must be able to take foreign policy decisions quicker… [and] this is why I want Member States to look at which foreign policy decisions could be moved from unanimity to qualified majority voting'.[37] Moreover, at the 2018 Munich Security Conference, the President of the Commission stated '[i]t is…unanimity that is keeping us from being able to act credibly on the global stage. Time and time again we find ourselves unable to reach the consensus needed for unanimous decisions'. Furthermore, there was a clear need to 'simplify these decision-making processes so that the European Union can also reach positions by qualified-majority voting'.[38] The Commission was not the only actor pushing for reform in 2018. The Franco-German Mesebery Declaration of June 2018 stated that possibilities should be explored to 'using majority vote in the field of the Common Foreign and Security Policy in the framework of a broader debate on majority vote regarding EU policies'.[39]

The 2018 State of the Union address by the President was coupled with a formal Commission Communication.[40] If the EU's Global Strategy was the political aim of moving EU foreign policy,[41] albeit more of 'a wish rather than a reality',[42] then the Commission's Communication on CFSP decision-making procedures was the

[35] Michael E Smith, 'What's Wrong with the CFSP? The Politics of Institutional Reform' in Pierre-Henri Laurent and Marc Maresceau (eds), *The State of the European Union: Deepening and Widening*, vol 4 (Lynne Rienner, 1998) p 167.

[36] 'State of the Union. The Hour of European Sovereignty'. Speech by President of the European Commission, Jean-Claude Juncker, 12 September 2018.

[37] 'State of the Union. Proposals for the Future of Europe That Can Be Implemented on the Basis of the Lisbon Treaty'. Speech by President of the European Commission, Jean-Claude Juncker, 13 September 2017.

[38] Speech by President [of the European Commission] Jean-Claude Juncker at the 54th Munich Security Conference. 17 February 2018 (Speech/18/841).

[39] Meseberg Declaration: Renewing Europe's Promises of Security and Prosperity – A Joint Franco-German Declaration Was Adopted during the Franco-German Council of Ministers, which took place 19 June 2018 in Meseberg, Germany.

[40] Communication from the Commission to the European Council, the European Parliament and the Council: A Stronger Global Actor: A More Efficient Decision-Making for EU Common Foreign and Security Policy. 12 September 2018 (COM(2018) 647 Final).

[41] Shared Vision, Common Action: A Stronger Europe. A Global Strategy for the European Union's Foreign and Security Policy (European Union) June 2016.

[42] Pieter Jan Kuijper, 'The Common Foreign and Security Policy and the Common Security and Defence Policy' in Pieter Jan Kuijper and others (eds), *The Law of the European Union* (Kluwer Law International, 2018) p 1263.

legal dimension to those intended aims. Remarkably, the 2018 communication of the Commission has noticeable similarities with the 1976 Tindemans Report.[43] Within it, it expressed scepticism of Member States' coordinating positions within the Council, and pointedly noted that 'European identity will not be accepted by the outside world so long as the [EU Member] States appear sometimes united, sometimes disunited'.[44] Even in the 1970s, common policies adopted by a majority of Member States was a proposition, but was not politically possible at the time. The Report had remarkable foresight, and yet, developments in CFSP matters have still not yet reached the stage whereby qualified majority voting (QMV) is the norm. The Commission in 2018, undertaking a revival of the Tindemans Report, therefore merits serious consideration, despite its proposition not being entirely new.

The method of CFSP decision-making and its attempt at exclusion of all other actors beyond the Council cannot be frozen in a time warp from the 1990s. Prior to the inclusion of EU foreign policy within the treaties, the European Council, in the run up to the eventual adoption of the Treaty of Maastricht, noted 'the need to review the procedures and mechanism for preparing, adopting and implementing decisions where foreign policy is concerned, so as to increase the coherence, speed and effectiveness of the [Union]'s international action'.[45] The European Council certainly had good intentions, but they have not substantially reviewed their own progress and instead, have left a political vacuum.

If the Commission's suggestions are to be taken seriously, it is very likely they would need to be tailored and narrow. The Commission's communication is targeted towards specific problems with CFSP decision-making, and was in no way a *carte blanche* effort to eradicate the CFSP decision-making regime absolutely. Yet this, in itself, raises some legal problems. With an activation of the passerelle clause,[46] syphoning off different types of CFSP decisions under Article 31 TEU, would begin to differentiate actions concluded on a CFSP legal basis between those that may be allowable through QMV, and those that will continue to be decided through unanimity. Such problems will eventually have to be settled through practice or through adjudication of the Court.

Much of the EU legal basis litigation in the EU legal order is fought on claims of an incorrect legal basis being used, such as between a CFSP legal basis and a non-CFSP legal basis; or between a CFSP legal basis and a JHA legal basis; and so forth. They are usually, but not always, inter-institutional debates over competence and power allocation. If the passerelle clause is used, the Court could be asked

[43] The Tindemans Report was discussed in Chapter 2 of this book. European Union. 'Report by Mr Leo Tindemans, Prime Minister of Belgium, to the European Council. Bulletin of the European Communities, Supplement 1/76' (the 'Tindemans Report')' (Office for Official Publications of the European Communities 1976).

[44] Ibid. p 15.

[45] Conclusions of the Presidency. European Council. Rome, 27 and 28 October 1990 (SN 304/90 REV 2) p 4.

[46] Discussed later in this Chapter.

about substantive questions that are predicated on a CFSP legal basis – a Decision – which may have utilised QMV and, in fact, might have been incorrectly adopted, when unanimity should have been used. This would arise when a Member State within the Council attempts to bring an action for annulment against the Council. This would inevitably bring the Court into the vortex of CFSP decision-making and pose some significant juridical issues.[47]

The Commission Communication was a far cry from what Member States had proposed when CFSP matters, as a legal and policy field, was created for it to develop on the international law spectrum, and 'not on the Union way'.[48] However, the time had clearly come for an open debate on the move of CFSP matters towards QMV. Having the passerelle clause within the treaties meant that the Member States did not want to be overtly constrained by the rigidity of CFSP decision-making. Thus, what the Member States foresaw as a possibility to move to QMV for CFSP matters, is now being presented as a viable reality.

For all the positive inclinations of the Commission's communication, it ultimately needs buy-in and endorsement from other institutional actors, namely the Council and European Council. Yet, it should be remembered that all the Commission can do is make suggestions;[49] in no way does it have legal leverage over the European Council to move away from unanimous decision-making for CFSP matters. The Commission appears to be involving itself in what is typically seen as a Council matter. The European Council has complete discretion on such modest Commission proposals such as activating the passerelle clause. It remains to be seen whether the Commission's call will be heard, but with no Franco-German objective in principle on the horizon, it is up to the other Member States to fall into line.

7.2.5. The Passerelle Clause

Whilst the norm is that unanimity applies in CFSP matters, QMV is conceivable for decision-making on a CFSP legal basis from a legal standpoint, with reform taking place within the existing treaty framework. Qualified majority voting in a very limited range of CFSP Decisions has already been possible, as defined by Article 31(2) TEU. This sets out exceptions to the normal procedure for CFSP decision-making that is governed by Article 31(1) TEU.[50] However, it is highly

[47] See Chapter 5 of this book.

[48] Eileen Denza, 'Forging Links between Legal Orders' (2016) 35 *Yearbook of European Law* 589 at 591.

[49] Strictly speaking, Commission Communications are soft law and are subject to potential actions for annulment. Case C-57/95, *French Republic v Commission of the European Communities*, ECLI:EU:C:1997:164.

[50] TEU, Article 31(1): 'Decisions under this Chapter shall be taken by the European Council and the Council acting unanimously, except where this Chapter provides otherwise. The adoption of legislative acts shall be excluded. When abstaining in a vote, any member of the Council may qualify its abstention

exceptional and given the overarching norm of unanimity, is of limited significance. No treaty change is needed to expand this qualified majority voting system, so an Intergovernmental Conference is not required.

Article 31(3) TEU is the all-important passerelle clause for CFSP matters and allows changes in decision-making procedures without recourse to treaty amendment. This passerelle clause provides elasticity away from unanimity, allowing for the adoption of certain CFSP Decisions by QMV in set areas as defined by the European Council. Also known as the enabling clause,[51] it was first introduced in the Treaty of Lisbon, but should be read alongside Article 48(7) TEU.[52] It allows the European Council to adopt unanimous decisions to clarify an area of CFSP decision-making in which QMV may be allowed within the Council.

However, the passerelle clause in Article 31(3) TEU has its limits. For QMV decisions that have a treaty basis within the articles on CFSP matters, Article 31 TEU contains two important limiting features.[53] Firstly, an emergency brake in Article 31(2) TEU that may be exercised by a Member State for 'vital and stated

by making a formal declaration under the present subpara. In that case, it shall not be obliged to apply the decision, but shall accept that the decision commits the Union. In a spirit of mutual solidarity, the Member State concerned shall refrain from any action likely to conflict with or impede Union action based on that decision and the other Member States shall respect its position. If the members of the Council qualifying their abstention in this way represent at least one third of the Member States comprising at least one third of the population of the Union, the decision shall not be adopted.' For more, see, Jean-Claude Piris, *The Future of Europe: Towards a Two-Speed EU?* (Cambridge University Press, 2012) p 77.

[51] Govaere (n 4) p 102.

[52] However as put, the 'two passerelles of Article 31(3) and Article 48(7) TEU seem to be in contradiction as they provide for different procedures for one and the same situation'. Robert Böttner, 'The Treaty Amendment Procedures and the Relationship between Article 31(3) TEU and the General Bridging Clause of Article 48(7) TEU' (2016) 12 *European Constitutional Law Review* 499 at 519. For further discussion on linking Article 31(3) with Article 48(7) TEU, see, Robert Böttner and Ramses A Wessel, 'Article 31 [Procedures for the Adoption of CFSP Decisions]' in Hermann-Josef Blanke and Stelio Mangiameli (eds), *The Treaty on European Union (TEU)* (Springer 2013) pp 1067–69.

[53] TEU, Article 31(2): 'By derogation from the provisions of paragraph 1, the Council shall act by qualified majority:

- when adopting a decision defining a Union action or position on the basis of a decision of the European Council relating to the Union's strategic interests and objectives, as referred to in Article 22(1) [TEU],
- when adopting a decision defining a Union action or position, on a proposal which the High Representative of the Union for Foreign Affairs and Security Policy has presented following a specific request from the European Council, made on its own initiative or that of the High Representative,
- when adopting any decision implementing a decision defining a Union action or position,
- when appointing a special representative in accordance with Article 33 [TEU].

If a member of the Council declares that, for vital and stated reasons of national policy, it intends to oppose the adoption of a decision to be taken by qualified majority, a vote shall not be taken. The High Representative will, in close consultation with the Member State involved, search for a solution acceptable to it. If he does not succeed, the Council may, acting by a qualified majority, request that the matter be referred to the European Council for a decision by unanimity.'

reasons of national policy'.[54] This is the 'Luxembourg Compromise' being appended to CFSP matters.[55] In such circumstances, however, the Council can act by qualified majority to send the matter to the European Council, which acts unanimously, thus re-enforcing the special character of CFSP matters. Secondly, Article 31(4) TEU ensures that the passerelle clause 'shall not apply to decisions having military or defence implications'. This excludes military CSDP missions from QMV, and therefore places a legal wedge on decision-making procedures between civilian CSDP missions and military CSDP missions. These two in-built safeguards within the passerelle clause ensure that CFSP decision-making does not turn from being a unanimity based area of the treaties to one of QMV in an instant, or without deserving consideration.

The Commission's 2018 Communication envisaged the move to QMV for CFSP matters only in specific areas and not in 'all areas of foreign policy', in the words of Article 24(1) TEU. First, for the Union's position on matters of human rights within other international organisations such as the United Nations Human Rights Council (UNHRC);[56] second, for decisions establishing restrictive measures (sanctions);[57] and third, to launch or implement civilian CSDP missions.[58] These three new areas would complement the existing legal possibility to use QMV in CFSP decision-making in limited treaty-defined circumstances as per Article 31(2) TEU.

CFSP decision-making has to date worked upon a practical philosophy of compromise. This culture, fostered over decades of negotiation will likely continue,

[54] Previously, this was 'important and stated reasons of national policy' at the Treaty of Amsterdam in Article J(13)(2), and retained at the Treaty of Nice as Article 23(2) of the Treaty of Lisbon amending the word 'important' to 'vital' suggests a higher threshold for a Member State to invoke it. Panos Koutrakos, 'The Decision-Making Process' in Robert Schütze and Takis Tridimas (eds), *Oxford Principles of European Union Law, vol 1: The European Union Legal Order* (Oxford University Press, 2018) p 1170. Moreover, Abstentions from Joint Actions, pre-Lisbon, were possible when a Member State faced a sudden change of circumstances. Steve Peers, 'National Security and European Law' (1996) 16 *Yearbook of European Law* 363 at 387. According to one view, this constructive abstention clause has been inspired by the OECD Convention, which contains a similar mechanism. Pieter Jan Kuijper, 'An Introduction to Union External Action, Its Scope, Its Institutions and Its Instruments' in Kuijper and others (n 42) p 1243.

[55] Robert Schütze, *European Constitutional Law* (Cambridge University Press, 2012) p 207.

[56] The Commission wants to see that the 'European Council unanimously adopts a decision based on Article 31(3) TEU providing that EU positions on human rights in international fora are adopted by qualified majority in the form of Council decisions'. Communication from the Commission to the European Council, the European Parliament and the Council: A Stronger Global Actor: A More Efficient Decision-Making for EU Common Foreign and Security Policy. 12 September 2018 (COM(2018) 647 Final) (n 40) p 11.

[57] The Commission also 'suggests that the European Council unanimously adopts a decision based on Article 31(3) TEU providing that decisions establishing a sanctions regime are adopted by qualified majority voting by the Council'.

[58] Finally, the Commission wants the European Council to 'unanimously adopt a decision based on Article 31(3) of the TEU providing that all decisions regarding Civilian Common Security and Defence Policy missions are adopted by qualified majority voting by the Council'. For the legal distinctions that are applicable between CSDP military missions and CSDP civilian missions, see, Chapters 5 and 6 of, Panos Koutrakos, *The EU Common Security and Defence Policy* (Oxford University Press, 2013).

even when there will be areas where the European Council has sanctioned use of the passerelle clause in limited areas within CFSP matters. To illustrate, special representatives can be appointed on a CFSP legal basis by QMV, but a vote within the Council has never been resorted to, which is a clear sign of CFSP decision-making being consensus-orientated, outside of strong points of contention.[59]

There are significant upsides to the Commission's Communication. Firstly, it would lessen the need for EU foreign policy to go at a slower pace than that of the Member States. Secondly, it would cement the progress of CFSP matters becoming more integrated with non-CFSP matters. Thirdly, it would align decision-making through QMV to the remainder of the treaties, procedurally making it more akin to non-CFSP matters. Fourthly, adversaries of the Union would no longer be able to pick off certain Member States in wielding their veto for EU foreign policy matters.

However, with the upsides are also downsides. A change to decision-making procedures will itself not resolve problems faced in CFSP matters. In particular, it falls short in correcting the institutional balance in that it does not open it to greater involvement or oversight of other EU institutional actors, such as the Parliament or the Court. Their position would still require other types of reform. Whilst the Commission's Communication was but a mere proposal, it is a concrete suggestions and deserves a debate as to how to improve the legal governance of the EU's foreign policy regime.

7.2.6. Handling Withdrawal

For activating the passerelle clause as the Commission suggested, certain Member States are constrained within the European Council as to how they might act. For example, the prior approval of national parliaments may in some cases be required.[60] Notably, the European Union Act 2011 – a domestic statute – contained a limit on a UK Government vote at the European Council on the utilisation of

[59] On a side note, special representatives (EUSR) are not fully housed with the EEAS. This is due to the fact it is the Council which defines their mandate and appoints them, and thus, they fall within the Council's remit, and not the EEAS's. However, special representatives are part of the EEAS's 'external machinery'. Steven Blockmans and others, 'EEAS 2.0: Recommendations for the Amendment of Council Decision 2010/427/EU on the European External Action Service' (Centre for European Policy Studies 2013) p 32. Placing the special representatives within the EEAS would subvert the ability of the Council to exercise its treaty-assigned prerogatives. For more on the Council perspective, see, Ricardo Gosalbo-Bono and Frederik Naert, 'The Reluctant (Lisbon) Treaty and Its Implementation in the Practice of the Council' in Piet Eeckhout and Manuel López-Escudero (eds), *The European Union's External Action in Times of Crisis* (Hart Publishing, 2016) pp 37–38. This minute but important point potentially undermines the abilities of EUSRs, disabling them for reaching their fuller potential.

[60] Jean-Claude Piris, *The Lisbon Treaty: A Legal and Political Analysis* (Cambridge University Press, 2010) p 262.

Article 31(3) TEU,[61] equivalent to the same lock the UK Parliament sought to apply to the use of Article 352 TFEU – the flexibility clause.[62] In the meantime, the European Union Act 2011 has been repealed by the European Union (Withdrawal) Act 2018, meaning any such parliamentary restriction on the national government is no longer applicable for activating the passerelle clause, when, or if, the United Kingdom withdraws from the Union.

The Commission has purposefully suggested the European Council adopt several decisions at the first European Council summit after the intended withdrawal date of the United Kingdom from Union in 2019.[63] After a withdrawal, a Member State can no longer participate in the EU institutional framework, nor can it be included in the EU's decision-making procedures. That applies regardless of whether the United Kingdom ratifies a withdrawal agreement with the Union. Moreover, with a transition period after leaving the Union, but before a future relationship agreement is concluded, a Member State has to fulfil obligations for CFSP matters, but without being part of the decision-making.[64] It is well-known that the United Kingdom has long held views against removing unanimity for CFSP matters.[65] With the United Kingdom no longer possessing any voting rights during the transition period, but still being bound by CFSP decisions,[66] during its transition period it will be a rule-taker, and not a rule-maker.

[61] Article 6(5)(a) of the European Union Act 2011 provides that '[a] decision under the provision of Article 31(3) of TEU that permits the adoption of qualified majority voting' may not be utilised by a Government Minister unless the draft decision is approved by an Act of Parliament.

[62] See, Graham Butler, 'The EU Flexibility Clause Is Dead, Long Live the EU Flexibility Clause' in Antonina Bakardjieva Engelbrekt and Xavier Groussot (eds), *The Future of Europe: Political and Legal Integration Beyond Brexit* (Hart Publishing, 2019).

[63] A Member State may unilaterally revoke the notice it gave under Article 50 TEU to leave the Union, right up to the date of withdrawal. See, Case C-621/18, *Andy Wightman and Others v Secretary of State for Exiting the European Union*, ECLI:EU:C:2018:999.

[64] In the words of the Commission in 2019 prior to a ratification of the agreed text of the withdrawal agreement: 'The Common Foreign and Security Policy will apply to the United Kingdom during the transition period.' 'The EU-UK Withdrawal Agreement Explained' (European Commission 2019) p 31.

[65] In response to the Commission's 2018 Communication, the UK Government said 'we think that EU foreign policy decisions made by consensus carry considerable weight because all Member States agree them'. 'Standard Form of Explanatory Memorandum for European Union: Communication from the Commission to the European Council, the European Parliament and the Council. A Stronger Global Actor: A More Efficient Decisionmaking for EU Common Foreign and Security Policy (12425/18) Submitted by the Foreign and Commonwealth Office on 5 October 2018 to the House of Commons European Scrutiny Select Committee'.

[66] There is one exception to this. According to Article 127(2) of the 'Agreement on the Withdrawal of the United Kingdom of Great Britain and Northern Ireland from the European Union and the European Atomic Energy Community, as Endorsed by Leaders at a Special Meeting of the European Council on 25 November 2018', '[i]n the event that the Union and the United Kingdom reach an agreement governing their future relationship in the areas of the Common Foreign and Security Policy and the Common Security and Defence Policy which becomes applicable during the transition period, Chapter 2 of Title V of the TEU and the acts adopted on the basis of those provisions shall cease to apply to the United Kingdom from the date of application of that agreement'. However, the United Kingdom appears to want to pursue a separate restrictive measures regime: 'While pursuing independent sanctions policies driven by their respective foreign policies, the Parties recognise sanctions as a multilateral

Despite the fact that non-EU Member States are barred from participating in CFSP decision-making, the likelihood is that the United Kingdom would like to continue full participation in EU foreign policy.[67] It could even be claimed that the United Kingdom's departure has forced it to rethink its relationship and bondedness to EU foreign policy – a commitment that has not always fully displayed as an EU Member State. As a policy field, CFSP matters have not been a reason for a Member State to withdraw. In fact, the quantifiable interests of the United Kingdom and Union with respect to the wider world have innate similarities. It is likely that the United Kingdom wish to retain a close partnership with the EU on CFSP matters covering not only practical matters of policy, but also some level of inclusion in the institutional structure.

There is some small precedent for United Kingdom involvement in CFSP matters post-Brexit. For example, in 2016, the US Secretary of State was involved in Council discussions on CFSP matters,[68] but not any form of decision-making. Furthermore, there is possibility for a non-Member State to contribute to CSDP missions.[69] However, no arrangement for a non-Member State is ever going to mimic that of EU membership. One modest proposal has been to allow for the creation of a 'European Foreign, Security and Defence Community',[70] to allow for post-EU membership states to continue to be a part of EU external action. However, a separate 'pillar'-like body dealing with EU foreign policy matters merely to include a departing Member State would be a colossal mistake. The pillarisation of the Union after the Treaty of Maastricht in and of itself threatened the nature of the Union.[71] There is no reason for it to bend and facilitate a voluntary choice of a Member State to withdraw, merely to ensure its inclusion in EU foreign policy decision-making.

Once the withdrawal of a Member State happens, the Commission and the said Member State will have to decide on their future relationship in respect of CFSP matters whilst the 'specific rules and procedures' of CFSP matters remain in EU primary law. However, some indications are already there. The notion of

foreign policy tool and the benefits of close consultation and cooperation.' 'Political Declaration Setting out the Framework for the Future Relationship between the European Union and the United Kingdom (BXT 111) (CO EUR-PREP 54)', para 99.

[67] Bruno De Witte, 'Near-Membership, Partial Membership and the EU Constitution' (2016) 14 *European Law Review* 471.

[68] Press, Release: 3482nd Council Meeting, Foreign Affairs, 11355/16 – Outcome of the Council Meeting.

[69] For example, the involvement of the former Yugoslav Republic of Macedonia in Operation Althea (EUFOR), as provided for by a CFSP Decision. L 188/9. Council Decision 2006/477/CFSP of 30 June 2006 Concerning the Conclusion of the Agreement between the European Union and the Former Yugoslav Republic of Macedonia on the Participation of the Former Yugoslav Republic of Macedonia in the European Union Military Crisis Management Operation in Bosnia and Herzegovina (Operation ALTHEA).

[70] Alan Dashwood, 'After the Deluge' (2016) 41 *European Law Review* 469 at 470.

[71] Notably, what occurred politically to bring about the Treaty of Maastricht and its lasting legal legacy threatened to see the Union 'being destroyed'. Deirdre Curtin, 'The Constitutional Structure of the Union: A Europe of Bits and Pieces' (1993) 30 *Common Market Law Review* 17 at 67.

'Political Dialogue' is on the table with the provisional aim of 'flexible consultation between the parties at different levels (ministerial, senior official, working)'.[72] Moreover, the High Representative 'may, where appropriate, invite the United Kingdom to informal Ministerial meetings of the Member States of the Union', which was a significant concession by the Union. Anticipating the eventual international agreement for the purposes of post-membership relations that the Union and the United Kingdom may have, it is assumed that until the international agreement provides otherwise, there will be no obligation for the departed Member State to be aligned to the direction of EU foreign policy in CFSP matters.

Involvement in EU foreign, security, and defence architecture have, until now, been predicated upon membership of the Union, yet both parties have an interest in maintaining levels of cooperation and coordination, where possible. This begs further questions about whether CFSP decision-making will continue, or whether there will be a need to develop new tools for a future special third country like the United Kingdom. A consultation mechanism for EU foreign policy cooperation could be established,[73] but it could be of political character, as opposed to being legally binding. Moreover, the future of the law on EU foreign policy will not be significantly affected by the withdrawal of a single EU Member State.

7.3. Abandoning the CFSP Legal Basis

Strong leadership can drive agendas forward that are in the best interests of a polity as a whole. What EU foreign policy needs are bold suggestions to ensure that external policies that the Union has, through its range of its legal bases for both CFSP matters and non-CFSP matters, are fit for the challenges it will face in the decades to come. The threat of continuing intergovernmentalist thinking is strong, and the Union through a form of outright intergovernmentalism would have significant consequences for the development of a more coherent external relations framework.

A wide reading of the Union's external powers can be made,[74] but not to the extent that it goes beyond the treaties. Accordingly, beyond minor technical issues like making use of a passerelle clause, treaty amendments ought to be considered. One way of improving and overcoming the discrepancies in CFSP matters is the combining of legal bases in EU primary law. The integration of CFSP and

[72] Political Declaration Setting out the Framework for the Future Relationship between the European Union and the United Kingdom (BXT 111) (CO EUR-PREP 54) (n 66), para 97.

[73] There is 'no obvious model of a cooperation framework readily available'. Paul James Cardwell, 'The United Kingdom and the Common Foreign and Security Policy of the EU: From Pre-Brexit "Awkward Partner" to Post-Brexit "Future Partnership"?' (2017) 13 *Croatian Yearbook of European Law and Policy* 1 at 2.

[74] Case T-306/01, *Yusuf and Al Barakaat International Foundation v Council and Commission*, ECLI:EU:T:2005:331 ('*Kadi I*'), para 155.

non-CFSP legal bases would contribute to a more coherent representation of the Union externally. Separating CFSP and non-CFSP matters into absolutely distinct, impermeable compartments has never been achieved. After its first number of years of CFSP matters being a legal and policy field, it 'neither improved visibility nor continuity of the Union's global external action'.[75] However, there are a number of problems with this, as already outlined in the previous chapters.

Due to the lack of any Intergovernmental Conference anytime soon to further align CFSP matters with non-CFSP matters, parliamentary and judicial practice is attempting to compensate for existing legal shortcomings. With its peculiar existence and a supranational procedure in place for non-CFSP external relations, the internal bipolarity of EU external action has persisted between CFSP and non-CFSP legal bases. As an integrated structure, the continued preservation of CFSP matters as a separate policy field has left the law of EU external relations fragmented. The absence of an efficient legal mechanism to establish consistency between CFSP and non-CFSP matters has been an issue that has been highlighted for some time,[76] which the High Representative has been charged with rectifying, minimising the legal warfare between the institutions. Such a trend might be measured as a mark of success.[77] Yet, as the legal distinction remains, the political possibilities for achieving greater consistency will be perpetually hampered.

The decision-making regime across the different areas of EU external action clearly presents the Union with problems of consistency.[78] From a Union perspective, the continued divide of CFSP and non-CFSP matters within the legal texts hampers the EU's ability to conduct effect external relations, thus ensuring less flexibility and disallowing a more unified approach to achieving foreign policy goals. The integration of CFSP and non-CFSP legal bases would boost the effectiveness of Union law and the coherence of EU external relations as a whole.

Eliminating the existence of CFSP legal bases, which are intergovernmentally rule-bound outside the normal decision-making procedures, has been attempted before. The negotiations leading to the creation of the Constitutional Treaty contained the proposal to transfer CFSP matters into normal EU external action. That is not to say the policy would have disappeared, but rather its specificity as a differentiated legal regime. Despite the fact that this would not

[75] Günter Burghardt, 'The Potential and Limits of CFSP: What Comes Next?' in Elfiede Regelsberg, Philippe de Schoutheete de Tervarent and Wolfgang Wessels (eds), *Foreign Policy of the European Union: From EPC to CFSP and Beyond* (Lynne Rienner 1997) p 327.

[76] Jörg Monar, 'The European Union's Foreign Affairs System after the Treaty of Amsterdam: A "Strengthened Capacity for External Action"?' (1997) 2 *European Foreign Affairs Review* 413 at 434.

[77] Alan Dashwood, 'Conflicts of Competence in Responding to Global Emergencies' in Antonis Antoniadis, Robert Schütze and Eleanor Spaventa (eds), *The European Union and Global Emergencies: A Law and Policy Analysis* (Hart Publishing, 2011) p 48.

[78] Mauro Gatti, 'Conflict of Legal Bases and the Internal-External Security Nexus: AFSJ versus CFSP' in Eleftheria Neframi and Mauro Gatti (eds), *Constitutional Issues of EU External Relations Law* (Nomos, 2018) p 107.

have removed the pillars,[79] it would have gone some way towards closely aligning EU external action into a more coherent EU legal framework.

Beyond the law, the distinction made between CFSP matters and non-CFSP matters in Union law 'does not reflect the reality of international relations and diplomatic practice'.[80] Yet, when the Treaty of Lisbon was billed as the Reform Treaty, it stood back from resolving some of the ongoing discrepancies over the delimitation of legal bases for EU external action. The continued separation of external action across CFSP and non-CFSP legal bases was important for some Member States, who sought to ensure that the autonomy of the second pillar was preserved in a newly depillarised Union. The United Kingdom in particular found this a 'conceptually' pressing point.[81] The UK's withdrawal from the Union[82] allows a rethink of the primary arrangements for overall EU foreign policy.

7.3.1. Justifying the Status Quo

With much of the Union's external action now incorporated into a unitary and integrated structure through the treaties, legitimate concerns can be raised regarding the competition between CFSP legal bases and non-CFSP legal bases. That being said, legal actions on a CFSP legal basis and a non-CFSP legal basis are predicated upon a single institutional framework.[83] The continuing separation of external action through each of these lenses brings challenges on a number of levels to the Union when acting externally. The Union would be better placed if conflicts between CFSP matters and other external policies were alleviated or eliminated completely.

[79] Juliane Kokott and Alexandra Rüth, 'The European Convention and Its Draft Treaty Establishing a Constitution for Europe: Appropriate Answers to the Laeken Questions?' (2003) 40 *Common Market Law Review* 1315 at 1325.

[80] Luigi Lonardo, 'Common Foreign and Security Policy and the EU's External Action Objectives: An Analysis of Article 21 of the Treaty on the European Union' (2018) 14 *European Constitutional Law Review* 584 at 606.

[81] House of Commons Foreign Affairs Committee, 'Foreign Policy Aspects of the Lisbon Treaty' (House of Commons 2008) HC120-II, Third Report of Session 2007–08, Volume II, p 31.

[82] See, Graham Butler, Mads Dagnis Jensen and Holly Snaith, '"Slow Change May Pull Us Apart": Debating a British Exit from the European Union' (2016) 23 *Journal of European Public Policy* 1278. The departure of the United Kingdom is causing a whole world of other complex legal issues, namely, the border on the island of Ireland. See, Graham Butler and Gavin Barrett, 'Europe's "Other" Open-Border Zone: The Common Travel Area under the Shadow of Brexit' (2018) 20 *Cambridge Yearbook of European Legal Studies* 252.

[83] Long before the Treaty of Lisbon, this was recognised in the General Court's *Kadi I* judgment: '[T]he Union is to be served by a single institutional framework which is to ensure the consistency and the continuity of the activities carried out in order to attain its objectives while respecting and building upon the acquis communautaire. The Union is in particular to ensure the consistency of its external activities as a whole in the context of its external relations, security, economic and development policies. The Council and the Commission are to be responsible for ensuring such consistency and are to cooperate to this end. They are to ensure the implementation of these policies, each in accordance with its respective powers.' Case T-306/01, *Yusuf and Al Barakaat International Foundation v Council and Commission*, ECLI:EU:T:2005:331 ('*Kadi I*'), para 126.

The division in EU external relations, between CFSP matters and non-CFSP matters, is a self-imposed division. If the Council is to continue to have superior powers in particular areas of Union law, as it does with respect to CFSP matters, then such powers must be justified. It is therefore argued that the executive dominance by the Council in CFSP matters can no longer be justified; and instead, the policy field will be levelled, institutionally, just like in every other normal area of Union policy. Alternatively, rather than extending the remit for non-Council institutions into CFSP matters as it presently stands, the bolder option would be to abolish CFSP legal bases altogether.

There are signs that Member States have begun to accept rules and procedures that are more alike across different areas of the treaties. Yet, the successful squaring of the circle has not yet happened in respect of CFSP matters.[84] Whilst the scope of CFSP matters can be labelled as broad, it has cynically been suggested that 'a narrow interpretation of CFSP [matters]...best served the corporatist interests of the officials who had to put it in practice'.[85]

For mixed international agreements, integrating CFSP and non-CFSP matters into a single legal regime would pose a systematic risk to the Union concluding ordely international agreements with third states.[86] Mixed agreements that, previously, the Union and Member States had to sign are gradually being replaced by agreements signed by the Union only, in what could be termed 'cross-pillar' mixity.[87] Whilst mixed agreements are a part of Union law, to include all elements from such agreements could 'encroach upon Member States' remaining foreign [policy] authority'.[88] Therefore, integrating the two legal regimes of CFSP matters and non-CFSP matters would require additional competence upon the Union to be conferred.

With CFSP matters on its own legal basis being relatively static, much is occurring elsewhere. The Union's Common Commercial Policy (CCP) is growing as the Union enters into ever-more sophisticated trade agreements with third entities, which in turn removes and absorbs the external dimension of the EU's internal market. Furthermore, JHA matters are also a growing field of law, but

[84] Alan Dashwood, 'The Relationship between the Member States and the European Union/European Community' (2004) 41 *Common Market Law Review* 355 at 365.

[85] Ramon Torrent, 'The "Fourth Pillar" of the European Union after the Amsterdam Treaty' in Alan Dashwood and Christophe Hillion (eds), *The General Law of EC External Relations* (Sweet and Maxwell, 2000) p 222.

[86] For some analysis of the problems this can create, pointing to the Italian strategy and tactics in the agreement the Union concluded with South Africa, see, Allan Rosas, 'The Future of Mixity' in Christophe Hillion and Panos Koutrakos (eds), *Mixed Agreements Revisited: The EU and its Member States in the World* (Hart Publishing, 2010) p 368.

[87] Christiaan Timmermans, 'Evolution of Mixity since the Leiden 1982 Conference' in Christophe Hillion and Panos Koutrakos (eds), *Mixed Agreements Revisited: The EU and its Member States in the World* (Hart Publishing, 2010) p 7.

[88] Rass Holdgaard, 'Principles of Reception of International Law in Community Law' (2006) 25 *Yearbook of European Law* 263 at 309.

CFSP matters are beginning to absorb some of its elements[89] as the external dimension of JHA matters and CFSP matters become more intertwined.[90]

If the 'specific rules and procedures' of CFSP matters are to be abandoned in favour of ordinary external relations decision-making, there will be calls for EU foreign policy measures that would continue to be responsive. Such potential flexibility has precedent. With respect to EU external aid, Article 213 TFEU can be used as a legal basis by the Council using QMV, without the Parliament.[91] Such derogations on institutional balance ought to be construed in a narrow sense to avoid abuses of the provisions. Moreover, the 2013 inter-institutional agreement between the Council, Parliament, and Commission on budgetary discipline permits the transferal of appropriations between items within the CFSP chapter of the treaties to allow the necessarily executive scope and speedy implementation of EU external action.[92] Structurally, confining such instances to a minimum would be best practice for the Union as a whole, but they are options for continued flexibility of EU foreign policy once the formal legal distinctions between CFSP matters and non-CFSP matters are abandoned.

Fully proceduralising all EU foreign policy decision-making akin to other decision-making fields has not yet come about. As the current structure of the treaties can be said to be 'at least pretending to preserve…a spacing for national decision-making' more generally,[93] given how many areas of public policy are in fact made at EU level. Member States' support for EU foreign policy is central for it to be anything more than a 'lame polic[y]'.[94] One practitioner has suggested that the sensitivities of some Member States need to be recognised when conducting foreign policy.[95] Abandoning the centrality of the Council in CFSP matters has

[89] Marise Cremona, 'External Competences and the Principle of Conferral' in Robert Schütze and Takis Tridimas (eds), *Oxford Principles of European Union Law, vol 1: The European Union Legal Order* (Oxford University Press, 2018) p 1139.

[90] For the example of CFSP matters taking on some JHA tasks, see, Graham Butler, 'EU Foreign Policy and Other EU External Relations in Times of Crisis: Forcing the Law to Overlap?' in Elżbieta Kużelewska, Amy Weatherburn and Dariusz Kloza (eds), *Irregular Migration as a Challenge for Democracy* (Intersentia, 2018). Furthermore, Panos Koutrakos, 'The Nexus between CFSP/CSDP and the Area of Freedom, Security and Justice' in Steven Blockmans and Panos Koutrakos (eds), *Research Handbook on the EU's Common Foreign and Security Policy* (Edward Elgar, 2018).

[91] Daniela Gauci, 'The European Parliament and EU External Aid: Measures of Response to Emergency Situations' in Antonis Antoniadis, Robert Schütze and Eleanor Spaventa (eds), *The European Union and Global Emergencies: A Law and Policy Analysis* (Hart Publishing, 2011) p 299.

[92] See, Section E, Financing of CFSP, C 373/1. Interinstitutional Agreement of 2 December 2013 between the European Parliament, the Council and the Commission on Budgetary Discipline, on Cooperation in Budgetary Matters and on Sound Financial Management (2013/C 373/01).

[93] Fernando Castillo de la Torre, 'The Court of Justice and External Competences After Lisbon: Some Reflections on the Latest Case Law' in Eeckhout and López-Escudero (eds), *The European Union's External Action in Times of Crisis* (n 59) p 130.

[94] Daniel Thym, 'The Intergovernmental Branch of the EU's Foreign Affairs Executive: Reflections on the Political and Security Committee' in Hermann-Josef Blanke and Stelio Mangiameli (eds), *The European Union after Lisbon: Constitutional Basis, Economic Order and External Action* (Springer, 2012) p 529.

[95] Ivan Smyth, 'Mixity in Practice – A Member State Practitioner's Perspective' in Christophe Hillion and Panos Koutrakos (eds), *Mixed Agreements Revisited: The EU and its Member States in the World* (Hart Publishing, 2010) p 318.

been warned against, as 'divisions in the foreign policy area are too profound to be overcome by simply introducing qualified majority voting, supremacy and direct effect'.[96]

Whilst significant weight lies with the uniformity and effectiveness of Union law,[97] erring too far in this direction at once has consequences. Therefore, the merging of CFSP and non-CFSP legal bases swiftly runs the risk of Member States wishing to undertake greater cooperation outside the Union's legal architecture to avoid the constraints imposed by the treaties. Activity in this sphere is already afoot,[98] so full buy-in from Member States for any major changes to the law of EU foreign policy will be needed. The unanimity requirement for a CFSP decision-making norm, as it stands, has gravitational pull to the Member States in the Council.

7.3.2. Parliamentarisation and Institutional Balance

If there was an award for an institution with the greatest determination to gain greater powers, the Parliament would win time and again. It has consistently argued there exists an uneven balance of powers when it came to CFSP matters, pushing back against the Council through litigation, and has demonstrated its fervent institutional credentials when it is not treated with the respect it thinks it deserves. Yet, the Council's central argument against an excessive role for the Parliament in EU external relations has been that parliamentary actors are not as capable of acting as swiftly as executive actors. Executives have long prevailed over parliamentary actors in foreign policy for as long as constitutional systems have been in place.

Such argumentation of excluding parliamentary bodies is based on the premise that foreign policy is fundamentally different to other types of policies that public bodies pursue. Attempts have been made to debunk the myth that the Parliament would be slow to respond in matters of foreign policy.[99] Moreover, since the Treaty of Lisbon, the Parliament is now a co-legislator in non-CFSP matters with respect to EU external relations. In this light, the Court has interpreted the Parliament's co-legislative powers as being expansive in nature.[100] International agreements are

[96] Maja Brkan, 'Exploring EU Competence in CFSP: Logic or Contradiction?' (2006) 2 *Croatian Yearbook of European Law and Policy* 173 at 198.

[97] Piet Eeckhout, 'Bold Constitutionalism and Beyond' in Miguel Poiares Maduro and Loïc Azoulai (eds), *The Past and Future of EU Law: The Classics of EU Law Revisited on the 50th Anniversary of the Rome Treaty* (Hart Publishing, 2010) p 220.

[98] 'L'Initiative européenne d'intervention (European Intervention Initiative (E2I))' (*French Ministère des Armées (Ministry of the Armed Forces)*, June 2018) As noted in, 'Editorial: A Stronger Common Foreign and Security Policy for a Self-Reliant Union?' (2018) 55 *Common Market Law Review* 1675 at 1683.

[99] With respect to example of external relations with Rwanda, Belarus, see, Geert De Baere, *Constitutional Principles of EU External Relations* (Oxford University Press, 2008) p 165.

[100] See, Joined Cases C-103/12 and C-165/12, *Parliament and Commission v Council*, ECLI:EU:C:2014:2400 ('*French Guiana*').

increasingly including characteristics akin to encompassing all matters of EU external relations – CFSP and non-CFSP matters alike. The Court in cases on non-CFSP matters has upheld the role that the Parliament plays under co-decision,[101] with an Advocate General noting that, institutionally, on decision-making procedures, the 'stakes…are high indeed'.[102] The typical arguments that the Parliament is in some way unsuited for inclusion in EU foreign policy no longer hold merit.

The balance between EU institutions has altered dramatically throughout the decades.[103] The borders and boundaries between the Union and Member States 'will need continual re-definition'.[104] This has been fought, for CFSP matters, principally, through institutional conflict. It is likely that the interinstitutional debates will continue to prevail while the specific legal character of CFSP matters are preserved in the treaties. Explicit reference to institutional balance was a late-comer to primary law. It was only inserted with the Treaty of Amsterdam through a Protocol, notwithstanding that the Court had referenced it as far back as the *Meroni* case,[105] before being elaborated on much later in *Chernobyl*.[106] The treaties did not always provide for the Parliament to litigate on acts of other institutions. Pre-Maastricht, when the *Chernobyl* case was lodged at the Court, the treaties stated '[t]he Court…shall review the legality of acts of the Council and the Commission other than recommendations or opinions. It shall for this purpose have jurisdiction in actions brought by a Member State, the Council or the Commission on grounds of lack of competence, infringement of an essential procedural requirement, infringement of this Treaty or of any rule of law relating to its application, or misuse of powers'.[107] The Parliament was deliberately omitted.

With the Parliament in a difficult position ensuring that its prerogatives were not encroached upon, the *Chernobyl* case was a creative way of underlining that institutional balance was fundamental for a functioning Union. The *Seat of Parliament* case some years beforehand,[108] in which the Court accepted that the Parliament could be a party to proceedings, was the beginning of the Parliament as a strong litigator at the Court. The Court is now regularly asked to annul acts and actions of various institutions for both substantive and procedural reasons.

[101] See, Joined Cases C-124/13 and C-125/13, *Parliament and Commission v Council*, ECLI:EU:C:2015:790 ('*Cod Stocks*').

[102] Opinion of Advocate General Wahl, Joined Cases C-124/13 and C-125/13, *Parliament and Commission v Council*, ECLI:EU:C:2015:337 ('*Cod Stocks*'), para 39.

[103] Jean Paul Jacqué, 'The Principle of Institutional Balance' (2004) 41 *Common Market Law Review* 383 at 387.

[104] Marise Cremona, 'The Common Foreign and Security Policy of the European Union and the External Relations Powers of the European Community' in David O'Keeffe and Patrick M Twomey (eds), *Legal Issues of the Maastricht Treaty* (Chancery 1994) p 249.

[105] Case C-9/56, *Meroni & Co, Industrie Metallurgiche, SpA v High Authority of the European Coal and Steel Community*, ECLI:EU:C:1958:7 ('*Meroni*').

[106] Case C-70/88, *Parliament v Council*, ECLI:EU:C:1991:373 ('*Chernobyl*') See, Koen Lenaerts and Amaryllis Verhoeven, 'Institutional Balance as a Guarantee for Democracy in EU Governance' in Christian Joerges and Renaud Dehousse (eds), *Good Governance in Europe's Integrated Market* (Oxford University Press, 2002) p 37.

[107] Then EC, Article 173.

[108] Case C-230/81, *Luxembourg v Parliament*, ECLI:EU:C:1983:32 ('*Seat of Parliament*').

The clinical legal practice of EU external relations is complicated, as has been proven by the cases before the Court. Interstate domination has upset institutional balance in particular policy fields, one manifestation of the financial crisis in Europe. During this crisis, executive actors can be criticised for bypassing the Parliament over and again.[109] Whereas institutional balance in the Union in times of crisis tends to favour those with strong executive credentials,[110] it is not just such times that reflect the role of institutions in EU policies. Rather, institutional balance is continuously distorted in CFSP matters. The divide between CFSP and non-CFSP matters means the intergovernmental-like and supranational nature of external action is not fully clear.

The very creation of the role of the High Representative and its upskilling with the EEAS may be a discrete attempt at bridging the divide. As Vice-President of the Commission, the High Representative chairs a subgroup of Commissioners that primarily deal with external issues of the Union. Collectively, this may allow the dividing line between CFSP and non-CFSP matters to become more difficult to separate as different instruments of EU external relations are put to use collectively. The actions of the High Representative and the accompanying EEAS show that the functions are similar to those of the Commission in external relations. The overlap between the EEAS and the Commission already occurs in several different fields, including political reporting and more response-related issues.

The absolute delineation of tasks assigned to the Commission and the EEAS, especially when operating within third states through one of its Delegations, can be exceptionally ambiguous. Given that as many as one-third of the EEAS's staff were originally Commission officials, or are still on secondment from the Commission, a merger is a distinct possibility. A battle for power allocation between the two is likely to be viewed as duplicated structures which may become more evident. Some members of the Parliament had previously advocated such an action,[111] and the proposal thus remains valid on its merits.

7.3.3. Loyalty

There is a sense of continued hesitation about the ultimate fate of CFSP legal acts and the applicable decision-making regime. However, the acknowledgment that the Union rests upon a single institutional framework makes bridging CFSP and non-CFSP matters an easier reality. For international agreements, Article 218 TFEU

[109] For example, with respect to establishing the Single Resolution Fund. See, Federico Fabbrini, 'On Banks, Courts and International Law: The Intergovernmental Agreement on the Single Resolution Fund in Context' (2014) 21 *Maastricht Journal of European and Comparative Law* 444.

[110] See, Deirdre Curtin, 'Challenging Executive Dominance in European Democracy' (2014) 77 *Modern Law Review* 1.

[111] European Convention. Letter from Giuliano Amato on Behalf of the Party of European Socialists, Elmar Brok on Behalf of the European People's Party, and Andrew Duff on Behalf of the European Liberal, Democrat and Reform Party. CONV 829/03 pp 17–18.

does much, given it covers international agreements based on either a CFSP or non-CFSP legal basis. However, it does not do much for internal decision-making for CFSP legal acts that are not linked with international agreements.

Whilst CFSP legal bases remain, a dual legal basis for certain EU actions may be a mature solution for institutional balance when it comes to CFSP matters. The recent Kazakhstan Enhanced Partnership and Cooperation Agreement (EPCA) was concluded on both CFSP and non-CFSP legal bases,[112] with Articles 31(1) and 37 TEU within the CFSP title, and Articles 91, 100(2), 207, 209, 218(5), and 218(8) TFEU outside of the CFSP title all being utilised. In *Commission v Council (Accord avec le Kazakhstan)*,[113] the ECPA itself was not contested, but the legal basis of a decision adopted within the Cooperation Council established by the international agreement was.[114] The Court said that CFSP matters were 'incidental to that agreement's two components constituted by the common commercial policy and development cooperation'.[115] It annulled the decision of the Cooperation Council. The judgment represents a 'high degree of integration of…CFSP [matters] with the standard operation of the EU legal order'[116] and fuels the notion that CFSP and non-CFSP matters are becoming increasingly intertwined.

The application of the duty of sincere (loyal) cooperation may be said to have application right across the breadth of the Union[117] and does not strictly apply only to non-CFSP matters. The Court has used it as a mechanism for tightening cooperative bonds between the Union and Member States.[118] In *Opinion 1/94*, the Court said 'the subject-matter of an agreement or convention falls in part within the competence of the Community and in part within that of the Member States, it is essential to ensure close cooperation between the Member States and the Community institutions, both in the process of negotiation and conclusion and in

[112] 'L 29/1. Council Decision (EU) 2016/123 of 26 October 2015 on the Signing, on Behalf of the European Union, and Provisional Application of the Enhanced Partnership and Cooperation Agreement between the European Union and Its Member States, of the One Part, and the Republic of Kazakhstan, of the Other Part'.

[113] Case C-244/17, *Commission v Council (Accord avec le Kazakhstan)*, ECLI:EU:C:2018:662. The Parliament did not intervene in this case in support of the Commission, despite it preferring non-CFSP legal bases for the Union's external action.

[114] L 73/15. Council Decision (EU) 2017/477 of 3 March 2017 on the Position to Be Adopted on Behalf of the European Union within the Cooperation Council Established under the Enhanced Partnership and Cooperation Agreement between the European Union and Its Member States, of the One Part, and the Republic of Kazakhstan, of the Other Part as Regards the Working Arrangements of the Cooperation Council, the Cooperation Committee, Specialised Subcommittees or Any Other Bodies.

[115] Case C-244/17, *Commission v Council (Accord avec le Kazakhstan)*, ECLI:EU:C:2018:662, para 46. For more on the overlap of CFSP and development cooperation, see, Morten Broberg, 'EU Development Cooperation and the CFSP: Mutual Encroachment?' in Steven Blockmans and Panos Koutrakos (eds), *Research Handbook on the EU's Common Foreign and Security Policy* (Edward Elgar, 2018).

[116] 'Editorial: A Stronger Common Foreign and Security Policy for a Self-Reliant Union?' (n 98) p 1681.

[117] TEU, Article 4(3): 'Pursuant to the principle of sincere cooperation, the Union and the Member States shall, in full mutual respect, assist each other in carrying out tasks which flow from the [t]reaties.'

[118] Robert Schütze, 'Parallel External Powers in the European Community: From "Cubist" Perspectives towards "Naturalist" Constitutional Principles?' (2004) 23 *Yearbook of European Law* 225 at 270.

the fulfilment of the commitments entered into',[119] thereby indirectly supporting the premise of streamlining EU actions, including those of EU external relations.

For CFSP matters, whether sincere cooperation is merely a symbolic measure, as opposed to a hard actionable instrument, is yet to be fully decided. Yet, some inclinations are there. In *Modjahedin I*, the General Court said the duty of sincere cooperation 'is of general application',[120] spreading across both CFSP and non-CFSP matters. This was reiterated by the General Court in *Mojahedin II*[121] and *Mojahedin III*.[122] This 'general application' of cooperation was endorsed by the Advocate General in the appeal of *Mojahedin III*,[123] but was not taken up by the Court,[124] given that the specific part of the General Court judgment dealing with it was not being appealed. Accordingly, a clear affirmation by the Court of the 'general application' of sincere cooperation in CFSP matters is still awaited. Nonetheless, the duty in itself for CFSP matters will inherently see resistance from Member States.[125]

7.3.4. EU Foreign Policy as Legal Acts

There is no doubt that CFSP legal acts could be seen, *prima facie*, as legislative acts, which they are not. Accordingly, their in-built characteristics make this a difficult realm to properly explore. The incremental changes to CFSP matters over the past 25 years have not been merely cosmetic. CFSP legal acts, which as has been correctly pointed out, are a lot more than 'adoption of foreign-policy positions and the making of diplomatic démarches'.[126] They are full-blown legal instruments for conducting actions.

The non-legislative understanding of CFSP legal acts – Decisions – may be eroding. In certain restrictive measures, there is an increased tendency for CFSP Decisions, adopted on the basis of Article 29 TEU, to be mirrored as non-CFSP Regulations on the basis of Article 215 TFEU. It can thus be argued that in such instances, CFSP Decisions start to become legislative in nature, despite their

[119] Opinion 1/94, *Competence of the Community to conclude international agreements concerning services and the protection of intellectual property*, ECLI:EU:C:1994:384 ('*WTO*'), para 108.

[120] Case T-228/02, *Organisation des Modjahedines du peuple d'Iran v Council*, ECLI:EU:T:2006:384 ('*Modjahedin I*'), para 123.

[121] Case T-256/07, *People's Mojahedin Organization of Iran v Council*, ECLI:EU:T:2008:461 ('*Mojahedin II*'), para 132.

[122] Case T-284/08, *People's Mojahedin Organization of Iran v. Council*, ECLI:EU:T:2008:550, ('*Mojahedin III*'), para 52.

[123] Opinion of Advocate General Sharpston, Case C-27/09 P, *France v People's Mojahedin Organization of Iran*, ECLI:EU:C:2011:482 ('*Mojahedin III*'), para 80.

[124] Case C-27/09 P, *France v People's Mojahedin Organization of Iran*, ECLI:EU:C:2011:853 ('*Mojahedin III*').

[125] For example, see, Stephen Hyett, 'The Duty of Co-Operation: A Flexible Concept' in Alan Dashwood and Christophe Hillion (eds), *The General Law of EC External Relations* (Sweet and Maxwell, 2000).

[126] Piet Eeckhout, *Does Europe's Constitution Stop at the Water's Edge? Law and Policy in the EU's External Relations* (Europa Law Publishing, 2005) p 18.

non-legislative character. As a result, in given circumstances, it could be argued that such CFSP Decisions violate the distinction that is supposed to apply to CFSP matters under Article 24(1) TEU. This has the effect of skewing the institutional balance. With this mirroring effect, the Court has had opportunities to clarify this,[127] but has not done so to date. However, it has been argued that in formal terms, 'CFSP [D]ecisons adopted pursuant to CFSP procedural rules could never be legislative acts',[128] despite acknowledging that they may be curiously similar from legislative acts on a non-CFSP legal basis.

Even if the divide between CFSP and non-CFSP legal bases was done away with, delegation of power would still be possible. Transforming CFSP legal acts from non-legislative to legislative acts would still allow scope for the Council within the treaties, but with enhanced political control by the Parliament. To place external competence together would provide additional coherence to EU foreign policy. Codifying all external relations provisions under one title in the treaties would, from a Union perspective, be an ideal scenario. Instead of CFSP Decisions, there could be 'European Decisions'.[129]

Even without such radical changes, it has been suggested that the treaties can be simplified, even with regard to CFSP matters.[130] The CFSP chapter in the treaties could be removed from the TEU altogether and pieced back together into the TFEU.[131] This would be desirable as CFSP matters are inherently about external relations collaboration and not the central principles of Union law for which the TEU is actually meant. Such progression in the Union legal order of relocating the CFSP chapter of the treaties would feed into a wider understanding of a single institutional framework that underpins the very existence of the Union.

7.3.5. Treaty Amendment

When the Union overcomes its prolonged period of constitutional stagnation, the treaties will inevitably have to be looked at once again with regard to EU external relations as a whole, including EU foreign policy matters. It would be an Intergovernmental Conference, under the provisions of Article 48 TEU, which will be composed of EU Member States that will draft, liaise, and finally agree upon the textual amendments for a revised set of treaties. In such an instance, the result

[127] Sara Poli, 'The Common Foreign Security Policy after Rosneft: Still Imperfect but Gradually Subject to the Rule of Law' (2017) 54 *Common Market Law Review* 1799 at 1832.

[128] Christina Eckes, *EU Powers Under External Pressure: How the EU's External Actions Alter Its Internal Structures* (Oxford University Press, 2019) p 139.

[129] Michael Dougan, 'The Convention's Draft Constitutional Treaty: Bringing Europe Closer to Its Lawyers?' (2003) 28 *European Law Review* 763 at 764.

[130] Steve Peers, 'The Future of EU Treaty Amendments' (2012) 31 *Yearbook of European Law* 17 at 100.

[131] As suggested in, ibid. p 100.

would be brought forward for ratification by each Member State, subject to their own domestic constitutional requirements. When such a move does take place, the foreign policy of the Union will be a part of the discussion. It is impossible to positively forecast the potential political choice that will be made at the next Intergovernmental Conference. Yet, given the developments in CFSP matters over the last number of years, when it comes to revising the treaties wholescale at Intergovernmental Conference level, it is irrefutable that the CFSP chapter in the TEU will be looked at. This begs the question of what will be a satisfactory outcome of any such treaty revision.

Pressures on the unity of the EU legal order are coming under increasing strain. Whilst calls for using the enhanced cooperation provisions of the treaties with respect to CFSP matters have not yet reached full fruition,[132] there is movement on this, particularly with regard to CSDP matters.[133] For the Union to remain relevant, change to its core legal document at some juncture will be necessary. Withering away is not an option. The Union has moved away from a process of 'semi-permanent' treaty revision,[134] and instead entered into a period of treaty stagnation. It would be a mishap if changes to the treaties were persistently avoided. It may very well be the case that the 'next time around' concept has prevailed.[135] Changes to the Union's legal framework are increasingly being conducted outside the framework altogether. The Treaty on Stability, Coordination and Governance (TSCG) and the European Stability Mechanism (ESM) illustrate this vividly.

The simplified revision procedures are not applicable to the TEU as Article 48(6) TEU stipulates revision can only occur to 'provisions of Part Three of the Treaty on the Functioning of the European Union relating to the internal policies and action of the Union'. Therefore, the CFSP chapter of the treaties is unreachable by the simplified revision procedures. An alternative option for treaty reform could be through an accession treaty, thus avoiding any full-scale revisional procedures.[136] Since 2009, the treaties have only been amended on one occasion through this method, on the accession of Croatia to the Union in 2013. With no accession on the horizon and the unlikelihood of such a process for treaty amendment, the scope for this considered method of revision is limited.

[132] It ought to be noted that the enhanced cooperation provisions for CFSP matters are located in the TFEU, and not the TEU. See TFEU, Art 329(2), TFEU, Art 331(2).

[133] This was of relevance when Permanent Structured Cooperation (PESCO) was launched in late 2017.

[134] See, Bruno De Witte, 'The Closest Thing to a Constitutional Conversation in Europe: The Semi-Permanent Treaty Revision Process' in Paul Beaumont, Carole Lyons and Neil Walker (eds), *Convergence and Divergence in European Public Law* (Hart Publishing, 2002).

[135] Joakim Nergelius, *The Constitutional Dilemma of the European Union* (Europa Law Publishing, 2009) p 103.

[136] Christophe Hillion, 'Widen to Deepen? The Potential and Limits of Accession Treaties to Achieve EU Constitutional Reform' in Steven Blockmans and Sacha Prechal (eds), *Reconciling the Deepening and Widening of the European Union* (TMC Asser Press, 2007) p 161.

7.4. The Steps Forward

Treaty change does not solve all woes, and law's problems cannot be solved through law alone.[137] Efforts to streamline Union activities through a more coherent legal framework will have to be strived for as the features of the Union become more attuned to becoming an ever-more-sophisticated polity. The inherent contradiction of EU external action is that both the Member States and the Union on the one hand signal a desire to make EU external action effective, operable, and consistent but, on the other hand, Member States also try to tightly control such action, and retain as much national competence as possible. Within this latter part, intergovernmentalism, as the 'most brutal form' of Member State bargaining,[138] has resulted in decades of slow progress that, in legal fields, has left legal carnage in its wake.

For all its downfalls, CFSP matters are now clearer, constitutionally speaking, than they ever have been. Going back in time, EPC was brought closer to the Union legal framework in the Single European Act,[139] thus, bringing it within the *acquis*, guaranteeing some role for the law. Whilst this 'formalised the practice of…EPC',[140] which was significant, it provided for later developments to occur at swifter speeds. Legally speaking and, diligently noted, distinctions have to be drawn between 'the efficiency of procedure to formulate a foreign policy' and 'the soundness of the policy as a matter of substance'.[141] Reform of the legal dimension to EU foreign policy does not in itself mean federalisation of foreign policy.[142] Instead of drastic measures being contemplated by any actor with an interest at stake, pragmatic decisive steps can be taken to ensure a harmonious approach.

Reforming the EU is a task wished upon nobody. For the next reform to be any way meaningful toward enhancing parliamentary involvement and judicial jurisdiction in EU external relations, the detachment between law and idealism will have to be bridged. Despite the clarity that an integration of CFSP matters and non-CFSP matters would bring, complete abolition of CFSP legal bases is highly unlikely in the short term given the Council's and Member States' preference for its use. The Union, over the past number of years, has been slogging through crisis periods, dealing with issues from the financial crisis, to the capacity to handle irregular migration from non-EU third states, to internal rule of law issues in a

[137] As put, 'not all legal problems can be solved legally'. Neil MacCormick, 'The Maastricht-Urteil: Sovereignty Now' (1995) 1 *European Law Journal* 259 at 265.

[138] Stephen Weatherill, *Law and Values in the European Union* (Oxford University Press, 2016) p 72.

[139] See Chapter 2 of this book.

[140] Mary T Robinson, 'Towards a European Foreign Policy – Legal Aspects' in Johan K De Vree, Peter Coffey and Richard H Lauwaars (eds), *Towards a European Foreign Policy: Legal, Economic and Political Dimensions* (Martinus Nijhoff Publishers, 1987) p 102.

[141] Eileen Denza, 'Groping towards Europe's Foreign Policy' in Deirdre Curtin and Tom Heukels (eds), *Institutional Dynamics of European Integration: Essays in Honour of Henry G. Schermers, Volume II* (Martinus Nijhoff Publishers, 1994) p 592.

[142] Thym (n 10) p 22.

select number of Member States. EU external relations have felt this pressure. Such lingering issues have halted any realistic expectations of reformed treaties coming forward for the foreseeable future. Major reforms would require the agreement of all Member States, ratification by their respective national (and in some cases, regional) parliaments, and even then, some Member States would hold or must hold a referendum before final ratification. One Member State failing to ratify renewed treaties would hold up the entire process.

7.4.1. Pace of Progress

Even in the late 1990s, moving from unanimity to QMV in CFSP matters was a 'pie in the sky' notion,[143] never mind further treaty change to bring about greater institutional balance. The Treaty of Maastricht in 1993 set out the first hints that the EU and WEU would eventually merge.[144] Small steps have been vital. It took three subsequent constitutional steps through the treaties of Amsterdam, Nice, and Lisbon over 16 years to ultimately abolish the WEU. The continuance of the WEU beyond this might have hampered the consistency and coherence of CFSP matters and overall external relations of the Union.[145] Yet, fundamental treaty change to CFSP matters has not been dared since it was properly introduced at the Treaty of Maastricht. Tinkering has arisen, but nothing on the scale that could be considered hugely relevant. Then, as now, however, arguments in favour of integration should not put at risk the consolidated gains of integration thus far.[146] With the techniques that have been developed by the Council to obfuscate power sharing with other institutions, the Union is a long way from normalised foreign policy decision-making. Any such reforms will continue to anchor the power base firmly at the heart of Member States' capitals.

It is never too bold in EU affairs to have high aspirations for the future. The process leading up to the Constitutional Treaty was filled with hope and desire for seeing Europe thrive further together. Touting the possibility of the distinctions between CFSP decision-making and non-CFSP decision-making being abandoned in favour of one coherent and suitable external relations legal framework will take significant political capital for any advocator to put forward. Enhancing Union external action by merging CFSP legal bases and non-CFSP legal bases may seem like a forced marriage, but in fact they were always destined for each

[143] 'Editorial: The Treaty of Amsterdam: Neither a Bang Nor a Whimper' (1997) 34 *Common Market Law Review* 767 at 771.

[144] Michael Smith, 'CFSP and ESDP: From Idea to Institution to Policy?' in Martin Holland (ed), *Common Foreign and Security Policy: The First Ten Years* 2nd edition (Continuum 2004) p 81.

[145] Martin Trybus, 'With or without the EU Constitutional Treaty: Towards a Common Security and Defence Policy?' (2006) 31 *European Law Review* 145 at 165.

[146] As analogised to the former multiple communities and their consolidation into a Union. Joseph HH Weiler and James Modrall, 'Institutional Reform: Consensus or Majority?' (1985) 10 *European Law Review* 316 at 332.

other anyway. The increasingly accepted formation of the Union as being federally grounded means CFSP matters and its continued ways are more legally suspect. Moreover, if the evolution of Union law slows, as it has in the past, it can raise questions about the Union's legitimacy.[147]

7.4.2. The Way of EU Foreign Policy Law

Multilateralism is a persuasive exercise for States and their external activities, bringing foreign policy more into line with one another. Naturally, such undertakings are onerous.[148] For the Austrian, Finnish, and Swedish accession processes, the class of 1995, CFSP matters were the first chapter dealt with in negotiations,[149] given the perceived problems with it that never manifested. Gradually, in practice, CFSP matters have been drifting towards the other EU institutions beyond the Council, one way or another. This is a positive development, and the only sustainable path for the EU foreign policy. The steady promotion of CFSP matters and its slow integration with the EU legal order have significance, even politically.[150] Concerns of it encroaching into particular policies of individual Member States have largely evaporated.

The law of EU external relations has to date contributed to the changing nature of Union law as a whole, and its ongoing practice will continue to shape the role of the legal order, both internally in the Union, and externally in the world at large. The United States of America has been the natural fallback for Europe to seek inspiration from. Not only was it a guarantor of European peace for the best and latter half of the twentieth century, but it has also provided Europe with legal ideals drawn from legal practice and scholarship. Whereas the states in the United States ceded foreign policy powers to the federal government, the total opposite is the case in the EU. Given its specificity, the EU remains an international construct, albeit with its own legal order.

The divide between CFSP matters and non-CFSP matters differentiates EU external action in terms of decision-making, procedures, substance, and justiciability. The legal basis arguments between different parts of the treaties are not merely academic commentary on hypothetical notions. The contestation of legal

[147] Ian S Forrester, 'L'Europe des Juges. Recent Criticism of ECHR and ECJ Judgments, the American Debate on Judicial Activism versus Judicial Restraint' in Carl Baudenbacher and Erhard Busek (eds), *The Role of International Courts* (German Law Publishers, 2008) p 277.

[148] Louis Henkin, *How Nations Behave: Law and Foreign Policy* (Pall Mall Press, 1968) p 55.

[149] Lykke Friis, 'Breaking the Waves: The European Union's Enlargement Negotiations with EFTA and Central and Eastern Europe' in Ole Elgström and Christer Jönsson (eds), *European Union Negotiations: Processes, Networks and Institutions* (Routledge, 2005) p 201.

[150] Antonio Tizzano, 'The Foreign Relations Law of the EU between Supranationality and Intergovernmental Model' in Enzo Cannizzaro (ed), *The European Union as an Actor in International Relations* (Kluwer Law International, 2002) p 144.

basis for EU external relations has much broader implications.[151] It has vast ramifications for the functioning of the EU governance regime, and thus affects how policies shape the EU's role in the outside world. From a bird's eye view, the EU's foreign policy system is 'unprecedented, unparallelled, and hybrid'.[152] Whereas the Union is typically called *sui generis*,[153] there is much debate as to whether it is or not, notwithstanding the legal workings of CFSP matters being labelled as 'very *sui generis*'.[154]

CFSP matters are still considered a derogation of unity.[155] Pragmatism has long outweighed theoretical concerns about its existence, with the law of its dynamics being completely crushed by political realities. The *common* element of CFSP matters has meant it has not become a *single* foreign policy.[156] That said, the call of a single policy 'would [be] welcome[d]…as a blessing'.[157] CFSP matters have typically been on the outer sphere of the EU legal orbit, along with JHA matters, as 'objects of European co-operation'.[158] The gravitational pull has been stronger for JHA matters, and it is likely that CFSP matters will fall next.

External relations of any description, according to one view, 'should be clear to others and should be consistent'.[159] The breadth of the Union's legal and practical capabilities and its ever-growing expansion lessen the need for a distinct legal field for CFSP matters. The Union still struggles to find its own consistency to ultimately have effect on foreign, security, and defence issues.[160] For EU external action to work externally, it must have substantive and procedural coherence and consistency internally. Without a coherent legal framework for external relations, with continued divisions of CFSP matters and non-CFSP matters, the cracks

[151] Peter Van Elsuwege, 'The Interface Between the Area of Freedom, Security and Justice and the Common Foreign and Security Policy of the European Union: Legal Constraints to Political Objectives' in Ronald L Holzhacker and Paul Luif (eds), *Freedom, Security and Justice in the European Union* (Springer, 2014) p 124.

[152] Stein and Henkin (n 27) p 78.

[153] This point is contested. For criticism of the 'sui generis' label and its applicability to the Union, see, Robert Schütze, 'On "Federal" Ground; The European Union as an (Inter)national Phenomenon' (2009) 46 *Common Market Law Review* 1069 at 1091.

[154] Ricardo Gosalbo-Bono, 'The International Powers of the European Parliament, the Democratic Deficit and the Treaty on European Union' (1992) 12 *Yearbook of European Law* 85 at 125.

[155] Deirdre Curtin and Ige Dekker, 'The European Union from Maastricht to Lisbon: Institutional and Legal Unity Out of the Shadow' in Paul Craig and Gráinne De Búrca (eds), *The Evolution of EU Law* (Oxford University Press, 2011) p 165.

[156] Denza (n 48) p 592.

[157] Giuseppe Federico Mancini, 'Europe: The Case for Statehood' (1998) 4 *European Law Journal* 29 at 39.

[158] Alicia Hinarejos, 'The Lisbon Treaty Versus Standing Still: A View from the Third Pillar' (2009) 5 *European Constitutional Law Review* 99 at 113.

[159] Henry G Schermers, 'The Main Issues in the Debate on the Further Development of European Foreign Policy' in Jürgen Schwarze (ed), *The External Relations of the European Community, in particular EC–US Relations* (Nomos, 1989) p 72.

[160] This was the case even before the Treaty of Lisbon. See, Panos Koutrakos, 'Security and Defence Policy within the Context of EU External Relations: Issues of Coherence, Consistency, and Effectiveness' in Martin Trybus and Nigel White (eds), *European Security Law* (Oxford University Press, 2007).

in the EU legal architecture are exposed. As EU external action becomes more developed, the sooner that the underlying primary law framework is adapted, the smoother the institutional legal process for executing EU external action will be.

7.4.3. An Objectionable Status Quo

There was a time when CFSP matters running along a light rules-based intergovernmentalist streak was acceptable, but not anymore. The Council should no longer act with impunity when handling CFSP matters despite its attempts at fully protecting individual Member States' interests, and not necessarily the EU's interest. With the Council using every trick in the book to circumvent the involvement of the Parliament and the Court wherever possible, stronger institutional protections are needed. Given that there are control and enforcement mechanisms within the primary law, it can be implied that Member States do not object to supranationalism in and of itself,[161] but rather, show hesitation towards accepting it.

Without further institutional reform, the Union's abilities to influence and shape global events will wane. Having no role for the Parliament in matters the same way as it would in non-CFSP matters is clearly a deficiency, in the same way the Court does not have full jurisdiction. The *Airport Transit Visas* case was a breakthrough on the pillars,[162] and the Court's conclusion meant the limited jurisdiction imposed on the pillars was not absolute.[163] The legal arrangements for CFSP matters have been complex, but nowhere as near as those or as hastily arranged as the former third pillar. In that sense, JHA matters wins that prize by a country-mile.[164] Yet, if the former third pillar can be moved to the ordinary legislative procedure under the TFEU, then there is no impediment to having the CFSP provisions of the treaties altered and moved to a TFEU legal basis. Both JHA and CFSP matters are sensitive areas for Member States, but if it can be done for JHA, then there is no reason why it cannot for CFSP matters.

There is no decided consensus for the future of European integration, never mind the future of EU foreign policy. An ultimatum for the continuing of CFSP as a legal regime will not merely depend on legal analysis, scholarly or otherwise, but will be made by officials and politicians at the upper echelons of political decision-making. EU external action through law is only going to flourish when a level of

[161] Ramses A Wessel, 'Towards a United Europe? A Legal Perspective on European Institutionalization and Integration' in Jaap de Wilde and Håkan Wiberg (eds), *Organized Anarchy in Europe: The Role of States and Intergovernmental Organizations* (IB Tauris Publishers, 1996) p 58.

[162] Case C-170/96, *Commission v Council*, ECLI:EU:C:1998:219 ('*Airport Transit Visas*').

[163] Angela Ward, 'Community Development Aid and the Evolution of the Inter-Institutional Law of the European Union' in Alan Dashwood and Christophe Hillion (eds), *The General Law of EC External Relations* (London, Sweet and Maxwell, 2000), p 47.

[164] Steve Peers, 'In a World of Their Own? Justice and Home Affairs Opt-Outs and the Treaty of Lisbon' in Catherine Barnard (ed), *Cambridge Yearbook of European Legal Studies 2007–2008: Volume 10* (Hart Publishing, 2008) p 383.

maturity is reached between the Member States and the Union.[165] Particularly, the Union's institutions will have to further alleviate potential interinstitutional wrangling.

CFSP matters, legally, are an 'esoteric area',[166] in which elites square off in pursuit of their institutional power. The Council has manned every wall of the CFSP castle, digging new trenches against the oncoming enemy; other EU institutions, such as the Parliament finding itself winning more procedural cases, and the Court delving into CFSP matters post-Lisbon. Yet, as a substantive policy domain, EU foreign policy is not as special as it may once have been considered. In the present era, it is no longer deserving of its own unique provisions catering for, amongst others, a specific decision-making regime. With no envisaged endgame, it is highly probable that legal disputes on EU foreign policy will continue until some overall lasting institutional settlement is reached between the key stakeholders.

Whereas the Treaty of Lisbon sought to streamline EU foreign policy and external relations to form a more coherent structure,[167] the potential for institutional litigation based on external action has increased. Whilst CFSP matters retain a distinct legal regime, it must be dealt with as issues arise. As CFSP legal acts have become more concrete and specific, far away from the vague and ambiguous Common Positions which are now a relic of the past, manoeuvre for the Court is greatly lessened, as should the fear be of its impact if granted full jurisdiction. It would be a matter in entrusting the Court with jurisdiction, whilst ensuring that it would not 'overshadow[] the authority of the political protagonists',[168] which to date, it has shown a high level of respect and caution. The most critical reading of the Court's case law is that it is difficult to accrue criteria upon which it adjudicates on finding an appropriate legal basis. Yet, the standard is not easily identifiable.[169] It is thus claimed that absolute criteria might not be a realistic prospect given the very nature of how CFSP matters have been legally structured, with external objectives of the Union to apply across all policies.

[165] For a fuller discussion on maturity, see, Inge Govaere, '"Setting the International Scene": EU External Competence and Procedures Post-Lisbon Revisited in the Light of ECJ Opinion 1/13' (2015) 52 *Common Market Law Review* 1277 at 1279.

[166] Adrian Hyde-Price, 'Decision-Making under the Second Pillar' in Anthony Arnull and Daniel Wincott (eds), *Accountability and Legitimacy in the European Union* (Oxford University Press, 2002) p 41.

[167] Or put another way, is now taking 'a more concrete shape'. Marise Cremona, 'The Position of CFSP/CSDP in the EU's Constitutional Architecture' in Blockmans and Koutrakos (n 90) p 5.

[168] Christophe Hillion and Ramses A Wessel, '"The Good, the Bad and the Ugly": Three Levels of Judicial Control over the CFSP' in Blockmans and Koutrakos (eds), ibid. p 86.

[169] Panos Koutrakos, 'Legal Basis and Delimitation of Competence in EU External Relations' in Marise Cremona and Bruno De Witte (eds), *EU Foreign Relations Law: Constitutional Fundamentals* (Hart Publishing, 2008) p 184.

7.4.4. Adaptation

EU foreign policy is constantly adapting to new global realities. Likewise, the treaties must change over time to match this global EU ambition. However, political issues, whatever they may be, regularly trounce legal arrangements.[170] Damage to the EU's external relations on legal grounds is not in the interest of any institution. The contextual interpretative means deployed adds further substance to the basic framework. The fear of dire consequences if CFSP matters were subjugated to ordinary Union decision-making processes is unfounded. Just because legal integration takes place in certain policy fields like trade, does not *de facto* mean that integration will go further in other areas like foreign policy. Indeed, economic integration has not naturally progressed to a political union.[171]

Incrementalism has proven to be the ultimate method for the EU's successes. This has led to the EU having 'quality of its international presence' as an international actor.[172] The great expectations placed upon the EU might be burdensome, and it must be recognised that the Union is nothing more than a giant compromise. CFSP decision-making is on the outer limits of European supranationalism and the Union's external action is conducted through a prism of appropriate legal choice, requiring adequate reflection and execution. Institutional actions by the Parliament, reactions by the Council, and adjudication of the Court have all contributed to the process of slow supranationalisation.

Fostering initiatives to integrate CFSP matters into the normal Union decision-making process is the way forward. Strict intergovernmentalism, as CFSP matters once were, is a thing of the past, and CFSP matters are now only necessary when it is possible. Yet it still possesses strong intergovernmental character, with rules, due to each Member State's continued possession of a formal veto over the pursuit of nearly all actions on a CFSP legal basis. That said, specific objectives for CFSP matters have been abolished. Inevitably, this act in time will likely be seen as one of a series of nails in the coffin of CFSP matters as a standalone field, as Union decision-making as a whole becomes even more communitarised and constitutionalised.

[170] Take for instance, the opting of Frankfurt as seat of the European Central Bank (ECB), as opposed to that of Luxembourg, which is where, according to a 1965 decision of Member States, it should have been located. See, Mathew Heim, 'The European Central Bank: Was It Not Bound to Go to Luxembourg?' (1994) 19 *European Law Review* 48.

[171] Pierre Pescatore, *The Law of Integration: Emergence of a New Phenomenon in International Relations, Based on the Experience of the European Communities* (A W Sijthoff, 1974) p 23.

[172] Christina Eckes, 'How the European Parliament's Participation in International Relations Affects the Deep Tissue of the EU's Power Structures' (2014) 12 *International Journal of Constitutional Law* 904 at 928.

7.5. Conclusion

No final ending point or destination for the law of EU foreign policy needs to be identified or achieved within a specific time period for how the law of EU foreign policy will develop. The enigma of 'who decides?' will consistently be at the fore. But to act on this new level of interconnectedness of EU external relations, law has to 'react'.[173] How this happens is an open question. Whilst the EU Global Strategy on Foreign and Security Policy of 2016 focused on sectoral areas of EU external relations as opposed to the legal instruments giving effect to the policies,[174] it did not fully recognise the division between CFSP and non-CFSP matters. This demonstrates that the Union's policies are becoming more integrated, and the law will have to catch up.

Executive power in CFSP matters is still abnormally strong and continues to expressively eclipse the parliamentary and judicial power within the Union. The day of reckoning for CFSP legal bases has yet to arrive, but it cannot be too far away. Intergovernmentalist tendencies have innate flaws which bypass the overall supranational character of Union law. This book has advanced the argument that the demarcation line between both CFSP matters and non-CFSP matters is problematic to define, and that the amalgamation of the law of EU foreign policy (CFSP matters) with the law of EU external relations (non-CFSP manners) is necessary. In the meantime, the constitutional importance of the legal basis for EU foreign policy acts shall remain an important question pondered under the treaties as they presently stand.

As a whole, EU external relations are slowly beginning to take shape. The entire array of legal actors with a stake in the process of European integration will need to come together at the right time to permanently resolve the legal issues of EU foreign policy. Such matters ought to include serious consideration of institutional reform of EU external relations law as a whole, driven by both administrative and political will. All this will lie on the premise that the Union is to become a true global actor. Where the Union goes next is a political choice, closely aligned between the legal tools and policy preference, which will ultimately have to closer work together to further its strength in the world at large.

[173] Waltraud Hakenberg, 'How to Square the Circle between Political Necessities and Constitutional Constraints? – An ECJ Perspective' in Thomas Giegerich, Oskar Josef Gstrein and Sebastian Zeitzmann (eds), *The EU between 'An Ever Closer Union' and Inalienable Policy Domains of Member States* (Nomos, 2014) p 548.

[174] 'Shared Vision, Common Action: A Stronger Europe. A Global Strategy for the European Union's Foreign and Security Policy (European Union) June 2016' (n 41).

BIBLIOGRAPHY

Literature

Abazi V and Hillebrandt M, 'The Legal Limits to Confidential Negotiations: Recent Case Law Developments in Council Transparency: Access Info Europe and In 't Veld' (2015) 52 *Common Market Law Review* 825.

Adam S, *La procédure d'avis devant la Court de justice de l'Union européenne* (Brussels, Bruylant, 2011).

——, 'The Legal Basis of International Agreements of the European Union in the Post-Lisbon Era' in Inge Govaere and others (eds), *The European Union in the World: Essays in Honour of Marc Maresceau* (Leiden, Martinus Nijhoff Publishers, 2014).

Albors-Llorens A, 'Changes in the Jurisdiction of the European Court of Justice under the Treaty of Amsterdam' (1998) 35 *Common Market Law Review* 1273.

Alemanno A, 'What Has Been, and What Could Be, Thirty Years after Les Verts/European Parliament' in Miguel Poiares Maduro and Loïc Azoulai (eds), *The Past and Future of EU Law: The Classics of EU Law Revisited on the 50th Anniversary of the Rome Treaty* (Oxford, Hart Publishing, 2010).

Allott P, 'Democracy, Accountability and Transparency (Discussant's Remarks)' in Alan Dashwood (ed), *Reviewing Maastricht: Issues for the 1996 IGC* (London, Sweet and Maxwell, 1996).

Ameller M, *Parliaments: A Comparative Study on the Structure and Functioning of Representative Institutions in Fifty-Five Countries* 2nd edition (London, Inter-Parliamentary Union by Cassell, 1966).

Armstrong KA, 'Citizenship of the Union? Lessons from Carvel and The Guardian' (1996) 59 *Modern Law Review* 582.

——, 'New Governance and the European Union: An Empirical Conceptual Critique' in Gráinne De Búrca, Claire Kilpatrick and Joanne Scott (eds), *Critical Legal Perspectives on Global Governance* (Oxford, Hart Publishing, 2014).

Arnull A, 'Does the Court of Justice Have Inherent Jurisdiction?' (1990) 27 *Common Market Law Review* 683.

——, 'Me and My Shadow: The European Court of Justice and the Disintegration of European Union Law' (2007) 31 *Fordham International Law Journal* 1174.

——, 'The Americanization of EU Law Scholarship' in Anthony Arnull, Piet Eeckhout and Takis Tridimas (eds), *Continuity and Change in EU Law: Essays in Honour of Sir Francis Jacobs* (Oxford University Press, 2008).

Azoulai L, 'The Europeanisation of Legal Concepts' in Ulla Neergaard and Ruth Nielsen (eds), *European Legal Method – in a Multi-Level EU Legal Order* (Copenhagen, Djøf Publishing, 2012).

Bagehot W, *The English Constitution* (Miles Taylor ed, Oxford University Press 2001).

Baquero Cruz J, *What's Left of the Law of Integration? Decay and Resistance in European Union Law* (Oxford University Press, 2018).

Barents R, 'Case C-316/91, Parliament v. Council, Judgment of 2 March 1994 (Full Court), [1994] ECR 1–653' (1995) 32 *Common Market Law Review* 249.

Barnard C, 'Where Politicians Fear to Tread?' (1992) 17 *European Law Review* 127.

Barrett G, 'Creation's Final Laws: The Impact of the Treaty of Lisbon on the "Final Provisions" of Earlier Treaties' (2008) 27 *Yearbook of European Law* 3.

——, 'European Economic Governance: Deficient in Democratic Legitimacy?' (2018) 40 *Journal of European Integration* 249.

Bebr G, *Development of Judicial Control of the European Communities* (The Hague, Martinus Nijhoff Publishers, 1981).

——, 'The Reinforcement of the Constitutional Review of Community Acts Under Article 177 EEC Treaty (Case 314/85 and 133 to 136/85)' (1988) 25 *Common Market Law Review* 667.

——, 'Case C-70/88, European Parliament v. Council, Judgment of the Court of Justice of 22 May 1990' (1991) 28 *Common Market Law Review* 663.

Beck G, *The Legal Reasoning of the Court of Justice of the EU* (Oxford, Hart Publishing, 2013).

Becker-Alon S, *The Communitarian Dimension of the European Union's Common Foreign and Security Policy* (Baden-Baden, Nomos, 2011).

Bello JH and Rudolf B, 'Commission of the European Communities v. Council of the European Union' (1997) 91 *American Journal of International Law* 349.

Benedetto G, 'Rapporteurs as Legislative Entrepreneurs: The Dynamics of the Codecision Procedure in Europe's Parliament' (2005) 12 *Journal of European Public Policy* 67.

Benedetto G and Hix S, 'Explaining the European Parliament's Gains in the EU Constitution' (2007) 2 *Review of International Organization* 115.

Bengoetxea J, *The Legal Reasoning of the European Court of Justice* (Oxford, Clarendon Press, 1993),

——, 'Rethinking EU Law in the Light of Pluralism and Practical Reason' in Miguel Poiares Maduro, Kaarlo Tuori and Suvi Sankari (eds), *Transnational Law: Rethinking European Law and Legal Thinking* (Cambridge University Press, 2014).

Berman P, 'The European Union – I: Development, Structure, and Decision-Making' in Sir Ivor Roberts (ed), *Satow's Diplomatic Practice* 6th edition, (Oxford University Press, 2009).

——, 'From Laeken to Lisbon: The Origins and Negotiation of the Lisbon Treaty' in Andrea Biondi, Piet Eeckhout and Stefanie Ripley (eds), *EU Law after Lisbon* (Oxford University Press, 2012).

Bermann GA, 'Competences of the Union' in Takis Tridimas and Paolisa Nebbia (eds), *European Union Law for the Twenty-First Century: Rethinking the New Legal Order – Volume 1: Constitutional and Public Law, External Relations* (Oxford, Hart Publishing, 2004).

Besselink LFM, 'The Place of National Parliaments within the European Constitutional Order' in Nicola Lupo and Cristina Fasone (eds), *Interparliamentary Cooperation in the Composite European Constitution* (Oxford, Hart Publishing, 2016).

Bicchi F and Carta C, 'The COREU Network and the Circulation of Information Within EU Foreign Policy' (2012) 34 *Journal of European Integration* 465.

Bickel AM, *The Morality of Consent* (New Haven, Yale University Press, 1975).

——, *The Least Dangerous Branch: The Supreme Court at the Bar of Politics* 2nd edition (New Haven, Yale University Press 1986).

Bieber R, 'Democratic Control of European Foreign Policy' (1990) 1 *European Journal of International Law* 148.

——, 'Democratic Control of International Relations of the European Union' in Enzo Cannizzaro (ed), *The European Union as an Actor in International Relations* (The Hague, Kluwer Law International, 2002).

Biondi A and Bartolini S, 'Recent Developments in Luxembourg: The Courts' Activities in 2013' (2014) 20 *European Public Law* 611.

Blockmans S, 'Between the Devil and the Deep Blue Sea? Conflicts in External Action Pursued by OCTs and the EU' in Dimitry Kochenov (ed), *EU Law of the Overseas: Outermost Regions, Associated Overseas Countries and Territories, Territories Sui Generis* (Alphen aan den Rijn, Kluwer Law International, 2011).

——, 'The EU's Modular Approach to Defence Integration: An Inclusive, Ambitious and Legally Binding PESCO?' (2018) 55 *Common Market Law Review* 1785.

——, 'EEAS 2.0: Recommendations for the Amendment of Council Decision 2010/427/EU on the European External Action Service' (Centre for European Policy Studies 2013).

Blockmans S and Spernbauer M, 'Legal Obstacles to Comprehensive EU External Security Action' (2013) 18 *European Foreign Affairs Review* 7.

Bobek M, 'On the Application of European Law in (Not Only) the Courts of the New Member States: "Don't Do as I Say"?' in Catherine Barnard (ed), *Cambridge Yearbook of European Legal Studies 2007–2008: Volume 10* (Oxford, Hart Publishing, 2008).

Boerger A and Davies B, 'Imaging the Course of European Law? Parti Ecologiste "Les Verts" v. Parliament as a Constitutional Milestone in EU Law' in Bill Davies and Fernanda Nicola (eds), *EU Law Stories: Contextual and Critical Histories of European Jurisprudence* (Cambridge University Press, 2017).
Bogdanor V, 'EC External Relations and the CFSP (Discussant's Remarks)' in Alan Dashwood (ed), *Reviewing Maastricht: Issues for the 1996 IGC* (London, Sweet and Maxwell, 1996).
Böttner R, 'The Treaty Amendment Procedures and the Relationship between Article 31(3) TEU and the General Bridging Clause of Article 48(7) TEU' (2016) 12 *European Constitutional Law Review* 499.
Böttner R and Wessel RA, 'Article 31 [Procedures for the Adoption of CFSP Decisions]' in Hermann-Josef Blanke and Stelio Mangiameli (eds), *The Treaty on European Union (TEU)* (Berlin, Springer, 2013).
Bovens M, 'Two Concepts of Accountability: Accountability as a Virtue and as a Mechanism' (2010) 33 *West European Politics* 946.
Bovens M, Schillemans T and Hart P 't, 'Does Public Accountability Work? An Assessment Tool' (2008) 86 *Public Administration* 225.
Bradley CA, 'Foreign Relations Law as a Field of Study' (2017) 111 *American Journal of International Law* 316.
Bradley CA and Goldsmith JL, *Foreign Relations Law: Cases and Materials* 4th edition, (New York, Wolters Kluwer Law and Business, 2011).
Bradley KSC, 'Maintaining the Balance: The Role of the Court of Justice in Defining the Institutional Position of the European Parliament' (1987) 24 *Common Market Law Review* 41.
——, 'The European Court and the Legal Basis of Community Legislation' (1988) 13 *European Law Review* 379.
——, 'The Variable Evolution of the Standing of the European Parliament in Proceedings Before the Court of Justice' (1988) 8 *Yearbook of European Law* 27.
——, 'Sense and Sensibility: Parliament v. Council Continued' (1991) 16 *European Law Review* 245.
——, '"Better Rusty than Missin"?: Institutional Reforms of the Maastricht Treaty and the European Parliament' in David O'Keeffe and Patrick M Twomey (eds), *Legal Issues of the Maastricht Treaty* (Chichester, Chancery, 1994).
——, 'The European Parliament and Comitology: On the Road to Nowhere?' (1997) 3 *European Law Journal* 230.
——, 'The Institutional Law of the European Union in 1998 (Incorporating Legal Developments in the European Parliament)' (1998) 18 *Yearbook of European Law* 477.
——, 'The European Parliament and Treaty Reform: Building Blocks and Stumbling Blocks' in David O'Keeffe and Patrick M Twomey (eds), *Legal Issues of the Amsterdam Treaty* (Oxford, Hart Publishing 1999).
——, 'The Institutional Law of the European Union in 1999' (1999) 19 *Yearbook of European Law* 547.
——, 'Halfway House: The 2006 Comitology Reforms and the European Parliament' (2008) 31 *West European Politics* 837.
——, 'Delegation of Powers in the European Union: Political Problems, Legal Solutions?' in Carl Fredrik Bergström and Dominique Ritleng (eds), *Rulemaking by the European Commission: The New System for Delegation of Powers* (Oxford University Press, 2016).
——, 'Legislating in the European Union' in Catherine Barnard and Steve Peers (eds), *European Union Law* 2nd edition, (Oxford University Press, 2017).
Breyer S, 'Judicial Review of Question of Law and Policy' (1986) 38 *Administrative Law Review* 363.
——, *The Court and the World: American Law and the New Global Realities* (New York, Alfred A Knopf, 2015).
Briggs A, 'The Death of Harrods: Forum Non Conveniens and the European Court' (2005) 121 *Law Quarterly Review* 535.
Brkan M, 'Exploring EU Competence in CFSP: Logic or Contradiction?' (2006) 2 *Croatian Yearbook of European Law* and Policy 173.

——, 'The Role of the European Court of Justice in the Field of Common Foreign and Security Policy After the Treaty of Lisbon: New Challenges for the Future' in Paul James Cardwell (ed), *EU External Relations Law and Policy in the Post-Lisbon Era* (The Hague, TMC Asser Press, 2012).

——, 'The Role of the European Court of Justice from Maastricht to Lisbon: Putting Together the Scattered Pieces of Patchwork' in Maartje De Visser and Anne Pieter Van Der Mei (eds), *The Treaty on European Union 1993–2013: Reflections from Maastricht* (Cambridge, Intersentia, 2013).

Broberg M, 'What Is the Direction for the EU's Development Cooperation after Lisbon? A Legal Examination' (2011) 16 *European Foreign Affairs Review* 539.

——, 'EU Development Cooperation and the CFSP: Mutual Encroachment?' in Steven Blockmans and Panos Koutrakos (eds), *Research Handbook on the EU's Common Foreign and Security Policy* (Cheltenham, Edward Elgar, 2018).

Broberg M and Fenger N, *Preliminary References to the European Court of Justice* (Oxford University Press, 2010).

Broberg M and Holdgaard R, 'Demarcating the Union's Development Cooperation Policy after Lisbon: Commission v. Council (Philippines PCFA)' (2015) 52 *Common Market Law Review* 547.

——, 'EU Development Cooperation Post-Lisbon: Main Constitutional Challenges' (2015) 40 *European Law Review* 349.

Brunkhorst H, 'Democracy under Siege: The Decay of Constitutionalization and the Crisis of *Public Law* and Public Opinion' in Poul F Kjaer and Niklas Olsen (eds), *Critical Theories of Crisis in Europe: From Weimar to the Euro* (London, Rowman & Littlefield, 2016).

Bruter M, 'Diplomacy Without a State: The External Delegations of the European Commission' (1999) 6 *Journal of European Public Policy* 183.

Burghardt G, 'The Potential and Limits of CFSP: What Comes Next?' in Elfiede Regelsberg, Philippe de Schoutheete de Tervarent and Wolfgang Wessels (eds), *Foreign Policy of the European Union: From EPC to CFSP and Beyond* (Boulder, Lynne Rienner, 1997).

Burrows N, 'COREPER, Competence and Conservation' (1997) 22 *European Law Review* 64.

Butler G, 'Pinpointing the Appropriate Legal Basis for External Action' (2015) 6 *European Journal of Risk Regulation* 323.

——, 'The Interparliamentary Conference on the CFSP/CSDP: A New Forum for the Oireachtas in Irish and EU Foreign Policy?' (2015) 26 *Irish Studies in International Affairs* 163.

——, 'The Ultimate Stumbling Block? The Common Foreign and Security Policy, and Accession of the European Union to the European Convention on Human Rights' (2016) 39 *Dublin University Law Journal* 229.

——, 'The Coming of Age of the Court's Jurisdiction in the Common Foreign and Security Policy' (2017) 13 *European Constitutional Law Review* 673.

——, 'The Court of Justice as an Inter-State Court' (2017) 36 *Yearbook of European Law* 179.

——, 'EU Foreign Policy and Other EU External Relations in Times of Crisis: Forcing the Law to Overlap?' in Elżbieta Kużelewska, Amy Weatherburn and Dariusz Kloza (eds), *Irregular Migration as a Challenge for Democracy* (Cambridge, Intersentia, 2018).

——, 'Implementing a Complete System of Legal Remedies in EU Foreign Affairs Law' (2018) 24 *Columbia Journal of European Law* 637.

——, 'In Search of the Political Question Doctrine in EU Law' (2018) 45 *Legal Issues of Economic Integration* 329.

——, 'Pre-Ratification Judicial Review of International Agreements to Be Concluded by the European Union' in Mattias Derlén and Johan Lindholm (eds), *The Court of Justice of the European Union: Multidisciplinary Perspectives* (Oxford, Hart Publishing, 2018).

——, 'The EU Flexibility Clause Is Dead, Long Live the EU Flexibility Clause' in Antonina Bakardjieva Engelbrekt and Xavier Groussot (eds), *The Future of Europe: Political and Legal Integration Beyond Brexit* (Oxford, Hart Publishing 2019).

Butler G and Barrett G, 'Europe's "Other" Open-Border Zone: The Common Travel Area under the Shadow of Brexit' (2018) 20 *Cambridge Yearbook of European Legal Studies* 252.

Butler G and Ratcovich M, 'Operation Sophia in Uncharted Waters: European and International Law Challenges for the EU Naval Mission in the Mediterranean Sea' (2016) 85 *Nordic Journal of International Law* 235.
Butler G, Jensen MD and Snaith H, '"Slow Change May Pull Us Apart": Debating a British Exit from the European Union' (2016) 23 *Journal of European Public Policy* 1278.
Cañamares ME, '"Building Coherent EU Responses": Coherence as a Structural Principle in EU External Relations' in Marise Cremona (ed), *Structural Principles in EU External Relations Law* (Oxford, Hart Publishing 2018).
Cannizzaro E, 'The Scope of EU Foreign Power. Is the EC Competent to Conclude Agreements with Third States Including Human Rights Clauses?' in Enzo Cannizzaro (ed), *The European Union as an Actor in International Relations* (The Hague, Kluwer Law International 2002).
——, 'Unity and Pluralism in the EU's Foreign Relations Power' in Catherine Barnard (ed), *The Fundamentals of EU Law Revisited: Assessing the Impact of the Constitutional Debate*, vol XVI/2 (Oxford University Press, 2007).
Cappelletti M, *The Judicial Process in Comparative Perspective* (Oxford, Clarendon Press, 1989).
Cardwell PJ, 'On "Ring-Fencing" the Common Foreign and Security Policy in the Legal Order of the European Union' (2013) 64 *Northern Ireland Legal Quarterly* 443.
——, 'The Legalisation of European Union Foreign Policy and the Use of Sanctions' (2015) 17 *Cambridge Yearbook of European Legal Studies* 287.
——, 'The United Kingdom and the Common Foreign and Security Policy of the EU: From Pre-Brexit "Awkward Partner" to Post-Brexit "Future Partnership"?' (2017) 13 *Croatian Yearbook of European Law* and Policy 1.
Cassese A, 'Preface' in Antonio Cassese (ed), *Parliamentary Control Over Foreign Policy: Legal Essays* (Alphen aan den Rijn, Sijtoff and Noordhoff, 1980).
Castillo de la Torre F, 'The Court of Justice and External Competences After Lisbon: Some Reflections on the Latest Case Law' in Piet Eeckhout and Manuel López-Escudero (eds), *The European Union's External Action in Times of Crisis* (Oxford, Hart Publishing, 2016).
Chalmers D, 'Post-Nationalism and the Quest for Constitutional Substitutes' (2000) 27 *Journal of Law and Society* 178.
——, 'The Politics of European Reason and New Reasons for European Politics: The European Union Fundamental Rights Agency' in Andrea Ott and Ellen Vos (eds), *Fifty Years of European Integration: Foundations and Perspectives* (The Hague, TMC Asser Press, 2009).
——, 'The Democratic Ambiguity of EU Law Making and Its Enemies' in Anthony Arnull and Damian Chalmers (eds), *The Oxford Handbook of European Union Law* (Oxford University Press, 2015).
Chalmers D and Tomkins A, *European Union Public Law: Text and Materials* (Cambridge University Press, 2007).
Chalmers D, Davies G and Monti G, *European Union Law: Text and Materials* 3rd edition (Cambridge University Press 2014).
Christiansen T, 'The European Union after the Lisbon Treaty: An Elusive "Institutional Balance"?' in Andrea Biondi, Piet Eeckhout and Stefanie Ripley (eds), *EU Law after Lisbon* (Oxford University Press, 2012).
Cini M, 'EU Decision-Making on Inter-Institutional Agreements: Defining (Common) Rules of Conduct for European Lobbyists and Public Servants' (2013) 36 *West European Politics* 1143.
Claes M and De Witte B, 'Competences: Codification and Contestation' in Adam Łazowski and Steven Blockmans (eds), *Research Handbook on EU Institutional Law* (Cheltenham, Edward Elgar, 2016).
Cohen JC, 'The European Preliminary Reference and U.S. Supreme Court Review of State Court Judgments: A Study in Comparative Judicial Federalism' (1996) 44 *American Journal of Comparative Law* 421.
Collins L, 'Foreign Relations and the Judiciary' (2002) 51 *International and Comparative Law Quarterly* 485.
Collinson DS, 'Foreign Relations Powers of the European Communities: A Comment on Commission v. Council' (1971) 23 *Stanford Law Review* 956.

Conway G, *The Limits of Legal Reasoning and the European Court of Justice* (Cambridge University Press, 2012).

Corbett R, 'The Evolving Roles of the European Parliament and of National Parliaments' in Andrea Biondi, Piet Eeckhout and Stefanie Ripley (eds), *EU Law after Lisbon* (Oxford University Press, 2012).

Corbett R, Jacobs F and Shackleton M, 'The European Parliament at Fifty: A View from the Inside' (2003) 41 *Journal of Common Market Studies* 353.

Corthaut T, 'An Effective Remedy for All? Paradoxes and Controversies in Respect of Judicial Protection in the Field of the CFSP under the European Constitution' (2005) 12 *Tilburg Foreign Law Review* 110.

——, 'Case C-166/07, European Parliament v. Council of the European Union, Judgment of the Court of Justice (Grand Chamber) of 3 September 2009' (2011) 48 *Common Market Law Review* 1271.

Craig P, 'Democracy and Rule-Making Within the EC: An Empirical and Normative Assessment' (1997) 3 *European Law Journal* 105.

——, 'Formal and Substantive Conceptions of the Rule of Law: An Analytical Framework' [1997] *Public Law* 467.

——, 'The Jurisdiction of the Community Courts Reconsidered' in Gráinne De Búrca and Joseph HH Weiler (eds), *The European Court of Justice* (Oxford University Press, 2001).

——, 'Competence: Clarity, Containment and Consideration' in Ingolf Pernice and Miguel Poiares Maduro (eds), *A Constitution for the European Union: First Comments on the 2003 Draft of the European Convention* (Baden-Baden, Nomos, 2004).

——, 'The Role of the European Parliament under the Lisbon Treaty' in Stefan Griller and Jacques Ziller (eds), *The Lisbon Treaty: EU Constitutionalism without a Constitutional Treaty?*, vol 11 (Vienna, Springer, 2008).

——, 'Institutions, Power, and Institutional Balance' in Paul Craig and Gráinne De Búrca (eds), *The Evolution of EU Law* 2nd edition, (Oxford University Press, 2011).

——, *The Lisbon Treaty: Law, Politics, and Treaty Reform* (Oxford University Press, 2011).

——, *EU Administrative Law* 2nd edition, (Oxford University Press, 2012).

——, 'Accountability' in Anthony Arnull and Damian Chalmers (eds), *The Oxford Handbook of European Union Law* (Oxford University Press, 2015).

——, 'Engagement and Disengagement with International Institutions: The UK Perspective' in Curtis A Bradley (ed), *Oxford Handbook of Comparative Foreign Relations Law* (Oxford University Press, 2019).

——, 'The EU, Democracy and Institutional Structure: Past, Present and Future' in Antonina Bakardjieva Engelbrekt and Xavier Groussot (eds), *The Future of Europe: Political and Legal Integration Beyond Brexit* (Oxford, Hart Publishing 2019).

Craig P and De Búrca G, *EC Law: Text, Cases and Materials* (Oxford, Clarendon Press, 1995).

Cramér P, 'Does the Codification of the Principle of Supremacy Matter?' in John Bell and Claire Kilpatrick (eds), *Cambridge Yearbook of European Legal Studies 2004–2005: Volume 7* (Oxford, Hart Publishing 2006).

Cremona M, 'The Doctrine of Exclusivity and the Position of Mixed Agreements in the External Relations of the European Community' (1982) 2 *Oxford Journal of Legal Studies* 393.

——, 'The Common Foreign and Security Policy of the European Union and the External Relations Powers of the European Community' in David O'Keeffe and Patrick M Twomey (eds), *Legal Issues of the Maastricht Treaty* (Chichester, Chancery, 1994).

——, 'The Draft Constitutional Treaty: External Relations and External Action' (2003) 40 *Common Market Law Review* 1347.

——, 'The Union as a Global Actor: Roles, Models and Identity' (2004) 41 *Common Market Law Review* 553.

——, 'The Union's External Action: Constitutional Perspectives' in Giuliano Amato, Hervé Bribosia and Bruno De Witte (eds), *Genesis and Destiny of the European Constitution: Commentary on the Treaty establishing a Constitution for Europe in the light of the travaux préparatoires and future prospects* (Brussels, Bruylant, 2007).

——, 'Case C-403/05, European Parliament v. Commission (Philippines Border Management Project), Judgment of the Grand Chamber of 23 October 2007, [2007] ECR I–9045' (2008) 45 *Common Market Law Review* 1727.

——, 'Coherence through Law: What Difference Will the Treaty of Lisbon Make?' (2008) 3 *Hamburg Review of Social Sciences* 11.

——, 'Defining Competence in EU External Relations: Lessons from the Treaty Reform Process' in Alan Dashwood and Marc Maresceau (eds), *Law and Practice of EU External Relations: Salient Features of a Changing Landscape* (Cambridge University Press, 2008).

——, 'Balancing Union and Member State Interests: Opinion 1/2008, Choice of Legal Base and the Common Commercial Policy under the Treaty of Lisbon' (2010) 35 *European Law Review* 678.

——, 'The EU and Global Emergencies: Competence and Instruments' in Antonis Antoniadis, Robert Schütze and Eleanor Spaventa (eds), *The European Union and Global Emergencies: A Law and Policy Analysis* (Oxford, Hart Publishing, 2011).

——, 'Values in EU Foreign Policy' in Malcolm Evans and Panos Koutrakos (eds), *Beyond the Established Legal Orders: Policy Interconnections between the EU and the Rest of the World* (Oxford, Hart Publishing, 2011).

——, 'The Two (or Three) Treaty Solution: The New Treaty Structure of the EU' in Andrea Biondi, Piet Eeckhout and Stefanie Ripley (eds), *EU Law after Lisbon* (Oxford University Press, 2012).

——, 'A Reticent Court? Policy Objectives and the Court of Justice' in Marise Cremona and Anne Thies (eds), *The European Court of Justice and External Relations Law: Constitutional Challenges* (Oxford, Hart Publishing 2014).

——, 'EU External Relations and the Law' in Dennis Patterson and Anna Södersten (eds), *A Companion to European Union Law and International Law* (Chichester, John Wiley & Sons, 2016).

——, '"Effective Judicial Review Is of the Essence of the Rule of Law": Challenging Common Foreign and Security Policy Measures Before the Court of Justice' (2017) 2 *European Papers* 671.

——, 'External Competences and the Principle of Conferral' in Robert Schütze and Takis Tridimas (eds), *Oxford Principles of European Union Law, vol 1: The European Union Legal Order* (Oxford University Press, 2018).

——, 'Structural Principles and their Role in EU External Relations Law' in Marise Cremona (ed), *Structural Principles in EU External Relations Law* (Oxford, Hart Publishing, 2018).

——, 'The Position of CFSP/CSDP in the EU's Constitutional Architecture' in Steven Blockmans and Panos Koutrakos (eds), *Research Handbook on the EU's Common Foreign and Security Policy* (Cheltenham, Edward Elgar, 2018).

Cross MKD, 'Secrecy and the Making of CFSP' (2018) 41 *West European Politics* 914.

Crum B, 'Parliamentarization of the CFSP through Informal Institution-Making? The Fifth European Parliament and the EU High Representative' (2006) 13 *Journal of European Public Policy* 383.

Crum B and Curtin D, 'The Challenge of Making European Union Executive Power Accountable' in Simona Piattoni (ed), *The European Union: Democratic Principles and Institutional Architectures in Times of Crisis* (Oxford University Press, 2015).

Cruz Vilaça JL da, *EU Law and Integration: Twenty Years of Judicial Application of EU Law* (Oxford, Hart Publishing, 2014).

Cullen H and Charlesworth A, 'Diplomacy by Other Means: The Use of Legal Basis Litigation as a Political Strategy by the European Parliament and Member States' (1999) 36 *Common Market Law Review* 1243.

Curtin D, 'The Constitutional Structure of the Union: A Europe of Bits and Pieces' (1993) 30 *Common Market Law Review* 17.

——, *Postnational Democracy: The European Union in Search of a Political Philosophy* (The Hague, Kluwer Law International 1997).

——, *Executive Power of the European Union: Law, Practices, and the Living Constitution* (Oxford University Press, 2009).

——, 'The Sedimentary European Constitution – The Future of "Constitutionalisation" without a Constitution' in Ingolf Pernice and Evgeni Tanchev (eds), *Ceci n'est pas une Constitution – Constitutionalisation without a Constitution?*, Vol 7 (Baden-Baden, Nomos, 2009).

——, 'Official Secrets and the Negotiation of International Agreements: Is the EU Executive Unbound?' (2013) 50 *Common Market Law Review* 423.
——, 'Challenging Executive Dominance in European Democracy' (2014) 77 *Modern Law Review* 1.
——, 'Overseeing Secrets in the EU: A Democratic Perspective' (2014) 52 *Journal of Common Market Studies* 684.
——, 'Democratic Accountability of EU Executive Power: A Reform Agenda for Parliaments' in Federico Fabbrini, Ernst Hirsch Ballin and Han Somsen (eds), *What Form of Government for the European Union and the Eurozone?* (Oxford, Hart Publishing, 2015).
——, 'Legal Acts and the Challenges of Democratic Accountability' in Marise Cremona and Claire Kilpatrick (eds), *EU Legal Acts: Challenges and Transformations* (Oxford University Press, 2018).
Curtin D and Dekker I, 'The European Union from Maastricht to Lisbon: Institutional and Legal Unity Out of the Shadow' in Paul Craig and Gráinne De Búrca (eds), *The Evolution of EU Law* (Oxford University Press, 2011).
Curtin D and Meijers H, 'The Principle of Open Government in Schengen and the European Union: Democratic Retrogression?' (1995) 32 *Common Market Law Review* 391.
Curtin D and Mendes J, 'Article 42 – Right of Access to Documents' in Steve Peers and others (eds), *The EU Charter of Fundamental Rights: A Commentary* (Oxford, Hart Publishing, 2014).
Curtin D, Mair P and Papadopoulos Y, 'Positioning Accountability in European Governance: An Introduction' (2010) 33 *West European Politics* 929.
Czuczai J, 'Mixity in Practice: Some Problems and Their (Real or Possible) Solution' in Christophe Hillion and Panos Koutrakos (eds), *Mixed Agreements Revisited: The EU and its Member States in the World* (Oxford, Hart Publishing, 2010).
Dankert P, 'What Parliament for Europe?' in Tom Heukels, Niels Blokker and Marcel Brus (eds), *The European Union after Amsterdam: A Legal Analysis* (The Hague, Kluwer Law International 1998).
Dann P, 'The Political Institutions' in Armin Von Bogdandy and Jürgen Bast (eds), *Principles of European Constitutional Law* 2nd edition, (Oxford, Hart Publishing, 2009).
Dashwood A, 'Editorial: April 1985: The Dooge Committee and Majority Voting on the Council' (1985) 10 *European Law Review* 85.
——, 'Democracy, Accountability and Transparency (Position Paper)' in Alan Dashwood (ed), *Reviewing Maastricht: Issues for the 1996 IGC* (London, Sweet and Maxwell, 1996).
——, 'EC External Relations and the CFSP (Position Paper)' in Alan Dashwood (ed), *Reviewing Maastricht: Issues for the 1996 IGC* (London, Sweet and Maxwell, 1996).
——, 'The Limits of European Community Powers' (1996) 21 *European Law Review* 113.
——, 'External Relations Provisions of the Amsterdam Treaty' (1998) 35 *Common Market Law Review* 1019.
——, 'External Relations Provisions of the Amsterdam Treaty' in David O'Keeffe and Patrick M Twomey (eds), *Legal Issues of the Amsterdam Treaty* (Oxford, Hart Publishing, 1999).
——, 'Opinion 2/00, Cartagena Protocol on Biosafety, 6 December 2001, Not yet Reported' (2002) 39 *Common Market Law Review* 353.
——, 'The Relationship between the Member States and the European Union/European Community' (2004) 41 *Common Market Law Review* 355.
——, 'Article 47 TEU and the Relationship between First and Second Pillar Competences' in Alan Dashwood and Marc Maresceau (eds), *Law and Practice of EU External Relations: Salient Features of a Changing Landscape* (Cambridge University Press, 2008).
——, 'The Law and Practice of CFSP Joint Actions' in Marise Cremona and Bruno De Witte (eds), *EU Foreign Relations Law: Constitutional Fundamentals* (Oxford, Hart Publishing, 2008).
——, 'Article 308 EC as the Outer Limit of Expressly Conferred Community Competence' in Catherine Barnard and Okeoghene Odudu (eds), *The Outer Limits of European Union Law* (Oxford, Hart Publishing, 2009).
——, 'What Can Be Salvaged If the Treaty of Lisbon Is Lost?' in Mielle Bulterman and others (eds), *Views of European Law from the Mountain: Liber Amicorum Piet Jan Slot* (Alphen aan den Rijn, Kluwer Law International, 2009).

——, 'Mixity in the Era of the Treaty of Lisbon' in Christophe Hillion and Panos Koutrakos (eds), *Mixed Agreements Revisited: The EU and its Member States in the World* (Oxford, Hart Publishing, 2010).
——, 'Conflicts of Competence in Responding to Global Emergencies' in Antonis Antoniadis, Robert Schütze and Eleanor Spaventa (eds), *The European Union and Global Emergencies: A Law and Policy Analysis* (Oxford, Hart Publishing, 2011).
——, 'The Continuing Bipolarity of EU External Action' in Inge Govaere and others (eds), *The European Union in the World: Essays in Honour of Marc Maresceau* (Leiden, Martinus Nijhoff Publishers, 2014).
——, 'After the Deluge' (2016) 41 *European Law Review* 469.
——, *Wyatt and Dashwood's European Union Law* 6th edition, (Oxford, Hart Publishing, 2011).
Davies G, 'The European Union Legislature as an Agent of the European Court of Justice' (2016) 54 *Journal of Common Market Studies* 846.
——, 'Does the Court of Justice Own the Treaties? Interpretative Pluralism as a Solution to over-Constitutionalisation' (2018) 24 *European Law Journal* 358.
Dawson M, 'The Legal and Political Accountability Structure of "Post-Crisis" EU Economic Governance' (2015) 53 *Journal of Common Market Studies* 976.
——, 'New Modes of Governance' in Dennis Patterson and Anna Södersten (eds), *A Companion to European Union Law and International Law* (Chichester, John Wiley & Sons, 2016).
De Baere G, *Constitutional Principles of EU External Relations* (Oxford University Press, 2008).
——, 'The Basics of EU External Relations Law: An Overview of the Post-Lisbon Constitutional Framework for Developing the External Dimensions of EU Asylum and Migration Policy' in Marleen Maes, Marie-Claire Foblets and Philippe De Bruycker (eds), *External Dimensions of European Migration and Asylum Law and Policy/Dimensions Externes du Droit et de la Politque d'Immigration et d'Asile de l'UE* (Brussels, Bruylant, 2011).
——, 'European Integration and the Rule of Law in Foreign Policy' in Julie Dickson and Pavlos Eleftheriadis (eds), *Philosophical Foundations of European Union Law* (Oxford University Press, 2012).
——, 'From "Don't Mention the Titanium Dioxide Judgment" to "I Mentioned It Once, But I Think I Got Away with It All Right": Reflections on the Choice of Legal Basis in EU External Relations after the Legal Basis for Restrictive Measures Judgment' in Catherine Barnard and others (eds), *Cambridge Yearbook of European Legal Studies 2012–2013: Volume 15* (Oxford, Hart Publishing, 2013).
——, 'EU External Action' in Catherine Barnard and Steve Peers (eds), *European Union Law* 2nd edition (Oxford University Press, 2017).
——, 'Subsidiarity as a Structural Principle Governing the Use of EU External Competences' in Marise Cremona (ed), *Structural Principles in EU External Relations Law* (Oxford, Hart Publishing, 2018).
De Baere G and Gutman K, 'Federalism and International Relations in the European Union and the United States: A Comparative Outlook' in Elke Cloots, Geert De Baere and Stefan Sottiaux (eds), *Federalism in the European Union* (Oxford, Hart Publishing, 2012).
De Baere G and Koutrakos P, 'The Interactions between the Legislature and the Judiciary in EU External Relations' in Philip Syrpis (ed), *The Judiciary, the Legislature and the EU Internal Market* (Cambridge University Press, 2012).
De Baere G and Van den Sanden T, 'Interinstitutional Gravity and Pirates of the Parliament on Stranger Tides: The Continued Constitutional Significance of the Choice of Legal Basis in Post-Lisbon External Action' (2016) 12 *European Constitutional Law Review* 85.
De Baere G and Wessel RA, 'EU Law and the EEAS: Of Complex Competences and Constitutional Consequences' in David Spence and Jozef Bátora (eds), *The European External Action Service: European Diplomacy Post-Westphalia* (Basingstoke, Palgrave Macmillan, 2015).
De Búrca G, 'The Principle of Subsidiarity and the Court of Justice as an Institutional Actor' (1998) 36 *Journal of Common Market Studies* 217.
——, 'The Constitutional Challenge of New Governance in the European Union' (2003) 28 *European Law Review* 814.

——, 'EU External Relations: The Governance Mode of Foreign Policy' in Bart Van Vooren, Steven Blockmans and Jan Wouters (eds), *The EU's Role in Global Governance: The Legal Dimension* (Oxford University Press, 2013).

——, 'International Law Before the Courts: The EU and the US Compared' (2015) 55 *Virginia Journal of International Law* 685.

De Búrca G and De Witte B, 'The Delimitation of Powers between the EU and Its Member States' in Anthony Arnull and Daniel Wincott (eds), *Accountability and Legitimacy in the European Union* (Oxford University Press, 2003).

De Waele H, *Layered Global Player: Legal Dynamics of EU External Relations* (Berlin, Springer, 2011).

——, *Legal Dynamics of EU External Relations: Dissecting a Layered Global Player* 2nd edition, (Berlin, Springer, 2017).

De Witte B, 'Chameleonic Member States: Differentiation by Means of Partial and Parallel International Agreements' in Bruno De Witte, Dominik Hanf and Ellen Vos (eds), *The Many Faces of Differentiation in EU Law* (Antwerp, Intersentia, 2001).

——, 'The Closest Thing to a Constitutional Conversation in Europe: The Semi-Permanent Treaty Revision Process' in Paul Beaumont, Carole Lyons and Neil Walker (eds), *Convergence and Divergence in European Public Law* (Oxford, Hart Publishing, 2002).

——, 'The Constitutional Law of External Relations' in Ingolf Pernice and Miguel Poiares Maduro (eds), *A Constitution for the European Union: First Comments on the 2003 Draft of the European Convention* (Baden-Baden, Nomos, 2004).

——, 'Legal Instruments and Law-Making in the Lisbon Treaty' in Stefan Griller and Jacques Ziller (eds), *The Lisbon Treaty: EU Constitutionalism without a Constitutional Treaty?*, vol 11 (Vienna, Springer, 2008).

——, 'Too Much Constitutional Law in the European Union's Foreign Relations?' in Marise Cremona and Bruno De Witte (eds), *EU Foreign Relations Law: Constitutional Fundamentals* (Oxford, Hart Publishing, 2008).

——, 'European Law as an Academic Discipline: Unity and Fragmentation' in Mielle Bulterman and others (eds), *Views of European Law from the Mountain: Liber Amicorum Piet Jan Slot* (Alphen aan den Rijn, Kluwer Law International, 2009).

——, 'Direct Effect, Primacy, and the Nature of the Legal Order' in Paul Craig and Gráinne De Búrca (eds), *The Evolution of EU Law* 2nd edition (Oxford University Press, 2011).

——, 'The European Union as an International Legal Experiment' in Gráinne De Búrca and Joseph HH Weiler (eds), *The Worlds of European Constitutionalism* (Cambridge University Press, 2011).

——, 'The Elusive Unity of the EU Legal Order after Maastricht' in Maartje De Visser and Anne Pieter Van Der Mei (eds), *The Treaty on European Union 1993–2013: Reflections from Maastricht* (Cambridge, Intersentia, 2013).

——, 'Near-Membership, Partial Membership and the EU Constitution' (2016) 14 *European Law Review* 471.

——, 'The Decision-Making Process' in Dennis Patterson and Anna Södersten (eds), *A Companion to European Union Law and International Law* (Chichester, John Wiley & Sons, 2016).

Dehousse R and Weiler JHH, 'The Legal Dimension' in William Wallace (ed), *The Dynamics of European Integration* (London, Pinter, 1990).

——, 'EPC and the Single Act: From Soft Law to Hard Law?' in Martin Holland (ed), *The Future of European Political Cooperation: Essays on Theory and Practice* (New York, St Martin's Press, 1991).

Delcourt C, 'The Acquis Communautaire: Has the Concept Had Its Day?' (2001) 38 *Common Market Law Review* 829.

Delgado Casteleiro A, *The International Responsibility of the European Union: From Competence to Normative Control* (Cambridge University Press, 2016).

Delgado Casteleiro A and Larik J, 'The Duty to Remain Silent: Limitless Loyalty in EU External Relations?' (2011) 36 *European Law Review* 524.

Demedts V and Chamon M, 'The Commission Back on the Leash: No Autonomy to Sign Non-Binding Agreements on Behalf of the EU: Council v. Commission' (2017) 54 *Common Market Law Review* 245.
Denza E, 'Groping towards Europe's Foreign Policy' in Deirdre Curtin and Tom Heukels (eds), *Institutional Dynamics of European Integration: Essays in Honour of Henry G. Schermers, Volume II* (Dordrecht, Martinus Nijhoff Publishers, 1994).
——, *The Intergovernmental Pillars of the European Union* (Oxford University Press, 2002).
——, 'Lines in the Sand: Between Common Foreign Policy and Single Foreign Policy' in Takis Tridimas and Paolisa Nebbia (eds), *European Union Law for the Twenty-First Century: Rethinking the New Legal Order – Volume 1: Constitutional and Public Law, External Relations* (Oxford, Hart Publishing, 2004).
——, 'Forging Links between Legal Orders' (2016) 35 *Yearbook of European Law* 589.
Devuyst Y, 'The European Union's Constitutional Order? Between Community Method and Ad Hoc Compromise' (2000) 18 *Berkeley Journal of International Law* 1.
——, 'The European Union's Institutional Balance after the Treaty of Lisbon: Community Method and Democratic Deficit Reassessed' (2008) 39 *Georgetown Journal of International Law* 247.
Diedrichs U and Tekin F, 'CFSP after the Constitutional Treaty: The Stakes for the Future' in Sergio Carrera and Thierry Balzacq (eds), *Security Versus Freedom? A Challenge for Europe's Future* (London, Routledge, 2006).
Dijkstra H and Van Elsuwege P, 'Representing the EU in the Area of CFSP: Legal and Political Dunamics' in Steven Blockmans and Panos Koutrakos (eds), *Research Handbook on the EU's Common Foreign and Security Policy* (Cheltenham, Edward Elgar, 2018).
Dougan M, 'The Convention's Draft Constitutional Treaty: Bringing Europe Closer to Its Lawyers?' (2003) 28 *European Law Review* 763.
——, *National Remedies Before the Court of Justice: Issues of Harmonisation and Differentiation* (Oxford, Hart Publishing, 2004).
——, 'The Vicissitudes of Life at the Coalface: Remedies and Procedures for Enforcing Union Law before the National Courts' in Paul Craig and Gráinne De Búrca (eds), *The Evolution of EU Law* (Oxford University Press, 2011).
——, 'What Are We to Make of the Citizens' Initiative?' (2011) 48 *Common Market Law Review* 1807.
——, 'Judicial Activism or Constitutional Interaction? Policymaking by the ECJ in the Field of Union Citizenship' in Hans-Wolfgang Micklitz and Bruno De Witte (eds), *The European Court of Justice and the Autonomy of the Member States* (Cambridge, Intersentia, 2012).
Doyle O, *The Constitution of Ireland: A Contextual Analysis* (Oxford, Hart Publishing, 2018).
Drieskens E, 'What's in a Name? Challenges to the Creation of EU Delegations' (2012) 7 *The Hague Journal of Diplomacy* 51.
Due O, 'Legal Remedies for the Failure of European Community Institutions to Act in Conformity with EEC Treaty Provisions' (1990) 14 *Fordham International Law Journal* 341.
——, 'A Constitutional Court for the European Communities' in Deirdre Curtin and David O'Keeffe (eds), *Constitutional Adjudication in European Community and National Law: Essays for the Hon Mr Justice T F. O'Higgins* (Dublin, Butterworths, 1992).
——, 'The Judicial System of the European Union in the Perspective of the 1996 Intergovernmental Conference' in Göran Melander (ed), *Modern Issues in European Law: Nordic Perspectives: Essays in Honour of Lennart Pålsson* (Dordrecht, Kluwer Law International 1997).
——, 'Report by the Working Party on the Future of the European Communities' Court System (the 'Due Report')' (Brussels, European Commission, 2000).
Duff A (ed), *The Treaty of Amsterdam: Text and Commentary* (London, Federal Trust, 1997).
Duke S, 'Consistency, Coherence and European Union External Action: The Path to Lisbon and Beyond' in Panos Koutrakos (ed), *European Foreign Policy: Legal and Political Perspectives* (Cheltenham, Edward Elgar, 2011).

Duke S and Vanhoonacker S, 'Administrative Governance in the CFSP: Development and Practice' (2006) 11 *European Foreign Affairs Review* 163.
Duquet S and others, 'Upholding the Rule of Law in Informal International Lawmaking Processes' (2014) 6 *Hague Journal on the Rule of Law* 75.
Dyrberg P, 'Current Issues in the Debate on Public Access to Documents' (1999) 24 *European Law Review* 157.
——, 'Accountability and Legitimacy: What Is the Contribution of Transparency?' in Anthony Arnull and Daniel Wincott (eds), *Accountability and Legitimacy in the European Union* (Oxford University Press, 2002).
Eaton MR, 'Common Foreign and Security Policy' in David O'Keeffe and Patrick M Twomey (eds), *Legal Issues of the Maastricht Treaty* (London, Chancery, 1994).
Eckes C, 'How Not Being Sanctioned by a Community Instrument Infringes a Person's Fundamental Rights: The Case of Segi' (2006) 17 *King's Law Journal* 144.
——, 'Case T-228/02, Organisation Des Modjahedines Du Peuple d'Iran v. Council and UK (OMPI)' (2007) 44 *Common Market Law Review* 1117.
——, 'Sanctions against Individuals: Fighting Terrorism within the European Legal Order' (2008) 4 *European Constitutional Law Review* 205.
——, *EU Counter-Terrorist Policies and Fundamental Rights: The Case of Individual Sanctions* (Oxford University Press, 2009).
——, 'European Union Legal Methods – Moving Away from Integration' in Ulla Neergaard and Ruth Nielsen (eds), *European Legal Method – Towards A New European Legal Realism?* (Copenhagen, Djøf Publishing, 2013).
——, 'EU Restrictive Measures against Natural and Legal Persons: From Counterterrorist to Third Country Sanctions' (2014) 51 *Common Market Law Review* 869.
——, 'How the European Parliament's Participation in International Relations Affects the Deep Tissue of the EU's Power Structures' (2014) 12 *International Journal of Constitutional Law* 904.
——, 'The CFSP and Other EU Policies: A Difference in Nature?' (2015) 20 *European Foreign Affairs Review* 535.
——, 'Common Foreign and Security Policy: The Consequences of the Court's Extended Jurisdiction' (2016) 22 *European Law Journal* 492.
——, *EU Powers Under External Pressure: How the EU's External Actions Alter Its Internal Structures* (Oxford University Press, 2019).
'Editorial: A Stronger Common Foreign and Security Policy for a Self-Reliant Union?' (2018) 55 *Common Market Law Review* 1675.
'Editorial: The CFSP under the EU Constitutional Treaty? Issues of Depillarisation' (2005) 42 *Common Market Law Review* 325.
'Editorial: The Treaty of Amsterdam: Neither a Bang Nor a Whimper' (1997) 34 *Common Market Law Review* 767.
Edward DAO, 'Is Art L of the Maastricht Treaty Workable?' in Georg Ress, Jürgen Schwarze and Torsten Stein (eds), *Die Organe der Europäischen Union im Spannungsfeld zwischen Gemeinschaft und Zusammenarbeit* (Baden Baden, Nomos, 1995).
Edward DAO and Lane R, *Edward and Lane on European Union Law* (Cheltenham, Edward Elgar, 2013).
Edwards DJ, 'Fearing Federalism's Failure: Subsidiarity in the European Union' (1996) 44 *American Journal of Comparative Law* 537.
Eeckhout P, *External Relations of the European Union: Legal and Constitutional Foundations* 1st edition (Oxford University Press, 2004).
——, *Does Europe's Constitution Stop at the Water's Edge? Law and Policy in the EU's External Relations* (Amsterdam, Europa Law Publishing, 2005).
——, 'A Panorama of Two Decades of EU External Relations Law' in Anthony Arnull, Piet Eeckhout and Takis Tridimas (eds), *Continuity and Change in EU Law: Essays in Honour of Sir Francis Jacobs* (Oxford University Press, 2008).

——, 'Bold Constitutionalism and Beyond' in Miguel Poiares Maduro and Loïc Azoulai (eds), *The Past and Future of EU Law: The Classics of EU Law Revisited on the 50th Anniversary of the Rome Treaty* (Oxford, Hart Publishing, 2010).

——, *EU External Relations Law* 2nd edition (Oxford University Press, 2011).

——, 'The EU's Common Foreign and Security Policy after Lisbon: From Pillar Talk to Constitutionalism' in Andrea Biondi, Piet Eeckhout and Stefanie Ripley (eds), *EU Law after Lisbon* (Oxford University Press, 2012).

——, 'Opinion 2/13 on EU Accession to the ECHR and Judicial Dialogue: Autonomy or Autarky?' (2015) 38 *Fordham International Law Journal* 955.

Eiselt I and Slominski P, 'Sub-Constitutional Engineering: Negotiation, Content, and Legal Value of Interinstitutional Agreements in the EU' (2006) 12 *European Law Journal* 209.

Emiliou N, 'Protecting Parliamentary Prerogatives' (1993) 18 *European Law Review* 56.

——, 'Opening Pandora's Box: The Legal Basis of Community Measures before the Court of Justice' (1994) 19 *European Law Review* 488.

Engel A, 'Delimiting Competences in the EU: CFSP versus AFSJ Legal Bases' (2015) 21 *European Public Law* 47.

Eriksen EO, *The Unfinished Democratization of Europe* (Oxford University Press, 2009).

Erkelens LH, *Institutional and Legal Aspects of EU's Judicial Policy to Fighting Piracy off the Coast of Somalia* (The Hague, TMC Asser Institute, 2014).

Fabbrini F, 'On Banks, Courts and International Law: The Intergovernmental Agreement on the Single Resolution Fund in Context' (2014) 21 *Maastricht Journal of European and Comparative Law* 444.

——, 'Austerity, the European Council, and the Institutional Future of the European Union: A Proposal to Strengthen the Presidency of the European Council' (2015) 22 *Indiana Journal of Global Legal Studies* 29.

——, 'The Relation Between the European Council and the Council: Institutional Arguments in Favour of an EU Senate' (2016) 22 *European Public Law* 485.

Fahey E, 'Challenging EU-US PNR and SWIFT Law before the Court of Justice of the European Union' in Patryk Pawlak (ed), *The EU–US Security and Justice Agenda in Action* (Paris, European Union Institute for Security Studies, 2011).

Feld W, *The Court of the European Communities: New Dimension in International Adjudication* (The Hague, Martinus Nijhoff Publishers, 1964).

Fennelly D, 'Crotty's Long Shadow: The European Union, the United Nations and the Changing Framework of Ireland's International Relations' in Eoin Carolan (ed), *The Constitution of Ireland: Perspectives and Prospects* (Dublin, Bloomsbury Professional, 2012).

Fennelly N, 'Reflections of an Irish Advocate General' (1996) 5 *Irish Journal of European Law* 5.

——, 'Legal Interpretation at the European Court of Justice' (1997) 20 *Fordham International Law Journal* 656.

——, 'Jurisdiction of the Court of Justice Following the Entry into Force of the Treaty of Amsterdam' [1999] European Parliament: Liberty, Security, Justice: An Agenda for Europe, Working Document, Civil Liberties Series, LIBE 106 EN 19.

——, 'The Area of "Freedom, Security and Justice" and the European Court of Justice – a Personal View' (2000) 49 *International and Comparative Law Quarterly* 1.

Fenno Jr. RF, *The Power of the Purse: Appropriations Politics in Congress* (Boston, Little, Brown and Company, 1966).

Fink-Hooijer F, 'The Common Foreign and Security Policy of the European Union' (1994) 5 *European Journal of International Law* 173.

Fletcher M, 'Extending "Indirect Effect" to the Third Pillar: The Significance of Pupino?' (2005) 30 *European Law Review* 862.

Foighel I and Gulmann C, 'Parliamentary Foreign Affairs Committees in Denmark' in Antonio Cassese (ed), *Parliamentary Foreign Affairs Committees: The National Setting*, vol 1 (Padova, Cedam/Oceana 1982).

Forman J, 'Case 16/88, Commission, Supported by Parliament v. Council, Judgment of 24 October 1989' (1990) 27 *Common Market Law Review* 872.
Forrester IS, 'L'Europe des Juges. Recent Criticism of ECHR and ECJ Judgments, the American Debate on Judicial Activism versus Judicial Restraint' in Carl Baudenbacher and Erhard Busek (eds), *The Role of International Courts* (Stuttgart, German Law Publishers, 2008).
Franck TM, *Political Questions Judicial Answers: Does the Rule of Law Apply to Foreign Affairs?* (Princeton University Press, 1992).
Friedmann W, *The Changing Structure of International Law* (New York, Columbia University Press, 1964).
Friis L, 'Breaking the Waves: The European Union's Enlargement Negotiations with EFTA and Central and Eastern Europe' in Ole Elgström and Christer Jönsson (eds), *European Union Negotiations: Processes, Networks and Institutions* (Abingdon, Routledge, 2005).
Fromage D, 'The European Parliament in the Post-Crisis Era: An Institution Empowered on Paper Only?' (2018) 40 *Journal of European Integration* 281.
Fursdon E, *The European Defence Community: A History* (London, Macmillan, 1980).
Gaja G, 'European Parliament and Foreign Affairs: (1) Political Cooperation among the Nine' in Antonio Cassese (ed), *Parliamentary Control Over Foreign Policy: Legal Essays* (Alphen aan den Rijn, Sijtoff and Noordhoff, 1980).
Gatti M, 'Diplomats at the Bar: The European External Action Service before EU Courts' (2014) 39 *European Law Review* 664.
——, *European External Action Service: Promoting Coherence through Autonomy and Coordination* (Leiden, Brill, 2016).
——, 'Conflict of Legal Bases and the Internal-External Security Nexus: AFSJ versus CFSP' in Eleftheria Neframi and Mauro Gatti (eds), *Constitutional Issues of EU External Relations Law* (Baden-Baden, Nomos 2018).
Gauci D, 'The European Parliament and EU External Aid: Measures of Response to Emergency Situations' in Antonis Antoniadis, Robert Schütze and Eleanor Spaventa (eds), *The European Union and Global Emergencies: A Law and Policy Analysis* (Oxford, Hart Publishing, 2011).
Gazzini T and Herlin-Karnell E, 'Restrictive Measures Adopted by the EU from the Standpoint of International and EU Law' (2011) 36 *European Law Review* 798.
Gestel R van and Micklitz H-W, 'Why Methods Matter in European Legal Scholarship' (2014) 20 *European Law Journal* 292.
Gianniti L and Lupo N, 'The Role of the European Parliament President in Parliamentary Diplomacy' (2016) 11 *The Hague Journal of Diplomacy* 144.
Ginsberg RH, 'The EU's CFSP: The Politics of Procedure' in Martin Holland (ed), *Common Foreign and Security Policy: The Record and Reforms* (London, Pinter, 1997).
——, 'Conceptualizing the European Union as an International Actor: Narrowing the Theoretical Capability-Expectations Gap' (1999) 37 *Journal of Common Market Studies* 429.
Glennon MJ, 'Foreign Affairs and the Political Question Doctrine' (1989) 83 *American Journal of International Law* 814.
Godmer L and Marrell G, 'The Creation of Institutional Expertise at the European Parliament: Legal and Political Resources of the Members of the Constitutional Affairs Committee' in Antoine Vauchez and Bruno De Witte (eds), *Lawyering Europe: European Law as a Transnational Social Field* (Oxford, Hart Publishing, 2013).
Goodhart M, 'Accountable International Relations' in Mark Bovens, Robert E Goodin and Thomas Schillemans (eds), *The Oxford Handbook of Public Accountability* (Oxford University Press, 2014).
Gormley LW, 'Reflections on the Architecture of the European Union after the Treaty of Amsterdam' in David O'Keeffe and Patrick M Twomey (eds), *Legal Issues of the Amsterdam Treaty* (Oxford, Hart Publishing, 1999).
——, 'Judicial Review – a New Dawn after Lisbon?' in Henning Koch and others (eds), *Europe. The New Legal Realism: Essays in Honour of Hjalte Rasmussen* (Copenhagen, Djøf Publishing, 2010).

Gosalbo-Bono R, 'The International Powers of the European Parliament, the Democratic Deficit and the Treaty on European Union' (1992) 12 *Yearbook of European Law* 85.
——, 'Co-Decision: An Appraisal of the Experience of the European Parliament as Co-Legislator' (1994) 14 *Yearbook of European Law* 21.
——, 'Some Reflections on the CFSP Legal Order' (2006) 43 *Common Market Law Review* 337.
——, 'The Significance of the Rule of Law and Its Implications for the European Union and the United States' (2010) 72 *University of Pittsburgh Law Review* 229.
Gosalbo-Bono R and Boelaert S, 'The European Union's Comprehensive Approach to Combating Piracy at Sea: Legal Aspects' in Panos Koutrakos and Achilles Skordas (eds), *The Law and Practice of Piracy at Sea: European and International Perspectives* (Oxford, Hart Publishing, 2014).
Gosalbo-Bono R and Naert F, 'The Reluctant (Lisbon) Treaty and Its Implementation in the Practice of the Council' in Piet Eeckhout and Manuel López-Escudero (eds), *The European Union's External Action in Times of Crisis* (Oxford, Hart Publishing, 2016).
Govaere I, 'The External Relations of the EU. Legal Aspects' in Dieter Mahncke, Alicia Ambos and Christopher Reynolds (eds), *European Foreign Policy: From Rhetoric to Reality?* (Brussels, PIE-Peter Lang, 2004).
——, 'EU Common Commercial Policy Throwing Off the Shackles of "Mixity"' in Inge Govaere, Reinhard Quick and Marco Bronckers (eds), *Trade and Competition Law in the EU and Beyond* (Cheltenham, Edward Elgar, 2011).
——, 'Multi-Faceted Single Legal Personality and a Hidden Horizontal Pillar: EU External Relations Post-Lisbon' in Catherine Barnard and Okeoghene Odudu (eds), *Cambridge Yearbook of European Legal Studies 2010–2011: Volume 13* (Oxford, Hart Publishing, 2011).
——, '"Setting the International Scene": EU External Competence and Procedures Post-Lisbon Revisited in the Light of ECJ Opinion 1/13' (2015) 52 *Common Market Law Review* 1277.
——, 'To Give or To Grab: The Principle of Full, Crippled and Split Conferral of Powers Post-Lisbon' in Marise Cremona (ed), *Structural Principles in EU External Relations Law* (Oxford, Hart Publishing, 2018).
——, 'Interconnecting Legal Systems and the Autonomous EU Legal Order: A Balloon Dynamic' in Inge Govaere and Sacha Garben (eds), *The Interface Between EU and International Law: Contemporary Reflections* (Oxford, Hart Publishing, 2019).
Granger M-PF, 'The Court of Justice's Dilemma: Between "More Europe" and "Constitutional Mediation"' in Christopher J Bickerton, Dermot Hodson and Uwe Puetter (eds), *The New Intergovernmentalism: States and Supranational Actors in the Post-Maastricht Era* (Oxford University Press, 2015).
Grevi G, 'The Institutional Framework of External Action' in Giuliano Amato, Hervé Bribosia and Bruno De Witte (eds), *Genesis and Destiny of the European Constitution: Commentary on the Treaty establishing a Constitution for Europe in the light of the travaux préparatoires and future prospects* (Brussels, Bruylant, 2007).
Griffiths RT, 'Europe's First Constitution: The European Political Community, 1952–1954' in Stephen Martin (ed), *The Construction of Europe: Essays in Honour of Emile Noel* (Dordrecht, Kluwer Academic Publishers 1994).
Griller S, 'External Relations' in Bruno De Witte (ed), *Ten Reflections on the Constitutional Treaty for Europe* (Fiesole, European University Institute, 2003).
——, 'The Court of Justice and the Common Foreign and Security Policy' in Allan Rosas, Egils Levits and Yves Bot (eds), *The Court of Justice and the Construction of Europe: Analyses and Perspectives on Sixty Years of Case-law – La Cour de Justice et la Construction de l'Europe: Analyses et Perspectives de Soixante Ans de Jurisprudence* (The Hague, TMC Asser Press, 2013).
Groussot X and Bogojevic S, 'Subsidiarity as a Procedural Safeguard of Federalism' in Loïc Azoulai (ed), *The Question of Competence in the European Union* (Oxford University Press, 2014).
Gulmann C, 'Methods of Interpretation of the European Court of Justice' (1980) 24 *Scandinavian Studies in Law* 187.
Gutman K, 'The Evolution of the Action for Damages against the European Union and Its Place in the System of Judicial Protection' (2011) 48 *Common Market Law Review* 695.

——, *The Constitutional Foundations of European Contract Law: A Comparative Analysis* (Oxford University Press, 2014).

——, 'Liability for Breach of EU Law by the Union, Member States and Individuals: Damages, Enforcement and Effective Judicial Protection' in Adam Łazowski and Steven Blockmans (eds), *Research Handbook on EU Institutional Law* (Cheltenham, Edward Elgar, 2016).

Haas EB, *The Unity of Europe: Political, Social and Economic Forces 1950–1957* (London, Stevens and Sons, 1958).

Habermas J, 'The Crisis of the European Union in the Light of a Constitutionalization of International Law' (2012) 23 *European Journal of International Law* 335.

——, 'Democracy in Europe: Why the Development of the EU into a Transnational Democracy Is Necessary and How It Is Possible' (2015) 21 *European Law Journal* 546.

Hakenberg W, 'How to Square the Circle between Political Necessities and Constitutional Constraints? – An ECJ Perspective' in Thomas Giegerich, Oskar Josef Gstrein and Sebastian Zeitzmann (eds), *The EU between 'An Ever Closer Union' and Inalienable Policy Domains of Member States* (Baden-Baden, Nomos, 2014).

Halberstam D, '"It's the Autonomy, Stupid!" A Modest Defense of Opinion 2/13 on EU Accession to the ECHR, and the Way Forward' (2015) 16 *German Law Journal* 105.

Halleskov Storgaard L, 'EU Law Autonomy versus European Fundamental Rights Protection – On Opinion 2/13 on EU Accession to the ECHR' (2015) 15 *Human Rights Law Review* 485.

Hartley TC, 'Consulting the European Parliament' (1981) 6 *European Law Review* 181.

——, *Constitutional Problems of the European Union* (Oxford, Hart Publishing, 1999).

——, *European Union Law in a Global Context: Text, Cases and Materials* (Cambridge University Press, 2004).

——, 'The European Union and the Systematic Dismantling of the Common Law of Conflict of Laws' (2005) 54 *International and Comparative Law Quarterly* 813.

Hautala H, 'The Role of Parliaments in the EU Constitutional Framework: A Partnership or Rivalry?' in Deirdre Curtin, Alfred E Kellermann and Steven Blockmans (eds), *The EU Constitution: The Best Way Forward?* (The Hague, TMC Asser Press, 2005).

Hay P, *Federalism and Supranational Organizations: Patterns or New Legal Structures* (Urbana, University of Illinois Press, 1966).

Heede K, 'Enhancing the Accountability of Community Institutions and Bodies: The Role of the European Ombudsman' (1997) 3 *European Public Law* 587.

Heim M, 'The European Central Bank: Was It Not Bound to Go to Luxembourg?' (1994) 19 *European Law Review* 48.

Heliskoski J, 'The Jurisdiction of the European Court of Justice to Give Preliminary Rulings on the Interpretation of Mixed Agreements' (2000) 69 *Nordic Journal of International Law* 395.

——, 'Small Arms and Light Weapons within the Union's Pillar Structure: An Analysis of Article 47 of the EU Treaty' (2008) 33 *European Law Review* 898.

——, 'Adoption of Positions under Mixed Agreements (Implementation)' in Christophe Hillion and Panos Koutrakos (eds), *Mixed Agreements Revisited: The EU and its Member States in the World* (Oxford, Hart Publishing, 2010).

Heliskoski J and Leino P, 'Darkness at the Break of Noon: The Case Law on Regulation No. 1049/2001 on Access to Documents' (2006) 43 *Common Market Law Review* 735.

Henkin L, *How Nations Behave: Law and Foreign Policy* (New York, Pall Mall Press, 1968).

——, *Foreign Affairs and the Constitution* (New York, Foundation Press, 1972).

——, *Constitutionalism, Democracy, and Foreign Affairs* (New York, Columbia University Press, 1990).

——, *Foreign Affairs and the United States Constitution* 2nd edition (Oxford, Clarendon Press, 1996).

Herlin-Karnell E, '"Light Weapons" and the Dynamics of Art 47 EU – The EC's Armoury of Ever-expanding Competences' (2008) 71 *Modern Law Review* 998.

Herrmann C, 'Gripping Global Governance: The External Relations of the EU Between the Treaty of Nice and the Convention on the Future of Europe' in Takis Tridimas and Paolisa Nebbia (eds), *European Union Law for the Twenty-First Century: Rethinking the New Legal Order – Volume 1: Constitutional and Public Law, External Relations* (Oxford, Hart Publishing, 2004).

Heukels T, 'Case C-65/93, European Parliament v. Council of the European Union, Judgment of 30 March 1995, (Full Court): Article 43 of the EEC Treaty – Obligation to Consult the Parliament' (1995) 32 *Common Market Law Review* 1407.
Hillion C, 'The Copenhagen Criteria and Their Progeny' in Christophe Hillion (ed), *EU Enlargement: A Legal Approach* (Oxford, Hart Publishing, 2004).
——, 'Widen to Deepen? The Potential and Limits of Accession Treaties to Achieve EU Constitutional Reform' in Steven Blockmans and Sacha Prechal (eds), *Reconciling the Deepening and Widening of the European Union* (The Hague, TMC Asser Press, 2007).
——, 'Tous Pour Un, Un Pour Tous! Coherence in the External Relations of the European Union' in Marise Cremona (ed), *Developments in EU External Relations Law* (Oxford University Press, 2008).
——, 'Mixity and the Coherence in EU External Relations: The Significance of the "Duty of Cooperation"' in Christophe Hillion and Panos Koutrakos (eds), *Mixed Agreements Revisited: The EU and its Member States in the World* (Oxford, Hart Publishing, 2010).
——, 'A Powerless Court? The European Court of Justice and the Common Foreign and Security Policy' in Marise Cremona and Anne Thies (eds), *The European Court of Justice and External Relations Law: Constitutional Challenges* (Oxford, Hart Publishing, 2014).
——, 'Fighting Terrorism through the Common Foreign and Security Policy' in Inge Govaere and Sara Poli (eds), *EU Management of Global Emergencies: Legal Framework for Combating Threats and Crises* (Leiden, Brill, 2014).
——, 'Decentralised Integration? Fundamental Rights Protection in the EU Common Foreign and Security Policy' (2016) 1 *European Papers* 55.
——, 'Overseeing the Rule of Law in the EU: Legal Mandate and Means' in Carlos Closa and Dimitry Kochenov (eds), *Reinforcing Rule of Law Oversight in the European Union* (Cambridge University Press, 2016).
——, 'The Protection of Fundamental Rights in the EU Common Foreign and Security Policy – "A Half Measure"?' (2016) 19 *Europarättslig Tidskrift* 45.
——, 'Conferral, Cooperation and Balance in the Institutional Framework of EU External Action' in Marise Cremona (ed), *Structural Principles in EU External Relations Law* (Oxford, Hart Publishing, 2018).
Hillion C and Koutrakos P (eds), *Mixed Agreements Revisited: The EU and Its Member States in the World* (Oxford, Hart Publishing, 2010).
Hillion C and Wessel RA, 'Restraining External Competences of EU Member States under CFSP' in Marise Cremona and Bruno De Witte (eds), *EU Foreign Relations Law: Constitutional Fundamentals* (Oxford, Hart Publishing, 2008).
——, 'Competence Distribution in EU External Relations after Ecowas: Clarification or Continued Fuzziness?' (2009) 46 *Common Market Law Review* 551.
——, '"The Good, the Bad and the Ugly": Three Levels of Judicial Control over the CFSP' in Steven Blockmans and Panos Koutrakos (eds), *Research Handbook on the EU's Common Foreign and Security Policy* (Cheltenham, Edward Elgar, 2018).
Hinarejos A, 'Judicial Control of CFSP in the Constitutional Treaty: A Cherry Worth Picking?' (2006) 25 *Yearbook of European Law* 363.
——, *Judicial Control in the European Union: Reforming Jurisdiction in the Intergovernmental Pillars* (Oxford University Press, 2009).
——, 'The Lisbon Treaty Versus Standing Still: A View from the Third Pillar' (2009) 5 *European Constitutional Law Review* 99.
Hix S, 'Constitutional Agenda-Setting Through Discretion in Rule Interpretation: Why the European Parliament Won at Amsterdam' (2002) 32 *British Journal of Political Science* 259.
——, 'Neither a Preference-Outlier nor a Unitary Actor: Institutional Reform Preferences of the European Parliament' (2005) 3 *Comparative European Politics* 131.
Hix S and Høyland B, 'Empowerment of the European Parliament' (2013) 16 *Annual Review of Political Science* 171.
Hix S, Raunio T and Scully R, 'Fifty Years on: Research on the European Parliament' (2003) 41 *Journal of Common Market Studies* 191.

HM Government, 'Review of the Balance of Competences between the United Kingdom and the European Union: Foreign Policy' (London, The Stationery Office, 2013).

Hoffmeister F, 'Curse or Blessing? Mixed Agreements in the Recent Practice of the European Union and Its Member States' in Christophe Hillion and Panos Koutrakos (eds), *Mixed Agreements Revisited: The EU and its Member States in the World* (Oxford, Hart Publishing, 2010).

Holdgaard R, 'Principles of Reception of International Law in Community Law' (2006) 25 *Yearbook of European Law* 263.

House of Commons Foreign Affairs Committee, 'Foreign Policy Aspects of the Lisbon Treaty' (House of Commons 2008) HC120-II, Third Report of Session 2007–08, Volume II.

Howe G, 'Towards a Common Foreign Policy' in Tom Heukels, Niels Blokker and Marcel Brus (eds), *The European Union after Amsterdam: A Legal Analysis* (The Hague, Kluwer Law International, 1998).

Howorth J, 'NATO and ESDP: Institutional Complexities and Political Realities' [2009] *Politique étrangère*, 95.

Huber K and Shackleton M, 'Codecision: A Practitioner's View from inside the Parliament' (2013) 20 *Journal of European Public Policy* 1040.

Huff A, 'Problems and Patterns in Parliamentary Scrutiny of the CFSP and CSDP' [2014] *Observatory of Parliaments after the Lisbon Treaty* 1.

——, 'Executive Privilege Reaffirmed? Parliamentary Scrutiny of the CFSP and CSDP' (2015) 38 *West European Politics* 396.

Hyde-Price A, 'Decision-Making under the Second Pillar' in Anthony Arnull and Daniel Wincott (eds), *Accountability and Legitimacy in the European Union* (Oxford University Press, 2002).

Hyett S, 'The Duty of Co-Operation: A Flexible Concept' in Alan Dashwood and Christophe Hillion (eds), *The General Law of EC External Relations* (London, Sweet and Maxwell, 2000).

Jacobs FG, 'Isoglucose Resurgent: Two Powers of the European Parliament Upheld by the Court' (1981) 18 *Common Market Law Review* 219.

——, 'Is the Court of Justice of the European Communities a Constitutional Court?' in Deirdre Curtin and David O'Keeffe (eds), *Constitutional Adjudication in European Community and National Law: Essays for the Hon Mr Justice T F O'Higgins* (Dublin, Butterworths, 1992).

——, *The Sovereignty of Law: The European Way* (Cambridge University Press, 2007).

Jacqué JP, 'The Principle of Institutional Balance' (2004) 41 *Common Market Law Review* 383.

——, 'Les Verts v The European Parliament' in Miguel Poiares Maduro and Loïc Azoulai (eds), *The Past and Future of EU Law: The Classics of EU Law Revisited on the 50th Anniversary of the Rome Treaty* (Oxford, Hart Publishing, 2010).

Jančić D, 'Globalizing Representative Democracy: The Emergence of Multilayered International Parliamentarism' (2015) 38 *Hastings International and Comparative Law Review* 197.

Joerges C, 'The Commission's White Paper on Governance in the EU – A Symptom of Crisis?' (2002) 39 *Common Market Law Review* 441.

Johansen SØ, 'Accountability Mechanisms for Human Rights Violations by CSDP Missions: Available and Sufficient?' (2017) 66 *International and Comparative Law Quarterly* 181.

Joliet R, 'Le remboursement des frais electoraux: un contentieux oublié' in Manuel Pérez González (ed), *Hacia un nuevo orden internacional y europeo: estudios en homenaje al profesor don Manuel Díez de Velasco* (Madrid, Tecnos, 1993).

Judge D and Earnshaw D, *The European Parliament* 2nd edition, (Basingstoke, Palgrave Macmillan, 2008).

'Judges as Diplomats in Advancing the Rule of Law: A Conversation with President Koen Lenaerts and Justice Stephen Breyer' (2017) 66 *American University Law Review* 1159.

Juncos AE and Reynolds C, 'The Political and Security Committee: Governing in the Shadow' (2007) 12 *European Foreign Affairs Review* 127.

Kapteyn PJG, 'The European Parliament, the Budget and Legislation in the Community' (1972) 9 *Common Market Law Review* 386.

Kapteyn PJG and VerLoren van Themaat P, *Introduction to the Law of the European Communities: After the Coming into Force of the Single European Act* (Laurence W Gormley (ed)) (Deventer, Kluwer Law and Taxation Publishers, 1989).

Kaunert C and Zwolski K, *The EU as a Global Security Actor: A Comprehensive Analysis Beyond CFSP and JHA* (Basingstoke, Palgrave Macmillan, 2013).

Keeling DT, 'In Praise of Judicial Activism. But What Does It Mean? And Has the European Court of Justice Ever Practiced It?' in Antonino Giuffrè (ed), *Scritti in onore di Giuseppe Federico Mancini: Volume 2* (Milan, Dott A Giuffrè Editore, 1998).

Keeling DT and Joliet R, 'The Reimbursement of Election Expenses: A Forgotten Dispute' (1994) 19 *European Law Review* 243.

Kelemen RD, 'The Court of Justice of the European Union in the Twenty-First Century' (2016) 79 *Law and Contemporary Problems* 117.

Kenneth J. Twitchett, 'External Relations or Foreign Policy?' in Kenneth J. Twitchett (ed), *Europe and the World: The External Relations of the Common Market* (New York, St Martin's Press, 1976).

Ketvel M-GG, 'The Jurisdiction of the European Court of Justice in Respect of the Common Foreign and Security Policy' (2006) 55 *International and Comparative Law Quarterly* 77.

Keukeleire S and Delruex T, *The Foreign Policy of the European Union* 2nd edition (Basingstoke, Palgrave Macmillan, 2014).

Kietz D and Maurer A, 'The European Parliament in Treaty Reform: Predefining IGCs through Interinstitutional Agreements' (2007) 13 *European Law Journal* 20.

Kiiver P, 'The Early-Warning System for the Principle of Subsidiarity: The National Parliament as a Conseil d'Etat for Europe' (2011) 36 *European Law Review* 98.

Kirchner E and Williams K, 'The Legal, Political and Institutional Implications of the Isoglucose Judgments 1980' (1983) 22 *Journal of Common Market Studies* 173.

Klamert M, 'Conflicts of Legal Basis: No Legality and No Basis but a Bright Future under the Lisbon Treaty?' (2010) 35 *European Law Review* 497.

Klein N and Wessels W, 'CFSP Progress or Decline after Lisbon?' (2013) 18 *European Foreign Affairs Review* 449.

Kleizen B, 'Mapping the Involvement of the European Parliament in EU External Relations – a Legal and Empirical Analysis', *Centre for the Law of EU External Relations* (The Hague, TMC Asser Institute, 2016).

Kokott J and Kaspar M, 'Ensuring Constitutional Efficacy' in Michael Rosenfeld and András Sajó (eds), *The Oxford Handbook of Comparative Constitutional Law* (Oxford University Press, 2012).

Kokott J and Rüth A, 'The European Convention and Its Draft Treaty Establishing a Constitution for Europe: Appropriate Answers to the Laeken Questions?' (2003) 40 *Common Market Law Review* 1315.

Komárek J, '"In the Court(s) We Trust?" On the Need for Hierarchy and Differentiation in the Preliminary Ruling Procedure' (2007) 32 *European Law Review* 467.

Konstadinides T, 'EU Foreign Policy under the Doctrine of Implied Powers: Codification Drawbacks and Constitutional Limitations' (2014) 39 *European Law Review* 511.

——, 'Book Review of Panos Koutrakos, The EU Common Security and Defence Policy' (2015) 21 *European Public Law* 395.

——, 'In the Union of Wine: Loose Ends in the Relationship between the European Union and the Member States in the Field of External Representation – Case C-399/12 Germany v. Council, Judgment of the Court of Justice of 7 October 2014' (2015) 21 *European Public Law* 679.

——, *The Rule of Law in the European Union: The Internal Dimension* (Oxford, Hart Publishing, 2017).

Koopmans T, *Courts and Political Institutions: A Comparative View* (Cambridge University Press, 2003).

Koskenniemi M, 'International Law Aspects of the Common Foreign and Security Policy' in Martti Koskenniemi (ed), *International Law Aspects of the European Union* (The Hague, Martinus Nijhoff Publishers, 1998).

Kostarakos M, 'The Role of the European Union Military Committee in EU External Relations' (2018) 23 *European Foreign Affairs Review* 435.

Koutrakos P, *Trade, Foreign Policy and Defence in EU Constitutional Law: The Legal Regulation of Sanctions, Exports of Dual-Use Goods and Armaments* (Oxford, Hart Publishing, 2001).

——, 'The Elusive Question for Uniformity in EC External Relations' in Alan Dashwood and others (eds), *Cambridge Yearbook of European Legal Studies 2001: Volume 4* (Oxford, Hart Publishing, 2002).

——, 'Constitutional Idiosyncrasies and Political Realities: The Emerging Security and Defense Policy of the European Union' (2003) 10 *Columbia Journal of European Law* 69.

——, *EU International Relations Law* (Oxford, Hart Publishing, 2006).

——, 'Security and Defence Policy within the Context of EU External Relations: Issues of Coherence, Consistency, and Effectiveness' in Martin Trybus and Nigel White (eds), *European Security Law* (Oxford University Press, 2007).

——, 'Legal Basis and Delimitation of Competence in EU External Relations' in Marise Cremona and Bruno De Witte (eds), *EU Foreign Relations Law: Constitutional Fundamentals* (Oxford, Hart Publishing, 2008).

——, 'Primary Law and Policy in EU External Relations: Moving Away from the Big Picture' (2008) 33 *European Law Review* 666.

——, 'The Application of EC Law to Defence Industries – Changing Interpretations of Article 296 EC' in Catherine Barnard and Okeoghene Odudu (eds), *The Outer Limits of European Union Law* (Oxford, Hart Publishing, 2009).

——, 'Current Developments: European Union External Relations' (2010) 59 *International and Comparative Law Quarterly* 481.

——, 'International Agreements in the Area of the EU's Common Security and Defence Policy' in Enzo Cannizzaro, Paolo Palchetti and Ramses A Wessel (eds), *International Law as Law of the European Union* (Leiden, Martinus Nijhoff Publishers, 2012).

——, *The EU Common Security and Defence Policy* (Oxford University Press, 2013).

——, 'Inter-Institutional Disputes and Treaty-Making' (2014) 39 *European Law Review* 599.

——, 'External Action: Common Commercial Policy, Common Foreign and Defence Policy, Common Security and Defence Policy' in Anthony Arnull and Damian Chalmers (eds), *The Oxford Handbook of European Union Law* (Oxford University Press, 2015).

——, 'Public Security Exceptions and EU Free Movement Law' in Panos Koutrakos, Niamh Nic Shuibhne and Philip Syrpis (eds), *Exceptions from EU Free Movement Law: Derogation, Justification and Proportionality* (Oxford, Hart Publishing, 2016).

——, 'Foreign Policy between Opt-Outs and Closer Cooperation' in Andrea Ott, Bruno De Witte and Ellen Vos (eds), *Between Flexibility and Disintegration: The Trajectory of Differentiation in EU Law* (Cheltenham, Edward Elgar, 2017).

——, 'The European Union´s Common Foreign and Security Policy after the Treaty of Lisbon' (Stockholm, Swedish Institute for European Policy Studies (SIEPS), 2017) 2017:3.

——, 'Judicial Review in the EU's Common Foreign and Security Policy' (2018) 67 *International and Comparative Law Quarterly* 1.

——, 'The Decision-Making Process' in Robert Schütze and Takis Tridimas (eds), *Oxford Principles of European Union Law, vol 1: The European Union Legal Order* (Oxford University Press, 2018).

——, 'The Nexus between CFSP/CSDP and the Area of Freedom, Security and Justice' in Steven Blockmans and Panos Koutrakos (eds), *Research Handbook on the EU's Common Foreign and Security Policy* (Cheltenham, Edward Elgar, 2018).

——, 'Institutional Balance and Sincere Cooperation in Treaty-Making under EU Law' (2019) 68 *International and Comparative Law Quarterly* 1.

Krajewski M, 'Foreign Policy and the European Constitution' (2003) 22 *Yearbook of European Law* 435.

Kreppel A, 'Moving Beyond Procedure An Empirical Analysis of European Parliament Legislative Influence' (2002) 35 *Comparative Political Studies* 784.

Krunke H, 'Development in National Parliaments' Involvement in Ordinary Foreign Policy and European Policy – Denmark' (2007) 13 *European Public Law* 335.

——, 'European Law as a Process between Constitutionalization and Democratization' in Hanne Petersen and others (eds), *Paradoxes of European Legal Integration* (Aldershot, Ashgate Publishing 2008).

——, 'Courts as Protectors of the People: Constitutional Identity, Popular Legitimacy and Human Rights' in Martin Scheinin, Helle Krunke and Marina Aksenova (eds), *Judges as Guardians of Constitutionalism and Human Rights* (Cheltenham, Edward Elgar, 2016).

Kuijper PJ, 'The Case Law of the Court of Justice of the EU and the Allocation of External Relations Powers: Whither the Traditional Role of the Executive in EU Foreign Relations?' in Marise Cremona and Anne Thies (eds), *The European Court of Justice and External Relations Law: Constitutional Challenges* (Oxford, Hart Publishing, 2014).

——, 'Litigation on External Relations Powers after Lisbon: The Member States Reject Their Own Treaty' (2016) 43 *Legal Issues of Economic Integration* 1.

——, 'An Introduction to Union External Action, Its Scope, Its Institutions and Its Instruments' in Pieter Jan Kuijper and others (eds), *The Law of the European Union* (Alphen aan den Rijn, Kluwer Law International, 2018).

——, 'Recent Tendencies in the Separation of Powers in EU Foreign Relations: An Essay' in Eleftheria Neframi and Mauro Gatti (eds), *Constitutional Issues of EU External Relations Law* (Baden-Baden, Nomos, 2018).

——, 'The Common Foreign and Security Policy and the Common Security and Defence Policy' in Pieter Jan Kuijper and others (eds), *The Law of the European Union* (Alphen aan den Rijn, Kluwer Law International 2018).

——, *The Law of EU External Relations: Cases, Materials, and Commentary on the EU as an International Legal Actor* (Oxford University Press, 2013).

——, *The Law of EU External Relations: Cases, Materials, and Commentary on the EU as an International Legal Actor* 2nd edition (Oxford University Press, 2015).

Kuisma M, 'Jurisdiction, Rule of Law, and Unity of EU Law in Rosneft' (2018) 37 *Yearbook of European Law* 3.

Kumm M, 'Who Is the Final Arbiter of Constitutionality in Europe?: Three Conceptions of the Relationship Between the German Federal Constitutional Court and the European Court of Justice' (1999) 36 *Common Market Law Review* 351.

Kutscher H, 'Methods of Interpretation as Seen by a Judge at the Court of Justice', *Judicial and Academic Conference 27–28 September 1976* (Luxembourg, Court of Justice of the European Communities, 1976).

Kuyper PJ and Wellens K, 'Deployment of Cruise Missiles in Europe: The Legal Battles in the Netherlands, the Federal Republic of Germany and Belgium' (1987) 18 *Netherlands Yearbook of International Law* 145.

Lacchi C, 'Multilevel Judicial Protection in the EU and Preliminary References' (2016) 53 *Common Market Law Review* 679.

Lalone N, 'Accountability in the EU's Common Foreign and Security Policy: Lessons from the Common Commercial Policy' in Esther Barbé and Anna Herranz (eds), *The Role of Parliaments in European Foreign Policy: Debating on Accountability and Legitimacy* (Barcelona, Office of the European Parliament 2005).

Lane R, 'New Community Competences under the Maastricht Treaty' (1993) 30 *Common Market Law Review* 939.

Larik J, 'From Speciality to a Constitutional Sense of Purpose: On the Changing Role of the Objectives of the European Union' (2014) 63 *International and Comparative Law Quarterly* 935.

——, *Foreign Policy Objectives in European Constitutional Law* (Oxford University Press, 2016).

——, 'EU Foreign Relations Law as a Field of Scholarship' (2017) 111 *American Journal of International Law* 321.

Lavenex S and Wallace W, 'Justice and Home Affairs: Towards a European Public Order?' in Helen Wallace, William Wallace and Marc Pollack (eds), *Policy-Making in the European Union* (Oxford University Press, 2005).

Lavranos N, *Jurisdictional Competition: Selected Cases in International and European Law* (Groningen, Europa Law Publishing, 2009).

Łazowski A, 'Advocates General and Grand Chamber Cases: Assistance with the Touch of Substitution' (2012) 14 *Cambridge Yearbook of European Legal Studies* 635.
Leino P, 'Case C-353/99 P, Council v. Heidi Hautala, Judgment of the Full Court of 6 December 2001, Nyr, Appeal Against the Judgment of the Court of First Instance of 19 July 1999 in Case T-14/98, Hautala v. Council, [1999] II-2489' (2002) 39 *Common Market Law Review* 621.
——, 'The Principle of Transparency in EU External Relations Law: Does Diplomatic Secrecy Stand a Chance of Surviving the Age of Twitter?' in Marise Cremona (ed), *Structural Principles in EU External Relations Law* (Oxford, Hart Publishing, 2018).
Lenaerts K, 'Constitutionalism and the Many Faces of Federalism' (1990) 38 *American Journal of Comparative Law* 205.
——, 'Some Reflections on the Separation of Powers in the European Community' (1991) 28 *Common Market Law Review* 11.
——, 'Some Thoughts about the Interaction between Judges and Politicians' (1992) *University of Chicago Legal Forum* 93.
——, 'Some Thoughts About the Interaction Between Judges and Politicians in the European Community' (1992) 12 *Yearbook of European Law* 1.
——, 'The Rule of Law and the Coherence of the Judicial System of the European Union' (2007) 44 *Common Market Law Review* 1625.
——, 'The Basic Constitutional Charter of a Community Based on the Rule of Law' in Miguel Poiares Maduro and Loïc Azoulai (eds), *The Past and Future of EU Law: The Classics of EU Law Revisited on the 50th Anniversary of the Rome Treaty* (Oxford, Hart Publishing, 2010).
——, 'EU Federalism in 3-D' in Elke Cloots, Geert De Baere and Stefan Sottiaux (eds), *Federalism in the European Union* (Oxford, Hart Publishing, 2012).
——, 'The Principle of Democracy in the Case Law of the European Court of Justice' (2013) 62 *International and Comparative Law Quarterly* 271.
——, 'Direct Applicability and Direct Effect of International Law in the EU Legal Order' in Inge Govaere and others (eds), *The European Union in the World: Essays in Honour of Marc Maresceau* (Leiden, Martinus Nijhoff Publishers, 2014).
Lenaerts K and Corthaut T, 'Of Birds and Hedges: The Role of Primacy in Invoking Norms of EU Law' (2006) 31 *European Law Review* 287.
Lenaerts K and De Smijter E, 'The Charter and the Role of the European Courts' (2001) 8 *Maastricht Journal of European and Comparative Law* 90.
Lenaerts K and Gerard D, 'The Structure of the Union According to the Constitution for Europe: The Emperor Is Getting Dressed' (2004) 29 *European Law Review* 289.
Lenaerts K and Gutiérrez-Fons JA, 'The Constitutional Allocation of Powers and General Principles of EU Law' (2010) 47 *Common Market Law Review* 1629.
——, 'The Place of the Charter in the EU Constitutional Edifice' in Steve Peers and others (eds), *The EU Charter of Fundamental Rights: A Commentary* (Oxford, Hart Publishing, 2014).
——, 'To Say What the Law of the EU Is: Methods of Interpretation and the European Court of Justice' (2014) 20 *Columbia Journal of European Law* 3.
Lenaerts K, Maselis I and Gutman K, *EU Procedural Law* (Janek Tomasz Nowak ed) 3rd edition, (Oxford University Press, 2014).
Lenaerts K and Van Nuffel P, *Constitutional Law of the European Union* (Robert Bray ed) (London, Sweet and Maxwell 1999).
——, *European Union Law* Robert Bray and Nathan Cambien (eds) 3rd edition (London, Sweet and Maxwell 2011).
Lenaerts K and Verhoeven A, 'Institutional Balance as a Guarantee for Democracy in EU Governance' in Christian Joerges and Renaud Dehousse (eds), *Good Governance in Europe's Integrated Market* (Oxford University Press, 2002).
Leopold PM, 'External Relations Power of EEC in Theory and in Practice' (1977) 26 *International and Comparative Law Quarterly* 54.

——, 'Community Law-Making: Opinions of the European Parliament' (1982) 2 *Oxford Journal of Legal Studies* 454.

Lindseth PL, 'Democratic Legitimacy and the Administrative Character of Supranationalism: The Example of the European Community' (1999) 99 *Columbia Law Review* 628.

'L'Initiative européenne d'intervention (European Intervention Initiative (E2I))' (*French Ministère des Armées (Ministry of the Armed Forces)*, June 2018).

Lonardo L, 'The Political Question Doctrine as Applied to Common Foreign and Security Policy' (2017) 22 *European Foreign Affairs Review* 571.

——, 'Common Foreign and Security Policy and the EU's External Action Objectives: An Analysis of Article 21 of the Treaty on the European Union' (2018) 14 *European Constitutional Law Review* 584.

Long D, 'Multilateralism in the CFSP' in Martin Holland (ed), *Common Foreign and Security Policy: The Record and Reforms* (London, Pinter, 1997).

Longo F, Fasone C and Delputte S, 'The Diplomatic Role of the European Parliament's Standing Committees, Delegations and Assemblies: Insights from ACP–EU Inter-Parliamentary Cooperation' (2016) 11 *The Hague Journal of Diplomacy* 161.

Lord C, 'The Political Theory and Practice of Parliamentary Participation in the Common Security and Defence Policy' (2011) 18 *Journal of European Public Policy* 1133.

MacCormick N, 'The Maastricht-Urteil: Sovereignty Now' (1995) 1 *European Law Journal* 259.

Mackenzie Stuart A, 'Subsidiarity – A Busted Flush?' in Deirdre Curtin and David O'Keeffe (eds), *Constitutional Adjudication in European Community and National Law: Essays for the Hon. Mr. Justice T. F. O'Higgins* (Dublin, Butterworths, 1992).

MacLeod I, Hendry ID and Hyett S, *The External Relations of the European Communities: A Manual of Law and Practice* (Oxford, Clarendon Press, 1996).

Madison J, 'Federalist No. 51: The Structure of the Government Must Furnish the Proper Checks and Balances Between the Different Departments', *New York Packet* (1788).

Maduro MP, *We the Court: The European Court of Justice and the European Economic Constitution: A Critical Reading of Article 30 the EC Treaty* (Oxford, Hart Publishing, 1998).

——, 'Legal Travels and the Risk of Legal Jet-Lag: The Judicial and Constitutional Challenges of Legal Globalisation' in Mario Monti and others (eds), *Economic Law and Justice in Times of Globalisation – Wirtschaftsrecht und Justiz in Zeiten der Globalisierung: Festschrift for Carl Baudenbacher* (Baden-Baden, Nomos, 2007).

——, 'Interpreting European Law – On Why and How Law and Policy Meet at the European Court of Justice' in Henning Koch and others (eds), *Europe. The New Legal Realism: Essays in Honour of Hjalte Rasmussen* (Copenhagen, Djøf Publishing, 2010).

Maher I, 'Economic Governance: Hybridity, Accountability and Control' (2007) 13 *Columbia Journal of European Law* 679.

——, 'Competition Law Modernization: An Evolutionary Tale?' in Paul Craig and Gráinne De Búrca (eds), *The Evolution of EU Law* 2nd edition (Oxford University Press, 2011).

Majone G, 'Europe's "Democratic Deficit": The Question of Standards' (1998) 4 *European Law Journal* 5.

Mancini GF, 'The Making of a Constitution For Europe' (1989) 26 *Common Market Law Review* 595.

——, 'Europe: The Case for Statehood' (1998) 4 *European Law Journal* 29.

——, *Democracy and Constitutionalism in the European Union: Collected Essays* (Oxford, Hart Publishing, 2000).

Mancini GF and Keeling DT, 'From CILFIT to ERT: The Constitutional Challenge Facing the European Court' (1991) 11 *Yearbook of European Law* 1.

——, 'Democracy and the European Court of Justice' (1994) 57 *Modern Law Review* 175.

Marias EA, 'Solidarity as an Objective of the European Union and the European Community' (1994) 21 *Legal Issues of Economic Integration* 85.

Marquardt S, 'The Conclusion of International Agreements Under Article 24 of the Treaty on European Union' in Vincent Kronenberger (ed), *The European Union and the International Legal Order: Discord or Harmony?* (The Hague, TMC Asser Press, 2001).

——, 'The Institutional Framework, Legal Instruments and Decision-Making Procedures' in Steven Blockmans and Panos Koutrakos (eds), *Research Handbook on the EU's Common Foreign and Security Policy* (Cheltenham, Edward Elgar, 2018).
Martinsen DS, *An Ever More Powerful Court? The Political Constraints of Legal Integration in the European Union* (Oxford University Press, 2015).
Matera C and Wessel RA, 'Context or Content? A CFSP or AFSJ Legal Basis for EU International Agreements' (2014) *Revista de Derecho Comunitario Europeo* 1047.
Mathis JH, 'How Much Democracy Can Economic Integration Bear?' (2017) 44 *Legal Issues of Economic Integration* 1.
Maurer A, 'The Legislative Powers and Impact of the European Parliament' (2003) 41 *Journal of Common Market Studies* 227.
McCown M, 'The European Parliament before the Bench: ECJ Precedent and EP Litigation Strategies' (2003) 10 *Journal of European Public Policy* 974.
McDonagh B, 'The Intergovernmental Conference: How the Deal Was Done' in Giuliano Amato, Hervé Bribosia and Bruno De Witte (eds), *Genesis and Destiny of the European Constitution: Commentary on the Treaty Establishing a Constitution for Europe in the light of the travaux préparatoires and future prospects* (Brussels, Bruylant, 2007).
McDonnell A, 'Farewell and Thanks to Alan' in Anthony Arnull and others (eds), *A Constitutional Order of States? Essays in EU Law in Honour of Alan Dashwood* (Oxford, Hart Publishing, 2011).
McGoldrick D, *International Relations Law of the European Union* (Harlow, Longman, 1997).
McLachlan C, *Foreign Relations Law* (Cambridge University Press, 2014).
Meissner K, 'Democratizing EU External Relations: The European Parliament's Informal Role in SWIFT, ACTA, and TTIP' (2016) 21 *European Foreign Affairs Review* 269.
Mendez M, 'The Enforcement of EU Agreements: Bolstering the Effectiveness of Treaty Law?' (2010) 47 *Common Market Law Review* 1719.
Mengozzi P, 'The EC External Competencies: From the ERTA Case to the Opinion in the Lugano Convention' in Miguel Poiares Maduro and Loïc Azoulai (eds), *The Past and Future of EU Law: The Classics of EU Law Revisited on the 50th Anniversary of the Rome Treaty* (Oxford, Hart Publishing, 2010).
Mény Y, 'De la démocratie en Europe: Old Concepts and New Challenges' (2003) 41 *Journal of Common Market Studies* 1.
Merket H, 'The EU and the Security-Development Nexus: Bridging the Legal Divide' (2013) 18 *European Foreign Affairs Review* 83.
——, 'The EU, Human Security and the Insulation of the CFSP: Comparing Recent Policy and Judicial Tendencies', in Aaron Matta and Tamara Takács (eds) *Human Security as a Tool for Comprehensive Approach for Human Rights and Security Linkages in EU Foreign Policy* (The Hague, TMC Asser Institute, 2014).
Mertens de Wilmars J and Steenbergen J, 'The Court of Justice of the European Communities and Governance in an Economic Crisis' (1984) 82 *Michigan Law Review* 1377.
——, 'The Court of Justice of the European Communities and Governance in an Economic Crisis', *The Art of Governance: Festschrift zu Ehren von Eric Stein* (Baden-Baden, Nomos Verlagsgesellschaft mbH & Co KG, 1987).
Miettinen S, 'Criminal Competence and the Choice of Legal Basis: Space in the Margins?' (2015) 5 *European Criminal Law Review* 222.
——, 'Annulment in Action: How Does the Court of Justice of the European Union Explain Maintaining the Legal Effects of Annulled Instruments?' in Jarna Petman (ed), *Finnish Yearbook of International Law 2012–2013: Volume 23* (Oxford, Hart Publishing, 2016).
Mills A, 'Private International Law and EU External Relations: Think Local Act Global, or Think Global Act Local?' (2016) 65 *International and Comparative Law Quarterly* 541.
Monaco R, 'The Limits of the European Community Order' (1976) 1 *European Law Review* 269.
Monar J, 'Interinstitutional Agreements: The Phenomenon and Its New Dynamics after Maastricht' (1994) 31 *Common Market Law Review* 693.
——, 'The European Union's Foreign Affairs System after the Treaty of Amsterdam: A "Strengthened Capacity for External Action"?' (1997) 2 *European Foreign Affairs Review* 413.

——, 'The Financial Dimension of the CFSP' in Martin Holland (ed), *Common Foreign and Security Policy: The Record and Reforms* (London, Pinter, 1997).
——, 'The Rejection of the EU-US SWIFT Interim Agreement by the European Parliament: A Historic Vote and Its Implications' (2010) 15 *European Foreign Affairs Review* 143.
Murray JL, 'The Influence of the European Convention on Fundamental Rights on Community Law' (2010) 33 *Fordham International Law Journal* 1388.
Naert F, 'European Union Common Security and Defence Policy Operations' in André Nollkaemper and Ilias Plakokefalos (eds), *The Practice of Shared Responsibility in International Law* (Cambridge University Press, 2017).
Naômé C, *Appeals before the Court of Justice of the European Union* (Oxford University Press, 2018).
Neergaard U and Wind M, 'Studying the EU in Legal and Political Sciences Scholarship' in Ulla Neergaard and Ruth Nielsen (eds), *European Legal Method – in a Multi-Level EU Legal Order* (Copenhagen, Djøf Publishing, 2012).
Neframi E, 'The Duty of Loyalty: Rethinking Its Scope through Its Application in the Field of EU External Relations' (2010) 47 *Common Market Law Review* 323.
——, 'Vertical Division of Competences and the Objectives of the European Union's External Action' in Marise Cremona and Anne Thies (eds), *The European Court of Justice and External Relations Law: Constitutional Challenges* (Oxford, Hart Publishing, 2014).
Nergelius J, ''De-Legalize It' – On Current Tendencies in EC Constitutional Law' (2001) 21 *Yearbook of European Law* 443.
——, *The Constitutional Dilemma of the European Union* (Groningen, Europa Law Publishing 2009).
Neuwahl N, 'Foreign and Security Policy and the Implementation of the Requirement of "Consistency" under the Treaty on European Union' in David O'Keeffe and Patrick M Twomey (eds), *Legal Issues of the Maastricht Treaty* (Chichester, Chancery, 1994).
Northedge FS, 'British Foreign Policy in a Community Context' in Kenneth J Twitchett (ed), *Europe and the World: The External Relations of the Common Market* (New York, St Martin's Press, 1976).
Nuttall SJ, *European Political Co-Operation* (Oxford University Press, 1992).
——, 'The Foreign and Security Policy Provisions of the Maastricht Treaty: Their Potential for the Future' in Jörg Monar, Werner Ungerer and Wolfgang Wessels (eds), *The Maastricht Treaty on European Union: Legal Complexity and Political Dynamic* (Brussels, European Interuniversity Press, 1993).
——, *European Foreign Policy* (Oxford University Press, 2000).
Öberg U, 'EU Citizens' Right to Know: The Improbable Adoption of a European Freedom of Information Act' in Alan Dashwood and Angela Ward (eds), *Cambridge Yearbook of European Legal Studies 1999: Volume 2* (Oxford, Hart Publishing, 2000).
O'Keeffe D, 'From Maastricht to the 1996 Intergovernmental Conference: The Challenges Facing the Union' (1994) 21 *Legal Issues of Economic Integration* 135.
O'Keeffe D and Schermers HG (eds), *Mixed Agreements* (Deventer, Kluwer Law and Taxation Publishers, 1983).
O'Leary S, 'Accession by the European Community to the European Convention on Human Rights – The Opinion of the ECJ' [1996] 4 *European Human Rights Law Review* 362.
Ott A, 'Between Pillars and Policies: The Quest for Consistency in EU External Relations Law' in Maartje De Visser and Anne Pieter Van Der Mei (eds), *The Treaty on European Union 1993–2013: Reflections from Maastricht* (Cambridge, Intersentia, 2013).
——, 'The Legal Bases for International Agreements Post-Lisbon: Of Pirates and The Philippines' (2014) 21 *Maastricht Journal of European and Comparative Law* 739.
——, 'The European Parliament's Role in EU Treaty-Making' (2016) 23 *Maastricht Journal of European and Comparative Law* 1009.
Ott A and Van der Loo G, 'The Nexus between the CCP and the CFSP: Achieving Foreign Policy Goals through Trade Restrictions and Market Access' in Steven Blockmans and Panos Koutrakos (eds), *Research Handbook on the EU's Common Foreign and Security Policy* (Cheltenham, Edward Elgar, 2018).

Palchetti P, 'Judicial Review of the International Validity of UN Security Council Resolutions by the European Court of Justice' in Enzo Cannizzaro, Paolo Palchetti and Ramses A Wessel (eds), *International Law as Law of the European Union* (Leiden, Martinus Nijhoff Publishers, 2012).
Passos R, 'Mixed Agreements from the Perspective of the European Parliament' in Christophe Hillion and Panos Koutrakos (eds), *Mixed Agreements Revisited: The EU and its Member States in the World* (Oxford, Hart Publishing, 2010).
——, 'The External Powers of the European Parliament' in Piet Eeckhout and Manuel López-Escudero (eds), *The European Union's External Action in Times of Crisis* (Oxford, Hart Publishing, 2016).
Passos R and Gauci D, 'European Parliament and Development Cooperation: Shaping Legislation and the New Democratic Scrutiny Dialogue' in Sandra Bartelt and Philipp Dann (eds), *Entwicklungszusammenarbeit im Recht der Europäischen Union – The Law of EU Development Cooperation* (Baden-Baden, Nomos, 2008).
Passos R and Marquardt S, 'International Agreements – Competences, Procedures and Judicial Control' in Giuliano Amato, Hervé Bribosia and Bruno De Witte (eds), *Genesis and Destiny of the European Constitution: Commentary on the Treaty establishing a Constitution for Europe in the light of the travaux préparatoires and future prospects* (Brussels, Bruylant, 2007).
Pech L and Ward A, 'Article 47 – Right to an Effect Remedy and to a Fair Trial (Effective Judicial Remedies before the Court of Justice)' in Steve Peers and others (eds), *The EU Charter of Fundamental Rights: A Commentary* (Oxford, Hart Publishing, 2014).
Peers S, 'National Security and European Law' (1996) 16 *Yearbook of European Law* 363.
——, 'Common Foreign and Security Policy 1998' (1998) 18 *Yearbook of European Law* 659.
——, 'Who's Judging the Watchmen? The Judicial System of the "Area of Freedom Security and Justice"' (1998) 18 *Yearbook of European Law* 337.
——, 'The New Regulation on Access to Documents: A Critical Analysis' (2001) 21 *Yearbook of European Law* 385.
——, 'EU Immigration and Asylum Competence and Decision-Making in the Treaty of Lisbon' (2008) 10 *European Journal of Migration and Law* 219.
——, 'Finally "Fit for Purpose"? The Treaty of Lisbon and the End of the Third Pillar Legal Order' (2008) 27 *Yearbook of European Law* 47.
——, 'In a World of Their Own? Justice and Home Affairs Opt-Outs and the Treaty of Lisbon' in Catherine Barnard (ed), *Cambridge Yearbook of European Legal Studies 2007–2008: Volume 10* (Oxford, Hart Publishing, 2008).
——, 'The Future of EU Treaty Amendments' (2012) 31 *Yearbook of European Law* 17.
Pernice I, 'The Treaty of Lisbon: Multilevel Constitutionalism in Action' (2009) 15 *Columbia Journal of European Law* 349.
Pernice I and Thym D, 'A New Institutional Balance for European Foreign Policy?' (2002) 7 *European Foreign Affairs Review* 369.
Pescatore P, *The Law of Integration: Emergence of a New Phenomenon in International Relations, Based on the Experience of the European Communities* (Leiden, A W Sijthoff, 1974).
——, 'Reconnaissance et contrôle judiciaire des actes du Parlement européen' (1978) 14 *Revue trimestrielle de droit européen* 581.
——, 'Contribution to the Discussion' in Christiaan Timmermans and Edmond LM Völker (eds), *Division of Powers between the European Communities and their Member States in the Field of External Relations* (Deventer, Kluwer, 1981).
——, 'The Doctrine of "Direct Effect": An Infant Disease of Community Law' (1983) 8 *European Law Review* 155.
——, 'Some Critical Remarks on the "Single European Act"' (1987) 24 *Common Market Law Review* 9.
Peters A, 'The European Ombudsman and the European Constitution' (2005) 42 *Common Market Law Review* 697.
Petersmann E-U, 'The Moral Foundations of the European Union's Foreign Policy Constitution: Defining "European Identity" and "Community Interests" for the Benefit of EU Citizens' (1996) 51 *Aussenwirtschaft (Swiss Review of International Economic Relations)* 151.

Piekutowska A, 'Towards the Democratization of the EU? Strengthening Prerogatives of the European Parliament in the Case Law of the Court of Justice of the European Union' in Elzbieta Kuzelewska and others (eds), *European Judicial Systems as a Challenge for Democracy, vol 3* (Cambridge, Intersentia, 2015).
Pijpers A, Regelsberger E and Wessels W (eds), *European Political Cooperation in the 1980s: A Common Foreign Policy for Western Europe?* (Dordrecht, Martinus Nijhoff Publishers, 1988).
Piris J-C, *The Lisbon Treaty: A Legal and Political Analysis* (Cambridge University Press, 2010).
——, *The Future of Europe: Towards a Two-Speed EU?* (Cambridge University Press, 2012).
Polakiewicz J, 'Accession to the European Convention on Human Rights (ECHR) – An Insider's View Addressing One by One the CJEU's Objections in Opinion 2/13' (2016) 36 *Human Rights Law Journal* 10.
Poli S, 'The Common Foreign Security Policy after Rosneft: Still Imperfect but Gradually Subject to the Rule of Law' (2017) 54 *Common Market Law Review* 1799.
Powell HJ, *The President's Authority over Foreign Affairs: An Essay in Constitutional Interpretation* (Durham, Carolina Academic Press, 2002).
Prete L, *Infringement Proceedings in EU Law* (Alphen aan den Rijn, Kluwer Law International 2017).
Ragnemalm H, 'The Community Courts and Openness within the European Union' in Alan Dashwood and Angela Ward (eds), *Cambridge Yearbook of European Legal Studies 1999: Volume 2* (Oxford, Hart Publishing, 2000).
Ramopoulos T and Odermatt J, 'EU Diplomacy: Measuring Success in Light of the Post-Lisbon Institutional Framework' in Astrid Boening, Jan-Frederik Kremer and Aukje van Loon (eds), *Global Power Europe – Vol. 1: Theoretical and Institutional Approaches to the EU's External Relations* (Berlin, Springer, 2013).
Ramsey MD, *The Constitution's Text in Foreign Affairs* (Cambridge, Harvard University Press 2007).
Rasmussen H, 'Docket Control Mechanisms, the EC Court and the Preliminary References Procedure' in Mads Andenas (ed), *Article 177 References to the European Court: Policy and Practice* (London, Butterworths, 1994).
——, *European Court of Justice* (Copenhagen, GadJura, 1998).
——, 'After Legal Pluralism and Integration: Could Disintegration Follow?' in Peter Blume (ed), *Legal Issues at the Dawn of the New Millennium* (Copenhagen, Djøf Publishing, 1999).
——, 'Present and Future European Judicial Problems after Enlargement and the Post-2005 Ideological Revolt' (2007) 44 *Common Market Law Review* 1661.
Rasmussen M, 'Revolutionizing European Law: A History of the Van Gend En Loos Judgment' (2014) 12 *International Journal of Constitutional Law* 136.
Raube K, 'The European External Action Service and the European Parliament' (2012) 7 *The Hague Journal of Diplomacy* 65.
——, 'Parliamentarisation Approach: Parliamentary Control in EU Foreign Policy' in Maciej Wilga and Ireneusz Pawel Karolewski (eds), *New Approaches to EU Foreign Policy* (Abingdon, Routledge, 2014).
——, 'Democratic Accountability and EU Governance: The EEAS and the Role of the European Parliament' in David Spence and Jozef Bátora (eds), *The European External Action Service: European Diplomacy Post-Westphalia* (Basingstoke, Palgrave Macmillan, 2015).
Raworth P, 'A Timid Step Forwards: Maastricht and the Democratisation of the European Community' (1994) 19 *European Law Review* 16.
Regelsberger E and Wessels W, 'The CFSP Institutions and Procedures: A Third Way for the Second Pillar' (1996) 1 *European Foreign Affairs Review* 29.
Reich N, 'Judge-Made "Europe a La Carte": Some Remarks on Recent Conflicts between European and German Constitutional Law Provoked by the Banana Litigation' (1996) 7 *European Journal of International Law* 103.
Riddervold M, 'Finally Flexing Its Muscles? Atalanta – The European Union's Naval Military Operation against Piracy' (2011) 20 *European Security* 385.
Riekmann SP, 'The Cocoon of Power: Democratic Implications of Interinstitutional Agreements' (2007) 13 *European Law Journal* 4.

Rittberger B, 'Institutionalizing Representative Democracy in the European Union: The Case of the European Parliament' (2012) 50 *Journal of Common Market Studies* 18.

Robinson MT, 'Towards a European Foreign Policy – Legal Aspects' in Johan K De Vree, Peter Coffey and Richard H Lauwaars (eds), *Towards a European Foreign Policy: Legal, Economic and Political Dimensions* (Dordrecht, Martinus Nijhoff Publishers, 1987).

——, 'Tendencies towards a European Foreign Policy' in Jürgen Schwarze and Henry G Schermers (eds), *Structure and Dimensions of European Community Policy* (Baden-Baden, Nomos, 1988).

——, 'Constitutional Shifts in Europe and the United States: Learning From Each Other' (1996) 32 *Stanford Journal of International Law* 1.

Rodríguez Iglesias GC, 'The Court of Justice, Principles of EC Law, Court Reform and Constitutional Adjudication' (2004) 15 *European Business Law Review* 1115.

Rosas A, 'The European Union and Mixed Agreements' in Alan Dashwood and Christophe Hillion (eds), *The General Law of EC External Relations* (London, Sweet and Maxwell, 2000).

——, 'The Future of Mixity' in Christophe Hillion and Panos Koutrakos (eds), *Mixed Agreements Revisited: The EU and its Member States in the World* (Oxford, Hart Publishing, 2010).

——, 'The Status in EU Law of International Agreements Concluded by EU Member States' (2011) 34 *Fordham International Law Journal* 1304.

——, 'EU External Relations: Exclusive Competence Revisited' (2015) 38 *Fordham International Law Journal* 1073.

——, 'Recent Case Law of the European Court of Justice Relating to Article 218 TFEU' in Jenö Czuczai and Frederik Naert (eds), *The EU as a Global Actor – Bridging Legal Theory and Practice: Liber Amicorum in Honour of Ricardo Gosalbo Bono* (Leiden, Brill, 2016).

Rosas A and Armati L, *EU Constitutional Law: An Introduction* (Oxford, Hart Publishing, 2012).

——, *EU Constitutional Law: An Introduction* 3rd edition (Oxford, Hart Publishing, 2018).

Rosén G, 'EU Confidential: The European Parliament's Involvement in EU Security and Defence Policy' (2015) 53 *Journal of Common Market Studies* 383.

——, 'A Match Made in Heaven? Explaining Patterns of Cooperation between the Commission and the European Parliament' (2016) 38 *Journal of European Integration* 409.

——, 'Contestation and Co-Optation: Why Secrecy in EU External Relations Varies' (2018) 41 *West European Politics* 933.

Rossi L and Vinagre e Silva P, *Public Access to Documents in the EU* (Oxford, Hart Publishing, 2017).

Rudden B and Phelan DR, *Basic Community Cases* 2nd edition (Oxford University Press, 1997).

Sajó A, 'Constitution without the Constitutional Moment: A View from the New Member States' (2005) 3 *International Journal of Constitutional Law* 243.

Sánchez-Tabernero SR, 'The Choice of Legal Basis and the Principle of Consistency in the Procedure for Conclusion of International Agreements in CFSP Contexts: Parliament v. Council (Pirate-Transfer Agreement with Tanzania)' (2017) 54 *Common Market Law Review* 899.

Sand I-J, 'European Legal Method: – A New Teleology, Law-in-Context, a New Legal Realism or Hybrid Law?' in Ulla Neergaard and Ruth Nielsen (eds), *European Legal Method – Towards a New European Legal Realism?* (Copenhagen, Djøf Publishing, 2013).

Sari A, 'The Conclusion of International Agreements by the European Union in the Context of the ESDP' (2008) 57 *International and Comparative Law Quarterly* 53.

——, 'Between Legalisation and Organisational Development: Explaining the Evolution of EU Competence in the Field of Foreign Policy' in Paul James Cardwell (ed), *EU External Relations Law and Policy in the Post-Lisbon Era* (The Hague, TMC Asser Press, 2012).

Sautter G, 'The Financing of Common Foreign and Security Policy – on Continuity and Change' in Hermann-Josef Blanke and Stelio Mangiameli (eds), *The European Union after Lisbon: Constitutional Basis, Economic Order and External Action* (Berlin, Springer, 2012).

Scannell D, 'Financing ESDP Military Operations' (2004) 9 *European Foreign Affairs Review* 529.

Scharpf FW, 'Judicial Review and the Political Question: A Functional Analysis' (1966) 75 *Yale Law Journal* 517.

Schepel H and Blankenburg E, 'Mobilizing the European Court of Justice' in Gráinne De Búrca and Joseph HH Weiler (eds), *The European Court of Justice* (Oxford University Press, 2001).

Schepel H and Wesseling R, 'The Legal Community: Judges, Lawyers, Officials and Clerks in the Writing of Europe' (1997) 3 *European Law Journal* 165.
Schermers HG, 'The Main Issues in the Debate on the Further Development of European Foreign Policy' in Jürgen Schwarze (ed), *The External Relations of the European Community, in particular EC–US Relations* (Baden-Baden, Nomos 1989).
Schermers HG and Slot PJ, 'Case C-65/90, European Parliament v. Council of the European Communities, Judgment of 16 July 1992' (1993) 30 *Common Market Law Review* 1067.
Schmidt-Radefeldt R, 'Article 36 [The Parliamentary Dimension of CFSP]' in Hermann-Josef Blanke and Stelio Mangiameli (eds), *The Treaty on European Union (TEU): A Commentary* (Berlin, Springer, 2013).
——, 'Article 41 [Financing the CFSP]' in Hermann-Josef Blanke and Stelio Mangiameli (eds), *The Treaty on European Union (TEU)* (Berlin, Springer, 2013).
Schrijver N, 'Case C-459/03, Commission of the European Communities v. Ireland, Judgment of the Court (Grand Chamber) of 30 May 2006, [2006] ECR I-4635' (2010) 47 *Common Market Law Review* 863.
Schütze R, 'Organized Change towards an "Ever Closer Union": Article 308 EC and the Limits to the Community's Legislative Competence' (2003) 22 *Yearbook of European Law* 79.
——, 'Parallel External Powers in the European Community: From "Cubist" Perspectives towards "Naturalist" Constitutional Principles?' (2004) 23 *Yearbook of European Law* 225.
——, 'The Morphology of Legislative Power in the European Community: Legal Instruments and the Federal Division of Powers' (2006) 25 *Yearbook of European Law* 91.
——, *From Dual to Cooperative Federalism: The Changing Structure of European Law* (Oxford University Press, 2009).
——, 'On "Federal" Ground; The European Union as an (Inter)national Phenomenon' (2009) 46 *Common Market Law Review* 1069.
——, 'Federalism and Foreign Affairs: Mixity as a (Inter)national Phenomenon' in Christophe Hillion and Panos Koutrakos (eds), *Mixed Agreements Revisited: The EU and its Member States in the World* (Oxford, Hart Publishing, 2010).
——, 'From Rome to Lisbon: "Executive Federalism" in the (New) European Union' (2010) 47 *Common Market Law Review* 1385.
——, '"Delegated" Legislation in the (New) European Union: A Constitutional Analysis' (2011) 74 *Modern Law Review* 661.
——, *European Constitutional Law* (Cambridge University Press, 2012).
——, 'EU Development Policy: Constitutional and Legislative Foundation(s)' in Catherine Barnard and others (eds), *Cambridge Yearbook of European Legal Studies 2012–2013: Volume 15* (Oxford, Hart Publishing, 2013).
——, 'External Union Policies: A Substantive Overview' in Robert Schütze (ed), *Foreign Affairs and the EU Constitution: Selected Essays* (Cambridge University Press, 2014).
——, 'External Union Powers: Competences and Procedures' in Robert Schütze (ed), *Foreign Affairs and the EU Constitution: Selected Essays* (Cambridge University Press, 2014).
——, 'The "Treaty Power" and Parliamentary Democracy: Comparative Perspectives' in Robert Schütze (ed), *Foreign Affairs and the EU Constitution: Selected Essays* (Cambridge University Press, 2014).
——, *European Constitutional Law* 2nd edition (Cambridge University Press, 2015).
——, *European Union Law* (Cambridge University Press, 2015).
——, 'Two-and-a-Half Ways of Thinking about the European Union' (2016) 53 *Politique européenne* 28.
——, 'Parliamentary Democracy and International Treaties' (2017) 8 *Global Policy* 7.
——, *European Union Law* 2nd edition (Cambridge University Press, 2018).
Schwarze J, 'Towards a European Foreign Policy – Legal Aspects' in Johan K De Vree, Peter Coffey and Richard H Lauwaars (eds), *Towards a European Foreign Policy: Legal, Economic and Political Dimensions* (Dordrecht, Martinus Nijhoff Publishers, 1987).

Sharpston E and De Baere G, 'The Court of Justice as a Constitutional Adjudicator' in Anthony Arnull and others (eds), *A Constitutional Order of States? Essays in EU Law in Honour of Alan Dashwood* (Oxford, Hart Publishing, 2011).

Shaw J, 'The European Union: Discipline Building Meets Polity Building' in Mark Tushnet and Peter Cane (eds), *The Oxford Handbook of Legal Studies* (Oxford University Press, 2003).

Simmonds KR, 'External Relations Power of the EEC: A Recent Ruling of the European Court' (1977) 26 *International and Comparative Law Quarterly* 208.

Sjursen H, 'Not So Intergovernmental After All? On Democracy and Integration in European Foreign and Security Policy' (2011) 18 *Journal of European Public Policy* 1078.

——, 'The EU's Common Foreign and Security Policy: The Quest for Democracy' (2011) 18 *Journal of European Public Policy* 1069.

Skordas A, 'Is Europe an Aging Power with Global Vision – A Tale on Constitutionalism and Restoration' (2005) 12 *Columbia Journal of European Law* 241.

Slaughter A-M, 'Are Foreign Affairs Different?' (1993) 106 *Harvard Law Review* 1980.

Smith M, 'CFSP and ESDP: From Idea to Institution to Policy?' in Martin Holland (ed), *Common Foreign and Security Policy: The First Ten Years* 2nd edition (London, Continuum, 2004).

Smith ME, 'What's Wrong with the CFSP? The Politics of Institutional Reform' in Pierre-Henri Laurent and Marc Maresceau (eds), *The State of the European Union: Deepening and Widening*, vol 4 (Boulder, Lynne Rienner, 1998).

Smyth I, 'Mixity in Practice – A Member State Practitioner's Perspective' in Christophe Hillion and Panos Koutrakos (eds), *Mixed Agreements Revisited: The EU and its Member States in the World* (Oxford, Hart Publishing, 2010).

Snell J, 'Free Movement of Capital: Evolution as a Non-Linear Process' in Paul Craig and Gráinne De Búrca (eds), *The Evolution of EU Law* 2nd edition (Oxford University Press, 2011).

Sørensen M, 'The Enlargement of the European Communities and the Protection of Human Rights' in Bartholomeus Landheer (ed), *European Yearbook, Vol. XIX* (The Hague, Martinus Nijhoff Publishers, 1973).

Spernbauer M, *EU Peacebuilding in Kosovo and Afghanistan* (Leiden, Brill, 2014).

Steenbergen J, 'Legal Instruments of External Policies of the EC' in Johan K De Vree, Peter Coffey and Richard H Lauwaars (eds), *Towards a European Foreign Policy: Legal, Economic and Political Dimensions* (Dordrecht, Martinus Nijhoff Publishers, 1987).

Stein E, 'The New Institutions' in Eric Stein and Thomas L Nicholson (eds), *American Enterprise in the European Common Market: A Legal Profile*, vol 1 (Ann Arbor, University of Michigan Press, 1960).

——, 'Lawyers, Judges, and the Making of a Transnational Constitution' (1981) 75 *American Journal of International Law* 1.

——, 'European Foreign Affairs System and the Single European Act of 1986' (1989) 23 *The International Lawyer* 977.

——, 'Foreign Policy at Maastricht: "Non in Commotione Dominus"' (1992) 29 *Common Market Law Review* 663.

——, *Thoughts from a Bridge: A Retrospective of Writings on New Europe and American Federalism* (Ann Arbor, University of Michigan Press, 2000).

——, 'International Integration and Democracy: No Love at First Sight' (2001) 95 *American Journal of International Law* 489.

Stein E and Henkin L, 'Towards a European Foreign Policy? – The European Foreign Affairs System from the Perspective of the United States Constitution' in Mauro Cappelletti, Monica Seccombe and Joseph HH Weiler (eds), *Integration Through Law: Europe and the American Federal Experience*, Vol 1: Methods, Tools and Institutions. Book 3: Forces and Potential for a European Identity (Berlin, De Gruyter, 1986).

Stein E, Hay P and Waelbroeck M, *European Community Law and Institutions in Perspective: Text, Cases and Readings* (Charlottesville, The Michie Company, 1976).

Stetter S, *EU Foreign and Interior Policies: Cross-Pillar Politics and the Social Constructions of Sovereignty* (London, Routledge, 2007).

Stewart P, 'Foreword' in Terrance Sandalow and Eric Stein (eds), *Courts and Free Markets: Perspectives from the United States and Europe*, vol 1 (Oxford, Clarendon Press, 1982).

Stone Sweet A and Brunell T, 'Constructing a Supranational Constitutions' in Alec Stone Sweet (ed), *The Judicial Construction of Europe* (Oxford University Press, 2004).

Sutherland PD, 'Joining the Threads: The Influences Creating a European Union' in Deirdre Curtin and David O'Keeffe (eds), *Constitutional Adjudication in European Community and National Law: Essays for the Hon Mr Justice T F O'Higgins* (Dublin, Butterworths, 1992).

Tamanaha BZ, *On the Rule of Law: History, Politics, Theory* (Cambridge University Press, 2004).

Temple Lang J, *The Common Market and Common Law* (Chicago, University of Chicago Press, 1966).

Terpan F, 'Financing Common Security and Defence Policy Operations: Explaining Change and Inertia in a Fragmented and Flexible Structure' (2015) 24 *European Security* 221.

Tervarent P de S de, 'EC External Relations and the CFSP (Summing Up)' in Alan Dashwood (ed), *Reviewing Maastricht: Issues for the 1996 IGC* (London, Sweet and Maxwell, 1996).

Thies A, *International Trade Disputes and EU Liability* (Cambridge University Press, 2013).

——, 'General Principles in the Development of EU External Relations Law' in Marise Cremona and Anne Thies (eds), *The European Court of Justice and External Relations Law: Constitutional Challenges* (Oxford, Hart Publishing, 2014).

Thym D, 'Reforming Europe's Common Foreign and Security Policy' (2004) 10 *European Law Journal* 5.

——, 'Beyond Parliament's Reach? The Role of the European Parliament in the CFSP' (2006) 11 *European Foreign Affairs Review* 109.

——, 'Parliamentary Involvement in European International Relations' in Marise Cremona and Bruno De Witte (eds), *EU Foreign Relations Law: Constitutional Fundamentals* (Oxford, Hart Publishing, 2008).

——, 'Foreign Affairs' in Armin Von Bogdandy and Jürgen Bast (eds), *Principles of European Constitutional Law* 2nd edition (Oxford, Hart Publishing, 2009).

——, 'The Intergovernmental Constitution of the EU's Foreign, Security and Defence Executive' (2011) 7 *European Constitutional Law Review* 453.

——, 'The Intergovernmental Branch of the EU's Foreign Affairs Executive: Reflections on the Political and Security Committee' in Hermann-Josef Blanke and Stelio Mangiameli (eds), *The European Union after Lisbon: Constitutional Basis, Economic Order and External Action* (Berlin, Springer, 2012).

——, 'Transfer Agreements for Pirates Concluded by the EU – A Case Study on the Human Rights Accountability of the Common Security and Defence Policy' in Panos Koutrakos and Achilles Skordas (eds), *The Law and Practice of Piracy at Sea: European and International Perspectives* (Oxford, Hart Publishing, 2014).

Tiili V, 'Transparency – An Everlasting Challenge for the European Union' in Pascal Cardonnel, Allan Rosas and Nils Wahl (eds), *Constitutionalising the EU Judicial System: Essays in Honour of Pernilla Lindh* (Oxford, Hart Publishing, 2012).

Timmermans C, 'The (in)Adequacy of Legal Instruments for a European Foreign Policy, a Co-Report' in Johan K De Vree, Peter Coffey and Richard H Lauwaars (eds), *Towards a European Foreign Policy: Legal, Economic and Political Dimensions* (The Hague, Martinus Nijhoff Publishers, 1987).

——, 'Evolution of Mixity since the Leiden 1982 Conference' in Christophe Hillion and Panos Koutrakos (eds), *Mixed Agreements Revisited: The EU and its Member States in the World* (Oxford, Hart Publishing, 2010).

Tizzano A, 'The Foreign Relations Law of the EU between Supranationality and Intergovernmental Model' in Enzo Cannizzaro (ed), *The European Union as an Actor in International Relations* (The Hague, Kluwer Law International 2002).

Tomkins A, 'Transparency and the Emergence of a European Administrative Law' (1999) 19 *Yearbook of European Law* 217.

Tonra B, *The Europeanisation of National Foreign Policy: Dutch, Danish and Irish Foreign Policy in the European Union* (Aldershot, Ashgate Publishing, 2001).

——, 'Constructing the CFSP: The Utility of a Cognitive Approach' (2003) 41 *Journal of Common Market Studies* 731.

Torrent R, 'The "Fourth Pillar" of the European Union after the Amsterdam Treaty' in Alan Dashwood and Christophe Hillion (eds), *The General Law of EC External Relations* (London, Sweet and Maxwell, 2000).

Toth AG, 'The Legal Status of the Declarations Annexed to the Single European Act' (1986) 23 *Common Market Law Review* 803.

Travers N, 'Access to Documents in Community Law: On the Road to a European Participatory Democracy' (2000) 35 *Irish Jurist* 164.

Tridimas T, 'Knocking on Heaven's Door: Fragmentation, Efficiency and Defiance in the Preliminary Reference Procedure' (2003) 40 *Common Market Law Review* 9.

——, 'The European Court of Justice and the Draft Constitution: A Supreme Court for the Union?' in Takis Tridimas and Paolisa Nebbia (eds), *European Union Law for the Twenty-First Century: Rethinking the New Legal Order – Volume 1: Constitutional and Public Law, External Relations* (Oxford, Hart Publishing, 2004).

——, *The General Principles of EU Law* 2nd edition (Oxford University Press, 2006).

——, 'Bifurcated Justice: The Dual Character of Judicial Protection in EU Law' in Allan Rosas, Egils Levits and Yves Bot (eds), *The Court of Justice and the Construction of Europe: Analyses and Perspectives on Sixty Years of Case-law – La Cour de Justice et la Construction de l'Europe: Analyses et Perspectives de Soixante Ans de Jurisprudence* (The Hague, TMC Asser Press, 2013).

Trybus M, *European Union Law and Defence Integration* (Oxford, Hart Publishing, 2005).

——, 'With or without the EU Constitutional Treaty: Towards a Common Security and Defence Policy?' (2006) 31 *European Law Review* 145.

——, 'The Vision of the European Defence Community and a Common Defence for the European Union' in Martin Trybus and Nigel White (eds), *European Security Law* (Oxford University Press, 2007).

Tsoukalis L, *In Defence of Europe: Can the European Project Be Saved?* (Oxford University Press, 2016).

Tuori K, 'The Relationality of European Constitution(s). Justifying a New Research Programme for European Constitutional Scholarship' in Ulla Neergaard and Ruth Nielsen (eds), *European Legal Method – Towards A New European Legal Realism?* (Copenhagen, Djøf Publishing, 2013).

Uerpmann-Wittzack R, 'The Constitutional Role of International Law' in Armin Von Bogdandy and Jürgen Bast (eds), *Principles of European Constitutional Law* 2nd edition (Oxford, Hart Publishing, 2009).

United Kingdom's House of Lords, 'House of Lords European Union Committee, 6th Report of Session 2003–04, The Future Role of the European Court of Justice: Report with Evidence (HL Paper 47)'.

Usher JA, 'The Primacy of Community Law' (1978) 3 *European Law Review* 214.

——, 'Variable Geometry or Concentric Circles: Patterns for the European Union' (1997) 46 *International and Comparative Law Quarterly* 243.

Valentine DG, 'The Jurisdiction of the Court of Justice of the European Communities to Annul Executive Action' (1960) 36 *British Yearbook of International Law* 174.

——, *The Court of Justice of the European Communities: Volume One: Jurisdiction and Procedure* (London, Stevens and Sons, 1965).

Van den Brink T, 'The Relationship between the European and the National Legislatures from the Perspective of Constitutional Integrity' in Fabian Amtenbrink and Peter AJ Van den Berg (eds), *The Constitutional Integrity of the European Union* (The Hague, TMC Asser Press, 2010).

——, 'The Substance of Subsidiarity: The Interpretation and Meaning of the Principle after Lisbon' in Martin Trybus and Luca Rubini (eds), *The Treaty of Lisbon and the Future of European Law and Policy* (Cheltenham, Edward Elgar, 2012).

——, 'Towards an Ever Clearer Division of Authority Between the European Union and the Member States?' in Ton Van den Brink, Michiel Luchtman and Miraslava Scholten (eds), *Sovereignty in the Shared Legal Order of the EU: Core Values of Regulation and Enforcement* (Cambridge, Intersentia, 2015).

Van Der Mei AP, 'EU External Relations and Internal Inter-Institutional Conflicts: The Battlefield of Article 218 TFEU' (2016) 23 *Maastricht Journal of European and Comparative Law* 1051.
Van Der Steen I, 'Mixity in Practice – A View from The Netherlands' in Christophe Hillion and Panos Koutrakos (eds), *Mixed Agreements Revisited: The EU and its Member States in the World* (Oxford, Hart Publishing, 2010).
Van Elsuwege P, 'EU External Action after the Collapse of the Pillar Structure: In Search of a New Balance between Delimitation and Consistency' (2010) 47 *Common Market Law Review* 987.
——, 'The Interface Between the Area of Freedom, Security and Justice and the Common Foreign and Security Policy of the European Union: Legal Constraints to Political Objectives' in Ronald L Holzhacker and Paul Luif (eds), *Freedom, Security and Justice in the European Union* (New York, Springer, 2014).
——, 'The Potential for Inter-Institutional Conflicts before the Court of Justice: Impact of the Lisbon Treaty' in Marise Cremona and Anne Thies (eds), *The European Court of Justice and External Relations Law: Constitutional Challenges* (Oxford, Hart Publishing, 2014).
——, 'Securing the Institutional Balance in the Procedure for Concluding International Agreements: European Parliament v. Council (Pirate Transfer Agreement with Mauritius)' (2015) 52 *Common Market Law Review* 1379.
——, 'Upholding the Rule of Law in the Common Foreign and Security Policy: H v. Council' (2017) 54 *Common Market Law Review* 841.
Van Gerven W, 'The Legal Protection of Private Parties in the Law of the European Economic Community' in Francis G Jacobs (ed), *European Law and the Individual* (Amsterdam, North Holland, 1976).
——, 'Two Twin-Principles of EU Law: Democracy and Accountability, Consistency and Convergence' in Ulf Bernitz and others (eds), *General Principles of EC Law in a Process of Development* (Alphen aan den Rijn, Kluwer Law International, 2008).
Van Hecke S and Wolfs W, 'The European Parliament and European Foreign Policy' in Knud Erik Jørgensen and others (eds), *The SAGE Handbook of European Foreign Policy* (London, SAGE, 2015).
Van Nuffel P, 'Case Law: Case C-65/93, European Parliament v. Council of the European Union, 1995 E.C.R. 1-643 (Extension of System of Generalized Tariff Preferences)' (1995) 1 *Columbia Journal of European Law* 504.
Van Ooik R, 'Cross-Pillar Litigation Before the ECJ: Demarcation of Community and Union Competences' (2008) 4 *European Constitutional Law Review* 399.
Van Rossem JW, 'The EU at Crossroads: A Constitutional Inquiry into the Way International Law Is Received within the EU Legal Order' in Enzo Cannizzaro, Paolo Palchetti and Ramses A Wessel (eds), *International Law as Law of the European Union* (Leiden, Martinus Nijhoff Publishers, 2012).
Van Vooren B, 'EU–EC External Competences after the Small Arms Judgment' (2009) 14 *European Foreign Affairs Review* 7.
——, 'The Small Arms Judgment in an Age of Constitutional Turmoil' (2009) 14 *European Foreign Affairs Review* 231.
——, 'A Legal-Institutional Perspective on the European External Action Service' (2011) 48 *Common Market Law Review* 475.
Van Vooren B and Wessel RA, *EU External Relations Law: Text, Cases and Materials* (Cambridge University Press, 2014).
Vara JS, 'The External Activities of AFSJ Agencies: The Weakness of Democratic and Judicial Controls' (2015) 20 *European Foreign Affairs Review* 118.
Viola DM, *European Foreign Policy and the European Parliament in the 1990s: An Investigation into the Role and Voting Behaviour of the European Parliament's Political Groups* (Aldershot, Ashgate Publishing, 2000).
——, 'The Genesis of the European Parliament: From Appointed Consultative Assembly to Directly Elected Legislative Body' in Donatella M Viola (ed), *Routledge Handbook of European Elections* (Abingdon, Routledge, 2016).
Von Bogdandy A, 'The Legal Case for Unity: The European Union as a Single Organization with a Single Legal System' (1999) 36 *Common Market Law Review* 887.

——, 'A Bird's Eye View on the Science of European Law: Structures, Debates and Development Prospects of Basic Research on the Law of the European Union in a German Perspective' (2000) 6 *European Law Journal* 208.
——, 'Founding Principles' in Armin Von Bogdandy and Jürgen Bast (eds), *Principles of European Constitutional Law* 2nd edition (Oxford, Hart Publishing, 2009).
——, 'Founding Principles of EU Law: A Theoretical and Doctrinal Sketch' (2010) 16 *European Law Journal* 95.
Von Bogdandy A and Bast J, 'The Federal Order of Competences' in Armin Von Bogdandy and Jürgen Bast (eds), *Principles of European Constitutional Law* 2nd edition (Oxford, Hart Publishing, 2009).
Von der Gablentz O, 'Luxembourg Revisited or The Importance of European Political Cooperation' (1979) 16 *Common Market Law Review* 685.
Vončina T, 'Speaking with One Voice: Statements and Declarations as an Instrument of the EU's Common Foreign and Security Policy' (2011) 16 *European Foreign Affairs Review* 169.
Walker N, 'Legal Theory and the European Union: A 25th Anniversary Essay' (2005) 25 *Oxford Journal of Legal Studies* 581.
——, 'Opening or Closure? The Constitutional Intimations of the ECJ' in Miguel Poiares Maduro and Loïc Azoulai (eds), *The Past and Future of EU Law: The Classics of EU Law Revisited on the 50th Anniversary of the Rome Treaty* (Oxford, Hart Publishing, 2010).
Walker N and De Búrca G, 'Reconceiving Law and New Governance Narrowing the Gap: Law and New Approaches to Governance in the European Union' (2007) 13 *Columbia Journal of European Law* 519.
Wallace W, 'European Foreign Policy since the Cold War: How Ambitious, How Inhibited?' (2017) 19 *British Journal of Politics and International Relations* 77.
Walsche AD, 'La procédure de conclusion des accords internationaux' in Jean-Victor Louis and Marianne Dony (eds), *Relations extérieures* (Brussels, Editions de l'Université de Bruxelles, 2005).
Ward A, 'Community Development Aid and the Evolution of the Inter-Institutional Law of the European Union' in Alan Dashwood and Christophe Hillion (eds), *The General Law of EC External Relations* (London, Sweet and Maxwell, 2000).
Weatherill S, 'Competence and Legitimacy' in Catherine Barnard and Okeoghene Odudu (eds), *The Outer Limits of European Union Law* (Oxford, Hart Publishing, 2009).
——, *Law and Values in the European Union* (Oxford University Press, 2016).
Weiler JHH, 'The European Parliament and Foreign Affairs: External Relations of the European Economic Community' in Antonio Cassese (ed), *Parliamentary Control Over Foreign Policy: Legal Essays* (Alphen aan den Rijn, Sijtoff and Noordhoff, 1980).
——, *The Transnational Setting: The European Parliament and Its Foreign Affairs Committees*, vol 2 (Padova, Cedam/Oceana 1982).
——, 'Community Member States and European Integration: Is the Law Relevant?' in Loukas Tsoukalis (ed), *The European Community: Past, Present and Future* (Oxford, Basil Blackwell, 1983).
——, 'The External Legal Relations of Non-Unitary Actors: Mixity and the Federal Principle' in David O'Keeffe and Henry G Schermers (eds), *Mixed Agreements* (Deventer, Kluwer Law and Taxation Publishers, 1983).
——, 'Pride and Prejudice: Parliament v. Council' (1989) 14 *European Law Review* 334.
——, 'Europe: The Case Against the Case for Statehood' (1998) 4 *European Law Journal* 43.
——, 'The Autonomy of the Community Legal Order: Through the Looking Glass' in Joseph HH Weiler (ed), *The Constitution of Europe: 'Do the New Clothes Have an Emperor?' and Other Essays on European Integration* (Cambridge University Press, 1999).
——, *The Constitution of Europe: 'Do the New Clothes Have an Emperor?' and Other Essays on European Integration* (Cambridge University Press, 1999).
——, 'The Transformation of Europe' in Joseph HH Weiler (ed), *The Constitution of Europe: 'Do the New Clothes Have an Emperor?' and Other Essays on European Integration* (Cambridge University Press, 1999).
Weiler JHH and Modrall J, 'Institutional Reform: Consensus or Majority?' (1985) 10 *European Law Review* 316.

Weiler JHH, Haltern U and Mayer FC, 'European Democracy and Its Critique' (1995) 18 *West European Politics* 4.
Wellenstein E, 'Twenty-Five Years of European Community External Relations' (1979) 16 *Common Market Law Review* 407.
Wessel RA, 'Towards a United Europe? A Legal Perspective on European Institutionalization and Integration' in Jaap de Wilde and Håkan Wiberg (eds), *Organized Anarchy in Europe: The Role of States and Intergovernmental Organizations* (London, IB Tauris Publishers, 1996).
——, 'The International Legal Status of the European Union' (1997) 2 *European Foreign Affairs Review* 109.
——, *The European Union's Foreign and Security Policy: A Legal Institutional Perspective*, vol 33 (The Hague, Kluwer Law International. 1999).
——, 'The Inside Looking Out: Consistency and Delimitation in EU External Relations' (2000) 37 *Common Market Law Review* 1135.
——, 'Good Governance and EU Foreign, Security and Defence Policy' in Deirdre Curtin and Ramses A Wessel (eds), *Good Governance and the European Union: Reflections on Concepts, Institutions and Substance* (Antwerp, Intersentia, 2005).
——, 'Differentiation in EU Foreign, Security, and Defence Policy: Between Coherence and Flexibility' in Martin Trybus and Nigel White (eds), *European Security Law* (Oxford University Press, 2007).
——, 'The Constitutional Unity of the European Union: The Increasing Irrelevance of the Pillar Structure?' in Jan Wouters, Luc Verheij and Philipp Kiiver (eds), *European Constitutionalism beyond Lisbon* (Antwerp, Intersentia, 2009).
——, 'The Dynamics of the European Union Legal Order: An Increasingly Coherent Framework of Action and Interpretation' (2009) 5 *European Constitutional Law Review* 117.
——, 'Cross-Pillar Mixity: Combining Competences in the Conclusion of EU International Agreements' in Christophe Hillion and Panos Koutrakos (eds), *Mixed Agreements Revisited: The EU and its Member States in the World* (Oxford, Hart Publishing, 2010).
——, 'Initiative and Voting in Common Foreign and Security Policy: The New Lisbon Rules in Historical Perspective' in Hermann-Josef Blanke and Stelio Mangiameli (eds), *The European Union After Lisbon: Constitutional Basis, Economic Order and External Action* (Berlin, Springer, 2012).
——, 'Reconsidering the Relationship between International and EU Law: Towards a Contents-Based Approach?' in Enzo Cannizzaro, Paolo Palchetti and Ramses A Wessel (eds), *International Law as Law of the European Union* (Leiden, Martinus Nijhoff Publishers, 2012).
——, 'Resisting Legal Facts: Are CFSP Norms as Soft as They Seem?' (2015) 20 *European Foreign Affairs Review* 123.
——, 'The European Court of Justice and External Relations Law' in *Constitutional Challenges*, Marise Cremona and Anne Thies (Oxford: Hart Publishing, 2014); (2015) 52 *Common Market Law Review* 1715.
——, 'The Legal Dimension of European Foreign Policy' in Knud Erik Jørgensen and others (eds), *The SAGE Handbook of European Foreign Policy* (London, SAGE, 2015).
——, 'Common Foreign, Security, and Defense Policy' in Dennis Patterson and Anna Södersten (eds), *A Companion to European Union Law and International Law* (Chichester, John Wiley & Sons, 2016).
——, 'Flipping the Question: The Reception of EU Law in the International Legal Order' (2016) 35 *Yearbook of European Law* 533.
——, 'Integration and Constitutionalisation in EU Foreign and Security Policy' in Robert Schütze (ed), *Globalisation and Governance: International Problems, European Solutions* (Cambridge University Press, 2018).
Wessels W, 'EPC after the Single European Act: Towards a European Foreign Policy via Treaty Obligations?' in Martin Holland (ed), *The Future of European Political Cooperation: Essays on Theory and Practice* (New York, St Martin's Press, 1991).
——, 'The EC Council: The Community's Decisionmaking Center' in Robert O Keohane and Stanley Hoffmann (eds), *The New European Community: Decisionmaking and Institutional Change* (Boulder, Westview Press, 1991).
——, 'Theoretical Perspectives. CFSP beyond the Supranational and Intergovernmental Dichotomy' in Dieter Mahncke, Alicia Ambos and Christopher Reynolds (eds), *European Foreign Policy: From Rhetoric to Reality?* (Brussels, PIE-Peter Lang, 2004).

Whitman R and Juncos A, 'The Lisbon Treaty and the Foreign, Security and Defence Policy: Reforms, Implementation and the Consequences of (Non–)Ratification' (2009) 14 *European Foreign Affairs Review* 25.

Wils W, 'Concurrent Liability of the Community and a Member State' (1992) 17 *European Law Review* 191.

Wisniewski E, 'The Influence of the European Parliament on the European External Action Service' (2013) 18 *European Foreign Affairs Review* 81.

Wouters J, 'Institutional and Constitutional Challenges for the European Union – Some Reflections in the Light of the Treaty of Nice' in Alfred E Kellermann, Jaap W de Zwaan and Jenö Czuczai (eds), *EU Enlargement: The Constitutional Impact at EU and National Level* (The Hague, TMC Asser Press, 2001).

——, 'The Organisation and Functioning of the European External Action Service: Achievements, Challenges and Opportunities' (Brussels, European Parliament Directorate-General for External Policies of the Union, 2013).

Wouters J and Cuyckens H, 'Festina Lente: CFSP from Maastricht to Lisbon and Beyond' in Maartje De Visser and Anne Pieter Van Der Mei (eds), *The Treaty on European Union 1993–2013: Reflections from Maastricht* (Cambridge, Intersentia, 2013).

Wouters J and Raube K, 'The Interparliamentary Conference on Common Foreign and Security Policy: A Quest for Democratic Accountability in EU Security Governance' in Nicola Lupo and Cristina Fasone (eds), *Interparliamentary Cooperation in the Composite European Constitution* (Oxford, Hart Publishing, 2016).

Wouters J, Coppens D and De Meester B, 'The European Union's External Relations after the Lisbon Treaty' in Stefan Griller and Jacques Ziller (eds), *The Lisbon Treaty: EU Constitutionalism without a Constitutional Treaty?* vol 11 (Vienna, Springer, 2008).

Wyatt D, 'Competence of the Community, Internal and External' (1977) 2 *European Law Review* 41.

Wyatt D and Dashwood A, *The Substantive Law of the EEC* (London, Sweet and Maxwell, 1980).

Official Journal

C36/32. Resolution on European Political Cooperation. European Parliament. Minutes of Proceedings of the Sitting of Thursday, 19 January 1978.

C83/210. Protocol (No 3) on the Statute of the Court of Justice of the European Union.

C95/1. Interinstitutional Agreement of 12 March 2014 between the European Parliament and the Council Concerning the Forwarding to and Handling by the European Parliament of Classified Information Held by the Council on Matters Other than Those in the Area of the Common Foreign and Security Policy (2014/C 95/01).

C139/1. Interinstitutional Agreement of 17 May 2006 between the European Parliament, the Council and the Commission on Budgetary Discipline and Sound Financial Management (2006/C 139/01).

C172/1. Interinstitutional Agreement of 6 May 1999 between the European Parliament, the Council and the Commission on Budgetary Discipline and Improvement of the Budgetary Procedure (1999/C 172/01).

C190/2. Decision of the Bureau of the European Parliament of 6 June 2011 Concerning the Rules Governing the Treatment of Confidential Information by the European Parliament (2011/C 190/02).

C201/1. Adoption of a Council Decision Establishing the Organisation and Functioning of the European External Action Service (2010/C 210/01) Draft Declaration by the High Representative on Political Accountability.

C212 E/37. Parliaments New Role and Responsibilities in Implementing the Lisbon Treaty (P6 TA(2009)0373) European Parliament Resolution of 7 May 2009 on Parliament's New Role and Responsibilities in Implementing the Treaty of Lisbon (2008/2063(INI)) (2010/C 212 E/08).

C286/80. European Parliament. Financing CFSP. Resolution on the Proposal for an Interinstitutional Agreement between the European Parliament, the Council and the European Commission on Provisions Regarding Financing of the Common Foreign and Security Policy (A4-0249/97) (16 July 1997).

C287/1. European Governance: A White Paper (COM(2001) 428) July 2001 (2001/C 287/01).

C298/1. Interinstitutional Agreement of 20 November 2002 between the European Parliament and the Council Concerning Access by the European Parliament to Sensitive Information of the Council in the Field of Security and Defence Policy (2002/C 298/01).

C324/219. European Parliament. Intergovernmental Conferences – Budgetary Control – Financing of the Communities. Resolution on the Intergovernmental Conferences in the Context of the European Parliaments Strategy for European Union (A3-270/90) 22 November 1990.

C338/1. Court of Auditors: Special Report No 13/2001 on the Management of the Common Foreign and Security Policy (CFSP), Together with the Councils Replies and the Commissions Replies (Pursuant to Article 248(4), Second Subparagraph, EC) (2001/C 338/01).

C373/1. Interinstitutional Agreement of 2 December 2013 between the European Parliament, the Council and the Commission on Budgetary Discipline, on Cooperation in Budgetary Matters and on Sound Financial Management (2013/C 373/01).

L29/1. Council Decision (EU) 2016/123 of 26 October 2015 on the Signing, on Behalf of the European Union, and Provisional Application of the Enhanced Partnership and Cooperation Agreement between the European Union and Its Member States, of the One Part, and the Republic of Kazakhstan, of the Other Part.

L29/3. Enhanced Partnership and Cooperation Agreement between the European Union and Its Member States, of the One Part, and the Republic of Kazakhstan, of the Other Part.

L39/44. Staff Regulations of the European Union Satellite Centre, 9 February 2002.

L42/92. Council Joint Action 2008/1247CFSP of 4 February 2008 on the European Union Rule of Law Mission in Kosovo, Eulex Kosovo.

L43/29. Council Decision (CFSP) 2015/260 of 17 February 2015 Extending the Mandate of the European Union Special Representative for Human Rights.

L52/1. Council Regulation (EEC) No 443/92 of 25 February 1992 on Financial and Technical Assistance to, and Economic Cooperation with, the Developing Countries in Asia and Latin America.

L62/37. Council Joint Action 2005/190/CFSP of 7 March 2005 on the European Union Integrated Rule of Law Mission for Iraq, EUJUST LEX.

L73/15. Council Decision (EU) 2017/477 of 3 March 2017 on the Position to Be Adopted on Behalf of the European Union within the Cooperation Council Established under the Enhanced Partnership and Cooperation Agreement between the European Union and Its Member States, of the One Part, and the Republic of Kazakhstan, of the Other Part as Regards the Working Arrangements of the Cooperation Council, the Cooperation Committee, Specialised Subcommittees or Any Other Bodies.

L108/1. Council Decision 2014/198/CFSP of 10 March 2014 on the Signing and Conclusion of the Agreement between the European Union and the United Republic of Tanzania on the Conditions of Transfer of Suspected Pirates and Associated Seized Property from the European Union-Led Naval Force to the United Republic of Tanzania.

L122/31. Council Decision (CFSP) 2015/778 of 18 May 2015 on a European Union Military Operation in the Southern Central Mediterranean (EUNAVFOR Med).

L123/7. Council Decision (CFSP) 2017/824 of 15 May 2017 Concerning the Staff Regulations of the European Union Satellite Centre.

L134/3. Council Decision of 14 May 2012 on the Signing, on Behalf of the Union, of the Framework Agreement on Partnership and Cooperation between the European Union and Its Member States, of the One Part, and the Republic of the Philippines, of the Other Part (2012/272/EU).

L139/9. Council Regulation (EC) No 881/2002 of 27 May 2002 Imposing Certain Specific Restrictive Measures Directed against Certain Persons and Entities Associated with Usama Bin Laden, the Al-Qaida Network and the Taliban, and Repealing Council Regulation (EC) No 467/2001

Prohibiting the Export of Certain Goods and Services to Afghanistan, Strengthening the Flight Ban and Extending the Freeze of Funds and Other Financial Resources in Respect of the Taliban of Afghanistan.
L145/43. Regulation (EC) No 1049/2001 of the European Parliament and of the Council of 30 May 2001 Regarding Public Access to European Parliament, Council and Commission Documents.
L154/1. Council Decision 2012/308/CFSP of 26 April 2012 on the Accession of the European Union to the Treaty of Amity and Cooperation in Southeast Asia.
L155/56. Council Decision of 17 November 2009 Concerning the Conclusion of the Agreement between the Government of the Russian Federation and the European Union on the Protection of Classified Information (2010/348/EC).
L157/51. Council Decision (CFSP) 2015/972 of 22 June 2015 Launching the European Union Military Operation in the Southern Central Mediterranean (EUNAVFOR Med).
L174/42. Council Decision 2014/349/CFSP of 12 June 2014 Amending Joint Action 2008/124/CFSP on the European Union Rule of Law Mission in Kosovo, Eulex Kosovo.
L183/16. Council Decision 2011/411/CFSP of 12 July 2011 Defining the Statute, Seat and Operational Rules of the European Defence Agency and Repealing Joint Action 2004/551/CFSP.
L187/1. Council Decision 2010/404/CFSP of 14 June 2010 Concerning the Signing and Conclusion of the Agreement between the European Union and the Principality of Liechtenstein on Security Procedures for Exchanging Classified Information.
L188/9. Council Decision 2006/477/CFSP of 30 June 2006 Concerning the Conclusion of the Agreement between the European Union and the Former Yugoslav Republic of Macedonia on the Participation of the Former Yugoslav Republic of Macedonia in the European Union Military Crisis Management Operation in Bosnia and Herzegovina (Operation ALTHEA).
L188/73. Council Decision 2014/401/CFSP of 26 June 2014 on the European Union Satellite Centre and Repealing Joint Action 2001/555/CFSP on the Establishment of a European Union Satellite Centre.
L191/1. Council Joint Action of 12 July 2002 on the European Unions Contribution to Combating the Destabilising Accumulation and Spread of Small Arms and Light Weapons and Repealing Joint Action 1999/34/CFSP (2002/589/CFSP).
L194/142. Council Decision (CFSP) 2018/1083 of 30 July 2018 Amending Joint Action 2008/851/CFSP on a European Union Military Operation to Contribute to the Deterrence, Prevention and Repression of Acts of Piracy and Armed Robbery off the Somali Coast.
L195/39. Council Decision of 26 July 2010 Concerning Restrictive Measures against Iran and Repealing Common Position 2007/140/CFSP.
L200/5. Council Joint Action of 20 July 2001 on the Establishment of a European Union Satellite Centre (2001/555/CFSP).
L200/21. Council Decision 2012/440/CFSP of 25 July 2012 Appointing the European Union Special Representative for Human Rights.
L201/30. Council Decision of 26 July 2010 Establishing the Organisation and Functioning of the European External Action Service (2010/427/EU).
L204/18. Council Decision of 21 December 2011 on the Signing, on Behalf of the European Union, and Provisional Application of Certain Provisions of the Partnership and Cooperation Agreement between the European Union and Its Member States, of the One Part, and the Republic of Iraq, of the Other Part (2012/418/EU).
L204/20. Partnership and Cooperation Agreement between the European Union and Its Member States, of the One Part, and the Republic of Iraq, of the Other Part.
L228/21. Council Joint Action 2004/523/CFSP of 28 June 2004 on the European Union Rule of Law Mission in Georgia, EUJUST THEMIS.
L229/1. Council Decision 2012/486/CFSP of 23 July 2012 Concerning the Signing and Conclusion of the Agreement between the Organisation for Joint Armament Cooperation and the European Union on the Protection of Classified Information.
L229/1. Council Regulation (EU) No 833/2014 of 31 July 2014 Concerning Restrictive Measures in View of Russia's Actions Destabilising the Situation in Ukraine.

L229/13. Council Decision 2014/512/CFSP of 31 July 2014 Concerning Restrictive Measures in View of Russia's Actions Destabilising the Situation in Ukraine.

L245/17. Council Joint Action 2004/551/CFSP of 12 July 2004 on the Establishment of the European Defence Agency.

L254/1. Council Decision 2011/640/CFSP of 12 July 2011 on the Signing and Conclusion of the Agreement between the European Union and the Republic of Mauritius on the Conditions of Transfer of Suspected Pirates and Associated Seized Property from the European Union-Led Naval Force to the Republic of Mauritius and on the Conditions of Suspected Pirates after Transfer.

L260/1. Council Decision 2010/587/CFSP of 14 June 2010 Concerning the Signing and Conclusion of the Agreement between the European Union and Montenegro on Security Procedures for Exchanging and Protecting Classified Information.

L266/55. Council Decision (CFSP) 2015/1835 of 12 October 2015 Defining the Statute, Seat and Operational Rules of the European Defence Agency.

L271/3. Council Regulation (EU) No 960/2014 of 8 September 2014 Amending Regulation (EU) No 833/2014 Concerning Restrictive Measures in View of Russia's Actions Destabilising the Situation in Ukraine.

L271/54. Council Decision 2014/659/CFSP of 8 September 2014 Amending Decision 2014/512/CFSP Concerning Restrictive Measures in View of Russia's Actions Destabilising the Situation in Ukraine.

L276/1. Council Decision 2009/747/CFSP of 14 September 2009 Concerning the Staff Regulations of the European Union Satellite Centre.

L278/16. Stabilisation and Association Agreement between the European Communities and Their Member States of the One Part, and the Republic of Serbia, of the Other Part.

L286/1. Council Decision of 8 November 1993 Concerning the Joint Action Decided on by the Council on the Basis of Article J.3 of the Treaty on European Union on Support for the Convoying of Humanitarian Aid in Bosnia and Herzegovina (93/603/CFSP).

L294/53. Council Decision (CFSP) 2015/2005 of 10 November 2015 Extending the Mandate of the European Union Special Representative in Afghanistan.

L301/33. Council Joint Action 2008/851/CFSP of 10 November 2008 on a European Union Military Operation to Contribute to the Deterrence, Prevention and Repression of Acts of Piracy and Armed Robbery off the Somali Coast.

L304/47. Interinstitutional Agreements: Framework Agreement on Relations between the European Parliament and the European Commission.

L317/3. Partnership Agreement between the Members of the African, Caribbean and Pacific Group of States of the One Part, and the European Community and Its Member States, of the Other Part, Signed in Cotonou on 23 June 2000.

L321/1. Council Decision (EU) 2016/2079 of 29 September 2016 on the Signing, on Behalf of the European Union, and Provisional Application of the Partnership Agreement on Relations and Cooperation between the European Union and Its Member States, of the One Part, and New Zealand, of the Other Part.

L322/22. Council Decision 2009/906/CFSP of 8 December 2009 on the European Union Police Mission (EUPM) in Bosnia and Herzegovina (BiH).

L325/35. Council Decision of 1 December 2009 Adopting the Council's Rules of Procedure (2009/937/EU).

L326/1. Council Joint Action of 10 December 2001 Concerning the Appointment of the Special Representative of the European Union (2001/875/CFSP).

L340/43. Council Decision of 20 December 1993 on Public Access to Council Documents (93/731/EC).

L346/42. Council Regulation (EU) No 1286/2009 of 22 December 2009 Amending Regulation (EC) No 881/2002 Imposing Certain Specific Restrictive Measures Directed against Certain Persons and Entities Associated with Usama Bin Laden, the Al-Qaida Network and the Taliban.

L347/884. Council Regulation (EU, EURATOM) No 1311/2013 of 2 December 2013 Laying down the Multiannual Financial Framework for the Years 2014–2020.

L349/20. Council Regulation (EU) No 129/2014 of 4 December 2014 Amending Regulation (EU) No 833/2014 Concerning Restrictive Measures in View of Russias Actions Destabilising the Situation in Ukraine, and Amending Regulation (EU) No 960/2014 Amending Regulation (EU) No 833/2014.

L349/58. Council Decision 2014/872/CFSP of 4 December 2014 Amending Decision 2014/512/CFSP Concerning Restrictive Measures in View of Russia's Actions Destabilising the Situation in Ukraine, and Decision 2014/659/CFSP Amending Decision 2014/512/CFSP.

L359/65. Council Decision 2004/833/CFSP of 2 December 2004 Implementing Joint Action 2002/589/CFSP with a View to a European Union Contribution to ECOWAS in the Framework of the Moratorium on Small Arms and Light Weapons.

L371/11. Council Regulation (EURATOM) No 3954/87 of 22 December 1987 Laying down Maximum Permitted Levels of Radioactive Contamination of Foodstuffs and of Feedingstuffs Following a Nuclear Accident or Any Other Case of Radiological Emergency.

Other Items

Agreement on the Withdrawal of the United Kingdom of Great Britain and Northern Ireland from the European Union and the European Atomic Energy Community, as Endorsed by Leaders at a Special Meeting of the European Council on 25 November 2018.

Annotated Summary of Bilateral Agreements between, on the One Party, the European Union, the Former European Community or Euratom, and, on the Other Part, Third States or International Organizations (Treaties Office, Legal Affairs Division) (European External Action Service 2018).

Annotated Summary of Multilateral Agreements to Which the European Union Is a Contracting Party (European External Action Service 2018).

Answers to the European Parliament: Questionnaire to the Commissioner-Designate, Federica Mogherini, High Representative of the Union for Foreign Affairs and Security Policy, Vice-President of the Commission.

Charter of the United Nations and the Statute of the International Court of Justice.

Communication from the Commission to the European Council, the European Parliament and the Council: A Stronger Global Actor: A More Efficient Decision-Making for EU Common Foreign and Security Policy. 12 September 2018 (COM(2018) 647 Final).

Communiqué Issued by the Heads of State or Government of the Nine after their Summit Conference in Paris.

Conclusions of the Presidency. European Council. Rome, 27 and 28 October 1990 (SN 304/90 REV 2).

Council of Europe and European Commission, Fifth Negotiation Meeting between the CDDH Ad Hoc Negotiation Group and the European Commission on the Accession of the European Union to the European Convention on Human Rights (Council of Europe 2013) 47+1(2013)008rev2.

Council of the European Union, Presidency Report on the European Security and Defence Policy (ST 14056 2000 COR 1) (4 December 2000).

——, CM 448/08.

——, CFSP Annual Report 2010. Main Aspects and Basis Choices of the CFSP (Point G, Paragraph 43 of the Interinstitutional Agreement of 17 May 2006) – 2010 – Annual Report from the High Representative of the European Union for Foreign Affairs and Security Policy to the European Parliament (12562/11) (Council of the European Union 2011) 12562/11.

——, CFSP Annual Report 2011. Main Aspects and Basis Choices of the CFSP (Point G, Paragraph 43 of the Interinstitutional Agreement of 17 May 2006) – 2011 – Annual Report from the High Representative of the European Union for Foreign Affairs and Security Policy to the European Parliament (14605/1/12) (Council of the European Union 2012) 14605/1/12.

——, CFSP Annual Report 2012. Main Aspects and Basis Choices of the CFSP (Point G, Paragraph 43 of the Interinstitutional Agreement of 17 May 2006) – 2012 – Annual Report from the High Representative of the European Union for Foreign Affairs and Security Policy to the European Parliament (14924/13) (Council of the European Union 2013) 14924/13.

——, CFSP Annual Report 2013. Main Aspects and Basic Choices of the CFSP (Part II, Point E, Paragraph 25 of the Interinstitutional Agreement of 2 December 2013) – 2013 – Annual Report from the High Representative of the European Union for Foreign Affairs and Security Policy to the European Parliament (12094/14) (Council of the European Union 2014) 12094/14.

——, CFSP Annual Report 2014. Main Aspects and Basic Choices of the CFSP (Part II, Point E, Paragraph 25 of the Interinstitutional Agreement of 2 December 2013) – 2014 – Draft Annual Report from the High Representative of the European Union for Foreign Affairs and Security Policy to the European Parliament (11083/15) (Council of the European Union 2015) 11083/15.

——, CFSP Budget Orientations for 2016 and 2017 (6383/16).

European Commission, C/97/243. Signing of the Interinstitutional Agreement on Financing of the CFSP.

European Commission, Budget, Multiannual Financial Framework, Figures and Documents. Financial Framework 2014–2020 as Established by Council Regulation No 1311/2013 (Excluding Adjustments).

European Convention, The Secretariat: Final Report of Working Group VII on External Action. From Working Group VII – "External Action" to Members of the Convention (CONV 459/02).

European Convention, The Secretariat: Draft Articles on External Action in the Constitutional Treaty. From the Praesidium to the Convention (CONV 685/03).

European Convention, Letter from Giuliano Amato on Behalf of the Party of European Socialists, Elmar Brok on Behalf of the European Peoples Party, and Andrew Duff on Behalf of the European Liberal, Democrat and Reform Party (CONV 829/03).

European Council, Presidency Conclusions: European Council Meeting in Laeken, 14–15 December 2001, SN 300/1/01 REV 1.

——, European Security Strategy – A Secure Europe in a Better World, 2003.

European Ombudsman, Decision of the European Ombudsman Closing His Own-Initiative Inquiry OI/12/2010/(BEH)MMN Concerning the Council of the European Union, the European Commission and the High Representative/European External Action Service.

——, Decision of the European Ombudsman Closing the Own-Initiative Inquiry OI/15/2014/PMC into the Way in Which the European External Action Service (EEAS) Handles Allegations of Serious Irregularities Involving the EU Rule of Law Mission (Eulex) in Kosovo.

European Parliament, Report on the Conclusion of an Interinstitutional Agreement between the European Parliament and the Council Concerning the Forwarding to and Handling by the European Parliament of Classified Information Held by the Council on Matters Other than Those in the Area of the Common Foreign and Security Policy (2012/2069(ACI)) (European Parliament 2012) A7-0245/2012.

——, Rules of Procedure – 8th Parliamentary Term (July 2014).

——, Rules of Procedure – 8th Parliamentary Term (January 2017).

——, European Parliament's approach to implementing Articles 9 and 10 of Protocol 1 to the Lisbon Treaty as regards parliamentary cooperation in the field of CFSP/CSDP 2011 [B7-0388/2011].

European Union, Report by Mr Leo Tindemans, Prime Minister of Belgium, to the European Council. Bulletin of the European Communities, Supplement 1/76 (the Tindemans Report) (Office for Official Publications of the European Communities 1976).

Framework Agreement on the Relations between the European Parliament and the Commission (15018/10).

Meseberg Declaration, Renewing Europes Promises of Security and Prosperity – A Joint Franco-German Declaration was Adopted during the Franco-German Council of Ministers, which took place 19 June 2018 in Meseberg, Germany.

Opinion of the Legal Service (Subject: Primacy of EC Law) (11197/07) (JUR 260).

Political Declaration Setting out the Framework for the Future Relationship between the European Union and the United Kingdom (BXT 111) (CO EUR-PREP 54).

Press Release: 3039th Council Meeting, 21 October 2010, 15172/10 – Relations between the European Parliament and the Commission – Council Statement.

Press Release: 3482nd Council Meeting, Foreign Affairs, 11355/16 – Outcome of the Council Meeting.
Press Release: Judges Forum: Celebration of the 60th Anniversary of the Signing of the Rome Treaties – March 2017.
Press Release: The Conference of Presidents on the External Action Service, 10 June 2010.
Report by the Foreign Ministers of the Member States on the Problems of Political Unification (Bulletin of the European Communities. November 1970, N° 11. Luxembourg) (Davignon Report).
Report of the Ad Hoc Committee for Institutional Affairs to the European Council (Brussels, 29–30 March 1985) (the Dooge Report) (ECSC-EEC-EAEC 1985).
Report of the Committee on Foreign Affairs and Security on Shaping the European Communitys Common Foreign Policy (A3-0322/92) (Rapporteur: Mr Josep Verde i Aldea) (European Parliament 1992) A3-0322/92.
Report of the Committee on Institutional Affairs on the Future Relations between the European Union, WEU and the Atlantic Alliance (A3-0041/94) (Rapporteur: Mr Karel De Gucht) (European Parliament 1994) A3-0041/94.
Report of the Committee on Institutional Affairs on the Structure and Strategy for the European Union with regard to its Enlargement and the Creation of a Europe-Wide Order (A3-0189/92) (Rapporteur: Mr Klaus Hänsch) (European Parliament 1992) A3-0189/92.
Report of the Court of Justice on Certain Aspects of the Application of the Treaty on European Union (Court of Justice of the European Communities 1995).
Report on Improving the Impact of Joint Actions Committee on Foreign Affairs, Security and Defence Policy (A4-0133/97) (Rapporteur: Mr Enrique Barón Crespo) (European Parliament 1997) A4-0133/97.
Report on the Annual Report from the Council to the European Parliament on the Common Foreign and Security Policy (12562/2011 -2012/2050(INI)) – 29 August 2012) (European Parliament 2012) A7-0252/2012.
Report on the Annual Report from the Council to the European Parliament on the Main Aspects and Basic Choices of CFSP, Including the Financial Implications for the General Budget of the European Communities – 2003 (8412/2004 – 2004/2172(INI)) (European Parliament 2005) A6-0062/2005.
Report on the Annual Report from the High Representative of the European Union for Foreign Affairs and Security Policy to the European Parliament (2014/2219(INI)) (European Parliament 2015) A8-0039/2015.
Report on the Role of the Union in the World: Implementation of the Common Foreign and Security Policy for 1998 (A4-0242/99) (European Parliament 1999) A4-0242/99.
Shared Vision, Common Action: A Stronger Europe. A Global Strategy for the European Unions Foreign and Security Policy (European Union) June 2016.
Speech by President [of the European Commission] Jean-Claude Juncker at the 54th Munich Security Conference. 17 February 2018 (Speech/18/841).
Standard Form of Explanatory Memorandum for European Union: Communication from the Commission to the European Council, the European Parliament and the Council. A Stronger Global Actor: A More Efficient Decisionmaking for EU Common Foreign and Security Policy (12425/18) Submitted by the Foreign and Commonwealth Office on 5 October 2018 to the House of Commons European Scrutiny Select Committee.
State of the Union, Proposals for the Future of Europe That Can Be Implemented on the Basis of the Lisbon Treaty. Speech by President of the European Commission, Jean-Claude Juncker, 13 September 2017.
State of the Union, The Hour of European Sovereignty. Speech by President of the European Commission, Jean-Claude Juncker, 12 September 2018.
Statement from the Paris Summit (19 to 21 October 1972).
The EU-UK Withdrawal Agreement Explained (European Commission 2019).

INDEX

Note: 'Treaties' is used to indicate the EU constitutional treaties as distinct from 'treaties', used to denote EU international treaties/treaties with third parties

www.ingramcontent.com/pod-product-compliance
Ingram Content Group UK Ltd.
Pitfield, Milton Keynes, MK11 3LW, UK
UKHW020906190926
475560UK00010B/296

9 781509 925940